C000175350

United Review

AN ILLUSTRATED HISTORY OF
MANCHESTER UNITED'S MATCHDAY PROGRAMME

Compiled and edited by Paul Davies

This book is dedicated to the eight journalists who lost their lives in the Munich Air Disaster on 6 February 1958: Alf Clarke, Don Davies, George Follows, Tom Jackson, Archie Ledbrooke, Henry Rose, Eric Thompson and Frank Swift.

And to David Meek (1930-2018) who was a much-loved and valued contributor to *United Review* for over 55 years.

Reach Sport

www.reachsport.com

Editor Paul Davies
Words Steve Bartram, Joe Ganley, Charlie Ghagan, Ian McLeish, Sean Mullan, Johnny Sharp
Sub-editing and production Simon Monk, Adam Oldfield
Design Mark Frances
Photography Manchester United FC, Getty, Mirrorpix
Thanks to Cliff Butler, Mark Wylie

Published in Great Britain and Ireland in 2020
by Reach Sport, a Reach PLC business,
5 St Paul's Square, Liverpool, L3 9SJ

www.reachsport.com
@Reach_Sport

Reach Sport is a part of Reach PLC.
One Canada Square, Canary Wharf, London, E15 5AP

Hardback ISBN: 978-1-911613-83-1

Printed and bound by Bell & Bain Ltd, Glasgow

Contents

Introduction **7**

Chapter 1 Front covers **10**
Chapter 2 Unforgettable games **28**
Chapter 3 Manager's notes **40**
Chapter 4 Cartoons **78**
Chapter 5 Columnists **120**
Chapter 6 The opposition **150**
Chapter 7 Adverts **166**
Chapter 8 Match action **186**
Chapter 9 Europe **206**
Chapter 10 Munich **228**
Chapter 11 Supporters **242**
Chapter 12 News & features **268**
Chapter 13 Other matches **304**

Introduction

Long before football clubs had websites and apps, television channels and multiple social media platforms, there was 'the programme' – which, for generations of supporters flocking to Old Trafford, meant *United Review*. Providing comment direct from the chairman and manager, rare insights into the lives of the players, crucial opposition details, plus all the latest news and ticketing information, the programme was the only place to hear the official voice of the club, a mine of information and a treasured souvenir.

Manchester United's programme, or rather Newton Heath's, did not start out like that. The first known matchday publication appeared in the late 1880s and was little more than a piece of card listing the team line-ups, as the curator of the Manchester United museum, Mark Wylie, explains.

"We've seen what look like flyers and posters advertising games that some people have said were programmes, but we're not sure there was a programme much before 1888," says Mark. "That's the earliest we've seen and it was a single sheet 'programme' for a friendly fixture on 6 October 1888 against a Canadian touring team who were simply referred to as 'The Canadians'. That was about the time that the league football began, when there started to be more organised matches, so that programme is probably among the earliest you'll find."

Above: Fans queue up at one of Old Trafford's many programme booths ahead of the game

During the 1890s, the Heathens (as Newton Heath were known) shared a programme with three other sports clubs: Broughton Rangers and Salford rugby league teams, as well as Manchester City FC. Each weekend the Official Football Programme – a 12 to 16-page publication – would include match reports from the previous week, that day's line-ups for all four matches, not to mention lots and lots of adverts.

After the club changed its name to Manchester United in 1902, the programme got its own magazine-style publication, edited by S W Gibbons. One of the earliest examples of this can be found in the Manchester United museum – an issue for a fixture against Blackburn Rovers in 1909, which is on loan from the family of former Reds half-back Alex Bell (who played 309 games for the Reds between 1903 to 1913). There are thousands more programmes in the archive, right up to the modern day, and many of them appear in this book.

At the start of the 1932/33 season, under editor Sidney F Wicks, the programme was given a substantial overhaul. 'I should prefer to sit back and see the team play,' wrote chairman James Gibson in an opening address to readers of the new-look publication (for the visit of Stoke City).

ALSO THIS PROGRAMME.

This Programme was also an inspiration of the Directors. There is no programme like it in the football world. Undoubtedly it has clinched the loyalty of many a supporter. Its pages took supporters into the confidence of the club, and made them feel that it was up to them to rally round, and if you who read these words want to carry on the good work—well, persuade your chums to buy a copy regularly. It costs money to produce, and every twopence helps.

'But the Editor insists a message from me shall preface the new Official Programme, which I hope will set a new standard in football programmes and form a handshake as it were, between the club and its supporters.'

By 1946, Gibson's metaphorical 'handshake' had taken on visual form on the front cover of the newly titled *United Review*: an illustration showing a fictional supporter and player shaking hands. The combination of the new name and distinctive masthead proved popular, and has since become the most recognisable matchday programme in football.

David Wicks – son of Sidney, and editor himself from 1956-74 – spoke to the club museum in the early 2000s, saying: "My father had the idea it would be nice to bring in the public [to the programme] and show that these matches were all about the people coming to watch. He had the idea of a footballer in his red and white strip having his right hand extended to a supporter, so that they shook hands in the middle. It was a bit sentimental perhaps, but it worked."

The happiest thing I shall write this Christmastide is this greeting to you!
Sidney F. Wicks

Above: Editor Sidney F Wicks was responsible for making big changes to the programme in the 1930s

The programme has undergone many changes in the decades since those immediate post-war years, but only for two seasons – 1977/78 and 1978/79 – has the name *United Review* been absent from the front cover. Then, for the 1981/82 season, the familiar look of the cover was back: black top, distinctive title and a modern illustration of the handshake.

Cliff Butler was *United Review* editor from 1989-2002, replacing previous incumbent Ken Ramsden. It was a proud honour for a self-confessed "fanatical supporter" who'd first got to know the programme when his father would leave a copy next to his bed after a night match for him to find in the morning. "I could talk about *United Review* all day," says Cliff, who describes his appointment as his own "Neil Armstrong moment".

Despite working on hundreds of issues of the *Review*, there's one in particular that stands out, and strangely it wasn't even for a match involving United.

"The one that gave me an awful lot of pride was the one that came on the back of tragedy, the Liverpool v Nottingham Forest FA Cup semi-final played at Old Trafford in 1989. It was the game rearranged because of the Hillsborough disaster and it felt a real privilege after such an awful event to be involved, to be doing my bit. I went to Anfield with a deputation from the club to pay our respects, and I was pleased to be able to then make a contribution in some way like producing the programme."

Other highlights of Cliff's time were also for poignant moments: the final game in front of the old Stretford End in May 1992 (v Tottenham) and the first match after the sad passing of legendary boss Sir Matt Busby in January 1994 (v Everton).

"There were two different covers for that Everton game – the new one with Sir Matt and the one we'd originally gone for, which showed an incredible

The Wolves programme from February 1958 is one of the most highly prized football programmes in the world

Former editor Cliff Butler was proud to edit the programme for the rearranged Liverpool v Nottingham Forest semi-final in 1989

save from Peter Schmeichel," Cliff reveals. "It was an incredibly sad time and meant us changing the programme really quickly but I always enjoyed the challenge of that and making sure we paid our respects the right way.

"The other one that really stands out was the final game of 1991/92 – the last game in front of the proper Stretford End. It was another sad day, but it had a silver-lining because I asked Denis Law if he would let me take his photograph on the famous terrace. And whilst we were together he told me that it was actually the first time he had ever stood on the Stretford End – what an honour!"

Those issues described are just two among the many over the years for which there's a special sentimental attachment to a great many supporters. But there are also those that have a large monetary value, too, as museum curator Mark Wylie explains.

"Probably the most valuable and sought-after programme is the Wolves one from February 1958,

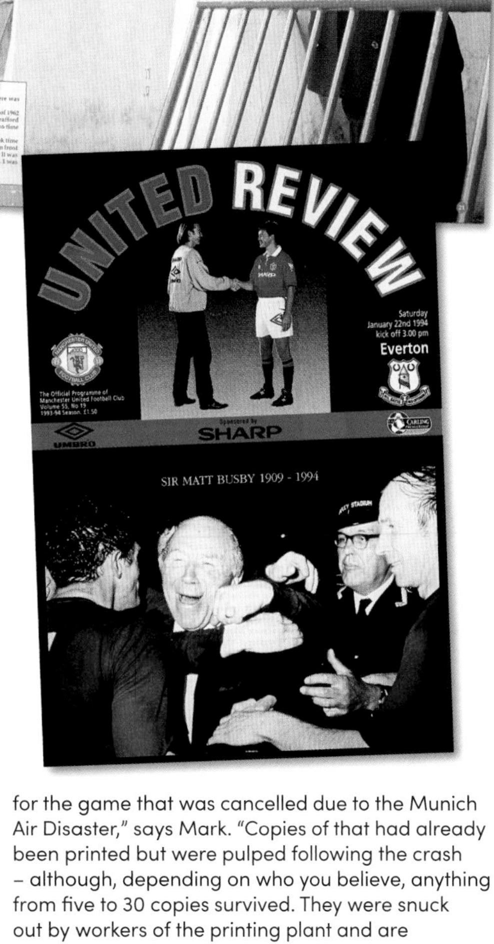

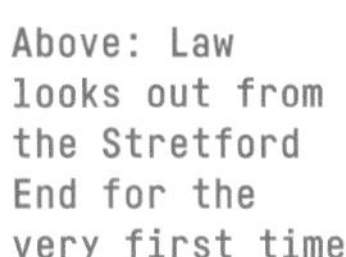
Above: Law looks out from the Stretford End for the very first time

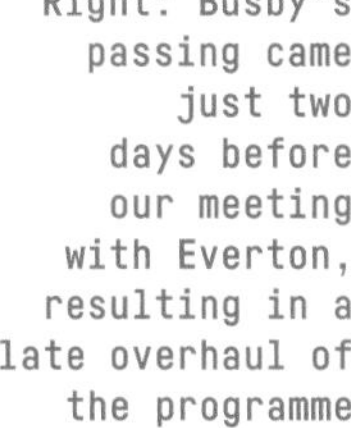
Right: Busby's passing came just two days before our meeting with Everton, resulting in a late overhaul of the programme

for the game that was cancelled due to the Munich Air Disaster," says Mark. "Copies of that had already been printed but were pulped following the crash – although, depending on who you believe, anything from five to 30 copies survived. They were snuck out by workers of the printing plant and are highly prized by programme collectors.

"In 1946/47, no programme was produced for the game against Blackpool due to a printers' strike, so there were 22 home matches in all competitions that season but only 21 programmes. There was also a very low print run for another game, against Stoke City in 1946/47. It was played on a Wednesday afternoon at Maine Road and attracted a crowd of only 8,456. It's another really tricky programme to get hold of."

In this book you'll find those rare issues and lots more fascinating content from over a century of Manchester United programmes, as we tell the story of the most famous club in football through the pages of its much-loved matchday publication.

CHAPTER 1

Front covers

The first port of call for fans as they pick up their programme, the *United Review* front cover has the job of setting the tone and sparking excitement – with some truly memorable offerings over the years...

Think of *United Review* and what immediately springs to mind for most fans is one thing: the supporter shaking hands with the player. First introduced in 1946, following the resumption of organised league football, the new-look publication and its distinctive front page quickly became the most instantly recognisable programme cover in British football.

The modern *United Review* has a cover that looks to set the tone for what follows within its pages, featuring a photo of an in-form player, a goal celebration from a recent fixture or a player about to pass a milestone for appearances or goals. There's occasionally some kind of message or retro approach to special issues or notable fixtures, with much thought given to what fans arriving at the ground would not only expect to see but also be drawn to when approaching the programme booths around the stadium. There's also a checklist of information and logos that simply have to be included on the front: United's club crest plus that of the opposition, the fixture information, logos for the competition, club sponsors, the price and the words 'Official Matchday Programme'.

From famous endorsements [top right] to the 2019/20 return to action in Old Trafford's first behind-closed-doors fixture [top left]

It's a far cry from the early days when advertisements would take up two-thirds of the programme cover, and the opposition name, date and competition would often be left off entirely. Those adverts could be for anything from theatre shows to men's ties to tobacco, with only the content on the inside pages changing from issue to issue.

It was at the start of 1948/49 that photographs first appeared as a matter of course on the cover, with FA Cup winning captain Johnny Carey featuring for the season opener against Derby County. The distinctive masthead was now well established, not to mention

UNITED REVIEW

MANCHESTER UNITED FOOTBALL CLUB

MANCHESTER UNITED v SHEFFIELD WEDNESDAY
Kick-off 7-30 pm

19th February
4d.
NUMBER 21
(F.A. CUP 5th ROUND)

1957-58

OFFICIAL SEASON PROGRAMME

UNITED WILL GO ON . . .

On 6th February, 1958 an aircraft returning from Belgrade crashed at Munich Airport. Of the twenty-one passengers who died twelve were players and officials of the Manchester United Football Club. Many others lie injured.

It is the sad duty of we who serve United to offer the bereaved our heartfelt sympathy and condolences. Here is a tragedy which will sadden us for years to come, but in this we are not alone. An unprecedented blow to British football has touched the hearts of millions and we express our deep gratitude to the many who have sent messages of sympathy and floral tributes. Wherever football is played United is mourned, but we rejoice that many of our party have been spared and wish them a speedy and complete recovery. Words are inadequate to describe our thanks and appreciation of the truly magnificent work of the surgeons and nurses of the Rechts der Isar Hospital at Munich. But for their superb skill and deep compassion our casualties must have been greater. To Professor Georg Maurer, Chief Surgeon, we offer our eternal gratitude.

Although we mourn our dead and grieve for our wounded we believe that great days are not done for us. The sympathy and encouragement of the football world and particularly of our supporters will justify and inspire us. The road back may be long and hard but with the memory of those who died at Munich, of their stirring achievements and wonderful sportsmanship ever with us, Manchester United will rise again.

H. P. HARDMAN, CHAIRMAN

The February 1958 cover v Sheffield Wednesday has become a piece of club history for tragic reasons

The biggest European nights always make for a prized match programme

popular, appearing on *United Review* (other than for cup ties, both domestic and European) with only slight tweaks up until 1967/68.

Various different looks were tried out thereafter, including a new landscape shape in 1977/78, before the original *United Review* design was returned to in 1981/82. There was a new illustration of the supporter greeting the player, but the overall look was the same and warmly received by fans – so much so that the next change of real note only came in 2002 when the programme changed its format again, with the handshake moving to the inside pages.

The iconic handshake shifted around the inside pages before appearing back on the cover by popular demand for the start of the 2010/11 campaign. In recent years dedicated supporters selected from the club's matchgoing fan base have taken centre stage, being illustrated shaking hands with a fictional player as part of the club's 'All Red All Equal' equality and diversity campaign.

Many covers across the programme's history have become synonymous with the matches they were created for. Most famous of all, for truly tragic reasons, was the cover of *United Review* for the FA Cup tie with Sheffield Wednesday in February 1958, just 13 days after the Munich Air Disaster. There was no photograph on the front on this emotion-charged evening, just words. 'United will go on...' it read, followed by a heartfelt eulogy to the fallen and a dedication to the future from club chairman Harold Hardman.

There's been no more recognisable programme cover in football than the one after Munich, but plenty more have meant a huge amount to a great many – conjuring not only nostalgia, but feelings of pride for Manchester United fans the world over.

THE EVOLUTION OF THE FRONT COVER, 1910-2020

1910/11-1927/28

1928/29-1930/31

1931/32

1932/33-1938/39

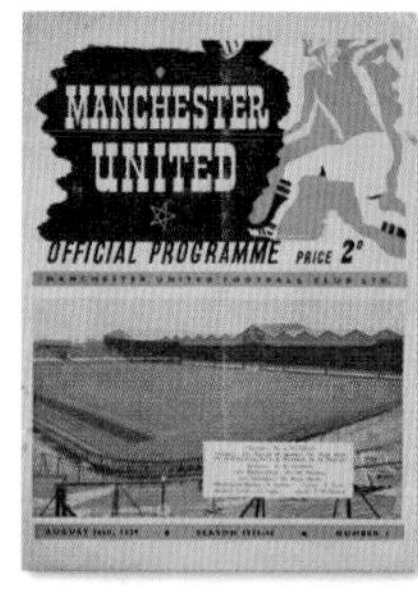
1939/40

1939-1946

1946/47-1950/51

1950/51-1958/59

1959/60-1965/66

1966/67

1967/68

1968/69

1969/70

1970/71

1971/72

1972/73-1973/74

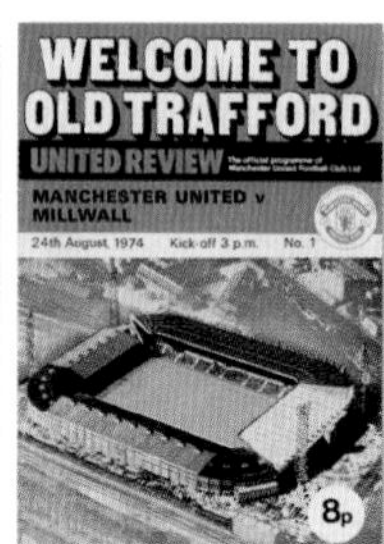
1974/75

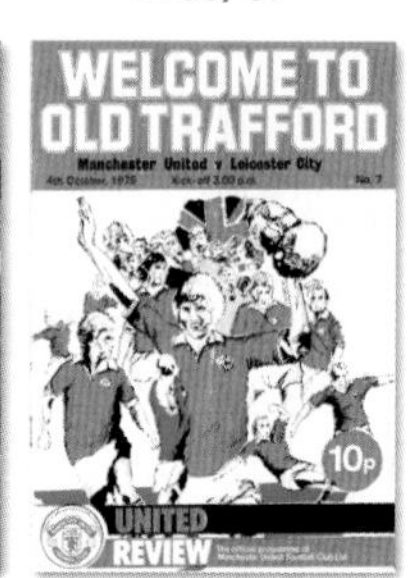
1975/76

1976/77

1977/78

1978/79

1979/80

1980/81

1981/82

1982/83-1985/86

1986/87-1987/88

1988/89-1989/90

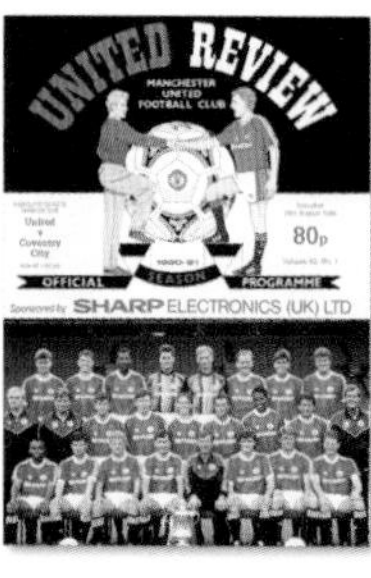

1990/91

1991/92

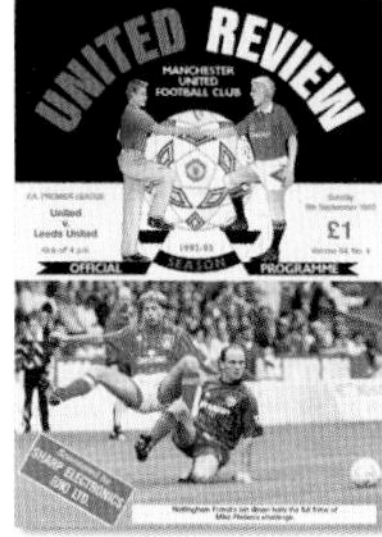

1992/93

1993/94

1994/95

1995/96

1996/97

1997/98

1998/1999

1999/2000

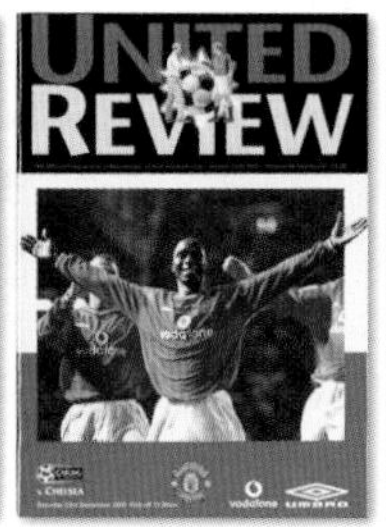

2000/01-2001/02

2002/03-2004/05

2005/06

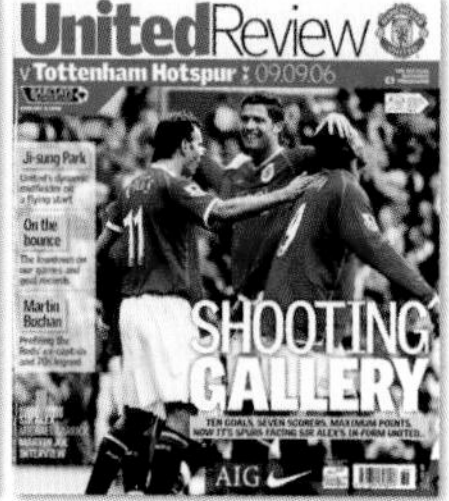

2006/07-2008/09

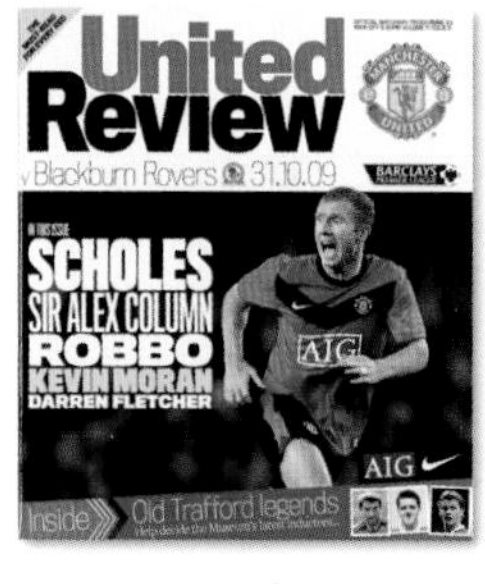

2009/10

2010/11-2011/12

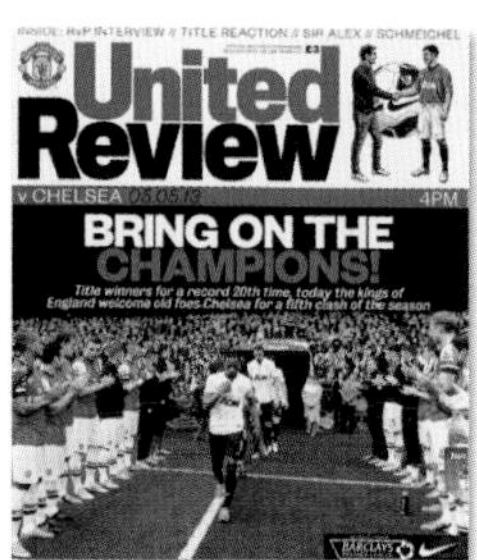

2012/13

2013/14

2014/15

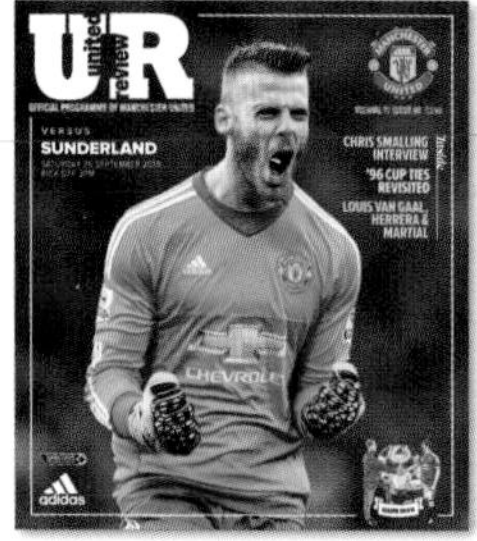

2015/16

2016/17

2017/18

2018/19

2019/20

Changing handshake: The programme's symbol of unity between the supporters and players has undergone numerous changes since first appearing in 1946...

The first handshake, with a fan wearing a suit and trilby hat, stayed on the cover for 13 years

When the handshake illustration was updated for the first time it reflected changing fashions

The handshake next changed in August 1966, with a new style of artwork and new font introduced

After a 14-year absence the handshake returned in August 1981, and remained on the cover until 2002

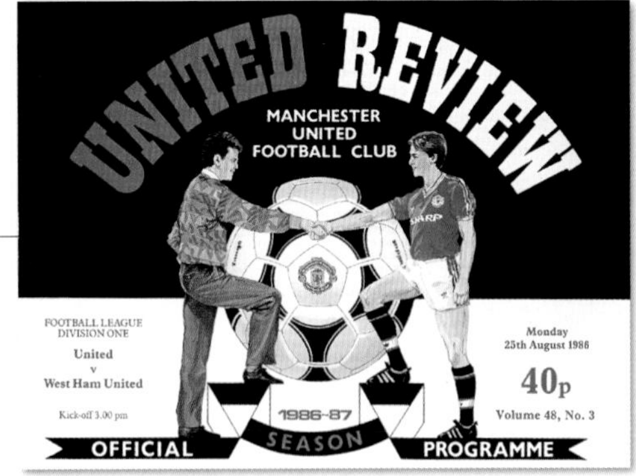

The player always wore the current home shirt, but the attire of the supporter changed less regularly

Bryan Robson remains the only actual player to appear in the *United Review* handshake, for the '93/94 season

Two actors posed for the handshake in '96/97, which stayed for two seasons, with the matchball in the background changing to reflect the new kit supplier

The new century brought about a new approach to the programme masthead, with the curved writing replaced by a bolder font and the illustration placed in the centre. This design was retained for two seasons

The handshake was moved from the cover to the inside pages of *United Review* in 2002/03, appearing in a number of locations across the programme before returning to the front for the 2010/11 campaign

In the 2012/13 illustration the fan wears a United scarf, while the player dons the latest-style boots

This retro-style cover, with a red background rather than traditional black, was introduced in 2013/14 and put a modern twist on the original 1946 design. *United Review*'s emblem then moved to the back cover in 2016/17 and stayed there for a couple of seasons

The modern handshake features an actual supporter, whose likeness is drawn alongside a fictitious player. The artwork better reflects the diversity of our global fan base and United's playing squad

There was no opposition name on the programme cover for this pre-Christmas match during the First World War, but Oldham Athletic were the visitors and United 3-2 winners of this War League fixture

Saturday, December 23rd, 1916. Price One Penny.

Don't Forget

THE GREAT MATCH

— ON —

BOXING DAY,

United v. City

KICK-OFF 2-40.

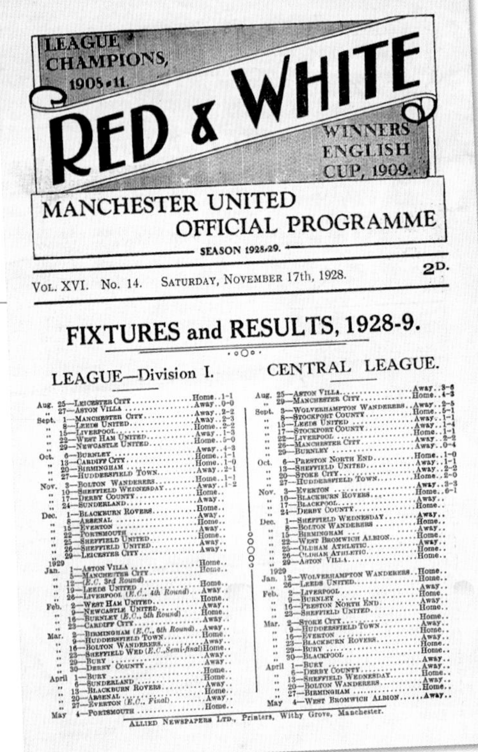

MANCHESTER UNITED OFFICIAL PROGRAMME

SEASON 1928-29.

VOL. XVI. No. 14. SATURDAY, NOVEMBER 17th, 1928. 2D.

FIXTURES and RESULTS, 1928-9.

LEAGUE—Division I.

Date	Opponents	Venue	Result
Aug. 25	Leicester City	Home	1-1
" 27	Aston Villa	Away	0-0
Sept. 1	Manchester City	Away	2-2
" 8	Leeds United	Away	2-3
" 15	Liverpool	Home	2-2
" 22	West Ham United	Away	1-3
" 29	Newcastle United	Home	5-0
Oct. 6	Burnley	Away	4-3
" 13	Cardiff City	Home	1-1
" 20	Birmingham	Home	1-0
" 27	Huddersfield Town	Away	2-1
Nov. 3	Bolton Wanderers	Home	1-1
" 10	Sheffield Wednesday	Away	1-2
" 17	Derby County	Home	
" 24	Sunderland	Away	
Dec. 1	Blackburn Rovers	Home	
" 8	Arsenal	Away	
" 15	Everton	Home	
" 22	Portsmouth	Away	
" 25	Sheffield United	Home	
" 26	Sheffield United	Away	
" 29	Leicester City	Away	
1929 Jan. 1	Aston Villa	Home	
" 5	Manchester City	Home	
" 12	(F.C. 3rd Round)		
" 19	Leeds United	Home	
" 26	Liverpool (F.C., 4th Round)	Away	
Feb. 2	West Ham United	Home	
" 9	Newcastle United	Away	
" 16	Burnley (F.C., 5th Round)	Home	
" 23	Cardiff City	Away	
Mar. 2	Birmingham (F.C., 6th Round)	Away	
" 9	Huddersfield Town	Home	
" 16	Bolton Wanderers	Away	
" 23	Sheffield Wed (F.C., Semi-final)	Home	
" 29	Bury	Away	
" 30	Derby County	Away	
April 1	Bury	Home	
" 6	Sunderland	Home	
" 13	Blackburn Rovers	Away	
" 20	Arsenal	Home	
" 27	Everton (F.C., Final)	Away	
May 4	Portsmouth	Home	

CENTRAL LEAGUE.

Date	Opponents	Venue	Result
Aug. 25	Aston Villa	Away	3-6
" 29	Manchester City	Home	4-3
Sept. 3	Wolverhampton Wanderers	Away	2-5
" 8	Stockport County	Home	5-1
" 15	Leeds United	Away	1-1
" 17	Stockport County	Away	1-4
" 22	Liverpool	Home	1-1
" 26	Manchester City	Away	2-2
" 29	Burnley	Away	0-4
Oct. 6	Preston North End	Home	1-0
" 13	Sheffield United	Away	1-1
" 20	Stoke City	Away	2-2
" 27	Huddersfield Town	Home	2-0
Nov. 3	Everton	Away	3-3
" 10	Blackburn Rovers	Home	6-1
" 17	Blackpool	Away	
" 24	Derby County	Home	
Dec. 1	Sheffield Wednesday	Away	
" 8	Bolton Wanderers	Home	
" 15	Birmingham	Away	
" 22	West Bromwich Albion	Home	
" 25	Oldham Athletic	Away	
" 26	Oldham Athletic	Home	
" 29	Aston Villa	Home	
1929 Jan. 12	Wolverhampton Wanderers	Home	
" 26	Leeds United	Home	
Feb. 2	Liverpool	Away	
" 9	Burnley	Home	
" 16	Preston North End	Away	
" 23	Sheffield United	Home	
Mar. 2	Stoke City	Home	
" 9	Huddersfield Town	Away	
" 16	Everton	Home	
" 23	Blackburn Rovers	Away	
" 29	Bury	Home	
" 30	Blackpool	Home	
April 1	Bury	Away	
" 6	Derby County	Away	
" 13	Sheffield Wednesday	Home	
" 20	Bolton Wanderers	Away	
" 27	Birmingham	Home	
May 4	West Bromwich Albion	Away	

ALLIED NEWSPAPERS LTD., Printers, Withy Grove, Manchester.

This was the cover for the visit of Division One leaders Derby County four months into the 1928/29 season. The Rams were 1-0 victors but eventually ended the season sixth in the table, while United finished back in 12th

SEASON 1931-32.

VOL. XIX. No. 34. GOOD FRIDAY, MARCH 25th, 1932. 2D.

THE ability to save will make all the difference in the part you play in the game of life. It will be your best defence against life's handicaps. The Manchester & Salford Savings Bank offers every facility to those who want to save. Get a Home Safe to-day. It will help you to save—help you in the great game of life.

J. W. JARVIS, Printer, 178 Stockport Road, Levenshulme.

This distinctive cover, for the Division Two visit of Charlton Athletic over Easter in 1931/32, displays an advert for a home safe

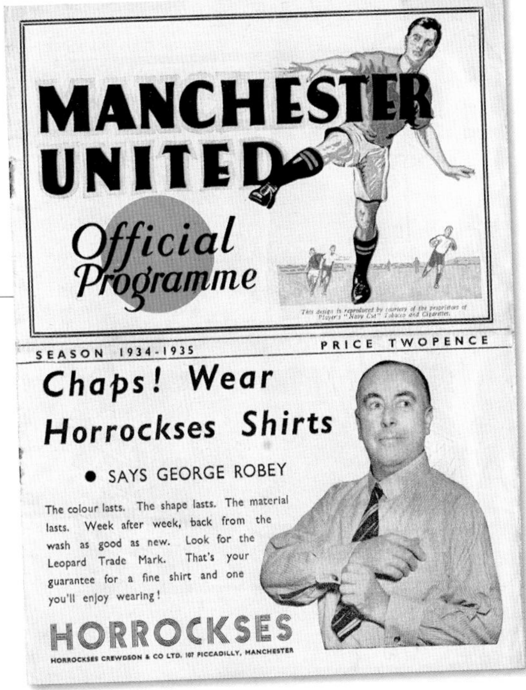

This was the cover for the visit of Barnsley to Old Trafford in September 1934 [a 4-1 United win] and features music hall star George Robey advertising shirts for a menswear store in Manchester city centre

The first programme of the 1939/40 campaign – for the visit of Grimsby Town – proved to be the only issue of the season as the Second World War brought a halt to competitive football. This 4-0 win against the Mariners, plus further league encounters with Charlton and Chelsea, were expunged from the records

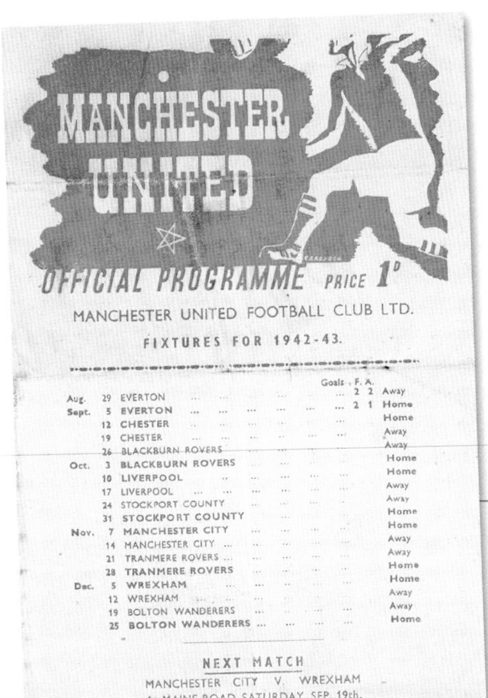

			Goals F.	A.	
Aug.	29	EVERTON	2	2	Away
Sept.	5	EVERTON	2	1	Home
	12	CHESTER			Home
	19	CHESTER			Away
	26	BLACKBURN ROVERS			Away
Oct.	3	BLACKBURN ROVERS			Home
	10	LIVERPOOL			Home
	17	LIVERPOOL			Away
	24	STOCKPORT COUNTY			Away
	31	STOCKPORT COUNTY			Home
Nov.	7	MANCHESTER CITY			Home
	14	MANCHESTER CITY			Away
	21	TRANMERE ROVERS			Away
	28	TRANMERE ROVERS			Home
Dec.	5	WREXHAM			Home
	12	WREXHAM			Away
	19	BOLTON WANDERERS			Away
	25	BOLTON WANDERERS			Home

NEXT MATCH
MANCHESTER CITY V. WREXHAM
At MAINE ROAD, SATURDAY, SEP. 19th.

Old Trafford's main stand was destroyed in a German air raid on 11 March 1941, rendering the ground unusable and forcing United to play wartime fixtures at Maine Road. A two-page programme was available for those matches, like this one for the visit of Chester City on 12 September 1942

Grimsby Town are the visitors to our temporary home, Maine Road - although there's no mention of them, the fixture date or kick-off time on the cover - as league football resumes after the Second World War. United win 2-0

The message on the front says it all: United are back at Old Trafford for the first time in a decade. The rebuilt stadium hosts the opening home game of the 1949/50 season and Matt Busby's side celebrate with a 3-0 victory over Bolton Wanderers

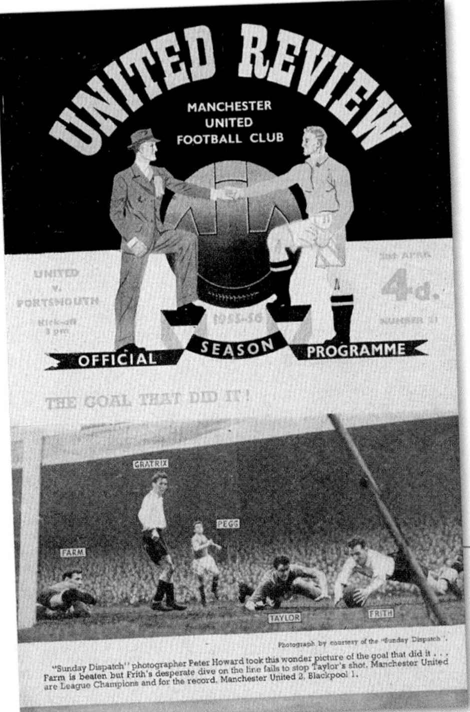

Matt Busby's 'Babes' are champions of England and this cover for the final fixture of the 1955/56 season shows the goal that sealed it: Tommy Taylor's scrambled winner against Blackpool

The Babes retain the title in April 1957 and the programme cover shares a message of thanks to supporters from United boss Busby, ahead of a 1-1 draw with West Bromwich Albion

Hollywood actor Charlton Heston (and his horse!) make a surprise appearance on the *United Review* cover, as the Reds take on Blackburn Rovers in a Division One fixture, played in October 1962

It's another big day at Old Trafford as the proud new kings of English football claim their 1966/67 crown in front of a 61,071 crowd. The game against Stoke was somewhat forgettable – a 0-0 draw – but it's the presentation of the trophy that fans have come to see

The European Cup takes pride of place on the *United Review* cover as the Reds return to competitive action for the first time since that famous Wembley night against Benfica in May 1968. George Best and Bobby Charlton – both scorers in the European final – get the goals in a 2-1 victory against the Toffees

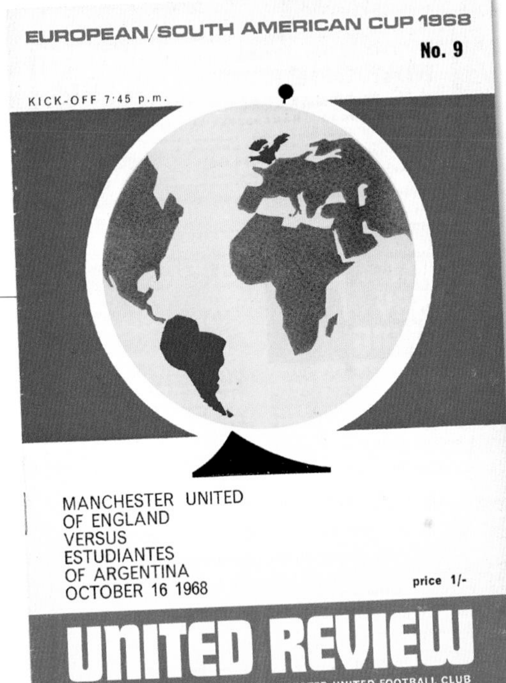

The programme had a striking front cover for the return leg of the Reds' Intercontinental Cup clash with Estudiantes, but sadly the South American champions achieved a 2-1 aggregate win to be crowned the world's best club side

United's defence of the European Cup took Busby's side to Milan for a semi-final tie, and this was the programme cover for the issue on sale at the big-screen showing of the first-leg away match

This illustrative design was in place on the *United Review* cover from August 1970 to April 1974, with slight variations for each of the three seasons it was used. This particular cover was for our opening fixture of the 1970/71 season, against Don Revie's Leeds

Cup ties were often given special treatment by the *United Review* team in the 1960s and 1970s, such as this one for the Manchester derby – a 3-0 win for the Reds against the Blues

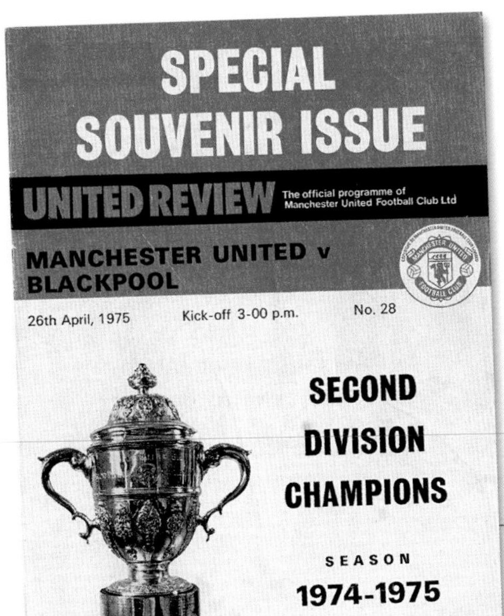

Dropping into the second tier of English football just six years after being European champions had been an ignominious experience for the Reds, but happily it proved to be only a one-season stay for Tommy Docherty's side

United Review's one-season experiment with a new size and shape wasn't to everyone's taste, but it did place the FA Cup trophy – won in May 1977 – front and centre of the new-look cover

United came out on the wrong end of a famous game against Ron Atkinson's exciting West Brom side in 1978, losing 3-5 – but at least the programme cover was suitably festive!

Old Trafford hosted the 100th Manchester derby in 1980 and there was a special issue of *United Review* to mark the occasion, complete with a cover collage of past derby programmes. Mickey Thomas scored as United beat City 1-0

'Whatever will be, will be...' and the Reds added further glory to our proud FA Cup record by beating Everton 1-0 in the sixth round, then going on to lift the trophy two months later

The curtain went up on a new season but thoughts were still firmly on the end to the previous one – a sixth FA Cup success thanks to Norman Whiteside's stunning Wembley winner against Everton in May 1985. The Northern Irishman was on target again in this game, a 4-0 Division One thumping of Aston Villa

Hello, boss! There was only ever going to be one man on the front of this particular programme, with Alex Ferguson taking charge of his first home game as the new United manager. The Reds beat QPR 1-0

A few club legends and one shiny trophy adorned the final programme cover of 1993/94, after United had clinched one half of what would become a first league and FA Cup Double. As for the game, it ended goalless

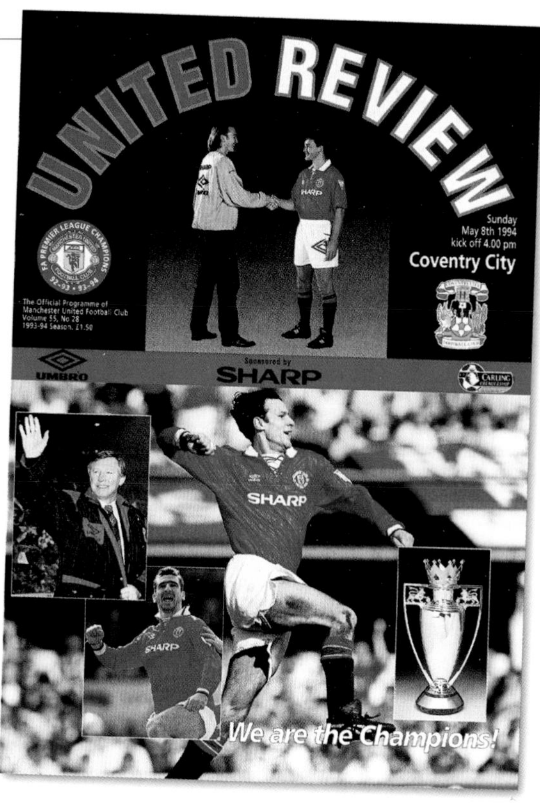

All eyes were on Eric Cantona the day he returned to action after a nine-month suspension for an altercation with a Crystal Palace fan, and he didn't disappoint. The Frenchman scored our second goal in 2-2 draw against Liverpool

Alex Ferguson led the Reds to an unprecedented Treble in 1998/99, and as a new home campaign began he proudly showed off the silverware collection. United beat the Owls 4-0

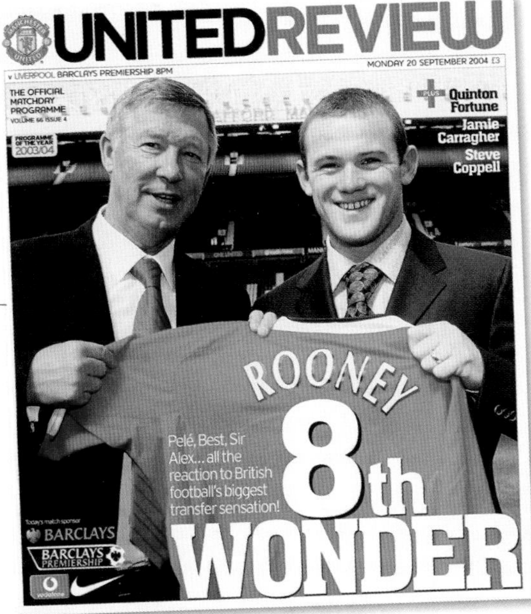

United Review reacted to the sad passing of the man widely regarded as the club's greatest ever player with this fitting cover. The Reds beat West Brom 3-1 in the League Cup tie, but this night was all about paying respects to a true Reds legend

United fans would have to wait a little longer to watch their new teenage hero – eight days to be precise – but *United Review* were happy to whet the appetite with this photo of English football's hottest young prospect

United Review raises a toast to the new English champions in 2007, with star of the season Cristiano Ronaldo suitably positioned on the celebratory cover

United Review reacts to the Reds winning the league title for a record 20th time in 2013, with an image from the previous week's game at Arsenal where the Gunners' players had given Patrice Evra and his team-mates a guard of honour

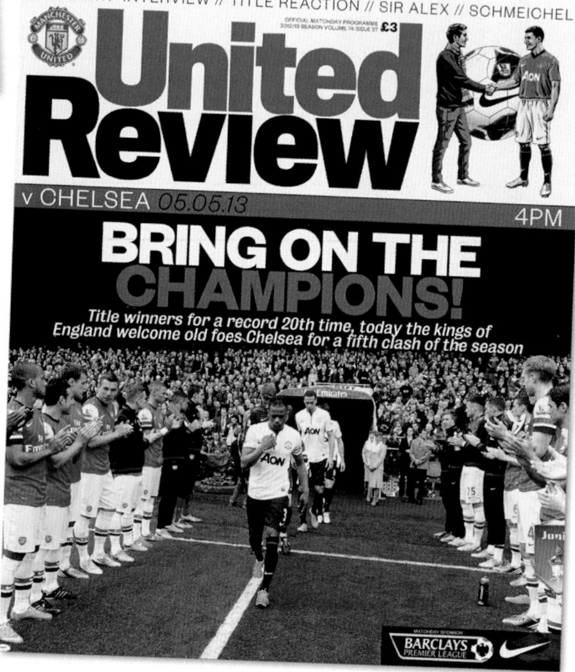

The 2008 cover image shows the joyous scenes after United's famous Champions League semi-final victory over Barcelona four days earlier, and there were more celebrations when the Reds defeated the Hammers 4-1. A week later Sir Alex's men retained the Premier League title, and 10 days after were champions of Europe for a third time

United Review ran a competition for fans to design the front cover of the programme for this visit of Man City in 2015, with the winning entry coming from Harri Lyons from Colwyn Bay, North Wales – a graphical depiction of the Manchester skyline

A reworking of Manchester's emblem, taken from the mosaic on the floor of the town hall, made for a striking cover as United and City met in the fourth round of the League Cup in 2016, a tie the Reds won 1-0 thanks to Juan Mata's second-half strike

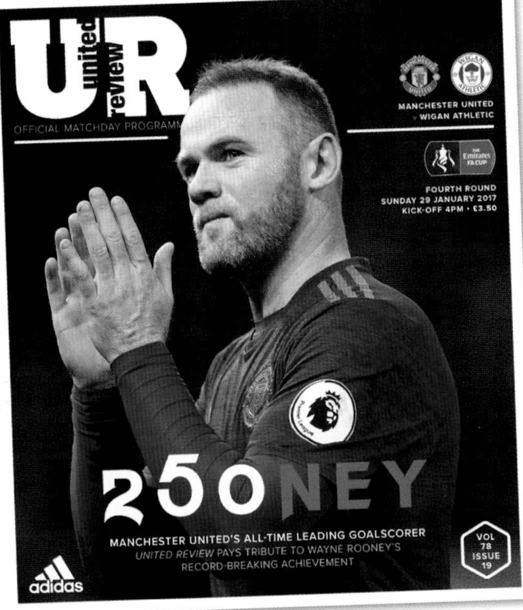

Take a bow! Wayne Rooney appeared on the cover of *United Review* quite often, but on this occasion it was to mark a very special achievement - becoming United's all-time leading goalscorer

It's the biggest rivalry in English football, often being referred to as the 'derby of England', and *United Review* took a creative approach to honour the 200th meeting of the old rivals

CHAPTER 2

Unforgettable games

Recalling 10 of the most magical, emotional and inspirational moments in the club's long history, as well as the front cover of that match programme. If you're lucky enough to own one of these issues, you've got yourself a collector's item...

Old Trafford is popularly known as 'the Theatre of Dreams' – a phrase first uttered by Sir Bobby Charlton during the 1980s. It's a nickname that acts as shorthand for the many miraculous feats of footballing drama that have blessed the stadium throughout its long history.

But regular matchgoing fans, many of whom consider Old Trafford a second home, will tell you that's not the half of it. Those lucky enough to have seen countless unforgettable matches in M16 know that the old place is special; know what it can inspire when magic and mood transport it into a realm few other venues can reach. But each and every home game is special to those who come every week. And that's not just because of the unforgettable games – of which there are hundreds – but because of the spirit and memories that Old Trafford harbours. The ghosts of the Busby Babes that Matt Busby claimed were "still hovering above the ground". The spectre of all the former greats that have graced this 110-year-old totem. Close your eyes briefly and you can still see them, flickering across the pitch.

Above: United's two-goal hero Bryan Robson is carried shoulder-high by jubilant supporters after our 1984 elimination of Barcelona in the Cup Winners' Cup

For supporters, it goes even further than that. Football matches are not just about 11 versus 11 out on the grass. For most people at the stadium each weekend, fixtures are events that encompass thousands of other little interactions.

When you think of the great goals, the great games, buried deep within your brain, you don't just see Eric Cantona's balletic poise or Ryan Giggs's effortless dribbling at pace. You remember the lad next to you, in tears, after a particularly euphoric last-gasp winner. The old, tired catchphrases garbled every week by the bloke behind you that everyone endures – but would miss

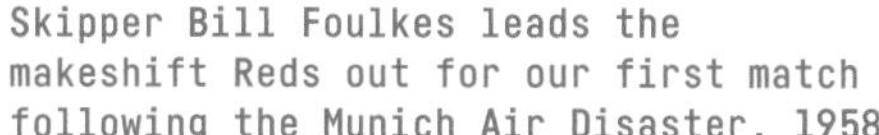

Skipper Bill Foulkes leads the makeshift Reds out for our first match following the Munich Air Disaster, 1958

Celebration time at the final whistle as United reach the 2008 Champions League final

FIVE THAT DIDN'T MAKE THE CUT...	United 10 Anderlecht 0 **26 September 1956**	United 5 Manchester City 0 **10 November 1994**	United 9 Ipswich Town 0 **4 March 1995**	United 3 Aston Villa 2 **5 April 2009**	United 8 Arsenal 2 **28 August 2011**

if he ever stopped coming to games. Then there are the links with your family and friends.

The chances are that, if you're a Red, Old Trafford is one of the few places you still go to that connects you to several generations of people who might no longer be with you. Even family members from distant, long-gone decades that you never even met. But when you take your place in those stands, and step into Old Trafford's chamber of images, memories and dreams, you're connected with them. That might feel beside the point when we're 3-0 down to a big rival, or someone shanks a gilt-edged chance into the second tier. But when you look back at your years of going to Old Trafford, these are the things that can mean something profound to you as a football fan.

United Review, of course, is part of that. Many collect *UR* and then hand their archive down to sons and daughters. Issues from the first match after the Munich Air Disaster, against Sheffield Wednesday, are treasured like heirlooms. For others, certain *UR*s become precious for personal reasons. Maybe last season saw a maiden visit with your first-born. Or the last with a beloved relative. Whatever the reason, each programme is part of someone's rich, personal Old Trafford tapestry.

But, of course, the game is ultimately what compels us; what drives us. It is the never-ending soap opera of Manchester United that seduces most. And when it comes to unforgettable moments, no other stadium in England can match Old Trafford.

Here are 10 games that stand out from its long and storied history of special home games (with one from our post-War temporary home, Maine Road). There are, of course, many that we couldn't find space for, regrettably. But it goes with the territory, when you're dissecting the best of this great club...

6 February 1957

Manchester United 3-0 Athletic Bilbao

European Cup quarter-final second leg, Maine Road, Att: 70,000

Exactly one year before a tragic day that threatened to destroy Manchester United came a seismic match that set the club apart from all others in England.

Our unprecedented foray into Europe had defied the FA and intrigued everyone else, but it wasn't until an epic to-and-fro with Spanish champions Athletic Bilbao that the full operatic sweep of the European Cup fully seduced a pre-*Coronation Street*, romance-ready public. Matt Busby's Babes had lost 5-3 in the Basque Country, amid snow-swept scenes fit for a Siberian spy thriller – as *UR*'s cover attests! Over 70,000 packed Maine Road for the return – Old Trafford was without floodlights – and both the atmosphere and the tie's denouement quickly became the stuff of legend.

Goals from Tommy Taylor and Dennis Viollet brought us level on aggregate and then, in the final minutes, Johnny Berry's clinching strike tore the roof off. Some claimed the racket made by fans could be heard in Oldham. Apocryphal, perhaps, but this was the night United were forever cast into concrete as the thrill-seeker's choice.

Busby's Reds were given an almighty scare in the San Mames snow (as pictured on the second-leg programme cover, right), but battled back in some style at Maine Road (top) to reach the semi-finals

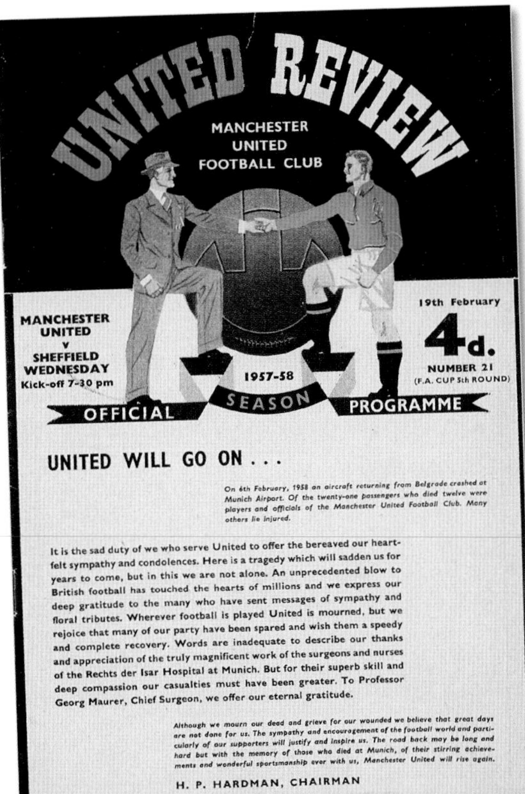

UNITED REVIEW

MANCHESTER UNITED FOOTBALL CLUB

MANCHESTER UNITED v SHEFFIELD WEDNESDAY Kick-off 7-30 pm

19th February

4d.

NUMBER 21 (F.A. CUP 5th ROUND)

1957-58

OFFICIAL SEASON PROGRAMME

UNITED WILL GO ON . . .

On 6th February, 1958 an aircraft returning from Belgrade crashed at Munich Airport. Of the twenty-one passengers who died twelve were players and officials of the Manchester United Football Club. Many others lie injured.

It is the sad duty of we who serve United to offer the bereaved our heartfelt sympathy and condolences. Here is a tragedy which will sadden us for years to come, but in this we are not alone. An unprecedented blow to British football has touched the hearts of millions and we express our deep gratitude to the many who have sent messages of sympathy and floral tributes. Wherever football is played United is mourned, but we rejoice that many of our party have been spared and wish them a speedy and complete recovery. Words are inadequate to describe our thanks and appreciation of the truly magnificent work of the surgeons and nurses of the Rechts der Isar Hospital at Munich. But for their superb skill and deep compassion our casualties must have been greater. To Professor Georg Maurer, Chief Surgeon, we offer our eternal gratitude.

Although we mourn our dead and grieve for our wounded we believe that great days are not done for us. The sympathy and encouragement of the football world and particularly of our supporters will justify and inspire us. The road back may be long and hard but with the memory of those who died at Munich, of their stirring achievements and wonderful sportsmanship ever with us, Manchester United will rise again.

H. P. HARDMAN, CHAIRMAN

19 February 1958

Manchester United 3-0 Sheffield Wednesday

FA Cup fifth round, Old Trafford, Att: 59,848

Old Trafford's first match since the Munich Air Disaster was, plainly, a night like no other. This ground had seen the bewitching, youthful Busby Babes dance to two league titles. But then, in a cruel, simple twist of fate, it was forced to endure the sight of its heroes being carried past in coffins.

'United will go on' insisted arguably *UR*'s most famous cover, ahead of a fifth-round FA Cup tie with Sheffield Wednesday. But inside there were blank spaces in place of the Reds' line-up. An eerie, shellshocked atmosphere abounded. However, two implausible goals from debutant Shay Brennan – who would score just four more times in his remaining 358 games – secured a poignant victory. With it came the first hints that a club fuelled with Babes' spirit could never be quelled. Here was the proof that United could go on, powered by a now unbreakable bond between a shattered club and its staunch support.

The message is clear, as the chairman outlines the club's determination to recover from our darkest hour. Top: captain Bill Foulkes shakes hands with opponent [and future Red] Albert Quixall before kick-off

21 March 1984

Manchester United 3-0 Barcelona

European Cup Winners' Cup quarter-final second leg, Old Trafford, Att: 58,547

The club's golden European history seemed to almost taunt United during the 1970s and 1980s – two long decades without a single entry into the European Cup. And when Diego Maradona and a star-studded Barcelona team touched down in M16 in 1984, buttressed by a 2-0 lead from the first leg of this Cup Winners' Cup tie, expectations were low.

But what came next seemed served up by the gods. Bilbao '57 might have set the template for classic European comebacks, but Barcelona '84 perfected it. Goals from our remarkable cover-star captain Bryan Robson (two) and Frank Stapleton turned the tie on its head, amid a white-hot atmosphere that is still hailed as the greatest Old Trafford has ever seen. The post-Busby, pre-Ferguson wilderness years were bleak, but here was some much-needed manna to remind the world that Old Trafford could make anyone – even Maradona – seem mortal.

The cover star for this Old Trafford encounter proved an inspired choice, as 'Captain Marvel' had arguably his finest game in a United shirt. Robson's second goal [top] levelled the tie, before Stapleton's winner

10 April 1993

Manchester United 2-1 Sheffield Wednesday

Premier League, Old Trafford, Att: 40,102

Over Easter weekend in 1992, United's latest agonising attempt to claim a first league title since 1967 had evaporated. So there was utter anguish when Stretford-born John Sheridan put Wednesday ahead in this vital home match during the run-in a year later.

But this time Alex Ferguson's burgeoning team didn't cave in. Two headed goals from captain Steve Bruce – in the 86th and 96th minutes – sent the crowd wild and drove Ferguson and his assistant Brian Kidd delirious (and on to the pitch). Most importantly, they turned what would have been a one-point deficit to Aston Villa at the top of the table into a two-point advantage, with just five games left. The end to a long, painful wait for domestic glory seemed closer than ever, and a confident, exciting team – with a penchant for late goals – seemed poised to take us back to the top.

This was the day Old Trafford realised it.

The cover features Andrei Kanchelskis's goal at Norwich five days earlier – a win that kick-started a run of seven straight victories to land the title, including Bruce's late show against the Owls (below)

3 May 1993

Manchester United 3-1 Blackburn Rovers

Premier League, Old Trafford, Att: 40,447

United's first top-flight championship for 26 years was confirmed at Villa Park the day before our final home game of the 1992/93 season, against Blackburn Rovers.

What could have been yet another panic-stricken evening for attendant Reds was turned into a mass party, after Oldham beat Aston Villa 1-0 to hand Ferguson's men the title. One of Old Trafford's greatest nights followed, as a slightly weary United side roared back from a goal down to beat Rovers 3-1, and in style. The reaction of a joyful, teary-eyed Sir Matt Busby said it all.

Everyone attending this match knew they'd leave Old Trafford having seen United lift the Premier League trophy; but no one could have known that the magical, celebratory night that lay ahead could soar to close to perfection. Twenty further years of domestic domination beckoned, but few, if any, titles delivered more satisfaction than Ferguson's first.

Aston Villa's shock loss to Oldham the previous night confirmed United as champions (below) – but that news came too late to appear in our programme, with Paul Ince's goal at Palace appearing on the cover

22 January 1994

Manchester United 1-0 Everton

Premier League, Old Trafford, Att: 44,750

Shortly after seeing the club he shaped reclaim its rightful place atop the English game, Sir Matt Busby passed away. Just two days later, United welcomed Everton to Old Trafford, for a league fixture which became a memorial and a tribute to the great man all rolled into one.

The tones of a lone bagpiper led the teams out, amid reverential silence from both sets of supporters. But when the whistle went, the champions leapt from the starting gate like a team determined to display what the great man had been all about: fast, daring, entertaining, attacking football.

Fittingly, it was Ryan Giggs – the latest great United youth product – who scored the game's only goal. But, in truth, the score could have reached five or six, given the verve and brio Cantona and co played with. It made for a mournful, moving day at Old Trafford, as the Reds' football stirred the soul in a fashion that would have made Sir Matt proud.

On a highly emotional afternoon at Old Trafford [above], the programme cover pays tribute to Busby with a striking photo from the Scot's finest hour: leading the Reds to a first European Cup in 1968

16 May 1999

Manchester United 2-1 Tottenham Hotspur

Premier League, Old Trafford, Att: 55,189

The first leg of an unprecedented and still unmatched Treble was delivered on the unforgettable final day of the 1998/99 league season. United needed to win and did so – just.

Les Ferdinand had put Tottenham ahead early in the game but, as so often in the Treble season, Ferguson's men came firing back to claim what was rightfully theirs. A sublime David Beckham equaliser unleashed an Old Trafford roar loud enough to rouse the dead, and Andy Cole's expert finish put us ahead in the second half, securing the vital three points that saw us finish just a solitary point ahead of Arsenal.

It was a fifth league title in seven years but, remarkably, the first time since the Busby era that we'd claimed the title on home soil. Ten days later the Treble was completed even more dramatically, but the triple triumph's only home leg will always rank highly among M16's most cherished and thrilling occasions.

Action shots on the cover were a regular sight during the Treble season, with this one coming from a tense 0-0 draw at Blackburn that left Dwight Yorke and his fellow Reds requiring a final-day win. Thankfully, we got it

10 April 2007

Manchester United 7-1 AS Roma

Champions League quarter-final second leg, Old Trafford, Att: 74,476

United had battered continental opposition before, and memorably too. Indeed our very first home game in the European Cup, way back in 1956, had been a record 10-0 mauling of Anderlecht.

But that was in the first round of the competition. This 7-1 goalscoring riot came at the quarter-final stage and, as easy as it is to forget now, United had lost the first leg! On the cover of *UR*, Cristiano Ronaldo urged Old Trafford to 'raise the roof', but the way the Reds played, the near-75,000 in attendance had no choice. We were 5-0 up and out of sight within 50 minutes, with Ronaldo scoring twice. Until Bayern Munich's 8-2 demolition of Barcelona in 2019/20, this was the competition's biggest margin of victory in a last-eight game. Old Trafford was a sea of joy, as endless waves of United attacks put the Romans to the sword over and over again, in one of the greatest exhibitions of attacking effervescence ever seen in M16.

There was a call to arms on the cover as the Reds aimed to turn this quarter-final around. As well as Ronaldo, fellow forward Alan Smith [top] ended the evening as one of our five goalscoring heroes

29 April 2008

Manchester United 1-0 Barcelona

Champions League semi-final second leg, Old Trafford, Att: 75,061

United won two European Cups in the 20th century, but never had they qualified for the biggest fixture in club football via a match at Old Trafford.

In 2008, they achieved that, with a nail-biting 1-0 victory over Barcelona that had echoes of the aforementioned 1984 success against the same opposition. This time Lionel Messi was the Argentinian superstar to be stifled, and once again the Old Trafford crowd rose to the occasion, applying pressure and driving United forward with every attack. Paul Scholes had missed the climax to the Treble in 1999, so his stunning long-range decider was an emotional, redemptive moment. But there were still 75 minutes remaining after Scholes had hit the net. What came next really defined this epic night: resolute defending from the team and unwavering support from the stands, where fans summoned the final whistle with twirling scarves and endless 'Viva Ronaldo' choruses.

This eye-catching design was based on the programme cover when Real Madrid came to Old Trafford in 1968, and once again it was a victorious night against a Spanish side, with Scholes our semi-final hero [below]

12 May 2013

Manchester United 2-1 Swansea City

Premier League, Old Trafford, 75,572

There were probably enough unforgettable Old Trafford games in the Alex Ferguson era alone to fill 10 of these lists. So it was little surprise that when the great man departed in 2013 – after 13 league titles, two Champions Leagues, five FA Cups and the rest – there was nary a dry eye in the house.

It's rare that football careers end at the top. And even rarer when an entire stadium can simultaneously mourn the end of an epoch and celebrate it. As the rain poured down in M16, Old Trafford did just that, honouring United's record-breaking 20th league title and the monumental achievements of our second legendary Scottish manager. Of course, there was the obligatory late winner, to earn Ferguson his final victory as United boss, but this was a day that was about so much more: a farewell to one of the sport's living legends, and a man who gave Old Trafford more unforgettable moments than anyone else in the club's history. The *UR* cover said it all, said it simply, and said it best: 'Thank you, Sir Alex.'

A studio portrait of Sir Alex adorned the cover for his final Old Trafford game, with the programme packed with tributes and memories of the legendary manager, who was also given a guard of honour [top]

CHAPTER 3

Manager's notes

Whether it's welcoming the opposition, whipping up the Old Trafford crowd or just getting the boss's message across loud and clear, the column in the matchday programme is a time-honoured tradition for any gaffer

As the figurehead for his club, a manager's role incorporates a great deal of front-line public relations. At Manchester United, that has long since included a column in *United Review*.

As Sir Matt Busby put it in his first ever open letter to supporters: 'To all United fans I say "how do you do?" This is my first opportunity of having a word with you since my arrival here, and what better means than by the club programme?'

The manager's notes are a direct line from author to reader; an opportunity for the man in charge to clearly and concisely outline his message to those in the stands his way, without filtration by the wider external media.

While Busby became the first United boss to utilise this outlet for his views on a regular basis, it was his predecessor, Scott Duncan, who blazed a trail by writing the first ever manager's notes (of sorts) when he penned a Christmas message to the supporters in 1932.

Above: Sir Alex Ferguson used his notes to instruct Old Trafford to raise the roof against Barcelona in 2008, with glorious results

Busby's first full season at Old Trafford marked the establishment of the manager's notes in each edition of *United Review*, and every one of the Scot's successors – bar Wilf McGuinness – saw fit to continue the column through the years.

The range and scope of the notes are wide and varied, starting with its audience. Sir Alex Ferguson used his column before the 2008 Champions League semi-final against Barcelona to urge supporters to 'raise the roof' in tandem with their side's efforts on the field; a move which undoubtedly contributed to one of the most rousing atmospheres Old Trafford has ever hosted.

While supporters are the ones who part with their hard-earned readies to buy a copy of the

Dutchman van Gaal salutes the home support pre-match, when many of the fans would have been reading his programme notes

Ferguson quickly realised the value of having a direct line to the United support

programme, usually on matchday, they aren't the only intended recipients of its message. Traditionally, the article has been a means of welcoming visiting opponents and their fans to Old Trafford, while more than one manager has utilised the column as a platform for addressing his players in public.

Dealing with the here and now of the day's fixture provides the main thrust of the notes' *raison d'être*, but they also give their author the chance to reflect on recent events and results or, when required, look ahead to the future.

When handed the opportunity to address readers for the first time ahead of the Reds' home meeting with QPR in November 1986, Sir Alex chose to look forward in a fittingly prescient tone.

'Success has a snowball effect as I found at Aberdeen,' penned the Scot, aided and abetted by ghost writer David Meek, who helped deliver Ferguson's column for the entirety of his Old Trafford reign. 'Instilling the right outlook will be my first priority. It's not something that can be built overnight... but that is what I shall work towards and I am going to love every minute of it here.

'A man is very fortunate if he gets the opportunity to manage Manchester United in his lifetime and I can assure you that I have no intention of wasting my opportunity.'

Since Sir Alex's retirement, the manager's column in *United Review* has continued unabated, penned by David Moyes, Ryan Giggs, Louis van Gaal, Jose Mourinho and Ole Gunnar Solskjaer, all of whom – despite their myriad media commitments in a position of such power – recognised the importance of utilising the platform offered by the official club publication.

GREETINGS
from A. SCOTT DUNCAN

On behalf of the United teams, I send to your readers my hearty good wishes for what Harry Lauder would call a " braw bricht " Christmas and a prosperous New Year. This is my first Christmas as a Manchester man, but the kindness and hospitality accorded to me makes me feel that I shall enjoy Yuletide even though so far from my native heath. As you know, the Christmas Season will be a strenuous one for the players. I hope to bring them back covered with glory. The men are in good heart and as keen as I am to win their way on and up.

Greeting to you all from,

A. SCOTT DUNCAN.

24 DECEMBER 1932, RESERVES v BIRMINGHAM CITY

For his Christmas message in 1932, the smiling Scots-born United boss evoked the spirit of his countryman, the world-famous music hall star Harry Lauder, to wish the fans from his new adopted home town all the best for the festive season.

MATT BUSBY
watches the field

Photo. : *Manchester Evening News*

To all United Fans I say " How do you do ? " This is my first opportunity of having a word with you since my arrival here last year, and what better means than by the Club programme ? This represents the written words and thoughts of the Manchester United F.C., and I am certain you and I have an equal interest in it. As it is intended that I have a regular article to discuss football from many view-points I hope it will bring us even closer together. You and I look forward to the opening of the 1946-47 season and what it has in store for us. How often have I felt that tingle run through me, known to all players on the first match of a new season, wondering in what form it would find me and how kindly the ball would run. I am finding all the same reactions as a manager.

A great number of people have asked me about our prospects for the coming season. To this I have replied that our boys are in good heart and excellent physical condition, and will hold their own. Others have remarked that the team should do very well if they start off as they finished last season. Yes, I would be a very happy man if they start off as they finished, but I realise from experience the number of things that can crop up to influence this. After all, each player is human and not a mechanical engine which, when you press a button, goes through its work every minute of the day. I do wish all followers of football would remember this very important point when a player has an " off day."

However, we must get on to the battle which starts this afternoon. We will all find the pace of the game stepping up, the tackling keener and the teamwork improved with a view to getting back to 1939 standards—which is all to the good of the game. Whether we start off on the right foot this afternoon or not, I do feel our boys will provide many happy afternoons for us all.

When I came here, I set out to have a team play methodical and progressive football. Without method a team gets nowhere. Without making progress after creating an opening or a position, the opportunity is lost and the team is back where it started. This will always be my policy, so I leave it to the players to supply the answer, and I hope you will have something good to shout about !

M. Busby

Manager.

The Reds attack at our temporary home of Maine Road, in the years after the war

31 AUGUST 1946, v GRIMSBY TOWN

The new United manager introduces himself to the fans in his opening column for our first post-war match, against Grimsby, held at our temporary home of Maine Road. True to his word, it wasn't long before Busby gave the fans 'something good to shout about!'.

MATT BUSBY TALKING

by the M.U.F.C. Manager

It's Old Trafford and Home again. In a way the start of this season brings with it something rather different in a number of ways from the start of recent years. As you all know our club has, since the ground at Old Trafford was bomb-damaged around eight years ago, been playing at Maine Road on alternate Saturdays. This position terminated at the end of last season and I am sure all at Old Trafford are grateful to the City club for the use of their ground. This means, of course, that we are playing this season at Old Trafford and whilst conditions are not what the club would like as regards covered accommodation for the main stand I feel sure our supporters will roll up despite this drawback. The only thing I hope for is that the weather behaves itself and we have not too many wet Saturdays! Another point is that we will be playing at home again. Quite a number of people have asked me do I think our boys will play as well at Old Trafford as they did at Maine Road. I really think that once we get settled in there will be an improvement if anything for the players will be playing on the ground they train and practice on and see most days of the week. Anyway, it is back at Old Trafford and back at home again and all the question points will be answered as we go on through the season.

Our Visitors

We have as visitors in our first two home games Bolton Wanderers and West Bromwich Albion. It is always a "Derby" game played in the friendliest spirit against the Wanderers. Again, I am sure we all welcome back the Albion to their rightful sphere in football.

24 AUGUST 1949, v BOLTON WANDERERS

A hugely important – and no doubt emotional – moment for Busby and the club in general, as he spoke of our return to Old Trafford following the three seasons lodging at Maine Road. The Reds rose to the occasion, defeating local rivals Bolton 3-0.

1 MAY 1948, v BLACKBURN ROVERS

There were still two league games to complete following the FA Cup final of 1948, but it provided Busby with an opportunity to thank his Cup-winning team who had just delivered the first silverware of his time in charge, and pay tribute to Blackpool, so gracious in defeat.

WATCHING THE FIELD

By **MATT BUSBY**, *Manager*

There can be few happier men in the country than I at this moment. It was a wonderful thrill when I gained a Cup Winner's medal at Wembley fourteen years ago, but I am sure that all the medals in the world could not have made me happier than when I saw my boys triumph last Saturday.

And what a great game it was! The critics have said it was the best Final for many years and I endorse that. Blackpool went down with flying colours and it must have been a terrific disappointment to them after holding the lead on two occasions to see the Cup slip from their grasp.

Blackpool have my sympathy. They fought magnificently and with scrupulous fairness all the way through. I know exactly how they must feel for I can honestly say that the biggest disappointment for any footballer is to be on the losing side at Wembley. I know this from personal experience.

But I did appreciate the splendid gestures of Joe Smith, Harry Johnston, Stan Mortenson, Stanley Matthews and the rest of the Blackpool team who came into our dressing room to pay tributes to United.

Yes, Blackpool showed sportsmanship both on and off the field, and I know that the players, too, appreciated their action in visiting the dressing room to pay their personal respects.

So we come to the season's end, and I would be failing in my duty if I did not say to all—players, directors, staff, and supporters—"Many thanks for everything."

MATT BUSBY talking . . .

By THE MANAGER, M.U.F.C.

Another season starts to-day. As League champions, Manchester United can anticipate keener games than usual. Every club takes a delight in beating the champions, or cup-holders, so the United players can be sure of even keener competition for season 1952-53.

Our immediate opening programme is as exacting as could be imagined with five away games out of the first eight matches, and including clashes with Arsenal (home and away), a call at Maine-road, and visits to Portsmouth, Derby, and Villa Park. A good start here, and maybe we shall be forgiven for anticipating League honours again coming to Old Trafford!

I think all who saw the United juniors in action last Saturday will appreciate that we have some of the greatest young players in the country. I am not going to individualize, but I do think we can feel delighted with the success of all the junior stars. Here are names with which to conjure, and a few years hence we shall, no doubt, be ready to welcome to-day's juniors as members of our senior side.

Good luck to all the players on the Manchester United books. Play good football, and the results are bound to be favourable!

Stan Pearson on United duty back in 1952

23 AUGUST 1952, v CHELSEA
This column for the opening match of 1952/53 not only gave Busby the opportunity to address the fans as manager of the champions for the first time, but it also provided an entincing glimpse into the future, with the boss mentioning the exceptional crop of youngsters coming through the ranks at United.

21 APRIL 1956, v PORTSMOUTH
Busby's pride in both the first team and reserves winning their respective championships was evident in these notes for the last game of the season against Pompey. The champions signed off with a 1-0 win, thanks to a Dennis Viollet goal, his 20th of the campaign.

MATT BUSBY talking

by THE MANAGER . . . M.U.F.C.

My hearty congratulations to the two senior teams on winning their respective championships. I was not with the first team at Sunderland, missing my second successive game, but I felt that, having already won the League championship and having three of the players in the England side, at Hampden, I should go over to Scotland to see that game. I was very pleased with the display of all the three United players.

We had to make several changes in our teams, both at Roker Park and in the Central League match, at Old Trafford, because of injuries and the international calls, but all's well that ends well, and the two teams were able to get a useful point. It was more than useful in the case of the second team, as it sufficed to give the boys the championship. How they have deserved it! I have had a stack of letters during the season from United supporters praising the young Central League eleven, and it is very gratifying to see how the "gates" have improved. To-day we close down on our senior League fixtures, and only one more record remains: to maintain our unbeaten home record, the only club in the senior League without a home defeat. Well played! My congratulations to you all. I am very proud of your successes.

MATT BUSBY talking

It gives me the very greatest pleasure to be writing in the "United Review" again, and first of all I want to thank all those good people who have sent me their good wishes for a speedy recovery during the past few months.

There were far too many to answer individually and some were anonymous. None the less, those messages of encouragement were a tremendous help in getting me well again.

So we have come to the start of a new season, and a momentous one in the history of the club. Can Manchester United rise once again to the top? I think they can, but we must be prepared to be patient, see how things go, and not hope for the moon to start with!

Photo by courtesy of the Manchester Evening News

It is a coincidence that our visitors in this first match should be Chelsea, managed by my friend Ted Drake.

Chelsea, like United, have placed their faith in youth, and their policy is already paying such rich dividends that before long they may be reaching for the very top themselves.

Players like Jimmy Greaves, Peter Brabrook, Tindall, the Sillett brothers and Cliss have already proved themselves crowd-pulling stars.

I am sure that they will give us a fine game to-day, and I hope that you all have a good season's entertainment.

23 AUGUST 1958, v CHELSEA
Another highly significent day as Busby returned to the Old Trafford dugout six months after Munich. A fine game was indeed to follow, the Reds beating Chelsea 5-2.

28 AUGUST 1963, v IPSWICH TOWN
The return of European football to United's calendar was very important to the boss, as outlined in his notes for the visit of the Suffolk side.

VOLUME XXV No. 1
28th AUGUST, 1963

MATT BUSBY *talking...*

Our F.A. Cup Final victory over Leicester City in May saw us qualify as England's representative in the European Cup Winners' Cup. This is something which will mean a great deal to players and fans alike.

It has always been our aim to provide the best possible football fare for our spectators. In my opinion, clashes against teams from Europe are the caviare, if you like, of a normal season.

Such games as these are invaluable in terms of experience for the players. I feel we can all learn something new from every game we take part in and this is particularly true of matches against Continental clubs.

That there is plenty of room for advancement in such matters as a common interpretation and understanding of the laws of the game there can be little doubt.

Most clubs who play abroad regularly appreciate this point, and I feel sure the powers that be will be giving this matter their early attention. A great deal of good will result when F.I.F.A. tackle this considerable problem in the near future.

This evening, we extend a warm welcome to Ipswich Town, our first visitors of the season. Ipswich have a remarkably good background and I am sure you will join me in wishing them well this winter under manager Mr. Jack Milburn, who has succeeded Alf Ramsey at Portman Road.

OUR COVER PICTURE . . .
Skipper Noel Cantwell is chaired by his team mates after their magnificent F.A. Cup victory at Wembley where they beat Leicester City by three goals to one. The date — 25th May, 1963.
An "Evening News" photo

MATT BUSBY TALKING

This afternoon, it is my very sincere pleasure to welcome my old club, Liverpool, to Old Trafford for this F.A. Charity Shield match, a clash which I hope will prove a fitting curtain-raiser to the new season.

As a former Liverpool player, I am always most anxious to do well against the famous Anfield club and in welcoming them I would like to take this opportunity of congratulating players and staff on their F.A. Cup success of last season and to wish them well in their next venture into Europe.

Everyone connected with the game appreciates the considerable prestige at stake in such tournaments. These matches are international affairs rather than club matches, a factor often lost sight of in the heat of "battle".

Liverpool, like ourselves, have had experience in Europe and will be all the better for it in the anxious months ahead when, for the first time, a Russian club, Dynamo (Kiev) will be competing in the Cup-Winners' Cup.

Today's match will be a useful guide as to prospects for **1965-66**, a year in which club strength will be taxed by increasing international calls as we prepare for the World Cup next summer.

I feel sure we can look forward to an enjoyable clash today and we all hope to hear an Old Trafford roar as well as the famous and so inspiring Mersey Sound, for which Anfield fans are so well-known.

Finally, may I add a personal wish to the supporters of both clubs – this the new season is full of fine football enjoyment and that your particular favourites add lustre to their outstanding reputations at home and abroad.

14 AUGUST 1965, v LIVERPOOL
Winning the title in 1964/65 meant that, as league champions, we hosted FA Cup winners Liverpool at Old Trafford for the Charity Shield curtain-raiser. Busby relished the chance to go up against his old club, who shared the trophy with United after an entertaining 2-2 draw.

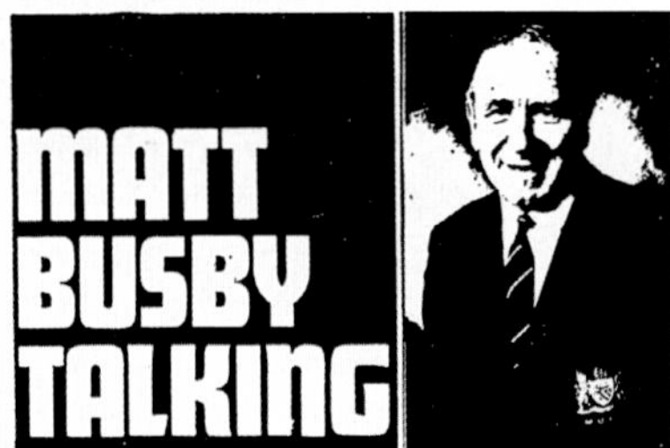

by Sir Matt Busby, C.B.E., *Manager, M.U.F.C.*

The long, long haul to what we have always regarded as the peak of soccer achievement was finally scaled on May 29th this year when, perhaps appropriately at Wembley, we became the first English club to win the much-coveted European Cup.

Our victory over Benfica represented the greatest moment of my life, the finale to eleven years of constant striving to bring the top prize in club football to Old Trafford.

It was a magnificent evening – probably the longest match I have ever sat through! – and our congratulations are due to everyone who played any part in the most thrilling victory in the history of Manchester United.

To our supporters let me say this: None of it would have been possible without your unstinting, uplifting encouragement over the years and particularly last season in bolstering the tremendous efforts of our entire staff . . . players and officials alike.

But we must keep on reminding ourselves that May 29th, **1968** was not the end; the very nature of this great game of ours demands that we must always be forward-looking, always striving to learn from our experiences, bitter and sweet, always ready to face up to the challenge of tomorrow.

And so as we set out on another season of football at home and abroad, we look forward to enjoying the magnificent support we have been fortunate to have had in the past in our constant aim to entertain and to bring the top teams in the world to this great city.

During the close season I received a wonderful personal tribute from Her Majesty, The Queen. Humbly, may I say that I regarded it more as a tribute to the club than to myself but I would like to say how very much I appreciated the very warm reception I received when the news was announced.

Now we must go forward . . . in the League, the F.A. Cup and the European Cup and in the lesser-known competitions that are still vitally important in building for a successful soccer future.

We look forward, as I have said, to meeting all our old friends this winter and we kick off against respected rivals in Everton, a club against whom we have had many memorable matches in the past.

To our visitors from Merseyside we extend a sincere welcome this afternoon and I feel confident in forecasting that we will see a top-class exhibition of football at Old Trafford today.

So join me in giving the two teams a warm welcome in anticipation of a fine beginning to this brand new season, a campaign that promises so much and which will signal the start of a new era in the history of Manchester United.

10 AUGUST 1968, v EVERTON
Not only was the manager able to address the supporters as the boss of England's first European champions at the start of the '68/69 season, he was also doing so as a knight of the realm, following his summer honour bestowed by the Queen – a tribute he shared with everyone involved with the club.

SIR MATT'S COLUMN

by Sir Matt Busby C.B.E., General Manager MUFC

We are now at the start of another new season and I am very glad to welcome you all back to Old Trafford. As you know Wilf McGuinness has taken over the responsibility of team matters and team selection and he will have the full support of the Directors, players and staff. I feel sure he will do a very good job and that the standard of football will continue to be of a high quality. I know I can count upon the continuation of the wonderful support you have given to us for so long and this is the best way you can assist the players to achieve further success.

I feel I must refer to the behaviour of those spectators responsible for the throwing at the Milan goalkeeper during the European Cup Semi-Final last May. This kind of behaviour is not in keeping with the reputation of our great club and I again appeal to all our supporters to help in stamping out incidents of this kind. Manchester United as a club and the vast majority of our spectators have a reputation for being modest in victory and sportsmanlike in defeat. We all know that it is impossible to win every match and when defeat comes we have to give credit to our opponents. In this way we can still gain maximum enjoyment from this great game of ours.

The Board has decided to defer the erection of fences behind the goals being strongly of the opinion that these are not necessary. I again ask for the co-operation of everyone to behave in a proper manner and not to give cause for the subject to arise again. We have confidence in our supporters and ask that you all show by your actions throughout the season that this confidence is not mis-placed.

This evening we begin our home League programme with a visit from old friends and close rivals, Everton, a club steeped in rich tradition and with an enthusiastic, whole hearted following all over the country.

In welcoming you all back to Old Trafford I know you will want to join me in wishing Everton and their supporters the very best of good fortune in 1969/70 as we look forward to a highly entertaining game tonight and one in keeping with standards set by our two clubs in previous meetings over so many years.

Bobby Charlton in 1969/70 - he'd remain an inspiration, regardless of who was manager

13 AUGUST 1969, v EVERTON

Sir Matt's first column of the '69/70 campaign saw him speaking in his new role of general manager, following the appointment of Wilf McGuinness as manager.

24 APRIL 1971, v IPSWICH TOWN

Sir Matt had returned to the dugout for four months following the dismissal of McGuinness, but used his notes for the final home game of the 1970/71 campaign to confirm that a new man would be appointed to take over in the summer.

SIR Matt Busby talking

by Sir Matt Busby C.B.E., General Manager MUFC

FOR THE PAST FEW YEARS UNTIL ARSENAL MADE THEIR PRESENCE KNOWN IN THE LEAGUE CHAMPIONSHIP, THE NORTH HAS RATHER DOMINATED THE QUEST FOR THE TOP HONOURS OF FOOTBALL.

Manchester has in fact been regarded by many people as the capital city of the game and I am proud of Manchester United's contribution over the years towards establishing that reputation.

At the same time I have always had a special regard for playing in London. Whatever the particular importance of the match involved I have always been aware of a special atmosphere in our visits to London.

After all London is the capital of the land and no-one, particularly of my generation, can be unaware of the special standing and tradition of clubs like Arsenal.

One is also conscious of the fact that the crowds are perhaps slightly more cosmopolitan with more critics and students of the game as opposed to simply supporters of the two sides.

Then of course London is the headquarters of the professional critics, the Press, television and radio journalists. You go to London and you go on show to a wider audience than anywhere else in the country.

Perhaps for all these reasons I have liked Manchester United to play well in London and I think over all we have usually managed to do this. Perhaps the players also catch this feeling and tend to try and rise to the occasion. I am sure that proud experienced men like Bobby Charlton, Denis Law and Pat Crerand all have this regard for playing in London.

I know I was very conscious of the fact that our game at Crystal Palace last weekend was my last visit to London as team manager, and not unnaturally I wanted to finish on a high note, perhaps even a game to remember.

When we were two goals down after only 25 minutes play I began to think it would be a game to remember all right . . . for all the wrong reasons!

Happily we pulled round and on the way towards finishing 5-3 winners showed the flair that I have always tried to make a special part of Manchester United.

I have aimed for this because I believe this is not only the kind of football that in the long run achieves success but is the way the spectators want to see the game played.

The team did not disappoint me against Palace; in fact they managed to cram into one game just about all the facets of football ranging from despair to elation.

It was an accurate reflection of my four months back in charge of team affairs. First we had that extremely encouraging run of good League results which lifted us to a respectable place in the First Division and gave us thoughts of Europe again in the Fairs Cup.

Then came a disappointing Easter which set us back and was a blow to our ambitions. But that of course is what football is all about and I have had 25 years of the emotional stress that this way of life involves.

It is the reason why I am ready to make way for a younger man to come and take charge of the team this summer and I wish him well. But as I step aside once more, I shall always cherish the memory of the outstanding flair that I like to associate with Manchester United and which the players showed me so convincingly on my last trip to London as team manager.

PAGE THREE

4 SEPTEMBER 1971, v IPSWICH TOWN
The new man in the Old Trafford hotseat was Frank O'Farrell, the Irishman previously catching the eye as manager of Leicester City. His first two 'home' games in charge were held at Liverpool's Anfield and Stoke City's Victoria Ground as punishment for crowd disturbances, and so his first game at Old Trafford came seven matches into the league season, for the visit of Ipswich Town.

Frank O'Farrell talking

I WAS A PROUD MAN WHEN I WAS APPOINTED MANAGER OF MANCHESTER UNITED. TO A CERTAIN EXTENT I WAS ALSO A WORRIED ONE, BECAUSE I AM VERY CONSCIOUS OF THE HIGH STANDARDS SET AT THIS CLUB FOR SO LONG BY SIR MATT BUSBY.

My task did not seem any easier with the events and disciplinary measures that brought the closure of Old Trafford and meant that the first six competitive games would have to be played away.

And although my football world last season lay in the Second Division with Leicester City, I had inevitably heard disturbing reports of the situation at Old Trafford. Finishing eighth in the First Division and all those cup semi-final appearances did not seem bad to me, but a lot of derogatory things were being said about the team.

The players were said to be temperamental and difficult to manage. In all it appeared I would have my hands full, and for a new manager especially, the sudden tightening up of behaviour by the referees created additional problems.

We felt the full weight of the new policy in our match against Chelsea at Stamford Bridge.

But now the first six matches are over and I am an even prouder manager of Manchester United.

For despite the problems and all the difficulties that were forecast for me with the team, I find I have had nothing but co-operation from everyone concerned. The response from the players has been marvellous. They have responded with hard work and they have responded to the suggestions made by myself and coach Malcolm Musgrove.

I never really doubted the ability at Old Trafford and as far as I am concerned now, I don't doubt any of the other qualities that go towards making a successful football club.

It is early days yet with a long way to go and a great many hard matches ahead. So don't construe this as an attempt to shout the odds about what we are going to accomplish.

At the same time we have completed a difficult first lap and come through with satisfying results. All credit to the lads for the way they have reacted to the challenge of not only the problems I have described but the basic one of a new boss.

Some of the players have known no other manager than Sir Matt, and for a while Wilf McGuinness, in all their football lives. Recent developments must have come as a fundamental change for them.

Every manager's ways are different, but it seems to me that without exception they have made a real effort to adjust and do their part in achieving the harmony between players and coaching staff so necessary if we are going to get anywhere.

For this I am grateful. The players deserve their good start, which while not everything, is so helpful and encouraging towards creating confidence.

A team needs good results in order to develop its full potential. We saw this especially in the way the team played against West Bromwich at Stoke. There was some beautiful football in that match.

I must also say how much we all appreciated the support in that game. I thought there was the right atmosphere at Stoke, something that did not quite catch on at Liverpool for the Arsenal game.

I was also delighted to see that there was hardly any trouble from the unruly element among our fans. For that I am also grateful because this problem of hooliganism is really the only factor that has disturbed and depressed me about coming to Manchester.

We have made a good start on the field of play and if we can eliminate the trouble that marred our opening games, I shall not only be a proud new manager of Manchester United but a happy one!

Tommy DOCHERTY Talking...

Mahager. Manchester United Football Club

FOR ME THERE IS ONLY ONE JOB IN FOOTBALL . . . MANAGER OF MANCHESTER UNITED, AND NOW I HAVE ACHIEVED MY ULTIMATE AMBITION, I AM AT OLD TRAFFORD.

I was happy as manager of Scotland and in that capacity I felt we had got something moving positively towards success in the next World Cup. Very few offers would have tempted me to leave the Scottish job, but when the opportunity of taking over Manchester United arose I had no hesitation.

I had been missing the day to day contact with footballers that is denied to the manager of an international team, but to get the chance of achieving this club life with United was more than I dared hope.

I have always had this love for Manchester United. It started when I was a player and of course my time at Preston brought me close enough to feel the greatness of Old Trafford.

My regard deepened when Matt Busby took charge of the Scotland team and I played for him. I realised why United were so great and were achieving so much. This man has done so much for football, not just for his club, and it is a privilege to follow him.

Some people talk about Sir Matt's great achievements and presence as a director as being some kind of handicap for his successor. Perhaps it's a matter of attitude on the part of the man taking over. For me there is no problem. I regard Sir Matt as an active director as being more of a help than a hindrance and I shall not hesitate to use him if I think he can help with a particular problem.

Sir Matt decided he had had enough of the day to day burden of running a team; but his experience and knowledge has not retired and I assure you it will be of great help in the big battle ahead.

And there is a tough fight ahead of course. I fully realise that although I have achieved a great personal ambition in my appointment as United manager, this is only the beginning! Achieving an ambition might suggest an easing up; far from it. For me it is merely the starting signal for a great deal of hard work to try and bring the success that was the regular hallmark of Manchester United.

It's going to be difficult but it is not impossible and this view is shared by the men I have gathered around me to tackle the first hurdle of retaining our place in the First Division.

My first call went to Tommy Cavanagh. I have known him since we were players together at Preston in 1949 and I helped to get him his appointment with Hull City. He is now our first team trainer.

But don't think this is an old pals' act! Tommy happens to be a terrific motivator of players with the terrible fault of being dedicated to football! He's not a Scot either so don't let me hear too much talk that I'm only interested in people from North of the border.

Pat Crerand is a Scot of course. There's no disguising that fact, but that's not why he was appointed assistant manager. I liked his style as a player and perhaps more to the point now he knows the game and I like his ideas on football. I knew very early on that Pat was the man for the job, but I wanted to work with him first and his appointment followed.

The third staff change was promoting Norman Scholes to chief scout. I didn't know him personally like Pat Crerand and Tommy Cavanagh, but he is held in such high esteem at the club that I felt it only right that he should be given the opportunity. Jimmy Murphy who has been scouting on a part-time basis for the club, will play a slightly more active role.

NOW WITH THE STAFF SETTLED AND NEW PLAYERS ARRIVING WE CAN GET DOWN TO THE MAIN JOB. LET'S ALL GET BUSY, INCLUDING YOU THE FANS WITH YOUR CONTINUED GREAT SUPPORT.

20 JANUARY 1973, v WEST HAM UNITED
O'Farrell's reign lasted just 18 months and the new man in charge – Tommy Docherty – used one of his early columns to admit he had 'achieved my ultimate ambition' by becoming United manager. His new assistant manager, Paddy Crerand, would still be a firm fixture in the pages of *United Review* four decades later!

Farewell to the top flight, but the Reds wouldn't be absent for too long

Welcome back to Old Trafford and our new life in the Second Division. You, the fans, gave us tremendous support in our fight against relegation and I am truly sorry that it did not bring a happier ending.

TOMMY DOCHERTY TALKING

Manager, Manchester United F.C.

But that battle is now history and I just hope that you will stay with us for the big challenge this season to win promotion. I think I can promise you that the staff and players will make every effort to give you more to cheer about this season.

Everyone at Old Trafford is deeply conscious of the debt we owe for your loyal support and it will be our inspiration in the months ahead.

The question I am constantly asked now is whether we shall win back our place in the First Division at the first attempt. I would dearly like to answer that with an unqualified yes, but soccer has a nasty habit of wrecking bold predictions.

So I am not going to tempt providence and say yes of course we will win promotion this season. What I can say is that everyone connected with the club will be working flat out to achieve it. I am also quietly confident because towards the end of last season I saw signs of real progress after a very unsettling period of rebuilding.

What must be remembered is that there were a great many changes that had to be made when I arrived as manager. For instance 34 players have left the club since my appointment; new men have been signed and young players have been brought forward to fill the gaps left by the heavy pruning of the playing staff.

It is very difficult to maintain winning results during extensive changes of this proportion, but now the major part of the upheaval is complete and we can settle down to producing the right blend of team. Man for man I think we can compare with every other team in the Second Division, but of course this is not the whole story. We must capture the right attitude and match the spirit and working rate of our opponents.

This is a hard division, certainly harder to get out of than to fall into. I have worked in the Second Division and know the problems. You have got to decide which teams you can play football against and those which require you to make increased physical effort.

Against some sides it is necessary to run, chase and work, and let the football flow if you can find the time!

It has always been fashionable to try and beat Manchester United. This will be especially so in the Second Division when we meet old friends who have fallen on hard times and when we play new faces anxious to impress against a club with probably the most famous name in the game.

Some of our games on away grounds will be like cup finals for atmosphere and motivated opponents. But I don't see this factor as a necessarily depressing one; it could make us play better ourselves. Our aim must be to match the spirit and aggression of our opponents. If we can ally this to our skill then we will be all right.

With the right attitude from our players, promotion can be won. I brought Chelsea back into the First Division and see no reason why I cannot be equally successful with Manchester United. Things are ticking over again at Old Trafford and I hope you will join us with your support in what I can certainly promise will be an exciting season.

The Chairman in his message today has referred to the people who cause trouble at away matches and I would like them to know that I agree fully with what he has said. We all appreciate the wonderful encouragement our genuine supporters give us at away games but a minority of hangers on, by getting involved in fights and causing damage to property and terrorising innocent people who happen to be in the vicinity, cause irreparable damage to the good name of Manchester United Football Club. I would just like to tell you that the players and myself and everyone at Old Trafford thoroughly deplore the activities of these people and if we had the choice we would prefer that they did not travel to away games if they cannot behave in a proper manner. I repeat, much as we want and appreciate the vocal support, we are prepared to do without this if those who cause the trouble will not think of the good name of the Club first and foremost. So I add my name to that of our Chairman and the players, who join me in saying, 'Behave yourselves and do not drag the Club's name in the mud or STAY AT HOME—WE DON'T WANT YOU'.

IMPORTANT

Please note that all outside vendors have NO club connection.

It has come to the club's notice that unofficial programmes purporting to come from the club are being sold at all away matches. We wish it to be known that these programmes and their vendors have no official standing or connection with Manchester United.

3

24 AUGUST 1974, v MILLWALL

By the time the start of the 1974/75 season had rolled round, the Reds had accepted relegation from the top flight and were adapting to life in Division Two. The Doc promised to repay the fans' loyal support and got off to a great start in this first home match, beating the Lions 4-0 and giving the near-45,000 crowd a glimpse of his side's new swashbuckling, attacking style.

Promotion was the big thing but I must say the championship is very rewarding.

TOMMY DOCHERTY TALKING

Manager, Manchester United F.C.

I am delighted that we shall be going back to the First Division with the title because it is the way Manchester United have tended to do things over the years.

Relegation was a big blow to a club with the pride and achievement of United, and how we would react to the set-back was the key to the future.

I wrote here a fortnight ago that it was the attitude of the players that had made all the difference in the successful promotion campaign. It was top-class and I am glad to see that it has been carried on all the way through to make sure of the title as well as promotion.

We are going back to the First Division as champions and at this stage, we can do nothing more. We have now established ourselves as the best team with a points total that cannot be reached by any rival.

I think we can be proud that we are not just the best in the division because we have taken more points than anyone else; I like to feel that we have proved the outstanding team in terms of the way we have played.

We have always attacked and put the emphasis on skill rather than rely unduly on a tactical formation. In other words we have entertained, which in the last analysis is what it is all about.

For without fans there would not be professional football and while it is easy to preach about the value of open, entertaining football when you have got a good side, it is nevertheless the goal that we should all be aiming for.

I think we can be satisfied on that score at Old Trafford, which is perhaps one of the reasons why we have received such tremendous support both at home and away.

Our attendances are about 5,000 up on last season and this is not just something that has come latterly when it was clear we were going to gain promotion.

The support was there right from the start. In other words our fans came with us into the Second Division.

It is easy enough to follow a winning team, but last season's League average of 42,712 during the fight for our First Division lives was tremendous.

And even when we were doomed for the drop they did not leave us because that was about the figure for our opening few games in the Second Division. Since then, when it became clear we meant business, the crowds have risen to an average of nearly 48,000.

I am sure the gate will be over 50,000 for our final home appearance. I hope so because I want to take this opportunity of speaking to as many of you as possible when I offer a sincere thank you on behalf of the club for your tremendously loyal and encouraging support.

It has definitely been one of the important factors that has spurred the team on in their bid for promotion. The players are always conscious that it is not just the manager they have to please . . . there is a huge following that is entitled to ask for nothing but the best and certainly demand a hundred per cent effort.

We intend to try to express our appreciation from the pitch this afternoon. The players, the directors and the staff want you to know we appreciate the part you have played in the past and will play in the future towards making this fine club strong and successful again.

I would add that we just as earnestly beg you not to let your excitement run away with you. Please do nothing silly or violent because we also want the reputation of our supporters to match the achievement of the players you have supported

The Doc toasts promotion at the first time of asking in 1974/75

26 APRIL 1975, v BLACKPOOL

Eight months later, the Reds had stormed to the title and were looking forward to a coronation party against Blackpool. The home campaign ended how it had began, with a 4-0 win.

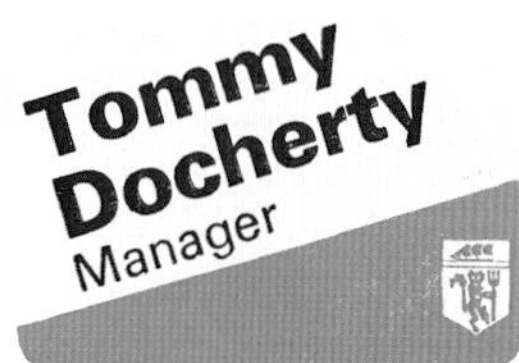

This afternoon's match winds up the season's football at Old Trafford and once again the curtain is coming down on a winter of mixed fortune.

Our big day is still to come with an F.A. Cup final against Liverpool next Saturday at Wembley. It is our chance to win a trophy and see some tangible reward for what I believe is our sound contribution to what is best in the game.

SPORTING SPIRIT

I am thinking of this club's willingness to strive for entertaining football played in the right sporting spirit. Even if we lose at Wembley for the second successive season, it won't change our outlook. At the same time I must admit that it would be nice to see a piece of silverware to prove to people outside that our way is the right way.

It has certainly brought us exciting progress in the F.A. Cup and until the thought of Wembley took the edge off our League games, I think we can claim to have made our mark in the championship race as well.

The most encouraging factor for me in our football this season has been the way we recovered from the bad time just before Christmas. We slipped right down the table and there were those who thought the skid was out of control.

Well I think we showed that although we were having a lean spell we weren't about to fold up. We battled back to fourth place and it is still possible for us to finish in the top six.

It took character on the part of the players to recover, and this is a quality we shall need not only next Saturday but in the seasons to come. It takes character as well as skill to survive the crowded, competitive life of a First Division club in English football.

I think we can claim to have a fair measure of both these ingredients in our present playing staff, which is something that heartens me for the future.

Of course there is plenty of room for improvement and from the football point of view we know there is still a lot of hard work ahead if we are going to continue to make progress.

There have been set-backs, the most heartbreaking of course the injury to Stewart Houston last weekend. As soon as I realised he had wrecked his ankle I lost all interest in the match against Bristol City.

Serious injury of this kind is a calamity for the player involved, but it is especially sad that it should happen on the eve of a Cup final. Stewart played a big part in getting us to Wembley again and I am sorry that he will have to miss the game.

All I can say is that he will have the best of medical care and attention to make sure he makes a full recovery which I hope will be in time for the start of next season.

We also leave this season with another cloud hanging over our heads, the ban on our supporters travelling to away matches. We saw how the restrictions bit deep into our support at Bristol last Saturday, and this state of affairs is going to be with us next season as well.

OUR ONLY HOPE

No time limit has been set, and it is obvious that the Government will impose the ban until such time as they think the hooligan element have learned their lesson.

continued on page 17

3

14 MAY 1977, v ARSENAL

The boss could look ahead to an FA Cup final against Liverpool after this final home game of the season... no-one would have predicted it was to be his final game as United manager at Old Trafford.

Docherty's crowning glory as the Reds beat Liverpool to claim the FA Cup

24 AUGUST 1977, v COVENTRY CITY

The latest man to attempt to bring the glory days back to United was Dave Sexton, who revealed in his first programme notes that he was on the verge of becoming Arsenal manager before he got an offer he couldn't refuse from Old Trafford, Manchester...

3

Dave Sexton
Manager

Manchester United are my kind of team. I suppose there is nothing particularly special about that because they appeal to people all over the country, indeed all over the world.

They are the best supported club in the business and have been for some years. Their name is an international by-word in football circles.

Even as a player and manager who has spent nearly all his career in and around London I was always well aware of the special qualities that go with the name of Manchester United.

PRIDE

So it is with particular pride that I have become manager at Old Trafford and an honour that I shall do my best to justify. I was on the point of joining Arsenal after leaving Queen's Park Rangers, and there is magic in working for the Gunners as well.

But when the vacancy suddenly materialised at Old Trafford it was an opportunity that I felt I could not miss. It was a chance that fired my imagination and I was delighted to be appointed.

It is my first job in the North, but that doesn't worry me. Frontiers at local or even international level don't mean very much to football people. We are travellers and football is a common language.

So I don't anticipate any problems settling in with United. After all there are already a couple of Cockney players at Old Trafford, and what with the Scotsmen and Irishmen around I don't exactly feel a foreigner!

Indeed I have been made to feel very welcome here in the North with friendly greetings from the supporters I have met which as the new boy at Old Trafford I would like to say I appreciate very much.

The question that undoubtedly seems to be in the minds of most of the fans I have spoken to is whether I am going to try and change United's style of play so I would like to take this early opportunity of putting your minds at rest.

I will not be making changes simply for the sake of change. I don't think I am one of those super ego people who must turn everything upside down just to let everyone know who is boss.

I hope I won't be afraid to change things if I feel it is right and necessary because after all I have a job to do and I would be letting the club down if I shirked it.

But United are a successful team with consistency in both Cup and League for the past couple of years. They have achieved this by producing an extremely attractive type of football.

I neither want to spoil the attractive nature of their game nor obviously do I want to do anything that will interrupt the run of success.

On the contrary I want to add something to Manchester United and I feel I may have something to offer after my experience with Queen's Park Rangers, Chelsea and Arsenal among other clubs.

SUCCESSFUL

The basics are clearly good. Tommy Docherty built this side and Tommy Cavanagh has coached them into good football habits. But you never stop learning in this game and there is always a new horizon.

United have evolved a pattern of play that has proved successful and entertaining. I don't want to alter it because it's good. I simply hope to add to it.

As I say, Manchester United are my kind of team, and if you look at the way Queen's Park Rangers play, I think you can see a lot of similarity.

Indeed some of the best games last season were between Manchester United and Queen's Park Rangers. That is perhaps my best credential for becoming manager at Old Trafford.

I shall do my best to uphold the proud traditions of this famous club.

MY VIEW

'. . . I haven't finished yet in the transfer market, though don't get the idea that I am a restless character who can't leave well alone.'

Welcome to Old Trafford for our first home game of the season, though perhaps the greetings should be the other way round. For I am really the new boy at Manchester United, while many of you are supporters of many years standing who have followed the club through the good years and perhaps the not-so-good.

All I can say is that I don't think it will take long to get to know each other because we have a common purpose, which of course is to put Manchester United at the top.

I think we have a few other things in common as well. Although I am the manager I am a fan of football at heart as well, and the last thing I want from my game is to be bored.

So along with my staff (who share my beliefs) and the players, we will be doing our best to entertain you with attacking football. This doesn't mean however, that in some games we may be obliged to defend for 90 minutes.

Football is about competition and we won't be able to dominate all the time. Mind you, we shall have a darned good go, and I think we have pulled off a transfer capture in Frank Stapleton which will enable us to back up those words with action.

I am excited about our attack with Frank alongside Garry Birtles and Steve Coppell. Garry has done well in the pre-season games and I think he will be starting the season with a renewed sense of confidence and purpose.

Steve has not been able to play in all the games because of an ankle injury, but hopefully all three will be playing this afternoon. It may take a week or two for them to develop the right understanding, but I am confident they will hit it off.

Because the signing of Frank Stapleton dragged on for a few weeks and involved a League tribunal, his arrival has tended to overshadow the signing of our other new player. John Gidman slipped quietly into Old Trafford some weeks ago, but don't be fooled by the lack of fuss.

John has settled down well and I think you are going to like the creative qualities he brings to his defensive game and will help us a great deal to improve the attacking level of our team.

In Frank Stapleton I believe we now have the best centre-forward in England, perhaps Europe, and for a fee which will perhaps enable us to continue to strengthen the squad.

I must be careful what I say here because we could be treading on dangerous ground. All I can say at this stage is that Manchester United should have the best players in the game, and that I shall endeavour to bring them here.

I haven't finished yet in the transfer market, though don't get the idea that I am a restless character who can't leave well alone. For instance after one very traumatic period with West Bromwich when four or five players left and we spent heavily on replacements, it was two years before I bought another senior man.

So Mick Brown and I do know how to get down to hard work and develop a team, once we are sure we have got the right make-up. So far I think we have made an excellent start and have improved the squad by 20 per cent. So we are starting with confidence and I hope you are able to share in the sense of excitement that grips me as I look ahead to the challenge of the new season.

11

**31 AUGUST 1981,
v NOTTINGHAM FOREST**

A brighter full-colour look was introduced to the programme around the time of the new incumbent's arrival, the suitably colourful and larger-than life figure of Ron Atkinson.

Frank Stapleton was an early Atkinson venture into the transfer market

One of the most significant transfers in United history as Robbo signs up

**3 OCTOBER 1981,
v WOLVERHAMPTON WANDERERS**

Big Ron used his notes for the visit of Wolves to herald the arrival of his new signing, Bryan Robson, from Atkinson's old club West Brom (with Robbo famously signing his contract on the pitch before the game), as well as mourning the recent passing of the legendary Bill Shankly.

MY VIEW

It's a pleasure to welcome Wolves to Old Trafford and renew links with the Midlands where I spent four exciting years with West Bromwich.

Whether we shall have the pleasure of seeing Britain's two most expensive players in Bryan Robson and Andy Gray in action on the same pitch remains to be seen.

At the time of going to Press we have had an offer for Robson accepted by the Albion, but it requires approval from their board and then we have to talk to the player and all this takes time.

What is certain is that as I said soon after I arrived at Old Trafford, Manchester United with their great following deserve the best players and I shall do my utmost to see that the club gets them.

This is why I pursued Bryan Robson ever since the Albion manager indicated that he would consider selling if the price was right.

I hope we can pull it off because he is a fine player and there is so much ability in this United team that it only requires just a fraction more to see us a very good team indeed.

We have put a very encouraging run together, unbeaten for the last five games. It puts us in a very healthy position on the grid as the championship race hots up.

But as we showed against Leeds, we still looked apprehensive and there was always the fear that they would score on the break.

They didn't manage to score which meant that Frank Stapleton's goal gave us a three-point haul. Incidentally four goals for Frank so far is wonderful.

There is still a lot more in our team that we have yet to show. There is a potential that needs bringing out and perhaps Bryan Robson would be the player to help do it.

But I cannot talk about the future without thinking about the passing of Bill Shankly.

When I was manager at Cambridge he was one of the people I used to phone for a chat and advice. He would always give you his forthright opinion which could be a big help if you were feeling baffled by a problem.

His last visit to Old Trafford was for the Swansea match just a couple of weeks ago. We had a cup of tea and another chat. I think he used to like coming to watch United.

Like many other people both in and out of the game I shall miss him.

Ron Atkinson

3

27 AUGUST 1983, v QUEENS PARK RANGERS

The Reds' manager approached the start of the 1983/84 league campaign in bullish mood, having seen his side lift the FA Cup at the end of the previous season and then defeat champions Liverpool 2-0 in the Charity Shield opener...

The Charity Shield victory helped buoy Atkinson ahead of the 1983/84 campaign

RON ATKINSON Talking

I welcome you all back to Old Trafford for the start of the new League season feeling very excited about the challenge ahead.

After the marvellous experience of winning the FA Cup last May we are naturally very confident about our prospects, particularly as we backed up the Wembley win by finishing third in the League and playing in the Final of the Milk Cup.

Beating Liverpool last Saturday to add the Charity Shield to our success was also a mighty good feeling.

After losing to Liverpool in the Milk Cup at Wembley the lads were particularly anxious to put one over the League Champions and I think we can safely say that in the end we did exactly that!

Naturally we were pleased for our own sakes to bring back a trophy to Old Trafford and then celebrate victory with the Charity Shield, but I can honestly say that every one of us at the club derive just as much satisfaction from knowing that we have been able to express our appreciation for the super support we enjoy at Manchester United in the way that we know you best want.

The trophy cupboard has not exactly been packed in recent years, and yet our fans have continued to make us the best supported team in the country. That's a heavy responsibility when things are not going well, but I can tell you that it makes success much more meaningful when you can bring back a trophy for such great supporters.

So thank you for your backing which helped us to success last season and which we look for again this year in an effort to go what we would all consider one better . . . and win the League Championship.

That will be our aim and I believe we have the staff and players capable of achieving it provided we all apply ourselves with the same dedication and enthusiasm.

The first important conclusion is to rid ourselves of the idea that beating Liverpool last week means we somehow become Champions. I wish it were that easy!

The Charity Shield result could so easily prove to be the worst for the rest of the First Division and the best for Liverpool. The Anfield pride will have been hurt and new manager Joe Fagan won't be too pleased. They could well start their season in angry mood and make us all suffer.

Our problem will be slipping into the idea that we have now arrived at the top and that everything else is a mere formality. I hope the players realise this before results spell it out for them.

Our aim as we great promoted Queens Park Rangers and congratulate them on their success is to start the season with the drive and application that enabled us to win the Cup and beat Liverpool last Saturday.

QPR could well turn out to be the surprise side of the First Division. They have style and we all have to visit that artificial pitch which will make enormous demands, as I saw for myself when our Youth team played there last season.

We must be right on our toes, starting this afternoon, if we are going to keep our name on the honours board.

RON ATKINSON Talking

I think we can safely say that Old Trafford will be buzzing tonight!

There is always something special about European football, particularly when one of the crack teams from the Continent are the visitors.

We were all thrilled to be involved in a match at the fabulous Nou Camp Stadium in Barcelona and we extend a sporting welcome to our opponents this evening.

No doubt our Spanish friends will be in confident mood after establishing a 2-0 victory in the first leg, but we are a long, long way from considering ourselves out of the running to reach the semi-finals of the European Cup Winners' Cup.

The battle in Spain may have been lost, but not the war!

Perhaps I shouldn't use those sort of terms because the first match was not at all warlike. It was competitive of course, but nothing like the cynical approach we met against Valencia in the UEFA Cup last season.

I was most depressed after that game because I felt that the whole point of European competition had been forgotten.

I was particularly sad because it was against the great Spanish side, Real Madrid, that Manchester United really put European football on the map.

The first leg of our quarter-final against Barcelona was played in the old tradition and I hope tonight that we will add further to the spirit that was first responsible for launching the great concept of European competition.

We could do with a touch of the never-say-die tradition from the old days as well, if we are to pull those two goals back. I am thinking of that memorable match 27 years ago when Manchester United came home from Spain after a 5-3 defeat against Bilbao in the quarter-final of the European Cup.

I am sure United supporters won't need reminding about the sterling performance that saw United win 3-0 at Maine Road.

Another of Sir Matt Busby's teams pulled off another remarkable performance in the Cup Winners' Cup 20 years ago when they beat Spurs 4-1 at Old Trafford after losing the first leg 2-0 in London.

So it can be done!

Those were among the outstanding games that set the standards of the time, and tonight we hope to make our own mark in the European theatre that I know means so much to United supporters.

The fans can be a big help to us and we are looking for some great vocal encouragement. We shall need it against a team so experienced in top competition that they have been involved in Europe every season for more than 20 years.

They have played in eight European finals, winning three of them, so they know what the big occasion is all about.

It's possible that under their present manager, Cesar Menotti, they are going to get even better. Certainly they have one of the most experienced and successful managers in the world at their helm.

He was manager of the Argentinian national team from 1975 until 1982. I well remember meeting him in London when he was with his country's team. You could sense he was a man of tremendous presence, once you had penetrated the cigarette smoke.

It was his chain-smoking with Argentina during the World Cup of 1978 that he will be remembered by millions of television viewers.

He is a character all right and a man of world stature. Nevertheless we hope to have him puffing anxiously on a few more cigarettes before we have finished tonight's match!

The official programme of Manchester United Football Club plc.
Edited by Ken Ramsden
Club statistics by Cliff Butler
Photography supplied by Manchester United Supporters Club
Printed by Hemmings & Capey (Leicester) Ltd.
Voted First Division Programme of the Year 1982-83 by the Football Programme Directory

Voted 'Best First Division Programme 1983-84' by Programme Monthly, the leading magázine for collectors of football matchday programmes, with a UK circulation in excess of 1,500. Magazine No. 36, containing all this season's programme awards is available, price 50p plus 16p sae from:
35 Gowing Road, Mulbarton, Norwich NR14 8AT.

21 MARCH 1984, v BARCELONA

A memorable night in United's history as we aimed to chase down Barcelona's first-leg lead in the European Cup Winners' Cup quarter-final decider. 'We could do with a touch of the never-say-die tradition from the old days if we are to pull those two goals back,' said Big Ron, prophetically.

RON ATKINSON

Looks forward to the new season

I welcome you back to Old Trafford this season at an anxious and worrying time for football.

Last season ended on such a tragic note, both home and abroad, with the terrible fire at Bradford City and the horror of events in Brussels at the European Cup Final between Liverpool and Juventus.

Obviously those kind of disasters cannot simply be shrugged off; it's only to be expected that everyone is now taking a long, hard look at the game of professional football.

The loss of life was so appalling on both occasions that we have inevitably come under the scrutiny of the Government as well.

Nevertheless it is only right that everyone connected with football should take a good, hard look at the game and resolve to work on the problems troubling us.

I believe the greatest contribution, and one that can be made by everyone from chairman to apprentice player, is to think about standards and how we apply ourselves to our jobs.

I know that as manager at the

sharp end and contact point with the public that I have a special responsibility in this critical season to work for the good of football as well as for the benefit of Manchester United.

STANDARDS

I know that the players are also well aware that the eyes of a critical outside world are on us; you may have read that our captain, Bryan Robson, is at the forefront of a drive to try and curb the small but troublesome hooligan element.

I won't find it difficult either to insist that our team continues to set a good example in terms of behaviour and standards both on and off the pitch.

Without being too smug, I believe that for some time Manchester United have been pointing the way ahead. Years ago the club took positive steps to shake off the unruly element, not easy when you have the biggest crowds in the game.

It wasn't popular either when we refused to take our own supporters to our away games in Europe; but we did it and I think that thanks to excellent Police work and the facilities developed at Old Trafford our ground is a safe place.

We will continue to work along those lines and I remain optimistic about the future of football.

I believe the game WILL recover . . . mainly because at the end of the day there is no finer entertainment than soccer. Other sports have their moments, but with the possible exception of the Olympics, which have a rarity value, nothing can compare with football for appeal.

17 AUGUST 1985, v ASTON VILLA

Atkinson sounded a sombre note in the first notes of the '85/86 season, but a mood of positivity was soon to sweep Old Trafford, with the Reds winning the first 10 league games in a row.

Robson was a key figure for Atkinson, although injuries restricted his games

United's inconsistent form in 1986 wasn't helping Atkinson's prospects as boss

1 NOVEMBER 1986, v COVENTRY CITY

With United at the wrong end of the Division One table the pressure was building on Atkinson, but in his programme notes he remained openly defiant that results would soon improve. Sadly, a 1-1 draw with the Sky Blues didn't help his cause and following a heavy midweek defeat at Southampton (1-4) he was replaced as United manager.

RON ATKINSON

It was maddening to find victory slipping through our fingers at Maine Road on Sunday.

The top five teams all lost, and it's on that kind of occasion when you want to win and narrow the gap.

But we had to be content with a 1-1 draw and we are still stuck in the basement, though hopefully not for much longer.

I think we are making steady improvement, and though disappointed with the result at Maine Road, we were at least able to complete October unbeaten in the League.

We drew at Nottingham Forest at the start of the month and finished with another draw sandwiching a couple of wins.

So it was not a bad month's work, especially considering our start to the season.

Certainly eight points from a possible 12 is better form than our League position would suggest! So we are confident that we will soon pull away and mount a serious challenge at the top end of the table.

An away derby was always going to be difficult, for while City are also struggling near the foot of the division, we knew they would raise their game for a tussle with their neighbours.

There was too much local prestige at stake for it to be otherwise, and new manager Jimmy Frizzell must have been delighted by the response of his players.

His new signings all did well, not least our recent export, John Gidman. Imre Varadi and Tony Grealish were also in top gear, and if they can all maintain the form they showed against us, City, too, will not be languishing in their present position for very much longer.

Overall I thought we handled City's pressure quite well.

They were the home side and they really came at us and gave us very little chance to settle.

I was a little dismayed at the way we let them in for Mick McCarthy's equaliser, and we were indebted to Chris Turner for a couple of particularly fine saves.

But we also created chances, and while a draw was probably a fair reflection of the play, I felt we had our moments. So I was not at all disheartened, and I feel sure that if we can maintain our recent momentum through November, we will soon begin to climb.

Mind you, it won't be easy against Coventry this afternoon. The Sky Blues flirted with relegation last season and we were able to notch a League double over them, winning 2-0 here and 3-1 away.

The game at Old Trafford was memorable for Jesper Olsen scoring both the goals.

But Coventry look an improved team this season. They picked up a very useful 2-2 draw at Sheffield Wednesday last weekend, and Hillsborough is never an easy place, as we know to our own cost.

They sit sixth in the League, and if they had taken full points last Saturday they could have been up in third place.

That's an indication of just how well they are going at the moment.

We have a couple of away trips after today's fixture, so it is important that we make home advantage count.

ALEX FERGUSON

Taking over a club of the magnitude of Manchester United is an awesome prospect. But ultimately a football club is a football club and I shall simply try to run things at Old Trafford in what I believe to be the right way.

I am not really interested in what has happened here in the past. I don't mean any disrespect to the great achievements of Manchester United over the years.

It's simply that now there is only one way to go, and that is forward.

The aim at this club must clearly be to win the championship. That is the only real way to lay the ghosts of the past. We must not allow a club of this stature to reach a quarter of a century without a League title on the honours board.

It quickly follows that I only want players here who are determined to achieve this for the club and for themselves.

Straight away they must rid themselves of any negative thoughts that it can't be done.

I am only interested in players who really want to play for Manchester United, and who, like me, are bad losers.

There always has to be a starting point, and I see the championship as the basis for Manchester United's future.

Success has a snowball effect as I found at Aberdeen when some people mistakenly thought that our first championship was a flash in the pan.

Belief and confidence are very important, and instilling the right outlook will be my first priority.

It's not something that can be built overnight, and it could take a few months before I can create a true relationship with the players.

But that is what I shall work towards and I am going to love every minute of it here.

There are so many things about Manchester United, not least the tremendous support for the club. Our average crowd at Pittodrie was 12,000, so I don't need to spell out what the huge audiences at Old Trafford mean to me.

The reputation of United's support is legendary. A man is very fortunate if he gets the chance to manage Manchester United in his lifetime and I can assure you that I have no intention of wasting my opportunity.

It's something that happens to very few people and I make no secret of the fact that the challenge excites me. It's very stimulating, and that's putting it mildly.

To greet you this afternoon for my first game at Old Trafford as manager is a special pleasure, and hopefully we can build on what we learned at Norwich last week.

Our performance at Carrow Road, though only a draw, convinced me that there is nothing seriously wrong with Manchester United.

The most important aspect was that there was a willingness and an appetite to play. The team perhaps wants some direction, but they will be alright.

I know we can depend on your full support and I look forward to meeting you this afternoon.

Alex Ferguson

22 NOVEMBER 1986, v QUEENS PARK RANGERS

The dawn of a new era. With Ron Atkinson sacked following a poor start to the 1986/87 season, this firebrand Scot who had been a huge success with Aberdeen had been tempted south of the border. 'There is only one way to go, and that is forward,' he wrote on the eve of his first home match, a 1-0 league win.

MANAGER'S VIEW . . .

I guess we all feel a lot happier as we return to League duty against Derby County this afternoon.
What a difference a result makes, particularly when it is in the third round of the FA Cup against a good team like Nottingham Forest. Everyone connected with Manchester United must feel a tremendous sense of relief, not least our supporters who must have wondered how much longer they had to wait for a win.
Obviously I was delighted to win at Nottingham Forest, not least for the sake of the fans who have stuck with us through the dry run and I must first express our appreciation.
For a while some sections of the media have been predicting doom and gloom for us, and indeed there was not a lot for the most loyal of supporters to be happy about, we had a hard core who never wavered.
I am thinking of the tremendous crowd who were in the freezing cold at Wimbledon and then the following which must have numbered nearly 7,000 who went over to Forest despite all the forecasts which had us fingered for defeat.
The fans were terrific right through the goalless first half and stayed right behind the team because I think it was crystal clear that we had people out there proud to wear the United jersey and determined to make it count.
Then when young Mark Robins gave us our goal they didn't let up with their encouragement. I think the lads inspired the fans who in turn inspired the players when we were under the cosh at the end and Forest were flinging everything at us.
The chemistry was terrific. Manchester United are an inspirational club, particularly in the Cup, but when things don't go right there can be a great backlash of depression.
But, as I say, our fans stuck with us and we were able to secure a very good result.
The attitude of the players was also first-class, and if I had to pick out a single factor for the success I think it would be the approach of the team to the tie. We were positive, and though playing away from home did not sit back.
We kept a lot of possession, defended well and broke dangerously. I think we were always a threat to them. It was never going to be easy after all sorts of criticism and dire predictions, but the players handled it magnificently.
The last 15 minutes put a few years on me, and perhaps we enjoyed a few breaks, but I don't think I need apologise for that because we have had plenty of tough moments lately when we have played well without getting wins.
So now when it really counted we have confounded the critics and though playing away from home cannot complain about a draw against Hereford, a Fourth Division team.
There is always the risk of an upset but it is up to us to play to our ability and make more progress. Indeed our priority now must be to cash in on our breakthrough and make sure that we get some consistency into our football.
One good Cup win doesn't make a season, and we have to get down to this problem of reaching the heights in one match only to fall away in the next.
We have done this once or twice this season and it's not good enough. I think the players realise it and will be on their guard today when they face Derby County, a team who on their day can beat the best. Add to that the fact that we have lost our last two games with them makes it quite clear that we have a big job on our hands.
But then with our fans behind us again I feel that we can build on our Cup success and start to climb back up the table.

13 JANUARY 1990, v DERBY COUNTY

For this league visit of the Rams, Ferguson used his programme notes to reflect on the recent FA Cup third-round win over Nottingham Forest, a result that would prove to be a springboard for greater success to come.

Lee Martin was the goalscoring hero as Ferguson claimed his first silverware

25 AUGUST 1990, v COVENTRY CITY

With the FA Cup back in the Old Trafford trophy room, Ferguson set about planning for even greater successes. 'I see the Cup as an important step in the development of the club,' he wrote. 'It will help the players acquire more belief in themselves and encourage them to realise their full potential.'

ALEX FERGUSON

Welcome to Old Trafford and if you are just half as excited as me then you will be itching for the new season to get under way.
Every manager approaches a fresh campaign with high hopes and I am no exception. For some it will be a fool's paradise, but not I am sure for Manchester United.
I am well satisfied with our pre-season preparation. Last year we asked a lot of the players when we took them to Japan. It was something we had to do because our sponsors are there, but at the same it was exhausting.
This time we had a less demanding but nevertheless extremely useful tour round Ireland, which also enabled us to meet a great many fans from one of the strongholds of support for Manchester United. Then we came home to face two harder games to lift us to the kind of level we must expect this afternoon from Coventry City. Glasgow Rangers gave us a good work-out and reminded us that we need to improve in certain areas, even if we did emerge 1-0 winners.
Wembley was a great day out again and I thought that taking everything into account a 1-1 draw was a fair result. We scored a good goal and I'll refrain from commenting on their penalty!
Liverpool are always a good test and a yardstick. I was pleased with our performance in many respects, though again it was an interesting exercise because the champions revealed one or two areas we need to work on.
That is what pre-season preparation is all about of course. You can never be sure you have got it right until the League competition actually starts, but I can tell you that the feeling in the camp is that we believe we can make a serious challenge for honours this season.
Winning the FA Cup last May was an important achievement. Most importantly it gave our supporters some return for their loyalty and patience and there is nothing to compare with winning a trophy.
But deeper than that I see the Cup as an important step in the development of the club. What it will particularly do is help the players acquire more belief in themselves.
It will encourage them to realise their full potential and express themselves in a more positive way.
For this team is still at the developing stage. We had five new players last season plus Mark Robins forcing his way into contention.
They added up to a lot of talented individuals, but I am well aware that we have yet to emerge as a team in the true meaning of the word.
We are capable of doing well in cup competitions, but it takes a well-rooted team to produce the kind of consistency that wins the League championship. That is the aim which is our target now and the priority is to find a better blend capable of real sustained success.
You will see a few changes but on the field of play with a sweeper system which I believe we are ready to take on board. Hopefully Bryan Robson will be back soon to control it at the back.
Meanwhile we hope for a good start this afternoon and I would like to take this opportunity to wish everyone a good football season.

ALEX FERGUSON

It is with great pride that we greet you this evening for our final match of the season.

To win in Europe was so special that I find it difficult to express my feelings. I think we have all been on cloud nine since our sterling victory in Rotterdam.

They say we had an easy route to the final of the European Cup Winners' Cup, and I wouldn't argue unduly with that, but we can look anyone in the eye now.

Football clubs just don't come any bigger than Barcelona and no-one can say we are lucky now. We met the best at Feyernoord and we beat them.

We have written another chapter of glorious history for the club and the players and staff can feel justifiably proud of their achievement.

To reach two Cup finals and finish in a challenging position in the League represents a satisfactory progress and has given us a solid platform for next season.

Tonight's game is our 60th competitive match of the season, and it is more for a considerable number of our players involved in international football.

So perhaps we are all due a break, and I include the fans in that, so that we can recharge our batteries in readiness for the next campaign. You see, I am already looking forward to August because I cannot conceal my excitement for the future of Manchester United.

I feel this is the dawn of a new era at Old Trafford and that we have steadily climbed into a position of striking out for the Championship.

It really is a mystery why this Club has endured 24 years without the title. There have been some close seasons. Indeed I was more than pleased with our runners-up place in my first full season as manager at Old Trafford.

Unfortunately that team, in my view, had gone to the limit of its capability and I had to make some sweeping changes. Inevitably we lost a little ground while new signings settled in and we coped with some savage set-backs on the injury front.

Eventually we picked up again and the FA Cup last May was the first evidence of an emerging team. This season we have gone up another notch and while it is always foolish in football to start shouting your head off about what you are going to do, I nevertheless will be approaching the future in a confident, positive manner.

With just one or two notable exceptions, we have an extremely young squad with players who have yet to deliver their full potential.

Arsenal have already arrived and I congratulate them on their second Championship win in three years. You can be assured that Graeme Souness will be ironing out Liverpool's problems and there will be plenty of ambitious clubs on the scene next season.

Our neighbours across at Maine Road are coming up fast while Crystal Palace have proved the shock side finishing in third place.

Spurs and Nottingham Forest showed their possibilities at Wembley on Saturday in the final of the FA Cup and will hope to translate their success into League football next season.

The challenge has never been wider, but that is not a bad thing from our point of view as we aim for even more consistency in our football.

Part of the Manchester United mentality inbuilt in the club seems to be that we can beat the best and lose to the worst. We must rid ourselves of that second bit which has hindered our efforts over the years.

I feel we are slowly doing so, though, and with the help of our magnificent supporters we shall continue to progress.

The warmth of the welcome home from Rotterdam was unbelievable and I would like to take this opportunity to thank all our fans for their truly great support throughout a long season.

Finally, a word of appreciation to Tottenham, their Directors and Terry Venables who so readily agreed to ease our fixture congestion by allowing us to play them tonight. It was a sporting gesture we won't forget as we close a memorable and exciting season.

20 MAY 1991, v TOTTENHAM HOTSPUR

A proud moment for Ferguson, who entered the final league match of 1990/91 with Spurs fresh from our Cup Winners' Cup triumph over Barça.

Ferguson takes the acclaim after the thrilling victory over Barcelona in Rotterdam in May 1991

2 MAY 1992, v TOTTENHAM HOTSPUR

A column filled with regret and sadness as the boss faces up to seeing his title dreams vanish at the tail end of the 1991/92 season, but also optimism and belief. 'We are determined we won't let you down again,' he wrote. 'We are going to rise again.'

United's title dreams were ended at Anfield in 1992

A MESSAGE FROM THE MANAGER

Alex Ferguson

One gets a lot of disappointments in life.

Every Saturday the supporters of perhaps half the football clubs in the country end up disappointed with their team's results. It's the nature of the game, indeed of all sport.

Normally you ride through it and think better luck next time.

Now and again, though, comes a setback which doesn't just numb you for a little while but hits you straight between the eyes and leaves a vacuum in your life, a void which at the time seems inescapable.

You wonder how you are going to get out of it and how long it will take to repair the damage.

I guess I have been down that road twice, once as a player and now as manager of Manchester United with the bitter disappointment of seeming to have the League championship in our grasp only to lose it at the death. And death is just about how I felt after seeing the title finally slip away at Liverpool last Sunday.

So I can fully understand how our fans felt going into work on the Monday morning after losing at Anfield of all places.

It cannot have been easy for them and you all have my sympathy on that score.

All I can say is that we tried our hardest and that God works in mysterious ways. Maybe this is the final lesson for us, the ultimate experience in humility and a reminder to our younger players of how it feels to lose.

At the moment I must confess that my overwhelming mood has been that I have let the fans down, betrayed them almost and my main concern is to find a way of repaying you, our supporters, who have been quite marvellous all season.

I have talked before about that terrific response we got at Queens Park Rangers and how I wanted to shake everyone by the hand. Now I wish I had because the encouragement given to us has been unbelievable.

With that very much in mind I know we will rid ourselves of this guilt feeling because it would be destructive to wallow in that kind of misery.

I just know that however difficult it has looked during this week we will find a way of rising again to meet the challenge.

I hope you all understand how we have been feeling. The thing is that we must not allow ourselves to think about the title failure over so many years as a curse.

We must not sink into a trough of believing that the world is against us because that way lies the thought that it is possible we will give in and I assure you that would be the very last thing.

If you give in once you will always give in and that is not going to happen at Manchester United. Maybe all the players riding high on the success of the last couple of years - and we musn't forget we have had our moments - will appreciate better the bitterness of defeat.

The experience could make them better men and true players of Manchester United. It might just be the final lesson creating a real team in the fullest meaning of the word.

Thank you for your support. We are determined we won't let you down again. We are going to rise again. The traditions built by Sir Matt Busby will not be allowed to waste. We are going to show we are bigger than that.

Sir Matt created the foundations of this place and produced a host of exciting players. We have their successors at the club right now and tomorrow at Old Trafford you will see one of the young men who have graced the pitch here.

We will be playing Everton in a testimonial for Norman Whiteside and I hope you will support him as a final gesture to the season that Manchester United can take defeat in the right spirit and come back all the stronger.

Alex Ferguson was talking to David Meek

6 DECEMBER 1992, v MANCHESTER CITY

The gaffer welcomed a new face to Old Trafford, as recent signing Eric Cantona prepared to make his debut in the 127th Manchester derby.

Ferguson professed himself pleased with his new signing from across the Pennines...

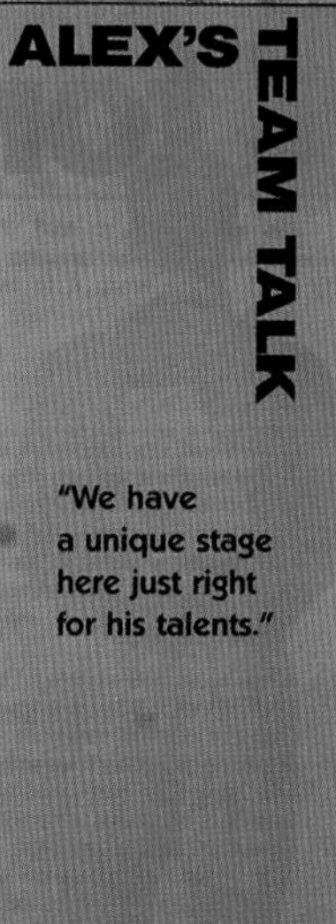

ERIC CANTONA is a highly experienced French international footballer who has been around, but I think we will be introducing him to something different when we entertain Manchester City here at Old Trafford this afternoon.

A Manchester derby is something special and I am sure Eric will savour the electric atmosphere and enjoy himself.

In fact I know he will like it because he is a great entertainer with a feel for the game. The reason why I am more confident about the success of this transfer than is being expressed in some quarters is that Manchester United are tailor made for a player of this Frenchman's temperament.

They don't call Old Trafford a theatre of dreams for nothing. We have a unique stage here just right for his talents.

People are worried about his temperament and a lot of the critics have been looking at the player's latest move with a very negative attitude.

I know he has had his moments in the past, but perhaps he has never been at a club big enough to cope with his particular character.

I believe he is smart enough and intelligent enough to realise that he is now at a club which can satisfy him emotionally and that it is more than worth his while to give of his very best because the satisfaction he will draw in return will be boundless.

I don't mind him having temperament. I like my players to feel passionately and care about the game and their club. Football and Manchester United are very important to me and I find nothing wrong with my players enjoying equally strong views.

It's no problem for me. This is an open club and I told Eric at our first meeting that I would always be honest with him, as I hope he will be with me. I'm not interested in all the tittle-tattle that has been flying about.

That's all in the past anyway and there are always two sides to everything. What concerns me is right now. As I say I hope he settles and enjoys himself because I can promise him that playing for Manchester United is an experience he will never forget.

We are all different and there have been many players with what people call temperament who have played for this club . . . and who have distinguished themselves. I am certain Eric Cantona will be no exception.

I know the fans will give him a warm welcome because there is a tradition at Old Trafford for the kind of football he plays.

I should add at this stage that writing early in the week makes it impossible for me to be absolutely sure of Eric's role against City. Certainly he will be involved but I have to bear in mind the goals our resident strikers have started to score and how things went in the game against Benfica in Lisbon in midweek.

What I do know was that I had to get another striker in because it is obvious that long term we have not scored enough goals to keep us in the championship frame.

Enough became enough. I had to create a competitive edge up front again. I did it with Dion Dublin of course but unhappily he was injured almost straight away.

Perhaps I should have moved immediately to make another signing, but at least we have got a player now who I know is going to make an important contribution.

I only sign players who are keen to join us and I was delighted when Eric did not hesitate to take the opportunity offered to him. He didn't wish to talk to anyone else or try to bounce other clubs off us. He was as keen as us to agree the move.

He is joining a big club with the biggest crowds. It's all made for him.

ALEX FERGUSON'S TEAM TALK

"I hope you all enjoy your summer..."

NOW it's the turn of our youngsters to take centre stage as we welcome Leeds United to Old Trafford for the first leg of the FA Youth Cup final

I suppose that winning the championship after a gap of 26 years has dominated all our thoughts this past week. It's the pinnacle of achievements and the celebrations have been joyously shared by players and supporters alike, not to mention the manager and his staff and directors!

But we come to an event this evening which in its way is just as important, because what we see on parade is the future of Manchester United.

I would like to congratulate the boys on reaching the final as they defend the crown they won so handsomely last season, and I wish both teams the best of luck in what promises to be an entertaining match.

Leeds have a good team, the result of Howard Wilkinson taking stock some time ago of his youth set-up at Elland Road, just as I did soon after my arrival at Old Trafford.

They are building an organisation and system to challenge us, as I am sure we shall see tonight and in the second leg in Leeds on Thursday.

Exceptionally gifted

But it will take a couple of very good performances by Leeds to stop our team who are an exceptionally gifted group of boys. I have never known their like before. They stand apart in my experience as a manager and play with a great sense of team without deserting their individual ability.

They show great composure and patience on the ball and have had a fine couple of years reflected in last season's success in the competition as well as winning this year's Lancashire League trophy and the Lancashire FA Youth Cup

They are being recognised internationally with six of them currently in England's Under-18 squad and the bonus is that they are a bunch of pleasant, well disciplined boys who will be able to handle success in professional football.

Eric Harrison and his staff have instilled good habits and brought them through to the point where they are beginning to knock on the senior door. I certainly have them very much in mind as I review our transfer policy because while we might need one or two experienced players to cope with selection for the European Cup I certainly don't want to shut the door on their careers.

I saw half a dozen of them in the tunnel immediately after we had beaten Blackburn and we had been presented with the Premier League championship and I asked how many would be helping me win it again in a year or two's time.

Euphoria

I am sure that if they ever need inspiration along what can be a hard road at times then they can think back to the euphoria of that wonderful celebration last Monday night.

Incidentally let me thank our supporters for the splendid way they co-operated by resisting the temptation to invade the pitch. With everyone staying in their places it meant we could all join in together for the presentation and walk round the pitch to say thank you for all the support we have enjoyed this season.

It was a wonderful climax to a historic year as we wait now for our super youth team to do their very best to put the icing on the cake!

I hope you all enjoy your summer and that we have given you enough happy memories to keep you going until we all meet again at this magnificent stadium for next season's excitements!

10 MAY 1993, YOUTH TEAM v LEEDS UNITED

Ferguson used the pages of the Youth Cup final first-leg programme for the visit of Leeds United to celebrate the first-team's inaugural Premier League triumph, which had been sealed the previous week, making reference to the 'celebrations that [have] been joyously shared by players and supporters alike!'.

The Manager

Firstly let me welcome you all back to Old Trafford for what will undoubtedly be a challenging but exciting season.

It's been a great summer, cherishing and celebrating that precious League championship which I know means such a lot to club and supporters alike.

Winning the elusive title after 26 years takes pressure off the club and eases the tension for the players who inevitably have had to shoulder the burden of why it has taken a club like Manchester United so long to find the consistency needed to win the League.

It is extra satisfying for me and the present-day players after the previous year's near-miss and the feeling that we had the trophy in our grasp only to drop it at the last moment.

The players have nothing to prove in that area, but of course there are other fields to conquer, and indeed wouldn't it be a fantastic achievement to keep the championship trophy?

So while nothing can take away the pride and satisfaction of becoming champions, we still have to lock it away in the memory cupboard, because everything is starting again. We have zero points in the League and we are back to square one for the Cup competitions.

In some ways the confidence that springs from winning the championship will help us. The albatross is no longer on our shoulders and the players know that whatever happens they have written a powerful chapter in the history of the club, but let's be under no illusion, clubs have always raised their game against us, and it will be even more so now as they strive to knock off our crown.

So it all comes down to what the players want from their careers now. Will they feel they have done enough, or do they want more?

I ask the question because it is important, but I would be very shocked and disappointed if the answer is anything but a burning determination to use the championship as a springboard for more success.

I know that I am certainly not prepared to settle for the easy life, and I don't think for one minute that the players have that kind of approach in their minds either. I am sure they want the challenge of last season and the thrill of coming out on top.

"There is a title to retain and the European Cup to be won"

It's very fitting that Benfica should be our visitors tonight, not only to celebrate the 25th anniversary of winning the European Cup in 1968, but to remind our present League champions that they still haven't matched the old glory days of Sir Matt Busby.

There is still the European Cup to be won, and when they look at our distinguished Portuguese visitors and see the United team of 1968 in the stands, they will know what is required of them now!

I would like to extend a very warm welcome indeed to our visitors and hope that they enjoy their stay in England as well as share in what I am sure will be a worthy and entertaining match.

I can think of no more appropriate opposition to bring up the curtain at Old Trafford.

Alex Ferguson

31 JULY 1993, v BENFICA

In an approach that would become his trademark, Ferguson used his notes for a pre-season friendly with Benfica at the start of United's first term as reigning Premier League champions to reset the club's ambition for more success, and use that first title as a launchpad for glory...

League champions again, but Ferguson was already looking forward to the next test

8 MAY 1994, v COVENTRY CITY

With a second title wrapped up with a game to spare, the boss was looking forward to an FA Cup final date with Chelsea and the chance to secure the club's first Double...

I must offer a doubly warm welcome to Coventry today after the favour they did us this week!

We are not too proud to accept any help that comes our way and of course it was their win over Blackburn that finally brought us the Championship again.

Of course their aim wasn't really to try and make Champions of us. They were playing for their own pride and satisfaction, just as they will be this afternoon.

And for the same reasons we can't be resting on our laurels. We would like to finish our home programme on a high note and play like Champions as a tribute to our marvellous support.

I want to acknowledge the really serious help we have had from our fans this season. Whenever the tickets have been available our supporters have travelled and given us marvellous encouragement at away fixtures.

Then when we had a bit of a wobble a few weeks ago for Blackburn to close the gap our fans stayed with us to give us the final shove over the finishing line.

It goes without saying that the players have done magnificently. During the short spell when we lost a couple of games at Blackburn and Wimbledon there was a lot of media talk about losing our "bottle".

Then when Blackburn faltered it was probably the same people who accused Rovers of lacking bottle. I find that expression unacceptable and indeed an insult to all players.

Players care about winning, they seek success for themselves and for their supporters, and when they lose it is probably because the other team have done slightly better or had the breaks. It is nothing to do with bottle.

I think the determination and commitment of our players has never wavered. They have lost at times, but not because their courage went or anything like that.

Exactly the same with Blackburn who I think have had a brilliant season. The way they closed the gap on us was quite superb and the fact that we were neck and neck for a spell is a tribute to their great tenacity.

They made a great challenge at the end, and if fact I think it worked for us because it kept an edge on our play which saw us produce some excellent performances at Ipswich, Leeds and against Manchester City.

The real break that worked for us was drawing at Wembley in the FA Cup semi-final against Oldham. Everyone immediately assumed that the replay gave us an extra fixture to squeeze in which we might find draining.

But I worked on the players to point out that the postponement of the Leeds fixture did, in fact, provide us with a more evenly spaced programme of League games.

It also had the advantage of giving Eric Cantona an extra League mach for us because the Cup replay absorbed one game of his five-match suspension.

I wouldn't have liked him to have gone back cold to Elland Road for his first match after the ban. As it was he scored twice in the 'Derby' and played well at Leeds so we did get a break there. We were always waiting for his return because he has been a key player for us in this season's Championship, as indeed he was last season.

Now after this afternoon's match we have the FA Cup Final against Chelsea to look forward to when we will be doing our best to bring off a League and Cup double.

The fact that we have got the League should help us because I think the players will be more relaxed and able to express themselves more freely. I know they will have a real crack at it and hopefully create a little more history for Manchester United by completing the first double; a feat which I think we are all agreed should be dedicated to the memory of Sir Matt Busby in the year which saw the great man leave us.

Alex Ferguson

ighlights of our
me back to the days
zled by the major

i couple of hours
mosphere in
heroes of football
ntracht Frankfurt and

he opportunity to see
s catching glimpses
ering to contemplate
your own ground.
: last World Cup are
o and Stoichkov and
ment just as much as

we put that kind of
ist we do in the
hat we have our own
e beat Johan Cruyff
nal of the European
jo.
lieving that we are
it them into
em carefully and
elona have three
they can be beaten if
we have our fans
g the team to play to

irday that we are
pporters tonight
he difference. As I

The Villa supporters roared their men home and I would like to think that our Old Trafford followers will do the same for us tonight.
I think you will find our players in the right frame of mind and worthy of encouragement. We have people like Paul Ince and Mark Hughes longing for the kind of platform they will enjoy tonight as well as our other internationals like Andrei Kanchelskis and Peter Schmeichel who will be bringing their experience of the top level to bear on this match.
We are all ready for it. The UEFA foreigner rule and limited runs in European competitions of late have restricted the players' education in Europe, but they are learning.
For instance I thought we handled the game in Galatasaray last month much better than the previous season against them in Turkey and we have, in fact, had the best return in our group with three points from the draw in Istanbul and the home win against Gothenburg.
Tonight is obviously a key game for qualification and I know we can perhaps expect a surprise or two from Johan Cruyff who is a great tactician. It is one of the things I enjoy as a manager at this level, pitting your wits against a rival manager you know is a born strategist.
We are all in fact involved tonight - players of course, the managers and most importantly you the fans who can prove the deciding factor. So let's hear it for the Reds tonight please!

Alex Ferguson

19 OCTOBER 1994, v BARCELONA
The United manager was excited to welcome some of the stars of the global game to Old Trafford in the 1994/95 Champions League group stage, not to mention the prospect of once again pitting his wits against 'born strategist' Johan Cruyff. The result was a thrilling 2-2 draw.

4 MARCH 1995, v IPSWICH TOWN
The boss was in forthright mood before the visit of Ipswich in March 1995, but he would have been in far finer spirits after the record 9-0 win that followed!

ALEXferguson ...talking

Abuse
The whole club has been under a lot of pressure lately, not least the controversy surrounding Eric Cantona and his appearance in front of an FA disciplinary commission.
When I say the club I include supporters because inevitably the abuse handed out to the players can also be aimed at the fans.
So I recognise that our own people have been feeling a backlash from rivals in recent weeks, but I was still bitterly disappointed to hear our own followers chanting at Norwich about hating Leeds United.
All of a sudden Leeds have come on to the agenda and we are not even playing against them.
To be quite frank I was appalled and I would most earnestly ask those responsible to cut it out.
I know a lot of people in and out of the game hate Manchester United because it is the way of things to dislike a club which enjoys more success than most, but that is no reason for us to reciprocate.
We have got to be bigger than that and not sink to the level of others. It is not always easy to ignore taunts and shrug off vile abuse as Eric Cantona has found to his cost, but players have to learn to bite the bullet and so do supporters.
We have got to be big and I don't want us to go down the road of singing that we hate other clubs. I believe that the vocal energy of our crowd would be better directed at supporting our own team.
Let's spend our time chanting the names of our own players. By all means let Eric know that he isn't forgotten and singing about our own heroes would be much more helpful and encouraging for the team than antagonising rival supporters.

Attitude
Everyone likes to have a chip at Manchester United. I thought Crystal Palace were out of order playing the 'Barcelona' song when we were down at Selhurst Park. Once might have been an accident, even amusing, but to put it over the public loudspeakers before the match and again at half-time I didn't consider very sporting.
But we must accept it, just as there is nothing we can do about the attitude of the media to us at times. Some of the papers turned the Cantona issue into a circus and milked it for all they were worth.
I am not suggesting that it could be ignored; of course it couldn't, but the way it was hammered in some of the tabloids blew the whole thing out of recognition and perhaps exerted undue influence on the commission who extended his suspension.
But the main point I want to make as we welcome Ipswich to Old Trafford this afternoon is that we have got to get on with the job and cut out this nonsense about hating other clubs.
Let's not descend to those depths ever again.....please!

Shock
Ipswich had the encouragement of a win last Saturday which we will respect, especially as we recall our defeat at Portman Road earlier in the season and the points we dropped in a goalless draw at Old Trafford with them last year.
George Burley has taken over at a difficult time, but he is a bright young man who will be hoping to provide the kind of shock Everton gave us last Saturday.
Our job now must be to put that defeat behind us and start another run, making sure we get the points this afternoon.

Alex Ferguson

There is always a special zing about the place when we play Liverpool and I don't have to tell you why. The rivalry between the two clubs has always been intense and when you look at our respective positions in the table today there is even more reason for a tremendous match and passionate support.

The particular fascination for me is that we have two clubs on show this afternoon who have gone down a similar road with their youth policies. What with transfers, injuries and suspension we have had the accent on youngsters in a very big way this season and the lads have done marvellously for us.

The same can be said of Liverpool who must be equally pleased with the way their younger players have come into the team and done so well that they have been making their mark at international level.

It takes courage sometimes to throw young players in at the deep end but it is exciting, too, and very rewarding when you find boys you have groomed at your own club progressing right to the top.

Roy Evans must be enjoying the success of his younger players. He showed great faith in them and has quietly and efficiently brought Liverpool back to the forefront with a good brand of quality football.

I am sure it is going to be a tremendous match because, apart from its significance as a tussle between two top teams striving to keep Newcastle in their sights both teams play exciting, attacking football.

I'm not surprised Sky plumped for the fixture for their live game - with the return of Eric Cantona obviously a bonus attraction.

I have to be honest and admit that our Frenchman's first public game of the season following his nine-month suspension is another reason for the air of excitement and expectation around Old Trafford, not just this afternoon but all week.

The media have homed in this week and really I had no option but to hold a Cantona open day to get the whole thing out of the way. Hopefully we have had the last two or three days in peace to concentrate on our preparations for a very important game.

Naturally I am delighted to have him back. Nine months without playing League football is a long time for a professional and Eric has been very quiet this week, no doubt making his own personal preparations.

There is no point opening up all the rights and wrongs of why he did what

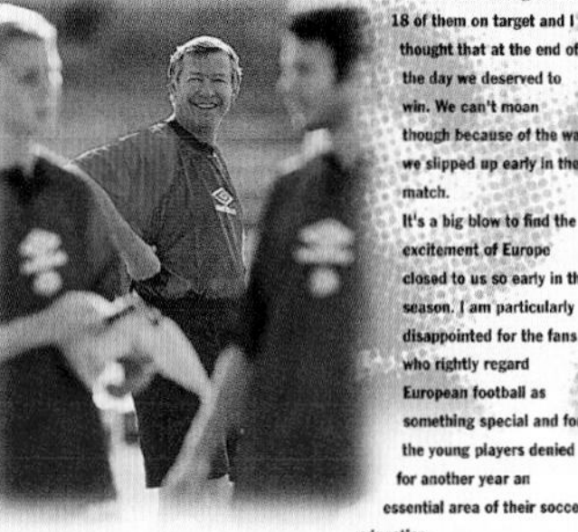

he did and the severe punishment he received. All I really want to say is that he has trained hard during his ban and he did well in his community service. He has served his punishment and all he needs now is some football.

So on with the show. Eric is back and part of our team again. I am sure all our supporters will welcome that because we have some stiff challenges ahead.

The League assumes even greater significance following our exit from the UEFA Cup in a crazy second leg against Rotor Volgograd. Our play in the first 25 minutes when we conceded our goals was appalling, yet it is a long time since I have experienced such a one-sided second half.

We had 33 strikes at goal with 18 of them on target and I thought that at the end of the day we deserved to win. We can't moan though because of the way we slipped up early in the match.

It's a big blow to find the excitement of Europe closed to us so early in the season. I am particularly disappointed for the fans who rightly regard European football as something special and for the young players denied for another year an essential area of their soccer education.

What it must do of course is increase our determination to pull our Coca-Cola Cup tie out of the fire at York on Tuesday and more immediately make sure we are at our very best against our friends from Liverpool.

1 OCTOBER 1995, v LIVERPOOL

The visit of our old rivals to Old Trafford in the autumn of 1995 also heralded the return of Eric Cantona following his long suspension. 'So on with the show. Eric is back…' wrote the gaffer.

I shook the hand of every Manchester United player as they came off the pitch at the end of our UEFA Champions League match against Juventus.

And if it had been possible I would have shaken the hand of every supporter as well because I thought it was a splendid effort both on and off the field.

The playing performance against the champions of Europe was superb and we had first-class backing from the fans. It all added up to one of those fantastic European nights at Old Trafford which we will look back on in years to come with pride and a thrill.

I know we lost and there was nobody more disappointed than me because it has taken qualification for the quarter-finals from our group down to the wire. Everything now depends on our result against Rapid Vienna in Austria on Wednesday with the added frustration of knowing that we also need a little help from Juventus in their game against Fenerbahce.

So we will all be on the rack next week and I admit that it is our own fault. We are paying the price for losing against Fenerbahce at Old Trafford after beating them in Istanbul.

But that's the way it can happen in football. We have never taken the easy route at Manchester United anyway!

I remain confident of a successful outcome though because I have taken great heart from that second-half display against the Italians. We showed what we could do and I simply don't go along with a lot of the critics who seemed to think we swamped Juventus through sheer endeavour rather than skill.

Powerful

Our local paper said it was determination versus class and I am sick of reading generally that Juventus had all the technique while we were apparently playing kick and rush stuff.

It's a nonsense. You don't slaughter the opposition and create nine good chances against the most powerful team in Europe by simply charging around. It's the old problem with the English Press that everything has to be stereotyped and given a label. Everything is black or white with no shade of grey.

I honestly believe that some of our football against Juventus was from the top drawer in terms of skill, control, passing and vision. I was impressed at the time and after watching videos of the game since I am even more convinced that we had just as much class as the opposition.

There are times when you lose a game of football and it is never easy to take. You go over where you went wrong to try to determine what needs to be done for next time but I have got to say that I couldn't fault either individuals or the teamwork. They were magnificent and with such whole-hearted vocal encouragement from the stands it was a night to remember and I would like our supporters to know that the players appreciate the way the fans rallied around.

Vibrant

It was a vibrant Old Trafford and I would like to think as we welcome Leicester City here this afternoon that that is how it is going to be in the future.

I have a friend in Parma who sends me clippings from the Italian newspapers and the Juventus players have made it quite clear in articles and quotes that they have the highest regard and respect for Manchester United. They were impressed by our performance that night.

Indeed they took off their attacking full-back and a midfield man in order to put on a centre-back and an extra defender to try to stop Ryan Giggs. So what does that tell you other than their alarm in the face of some devastating play in attack?

One wonders how it would have been if we hadn't had the unfortunate early injury to Phil Neville which meant I had to pull Roy Keane out of midfield to play at the back. We adjusted and by the second half we had become irresistible.

We have had our problems lately, both from injuries and loss of form, but we are not far away again and of one thing I am convinced: if we get through in Vienna next week and qualify for the knock-out phase I believe we will do extremely well.

three

Cantona's return to the side after suspension was to be a memorable one

30 NOVEMBER 1996, v LEICESTER CITY

These notes were for the domestic visit of Leicester, but Ferguson's mind was very much still on Europe after a rousing match with Juventus.

Alex Ferguson

Some supporters may have preferred to see us win the Championship in live action against Newcastle on Thursday, or even today against West Ham, but personally I have no complaints because the way the title arrived meant it was not decided by a test of endurance.

I made no secret of my dislike of being asked to play four games in eight days which of course is why I pressed for an extension to the season. That wasn't forthcoming, as we all know, and we had readied ourselves for a very testing week.

In the event, Wimbledon and West Ham decided the issue for us on Tuesday night which immediately took the pressure off us and, as I say, I am not sorry because putting players into a pressure cooker of playing too many games too quickly is no way to decide a Championship which should always be an examination of skill and commitment over a full season.

And in that respect I think we have answered all the questions. Winning the League is a wonderful achievement. The first time we did it was a precious moment for everyone connected with Manchester United, but after that, each time has got better because the expectation has become higher and four times in the last five years we have lived up to that expecation and delivered. The ultimate, of course, would have been to win in Europe, too. That sadly was not to be but I still draw great satisfaction from reaching the semi-final stage because it proved that we are capable of handling the twin challenges of competing at both home and abroad.

The progress and improvement we showed in the course of our campaign in the UEFA Champions League pleased me and I believe we are very close now to winning the ultimate European trophy. We need just one more step and we have an outstanding chance.

Clean sweep

This particular year has also produced an achievement which more than compensates for failing to reach the Munich final and that has been to see all four of our teams win their leagues.

The A and B sides won their respective divisions in the Lancashire League and the reserves won the Pontin's League, so this year of the clean sweep is very special and I am sure you will show your appreciation when the trophies are all presented here at Old Trafford this afternoon.

I am particularly pleased for the coaching staff who have steered their players to the titles. There is a good quality of player at Old Trafford at all levels and a lot of people work very hard to bring this about.

Support

There are the people who have put a good deal of time and money into making this a very special club and I am referring to the supporters who have backed us all the way. This is a team game, both on and off the field, and I am glad the name of the club includes the word "United" because I feel there is a unity which very much includes the fans.

Even on our worst days the supporters have stayed true. Of course they have shown their anxiety in games and I have screamed my frustration and anger with the best of them at times.

That's OK and I doubt it will ever be any different at this club because when you pledge yourself to Manchester United you are buying a ticket for a roller coaster ride.

We have had a share of shocks and some might say we have kept our Championship despite winning fewer points than usual, but I believe the League is getting closer and more competitive. Liverpool are always a threat of course, but clubs like Chelsea and Newcastle have spent a lot of money while Arsenal have brought in new players to help make it an extremely exciting season.

I still believe we have the best in the country and what made the difference was going to places like Liverpool and Arsenal and winning.

I believe we are worthy Champions.

three

11 MAY 1997, v WEST HAM UNITED

With a fourth title in five seasons secured, Ferguson began to set his sights even higher: 'I believe we are very close to winning the ultimate European trophy.'

Juventus were fast becoming our familiar foes on the European stage

1 OCTOBER 1997, v JUVENTUS

Another season, another Champions League meeting with the Italian giants and 'a chance to measure ourselves against the best'.

Alex Ferguson

There were perhaps a few Manchester United supporters who groaned when we were drawn again in the same group as Juventus for this season's UEFA Champions League.

Their misgivings are based of course on the fact that we lost both our group games against the Italian champions last season.

My reaction, though, was more one of elation because we now have the opportunity to set the record straight. Life doesn't always give people a second chance; but here in European competition at least, that is exactly what this year's draw has given us.

This is our opportunity to make up for the mistakes that saw us beaten, albeit on both occasions by the narrow margin of 1-0, and make it plain that we consider we have gone up a gear since then.

Our aim now is twofold, obviously to do well, but perhaps even more importantly make it clear that we have the ability to learn.

This is not just a matter of whistling in the wind because I think there was evidence even last year as the competition progressed that out players are prepared to absorb experience and use it to emerge a better team.

As the first game against Juventus in Turin wore on, we were better in the second half than we had been in the first, and by the time we were playing them at Old Trafford, I thought we had nothing to fear.

We lost, but that sometimes happens in football, and I think it would be fair to say that Juventus felt that on the night they had the touch of luck that makes all the difference.

So I certainly welcome this opportunity to play then again and I extend the warmest of welcomes to their players and Marcello Lippi, a coach for whom I have the greatest respect.

We cannot at the moment put up a record in Europe to compare with Juventus, but he knows we are an emerging team and I think he will know that he will be taking on a slightly harder task this year.

Juventus will be feeling pretty confident themselves of course after opening with a 5-1 win at home to Feyenoord, but I was certainly happy enough to open our own account with an away win to the tune of 3-0 against Kosice in Slovakia.

We were good in the first half, perhaps a little patchy in the second, but you cannot control a game all the time. It was a very good result for us and hopefully tonight we will have one or two of our injured players back in action to give me more options.

So, on to this evening's game and it's great to have Juventus again with the chance to measure ourselves against the best. This is what the game is all about, especially in Europe, and I am really looking forward to it.

ALEX FERGUSON

Roy Keane is the heart-beat of Manchester United and as we launch into the new League season this afternoon I have got to say that it is good to have him back.

After being without him for most of last season following his injury and rehabilitation from a cruciate ligament operation, it's like signing a new player. I said at the time that he could expect to make a full recovery and that we would resist any temptation to rush him back into action.

We stuck to that and driven by his own highly motivated discipline he has been looking as good as new. There were games last season when he was badly missed and he will definitely bring an increased urgency to the team, especially at those times when you are looking for inspiration and something extra.

Yes, we know all about Roy's tendency to get carried away from time to time but that's just a small downside of the enthusiasm and conviction that he brings to the team.

I think being captain during the time he played helped him become a more responsible player. Whether we should ease him back into the action without being skipper this season is something which at the time of writing I haven't decided.

Perhaps we should get him playing again without any extra pressure by leaving the captaincy with Peter Schmeichel who did a splendid job for us last season, both on and off the field. Peter is very much our senior professional now and I wouldn't want him to feel that he had let us down in any way as skipper because in fact he did a great job.

I an fortunate to have two such obvious candidates for the job. So it's welcome back to Roy who I am sure will play an important part in helping our newcomers, Jaap Stam and Jesper Blomqvist, settle into the side. Jaap has a key role taking over from Gary Pallister, a player who won more medals with Manchester United than any other player in the club's history.

He has set a standard for others to strive to reach. Ryan Giggs is the closest in the medal department and I hope he and the rest of the players will regard it as an achievement to match. Ryan can make a vital contribution, too, and I am sure that after watching so many of his colleagues perform on the world stage in France, he will be eager to compensate for his club.

The arrival of Jesper Blomqvist means he can be freed to operate in other more central areas and it is an option I welcome. We were short of a left-sided attacking player last season and when Ryan was injured I tried a succession of players on the left flank. Ole Gunnar Solskjaer, Phil Neville, Nicky Butt and Ben Thornley all had a go, most of them playing out of position of course, and I was particularly pleased when I finally secured Jesper. I am sure he will prove a key man for us.

> **Roy Keane is the heart-beat of Manchester United**

The bookmakers have made us favourites for the Championship again, but we know after last season's disappointments that they are not always right, and the opposition is looking stronger than ever.

Arsenal as reigning champions will play with that extra degree of confidence, but it's Chelsea who have taken centre stage with four more foreign signings in Brian Laudrup, Marcel Desailly, Pierluigi Casiraghi and Albert Ferrer.

Liverpool had problems last season but still finished third and they will be there or thereabouts again this winter. There will be other challengers, too, perhaps our visitors today. We know at personal cost that Leicester City are a difficult team to beat and as we welcome then to Old Trafford I am sure they will be out to prove that they can become a major force in the Premiership.

Enjoy the game and have a safe journey home

Alex Ferguson

Alex Ferguson was talking to David Meek

15 AUGUST 1998, v LEICESTER CITY

The beginning of a season that would never be forgotten. Ferguson welcomed back Roy Keane from injury, introduced new signings Jaap Stam and Jesper Blomqvist, and set about regaining our Premier League crown from champions Arsenal...

ALEX FERGUSON

When I first became manager of Manchester United I had two big ambitions. The most pressing was to bring the League Championship back to Old Trafford for the first time in 26 years and get rid of an albatross which had hung round the neck of the club for far too long. I always knew that I wouldn't be acknowledged as a successful manager until I had won the League.

The other desire I nursed was in addition to winning the Championship I relished the prospect of clinching the title in our own stadium, in front of our own fans and ideally on the last day of the season.

Well, it's not in the bag yet and there is a lot of hard graft ahead for the players before I can complete a dream I have cherished for nearly 13 years, but at last there is the chance. It's just something that for me would complete a glorious season in the League, and I would hazard a guess that most supporters would also dearly like to see us sign off with that kind of flourish.

I won't really add anything in terms of the achievement but it would be highly significant for me because in my four Championship wins at Old Trafford they have all been clinched on someone else's ground or courtesy of another result. This time I hope we can do it here, but perhaps I shouldn't allow my thoughts to run so far ahead because as we welcome George Graham and Spurs to Old Trafford I know it is going to be a very difficult match.

George and I go back a long way as rivals and friends and the last thing I expect is a favour. There just isn't such a thing in football, which of course is the only way, and why you found Leeds beating Arsenal the other day followed by Blackburn Rovers holding us to a draw.

At least I got it right when I said a little while ago that the Premiership would probably go to the very last game of the season.

> **"I would like to express the appreciation of myself and the players for the way you have supported us throughout the season"**

I certainly didn't get it right on television after our match at Blackburn on Wednesday when I said that I thought the draw would give Rovers a lifeline to stay up. But that embarrassing moment should also tell you something about me and about my players in the sense that it makes clear that our focus is totally on our own efforts as we enter this momentous last phase of the season.

For some time now I have stressed to the players that our destiny is completely in our own hands and that they should not concern themselves with what is happening elsewhere. You may say this is a self-centred, blinkered attitude, and you would be right, but if you are going for the big prizes, then this is how it has to be.

It's a waste of energy and a huge distraction if you are forever calculating what the opposition is doing, or if you concern yourself with the plight others might be in. It's an approach that can perhaps leave you floundering on television for a few moments but so be it. There will be plenty of time later for tea and sympathy with guys like Brian Kidd, and let me say here and now that I know he will pull things round once he has had a proper chance to sort out what has to be done at Blackburn.

In the meantime, back to this afternoon's challenge as I ask the players to make a mighty effort to land the Championship on our own ground to give our supporters something that they will remember for the rest of their lives.

The fans, as usual, have a part to play as well, and I would like them to leave a part of themselves in the stadium because I know the players will leave their sweat and commitment on the pitch. I cannot think of a more honest bunch of players, and whatever the outcome today, I hope you will give them the welcome they deserve and the encouragement they need to help them through to victory.

On this last day of the League season and my final opportunity to talk to you, I would like to express the appreciation of myself and the players for the way you have supported us throughout the season. It's been magnificent and perhaps in keeping with what the players have given in return.

I still find it difficult to comprehend that we have what amounts to three Cup finals in 10 days, an incredible achievement already, regardless of what happens in those games. I salute the players for their superb efforts on such a wide front and just hope that they will be rewarded in terms of actual trophies.

Our focus demands that we think solely today about our task in the Premiership and so all I will say about the FA Cup final and the Champions League final in Barcelona is that those of you who have been fortunate enough to get tickets have great days out and enjoy what are fantastic occasions.

I am disappointed that I now have to end on a sad note, but I really cannot allow the BBC's programme on Sir Matt Busby, due to be screened tomorrow night, to go ahead without saying that I cannot understand why they feel it is necessary to pick holes in the great man's reputation.

In my time at United I have never heard one of his players say a bad word about him and I think that tells you the real story.

16 MAY 1999, v TOTTENHAM HOTSPUR

The visit of Spurs for our final league outing, and the chance to secure the first stage in an unprecedented end to any season. 'I still find it difficult to comprehend that we have what amounts to three cup finals in 10 days, a incredible achievement regardless of what happens...'

Suddenly, and after what seems such a brief time, we are plunged back into another season. FA Charity Shield and Everton already, and now this evening we welcome Sheffield Wednesday to Old Trafford for our first home game of the new campaign.

It's all happening again, the fierce competition as we set out to defend our hard-won titles, more controversy than ever with the saga of our FA Cup withdrawal, the onset of injuries and of course getting down to the core business of striving to bring more success to Manchester United.

Yet as far as I am concerned, no matter the issues swirling about us, my mind repeatedly flashes back to Barcelona and the splendid night that saw our long cherished European dream become reality.

I need no reminding about the dangers of living in the past. I am well aware that beating Bayern Munich last May doesn't earn us a single point in this season's Premiership race, nor will it guarantee us safe passage in the next Champions League match!

But I am still not ready to regard our achievement in Europe as simply history, to consign it to the record books as something that must be dismissed from our minds lest it weakens our resolve for the challenges ahead.

Certainly at the moment I can't bring myself to wipe out the memory of that great night in the Nou Camp stadium. It was such a fateful and romantic odyssey which is now part of Manchester United folklore and to my mind it doesn't deserve to be locked away in the cupboard. Not yet anyway!

Impression

Like most supporters, I imagine, I went away on my summer holiday ready to enjoy myself, but the moment I started to relax by the swimming pool my mind would replay all the high drama of our victory. I only watched the complete video of the final when we reported back for pre-season training, an experience that confirmed my initial impression that we fully deserved to be the victors.

I concede that for most of the match we did not play particularly well, certainly not as well as we had done in the earlier rounds against Internazionale and Juventus. It could also be argued that we enjoyed moments of luck when the Germans hit the woodwork of our goal.

But my firm conviction is that we deserved to win because, unlike our opponents, we **tried** to win it. We took the game to Bayern. The players were bold and I think it right that fortune should favour the brave.

So how should we reconcile the pride, satisfaction and wonderful memories of last season's triumphs, not just in Europe, but in the Premiership and the FA Cup, with the need to focus on starting all over again?

Do we need to banish last season's achievements from our minds?

Part of me last May said that very quickly we must forget the glory, but reflecting over the summer, I have come to the conclusion that the treble, especially the European part, was so monumental that it would be cavalier to regard it so soon as just another statistic, just another item for the record book.

Marvellous

I certainly cannot praise the players enough. Their whole campaign in Europe was fantastic, their team spirit and will to win was so marvellous, that I believe we should keep the value of those qualities clearly in our minds so that they can act as an inspiration for the battles ahead.

I want players and supporters alike to continue to celebrate last season's successes so that they will serve as a yardstick for the future, that rather than banish our memories to the attic we will keep our best performances at the ready to remind us that standards have been set and that that is what must be produced all over again.

That is what playing for Manchester United is all about.

Although we had an arduous but encouraging pre-season tour, we perhaps didn't quite reach those standards against Arsenal in the FA Charity Shield. The players knew it as well. I could see the disappointment written on their face in the dressing room afterwards. I liked that because it showed they knew and that they cared.

They certainly tried hard enough to make amends at Goodison Park on Sunday, but we failed to take our chances while Everton kept going to enjoy a moment of luck with an own-goal and hold us to a draw.

I trust our players though and long-term I know they won't let us down. I hope they continue to remember and enjoy last season's achievements because that way they will know exactly what is required of them as the new season unfolds.

Thank you all for your loyal and continued support.

Alex Ferguson

Sir Alex Ferguson was talking to David Meek

One of the rewards from a genuinely historic season for Ferguson's men

11 AUGUST 1999, v SHEFFIELD WEDNESDAY

Now with three letters added to the front of his name, Sir Alex started the 1999/00 season by reflecting on what his remarkable team had achieved at the end of the previous campaign.

3 MAY 2003, v CHARLTON ATHLETIC

As the 2002/03 season came to a dramatic close, Sir Alex was able to reflect on a disappointing Champions League exit to Real Madrid, while eyeing another title triumph...

SIR ALEX FERGUSON

I have been scared to go to sleep lately in case I missed anything! It's a tremendous time for us all; management, players and supporters alike, as the season comes to its dramatic climax. Not everything has gone our way, of course. It was certainly very satisfying last weekend to see us take a five-point lead for the Championship, albeit having played a game more than Arsenal, but we had to accept disappointment in the Champions League.

It was a truly demanding week and four things will stay with me for a long time. First was the manner and spirit of our match against Real Madrid at Old Trafford, with both teams putting their reputations on the line with no fear, to produce as good a game of football as you are likely to see. Although the stakes were so high, with a place in the semi-finals as the prize, both Real Madrid and ourselves stayed true to each club's traditions and played to win with football of incredible imagination. The emotion and exhilaration of it was quite moving. Coming from behind after losing 3-1 in Madrid, I was so pleased with the belief of the players. They really had a go and to win 4-3 on the night was a great achievement - if not quite good enough to come through on aggregate. I always knew we would score goals and we did that tremendously well, but it is difficult to legislate for someone like Ronaldo, who sank us overall with his superb hat-trick.

That brings me to my second lasting memory of that unforgettable week, the way that our support applauded Ronaldo as he walked off the pitch to be substituted. That spontaneous burst of appreciation was the essence of sport and I felt proud of our fans. It tells you a lot about them. Mind you, I don't want to see it happening too often - there is a limit to the number of times you want to see the opposition turning you over!

Incidentally, it is not the first time that our supporters have generously acknowledged the achievements of an opponent. I remember our crowd giving Gary Lineker a standing ovation when he played his final game at Old Trafford. That was good to hear as well.

As we welcome Charlton Athletic, and this being our last home game of the season, I would like to take the opportunity of thanking you all for your support, especially these last few weeks when the players have found the encouragement you have given them quite inspiring. It's why I made a point of going across to the visitors' enclosure at the end of our game at Arsenal the other week, and the backing was top class again at Tottenham. All our players were talking about it on the train coming home from London. We were all tested last Sunday, with Kasey Keller having one of those days when everything came to hand and it looked as if we would never score. It was a situation which called for patience and perseverance, a very trying scenario for supporters, not to mention the manager. And this brings me to the third unforgettable impression of these exciting times - the character of the team, which came through strongly once again.

"I ALWAYS KNEW THAT WE WOULD SCORE GOALS AGAINST REAL MADRID, BUT IT IS DIFFICULT TO LEGISLATE FOR SOMEONE LIKE RONALDO"

This club needs people of substance who show their colours when the going gets tough. Happily we have always had people like that, dating back to the era of Nobby Stiles, Pat Crerand, Bobby Charlton and Denis Law, through to players like Bryan Robson, Mark Hughes, Steve Bruce and on to today's crop of monsters! That's why Manchester United have enjoyed so much success over the years and why we are in the thick of the action right now.

Highbury, Anfield and St James' Park are not places for the faint-hearted, but the boys have come through and faced it out once more at White Hart Lane when it just didn't seem to be our day. Paul Scholes turned it for us after a sweeping move typical of our football and Ruud van Nistelrooy was the coolest man in the place despite not being able to get a string of chances past Keller. While we were all stewing in the dug-out, and our following were no doubt on the edge of their seats, our incomparable Dutchman stayed composed, as if to say, don't worry, I'll get another chance and next time I will score - as indeed he did, his 40th of the season, certainly a landmark memory!

Finally among my memorable moments was winning the FA Youth Cup. From the days of Sir Matt Busby, when United won the trophy the first five years it was played, the club has never lost sight of the importance of cultivating its own players. While never afraid to buy, and buy big, we spend a lot of time and energy educating our own youngsters. And when the media is bursting with speculation on who we're going to buy or sell, the FA Youth Cup is a timely reminder that we're still working hard at the grass roots. As for the transfer market, all in good time... and this is not the time! We have a Championship to win with two fixtures remaining and everything to play for - so on with the game...

Alex Ferguson

TODAY'S MATCH

Sir Alex Ferguson

As you are well aware, Manchester United and Roy Keane have parted company, a decision we consider to be in the best interests of club and player. As I said at the time of the announcement, Roy has been a fantastic servant for Manchester United. The best midfield player in the world of his generation, he is already one of the great figures in our club's illustrious history.

Roy has been central to the success of the club in the last 12 years and everyone at Old Trafford wishes him well in the rest of his career and beyond. It's always sad when a great player departs the scene of his triumphs, but football doesn't stand still and I know Roy would be the first to agree we must all focus now on tonight's match as a crucial moment in our bid to reach the knockout stage of the UEFA Champions League.

We know we must deliver the kind of performance that beat Chelsea in our last home game and, given our excellent home record in European football, I'm sure we have a great chance of getting back on track to qualify from our group.

The pressure will help, just as it did for the Chelsea game when the bookies and all but our stoutest fans had us down for a drubbing. I'm not being clever after the event, but I wasn't surprised with the way we responded to the challenge. Expectations were high, but I knew the players would rise to the occasion and that our form had not been a true reflection of their ability.

Yes, they'd been caught short, but because of our injuries we had been playing with a very young side. Five of them were 21 or under and it's asking a lot to get consistency with such a raw team.

When you're at full strength you're able to give the younger people a break, pull them out and keep them fresh. As it was I had to keep playing them and from time to time, in certain matches, it showed. Against Chelsea they made a supreme effort. We were asking a lot of them, but they responded and delivered a major result for us.

There has always been strength of character within this club. It was there in the time of Sir Matt Busby when he had a team destroyed in the Munich disaster, but rebuilt and won the European Cup just 10 years later, an incredible achievement.

When they put the phoenix on their shirt badge to symbolise rising from the ashes it set a standard. Of course, coming back from a bad defeat doesn't compare with the tragic circumstances of the air crash but nevertheless there is a strong sense of family within Manchester United, with players prepared to dig deep when they realise we are looking to them for a special effort.

> "I know Roy would be the first to agree we must now focus on tonight as a crucial moment in our bid to reach the knockout stage of the competition"

Now we have to take the Chelsea performance as a barometer for the future. It's no use beating Chelsea, even though it was a magnificent effort, if we then fail in subsequent games. I hope, for instance, that things went well at Charlton at the weekend – though tonight is when it really matters again within a group so tight everyone has a chance of going through. Just two points separate Villarreal at the top of the table from Benfica at the bottom. We lie

22 NOVEMBER 2005, v VILLARREAL

The manager tackles a tumultuous period in United's recent history and the shock departure of captain Roy Keane after 12 years at the heart of the club's successes: 'The best midfielder in the world of his generation.'

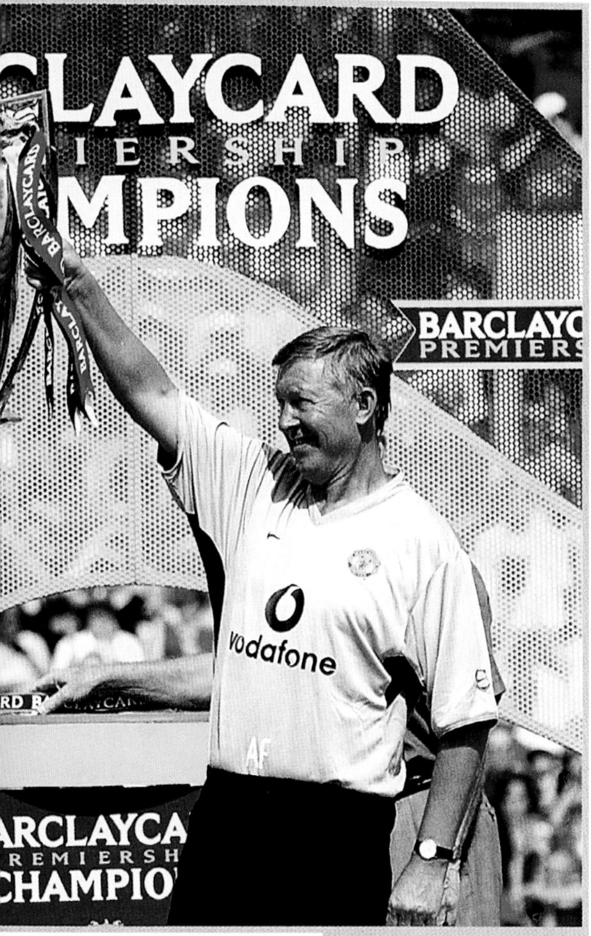

Twin peaks: Roy Keane and Sir Alex parade the Premiership trophy at Old Trafford in 2003, the last of the Irishman's seven title triumphs

between them, level with Lille, so this is a significant match for us.

Villarreal gave us a hard time in Spain. We lost Gabriel Heinze to a cruciate ligament injury requiring an operation that will keep him out for the rest of the season. We also had to play the last 25 minutes with 10 men following Wayne Rooney's dismissal. So, we were up against it, and in the circumstances I was satisfied with a point. I said at the time our results at home would be the key factor, and that's exactly how it's working out.

Dropping two points at home to Lille has put us under pressure, but it's not irredeemable if we do the business this evening. We could even go back to the top of the table, a nice position to be in for the final group game against Benfica in Portugal. So I'm looking for another special effort tonight – from the players of course, but also from you, the fans. I thought the support against Chelsea was unbelievable and made a big difference. I know we were under the cosh at the end, but our supporters stayed with us for what I thought was a deserved success in a fine match.

There was nothing petty in the game and I thought the reactions of Alan Smith and John Terry when they tore into each other for a 50-50 ball summed up the spirit. It was tough, but they hugged each other immediately.

From Chelsea's point of view their defeat was obviously a big blow, but I thought they acknowledged our victory with good grace. Jose Mourinho was fine and still presented me with a very nice bottle of wine.

In terms of the Premiership, I believe we'll get stronger as we get some of our more experienced players back. Hopefully, other teams will be encouraged by our success and Chelsea will find the going gets tougher. Maybe their luck will dry up a little. I think they have had a few breaks. I know we did when we were storming along in our Treble-winning year.

Things change fast in football, though, and the championship race is far from over. Tonight, though, it's all about progressing on the European front, and hopefully another good performance from our guys that brings three more points!

Alex Ferguson

HONOURS&TROPHIES

European Champions Clubs' Cup 1968, 1999
European Cup Winners' Cup 1991
FA Premier League 1993, 1994, 1996, 1997, 1999, 2000, 2001, 2003
Football League Division One 1908, 1911, 1952, 1956, 1957, 1965, 1967
FA Challenge Cup 1909, 1948, 1963, 1977, 1983, 1985, 1990, 1994, 1996, 1999, 2004
Football League Cup 1992
Inter-Continental Cup 1999
UEFA Super Cup 1991
FA Charity/Community Shield 1908, 1911, 1952, 1956, 1957, 1983, 1993, 1994, 1996, 1997, 2003
Joint Holders 1965, 1967, 1977, 1990
FA Youth Cup 1953, 1954, 1955, 1956, 1957, 1964, 1992, 1995, 2003

MANCHESTER UNITED LIMITED

Directors Joel Glazer, Avram Glazer, Bryan Glazer
Chief executive David Gill
Group finance director Nick Humby
Commercial director Andy Anson
Manchester United Football Club directors David Gill, Nick Humby, Michael Edelson, Sir Bobby Charlton, Les Olive, Maurice Watkins
Manager Sir Alex Ferguson CBE
Secretary Ken Merrett
Honorary president Martin Edwards

EDITORIAL TEAM

Editor-in-chief Ian McLeish
Art director Liz Wallace
Contributing editor Rob Ganley
Editor, ManUtd.com Adam Bostock
Design editor Emma Howcutt
Managing editor Stewart Williams
Associate editor Sarah Dyson
Chief sub-editor Steve Morgan
Senior staff writer Paul Davies
Staff writers Ben Hibbs, Gemma Thompson, Steve Bartram
Sub-editor Caroline Hunt
Senior designer Andy Martin
Designer Sam Scott
Picture editor Richard Lawrence
Contributors Tony Bugby, Pat Crerand, Alan Eldridge, José Manuel Garcia, Mike Hammond, Jon Hotten, Tim Kahane, John Leach, David Meek, Andy Mitten, Rob Wightman
Editorial consultant Cliff Butler, Manchester United
Photography John Peters, Matt Peters, Tom Purslow, Chris Coleman, Action Images, Empics, Getty Images, Popperfoto, Offside
Group editor Johnny Aldred
Group art director Martin Tullett
Account director Cormac Bourne
Account manager Rachel Marks
Group production manager Jane Emmas
Production manager Trevor Simpson
Production controller Alex Maison
Kevin Costello Chairman Haymarket Network
Simon Kanter Publishing director
Patrick Fuller MD Haymarket Network
Repro by Colour Systems
Printed at Garnett Dickinson Prints Ltd
Subscribe: UK: £38.25 (15 issues by direct debit) Europe: £95 (24 issues) Rest of world: £120 (24 issues)

TO SUBSCRIBE CALL: +44 (0) 845 677 7801 (lines open weekdays 9am - 5.30pm)

SIR ALEX FERGUSON

United's Premiership triumph has been built on the bedrock of a solid team ethic and fantastic support from you, the fans

Well, you helped get us over the line and now we stand proudly as champions with the possibility of an even more glorious finale of a League and FA Cup double.

The Cup final at the new Wembley beckons, and of course pits us against Chelsea, our main rivals in the League contest. But before we go any further, I want to thank you, the supporters, for your patience – and especially for the way you got behind the team over the last few weeks. I know your encouragement was much appreciated by the players and that it made a difference.

Everything is so tight and competitive in football these days that every aspect of preparation and the degree of enthusiasm from the crowd can make a real difference. You certainly made your presence felt and kept the lads going because those last few matches were highly demanding. Injuries seriously depleted our squad and in the latter stages we were down to 14 senior players, so there was little scope for resting players and bringing in fresh legs.

I think this was evident when we played the second leg of our Champions League semi-final against Milan in the San Siro. The Italians were much fresher and sharper and I felt that we had left something on the field at Everton in our previous league game.

I was very concerned about the mental and physical fatigue in the closing stages and when we squeezed home 1-0 at Manchester City in what turned out to be the fixture that clinched the title for us, I thought the team were running on empty.

As you would expect in a Manchester derby, it was a tough game but the boys dredged something up from somewhere to see us home. It was rather fitting that the winner came from Cristiano Ronaldo. City roughed him up a bit, but typically he picked himself up and kept running at the opposition to pick up a penalty that he tucked away for the winner.

It was Cristiano's 23rd goal of the season, an amazing tally for a winger and of course just one reason among many why he is undoubtedly the season's outstanding player.He swept the board as the choice of both the Professional Footballers Association and the Football Writers with a third trophy due to come his way on Monday night, when he will find himself the winner of the vote among his own team-mates.

Didier Drogba was probably the favourite to win the vote from his fellow professionals and football writers, with his goals repeatedly helping Chelsea to stay on our tails, but since the turn of the year Ronaldo emerged the more emphatic player, getting better and better. But though he has scored heavily in the individual stakes, I cannot emphasise too heavily that the key to success this season has been based on the team ethic.

Job done: Sir Alex and his backroom staff kick off the celebrations at Carrington

> "I want to thank you, the supporters, for your patience, and the way you got behind the team over the last few weeks. You kept the lads going"

We have a lot of major stars and strong personalities at the club these days but we don't have any inflated egos. I have said repeatedly during the season that there is a good spirit in the dressing room and it stood us in good stead as we approached the finishing line with the tanks running low.

Everyone has contributed, ranging from senior players such as Ryan Giggs and Paul Scholes to newcomers Michael Carrick and Nemanja Vidic and including youngsters like Darren Fletcher and John O'Shea. Some folk forgot how young they were when they started coming into the side, and

13 MAY 2007, v WEST HAM UNITED

The Reds were back on top of the Premier League pile after a four-year gap, in a success driven by Player of the Year Cristiano Ronaldo. Sir Alex was able to pay tribute to all before the last league game of the season.

we still haven't seen them in full bloom yet because they are only just starting to mature. Indeed, I would go as far as saying that if they stay together the whole team is going to get better.

They have already proved themselves by winning the championship and hopefully will underline their quality by making it a Double next weekend. But in my view they have the potential to go on to even greater heights. This is why you shouldn't be too downhearted about Europe. Yes, I thought we were capable of going all the way but don't believe the doomsters who are suggesting Milan's brilliant win against us means that we have no chance of equalling them.

You have to keep things in perspective: just as our super victory against Roma doesn't make us world-beaters, so Milan's performance doesn't make them light years better than us.

Every team has its day and in Italy they are saying that the display against us was Milan's best for years.

So don't worry, it will come, especially if you keep on supporting us the way you have done this season with patience while I was rebuilding the squad.

Now, this afternoon, we welcome West Ham to Old Trafford for a game of vital interest to the clubs scrapping for survival in the Premiership. I rested players for the midweek fixture at Chelsea because, as I say, we have had a few tired bodies, but today I shall pick my strongest possible team.

Alan Curbishley is a friend of mine but he wouldn't expect me to do anything less in fairness to rivals at that end of the table and regardless of preparations for our Cup final next Saturday.

That's going to be some game with the chance of a rare League and Cup Double for us, and a Cup Double for Jose Mourinho following their Carling Cup success earlier in the season.

A fierce rivalry has developed between us after our neck-and-neck battles with them in recent seasons, and it's not going to change, but I think tired bodies will take on a new lease of life and that we shall see a fine spectacle between two outstanding teams that will set the standard for Wembley in all its new glory.

Finally, as this is my last programme piece of the season, thanks again for your support, enjoy your summer and come back in good voice for the next campaign.

One voice of the club who won't be returning is our secretary, Ken Merrett, who is taking a well-deserved retirement. Like the man before him, Les Olive, Ken always represented the core values of Manchester United in terms of integrity and concern for supporters.

Although football is global big business these days, we have always striven to remain a family club and retain a sense of values in keeping with our history. That this has been possible has been down to people like Ken.

He was with United for 41 years, starting in the office before becoming assistant secretary and then secretary for the last 18 years to contribute considerably to the success we have enjoyed over the years.

I'm sure you will join me in wishing him well in his retirement.

Alex Ferguson

HONOURS & TROPHIES

European Champions Clubs' Cup 1968, 1999
European Cup Winners' Cup 1991
FA Premier League 1993, 1994, 1996, 1997, 1999, 2000, 2001, 2003, 2007
Football League Division One 1908, 1911, 1952, 1956, 1957, 1965, 1967
Football League Division Two 1936, 1975
FA Challenge Cup 1909, 1948, 1963, 1977, 1983, 1985, 1990, 1994, 1996, 1999, 2004
Football League Cup 1992, 2006
Inter-Continental Cup 1999
UEFA Super Cup 1991
FA Charity/Community Shield 1908, 1911, 1952, 1956, 1957, 1983, 1993, 1994, 1996, 1997, 2003
Joint Holders 1965, 1967, 1977, 1990
FA Youth Cup 1953, 1954, 1955, 1956, 1957, 1964, 1992, 1995, 2003

MANCHESTER UNITED LIMITED

Directors Joel Glazer, Avram Glazer, Bryan Glazer, Kevin Glazer, Edward Glazer, Darcie Glazer
Chief executive David Gill
Manchester United Football Club directors David Gill, Michael Edelson, Sir Bobby Charlton, Maurice Watkins
Manager Sir Alex Ferguson CBE
Secretary Ken Merrett
Honorary president Martin Edwards

EDITORIAL TEAM

Editor-in-chief Ian McLeish
Editor, United Review Paul Davies
Managing editor Alan Beck
Features editor Steve Morgan
Group art editor Mark Wheeler
Deputy art editor Andy Martin
Associate art editor Aubrey Smith
Editor, ManUtd.com Adam Bostock
Staff writers Ben Hibbs, Gemma Thompson, Steve Bartram
Chief sub-editor Frankie Theobalds
Sub-editor Caroline Hunt
Picture editor Richard Lawrence
Contributors Pat Crerand, Alan Eldridge, David Meek, Toby Leigh, Kevin Affleck, Nick Coppack, Johnny Sharp, Scott Morgan
Editorial consultant Cliff Butler, Manchester United
Photography John Peters, Matt Peters, Tom Purslow, Chris Coleman, Empics, Getty Images, Popperfoto, Colorsport, Offside
Group editor Johnny Aldred
Group art director Martin Tullett
Director (Sporting division) Cormac Bourne
Account director Ruth Dodson
Group production manager Jane Emmas
Production manager Trevor Simpson
Production controller Danny Norman
Kevin Costello Chairman Haymarket Network
Simon Kanter Publishing director
Juliet Slot MD Haymarket Network
Repro by Haymarket Pre-press
Printed at Garnett Dickinson Prints Ltd
Subscribe: UK: £38.25 (15 issues by direct debit) Europe: £95 (24 issues) Rest of world: £120 (24 issues)

TO SUBSCRIBE CALL: +44 (0) 845 677 7801
(lines open weekdays 9am – 5.30pm)

THE MANAGER'S COLUMN

SIR ALEX FERGUSON

What a night! A spirited team performance and a wonder strike have put us into the Champions League final, now let's go all-out for the title

Tevez faces his old club, whom he helped to avoid the drop last season with a winner at OT

WELL, WE DID IT, we are going to the Champions League final in Moscow with the chance to write another great chapter in the history of Manchester United.

It was a gripping second leg in our semi-final against Barcelona on Tuesday but I think we deserved our 1-0 victory that sees us paired now against Chelsea in an all-England final that is clearly a great boost for the Premier League. We needed a fantastic performance to beat Barcelona and that's what we delivered with a superb goal from Paul Scholes to cap a super all-round team effort. These days, Paul doesn't get the dozen or so goals he used to score each season as a youngster but my word, he dug out one of his best for this match. I always intended to play him in the final if we made it after missing out the last time against Bayern Munich because of suspension, and now it can't be said that I'm getting sentimental in my old age.

He is more than worth his place, as indeed is everyone who has helped us through a pretty solid campaign that to my mind has shown us in a more mature light for Europe. We didn't go hell for leather all the time against Barça but I think we won the tactical battle as well as the actual contest.

We were a little nervous in the first half but played with more confidence and conviction in the second. Yes, we had anxious moments towards the end but that's not surprising because Barcelona are a good side and a great club as they showed in their dignified acceptance of defeat at the end. Now we go for a double as we welcome West Ham to Old Trafford today on the last lap of an enthralling race for the domestic title.

People have been saying for some time now that the Premier League is the best football championship in Europe, if not the world, and I think this season's title race simply underlines the point. It's so dramatic, so cut-throat, exciting, skilful and fast, and it's going right to the finishing line. The nature of the league is murder for managers like me and Avram Grant at Chelsea, and it's nerve-wracking for our players and supporters as well, but if we can detach ourselves from the turmoil for a moment, we have got to concede that it is fantastic for the game of football in this country.

It would be impossible to make the Premier League any more exciting than it is, which is why more than 200 countries take our top matches on television. I'm told the figure was 230 when we played Arsenal recently. To be honest, I don't think I knew there were that many countries in the world.

Essentially, it's the way we play the game that makes it so attractive, and I also believe that the increasingly competitive nature of the league is a big factor, too. There just isn't a 'dead cert' outcome when it comes to predicting results.

The turmoil of the league can take its toll on the likes of Avram Grant (top) and Sir Alex

Some say that the big clubs with their cash are squeezing the others into becoming also-rans, but I don't see it. There has been a definite tightening up in the Premier League.

It's a two-horse race on the home straight between us and Chelsea, but Arsenal were right up there until lately and Liverpool were always a threat with several other sides close to breaking into the leading group at one point. Everton and Aston Villa have narrowed the gap on the so-called top four. Certainly the days of a long, two-horse race for the title have gone and, in fact, there are a number of teams in the division who have had a vital say in the destination of the Premier League title this season.

Manchester United v West Ham United

3 MAY 2008, v WEST HAM UNITED

Another Old Trafford campaign completed by the visit of the Hammers and another title within our grasp, but this time thoughts were also drawn to a Champions League final in Moscow, after a dramatic night against Barcelona.

THEMANAGER'SCOLUMN

League title this season. Bolton took three points off us and Derby gave us a fright at their place.

Middlesbrough have taken points off Arsenal, Chelsea and Liverpool as well as a couple off us. So there are no easy games and who knows what is going to happen in the remaining fixtures that line us up against West Ham and Wigan while Chelsea take on Bolton and Newcastle?

These are the clubs who could decide the destination of this season's title and I am very mindful that West Ham beat us 1-0 in the final game of last season.

I don't imagine Carlos Tevez will ever forget it because he was the scorer who capped a sparkling run of results that kept the Hammers up. Neil Warnock, the boss of Sheffield United who were relegated as a result of that win, had a go at me for fielding what he considered a weakened team. However, we had an FA Cup final to plan for and the side that played was good enough to win. West Ham were on a roll, and had triumphed in seven of their last nine games – that's title-winning form. They deserved to keep their place after a revival like that and they have justified their Premier League place this season with a solid mid-table position.

Our job this afternoon is to put the Chelsea defeat behind us in the knowledge that victory will take us to the very brink of winning the title. We couldn't ask for a greater incentive for the players, and nor for our supporters, who I hope will crown a good season of unstinting support with really rousing encouragement today. I'm not interested in what Chelsea do now. It's down to us and I look on our game with them at the weekend as one of those days when the decisions didn't go our way.

"We have played some outstanding football that is as entertaining as anyone else's in the country"

We have had a little run like that in recent games and there is nothing you can do about it except to play so well in your next match that nothing can hold you back.

I'm certainly happy with the form we are taking into the fixture. We have had a good season and played some outstanding football that has been as entertaining as anyone else's in the country. We have a young squad that is going to be even better next season. Our new players have done well and the future is very positive for us.

Thank you for your fantastic support against Barcelona and if it is not too much to ask, let's hear that level of noise again this afternoon, please.

Alex Ferguson

The support the fans gave against Barcelona was incredible and a repeat showing today will help United finish the job

The manager's column

// CHAMPIONS – AND WE'RE HERE TO STAY!

// OUR SQUAD IS GOOD ENOUGH AND YOUNG ENOUGH TO IMPROVE

// ROBIN VAN PERSIE GETS MY VOTE, BUT ONLY JUST

// NO DULL FINALE AS WE WELCOME CHELSEA TO OLD TRAFFORD

SIR ALEX FERGUSON

This team of champions is not going away – we are here for the long ride! We will get better and if we apply ourselves in our normal fashion I see our 20th league title as nothing but the start of another decade of success.

Whether I will be here to oversee another 10 years remains to be seen, but I certainly don't have any plans at the moment to walk away from what I believe will be something special and worth being around to see!

It's always difficult in football to be absolutely sure of the future because the game has a habit of tripping you up, but I don't live in a fantasy world and believe we have every reason to feel confident about the future of Manchester United.

My view stems not from the euphoria of winning back the league title we lost so narrowly last season, but on the way we did it and the make-up of our playing personnel.

We had the right focus that gave us a consistency that was simply too much for our rivals.

We had a relatively rocky start to the season, losing on the opening day, and it took us some time to get into our stride. The reason for that I think is quite obvious – we had an injury blitz among our central defenders that forced us to make repeated changes and switch players into the back line to play out of position.

Once we had some stability and continuity in the defence we improved beyond all recognition and we did particularly well in that department during the crucial closing stages of the season.

But the biggest factor behind my optimism for the future lies in a squad of players who are both good enough and young enough to improve. I am thinking of players such as David De Gea, Rafael, Danny Welbeck, Phil Jones, Jonny Evans, Tom Cleverley, Chicharito, Chris Smalling, Shinji

The ever-improving Rafael is one of many at OT with immense potential

05.05.2013, v CHELSEA
Sir Alex was full of optimism for the future having seen his side clinch a 20th league title, and gives no indication of his impending retirement. Was he just trying to throw fans off the scent?

RvP took the headlines as United clinched the title; (left) Rio and co savour the moment

Kagawa and Alex Büttner whose ages all fall between 21 and 25.

They are still on their learning curves and their potential is immense. Most of them, too, have been with us from a young age and I think growing up with us builds a loyalty base that is good for the club spirit and the family ethos of Old Trafford.

So all that for me augurs well for the future, though I would be the first to concede that I knew what Alan Hansen had in mind when he famously said that you don't win anything with kids. It was a hopeless exaggeration, well wide of the mark with the especially talented group who were coming through at the time, but you do need to have a balance of maturity and experience in your side and I think we have that as well.

They don't come any more experienced than Ryan Giggs and Paul Scholes of course, with a solid core of people behind them who have been there and done it such as Robin van Persie, Wayne Rooney, Michael Carrick, Rio Ferdinand, Patrice Evra and Nemanja Vidic. We have a few other players to slot in there behind them like Antonio Valencia, Ashley Young, Nani and Anderson. It all adds up to a nicely balanced squad that, as I say, is going to get better.

"Growing up with us builds a loyalty base that's good for club spirit and our family ethos"

I like the cockiness of the young element and I like the wisdom of the older guys to keep it in check and set the right example as, say, Robin van Persie has done for us this season.

I don't think there is much argument about our player of the year after he breathed new life into us with his torrent of goals in the first half of the season, capped with a marvellous finish. I shall never forget his brilliant second goal in the hat-trick that clinched us the championship against Aston Villa a fortnight ago.

I must quickly add, though, that in my book he only gets top spot by a short head from Michael Carrick (far left), who has had a brilliant season for us, the best since he joined us, not only so cool, calm and collected but consistent with it.

It is always slightly invidious to pick out individuals in a team game, but I must make exception for some of our youngsters who have made so much progress that it would be unfair not to acknowledge it.

David De Gea came through an early baptism of fire that worried a lot of supporters, but we had faith in him and he responded. The new young goalkeeper has produced stronger performance levels to mature and stand on the threshold of becoming a truly great player. Phil Jones is another who has all the makings to become an outstanding performer with the option of playing several roles, and as for young Rafael, he has been phenomenal.

This afternoon we welcome Chelsea to Old Trafford in the knowledge that in addition to their involvement in the Europa League they are desperate to beat us as they scrap to hold off Arsenal and Spurs for a place in the top four to qualify for next season's Champions League. We got a taste of the fierceness of this top-four battle in our 1-1 draw with Arsenal last Sunday, and this is certainly no dull finale to the season.

So no winding down just yet! I want a good performance from us in keeping with our returned status as champions – one that I hope you will enjoy.

Alex Ferguson

The manager's column

4 Manchester United v Swansea City

12 MAY 2013, v SWANSEA CITY

Time to say goodbye. After 26 years at the helm, and 38 trophies won, SIr Alex Ferguson's last game in the Old Trafford dugout as Manchester United manager – and his final programme notes – was against Swansea City in May 2013.

The manager's column

SIR ALEX FERGUSON

The decision to retire is one that I have thought a great deal about and one that I have not taken lightly. It is the right time.

It was important to me to leave an organisation in the strongest possible shape and I believe I have done so. The quality of this league-winning squad, and the balance of ages within it, bodes well for continued success at the highest level whilst the structure of the youth set-up will ensure that the long-term future of the club remains a bright one.

Our training facilities are amongst the finest in global sport and our home Old Trafford is rightfully regarded as one of the leading venues in the world. Going forward, I am delighted to take on the roles of both Director and Ambassador for the club. With these activities, along with my many other interests, I am looking forward to the future.

I must pay tribute to my family, their love and support has been essential. My wife Cathy has been the key figure throughout my career, providing a bedrock of both stability and encouragement. Words are not enough to express what this has meant to me.

As for my players and staff, past and present, I would like to thank them all for a staggering level of professional conduct and dedication that has helped to deliver so many memorable triumphs. Without their contribution the history of this great club would not be as rich.

In my early years, the backing of the board, and Sir Bobby Charlton in particular, gave me the confidence and time to build a football club, rather than just a football team.

Over the past decade, the Glazer family have provided me with the platform to manage Manchester United to the best of my ability and I have been extremely fortunate to have worked with a talented and trustworthy Chief Executive in David Gill. I am truly grateful to all of them.

To the fans, thank you. The support you have provided over the years has been truly humbling. It has been an honour and an enormous privilege to have had the opportunity to lead your club and I have treasured my time as manager of Manchester United.

A WORD FROM THE BOSS

DAVID MOYES

I HAVE TO SHOW YOU I'M THE RIGHT SUCCESSOR TO SIR ALEX

PLAYERS SHOWING HUNGER TO KEEP WINNING TROPHIES

A WARM WELCOME BACK TO ENGLAND FOR JOSE MOURINHO

"Welcome to Old Trafford tonight, as I take charge of my first competitive home game. I've been looking forward to this ever since Sir Alex told me I would be the new Manchester United manager at the end of April.

Taking over the job as manager of Manchester United is one that everybody in football would want, but I'm not sure there would necessarily be that many wanting to follow Sir Alex. But after speaking to him, and him telling me all about the club, it was obvious to me that I could not turn down this opportunity.

Sir Alex is someone that I greatly admire, everybody in football does, and I'm pleased to know that he'll be joining the board here and will remain very much a part of the club. He is someone I know I can go to when needed.

I'm very honoured to be in this position and have worked hard since my early days in management to be as successful as I possibly can, for both Preston North End and Everton. It was a big wrench to leave Everton but the lure of Manchester United was too strong. I have a great deal of respect for my former club and the people I worked with there. My aim now is to continue all the good work the previous manager did before me, and I want to build upon it.

I've brought several of my own staff with me from Everton and they have integrated well with the existing Manchester United staff – I know they already feel very much a part of it here.

My main focus at the moment is the playing squad and what is left of the transfer window. I always knew this would be a tough transfer window, mainly because my appointment started on 1 July, and we'll be doing everything we can to improve the team and squad.

I've only been in the job for six or seven weeks, which isn't a lot of time, but I've taken a lot of advice from Sir Alex and from people like Rene (Meulensteen), and Mick (Phelan) before they left. I'd like to thank them both for their efforts in the past and for their understanding of me coming into the job.

I've had to get to know the players, to find out more about them, and to find out the kind of player we needed to bring in. In time I'll be looking at all departments, to continue to make progress and to see if there's any improvements that can be made.

In my short time here I've already travelled halfway around the world, and the level of support I've seen has been incredible. To see thousands come to watch training, people waiting outside our hotels at all hours, huge crowds at the matches, and the level of interest in the Premier League, in Asia especially, has been amazing. I'd also like to thank all those fans who have sent letters wishing me good luck. I won't be able to respond to all of them but I've appreciated the kind sentiments. I've no doubt those supporters will be among the many millions watching this game around the world tonight.

Closer to home we enjoyed similar levels of support at Wembley for the Community Shield and at Swansea last week for the start of the Premier League season. I have to thank all the fans who were there for the encouragement they gave me and the team. I won't be taking that support for granted. I know I have to earn it. I know I have to go out there and show you fans, and everyone at Manchester United, that I'm the right successor.

Having a big atmosphere at Old Trafford will be really important. Myself and the team will do all we can to help create that, but in a year when some people are discounting Manchester United your backing can also play a big part. We'll certainly be using that in a positive way.

As a football manager you can never ask for time in the job, but you're always looking for a little bit of patience. There's no doubt we're in a transitional period at the club – most people recognise that when a new manager joins – but I'm hoping that it's going to go smoothly and that there won't be too many bumps along the way.

I have been impressed by the club's owners, the Glazer family, both for their strength of decision-making and their plans for building on the success here. I'm excited by what they've told me about their plans for the future and for continuing the club's success.

For this first home league fixture of the season we welcome Chelsea and their manager Jose Mourinho. Chelsea have undoubtedly got themselves a great coach who they know well from his first spell at Stamford Bridge. In the modern era of managers, Jose has been one of the most successful of what I regard as the new breed of young managers. He is back where he feels happy and I think everyone in the Premier League will be pleased to see his return. I think Jose's return will make for a really competitive league this year.

We couldn't have had a harder start to the Premier League season but after a great win at Swansea we're in good condition and ready to take on the challenge. I've been really pleased with all the players. I'm still getting to know many of them but they've certainly, in the main, got in a good pre-season. They've all been great to work with and I've been really impressed by their competitiveness, their level of professionalism and the hunger they've got to keep winning trophies. I share their hunger.

Enjoy the game tonight.

David Moyes"

04 Manchester United v Chelsea

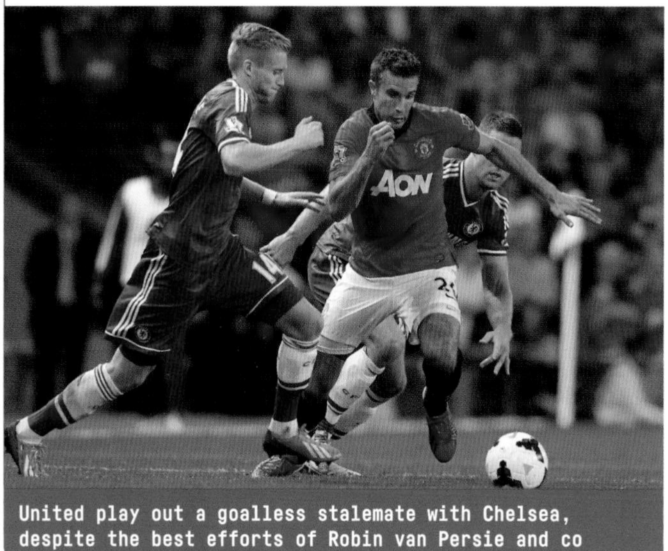

United play out a goalless stalemate with Chelsea, despite the best efforts of Robin van Persie and co

26 AUGUST 2013, v CHELSEA

The new man in charge had enjoyed a winning start to life as United boss with a Community Shield victory over Wigan Athletic and faced Chelsea in his first home match, who had recently reappointed Jose Mourinho as boss.

A WORD FROM THE BOSS

LOUIS VAN GAAL

"I ALWAYS KNEW THIS WAS A BIG CLUB BUT IT WAS INCREDIBLE TO WITNESS AS THE MANAGER"

Wayne Rooney will lead by example with the armband this season

Hello and welcome to Old Trafford for the first match of the new Premier League season, and a day I have been looking forward to since I accepted the job as Manchester United manager. I feel a huge sense of pride to be the manager of this wonderful football club, and it was a proud moment for me to walk out of the tunnel for the first time as United manager on Tuesday for the friendly match with Valencia. The fans were fantastic – what a welcome – and it gave me goosebumps when everyone was singing my name. We didn't play too well against Valencia, but in spite of that we won the game through our determination and fighting spirit.

FANTASTIC FANBASE

As I mentioned in my notes for the Valencia programme, I saw first-hand on tour in the United States how big this football club really is. The fanbase is just incredible – at every match most of the fans were wearing red shirts. Of course, I always knew this was a big club but it was incredible to witness as the manager. I have had a lot of contact with so many supporters who seem very happy for me to be here, and that is nice to see. I hope they have enjoyed what they have seen so far in pre-season but I know those matches will not be so important to them; it will be today's match against Swansea City that will be important. Today is when it really begins. I have admired the Premier League for a number of years – it being very fast and very physical – and know it is a very hard league to win.

Swansea are a very good footballing side and I put a lot of that down to Michael Laudrup's time at the club. He is a very good trainer and coach, and I'm sure the good work he did at the club will be continued with Garry Monk. Swansea will provide us with a big test today, and we must make sure that we are ready for that.

PLAYER ASSESSMENTS

After the US tour we returned to Manchester to continue preparations at the Aon Training Complex, where training has been going well. We really only started on the physical work when we got back from the tour as we could not do that in the States, because of the climate and also the travelling and the number of matches that we had. We have to be ready, but not everyone will be. All of the players are at different stages and we have picked up a few injuries, but that is always the case after a World Championship. However, every club which has a lot of international players will have the same problem.

It has also been an important time for me to try and get the players to understand my footballing philosophy. That is based on good communication and structure, in terms of a strategy to play football against an opponent. You have to take into account the qualities of the opponent and give your team structure to do that, plus the team has to perform as a team and not as individuals. I always train in the brains and not in the legs. The most important thing they have to know is why we do things. A lot of players are playing intuitively – but they have to think and know why they have to do certain things, rather than just doing it intuitively. It's a process that

04 Manchester United v Swansea City

16 AUGUST 2014, v SWANSEA CITY

The 2014/15 season heralded the arrival of Louis van Gaal, with the legendary Dutch coach beginning to realise how popular United is on the global stage.

MANAGER'S NOTES

JOSE MOURINHO

We've overcome some big challenges, but I'm so proud of my boys' efforts as we prepare for the most important week of the season

Good afternoon and welcome to Old Trafford. Today we welcome Sam Allardyce and Crystal Palace and I must congratulate Big Sam for another amazing victory in the battle against relegation. He has done a great job once again. Welcome also to the travelling Palace supporters who always provide an amazing support at Selhurst Park.

Like everyone else we played 38 Premier League matches this season, but as well we have played every possible match in the Europa League – next Wednesday's final will be our 15th in the competition – and we played the Community Shield, every possible match in the EFL Cup, every match in the FA Cup except the semi-final and final, so this season we will have played a total of 64 games. The maximum we could have possibly played is 66!

I have seen in the football media that certain pundits cannot understand why our players are tired. A pundit is not honest if they cannot forget their colours or if they try to hide the truth from their audience. It's not my fault if their managerial career was very poor.

Our main goalscorer, Zlatan, has had major knee surgery, as has a top central defender in Marcos Rojo. Luke Shaw has had surgery at a time when he hit his best form.

Phil Jones and Chris Smalling had important injuries at the same time. Our postponed fixtures accumulated to the last month of the season, and in the last two months of the season we have played 16 matches. Don't we deserve respect for that? Don't we deserve to be analysed in this context? Didn't this team fight every second of every match? Didn't this team win the Community Shield and League Cup? Didn't this team beat the club record of 25 Premier League matches unbeaten in the same season? Isn't this team going to play a European final next Wednesday?

I have to stand up and say that my boys deserve all my respect, and with my boys I will walk to Stockholm. We will go together, some on crutches, others limping, but 11 starting and another seven substitutes will go to the field of battle representing and fighting for our group of brothers, for the Manchester United family.

Before then, today is a big match for many young boys. One thing is an isolated debut surrounded by experienced players, another thing is a collective debut of many young players, so they all need your support today.

Enjoy the game.

"WE WILL GO TOGETHER TO STOCKHOLM, SOME ON CRUTCHES, OTHERS LIMPING, REPRESENTING AND FIGHTING FOR OUR GROUP OF BROTHERS, FOR THE MANCHESTER UNITED FAMILY"

04 • Manchester United v Crystal Palace

21 MAY 2017, v CRYSTAL PALACE

With Mourinho installed for the 2016/17 season, he used his notes for the final home game against Palace to highlight his team's achievements in his debut season – two trophies, and a Europa League final to come.

CARETAKER MANAGER'S NOTES

1

It's an exciting return to Old Trafford for the caretaker boss, and while three points is the main aim today, he's keen to remind fans what this great club is all about...

Hello and welcome to Old Trafford. I should start by underlining how excited I am to be back at Manchester United. I feel like I have come home. From the moment I found out that I was doing this role, today is the day that I really couldn't wait for. To walk out at Old Trafford means so much to me and I want to thank you all for making me feel so welcome. Walking into the training ground on that first day last week was quite something, to see all the staff, many of whom I knew and a few new faces too – it was something special.

After today's game against Huddersfield Town, we will be halfway through the Premier League season and I am under no illusions as to the scale of the job ahead. We all have a lot of work to do in order to get this club back towards where it should be. Not only do we have to improve our results, we have to remind people what Manchester United is all about. We have to show everybody who we really are.

This is a club built on entertainment and excitement, on giving young players the opportunity to express themselves. These players have shown that they have the never-say-die spirit that United has always had. There is a lot of talent in our squad and this is a big opportunity for these players to demonstrate that and show everybody why they play for this great club. I want Old Trafford to see that today.

It has been a difficult season so far, of course, but throughout it all, our supporters have been incredible. This is how I remember the fans from my previous time at the club: home and away, the players are always able to count on your backing. It is time for that faith and support to be repaid.

There are plenty of games left this season and lots to be optimistic about. We still have a lot of games to play in the Premier League and ground to make up on the teams above us; we have an FA Cup campaign starting next month and, of course, there is a very exciting Champions League tie with Paris Saint-Germain to look forward to.

We have a huge challenge ahead over the rest of the season, but this is a club which rises to challenges and relishes them. It will require hard work from every single person associated with the club, but it can be done and I am very excited to be involved.

I hope you all enjoy the game.

"This is how I remember the fans from my previous time at the club: home and away, the players are always able to count on your backing"

04

26 DECEMBER 2018, v HUDDERSFIELD TOWN

A United legend from his playing career, Ole was very proud to be handed the opportunity to manage the Reds, initially on a temporary basis, with his first game back at Old Trafford on Boxing Day 2018. He celebrated with a 3-1 win.

CHAPTER 4

Cartoons

For many years the regular cartoon strip was a staple favourite in *United Review*, with some of the nation's most talented illustrators contributing regularly, all in the name of sparking laughter (as well as making some serious points...)

From the early 1930s to the mid-1990s there was rarely an issue of the Manchester United programme without some form of artistic satire within its pages.

From the Gee Bee comic strip to the Bricks and Bokays cartoon, the hugely popular Thick and Thin series to the Footballing Antics of Fred the Red, the matchday programme's cartoon or comic strips have, for a large portion of the publication's history, had fans quietly chuckling in the stands.

Many of the columnists within the pages of *United Review* were journalists working for the regional and national press, and so too were the cartoonists. George Butterworth of the *Evening Chronicle* was the first of them, introducing his Gee Bee comic strip to fans at the start of the 1932/33 season. A contributor to many national publications during his career, his humorous take on events at the club – on the pitch and off it – made for the perfect light-hearted read for those stood on the Popular Side terraces or seated in the relative comfort of the Grand Stand. Alternating between multi-frame cartoons or the so-called one frame 'single gag', Gee Bee and later Bricks and Bokays (the latter also drawn by Butterworth) always reflected the mood around the club.

Nobody was safe from his ribbing – not the owner, club secretary, manager or a poor unfortunate misfiring centre-forward. It's doubtful the Chorley-born artist would have fretted too much about the views of the easily offended, having made it on to Adolf Hitler's 'Death List' for his less-than-flattering depictions in the UK press of the Nazi leader during the Second World War.

Above: United return to Old Trafford in 1949 after a lengthy absence due to the Second World War

A cartoon with a kick to it; from 1932/33 [left] while the adventures of Thick and Thin [below] kept supporters entertained for many years

While the humour was often aimed at grown-up Reds, the cartoons proved popular with younger fans

George Butterworth's contribution to *United Review* came to an end following the Munich Air Disaster – after losing so many friends and colleagues in the tragic accident, his heart was 'no longer in the job'. A man of great talent and rare humour, he passed away in 1988.

Spike's Soccer Smiles and Smart's Cartoon Commentary attempted to fill the gaps but it was only when *Daily Mirror* cartoonist David Rowe contributed the Thick and Thin strip in 1981 that a true successor to Butterworth was found.

This tale of two fictitious, hugely loyal United fans gave a contemporary view of life on the Old Trafford terraces, covering issues such as the ID card scheme, plastic pitches and the dash for cup final tickets. There were occasional star cameos, too, like a basketball-playing Diego Maradona in 1986 and, later, Ruud Gullit for a high-profile friendly fixture against the all-conquering AC Milan side in 1989.

Some of the content may now seem a little dated these days, but at the time it was a favourite section of *United Review* for a great many readers. Thick and Thin last appeared in 1990, with Rowe retiring as a freelance cartoonist in 1994 and sadly passing away in 2004.

Later cartoons were very much aimed at young fans, with club mascot Fred the Red featuring from the mid-to-late 1990s in the kids section of the programme.

There was also a short-lived strip entitled Norm and Ec that featured around the same time, but none of these later contributions could match up to those of earlier decades.

15 OCTOBER 1932: STARS IN STRIPES

United introduced a hooped change strip for the 1932/33 season, which some felt resembled a rugby shirt. Still, it gave the Second Division Reds their only two wins so far that campaign, away to Charlton and Burnley. As Bradford Park Avenue arrived at Old Trafford (to be beaten 2-1), 'Gee Bee' (aka renowned newspaper cartoonist George Butterworth) mused on other sartorial options...

3 DECEMBER 1932: CARTOON CALEDONIANS
With United's squad now featuring eight Scottish players, Gee Bee made light of this relatively multi-national (for the 1930s) line-up with a barrage of not entirely original Scot-related jokes. Sadly, history does not record whether United's contingent from north of the border saw the funny side.

1 FEBRUARY 1936: LOCAL LOYALTIES

Cartoonist George Butterworth also turned his hand to single-pagers. Here he expressed Reds' hopes that after our defeat in the 1935/36 FA Cup against Stoke, Manchester City would fare better in the competition. Back then, many Reds would happily watch City at home whenever United were playing away, with fierce cross-city rivalry very much a post-war phenomenon.

When Greek meets Greek . . .

Mancunia: "Let th' battle begin—Glory's mine anyhow!"

MANCUNIA

COTTON

UNITED

MANCHESTER'S BLUE RIBAND

CITY

GEE BEE

Page 5

12 SEPTEMBER 1936: TUG OF WAR

Newly promoted United faced that season's eventual champions Manchester City in our third home outing of '36/37 – a campaign that would eventually see us relegated. Gee Bee references a 'Mancunia' built on the cotton trade for which the city was so well known at the time. The Red underdog would prevail in this battle, with United's 3-2 win a rare highlight in a season of struggle.

25 DECEMBER 1936: SEASONAL STRUGGLES

United hosted Bolton on Christmas Day 1936 after 11 league games without a win. In this new series of cartoons (referring to the brickbats and bouquets metaphorically launched from the terraces) Gee Bee hoped Santa would bring luck – and indeed he did, as United chalked up a much-needed 1-0 victory against the Trotters, with 47,658 fans there to witness it.

26 AUGUST 1939: WAR FOOTING

United would play only once at home before the Second World War ended the season prematurely. Craddock, another newspaper cartoonist freelancing on the side, was bound to pick up on the military theme as the prospect of international conflict loomed large heading into this game against Grimsby Town.

31 AUGUST 1946: BACK WITH A BANG

The artist formerly known as Gee Bee was back at the start of 1946/47, and in a decidedly gung-ho mood. Barely a year after the war had ended with atomic bombs laying waste to Japan, he urged the Reds to 'atomise' our Division One rivals with this United bomb. Hmmm...

BRICKS AND BOKAYS

By BUTTERWORTH

ATOMISE 'EM!

UNITED

WOLVES

VILLA

ARSENAL

CHELSEA

THE BOLTON TROTTER

DERBY RAM

PRESTON

1ST DIVISION SHIP

POMPEY

OUR OWN LITTLE ATOM BOMB DROPS TO-DAY

PAGE FIVE

14 SEPTEMBER 1946: EYE FOR THE MAINE CHANCE

With Manchester City letting United play at Maine Road while bomb-damaged Old Trafford was rebuilt, Butterworth saw the potential for amusement from the new situation. He also refers to United having rather more refined tastes than our neighbours – could this be true?!

BRICKS AND BOKAYS

By BUTTERWORTH

IN SAYING "WELL DONE, UNITED," MAY I OFFER A LITTLE ADVICE TO OUR CUP CHAMPIONS?

WE'D BETTER NOT CHARGE 'EM FOR USING OUR GROUND NOW

FIRST OF ALL, AS A MARK OF APPRECIATION, LET CITY HAVE THE LID.

SO THAT'S UNITED!

PRESENT THE STAND TO WALTER CRICKMER SO THAT HE CAN SEE HIS FIRST FOOTBALL MATCH.

SEND PHOTOGRAPHS OF THE CUP TO ARSENAL AND CHARLTON AND TELL THEM

THA CAN KEEP T'LIONS!

WE'LL PLAY 'EM FOR NELSON'S COLUMN SOME EVENING.

THIS'LL DO FOR YOU LOT. FIVE GUINEAS A DAY—CASH DOWN

AND ABOVE ALL, DON'T GO TO BLACKPOOL FOR A HOLIDAY THIS SUMMER!

1 MAY 1948: CUP WINNERS COME HOME

The weekend after winning the FA Cup at Wembley with a 4-2 win over Blackpool, United played our final game of the league season against Blackburn Rovers. Cartoonist Butterworth was in ebullient mood and only too happy to have fun making light of other clubs' misfortunes.

2 SEPTEMBER 1950: DRAWING ON RICH HERITAGE

The 1950/51 season saw *United Review* chart the Reds' history in beautifully illustrated form. This first instalment, commissioned for the programme sold at our league game against Blackpool, traced the club's history back to Newton Heath's railway roots.

THE HISTORY OF MANCHESTER UNITED—No. 1

By A. S. MELLOR

This is the first of a series of pictorial pages from the History of Manchester United specially contributed by A. S. Mellor. An expert in the club's history, A. S. Mellor has been a United supporter for many years. These unique histories will appear regularly throughout the coming season.

28 APRIL 1951: TO BE CONTINUED...

The illustrated history continued throughout that season, often focusing on key figures in the United story. In this case the spotlight was on long-time club administrator, legendary scout and the man who claimed to have suggested the name 'Manchester United', Louis Rocca, who had passed away the previous June.

3 SEPTEMBER 1952: THE KIDS ARE ALRIGHT

For the programme on sale early in 1952/53, against Arsenal, Butterworth noted how Matt Busby's champions were also about to blood a bunch of exciting young talent – the characters here look so young, you could even call them 'Babes'.

21 APRIL 1956: BUOYED BY THE BABES

With United having already been crowned champions again in 1956, Butterworth chose the occasion of the season's final game, against Portsmouth, to imagine the boss grabbing a new handful of youngsters for the following season...

22 SEPTEMBER 1956: DON'T BE BLUE

With FA Cup holders Manchester City visited the reigning league champions United, Butterworth again refers to a curious perception that City are the more flat-capped relations, and also to United's lofty league position in 1956/57. The Reds duly saw off the neighbours 2-0 during a run of 10 wins from our first 12 games, en route to defending the title.

6 FEBRUARY 1957: SPANISH VISITORS
As United welcomed Athletic Bilbao in a challenging European Cup quarter-final second leg, Butterworth dusted off his book of national stereotypes to reflect on United's tough trip to Spain two weeks previously (where we lost 5-3 after being surprised to find snowy conditions in the Basque Country).

29 APRIL 1957: CHAMPIONS AGAIN

As United celebrated sealing back-to-back league titles before the final game against West Brom, the programme's cartoonist reflected on a season that saw foreign travel, the advent of the timeless *United Calypso* song and a run to Wembley for the FA Cup final (where we would unfortunately lose 2-1 to Aston Villa the next weekend).

3 JANUARY 1959: A NEW PERSPECTIVE
After the Munich Air Disaster, Butterworth admitted he couldn't find the humour required for a regular United cartoon. One successor in *UR* was 'Spike', who opted for a less topical approach like this example in the Blackpool programme.

12 SEPTEMBER 1959: A SMARTER APPROACH

Another new cartoonist offered his angle on footballing matters in the 1959/60 season. In this issue of *UR*, on sale at the Tottenham league fixture, he used stories from the wider world of football as the hook for his humorous musings. The final panel didn't seem quite so amusing after United were crushed 5-1 by Spurs that day.

19 DECEMBER 1959: FESTIVE FUN

Several years before *Private Eye*, *Viz* et al perfected the art of the spoof advert, Smart raised a few smiles with these football-themed parodies of magazine and newspaper small ads. With United struggling in the lower half of the league and about to go down 3-2 at home to West Bromwich Albion, any comic relief was welcome...

16 JANUARY 1960: NEW DECADE, NEW HOPE

As United prepared to face Birmingham City at home, Smart offered an optimistic message, trusting in young Red talent to lead United into a brighter future following the tragic events of the late '50s. Smart's faith would be rewarded in the years to come.

KNOW THE GAME
by JACK CLOUGH
THE EX-FOOTBALL LEAGUE, INTERNATIONAL AND CUP FINAL REFEREE

KNOW THE GAME . . . . . METHOD OF SCORING No. 2

A goal is scored when the WHOLE of the ball has passed over the goal-line, between the goal-posts and under the cross-bar. Always providing that the ball has not been thrown, carried or propelled by hand or arm, by a player of the attacking side. That is the law but should the cross-bar become displaced during a game and the ball crosses the line at a point which the referee considers would have been beneath it, he shall award a goal.

Maybe we could consider an unusual occurrence. It could happen that a player lying on the ground notices the lace protruding from the football casing and taking it between his teeth he runs with the ball into goal. As the player has carried the ball a goal could not be awarded.

Quite often we have instances of outside interference associated with the game which can present problems. Dogs are a common source of annoyance and if it so happens during the normal course of play that a dog stops the ball from passing into goal, a goal cannot be awarded. It could also be that a spectator enters the field and stops what is considered to be a certain scoring shot, but again it is not a goal. In cases where any outside agency restricts or interferes with the play, the referee must stop the game and restart by dropping the ball at the point of interference.

Illustrated by Syd. Robinson.

PAGE FIVE

26 AUGUST 1961: FUNNY OLD GAME

A new cartoon, accompanying the writing of a former ref, gently satirises familiar guides to the game found in newspapers by envisaging faintly ludicrous scenarios and considering how the game's laws would apply.

28 AUGUST 1963: PICTORIAL HISTORY

A more serious style of illustration was adopted for the first home game of the 1963/64 season, against Ipswich Town, as *United Review* chose to educate readers about the club's past. Peter Slingsby was a columnist for *The Guardian*, and he scripted *Cecil Rigby*'s elegant sketches that soon became very popular with matchgoing supporters.

31 AUGUST 1963: MR DAVIES AND THE DOG

The strip in the programme for the Everton league game made reference to the now famous yarn of the near-bankrupt club's fortunes being fortuitously saved by a United mascot dog – and John Henry Davies, who invested in the club on the condition he could have the pooch to give to his daughter, back in 1902.

27 FEBRUARY 1965: THE BELFAST BOY

By the time United faced Wolves in the League the following season, our on-field form had seen a significant upturn, due in no small part to the emergence of a young Ulsterman. Less than 18 months since George Best's debut for the club, Slingsby and Rigby were drawing him into United history.

THE UNITED STORY *An illustrated history of United by Peter Slingsby and Cecil Rigby*

* Signed for M.U.F.C. May, 1963

PAGE FOUR

15 MARCH 1965: THE RULE OF THE LAWMAN

With the Reds looking like serious contenders to win the league title for the first time in eight years, the programme for the Fulham league fixture focused on the importance of another future member of the Reds' famed Trinity. Denis Law's goals (39 in all competitions over the course of the season) were proving indispensable.

THE UNITED STORY *An illustrated history of United by Peter Slingsby and Cecil Rigby*

30 AUGUST 1969: WHERE THERE'S A WILF...

With Matt Busby's retirement, Wilf McGuinness had the daunting task of taking over from a legend. Uninitiated United fans got an introduction in *UR* against Sunderland, as the story of Wilf's career so far was sketched out.

PRESENTING . . . WILF McGUINNESS

CHIEF COACH MUFC

COMPILED AND DRAWN EXCLUSIVELY FOR THE UNITED REVIEW
BY MARTIN F. DONOGHUE

MOUNT CARMEL SCHOOL MANCHESTER - TWO YEARS WITH THE CITY BOYS' TEAM THE DISTINCTION OF TWO YEARS WITH THE ENGLAND BOYS' TEAM AND UNIQUE DISTINCTION OF BEING CAPTAIN IN ALL THESE TEAMS DURING 1952 AND 1953

AT 17 YEARS OF AGE MADE LEAGUE DEBUT AGAINST WOLVES AT OLD TRAFFORD 8TH OCTOBER 1955 - UNITED WON 4-3

ENGLAND YOUTH TEAM & ENGLAND U/23 TEAM HONOURS FOLLOWED

FULL INTERNATIONAL CAPS VERSUS IRELAND AND MEXICO 1958

THE END OF A DISTINGUISHED PLAYING CAREER - A BROKEN LEG - WHILST PLAYING AGAINST STOKE CITY RESERVES AT OLD TRAFFORD 12TH DECEMBER 1959

APPOINTED ENGLAND YOUTH TEAM TRAINER, THEN IN 1968 MANAGER OF THE INTERNATIONAL YOUTH TEAM

ONE OF SIR ALF RAMSEY'S ASSISTANTS DURING THE WORLD CUP SERIES 1966

SPECTATOR'S VIEW OF THE RESERVE TEAM'S TRAINER

CHIEF COACH 1969

PAGE FOUR

11 OCTOBER 1969: THE BACKROOM LEGEND

In the same series of illustrated stories, Jimmy Murphy's role was highlighted in the programme for the Ipswich Town league game. His most memorable contribution to the club was of course standing in for Matt Busby after Munich, but Murphy had also been an indispensable part of the youth development set-up.

PRESENTING . . . JIMMY MURPHY

ASSISTANT MANAGER MUFC

COMPILED AND DRAWN FOR THE UNITED REVIEW BY MARTIN F. DONOGHUE

TON PENTRE SCHOOLS · RHONDDA 1922/23 WELSH SCHOOLBOY INTERNATIONAL 1924 - DEFEATED ENGLAND BOYS 3-2 AT CARDIFF

JOINED WEST BROMWICH ALBION 1928 · DEVELOPED INTO STRONG FORCEFUL WING-HALF - EARNED FIRST FULL INTERNATIONAL CAP AT 20 - AGAINST ENGLAND.

1935 REACHED F.A. CUP FINAL WITH W.B.A LOST TO SHEFFIELD WEDNESDAY 4-2

SERVED IN THE R.A. DURING 1939-45 WAR - 3YRS. WITH EIGHTH ARMY - MET SIR MATT IN BARI ITALY 1945 AND WAS ASKED TO JOIN UNITED AS SIR MATT'S ASSISTANT IN RE-BUILDING THE CLUB AND GROUND

TO SUCH EFFECT THAT FROM 1946 TO 1957 THE LEAGUE CHAMPIONSHIP HAD BEEN WON 3 TIMES AND RUNNERS UP 4 TIMES F.A. CUP FINALISTS TWICE WINNING ONCE PLUS 2 CHARITY SHIELD WINS

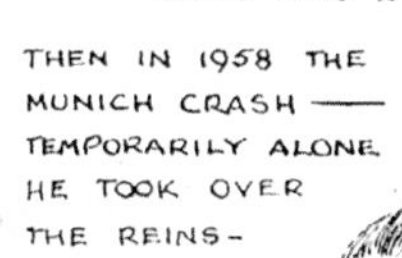

THEN IN 1958 THE MUNICH CRASH —— TEMPORARILY ALONE HE TOOK OVER THE REINS -

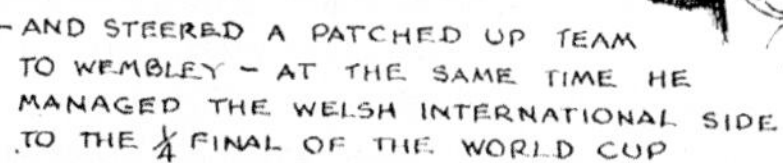

- AND STEERED A PATCHED UP TEAM TO WEMBLEY - AT THE SAME TIME HE MANAGED THE WELSH INTERNATIONAL SIDE TO THE ¼ FINAL OF THE WORLD CUP

THE 'BOSS' RETURNED AND TOGETHER THEY REACHED FURTHER HEIGHTS - TWO MORE CHAMPIONSHIPS, A FURTHER CUP SUCCESS, ALL CULMINATING IN THAT SUPREME TRIUMPH - THE EUROPEAN CUP WIN AT WEMBLEY 1968 - THE STORY HAS NOT YET ENDED FOR THE

ASSISTANT MANAGER

PAGE FOUR

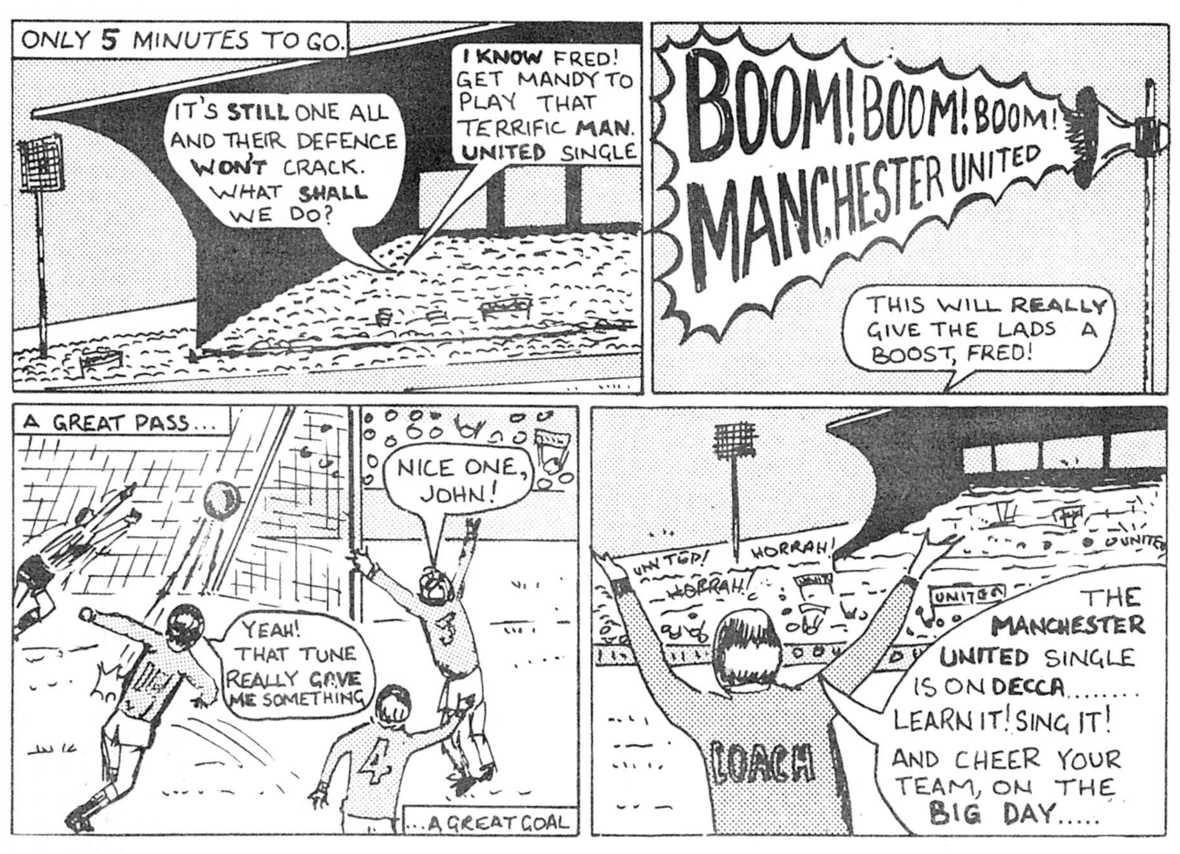

7 MAY 1979: SING UP, LADS!

Cartoons were a rarity in *UR*s of the 1970s, but when United reached Wembley in 1979, the Decca record label chose this format to remind readers of the club's 1976 FA Cup final song *Manchester United* (catchy title). Unfortunately neither this, nor our 1979 tune *Onwards Sexton Soldiers* could serenade the Reds to victory at the national stadium.

WOTSISNAME by David Rowe

31 AUGUST 1981: THE NEW BOYS
Daily Mirror cartoonist David Rowe was handed a regular slot in *UR* in the early 1980s. Originally called *Wotsisname* then *Thick and Thin*, it focused on the titular United fans. Here they were cheering on captain Martin Buchan before the first home game of the season, against Nottingham Forest.

THICK AND THIN by David Rowe

28 NOVEMBER 1981: THE HARD SELL
Advertising was becoming ever more prevalent in football, with shirt sponsors now commonplace. Thick and Thin had their satirical say before the Brighton league fixture at Old Trafford in 1981/82.

26 DECEMBER 1981/ 6 FEBRUARY 1982: CAPTION COMPETITION
Slightly belatedly, at the Everton Boxing Day game, readers got the chance to win a tidy sum for the best caption to the above festive cartoon. The winning entry (right) was published for the Villa game a few weeks later, with £500 as the prize.

27 FEBRUARY 1982: DERBY DAY
As United prepared to take on Manchester City, the pair expressed a fairly gentle sense of rivalry with our neighbours, wishing them no ill... other than when they're up against the Reds, naturally.

17 APRIL 1982: CROWD-SOURCING
Rowe loved tapping into terrace humour in his strips, as he did on this occasion for the Spurs matchday programme towards the end of the 1981/82 campaign.

11 SEPTEMBER 1982: MAMA MIA!
United had enjoyed a strong start to the 1982/83 season, and for the Ipswich Town league programme Thick and Thin chose to celebrate it with the kind of mother-in-law gag that was all too familiar in those days...

24 SEPTEMBER 1983: TOPICAL TWOSOME
Thick and Thin often chewed over recent events. In this case, they referred to the recent Charity Shield win over Liverpool, that matchday's league opponents.

THICK AND THIN by David Rowe

19 NOVEMBER 1983: ROUTE 1 UNITED 4
Visitors Watford were known as a long-ball team, even though they had been league runners-up the previous season. United had their number, though, beating Graham Taylor's Hornets 4-1 at Old Trafford.

21 MARCH 1984: BARÇA BEWARE!
After losing the European Cup Winners' Cup first leg 2-0 to a Diego Maradona-led Barcelona, United had an uphill task back at Old Trafford, as Thick and Thin acknowledged. Of course, the Reds would pull it off, winning 3-0 on a famous night.

Thick and Thin by David Rowe

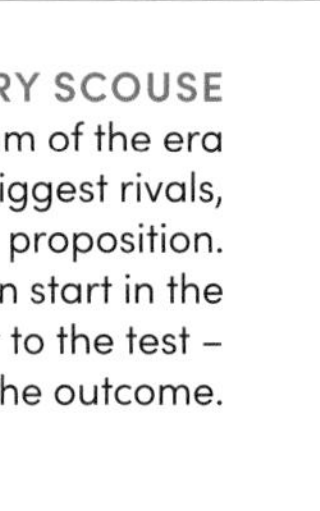

19 OCTOBER 1985: SCARY SCOUSE
Liverpool, the dominant team of the era and arguably United's biggest rivals, always proved a difficult proposition. United's unbeaten start in the league was to be put to the test – a 1-1 draw was the outcome.

17 AUGUST 1986: A REAL TEST

The first home game after the 1986 World Cup was a friendly against Spanish side Real Sociedad. Meanwhile, Argentina's World Cup hero Maradona was still *persona non grata* in England after the 'Hand of God' goal.

22 NOVEMBER 1986: FESTIVE FERGIE CHEER

With Alex Ferguson newly unveiled as United's new manager, Thick was getting excited about the team's prospects with Christmas around the corner and QPR arriving for the new boss's first home league game.

UNITED REVIEW

Thick and Thin by David Rowe

31 AUGUST 1987: MEMBER, ME?
Before the first home game of the 1987/88 season, against Chelsea, the prospect of compulsory membership cards for football fans was becoming a big talking point within the English game.

Thick and Thin by David Rowe

17 MAY 1988: ITALIAN STYLE
Excitement surrounded this friendly clash against Italian champions AC Milan – Ruud Gullit was in town, linchpin of probably the coolest football team in the world at the time, and one of the best.

30 AUGUST 1989: CANARIES COMING
A slightly different look to the cartoon greeted the new season. Former Norwich men Steve Bruce and Mick Phelan featured as United played host to the men from Norfolk.

12 NOVEMBER 1989: CLOUGH FIXTURE
United prepare to face Nottingham Forest, with their long-serving, much-loved but outspoken boss Brian Clough in charge of the visitors.

UNITED REVIEW

3 FEBRUARY 1990: BLUE TOUCHES
Manchester City had been promoted back to Division One, so this was the first Old Trafford derby in nearly three years. A rare appearance of blue colours in the cartoon greeted the occasion.

UNITED REVIEW

THICK and THIN

BY DAVID ROWE

5 MAY 1990: FINAL FEVER
As United ended our league campaign against Charlton, with one eye on the Cup final against Palace the following weekend, Wembley tickets were at a premium. Meanwhile, Thick and Thin were approaching the end of their long run in *United Review*.

1 JANUARY 1994: NEW YEAR MESSAGE
On the day Leeds rolled up to Old Trafford, this one-off cartoon offered a New Year's message, apparently hoping old Father Time would be kind on the Reds. We're not quite sure what his role was in proceedings, but of course Alex Ferguson's men were already en route to a first league and Cup Double that season.

27 DECEMBER 1995: RIGHT SAID FRED

The next cartoon character to regularly grace the *United Review* pages was club mascot Fred The Red, who was first tasked with entertaining younger fans in the early '90s. So down with the kids was he that in this issue, on sale at the Newcastle United game in 1995/96, Fred even nodded to some of the facial hair trends of the time!

20 MARCH 1996: COMICAL CAPERS

Fred The Red's antics continued to be faithfully documented through the Double-winning season of 1995/96, although in this issue, published for Arsenal's midweek league visit, he wasn't afforded quite as much space as earlier in the season.

1 NOVEMBER 1997: NORM & EC'S CAMEO

From time to time *United Review* would feature different cartoons, but sometimes they were short-lived, as was the case with this single-strip affair, which appeared in the issue published for the Sheffield Wednesday league fixture in the 1997/98 season.

TWENTY MINUTES LATER, AT THE CLIFF...

NOW, FRED, I WANT YOU TO SET A GOOD EXAMPLE TO THESE KIDS, AND SHOW THEM A FEW TRICKS. MAKE THE GRADE TODAY, AND I'LL GIVE YOU A TRYOUT IN THE NEXT RESERVE GAME!

FRED'S A NATURAL WITH THE KIDS, BUT WILL HE MAKE THE GRADE? TO BE CONTINUED...

MANCHESTER UNITED FOOTBALL COURSES ARE RUN THROUGHOUT THE HOLIDAYS FOR YOUNGSTERS OF ALL AGES. FOR FURTHER INFORMATION, WRITE TO: DAVE RYAN, FOOTBALL COMMUNITY OFFICER, MANCHESTER UNITED SOCCER SCHEME, OLD TRAFFORD, MANCHESTER M16 ORA
IF YOU'D LIKE MORE INFORMATION ON JOINING FRED THE RED'S JUNIOR DEVILS, SEE THE NEXT PAGE FOR DETAILS!

15 AUGUST 1998: MASCOT'S GOT TALENT

Fred the Red was back with a new look for the 1998/99 Treble season to greet our first opponents, Leicester City. Here, the club's football courses get a plug from the boss, while Fred appeared to be the club's hot new signing... 20 years or so before we signed the human Fred!

11 AUGUST 1999: RED DEVIL DOWN UNDER

In the issue on sale at the first home game of the new season, against Sheffield Wednesday, another kids' cartoon co-opted the name of the Antipodean soap opera to hang a Fred adventure around the recent signing of Aussie international keeper Mark Bosnich from Aston Villa. Nicely done.

CHAPTER 5

Columnists

A plethora of distinctive voices have helped shaped *United Review* down the decades, from the all-seeing eye of 'The Editor' to the impeccably biased Paddy Crerand, without forgetting the epoch-defining David Meek...

Here in the 21st century, *United Review* is full of different voices. Players, legends and fans all get their say, as does the manager, of course. But it wasn't always like that.

Back in the 1920s, there was just one lone columnist: 'The Editor'. Their real name was unknown – or at least undeclared – but he/she was the voice that rounded up all the latest goings-on at the club in a column entitled 'Play and Players'. Very little was left on the cutting-room floor: if it was news, then it went in the column, which meant that 'Play and Players' could often include honest reports of what would be deemed sensitive information by modern-day standards.

By the 1930s, the column had been reshaped into 'Between You and Me' – a more pithy, opinion-based piece of raconteuring. And while you might imagine the inter-war years as prim and proper, there were plenty of no-nonsense assessments laid out on the table. If you weren't performing on the pitch, 'The Editor' wouldn't spare you from a good panning!

Above: The Munich Air Disaster was to claim the lives of a number of great journalists

But this was also the decade when officials at the club assumed a greater position of authority. The chairman might include a new message for the season in the first issue of the campaign, or a goodwill greeting at Christmas time, or important notices about tickets, attendances or a new managerial appointment.

After the Second World War, local newspapermen were given columns. Tom Jackson (*Manchester Evening News*) and Alf Clarke (*Manchester Evening Chronicle*) were the most regular contributors, but many other journalists also featured. Sadly, several of these great passionate football men met a tragic end at the Munich Air Disaster of 1958. It's an often overlooked aspect of the

David Meek was a constant voice in *UR* for more than five decades

Journalists Alf Clarke (left) and Tom Jackson (right) brought expert opinions to the pages of the programme

accident that journalism was also robbed of a great generation of talents – not just football.

Following Jackson's death at Munich, the legendary David Meek assumed his job covering the Reds for the *MEN* – and also began a column in *United Review.* It was the start of a long and fascinating relationship, which would see Meek contribute to the programme for 55 years, writing not only his own column but also Sir Alex Ferguson's, until the latter's retirement in 2013.

'I shall never forget of course the highly charged days of despair that followed the disaster at Munich which not only destroyed what seemed likely to become the best football team ever created but left such agony of mind for so many people,' wrote Meek in 1979. 'I knew well what was involved in becoming a one-club reporter, though I hardly guessed at the scale of world-wide interest inescapable with Manchester United.'

Little did Meek know just how that worldwide interest would grow in the subsequent decades, as Ferguson-led success further enshrined United as a sporting and cultural juggernaut.

As opinions continued to proliferate, columns increasingly became the preserve of club legends like Paddy Crerand, rather than journalists. The famously red-eyed and belligerent Scot is among the most beloved of former Reds, and his forthright, uncompromising views are the perfect tonic for supporters – whether we're celebrating success or railing against injustice.

It's a far cry from the anonymity of the 'The Editor' and those simple club bulletins. But the progression of *United Review*'s columns displays a neat timeline of the club's ever-changing relationship with media coverage and public opinion.

Clubs and Players

THE United forwards are not expected to consider the feelings of any commentator on their doings, but it was unkind of them to give away the writer of these notes as completely as they did on Saturday last. On the morning of the match with Tottenham Hotspur there appeared in these columns a prediction to the effect that the United forwards would not play worse than they did against Burnley if they stuck the game for another twenty years. That shows how little a critic knows of the capacity of the United vanguard, or at least a portion of it. On Saturday it was demonstrated beyond contradiction that the United attack can do worse even than against Burnley, but it must be almost impossible for them to fall lower than the standard exhibited in the match with Tottenham Hotspur. Of course, the question is not now how much worse, but how much better they can play, for in the absence of any improvement it is certain that only a miracle can save us from a descent into the Second Division. Six points from the remaining engagements would probably make us secure, but echo is silent as to where these are to be obtained. If we had the pointage of Liverpool we should consider ourselves safe, but the Merseyites hold other views, and they will fight hard enough this afternoon to lift themselves even clearer than they are from the danger zone. The advantage to us is that of playing at home, and if our men fail to turn that to good purpose, then our state is indeed parlous. Our team were able to force a draw at Liverpool in the first engagement, and a victory therefore to-day should not be beyond their powers.

Despite our splendid record of successes at Newcastle, and, in a lesser degree, at Oldham, the prospects of points gained from the away Easter matches are decidedly slender. Newcastle are almost as desperately placed as ourselves, and Oldham Athletic have good warrant for holding the belief that the League championship is theirs for an extra effort. Bradford, too, are a good side, and, generally speaking, our men will have to revert to their away form of December and January, when they drew five successive "out" fixtures, if any result should accrue from their visits to the clubs mentioned.

Dependence upon the shortcomings and possible failures of other clubs in the threatened area is hardly a heroic proceeding, but it is at least consoling to know that a few of our present company at the foot of the League have no better outlook than ourselves. We don't really enjoy the sight of other clubs floundering about at the bottom of the table, but we can't help feeling a little the better for it in our own lamentable state. Where the submerged have to meet each other nothing but good can happen to our prospects, and Newcastle United are not to be envied in having to visit Tottenham, Bolton, and Nottingham. Notts County have five of their remaining six matches at home, and two of these are with Newcastle and Chelsea, and the chances of the "Magpies" dodging relegation are brighter than appears on the surface. We have to visit Chelsea on April 19, and the "Pensioners" will not allow their Cup final engagement of five days later to blind them to the necessity of going all out in the League engagement with Manchester United.

In the course of the match on Saturday Allman had the ill-luck to be injured and may not recover in time for the game this afternoon. In his absence, Hodge will fill his old accustomed position in the team, and if he reaches his best standard his presence will be a big factor in the contest. Woodcock has played himself to a standstill in recent matches, and is obviously in need of a rest. Since the introduction of he and Potts to the team, the pair have scored ten of the fourteen goals credited to the club, and have thoroughly justified their promotion. Anderson will lead the attack, and a repetition of one of his graceful goal-scoring days would be a welcome Easter egg for his directors and our supporters.

Lancashire has every reason to be proud of itself over the selection of the venue for the Cup final. The Old Trafford enclosure is honoured by the first choice, and if the "gate" does not exceed that of the memorable replayed final of four years ago, it will, doubtless, reach a figure considered ample in these straitened times. It is worth repeating, that all the records for the F.A. Cup competition outside the Crystal Palace are held by Old Trafford, and it can be said even now that a minimum attendance of 50,000 may safely be relied upon. Goodison Park will house the replay, if one is considered necessary, and Lancashire may feel flattered that one of the semi-finals and the final has been decided within its borders. Even in appointing the referee, the F.A. have displayed a keen sense of the fitness of things, for Mr. H. H. Taylor hails from Altrincham, and can be considered almost at home on the Old Trafford ground.

Harold Halse may have fallen a little from his best form, as some of the critics allege, but his knack of scoring goals in Cup-ties has not yet deserted him. He was a big factor in the success that led to Manchester United appearing in the final in 1909, and two years ago he fulfilled a similar office for Aston Villa, whilst his goal on the Villa ground on Saturday completely settled the pretensions of Everton to figure in the last round of all. Other players have appeared in the final oftener than Halse, but if the old United player toes the mark on April 24 he will create a record of having represented three different clubs in three finals.

The difference between the League tourney and the Cup competition is reflected in the fact that while Chelsea have failed to win a solitary away League match, the Londoners have removed from the knock-out competition, on foreign soil, three strong teams in Manchester City, Newcastle United, and Everton. Chelsea is the first London club in fourteen years to appear in the Final, and it is curious that the opposition to the Pensioners will be provided by Sheffield United, the club Tottenham Hotspur defeated when they recovered the trophy for the South in 1901, after a long exile in the north.

Formed in 1905-6, Chelsea have always been extraordinarily successful as a gate-drawing club, but have rarely fulfilled expectations as a side, and in the League they have generally been nearer the bottom than the top of the table. Now they are in the anomalous position of being Cup finalists and the bottom of the League table. Sheffield United have appeared thrice in the Final, and have carried off the trophy on two occasions. In 1899 they defeated Derby County, and in 1902 they beat Southampton. They were also in the final won by Tottenham Hotspur in 1901, at Bolton, after a draw at the Crystal Palace.

The instruction from the League that May 1 should be pressed into service for the purpose of playing matches postponed owing to the Cup-ties can be said to apply to the Manchester United v. Aston Villa fixture, which was due for decision on April 24, at Old Trafford, but, of course, cannot be played on that date owing to the ground being requisitioned for the Final tie. The Villa are a good draw at Old Trafford any time, and their welcome will be none the less hearty because it is a week later than arranged originally.

The Everton centre forward, Parker, is now in advance of the average rate of scoring which will enable him to eclipse Bert Freeman's League record of 38 points in 1908-9. In 31 games Parker has scored 33 goals, and has seven matches in which to get the six points that will better Freeman's splendid performance. Freeman, of course, put up his record whilst wearing the Everton uniform, and it is perhaps only appropriate that one of his successors in the Goodison team should be instrumental in setting up higher figures.

At the League Management meeting on Monday last, it was decided that Spratt should remain a Manchester United player on Brentford receiving £175 for his transfer.

2 APRIL 1915, v LIVERPOOL
The programme editor doesn't hold back in his criticism of United's forward line, and although they improve against the 'Merseyites', winning 2-0, the match is later found to have been fixed.

CLUB CHATTER

MR. GIBSON—SPORTSMAN.

UNITED'S FUTURE IN THE HANDS OF THE PUBLIC.

"Let us now praise famous men."

By that I mean let us talk of Mr. James W. Gibson, the Manchester business man, who has very sportingly come to the aid of Manchester United at a time when the future of the club hung in the balance.

Maybe the general public did not realise the serious financial position of the club, but happily Mr. Gibson was acquainted with the facts and then decided that he would take on the responsibilities of the club until January 9th. In all probability, and especially at this time of the year, Mr. Gibson will have his own private worries, and therefore his action is all the more to be admired, and I hope that the people of Manchester will see to it that his call for better support will not be in vain.

It must be realised that Mr. Gibson's sporting action will have been nothing more than a waste of time and money unless his efforts are backed up by the thousands of people who once—not many years ago—were fervid supporters of the United.

Mr. Gibson has intimated that if these people return to Old Trafford on Saturday afternoons he is prepared to put the club on its feet again by appointing a manager and acquiring new players. That he also has the welfare of the shilling spectators at heart is proved by the fact that he is going to consider erecting covered accommodation on the popular side. This gentleman takes the view that the City of Manchester cannot afford to lose Manchester United, and I agree with him, and furthermore, think that not only the club but the City itself owe a debt of gratitude to him that can never be repaid. Probably it will not interest him in the least, I don't think it will, but, Mr. Gibson has made himself famous in football circles by his big-hearted action, and has certainly proved himself to be that epitome of sportmanship, "A Man's Man."

Everything now depends on the public. If they want Manchester United to be the Arsenal of the North they must give Mr. Gibson the support that he asked for, and show him that all his enterprises will have the backing of thousands of his fellow citizens. If you want to see your club in the forefront once more, prove it to Mr. Gibson in a practical manner by turning up in thousands at next Saturday's game with Bradford.

The present board will strive their utmost to co-operate effectively with Mr. Gibson, and will do everything in their power to bring his schemes to fruition. If the spectators will only adopt the same attitude, then better times are ahead for Manchester United.

By the way, the Central League game with Everton Reserves has been re-arranged, and they will visit Old Trafford on January 9th, and during the game frequent messages will be sent round the ground pertaining to the state of affairs at Plymouth and Millwall. In conclusion, on behalf of the club, I wish every one a Very Merry Christmas and a most happy and prosperous New Year.

THE EDITOR.

25 DECEMBER 1931, v WOLVES
There's plenty of praise for the new United chairman James W Gibson, with the editor calling for fans to heed the calls for bigger crowds at Old Trafford.

Time : Friday, before the Cup Game.

Tommy : " It's all right, Editor. I had a dream last night."

Editor : " Do dreams come true ? What about the football writers who tell us that United faces almost a hopeless task in fighting a team unbeaten on their own ground this season ? "

Tommy : " Well, I'm backing my dream. I saw Mutch as clear as daylight scoring a goal ! "

Editor : " And did you see how many Reading forwards scored ? "

Tommy : " All right, you'll see."

* * *

Scene : London Road Station, Friday, 5.30 p.m. Editor shakes hands with Casual and Tom Jackson. " Good luck, send back a good story. Sorry I can't come. Doctor forbids ! "

Editor greets Mr. Scott Duncan : " The best of luck. I'm afraid you've got a hard task."

A. S. D. : " Yes, a hard task ; but I'm hopeful—I'm hopeful."

Editor gives George Mutch a parting handshake. " All the best for a great game. At least bring back a replay at Old Trafford next Wednesday."

G. M. (with a vigorous shake of the head) : " No, we'll do better than that."

* * *

Wireless : Sports Results, 6 p.m.

" Good heavens—Sunderland."

" Ah, City through."

" By jove."

" Good."

" Here it is—hush ! . . . Reading 1—Manchester United (hurry, man) 3 ! ! ! "

Three cheers for the team !

* * *

Well, fellow supporters, we have had some exciting times since we last prepared a programme a few days before Christmas. There was that keen disappointment about Barnsley on the home ground ; and the brilliant hit-back on Barnsley ground ; there was the sensational change of making Mutch the centre-forward with Gardner on his right ; and also the daring experiment of placing Bamford on the right wing. The Mutch-Gardner combination immediately justified itself. On general grounds Bamford on the wing succeeded—although I wait to hear what Casual says.

There was a stage when supporters began to wonder whether Mr. Scott Duncan was over-optimistic when he said, at the beginning of the season, that all positions were strongly duplicated. It looked as if it were not so. But then came the discovery of Gardner, and in my humble judgment the present forward line looks a pretty good one. If Bamford shows as much persistence as he did at centre-forward and is a thought quicker, he might prove a great success. Here's wishing him luck.

We are still in a good position with a game in reserve. Reading shows that we can win difficult games away. Away wins we want. Let our boys give us away wins, and anything may happen. May they come up to our brightest hopes. If Southend can draw with the Spurs, why can't we beat them ?

Now then, what about the next draw ?

MONDAY.

No, we do not get much luck in the draw. Another away game—and by the time this is in print you will know whether it is to be Millwall or Stoke City. We had hoped for a good home draw—Arsenal or City for preference—what ? But still, uncertainty is the thing that puts spice in the Cup ; as Sunderland now know. Neither Millwall nor Stoke City are to be feared under normal conditions. Some of you once cheered United out of a nasty spot of bother on the Millwall ground ; and you have seen us beat Stoke City. Naturally, Port Vale's twin club will be anxious to do the Sunderland trick on us—but we're not Sunderland ; and you cannot always have ice-frozen ground. One good thing—if it's Stoke City, there will be a mighty invasion of the Red and Whites into the Potteries. And so, though I like the Millwall men, I'm hoping that Stoke City will win. Am I right ?

And now—what will Robertson and Owen think of Gee Bee's cartoon ? Good luck to them.

Page 5

18 JANUARY 1936, v NEWCASTLE UNITED
The 'Between You and Me' column took on various formats during its spell as a column within the matchday programme, this one being a cross between the script of a play and a direct conversation with the reader. The upshot? United beat Reading in the FA Cup third round and the editor being rather pleased about it.

19 SEPTEMBER 1936, v SHEFFIELD WEDNESDAY
A week on from United beating City 3-2 in a first league derby in five years, it's thanks all round from chairman Gibson after a thrilling afternoon for the Reds.

United were promoted back to Division One in 1935/36, with this photo showing the Reds' promotion clash at West Ham

TELEPHONE TRAFFORD PARK 1661 & 1662

MANCHESTER UNITED Football Club Ltd.

1936—1937

OLD TRAFFORD MANCHESTER

Chairman : Mr. J. W. GIBSON
Directors :
Mr. MATHEW M. NEWTON, Mr. HUGH SHAW, Mr. H. P. HARDMAN, Mr. G. E. WHITTAKER, Dr. W. MacLEAN
Secretary : W. R. CRICKMER
Manager : A. SCOTT DUNCAN

September 19th, 1936
NUMBER 4

Official Programme

Price TWOPENCE

Editor : Sidney F. Wicks — Manchester Guardian Buildings, Pall Mall, Manchester

A Tribute from our Chairman

Dear Friends,

I wish to place on record my tribute to all those who helped to make last Saturday one of the greatest days in the history of Manchester United.

I would thank . . . .

The Police for their wonderful tact, good humour and efficient control of a vast crowd.

The St. John's Ambulance men for their willing and expert service.

The stewards for their wonderful marshalling of the 69,000.

All the spectators for their fortitude and patience in trying conditions, for their good spirits and supreme sportsmanship.

The two teams for the spirit in which they fought a game which imposed such a strain on nerves and body. The twenty-two men were splendid.

Yours faithfully,

J. W. Gibson

Page 3

BETWEEN YOU and ME

By the EDITOR

From some points of view it was unfortunate that we had to play three difficult away games in succession, while the team as a whole was trying to find its form. It is an expensive lesson but it is better learnt now than later on. The game last Saturday at Stoke definitely showed that the team is remedying weaknesses in play and regaining that brilliance of which the game against Birmingham gave a hint. I am glad there has been no panic just as there was no boasting at the beginning. Both directors and players have quietly persevered. That will bring its reward.

What material for arguments has been provided by Manchester football this season! I can imagine many a dart board has suffered. There is the old argument as to whether a man who is below form should be immediately replaced or persevered with. If you replace him you weaken his self-confidence and stop him from staging a come-back. If you let him go on there is the danger of losing vital points. How is the management to decide? The answer is that you cannot decide the question on paper. You have to know the man. Directors may know of influences affecting him of which we are ignorant. Talking to him they may recognise a determination to succeed which they are bound to respect.

Always learn to allow for the human side. Put yourself in the place of a man who has done brilliantly last season and cannot just find his form with a new club. He believes in himself and any moment he may come bang to the front. Then put yourself in the place of the chairman of a club. He wants to please his loyal supporters; he wants to score vital points. If he replaces the player he may be doing harm to a man. If he does not replace him, he may be keeping some ambitious player back. Not easy, is it? What would you do?

One fact emerges—the perseverance shown in playing the same forwards shows that the directors have faith in them. This is heartening to them. It is a grand thing when faith is justified.

Let us try not to be just a mob which looks upon a team as a penny in the slot machine to produce victories. Look upon them as men and fellow sportsmen.

Then think what a team is when it is carrying all before it. It means something has clicked—the machine has become perfect. For how long? I make bold to say that perfection is impossible to maintain. A team is either approaching good form or it is falling away from good form. Men change from week to week and there are accidents. After all, isn't it this unaccountable reaction of human nature that makes football fascinating? There is always hope but there should never be panic; and as for boasting—not at all!

MUJAC! May I add a note about this mystic word: It stands for Manchester United Junior Athletic Club. Within a seven mile radius of United ground there are over 250 schoolboy soccer teams with upwards of 3,000 players. These mostly owe their life to the enthusiasm of school-teachers. In order that promising players might not be wasted MUJAC scheme was placed under the patronage of Manchester United Directors with a committee composed of teachers and other experienced friends. The Club nights definitely encourage the lads to do well in their everyday occupations as well as in football. It is a splendid experiment, and in the next number we shall tell you more about it.

SMILE!

A candidate rushing to address a meeting at an election was accosted by a friend.

"What do you think about the political situation now?" the friend asked.

"Don't bother me!" replied the candidate. "I've got to talk. This is no time to think."

* * *

It was three o'clock in the morning. Heavy rolls of smoke billowed into the night sky. Angry tongues of flame shot from the various windows of the blazing hotel.

Below an army of firemen fought valiantly to check the fast-spreading blaze. On the second floor two drunks were awakened by the commotion. One of them staggered out of bed. He walked to the window and threw it open. A powerful stream of water from a fireman's hose caught him flush in the face.

The second drunk propped himself up on a pillow. "What ish it?" he inquired. "No good," hiccoughed the other. "'S'only water!"

MUSIC PROGRAMME

L.N.E.R. (M/c. District) SILVER PRIZE BAND

March	"The Middy"	*K. Aldford*
Selection	"The Golden Age" ...	*J. Greenwood*
Trombone Solo ...	"The Mosquito"	*H. Moss*
	Soloist, W. Schofield	
Spanish March ...	"The Ballerina" ...	*G. McKenzie*
	"The Blackpool Walk"	
Fox-Trot ...	"You can't Stop me from Dreaming"	*G. McKenzie*
Euphonium Solo	"Kentucky Home" ...	*arr. Rimmer*
Half-time March ...	"Colonel Bogey"	—

Bandmaster. Mr. J. R. Donbavand.

Secretary: Mr. H. Potter, L.N.E.R. Works, Cornwall St., Openshaw.

24 SEPTEMBER 1938, v CHELSEA
The mysterious 'Editor' discusses the part confidence plays in football and makes reference to the recently created Manchester United Junior Athletic Club, the club's first-ever youth system. The brainchild of chairman Gibson and secretary Walter Crickmer, the aim was to find the best young players in the local area and turn them into first-team footballers.

Also in this issue, sports writer Stacey Lintott has a suggestion for avoiding kit clashes, promotes the idea of shirt numbers and admires United's striking new 'stockings'.

Stacey Lintott's Column

For the third time in four away matches I read that Manchester United have had to change their colours in order to avoid clashing with those of the home team.

Is it not about time that we standardised colours of football jerseys, say red with white knickers for home teams and white with black knickers for visiting teams?

There would be an outcry from the supporters? I doubt it. Of course, we have got to associate certain colours with certain clubs, but hardly any is really distinctive. United have always played in red? But then so do Arsenal, Liverpool, Nottingham Forest and various other clubs. And look at the number of clubs who play in the "England" colours, white and black. Even the famous claret and blue of Aston Villa are no longer really distinctive.

Clubs have shown very little enterprise and initiative in their choice of colours. Nearly all red or white, black or blue. And some clubs have changed and changed again, like Blackpool and Bradford. Remember, too, that even in these days the whole team cannot be dressed in the familiar colours. Goalkeepers must always wear a distinctive jersey with certain colours rigidly enforced.

Clubs to-day study appearances on the field far more than they did. Which is good. The bigger clubs, at least, no longer wear jerseys discoloured, washed out, so that they look more fit for the rag-bag.

And look at the stockings. How smart and neatly ringed many of them are. Once such stockings were associated only with the "old school tie." These distinctive stockings, of course, are not merely decorative. They are of practical advantage. Catch the eye of a player anxious for a colleague to pass to. Footballers cannot go about with their eyes always turned heavenwards.

Many players will tell you that they don't care for repeated changes in their jerseys. When you are used to looking out for a colleague in a red shirt, it can be disconcerting to have to remember that, for a change, you must look for a blue one.

And why not number players? The average football fan needs no such help with his own men. But he has a job to pick out and identify visitors. Particularly in these days of "switches" and interchange of positions. And spectators, say what you will, do take some interest in the other side, like to know who has scored and so on. To-day, thousands have to wait for the evening papers before they are certain of that. I can see no real objection, save prejudice, but many obvious advantages.

United's 1938/39 squad show off their striped socks, much admired by one particular programme columnist

26 AUGUST 1939,
v GRIMSBY TOWN

The spectre of war hangs over the country but the editor of the programme remains in upbeat mood on the first day of the 1939/40 season - what he describes as a 'day of hullos and handshakes'. This would be the only programme of the season, with Britain declaring war on Germany eight days later.

BETWEEN YOU and ME

BY THE EDITOR

To-day is a day of hullos and handshakes. After a dismal summer a new interest leaps into life with the first blast of the football referee's whistle. Now for weekly debates on the ups and downs and thrills of the game. It is good to meet old chums again and good to see the solid phalanx of the most loyal supporters any club ever had.

A word of thankfulness that we are still at peace (written August 22nd). A word of remembrance for the lads doing their military training. Should the worst ever happen the nation will be none the less prepared because of our keenness about sport.

The Practice Match was a real picture—like a stage play. Golden sunshine, emerald green turf, bright red and blue shirts. Of course it was not a real game. Perhaps that is why the Blues won. They had the advantage of being the side with something to attack. The First Team cannot be judged until they are in the grip of a dour League struggle.

The youngsters' game deserved a better gate ; it was full of interest to the student of football and of the future of the game. Tons of technical skill ; wonderful eagerness. Here are lads destined, one of these days, to write their name in the annals of football.

Our hope to see Manchester City back in the First Division seemed almost realized in the friendly game. A keenly contested game with a good spirit in it. Here again City had the advantage of having something to attack.

A hot game in every sense ; light ball, blazing sun, hard ground. A draw pretty fairly expressed the game. We waited to see if any paper would use the tag—"Wait and see" with regard to Asquith. One did !

We welcome the Chairman's message to Supporters in this number and sincerely congratulate him on his splendid speech. It was full of confidence in the future and expressed determination to win honours for the team. The Directors are ready for any of those emergencies which so often arise during the season. There were notable sayings in the speech. "We have no intention of buying mediocrities" . . . . . if a man has not got football ability in him ; gland treatment will not give it to him" . . . . . the reserve and junior sections of the club are so rich in promise that the creation of an all-Manchester team is a not impossible goal at some future period" . . . . . wise and shrewd words.

And so coats off to-day and let the battle begin. As the dear old red shirts come on the field give them a great encouraging and confident cheer. There are no big stars but a team of good men and true, who will twinkle steadily in the football sky.

Hullos and handshakes all round ! And here's to England !

SCORE BOARD KEY page 14

Charlie Roberts played for United from 1904 to 1913

Stacey Lintott's Column

Those of you who cannot recall the playing days of the late Charlie Roberts, at least recall his name, so perhaps a little intimate pen sketch may interest you.

Charlie Roberts was one of the greatest centre half-backs who ever wore the colours of Manchester United—or any other club. He was a giant physically and a giant in ability. In the days when the centre half was the hardest-worked man on the field, Charlie never seemed in a hurry, never "all out." He strolled through the game.

An uncanny gift for positional play was the secret of his great success. He used his height to great advantage when the ball was in the air, but it was skill not strength which served him when it was on the ground. His ball control was almost perfect, his feeding as good as his defence.

Yet Charlie only played in one season for England, in three matches. A mystery ? Well, hardly that. Charlie was something of an agitator by nature, a fighter. In the thick of things in the early days of the Players Union, a leader of men, the Football Association looked upon him with suspicion and even worse. The Players Union was regarded as a menace to the game and to the governing body of the game. Charlie, because he believed in himself and in the justice of his fellow-players' demands, fought on—and lost his caps.

The Football Association declared little "Fatty" Wedlock to be the better centre half. Now that we have mellowed with age, that looking back our judgment is less clouded, how many of us believe that now ? Not that I ever did.

The Football League were more appreciative of his qualities and less critical of his "faults." They knew a real footballer when they saw one and "capped" him many times.

Elsewhere, columnist Lintott takes a trip down memory lane, recalling the late, great Charlie Roberts just a few weeks after his sad death at the age of just 56.

THIS IS THE OFFICIAL PROGRAMME OF

MANCHESTER UNITED FOOTBALL CLUB LIMITED

Chairman: Mr. J. W. GIBSON.

Directors: Mr. M. M. NEWTON, Mr. H. P. HARDMAN, Dr. W. MACLEAN, Mr. G. E. WHITTAKER

Secretary: Mr. W. R. CRICKMER. Editor: Mr. SIDNEY F. WICKS. Manager: Mr. MATTHEW BUSBY

AUGUST 31st : SEASON 1946-47 : NUMBER 1

Our Chairman's Greetings

Photo: Lafayette

Dear Friends,

May I offer my greetings and a welcome to our Supporters on the return to normal first division football after the interlude of watching teams comprised of strange personnel, weary war-workers and travel stained service-men, who, despite numerous difficulties, gallantly succeeded in keeping our grand game alive through the darkest days of a world war. Yes, I think you will agree, everybody did their best to keep the "United" flag flying, all anxiously waiting and looking forward to this day when we embark on the first post-war season of serious competitive football. It is indeed gratifying to know practically all our service players are with us once more, fully trained and fit to do battle with the best. I was with them on an occasion during training and was really impressed with their activities. Mr. Busby, our manager, tells me he is satisfied the team will do well, so we open up full of confidence. A number of the 1939 older players are no longer with us—six years is a long time and changes were imminent, but as you will see, our policy in fostering junior talent is now proving its worth.

A lump rises in my throat when I think of our premises at Old Trafford damaged beyond repair by fire and blast in March 1941, and still looking a sorry spectacle owing to the Government policy of issuing only limited licences for building materials whilst the housing problem is so manifest. As against this, we are fortunate that our neighbours, Manchester City, to whom we are greatly indebted, came to the rescue and offered us a temporary home, which we still enjoy.

In conclusion I must say how much I appreciate your loyalty during the past war-years and sincerely trust you will be rewarded with real, enterprising football.

Yours faithfully,

J W Gibson

31 AUGUST 1946, v GRIMSBY TOWN
League football resumes after the Second World War, and chairman James W Gibson sets the scene ahead of a new campaign under a new manager (Matt Busby) and at a new venue (Maine Road). He also gives thanks to those who 'kept the "United" flag flying' after Old Trafford had been put out of action by the Luftwaffe.

The Editor's Note Book

Since the dark day when War shattered our old way of life (and put paid to football) I have often turned over the pages of the old Manchester United Magazines, thinking of the grand games, of our hopes that went up and down, of the throng that milled through the turnstiles. Couldn't help giving a sigh either; for one lad who used to write clever stuff for the magazine lies quiet in Italy.

Aye, many a man who used to yell "Goal" at Old Trafford will never come back. These chums, these sportsmen, played a bigger game than football—and heard the referee's whistle at the end of the final game.

All the more warmth in our welcome to you ex-service men who gather again to cheer Manchester United. It's not easy to settle down after all that. And things are not too easy for anybody. We hope that entering into the spirit of the old game and the old team will do you a bit of good.

It's strange for our team to be playing at Maine Road, isn't it? Poor Old Trafford surely got a packet when the stands went up in flames. There's little hope of getting back to the familiar ground in a hurry. It takes a lot of material to build stands and the permit is not yet available. Never mind, the game goes on. We say "well done" to Manchester City for their sporting comradeship and we hope United and City supporters will mix it in a new fellowship. That will give all the more zest to the rival game between the two clubs when it comes.

To-day it is my privilege to greet you in this new magazine—the United Review. This we owe to the keenness of our staunch Chairman, Mr. Gibson, to have once more a magazine which shall form a meeting ground of the club, the team and the supporters. May all his hopes for the club be realised! We have had to overcome tremendous obstacles to get the Review going, but here it is and we hope you like it. It will grow better as we go along.

Isn't it astonishing how old friends have kept together—tried and trusted directors, Walter Crickmer and his helpers, and the football writers Alf Clarke and Tom Jackson, all as young as ever. We give a hearty hand to a new friend to the Magazine—our Manager, Matt Busby. Good luck to him!

One word of appeal. The success of this Review depends entirely upon your loyal backing. Tell your chums who missed buying a copy that it's up to them to support the Review. It's first class reading for sportsmen. Please do your best.

I have been over in Alsace-Lorraine investigating ruined and looted villages. It's grand to see the sturdy provincial French folk working twelve hours a day to rebuild the liberty of France. And how they want friendship with Britain, the country that stood alone! But I saw no signs of sport. Perhaps that is a pity. Sport has played a big part in keeping British people steady and good humoured. We are poor haters but lovers of fair play. Sport keeps us from getting all heated up over theories. So good luck to football and good luck to Manchester United.

Editor Sidney F Wicks introduces the new-look programme, renamed *United Review*, describing it as a 'meeting ground of the club, the team and the supporters'.

our guest sportswriter—No. 5

H. D. DAVIES

(OLD INTERNATIONAL)

OF "THE MANCHESTER GUARDIAN"

Football crowds develop personalities every whit as clear and unmistakable as those of the players themselves. That is quite understandable. People living in the same locality naturally possess some common attribute or other which sticks out a mile as soon as those people collect in the mass. Thus, "Owdham Roughyeds"; "Yewwood Monkeys"; "Middleton Moonrakers"; "Rochda Bulldogs" are names denoting qualities which, rightly or wrongly, the inhabitants of those parts long ago believed were held in common.

All crowds are vocal, let there be no mistake about that, but to the person whose job it is to travel round from ground to ground there is a marked difference in the quality of the sounds produced. The shrillest crowd I know is at Anfield; the most excitable at Aston Villa; the most thunderous at Hampden Park (International Match); the best behaved at Wembley; the most terrifying at Merthyr Tydvil; the most partisan at Leeds or Preston; the most indulgent at Chelsea; the most good-humoured at Manchester. But for forth-rightness, plain speaking and a mastery of local idiom as rich in colouring as any of Turner's canvasses, is there anything to beat the tacklers at Oldham?

The differences between crowds internationally are even more plainly marked than between localities. Only those who have experienced at first hand the wild excitability of the French crowds; the hissing and stamping of Hungarian crowds; the turbulence of the Viennese and so on can appreciate the dignity, restraint and even-tempered tolerance of crowds at home. You may remember the visit of the Italian team to Highbury before the war, when Mussolini sought to add a victory over English football to the blood-stained trophies of his Abyssinian triumphs. At one time there was the possibility of as much blood flowing at Highbury as on any Abyssinian battlefield, almost. Ask any of the English players who were kicked black and blue by Mussolini's hirelings and yet stood firm to their undertaking not to retaliate. At one time the situation on the field took an ugly turn, and officials began to fear the worst. Suddenly the crowd saw the funny side of things and began to laugh, and immediately the English players recovered their balance. Thus, as Evelyn Montague wrote, a threatening situation was saved by the instinctive humorous sanity of the British crowd. Those are fine words "instinctive humorous sanity," may they always be characteristic of the watchers at Maine Road.

H. D. DAVIES.

26 DECEMBER 1946, v BOLTON WANDERERS
H.D. Davies, or 'Donny' to his friends, who also wrote under the pseudonym 'Old International', discusses football crowds in this guest columnist from Boxing Day 1946. Sadly, Donny was one of the eight journalists killed in the Munich Air Disaster.

OUR GUEST SPORTSWRITER—**No. 1**

HENRY ROSE

SPORTS EDITOR OF "THE DAILY EXPRESS"

Austerity, ersatz rations, lack of clothing coupons and other headaches notwithstanding, soccer will boom again this season.

Practically every club made a profit last season and my guess is that they will all do so again.

Once again will secretaries of successful clubs experience the ticket nightmares before big games. So will anyone connected with the F.A., and Wembley Stadium on the eve of the big cup games and international matches.

The precious pasteboards last season were sold out almost before they were printed. And until some genius comes across with a gadget that will make big grounds elastic, that will be the situation for years to come.

English soccer prestige had a few hefty kicks in the pants last time round, but drooping chests were restored to an upright position when Great Britain trounced the might of the Rest of Europe.

But we mustn't be smug about that. The lesson that the continentals have taught us (we taught them first and then forgot) is that coaching, training and mental approach to the game are important.

Gone is the time when to throw a ball at the foot of a youngster was sufficient. I have been delighted with the numerous coaching schools that have been doing their stuff in recent weeks. The dividends will not be shown next week or next year, but they will be in the times to come.

I am not going to stick my neck out (one of my favourite pastimes, you may remember) and give you a list of the teams who may win the honours with the season just begun.

Soccer fans have a nasty habit of cutting out the printed word and throwing back in the critic's face at awkward times.

But I will hazard what shred of reputation is left to me and predict that your own Manchester United will be bang there at the finish, as the racing boys have it.

I have seen them in training and have been impressed by their extreme loyalty, their obvious "raring to go" style and the concord between young and old players regardless of prospects of a place in the senior eleven.

To manager Matt Busby, Walter Crickmer, Jimmy Murphy, Tom Currie, Louis Rocca, Ted Connor and every man-jack behind the organisation is extended my sincere wishes for a successful season.

Matt Busby is a straight shooter. If all managers were like him, the job of the sports journalist would be a paradise instead of the strain it is. He is the man with a thousand friends and not a single enemy.

One comes across a great deal of insincerity mixing back stage in soccer, but I think I am safe in saying that if Manchester United happened to realise the dream of all clubs and win both League and Cup this season, Matt Busby (and I must not forget his charming wife, Jean) would not be begrudged the great honour by anyone in the game.

30 AUGUST 1947, v CHARLTON ATHLETIC
Henry Rose was one of the most respected sports writers in the country and another of those killed in Munich. Here he kicks off another season of guest columns with the prediction of an impressive campaign ahead for the Reds.

CASUAL COMMENTS

By **ALF CLARKE**

OF THE "MANCHESTER EVENING CHRONICLE"

The scene is the dining-room in the London Press Club. The occasion: the presentation of the Statuette to Johnny Carey, "the footballer of the year" by the Football Writers' Association, of which I am a member. There is a full gathering. It is Cup Final eve, and the guest of honour is the United captain. I have talked to him before the dinner. I have had a chat to Matt Busby, to Walter Winterbottom, to Scott Duncan (former United manager) to Mr. Vernon Stokes, chairman, Portsmouth football club (the champions, to whom I had offered congratulations). There is Mr. R. Smith, the City chairman accompanied by Mr. Eddie Gill; Mr. H. P. Hardman (acting chairman of United) along with Walter Crickmer (secretary), are also among the V.I.P.s gathered together on this important occasion. Sir Stanley Rous, Col. J. J. Aston, Sir Norman Birkett, P.C., Mr. Brook Hirst, F.A. president, and scores of others. All have come to honour this occasion.

It is a happy gathering. I look at Johnny Carey. In a few hours he and Matt Busby will be making their way to the train, settle down in their "sleepers" and be on the way to Newcastle for the game to-morrow.

But my mind goes back to the days, just before the war, when Johnny Carey came to Manchester as a youngster from St. James's Gate, Dublin. Little did he realise, then, that he was going to enjoy such a wonderful career with Manchester United.

I see no trace of nervousness in Johnny's make-up. But, inwardly, he must feel that this is the greatest day in his life. He may have felt embarrassed when Ivan Sharpe, my colleague, who is president of the F.W.A. this year, tells the large gathering, in eulogistic terms, what he thinks of Johnny Carey. He has just made reference to stars of the past. "Those outstanding players I have mentioned were also gentlemen as well as footballers, and, in that category, I place John Carey," he continues. He relates how the United captain, though a native of Eire, served in the British Army, and then: "I have never seen him do an action on the field that was suspect, and I hope I never shall. He has always been as cool as a cucumber, and I hope he continues to grace the game for many years to come, to set an example to the other players, and to the schoolboys looking on."

So that's what was thought of Johnny Carey. I could endorse every word of it, for few have seen him play so often as I have. Then it came Johnny's turn. "I had hoped to start off by saying I did not feel a bit nervous because I am amongst friends. I still start off amongst friends, but still I am very nervous," said Johnny. Well, he did not look like it. He continued with a speech which, afterwards, Sir Norman Birkett described as: "It is a long time since I enjoyed a speech as good as that one."

He went on to tell of the Cup Final of a year before, and concluded his speech: "I have won this wonderful trophy. Now I have one greater ambition—to bring honour and dignity and prestige to this and I shall do that as long as I live because this is an honour I shall treasure all my life."

Well done, Johnny! You have brought honour to yourself, Manchester United and soccer in general.

PAGE THREE

7 MAY 1949, v PORTSMOUTH
Alf Clarke was a columnist for *United Review* from 1946 until his death in the Munich Air Disaster in 1958. Here he heaps the plaudits on Reds skipper Johnny Carey.

the editor's notebook

When the report was published that Ryder Cup Captain Cotton, after the defeats of 2nd October, had said "I have been kicking them all round the dressing room for their play to-day" many wise old heads were shaken. There seemed to be an idea that this was not the best way to re-establish confidence and to create the winning spirit. That depends whether it was said in fun or not. In any case I liked Tommy Taylor's interview with Archie Ledbrooke in which he told of the way his Boss discussed the lessons of the previous game. It was interesting to learn of the brilliant way in which Matt Busby analyzed the players and the problems they presented. Tommy said that the last word from the Boss would be: "Keep playing football. Play football all the time; the results will come eventuaally". There is typical wisdom in that. But remember that all the wisest manager can do is to try to bring out the best that is in every player. The fact is that miracles cannot be done. If two teams meet and each has been given the wisest coaching possible and every player does his best, why is it that one side wins? There you have the mystery which constitutes every game. If one club possessed eleven ideal and invincible players, who would want to go and witness the inevitable result? Of course it was disappointing when United were beaten by Burnley. All I know is that in the long last, steady pressure of will and fitness and management will bring its reward.

However, a glance at the performances of our junior teams gives encouragement for the future. All the teams are playing extremely well, so come along and watch the boys and really support the **Club.**

10 OCTOBER 1953, v SUNDERLAND
Editor Sidney Wicks explains why he prefers Matt Busby's style of man-management to that of Great Britain's Ryder Cup captain Henry Cotton.

UNITED TOPICS

By **TOM JACKSON**

OF THE "MANCHESTER EVENING NEWS"

The football "specials" which chug merrily between Central Station and Old Trafford take only a few minutes to complete the journey—but what crowded memories they arouse in those fleeting moments!

Every soccer topic under the sun must have been discussed at some time or other within those packed compartments, and the light-hearted banter of the spectators has more than once compensated me for an afternoon's dull entertainment on the field.

Not many weeks ago, a friend who has been abroad nearly 15 years accompanied me to a game at Old Trafford—his first real glimpse of England's premier sport in all that time. The match—it was Middlesbrough's visit here—was exciting and full of good football, but I wasn't really surprised when my friend commented "I enjoyed the football, but best of all I liked the train journey to and from the match. It was an entertainment in itself."

This, I like to think, was a tribute to the bon homie and easy knack of making friends which is an integral part of the make-up of the ordinary football enthusiast. Sport is a great leveller, we are told, and whether your spectator is a doyen of the "grand stand" or the man who queues at the popular-side turnstile his views on football, its personalities and the club he regularly follows, are equally worth hearing.

Take Weymouth's Cup visit a week ago as an example of the sportsmanship which, despite all that may be said to the contrary, does exist to-day. We were a mixed crowd in our particular carriage on the way to the ground; a few "red-hot" United fans, a couple of neutrals who had obviously mis-fired with their arrangements to see the City-Derby tie, and lastly a benevolent-looking man accompanied by his wife and young son, all wearing the green and white colours of Dorset.

Some-one mentioned that Weymouth were 5,000-1 "outsiders" for the Cup, and that United ranked as 7-1 favourites. "Jack Rowley should get a dozen" voiced a United partisan. "It'll be like shelling peas for our lads. I don't arf fancy my chance with United in the club sweep."

Everyone sat uneasily for a few moments, casting sympathetic glances in the direction of Mr. and Mrs. Weymouth and their off-spring who had a picture-brooch of his pride and joy, Patsy Gallacher fastened to his lapel.

Then it happened. "There are no one-horse races in the Cup and more surprising things have happened than Weymouth giving United a run for their money" ventured one of the United enthusiast's companions. Which remark immediately put everyone at ease, gave a ray of hope to the Weymouth contingent, and better still, brought forth ringing cries of "Good luck to your boys" from the Old Trafford enthusiasts as we parted company on the platform.

I'll wager that at least three people who had travelled eight hours from the Dorset seaside resort to Manchester for the tie went away with a high opinion of the sporting attitude of Old Trafford crowds. And the fact that their team held United to four goals, and never at any time looked like football minnows, should make their recollections all the happier.

I wonder what the crowds will be saying on the 1-30 p.m. "up train" this afternoon? It's bound to be entertaining!

14 JANUARY 1950, v CHELSEA

Tom Jackson's columns in *United Review* were always fascinating reads, like this one recalling his train journey to Old Trafford the previous week for the Reds' FA Cup tie with Weymouth (a 4-0 win).

28 APRIL 1951, v HUDDERSFIELD TOWN
Clarke's column reflects on what might have been for the Reds as Tottenham make the most of games in hand to win the league title by four points. Still, Alf remained positive for the future and accurately predicted that the title was just 12 months away.

CASUAL COMMENTS

By **ALF CLARKE**

OF THE "MANCHESTER EVENING CHRONICLE"

League Champions or runners-up? That is the question now. The latter position is already a certainty for United, but Tottenham Hotspur have a lot in hand and it may be that we shall have to accept second position after to-day's games. You never know, of course, and United will fight to the last minute. Oh, to eliminate those Christmas blunders which have cost United so dearly.

There's next season, of course, and my vote is that the championship label will be pinned at Old Trafford. But four times runners-up in five seasons, the other occasion in fourth place, plus a Cup Final victory, is consistency which makes the United team proud of its distinctions.

To-day I shall be watching the Cup Final at Wembley and interested in seeing whether this Blackpool-Newcastle United game approaches in brilliance that of 1948 when United defeated Blackpool. Could any match be more impressive than that? I doubt it, really; but I do feel that this time it will be Blackpool's Cup—if Newcastle's form last week is a true criterion.

Of course Newcastle United were only allowed to play as well as Manchester United permitted them, at St. James's Park, where the Old Trafford team won 2—0. The fact emerges that Newcastle United were defeated by a much better side; and we should take pride in that Manchester United have, this year, accounted for clubs like Tottenham, Middlesbrough, Arsenal, Wolverhampton, Burnley and Newcastle United. That is consistency, and deserves more than runners-up prize.

Do you know that United have a post-war record? They are the only club to secure 50 points or more five years in succession—and the only team to secure bonus money five successive seasons. These are proud records.

United entertain Aberdeen next Wednesday evening, and I hope we have a big gate for the return of Jimmy Delaney, Tommy Lowrie and, in all probability, Tommy Bogan, ex-United stars now with Aberdeen. The kick-off is at 6-30 p.m. Then we have the Festival of Britain visit of Red Star, Jugoslavia, on May 12th (7 p.m.).

After the match against the Continental side United go to Denmark, on a 14-day tour embracing five games, two in Copenhagen, and in Odense, Aalborg and Aarhus. I have made arrangements to travel with the United team to cover their matches in Denmark.

Meanwhile, United affairs show that the policy of bringing in the young stars into the Central League side is to be admired. Though the reserves lost last week-end, the occasion marked the debut of 16 year-old E. Lewis, an inside left, who looks destined to make a name for himself. Indeed, the United Reserve team on duty last week-end was probably the youngest ever to represent the club. It was: Wood; Killin, Byrne; Whitefoot, Jones, Blanchflower; Birkett, Viollet, Cassidy, E. Lewis, Bond. Three 17 year-olds at half-back, two in attack and Lewis, aged 16. They are being groomed to stardom. In a few years' time they will be names with which to conjure.

14 APRIL 1952, v BURNLEY

A year on from his prediction that the 'championship label would be pinned at Old Trafford' at the end of 1951/52, Clarke is getting worried that more disappointment is headed United's way after recent slip-ups. However, a 6-1 win against Burnley would have done much to help settle his nerves.

CASUAL COMMENTS

By ALF CLARKE

OF THE "MANCHESTER EVENING CHRONICLE"

It could well be that, when Saturday 26th April comes around, Burnley could do United a good turn. A championship gesture, in fact. For, on that day, Portsmouth are at Turf Moor and United entertain Arsenal. Now supposing the championship flag rests on (1) the outcome of United's home game with Arsenal, or, (2) Burnley's meeting with Portsmouth. Well, I am sure that Burnley would like to see the championship label coming to Lancashire. . . .

I write before knowing the Easter results against Burnley (Good Friday) and Liverpool (last Saturday). If United have not helped themselves in these two games then it may well be we shall have again to be satisfied with a position in the first four. I have never been unduly pessimistic, and I think United can still lift the championship, but we must not have slip-ups like we saw at Huddersfield and Portsmouth. You don't often see United sustaining two away defeats in succession; rather is it a question of how long they will go before their colours are lowered. Is it getting too big a strain this continual racing for the championship?

Players are only human. But how disappointed we shall be if United fail this time! Errors have been made when we least expected them. This refers to defensive lapses and, perhaps ever more glaring, failure to take goal scoring openings which, normally, would be accepted.

Take the Portsmouth game. I had been talking to Mr. Bob Jackson, the Pompey manager (he's a Lancashire man, from Bolton, by the way), who has done grand work for Portsmouth. But he was certain that Portsmouth would beat United, at Fratton Park. I begged to differ with him — I usually do when it is suggested United might lose! — but Mr. Jackson was not at Fratton to see the match. He had apparently made a decision, on Friday noon (just after I had phoned him) to go to Hampden to see the international, so I was not able to offer "humble apologies" — with the opinion that Portsmouth were lucky to win! Lucky? I'll say they were. The game could have been in United's keeping by half-time had the forwards been on the mark.

So Pompey became the first team this season to complete the "double" over United, and it was United's first defeat at Fratton Park in post-war football.

Meanwhile, United are now busy preparing to make a six-weeks close-season tour of America. They were there two seasons ago and created such a tremendous impression that, though America is not soccer conscious like we are here, the visit of United has already resulted in big bookings at some of the places where they will play. In Los Angeles, for instance, I have had word that one match there — either against Tottenham Hotspur or the Mexican All-Star XI — is an assured sell-out. They recall United's 6-6 hectic draw two years ago with the Mexican side.

5 NOVEMBER 1955, v ARSENAL

Tom Jackson has another tale to tell – this one about his stay at the United team's hotel, in Porthcawl, ahead of playing Cardiff City.

UNITED TOPICS

by TOM JACKSON

of the "MANCHESTER EVENING NEWS"

Whenever United are playing at the famous Ninian Park ground they invariably stay overnight at the quiet, but extremely pleasant seaside resort of Porthcawl, which is within comfortable distance of Cardiff City's headquarters.

And thereby hangs a tale . . . It concerns United's latest visit to Wales a week ago which resulted in a forty-third minute goal notched by Tommy Taylor sufficing to give United full points and a new-look at the top of the First Division table.

An hour or so before the party was due to leave the hotel for the Cardiff ground and while the players were having their usual tactics talk with Matt Busby, a small group of officials headed by Mr. Harold Hardman, the United Chairman, and fellow-director Mr. George Whittaker, sat down to lunch. Naturally the conversation turned to match prospects, but it was suddenly stilled when the waitress, a trim little Welsh lass, piped up with the remark: "I'm sorry for your boys this afternoon. Do you know, the last four teams which have stayed here all lost. And that includes the England team who were here last week."

For a few moments there was an awkward silence. Then Mr. Hardman came to the rescue. Jokingly he called the young lady aside and in a kind of stage whisper he told her: "Don't worry, miss. Everything is going to be changed this afternoon. I can tell you confidentially that United have come here specially to win this match. You can tell your friends, if you like."

The girl seemed bucked by the confident forecast. She waltzed round the table giving tip-top attention to all and sundry and when the coffee stage was reached, her parting shot was: "I'm so glad your boys are going to win. You see, they're the nicest-looking football players we've had in the hotel for a long time!"

So much for the lighter side of the Cardiff story. The points came to United all right, but it all turned out to be a tremendous struggle, simply because several excellent scoring chances were allowed to go astray. At one point, with a little more certainty in their finishing, United might have had a lead of at least three goals.

This victory, coinciding with Sunderland's forfeiture of a home point and Blackpool's shock at the hands of Preston North End, now gives United a one-point lead at the head of the table. But there's no room for complacency. Roger Byrne really hit the nail right on the head on the homeward journey in the small hours of Sunday morning when he remarked: "It's been a fight to get to the top of the League, but our hardest task now will be to stay there. Everybody will be out to spike our guns."

Well spoken, Roger! But I can add that United are not lacking in fighting spirit or determination. The defence put up a great barrier at Ninian Park, Mark Jones responding brilliantly against the dashing Trevor Ford, and both wing-halves Duncan Edwards and Jeff Whitefoot rarely yielding an inch of ground.

Then, when Cardiff went all out to save a point in a grandstand finish, Ray Wood marked his return to the team with a "wonder" save from inside-left Ron Stockin. It had England class written all over it.

It all makes such an inspiring picture for United in view of the way the young Central League side is also keeping the flag flying. Results speak for themselves.

PAGE EIGHT

The Busby Babes were champions in 1955/56 and retained the title the following season

UNITED TOPICS

by TOM JACKSON

of the "MANCHESTER EVENING NEWS"

Roger Byrne, the Manchester United captain, went on record at the beginning of the season with the statement that the champions were not only aiming to retain the League title, but were setting their sights on the F.A. Cup and European Cup targets as well!

Such optimism, even by a captain so sure of the abilities of his team to maintain the exacting pace in all three competitions at the same time, was almost tantamount to naming the Derby, Grand National and St. Leger winners a year in advance.

It's no racing certainty by a long chalk that even now, exactly seven months later with United still vitally involved in this great treble-chance bid, that Roger Byrne's bold prophecy will come true. But whether or not one "leg" goes down against the F.A. Cup challenge of Everton here to-day or whether United fail at the final League and European Cup hurdles, the attempt will be committed to the records as a glorious chapter in United's already colourful history.

Those who have followed United's fortunes at home and on the Continent this season have had more thrills, excitement and quality football than one could have reasonably expected from a team with so many irons in the fire. The amazing point, to my mind, is that despite occasional setbacks such as those sustained in the League matches with Bolton, Sheffield Wednesday and, yes, Everton, the pressure has never slackened.

Like me, you probably expected some reaction from the strain of that never-to-be-forgotten battle for supremacy against Bilbao in the European Cup at Maine Road, when the championship test came with Arsenal here last week. And also like me, those who watched this ding-dong League game, must have wondered from just where the United players got their remarkable stamina.

This 6-2 victory over an Arsenal team which came to Old Trafford riding on the crest of a wave of successes capped a great soccer week for Manchester. So many words have been poured out on the Bilbao epic that further comment is unnecessary, but suffice to say that this was a football match which more than justified the tremendous advance "billing" it received.

Now the Spanish captain, "Piru" Gainza, who led a great sporting Bilbao side, has joined forces with Jeff Mermans (Anderlecht) and Alfred Preissler (Borussia Dortmund), previous captains of champion sides defeated by United in the European Cup.

All three are unanimous in the view that United will go on to win the European trophy, although Belgian international Mermans qualifies his forecast by saying that Real Madrid, the holders, will prove a mammoth test for United if they are paired in the final. The advantage will be with Real Madrid, in that event, because the final of the competition is a one-match decider to be staged in the Spanish capital this summer.

Draw for the semi-finals will be made in Cologne, Germany, on February 28th, and the ties have to be decided between March 1st and April 30th. These dates should allow United to stage their home "leg" at Old Trafford under the new floodlights which are nearing completion.

United, by the way, are the first team to win through to the semi-finals. Their opponents? Well, they could be one of six teams still fighting it out — Real Madrid, Nice (France), Zurich (Switzerland), Florence (Italy), Red Star, of Belgrade (Yugoslavia) and Sofia (Bulgaria).

16 FEBRUARY 1957, v EVERTON

The Babes were still chasing the 'great treble-chance' of league title, FA Cup and European Cup with just less than three months of the season to go – and columnist Jackson is feeling optimistic.

Crash survivor Frank Taylor unveils a plaque at Old Trafford to the journalists killed in Munich

8 FEBRUARY 1958, v WOLVES

This is the last column written by Tom Jackson, submitted ahead of the ill-fated flight back from Belgrade for the weekend's league clash with table-topping Wolves. Following the air crash the game was postponed and all but a handful of programmes destroyed, with the few remaining issues now very much prized by collectors. Tom was among the 23 people who lost their lives in Munich and one of the eight journalists who perished.

UNITED TOPICS

by TOM JACKSON

of the MANCHESTER EVENING NEWS

Now the heat is really on full blast in the First Division championship race and to-day's visit of the League leaders, Wolves, to Old Trafford marks the beginning of yet another vital match period for United. There are only eleven weeks to go in the League campaign, but now, more than at any other stage in the season, every point won or lost assumes double importance.

United face the challenge of the Wolves this afternoon having barely had time to shake the travel-dust off their boots after a near 2,500-mile trip to Yugoslavia and back for the mid-week European Cup quarter-final return match with Red Star in Belgrade.

By the time these notes are in print, the outcome of that intriguing European Cup adventure will have been entered into the record books, but whatever the result I am sure United will have made many new friends in a corner of Europe which is unfamiliar territory for British club sides.

There is no doubt at all that from the viewpoint of spreading the British soccer "Gospel", United's excursions abroad in the European Cup since they first entered the tournament last season have been outstanding successes. That's why clubs in Germany, Spain and Czechoslovakia, previous Cup rivals over the last eighteen months or so, have been well to the fore among the foreign sides anxious to welcome United back to their shores for friendly matches this close-season.

In most of the post-war summer breaks from competitive football United have ventured far and wide on friendly-match tours—twice to the United States and Canada and three times to Scandinavia. But this summer may have to be the exception in view of the World Cup finals in Sweden in June when so many United players will be on call by their countries and club officials Matt Busby (Scotland) and Jimmy Murphy (Wales) will be in charge of their national teams.

When the World Cup parties are announced it seems almost certain that England will include at least three United players — Roger Byrne, Duncan Edwards and Tommy Taylor. Northern Ireland will want Harry Gregg and Jackie Blanchflower, and Wales, assuming they made certain of World Cup qualification by defeating Israel in mid-week, are likely to require the services of Colin Webster, who has already been capped once, and young Ken Morgans, who has come into the reckoning by his displays at outside right.

Whether all or more than the players I have mentioned are honoured by their native countries remains to be seen, but the fact remains that United's link with British international football is really predominant this season, quite apart from the number of players who have gained further caps.

Look at it this way: Matt Busby and his second-in-command at Old Trafford, Jimmy Murphy, are team managers of Scotland and Wales respectively. In the England "camp", a former United player, Walter Winterbottom is in control, while we also have another ex-United player in Johnny Carey guiding the fortunes of Eire. And to complete the picture, we must remember that Peter Doherty, the team manager of Northern Ireland, also has close associations with Manchester, having been a renowned City player before the war.

It's a record that may never be equalled for one club and one city to provide the key-men guiding the fortunes of so many countries in the international field.

CLUB COMMENTS

by

KEITH DEWHURST

of the "Evening Chronicle", Manchester

The damage done to English football as a whole by the Manchester United air disaster is much deeper than it seems, and extends far beyond the loss to the international team of Byrne, Edwards and Taylor.

This in itself is bad enough. England, drawn in the same group as Russia and Brazil, has a very tough task in the World Cup, and there is very little time now to find a new blend. But even though many of the reserves in the England World Cup party would have come from United, the blow is not so crippling to our country as that suffered by Italy when the Turin team was wiped out in 1949. Turin provided more than half the national team, which has not recovered to this day.

It is none the less tragic because it has destroyed the team which was the spearhead of the revival of English football. In the past the curse of English football has been its insularity, its refusal to recognize the importance of what was happening beyond these shores.

United were great not only because they played great football, but also because they looked beyond domestic supremacy to European and even world horizons. If they had beaten Real Madrid in this year's European Cup they really would have been the greatest team in the world.

Who can take their place? Wolves and West Brom are the only candidates. Frankly, their performance in friendly games are no guide. It is a different matter when the chips are down, as Real Madrid showed when they hammered Seville 8-0 recently.

I think that Wolves, West Brom or Preston (one of them must surely be our European Cup candidate next season) will fight hard, and I wish them luck. But none of them look quite good enough to go far.

This, together with the fact that United were crippled by an air accident, is bound to have its effect. I hope and pray that it will not cause a swing back to the old insularity.

Ultimately the future of football lies in more international competitions. The vast crowds who have watched United in the European Cup at Old Trafford and on television prove that the public is ready for it.

We have lost a superb team and a great example. But the inspiration that created United is still there, and I do not think it will be very long before it is felt again.

22 FEBRUARY 1958, v NOTTINGHAM FOREST

Keith Dewhurst wrote this column for *United Review* for the first league game since Munich, reflecting on the devastating impact of the crash on not just the club and England, but the whole of football.

23 AUGUST 1958, v CHELSEA

David Meek had replaced Tom Jackson as the United correspondent at the *Manchester Evening News* after the crash, and he also stepped up to write a column for the matchday programme. It was an association that was to last for over 50 years.

UNITED JOTTINGS

by DAVID MEEK

of the "MANCHESTER EVENING NEWS"

Welcome back Albert Scanlon and Ray Wood . . . two more crash survivors to make a come-back into football.

Altogether eight survivors went back to Munich on United's pre-season tour of Western Germany and I think one of the most heart-warming features of this very successful tour was the top priority job listed by the United players.

Almost immediately on arrival, Albert Scanlon, Dennis Viollet, Ray Wood and Ken Morgans made a bee-line for the Rechts der Isar Hospital armed with huge bunches of flowers for the sisters and staff who nursed them back to health.

Hot on their trail were the rest of the survivors including Manager Matt Busby who was only sorry that Professor Maurer was away in Italy on holiday.

Albert Scanlon made his return to United's team. He tells me that it was quite an ordeal and that he was terribly nervous and out of touch after such a long lay-off without a competitive game.

I'm glad the knee he twisted in training — not the leg ironically enough injured in the crash — mended in time for the tour games to allow him to make his come-back before the League programme opens.

The tour, with a match against a combined Bayern F.C. and Munchen 1860 team in Munich and another in Hamburg against Hamburger S.V. was a great success despite the fact that both games were lost to the home sides. The tour not only gave Manager Matt Busby two valuable matches in which to weigh up prospects for this season, but gave the players the opportunity to start the League programme on their toes, for practice matches are a poor substitute for competitive games.

The hospitality extended was tremendous. We were wined and dined by our host clubs and in Munich we were entertained by the Munich Burgermeister in his beautiful city and also by the Bavarian Football Association at their lakeside hotel about 25 miles from Munich.

The journey was a long one — overnight by sleeper-train from Ostend to Munich and then a 10-hour day trip by rail from Munich to Hamburg. But the decision to go by land and sea rather than fly was the right one in spite of the fact that many of the players did not get much sleep on the journey!

There are still a number of crash survivors who do not relish the thought of air travel for a while yet. United's policy of not making a decision until circumstances — such as a trip to Helsinki in the European Cup — force them. With a bit of luck, that should postpone the issue until next season when nightmare memories may have faded.

United will fly again one day — but in my view — they should fly only when they feel themselves ready.

MUSIC PROGRAMME

March	**Col. Bogey**
Selection	**South Pacific**
Waltz	**Belle of the Ball**
Selection	**My Fair Lady**
Vocal	**Selected** (Vocalist Sylvia Farmer)
March	**On the Quarter Deck**

Conductor: A. Risby.
Secretary: C. W. Daly.

PAGE TEN

Albert Scanlon was injured in Munich but returned to the team at the start of 1958/59

23 FEBRUARY 1963, v BLACKPOOL

Arctic conditions in England decimated the 1962/63 winter calendar, and David Meek reveals how some clubs travelled to Ireland for some much-needed match practice.

Man of the moment for me tonight is Manchester United right-half Nobby Stiles, the youngster who shuffles in and out of the side in the shadow of Pat Crerand.

Crerand is Cup-tied until the Sixth Round because of the 14-day waiting period before a transferred player becomes eligible to play in the F.A. Cup for a new club.

So Crerand is in for League matches and out for the Cup ties, with Stiles filling the appropriate gaps.

It must be a nerve-wracking experience to step up for vital Cup games and then drop back into the reserves.

But Stiles has taken his new role in his stride, and he played an excellent part in United's Third Round win against Huddersfield Town.

The Club are fortunate to find that the player in this yo-yo situation has the right outlook.

Manager Matt Busby tells me that it must be the first time in his career that he has had to drop an uninjured player after a 5-0 Cup win!

But that was what was due to happen for the game against Tottenham on Saturday.

Crerand was available again and as a world-class player had to come into the team.

He is out again tonight, so in strides young Norbert determined to give of his best once again.

And I think I am pretty safe in writing before the match that that is exactly what he will do.

No moody player this! In fact I understand Crerand has been more disturbed about the situation than Stiles.

However, it is a very healthy position for the Club.

Now that the grounds have unfrozen, matches are coming thick and fast. Injuries will be inevitable with little time for recovery.

The Cup and League championship could well be decided this season by the club which proves to have the best reserves.

United can certainly claim good reserve cover at the moment.

The Central League side are still fighting it out near the top of the table and in their last three outings have rattled up a tally of 15 goals.

The reserves speak for themselves when you note that Arsenal, Sheffield Wednesday, Blackburn, Bury, and Preston were all represented at their game against Chesterfield at Old Trafford on Wednesday.

Other clubs also obviously share the regard for United's reserves!

***

PAGE TWO

It is an ill wind that blows no good and certainly Irish football fans could hardly grumble at the freeze-up in England.

Some of the most expensive footballers in the business played in the Republic of Eire as their clubs flew in search of playable pitches.

Funnily enough, Manchester United twice played on grounds which the local referees said they would not have passed for proper League matches.

But the Reds were unlucky. The first time a keen frost the night before the game hardened a ground that had been in perfect shape all week.

The next time, pouring rain for 24 hours before and during the game made the pitch ankle deep in mud in places.

But despite tough conditions, there is no doubt both ventures were successful and extremely valuable.

United opened their Irish season with a friendly against Coventry City in Dublin. The players adapted themselves well on the frozen ground.

They were sensible in the tackle but keen enough to make for an extremely attractive match and a 2-2 draw.

The match brought United into contact with that bearded Soccer character, Mr. Jimmy Hill, former Chairman of the Professional Footballers Association, now manager of Coventry.

He admits he has many additional and different problems now he is at the helm, but insists that he is NOT on the other side. He says: "For years as a player I tried to get results for my club. Now as manager I am still trying to do exactly the same thing. Surely we are all on the same side!"

United's next trip over the Irish sea was to Cork where there was a great personal welcome for Noel Cantwell on his return to his native town.

He captained the team to a useful 4-2 win over Bolton who had been without a game for 10 weeks.

New signing Pat Crerand made his debut and got off on the right foot — by scoring!

United returned to Dublin the following week to play a combined Irish XI.

All the games helped bridge the frustrating gap to the return of normal League football, and if in the process it has helped entertain Irish soccer fans, so much the better.

***

PAGE TWO

11 MARCH 1963, v ASTON VILLA

Here Meek discusses the battle for places at Old Trafford, with Matt Busby's rotation of Paddy Crerand and Nobby Stiles catching his eye.

28 AUGUST 1963, v IPSWICH TOWN

Peter Slingsby was a stats man almost ahead of his time and in the first programme of the 1963/64 season he assessed the myriad positional changes made by Busby's side in the previous campaign.

Manchester United's pulsating performance at Wembley in last season's F.A. Cup Final was a fitting finale to a winter punctuated by so many disappointments in the League.

The reasons for the slump in the First Division—United's final League table position was the poorest in the club's post-war history—are well known.

One of them undoubtedly was the continual striving for the match-winning blend. But it all came right at wonderful Wembley as United romped to their second Cup Final success under the guidance of manager Matt Busby.

Some indication of United's search for the best combination from the considerable talent available at Old Trafford can be found in a positional breakdown and the large number of changes and positional switches made during 1962-63.

These amounted to 89. The number shown in brackets is the number of changes made in that position in League and Cup games:

Goal: Gregg, Gaskell (4)
Right-back: Brennan, Dunne (3)
Left-back: Cantwell, Dunne (6)
Right-half: Stiles, Nicholson, Lawton, Crerand (10)
Centre-half: Foulkes, Haydock (1)
Left-half: Setters, Lawton, Nicholson, Stiles, Brennan (13)
Outside-right: Giles, Moir, Quixall (8)
Inside-right: Quixall, Pearson, Chisnall, Setters, Lawton, Law, Giles (15)
Centre-forward: Herd, Quixall (8)
Inside-left: Law, Pearson, Chisnall, Lawton, Charlton, Quixall, Giles (13)
Outside-left: Moir, McMillan, Cantwell, Charlton, Walker (8)

We have received numerous requests for a full and complete "Roll Call" for last season, especially from readers of the United Review abroad.

Here then is the first half of "Roll Call" for last season showing the appearances and goal-scorers:

	League		F.A. Cup		Senior Friendlies		Central League	
	Appearances	Goals	Appearances	Goals	Appearances	Goals	Appearances	Goals
E. Ackerley	0	0	0	0	0	0	7	0
W. Anderson	0	0	0	0	0	0	5	1
S. Brennan	37	0	4	0	7	0	2	0
R. Briggs	0	0	0	0	0	0	12	0
N. Cantwell	25	1	5	0	7	0	10	1
R. Charlton	28	7	6	2	4	2	0	0
P. Chisnall	6	1	0	0	4	1	32	14
P. Crerand	19	0	3	0	5	1	0	0
W. Donaldson	0	0	0	0	0	0	10	0
A. Dunne	25	0	3	0	7	0	14	0
E. Dunphy	0	0	0	0	0	0	5	0
W. Foulkes	41	0	6	0	10	0	0	0
B. Fry	0	0	0	0	0	0	8	2
D. Gaskell	18	0	2	0	3	0	22	0
J. Giles	36	4	6	1	10	2	1	0
B. Grayson	0	0	0	0	0	0	4	1
H. Gregg	24	0	4	0	7	0	7	0
F. Haydock	1	0	0	0	0	0	40	1
D. Herd	37	19	6	2	9	6	0	0
A. Kinsey	0	0	0	0	0	0	5	1
D. Latham	0	0	0	0	0	0	15	4
D. Law	38	23	6	6	9	4	0	0
N. Lawton	12	0	0	0	2	0	13	2

"Senior Friendlies" includes United's tour games in Italy. Substitutes are also included.

To be continued in the Everton programme, 31st August, 1963

The last time Stanley Matthews played at Old Trafford a few misguided fans booed him.

It was in his Blackpool days of course, and if I remember aright, a bunch of fans took it out on Stanley because they did not agree with the referee's decisions against Joe Carolan, the United left back lined up against the maestro.

It sticks in my mind because the last thing I ever expected to hear was Matthews booed. If he is playing today I sincerely hope he will receive a more sporting and more typical Old Trafford reception.

For this man Matthews is a remarkable player. Last May the Football Writers Association elected him Footballer of the Year for the second time in his career. And what an appropriate choice, too, when you consider Stoke City's championship-clinching match of the season.

Even his best friends would not call Stanley Matthews a prolific scorer, yet in their last home match he suddenly and dramatically scored against Luton to give Stoke the two points they needed to become Second Division champions.

Jackie Mudie's earlier goal was just as important of course, but no one would wish to deny the splendid timing of Stanley's score.

It was his first League goal of the season—and what an ideal moment he had waited for!

He was 48 and the wheel had come full circle because 30 years previously he had been in the last Stoke Second Division championship side.

I hope he is playing today along with former United international Dennis Viollet. For that also would be appropriate because Matthews has been one of the people responsible for Viollet's new lease of life with Stoke.

He has converted Dennis to his rather Spartan dieting beliefs and has helped him gain a new confidence which obviously must have been at a low ebb when he left Old Trafford.

The other player I am anxious to see in action is John Ritchie, the centre forward discovery at Stoke who has been scoring freely despite moderate results by the team. His two goals against Birmingham last week brought him a tally of 19 in only 12 games.

Meanwhile United are quietly preparing for their return leg with Spurs in the European Cup Winners Cup at Old Trafford on Tuesday.

Certainly the Reds had every encouragement for last Tuesday's opening leg at White Hart Lane after their return to the winning trail at Sheffield United last Saturday.

Although the team had failed to score in the two previous League games, they always looked good for goals at Bramall Lane and were worth their 2-1 win. Denis Law was the hero by scoring them both and he delighted United followers by so showing that he could be a major force in a match despite the disciplinary case hanging over his head.

The game saw a last-minute change of goalkeeper. David Gaskell was unexpectedly given an all-clear by the specialist who examined the X-rays on the broken wrist bone.

It seemed tough luck that Ronnie Briggs who had been selected to play had to stand down—particularly as he was set for a come-back at White Hart Lane three days previously until the fog clamped down.

But with Tuesday's postponed Cup-tie coming up, manager Matt Busby had no option but to give Gaskell a full-scale try-out.

Briggs was bitterly disappointed; even in these days of big money, a professional footballer's life is not all beer and skittles!

FOUND

Black donkey jacket. Apply Club offices.

Stanley Matthews (left) leaves the field after United's 5-2 win against his Stoke City side

7 DECEMBER 1963, v STOKE CITY

The great Stanley Matthews was the main focus of the United Jottings when the Potters came to Old Trafford in December 1963, but the player fans were talking about after the match was four-goal Denis Law (in a 5-2 win).

UNITED
JOTTINGS

by **David Meek**
Manchester Evening News and Chronicle

They often say in football that a team is as good as the last game. So I suppose a few people will be thinking of Manchester United in terms of their last fixture which was of course a 2–0 defeat at Chelsea.

But it will be a long time in my mind before the European Cup battle of the previous Wednesday fades from my memory. This was a match which I think time will prove to be one of the key happenings in the Old Trafford club's quest for the game's major honours.

It was the opportunity for Manchester United to put themselves to the test against a world-class team, not only in terms of the skills of soccer but in temperament and approach to the game.

It can sometimes be dangerous to draw too hard a conclusion from a couple of games; after all, football is studded with giant-killing acts.

But United hardly fall into this category, for their display was not one of underdogs stampeding the opposition out of the game, but rather a cool and composed exhibition matching the Portuguese champions skill for skill in every department.

Benfica have the European Footballer of the Year and Eusebio showed the merit of his election in the first leg at Old Trafford. But Eusebio was overshadowed in the Estadio da Luz by 19-year-old George Best who rose superbly to the occasion, not only by scoring the first two goals, but with his wide range of trickery with the ball.

The whole forward line blended beautifully and of course flourished on the strength of their defence. Perhaps Nobby Stiles should be singled out here for the way he helped make Best the star of the night by completely containing Eusebio.

With Bill Foulkes also devoid of nerves in a personal victory against the towering Torres and a commanding display in goal by Harry Gregg, the team was in magnificent shape.

They swept to a 5–1 win, the first time Benfica had been beaten on their own ground in the European Cup and their heaviest defeat in all competitions.

But it was not just the size of the score that impressed, but the way they did it, the bold attacking football, the blend of skill and strength that used to belong to Benfica, Real Madrid and such teams. Such a high standard may be just a momentary peak, but I doubt it.

United's football that night had the look of a team turning on that level of play naturally and with the kind of familiarity that given an equally notable occasion they could do again.

Certainly Lisbon have taken United to their hearts. In the space of the match they overcame the disappointment of seeing their own team beaten and they finished as admirers of United. This is not easily achieved in Continental countries where football is debated with the passion of politics.

But the people of Lisbon have been won over in support of "El Beatle" and a team which played so much pure football that their instinct for appreciating what is best in the game had no option but to respond.

If United can win through the semi-final and reach the final which will be played in Lisbon on May 11th, they will find themselves almost home from home.

The football followers of Portugal will be firmly rooting for the Reds. The fans and their newspapers are probably best summed up by "A Bola" who said after the game: "We wait for the final in May to salute Manchester United."

19 MARCH 1966, v ARSENAL

David Meek reflects on the night the world woke up to the genius of George Best, United's brilliant teenager inspiring a 5-1 thrashing of the mighty Benfica in their own back yard.

Best was labelled 'El Beatle' by the Portuguese press after a stunning display against Benfica

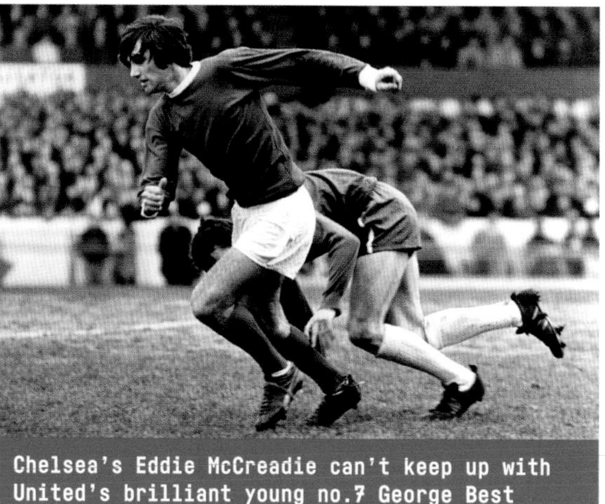

Chelsea's Eddie McCreadie can't keep up with United's brilliant young no.7 George Best

27 APRIL 1966, v BLACKPOOL

Arthur Walmsley talks George Best as the 1965/66 season draws to a close, comparing him to many of the true greats of the game, but says there's much more for the young Northern Irishman to learn.

TALKING
SPORT

by **Arthur Walmsley**
of THE SUN

When George Best limped off the field in Belgrade a couple of weeks ago and it was confirmed that he would be out of competitive Soccer for the rest of the season a bright flame of dazzling footballing radiance was temporarily snuffed and some of the savour of the end-of-season excitement at Old Trafford was lost for scores of thousands of fans.

Throughout the history of Soccer it has been given to few players to make such a nationwide impact on the game at such a tender age as young Best. Even the abundantly talented Bobby Charlton had not made such a mark as early.

Looking for a comparable case one's thoughts turn almost automatically to Duncan Edwards who was a colossus in the game before he was twenty, although a player of different style than Best.

But, in trying to assess Best against the greats of the past we quickly run up against the first poser – With whom do we try to compare him – great inside forwards or great wingers? For although Best is nominally a winger on the team sheet he is given that freedom of movement by his club which his astonishing talents merit, and in practice operates as much at inside as outside forward.

It is perhaps testimony to Best's ability that one can speak of him in the same breath as Matthews and Finney or Peter Doherty, Wilf Mannion or Raich Carter. Certainly I do not believe it is an exaggeration to claim that none of them were more blessed in the natural gifts of the game than Best. The difference, at this stage of Best's career, lies in the application of those gifts.

Let me take Peter Doherty as my inside forward example. I rate Doherty the greatest inside forward I have ever seen – and that includes the Peles, Eusebios, Puskases as well as our home produced players.

Like Best, Doherty was a brilliant ball player with a lazy, deceptive swerve and turn of pace. But when Doherty was beating men it was always to some clear-cut purpose and he was a master at bringing his fellow forwards into the game or creating openings for them. I always felt that playing alongside Peter kept the great-hearted Eric Brook in the game a season or two longer than might have been the case – so easy was his left wing task made for him by the tireless, scheming Irish genius.

Thus, Doherty's game whilst being vastly entertaining at individual level, always somehow seemed integrated to the broader team pattern with his genius the very heart of the side rather than a dazzling appendage to it.

Could one say the same about Best at present? Without being unkind – I think not. Indeed, at such a young age one could hardly expect that Best could have harnessed his fantastic ability to mature application. I did not see Peter Doherty playing in his teens but I am sure he was not the complete player he was in his great years with Manchester City when in his middle 20s.

At present Best is largely an extempore player – with the almost unbelievable ability in his feet ruling the football brain in his head. If there are men to beat then Best incredibly just goes on beating them without prior regard, one feels, for the end product.

It is breathtaking to watch and makes Best one of the most thrilling players in the game. But if that were all it would be a fairy story tinged with tragedy. It would be genius denied the full flower.

Yet, happily, there are already signs that Best's game is developing beyond sheer individualism, that the ebullient, youthful urge for the mazy solo run is being tempered by the experience of expedience.

The signs may still be infrequent – but they are there where they were not a season ago. Certainly I would not wish to impose any tactical discipline on a player of Best's ability or curb his self-expression. That could be ruinous.

If such discipline is to have any value it must come from the player himself – and I am convinced that this is now happening. If and when that development reaches full maturity I could well be ready to revise my opinion about the best inside or wing forward I have ever seen.

For the present it is enough to have been privileged to see this frail-looking youngster bringing his own priceless brand of heart-stopping football to a game sadly in need of his kind and to wish him a swift and full recovery from his knee operation.

Greetings from *THE CHAIRMAN*

LOUIS C. EDWARDS

It is once again my very pleasant duty, on behalf of my colleagues, to welcome you all back to Old Trafford at the start of yet another season and one which, as always, is full of promise of first-class football entertainment.

The summer, of course, proved a wonderful one for English soccer prestige in which England won the World Cup on the first occasion the tournament had been staged here. It was a considerable achievement and I would like to congratulate all those who played any role in that success.

We were privileged to supply three players to the England squad in Bobby Charlton, Nobby Stiles and John Connelly. All did extremely well and their performances reflected great credit not only on them but on the Club, too.

For the World Cup ties here at Old Trafford, we carried out certain ground improvements. These were specifically designed for the comfort and well-being of our patrons—a matter which is constantly in the minds of the Club's directors.

In all, something over £350,000 represents the Club's outlay on the ground in the last two years and this sum does not take into account any contribution from the Government or the Football Association.

But, despite these vast payments and the added financial burden of the Selective Employment Tax which has to be borne by all clubs, there will be no increase in admission charges this season.

It is our hope that all these items of increased expenditure can be met out of income.

I think we can now reasonably claim to have one of the finest grounds in the country; certainly no other club has carried out, since the war, as we have done, the entire re-building of stands and the renewing of so many amenities.

Now we look forward to the new season, in which every effort will be made to provide a successful team and to play the attractive football we all wish to see.

In conclusion, on behalf of the Directors, Players and Staff, I would like to thank you all for your wonderful support in the past and to assure you we will do our best to continue to deserve it in the future.

Nobby Stiles [far left] and Bobby Charlton [far right] helped England to World Cup glory in 1966

20 AUGUST 1966, v WEST BROMWICH ALBION
Chairman Louis Edwards often started the season with a column in the first programme and here he congratulates the three United men who helped England to win the World Cup.

TALKING SPORT

by **Arthur Walmsley** *of* **THE SUN**

One of my earliest Soccer memories is of being snatched from a forest of legs on the Maine Road terraces and raised high over the crowd before being rolled over a billowy sea of outstretched arms and finally deposited for safety over the wall on to the cinder track around the pitch.

I was about seven at the time. The occasion was City v. United and the crowd in excess of 70,000. I remember nothing of the game in detail but the feeling of occasion remains with me vividly—especially that rolling ride down the terraces and the delight of finding myself sitting with my back to the wall with a secure, uninterrupted view of the whole field.

That is more years ago than I now care to remember, yet in a rapidly changing world in which the bulldozer and the demolition workers are tearing down so many memories for those of us well past the first—and last—blush of youth it is good to know that just a few things are seemingly unchanged.

The United—City match is one. Today's game was a sell-out a fortnight ago, proving that the appetite for the "derby" game has not staled over the years. True, the passing parade of players "strutting their brief spell" is in continual change, but the traditional loyalties and interest remain as strong as ever, proving if proof were needed that the club is greater than the player.

I wonder if the younger fans at today's game realise what a rich sporting inheritance is theirs in these "derby" matches and whether they can prove worthy of it. For the rivalry between Red and Blue down the years has done far more to bring credit than discredit to football.

Games between the two clubs have been remarkably free from serious unpleasantness both on the terraces and on the field. Inevitably in such fiercely partisan atmosphere there have been isolated incidents, yet by their very infrequency and comparative triviality they have served more to emphasise the general good humour of these contests rather than bring them into disrepute.

Indeed, when poor Allenby Chilton was sent off in the Maine Road match in 1956 the City players, led by Don Revie, swarmed round the referee pleading that Chilton be allowed to remain. That one example says everything for the spirit of sportsmanship in which "derby" games have been played AND WATCHED—and one fervently hopes that today's players and spectators will live up to the long tradition.

For if ever Soccer needed a lead in controlled, sporting behaviour it is NOW. Each week seems to bring an increasing crop of unsavoury crowd incidents up and down the country which are a slur not only on football but on our whole national character.

It would be hypocritical to pretend that Manchester has not got its rash of Soccer sinners—they seem to be an inescapable part of the sickness of our times—but so far, at least, they seem to be in smaller numbers than in other less fortunate centres.

What a feather in Manchester's sporting cap if, in these troubled Soccer times, we could show the rest of the country that an emotion-charged, capacity crowd of more than 60,000 split almost down the middle in its loyalties can still harness fierce rivalry and enthusiasm to the greater cause of good sportsmanship.

I fancy there is little danger to the "derby" tradition from the folk in my age group. The challenge is to the young ones. Maybe it will help if they remember it takes a bigger man to swallow disappointment or defeat than to throw a bottle at the back of an unprotected goalkeeper. If they remember and act on that then there will be no losers—only winners this afternoon.

HOSPITAL COMMENTARIES

Manchester and District Hospital Commentaries Association will be collecting outside Old Trafford today. They now have 35 hospitals on their network for live commentaries on the United v. City matches and are delighted to see the return of a Manchester "Derby" to help them finance their entirely voluntary work which is now in its 15th year.

17 SEPTEMBER 1966, v MANCHESTER CITY
Arthur Walmsley fondly recalls his first experience of the Manchester derby and, with football hooliganism on the rise, calls on supporters to show the sporting spirit of bygone years. For the record, 62,085 saw United beat City thanks to a goal from Denis Law.

United's players raise a glass to winning the title for the second time in three seasons

13 MAY 1967, v STOKE CITY

David Meek hails the new champions and marvels at the style in which it was confirmed by a 6-1 thrashing of West Ham at Upton Park.

UNITED JOTTINGS

BY DAVID MEEK

MANCHESTER EVENING NEWS & CHRONICLE

What a triumphant way to take the title! The previous few weeks we had been busy working out goal averages and wondering if and when Nottingham Forest or Leeds United would drop the point Manchester United needed to win the championship.

But this was no championship by default! This was an all-out effort as the Reds took the match against West Ham by the scruff of the neck and shook six goals, their highest score of the season, out of the Londoners.

They were in relentless mood, even to the end. As Nobby Stiles described to me afterwards: "Just after we had scored our sixth goal I trotted over to Bill Foulkes and congratulated him on winning his fourth championship medal. All I got in return was a blasting to concentrate on the game."

This was rather typical of United's whole approach to the match. "I knew everyone was pretty keyed up, but this was great," said Bill Foulkes. "We worried West Ham all the time, never let up on them for a minute.

The tension disappeared for us when we beat Aston Villa the previous week at Old Trafford. That was the game that worried us. Once we had won that we knew we could do it and it was simply a question of finishing off the job."

United finished off the job with a little more flair than that kind of workmanlike phrase would suggest. Bobby Charlton started the ball rolling in only the second minute after sheer determination by Nobby Stiles had won possession just inside the West Ham penalty box.

Stiles, who had a wonderful match personifying United's determined play, thrust towards goal and although his shot was blocked he was following up so fast that the West Ham defence was helpless as the ball spun across. Charlton, showing the same sharpness and determination, was through between two players like a flash to hammer home the first goal.

Aston, playing with the skill too few fans have given him credit for, crossed a delightful centre in the sixth minute for Pat Crerand to head United's second goal past Colin Mackleworth, the Hammers' teenage goalkeeper playing in only his third League game.

Bill Foulkes, the defence top scorer with four goals this season, once again found his policy of coming up for corners paying off. He hustled Mackleworth from Aston's corner-kick to score the third goal in the 10th minute.

Stiles put George Best through for the fourth goal after 25 minutes. John Charles the West Ham full back pulled a goal back for the Londoners a minute after the interval but United absorbed their rally and swung back with first a penalty scored by Denis Law and then a typical opportunist Law goal from Best's centre.

So United clinched their fifth post-war championship, their seventh in all which equals the record held jointly by Liverpool and Arsenal.

Bobby Noble's father has asked me to pass on his appreciation to the scores of people who have written expressing their sympathy and good wishes for Bob's recovery. He says there are too many to reply to individually and he would like to say thank you through the United Review. David Herd – his leg still in plaster – was able to join the team for the journey to West Ham and take part in the subsequent celebrations.

Good luck to both David and Bobby and we look forward to seeing you both in top form next season.

When you collect your favourite newspaper tomorrow morning the main sports page will contain a once-yearly piece of news that is always eagerly awaited (and argued about) by football fans the length and breadth of the country.

The item will give you the name of the Footballer of the Year, the result of the 21st nationwide poll of members of the Football Writers Association. It is a ballot that has become an integral part of a soccer season.

Traditionally – or so it has seemed over the years – the recipient of the game's most coveted individual trophy has been associated with one or other of the Cup Final teams.

So the performances of Everton and West Bromwich Albion players as they have travelled the Wembley trail will have been carefully examined in the last few days. It is a tricky task . . . but I must admit I did not lose any sleep over my vote.

As it is very much a private ballot, I won't give you the name of my top player for 1967-68, but the men who will have had tons of support are Albion stars like goalkeeper John Osborne and striker Jeff Astle, and Everton's bang-in-form pair Brian Labone and Howard Kendall.

There will be others too from both Cup camps, but I have a shrewd suspicion, as has happened in the last two years, the critics will look beyond the Wembley rivals and go for a young man who has been consistently in the soccer spotlight at club and international level these last few months.

As I've been tipping Everton and West Brom for Wembley since the Fifth Round, you'll gather I'm in sound forecasting form, and my feeling is that George Best will end up with the award and so complete a novel hat-trick of "wins" for Manchester United, following in the footsteps of Johnny Carey (1948-49) and Bobby Charlton (1965-66).

With shooting stars like David Herd and Denis Law unfit and unavailable for many key matches, Best has accepted the obvious but difficult challenge like the true professional he is and, with a little luck, could end the campaign in a high position in the 'national marksmanship table in the League.

As I pointed out here recently, the modest Irishman has already doubled his previous highest goal haul for one season in the First Division, and I will certainly never forget his match winner against Real Madrid ten days ago.

That night George had a television audience of something like 150 M. – the largest ever, I understand, for a club match – and if he can "turn it on" in Madrid he could be in line for a European Player of the Year award in the near future.

It hardly bears thinking about that for a few hours in July, 1961, homesick for family and friends in Belfast, he turned his back on football in England and but for Matt Busby's powers of persuasion Best's brand of pure magic could have been lost to Old Trafford and, indeed, the game in general.

CLUB COMMENTS

BY PETER SLINGSBY

THE NEWS OF THE WORLD

But now we'll have to wait and see for a few hours longer. The votes have all been cast, even counted by now and certainly I'll be more anxious than usual for the arrival of my Sunday newspaper tomorrow morning.

Somehow, I think George Best will be, too.

I have been asked to give a complete list of those who have won the "Footballer of the Year" award since it was first offered in 1947-48.

Here it is:

1947-48 Stanley Matthews (Blackpool)
1948-49 Johnny Carey (Manchester United)
1949-50 Joe Mercer (Arsenal)
1950-51 Harry Johnston (Blackpool)
1951-52 Billy Wright (Wolves)
1952-53 Nat Lofthouse (Bolton Wanderers)
1953-54 Tom Finney (Preston North End)
1954-55 Don Revie (Manchester City)
1955-56 Bert Trautmann (Manchester City)
1956-57 Tom Finney (Preston North End)
1957-58 Danny Blanchflower (Tottenham H.)
1958-59 Syd Owen (Luton Town)
1959-60 Bill Slater (Wolves)
1960-61 Danny Blanchflower (Tottenham H.)
1961-62 Jimmy Adamson (Burnley)
1962-63 Stanley Matthews (Stoke City)
1963-64 Bobby Moore (West Ham United)
1964-65 Bobby Collins (Leeds United)
1965-66 Bobby Charlton (Manchester United)
1966-67 Jackie Charlton (Leeds United)

PAGE NINE

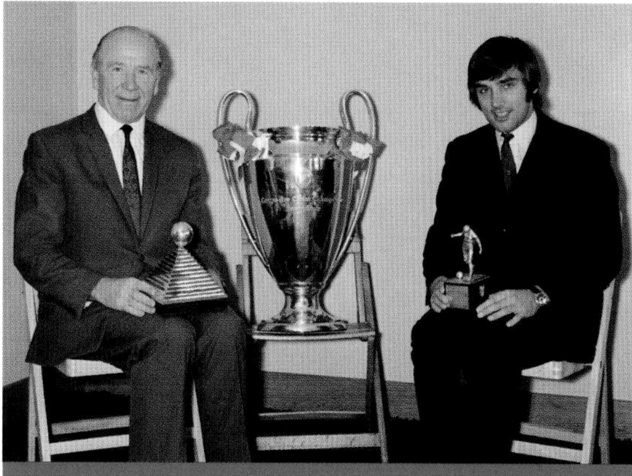

What a year for Busby and Best - individual awards plus winners of the 1968 European Cup

4 MAY 1968, v NEWCASTLE UNITED

Peter Slingsby predicts that George Best will be named Footballer of the Year for 1967/68, and even tips him for the European award too. He was right, of course, with Best winning both awards after a stunning season for the Reds.

A dream made real: Matt Busby leads United to European Cup glory in 1968

10 AUGUST 1968, v EVERTON

News of the World journalist Peter Slingsby reflects on the 1968 European Cup final and delights in how his press colleagues had reported on the Reds' night of nights at Wembley.

Peter SLINGSBY
THE NEWS OF THE WORLD

CLUB COMMENTS

The orchestra struck the right note from the outset. Under the baton of the incomparable Joe Loss, they "borrowed" the Top Twenty hit, "Congratulations", and with some rapid, ingenious, re-writing and a couple of rehearsals we all saluted the new Champions of Europe.

The date was May 29th, 1968. The occasion the Club's post-Wembley celebration at the Russell Hotel and the salute greeted the team's arrival complete with the most-coveted trophy in club football.

And, of course, the European Cup was given a place of honour in the stately suite as the players, directors, officials, wives, sweethearts and official guests danced until dawn.

Those who were there thoroughly enjoyed every minute of that lavish reception on a night when, all over the football world, the toast was "Manchester United".

For those of us with a professional interest, the arrival of the early editions of the newspapers was awaited with greater interest than usual. No one was disappointed.

The photographers had had a ball, as they say, and the writers excelled themselves, too, on a night of triumph for United and, indeed, for English football as a whole.

I must confess I did not see Frank McGhee's story in the "Daily Mirror" until two days after the event, but of them all I found it the most enthralling, headed:

PAGE FOURTEEN

"UNITED'S HEART, VITAL TRUMP".

It was a brilliant piece of writing – like this, "They won it because they produced something important, something marvellous, something memorable . . . something the man for whom they did it, manager Matt Busby, summed up in one word – Heart".

"The Guardian" cast tradition to the winds and gave Eric Todd's beautifully-written report two columns on their front page, giving it precedence over everything that had happened throughout the world on May 29th.

Todd's account was really superb, beginning "The football might of Benfica, indeed of Portugal, was brought low by Manchester United at Wembley last night" and ending, appropriately enough, "Home are the hunters, home from the hill. At last".

The "Daily Mail" via Ronald Crowther dubbed United "Masters of Europe". Most of us agreed with this Crowther comment, "No club could have deserved it more; no victory was ever bought at so great a cost in terms of human endeavour".

Alan Thompson in the "Daily Express" wrote, "In an eight-minute flash of brilliance that produced three magical, wonderful, and almost unbelievable goals, Manchester United, the pioneers, became England's first European champions".

Eric Cooper, in the same paper, called it "a day to remember in a football life-time", adding "Surely this epic is Busby's greatest qualification for a place in Soccer history . . . something the fans made clear even before the match with a reception for the manager which was not excelled even during it".

In the "Daily Telegraph", Donald Saunders coined a classic second paragraph thus: "Derby Day has produced many fine thoroughbreds over the years. None has been greater, I suspect, than the team that made Matt Busby's dream come true".

Peter Lorenzo ("The Sun") made Bobby Charlton "a soccer prince", and linked United's win with that England in the World Cup . . . "It was like the World Cup Final all over again at Wembley last night when, as with England, character and skill triumphed in the demanding minutes of extra time".

So ended the tributes in print, but the most lasting and poignant memory for yours truly was the sight of Sir Matt Busby embracing the trophy as the hearty strains of "Congratulations" finally died in our throats . . . it was completely unforgettable.

Joe Mercer talking (Manager of Manchester City F.C.)
...to Denis Lowe of the Daily Telegraph

A MAN OF TREMENDOUS CHARACTER, BLESSED WITH A WONDERFUL PHYSIQUE AND FINE TEMPERAMENT. THE TYPE OF FOOTBALLER ALL MANAGERS WANT TO HAVE IN THEIR SIDE.

That's how I rate Bill Foulkes, who gets a richly-deserved reward tonight for 20 years of loyal, dependable service as a Manchester United player.

I'm sure I'm stating the obvious when I say that we at Manchester City are delighted to provide the opposition and share in this notable occasion.

I played against Bill during the closing stages of my career with Arsenal, and his attitude and approach to the game hasn't altered one bit since those days. He believes in giving his manager everything he has in the way of effort.

Matt must have appreciated Bill's many qualities in hundreds of important games, and it's a fact that players like this are becoming more and more difficult for clubs to find. All too few people notice players like Bill Foulkes and give them the credit they deserve.

Bill didn't find the First Division an easy business when he first won a regular place for United, but he kept working, improved his skills and by making the most of his assets became a great competitor and fine defensive player.

Like Leslie Compton and Billy Wright, two other converts to the position, Bill played some of his finest games after the switch from full-back to centre-half.

Dominant in the air, powerful in the tackle, and supremely fit, he has always had a good football brain. In later years he was the perfect example of the fact that there's no substitute for experience in top-class football and I shall always remember his great performance against Benfica in the European Cup Final at Wembley.

Bill has played with all the Old Trafford greats during his 600 senior matches . . . from the days of Carey and Byrne, Colman and Taylor, Viollet and Charlton . . . to the men of today, Law, Crerand and Best.

Now he's showing the youngsters how it's done as a coach, a side of the game in which he can make just as big a contribution in the future.

Best wishes from

A. Pavion,
50 Bury Old Road, Prestwich.

Tony Book.

Brian Cash,
Hotel Piccadilly, Manchester.

Eric Richardson,
17 Chorlton Street, Manchester 1.

Archie Thornhill Limited,
Warburton Street, Didsbury.

Arturo Mascaro,
51 Faulkner Street, Manchester.

Foy Brothers,
Wood Street, Middleton.

F.A. Cup, League Championship, European Cup – 100 per cent for a 100 percenter. Congratulations on a great Medal Round.
Alan Thomson, Daily Express.

Searchlight Electric,
Middlewood Street, Salford.

Thanks Bill for many hours of sporting enjoyment –
Tom Henry.

PAGE TWELVE

10 NOVEMBER 1970, BILL FOULKES TESTIMONIAL

City boss Joe Mercer speaks affectionately of the stalwart United defender – who is by now a youth team coach at Old Trafford – ahead of a testimonial game that features eight reserves for the Reds due to international call-ups and injuries. City win 3-0.

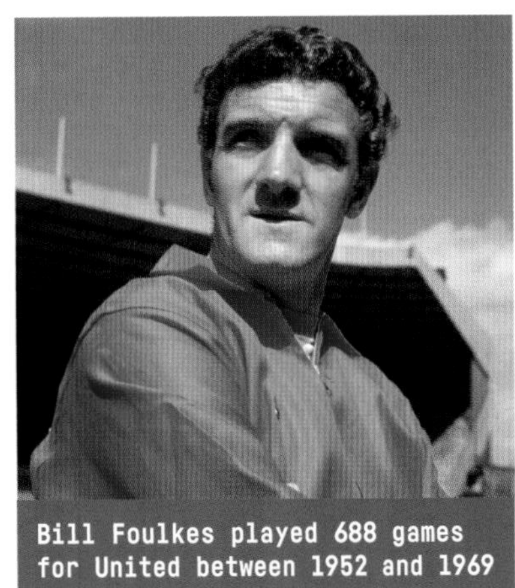

Bill Foulkes played 688 games for United between 1952 and 1969

CLUB TOPICS

By DAVID MEEK
of the Manchester Evening News

Manchester United will go back to the First Division with plenty of cheers ringing in their ears.

The title-winning Reds will reach the magic million against Blackpool at Old Trafford this afternoon.

Only one club will have been watched by over 1m spectators in their home League games this season.

Liverpool, United's traditional rivals for top attendance, will fall at least 20,000 short of the million mark when they tot up the figures for their 21 League games at Anfield this year.

United on the other hand will sail past the million. They need just 42,646 spectators today to top the million and the indications are for an attendance of at least 50,000.

All reserved seating was sold nearly a fortnight ago and there is sure to be a massive salute from the terraces as the Reds return to the First Division as champions

United's average League attendance at Old Trafford this season is running at 47,867 and it adds up to the magic million watching their League home games. Throw in Cup ties as well and the total attendance figures at home are nearer one and a half million

It is further cause for satisfaction for chairman Louis Edwards as he sees his club rebuilding and reclaiming their premier place in the game.

The financial situation is certainly very healthy. A year ago the club had an overdraft of £300,000, an undoubted burden when they faced up to their life in the Second Division.

It meant a much more careful approach to the transfer market and though he was always told that more money was available if he needed it, I know manager Tommy Docherty was determined to try to balance the transfer books.

The result is that after signing Stuart Pearson last summer the United manager has turned his back on any major signing—such is his confidence in his staff and the youngsters in the junior teams.

The outcome is the record-making profit which will be revealed in detail at the annual meeting early next season.

Manchester United are returning to the First Division in very good shape for the challenge of the future.

SEVENTH

Stewart Houston is certainly finishing the season on a high note. After winning his first international cap for Scotland in midweek, it was Houston who opened the scoring in the title-clinching 2–2 draw at Notts County. It was his seventh League and Cup goal of the season, a splendid return for a full back.

BOOST

Steve Coppell also came back from Meadow Lane with a boost. Don Revie watched the game and I understand that the England manager spoke very highly of the winger's ability to cross the ball quickly and dangerously. Perhaps he could have done with more of that kind of action against Cyprus.

BARON

It doesn't look as if the Baron is getting any better as a penalty taker! The Radio Manchester disc jockey scored four out of 10 against Alex Stepney last year. Then in a repeat competition with Gerry Daly this week his tally out of 10 penalties was . . . four again. Spot-kick king Daly scored seven

8

26 APRIL 1975, v BLACKPOOL
There was plenty to discuss in the programme on the day United were presented with the Division Two trophy, such as the impressive crowds the Reds had attracted throughout the campaign.

Martin Buchan receives the Division Two trophy in front of 58,769 supporters

24 AUGUST 1977, v COVENTRY CITY
Another season, another David Meek column. This one focuses on United's fortunes on pre-season tour in Germany and Norway under new boss Dave Sexton.

9

Club Topics

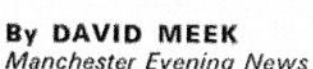

By DAVID MEEK
Manchester Evening News

It was second time lucky for Manchester United when they offered Dave Sexton the job of manager at Old Trafford.

For the Reds tried once before—and failed.

For United's new boss does not lightly change jobs. He believes contracts are there to be honoured and he refused Old Trafford a few years ago because he was in the middle of an exciting period with Chelsea.

"I was very tempted to join United the first time but we had got something good going at Chelsea and I just felt I wanted to see it through," he admitted to me.

It was a similar story when Ajax and other clubs tried to tempt him away from Queen's Park Rangers. They were turned down because he preferred to stay and see whether his work at Loftus Road would land a trophy.

United caught him this time between jobs . . . departing from Q.P.R. because he believed it was time for a change and before he had taken up the invitation to become coach at Arsenal.

So a bad summer finished with a lucky break for the Reds!

STEWART SAYS

One of the hardest working players on the club's pre-season tour of Norway didn't get a game!

But there were no complaints from odd-man-out Stewart Houston on that score. The Reds' defender was only too happy to be back in training with the first-team squad after his unlucky ankle injury at Bristol last May.

He trained almost every day with physiotherapist Laurie Brown and went back a much fitter player after his strenuous Scandanavian work-outs.

His ankle with torn ligaments and chipped bone has mended well and he was running freely by the time the team flew home from Oslo for the Charity Shield.

He aims to be playing again by the middle of September and in the meantime has asked me to pass on a message of appreciation to the United supporters who have written to him.

He says: "I have received so many letters, cards and good wishes for a speedy recovery from fans that it would be impossible for me to answer them all. So I would like to thank everybody who took the trouble to write to me. It was a great encouragement to try and get fit again. Injury to a professional footballer is very disheartening because you slip so far behind everyone else. I'm catching up again now—and the get-well messages helped me a lot."

JIM'S GOALS

It was Jimmy Greenhoff's turn for a slice of bad luck in the Charity Shield match at Wembley when he damaged the ligaments below his right knee.

For the Reds' striker had just completed the most successful warm-up to a season in his career.

Jimmy was the top scorer on the pre-season tour of Germany and Norway, hitting seven goals in four games. He was the only player to score in all three Norwegian games, notching five in the last game against Stromsgodset in Drammen.

That was a record haul for the former Stoke player. His previous best was four for Birmingham City against Fulham.

TOUR RECORD

The pre-season tour of Germany and Norway record reads:

Aug. 1—Bremen 3, United 2 (Pearson, McIlroy).
Aug. 3—Rosenborg 0, United 8 (Forsyth, Hill 2, McIlroy, McCreery, J. Greenhoff, Buchan, Muri o.g.).
Aug. 8—Ham Kam 0, United 4 (J. Greenhoff, McCreery 2, Pearson).
Aug. 10—Stromgodset 2, United 9 (J. Greenhoff 5, Macari 2, McGrath, Pearson).

Busby with his squad ahead of the '58 Cup final, when Meek was a rising reporter

22 DECEMBER 1979, v NOTTINGHAM FOREST

Over two decades on from the Munich Air Disaster, David Meek reflects on how his relationship with Manchester United began – in the dark days immediately following the tragic accident.

DAVID MEEK REMEMBERS...

In a few weeks time will dawn another bleak February, the month which will forever be associated in the minds of many Manchester United supporters with the terrible tragedy of Munich.

For me it also marks my starting point as the reporter covering Manchester United for the Manchester Evening News.

The directors of the club kindly acknowledged my 21-year connection with Old Trafford this season by presenting me with a suitably inscribed watch.

Now the programme Editor has asked me to cast my mind back over the years to note some of the changes in an era that has ranged from tragedy to triumph and from strife to success.

I shall never forget of course the highly charged days of despair that followed the disaster at Munich which not only destroyed what seemed likely to become the best football team ever created but left such agony of mind for so many people.

The Manchester Evening News had also suffered its own loss with the death of Tom Jackson who had been one of the top sports journalists also killed in the air crash on February 6, 1958.

I was the paper's political and leader writer at the time but had always had an involvement with soccer. My father for instance was well on his way at the time towards completing an incredible 45 years reporting the affairs of York City for the local evening newspaper.

So I knew well what was involved in becoming a one-club reporter, though I hardly guessed at the scale of world-wide interest inescapable with Manchester United.

The particular difficulty after Munich was to try and hold a balance between intruding too deeply on people still suffering from the shock of losing their friends and comrades while still trying to supply news to readers anxiously wanting to know what was happening.

The main burden on the playing side fell to Jimmy Murphy, the assistant manager who had missed the trip to Belgrade because of a commitment with the Welsh team. He was helped by Joe Armstrong, the old faithful chief scout and he had an ally in Ted Dalton, the physiotherapist and a man of good counsel, but the management team had been decimated with Matt Busby critically ill in hospital and Bert Whalley the coach along with Tom Curry the trainer both killed.

It's incredible now looking back that Jimmy Murphy was able to turn out a team just eight days after the accident. He was a man in torment gathering young reserves around him, trying to sign new players and coping with the continuing grief of Munich as Matt Busby fought for his life, Duncan Edwards lay dying and other players recovered from their injuries.

He retreated to the Norbreck Hydro at Blackpool with the remnants of his playing staff and it was there that we of the Press kept in touch with developments.

Back in Manchester chairman Harold Hardman a tough old bird vowed that Manchester United would carry on. "Manchester United is bigger than any of us," he declared in a moving statement to the Press.

But most of the time we spent at Blackpool and I shall always associate the smell of chlorine from the hotel swimming pool as Jimmy Murphy announced the team that would play at Old Trafford against Sheffield Wednesday in the fourth round of the F.A. Cup.

Reporting was difficult because everything was set against the emotion and drama of Manchester United's plight. Murphy's makeshift marvels were such heroes that it almost made their first opponents like Sheffield Wednesday into villains, which hardly was fair of course.

So from the Press point of view we tried to stick to straight reporting and just give the facts about the "unknowns" like Shay Brennan, Alex Dawson and Mark Pearson who were overnight shot from the A team into First Division football.

Matt Busby returned later that season and I met him for the first time sitting in the sun outside the Norbreck Hydro. He was still in pain and could move only slowly on sticks.

Sir Matt not only had a new team playing for him he had a new Press corps to deal with, for eight senior journalists had also perished in the crash.

He dealt just as sympathetically with us new boys even though our presence must have been almost as painful a reminder to him as to see the ghosts of his beloved players every time he looked across the Old Trafford pitch.

behind the news

Manchester United helped ring up the curtain last week on the first all-seater stadium in the country.

Coventry City believe the visit of United, with their large following of fans, provided a good guide to the prospects of their venture being a success.

Certainly the indications are favourable. United fans boosted the attendance to a near capacity of 20,050 and played a big part in allaying the first fear that there would be a lack of atmosphere.

Sitting down didn't stop the Manchester supporters giving good vocal encouragement and the home fans were also in good voice.

But the main success of course was in the fact that there was no trouble at the match. Of course United fans are much better behaved now than a few years ago and the hooligan minority seems to have been weeded out.

It will be interesting to see if the visit of Leeds United – whose fans I rate the most aggressive nowadays – is as peaceful.

Nevertheless it was a good opening for the Sky Blues whose chairman, Jimmy Hill, is convinced that the most practical step a club can take towards eliminating hooligans at football is to get all the customers sitting down.

But United fans were not so happy with the price they had to pay for admission . . . a massive £6. This was the price of the tickets sent to Old Trafford for distribution to Manchester fans.

The rub is that the visitors were paying double for the kind of seats sold locally. And it was no use waiting to the day of the game either because on match days all admission goes to £6.

It's all part of the plan to stamp out the trouble-makers of course by pricing them out of the market. It's a bit steep for the hundreds of de-

By DAVID MEEK
The Voice of Football

cent supporters, though, and I think the situation lends itself to ticket spivs.

They were out in force on the approaches to Highfield Road and by solving one problem Coventry may have fuelled another.

SMILING SEXTON

Dave Sexton was probably the happiest man at Highfield Road after seeing his new club best his last one!

He conceded that the victory had meant a little more to him than normal, and also admitted that at times he had found it difficult to remember which side he was supposed to be supporting!

'Just occasionally in the exciting moments it almost caught me out,' said the manager who seems to have settled well in his new set-up at Coventry.

CHAMPAGNE CELEBRATION

United boss Ron Atkinson has naturally attracted a lot of media attention since taking up his post at Old Trafford.

And there is one picture in particular that seems to be following him around to illustrate his inclination to relax in party mood after a game.

It shows him standing behind a bar with a bottle of champagne in his hand and the glasses all lined up. In fact you could be forgiven for thinking that he spends a lot of his time dispensing champagne.

But while Old Trafford's new boss would not deny that he takes the occasional glass, it's perhaps worth pointing out that the photograph that has gone round the football world was taken some years ago when Albion were celebrating a Cup-tie success.

He went along to the Press room and on an impulse asked for a bottle of champagne for the media men. He was pictured pouring it for Press . . . and now he is paying for it!

EMERGENCY CALL

The man helping to fill the gap caused by the tragic death of physiotherapist Jim Headrige is no stranger to the Manchester soccer scene.

Peter Blakey is a remedial gymnast who has been working in recent years at Bury Hospital.

He was of course with Manchester City for several years after originally playing for Burnley and coaching their youth team.

Then he joined Bertie Mee in the medical room at Arsenal before his transfer to City. Family circumstances now make it difficult for him to work full time in football, but he answered an emergency for Nottingham Forest for a season before helping United in their present predicament.

5 SEPTEMBER 1981, v IPSWICH TOWN

The *Manchester Evening News* reporter has his say on Ron Atkinson's start as United boss, a 1-2 defeat to Coventry City at the new (and unpopular) all-seater Highfield Road.

Big Ron toasts a win while he was West Brom boss, in a photo mentioned by Meek

DAVID MEEK'S NOTEBOOK

United's interest in the transfer-listed Alan Brazil seems to have cooled lately and it's not very difficult to find the reason.

The last thing Ron Atkinson wanted to do was put pressure on Norman Whiteside by constantly reiterating admiration for the Ipswich Town striker, but obviously a great deal depended on his youngster's progress.

However brilliant a start or full of promise a player might be, there must always be a query about the ability of a 17-year-old to settle into the First Division on a permanent basis.

But the longer this season goes the stronger Whiteside gets and the bigger the game the more he seems to blossom.

The first leg of the Milk Cup semi-final at Arsenal for instance was a particularly tense and important match; one would have expected a teenager's nerves to jangle a bit.

AN IMPACT

But the boy from Belfast made an immediate impact on the game. He scored the first goal, laid on the second for partner Frank Stapleton and was going just as powerfully at the end. In fact it was Whiteside who put Steve Coppell in for the final goal.

Four days later he put the Reds through to the quarter-finals of the FA Cup by scoring six minutes from the end of the game at Derby County. It was a cool clinical finish from Steve Coppell's pass to complete a great week for the young Irishman.

Although he had a lean scoring spell after a four in five games start to the season, the goals are coming steadily now and he is clearly going to finish with a tidy total as well as a high tally of assists, as the Americans would describe it.

The manager said a few weeks ago that he had seen enough to wait until the end of the season before making a final decision about Brazil.

He explained: 'I shall take stock in the summer. Norman has had a splendid season already, though I must say I am not surprised. He will never be a flying machine, but he has good solid basics with good control and awareness. He has certainly proved that he is no flash in the pan and I am well satisfied with his progress.'

NO HEATING

Postponement of the Luton League fixture was very frustrating — particularly when under-soil heating would have solved the problem. It's a situation that has again puzzled people who cannot understand why a club like Manchester United have been reluctant to spend a relatively modest sum on trying to beat the freeze-up which affects football every winter.

But there are reasons — mainly the fact that the pitch at Old Trafford has been giving the club a lot of worries in recent seasons. The once immaculate turf suddenly deteriorated, with a clogging up of the drainage system probably the chief cause.

The Board wanted to see the problems sorted out before installing a heating system underground which would make any future drainage work very difficult and costly.

They are also reluctant to stage matches if the weather is so bad that it makes travel difficult for their supporters, many of whom come from a long way away.

The perfect system has not been invented yet either. United for instance played at Arsenal in the Milk Cup semi-final in the ridiculous situation of one flank muddy where the hot air reached and the other wing frozen solid.

CUP DRAW

United got what they wanted in the FA Cup draw for the quarter-finals . . . a home tie.

A game against a team they have already beaten at Old Trafford this season shouldn't frighten them either — except Everton have a good track record in the Cup, at least as far as the semi-finals, in recent years.

Manager Howard Kendall says: 'You can't say it's easy when you have to play the favourites away. We have lost at Old Trafford this season but that was some time ago and we can do better than that. We will certainly give it a go.'

7

Whiteside made a stunning impact in his first full season for the Reds

26 FEBRUARY 1983, v LIVERPOOL
David Meek puts his focus to breakthrough star Norman Whiteside, expresses surprise at interest in signing Alan Brazil from Ipswich, and bemoans the unreliability of undersoil heating.

United won the first 10 matches of 1985/86 but the title remained elusive

UNITED REVIEW

DAVID MEEK

So the Spurs super start to a season of 11 wins still stands as a record!

But Manchester United have still a lot going for them . . . not least a 10-point lead at the top of the table.

Their opening burst of 10 wins on the trot is certainly a club record. The best the pre-Munich team managed was five successive wins while after Munich eight wins were the most a team strung together.

Ten on the trot also equals the longest winning sequence at any stage of a season in the First Division and you have to go back to season 1907-08 to find a United team putting 10 victories together in the First Division.

So congratulations to the latter-day Reds . . . even though they did just fail to join Spurs in the record books!

A FOUNDATION

The opening burst has laid an excellent foundation for winning the Championship, though you won't find manager Ron Atkinson thinking that far ahead. All he will say is that to win the League you require a good start, you must accelerate in mid-season and finally finish with a strong burst.

There is also another important record to aim at . . . the Leeds United achievement of going 29 matches unbeaten from the start of season 1973-74.

BETTER BALANCED

Joe Jordan, who spent four seasons at Old Trafford before playing in Italy, thinks United will win the Championship.

After playing against United for Southampton he told me: 'The present team is better than the ones I played in. There is a better balance about the side now and it's stronger in midfield.

'Gordon Strachan is a major asset as well. He plays with great intelligence as well as skill, and when he is fit again I can see United launching into another long winning run.'

STRENGTH

David Pleat, the Luton manager, singled out an unusual quality which he believes makes United such a formidable team.

He said after last Saturday's game: 'I watched United training on our pitch before the match and I was struck by the strength of their players individually.

'From the waist down they nearly all seemed to be so strong physically with good muscled legs. At the end of the day in the competitive spirit of our football it makes an important difference.

'It makes them very resilient in the challenge, and when United took a grip on the game in the second-half I could see several of our players fading.'

FIT AGAIN

One of the spectators at Luton was former United player Ashley Grimes.

The Irishman has played only one League game for the Hatters this season after joining them a year ago from Coventry.

He has been hard hit by injuries, but tells me: 'I am fit now and ready to start playing again. I had an operation on my knee during the summer and since then I have had a back injury.

'But hopefully all that is behind me now.'

Grimes had six seasons of first-team football at Old Trafford where he was first tried in a left-back position which seems to be his regular role these days.

WANTED

European football may be out of sight and out of mind these days, but the English contribution has not been forgotten abroad.

Chairman Martin Edwards had a visit the other day from an Italian businessman, Pino Curotto, who now lives in this country.

Pino had been home to Italy and discovered that his countrymen hold nothing against the English for the tragedy of the Brussels European Cup Final when so many Juventus fans died.

He told the chairman that the Italians wanted the English teams, especially Manchester United, back in European competition.

In fact a local team near his home town had added the name of United to their playing title and wanted to play in Old Trafford's colours.

The chairman promptly presented Valle Sturla United with a complete set of club strip . . . something to represent Old Trafford in Italy until the day Manchester United can play in Europe again themselves.

5

12 OCTOBER 1985, v QUEENS PARK RANGERS
The programme's regular columnist reflects on United's start to the season, and highlights the admirers Ron Atkinson's side have gained in the first three months of the season.

Manchester United don't need any reminding of the need to solve the problem of hooliganism.

Born from the bitter experience of finding themselves in the front line 10 years ago with a wild element among their own supporters, they know how easily a good name can be blackened.

Happily, thanks to the development of the ground, a few counter measures at the time and the good work of the Police, Old Trafford is a safe place again.

United would readily co-operate in any plan that would bring law and order back at other grounds presently afflicted by the curse of those who use football as a platform for assault.

But they do have a problem, for one of the proposals under active consideration at the moment is the introduction of an identity card system.

RAMPAGE

Indeed it seems to be the main concern of the Government following the Liverpool rampage in Brussels which led to so many deaths.

So it makes it all the more difficult to come out in opposition to the idea; the last thing United want to do is to appear to be standing in the way of any attempt to get rid of the undesirables.

But Manchester United sincerely believe that identity cards are simply impractical and would lead to more problems than they solve.

I believe they are right. I just don't think it is feasible to get a crowd of 42,000 — United's average last season — through the turnstiles if every spectator

DAVID MEEK

has to have his photograph inspected as well as his money taken.

Anyone who has been through a country's Passport Control will know it takes time to deal with just one plane load of passengers.

And what happens if the turnstile operator is not satisfied with the identity card?

A FARCE

Unless the system becomes a farce he would have to be on the alert to deal with forgeries, stolen cards and ones simply borrowed.

But if you have ever been through a turnstile in a crush you will know that it is almost impossible to turn round and go back — especially if you don't particularly want to!

Turnstiles would certainly have to be redesigned because the villains would simply dive in over the top of the existing ones . . . or would there have to be a Policeman at every entry?

I could see a whole black market in identity cards springing up and the turnstiles becoming extra troublespots.

An awful lot of innocent people would have to suffer like the groups, parties and casual visitors who are attracted to the big clubs.

United reckon that to reach their 42,000 average they probably see 100,000 different faces in the course of a season.

An identity card system would decimate their gates to the point where you would wonder if they could continue to function.

And that would hardly seem right at a club where the problem has been virtually eliminated.

It has been suggested that there could be a section for occasional visitors specially supervised by the Police, but obviously segregation would have been sacrificed and you would have a powder keg.

EFFECTIVE

I still think that the simplest and most effective way is to make potential trouble matches, or where clubs with a bad record are involved, all ticket.

Then you simply limit or refuse the visiting club any tickets while carefully monitoring your own sales. In other words you don't sell large blocks to unknown faces.

It's the system that was introduced when United were in trouble and it succeeded in breaking up the huge Red Army that was travelling to away games and causing conflict in places like Norwich.

It hits gate revenue of course . . . but not as much as an identity card system which is too cumbersome to have any value anyway.

17 AUGUST 1985, v ASTON VILLA

David Meek lays into the government's plan for a nationwide identity-card scheme for all fans, an idea partly resulting from the deaths of 39 football supporters at the Heysel Stadium disaster in May 1985.

7 MAY 1989, LIVERPOOL v NOTTINGHAM FOREST

In the month after the Hillsborough disaster, Old Trafford hosts the rearranged FA Cup semi-final (see cover, above), and United chairman Martin Edwards outlines the measures taken to allay safety concerns ahead of the tie.

WELCOME TO OLD TRAFFORD

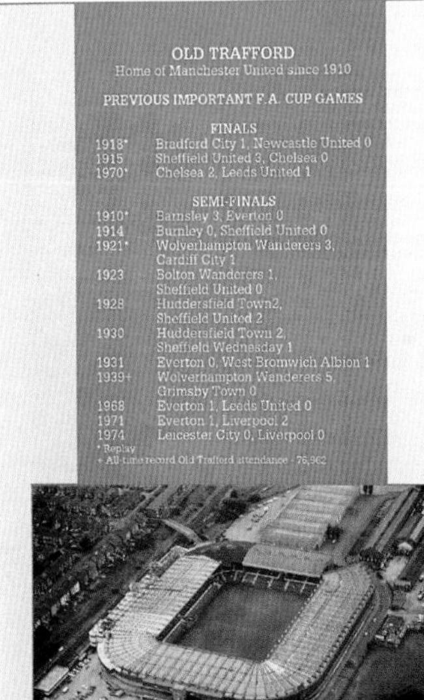

OLD TRAFFORD
Home of Manchester United since 1910

PREVIOUS IMPORTANT F.A. CUP GAMES

FINALS

1918*	Bradford City 1, Newcastle United 0
1915	Sheffield United 3, Chelsea 0
1970*	Chelsea 2, Leeds United 1

SEMI-FINALS

1910*	Barnsley 3, Everton 0
1914	Burnley 0, Sheffield United 0
1921*	Wolverhampton Wanderers 3, Cardiff City 1
1923	Bolton Wanderers 1, Sheffield United 0
1928	Huddersfield Town2, Sheffield United 2
1930	Huddersfield Town 2, Sheffield Wednesday 1
1931	Everton 0, West Bromwich Albion 1
1939+	Wolverhampton Wanderers 5, Grimsby Town 0
1968	Everton 1, Leeds United 0
1971	Everton 1, Liverpool 2
1974	Leicester City 0, Liverpool 0

* Replay
+ All-time record Old Trafford attendance - 76,962

On behalf of everyone connected with Manchester United, I extend a very warm welcome to the supporters, players and officials of Liverpool and Nottingham Forest.

The words of welcome originally prepared for a possible replay, are wholly inappropriate for they were written before the terrible tragedy at Hillsborough. So many words and expressions of sympathy have already been written and shown, that anything I say here may seem superfluous - I think not however. For we want those who lost loved ones and friends to know how much we feel for them.

I could say that we know what you are going through, for Manchester United also suffered great sadness at Munich Airport in 1958. To say that though, would be a mistake for your grief is personal to you and no-one else truly knows how you feel. All we, in the rest of football, can do in the short term, is offer whatever practical help is required and in the longer term continue to extend the hand of friendship. These thoughts are not just directed at Liverpool but to Nottingham Forest also, for they too have had to come to terms with the shock and grief of Hillsborough.

In practical terms, we have done everything humanly possible to minimise the trauma that this afternoon's match will, for some, inevitably produce. The information printed on the back of all standing tickets was done quite deliberately in an effort not only to reassure spectators but, equally important, their families and friends at home.

Whilst on the subject, it is appropriate that we think of those supporters who still feel unable to attend this semi-final. We hope that in the fullness of time they will feel able to once again, return to the ground of their favourite club.

We have invited Liverpool Social Services staff to attend so that they may offer their services to anyone who may be overcome by the occasion.

Additional medical facilities have also been rbough in, not because we are usually undermanned - far from it - it has been done simply as a gesture of re-assurance.

For the same reason, we have deliberately issued less tickets for the standing accommodation than our ground safety license permits. Again, we want supporters to feel comfortable on what for some, may be a very difficult day.

Having said all that, I am sure that it is good for everyone that we, in football, are attempting to return to some sort of normality. We are told that Liverpool's decision to play is very much a reflection of the wishes of the bereaved and injured. That being the case, I am sure that they would want a match worthy of the occasion. Hopefully, both teams will go all out from the first to last in order to secure a Cup final place. To play the game in any other way would be to abdicate their responsibilities - not only to the 50,000 present this afternoon, not only to the countless millions watching on television - but most importantly to the 95 supporters who cannot be with us today. They deserve a cup-tie played in the best traditions of the game.

May the best team win.

C.M. Edwards
Chairman,
Manchester United

UNITED REVIEW

UNITED THE WORLD OVER

by Cynthia Bateman of The Guardian

There was one move at United last week that you might have missed, amid all the activity in the transfer market Ken Ramsden, the club's Assistant Secretary, who has compiled the *United Review* for the last eight years, handed over his editorship, although he retains overall responsibility for producing the magazine, which sells 47,000 copies - more than many local newspapers.

After each home game, more than 200 are mailed to Unitedites in 60 different countries. As you read this, one supporter in Mauritius is waiting for his copy of the Arsenal match day review to drop through his letter box. The Australian fans have a longer wait, but the *Review* must be one of the few Western publications uncensored behind the Iron Curtain, with readers in Russia, Bulgaria and Rumania. The Scandinavians read the review when they are not watching United videos, and the interest in United is so keen in Europe that after home games the Old Trafford switchboard is jammed with Continental calls demanding the result.

One copy of the Review goes to the Falklands - that expensive new airport had to be good for something - and a Falklands' broadcaster was at Old Trafford to see United beat Arsenal. It was one of the longest trips made by any supporter, although many of the Irish contingent, among United's most faithful followers, have to leave home on Friday mornings to reach Old Trafford for Saturday afternoon.

"I am convinced Ireland rises 3 ft out of the water every time we have a home game," said Ken. He remembers seeing two Irishmen on the pitch one day, one of them down on all fours. "He was actually eating the grass," said Ken. "We wouldn't want to encourage that." But he can understand the effect Old Trafford has on supporters.

Many fans returning on Monday to buy tickets for the next match, even though they have been to a game here on Saturday, ask if they can just have a look at the stadium. "If you ask why, and point out there is nothing going on inside, their response is: "We just want to look," said Ken.

Bobby Charlton tells the story of arriving one day to find a coachload of people looking round an empty ground. "I asked them why they were here since there was no match on," he said. "And it turned out they had just come to see the new floodlights being erected."

Old Trafford worked miracles for Cam Erskine and his son Nigel, who was severely handicapped and believed he had noting to live for.

A visit to United gave him a new lease of life, and he and his father have made what is for them an arduous journey from Cardiff for every home match for the last 14 years.

More than 100 coaches bring supporters from all over the country to Old Trafford on match days, with at least one from each of the 60 areas that has a supporters club branch.

Nobody went home happier last week than those from the four London branches . . . except perhaps the manager and the chairman, and if you can talk about Manchester United, you can make friends anywhere in the world, with one or two notable exceptions, one of them just down the Ship Canal.

A Brit crossing the Sahara, who arrived dying of thirst at a desert oasis - although I have to say it was a pint of bitter he was gasping for - found the natives spoke only two words of English - "Manchester United".

"Building friendships is what the membership scheme is about," said Ken, "We recognise at Manchester United that people want to feel part of the club. It would be easy to become blase, but we have had a strict upbringing here, and we realise this place is food and drink to the supporters."

United is firmly established on the tourist trail, and visitors from 62 countries have been to the museum. Its curator, Cliff Butler, who is also club photographer, historian and statistician, is taking over as editor of the *Review*. "Cliff has a similar knowledge of United's history," said Ken. "If you ask him what size boots, the number nine wore in 1903, chances are he'll be able to tell you.

27

30 AUGUST 1989, v NORWICH CITY

There's a change in editor at *United Review*, Cliff Butler replacing Ken Ramsden, and the outgoing man discusses the Reds' growing global appeal with *The Guardian*'s Cynthia Bateman.

2 MAY 1992, v TOTTENHAM HOTSPUR

United skipper Bryan Robson cannot hide his disappointment at the Reds being pipped to the league title by Leeds, plus he wishes Gary Lineker well ahead of his final game in English football and ends speculation about his own immediate future.

Gary Lineker with a parting gift as he bids farewell to English football

A FEW WORDS FROM OUR CAPTAIN

Disappointment is not a strong enough word to sum up the players' feelings at the failure of our bid to win the League Championship. I know exactly how the fans are feeling now. But once again success has been punished and been a major factor in failure. It is crazy fixture planning to be faced with four games in seven days at the most crucial phase of the season. It is comparable to an athlete being asked to produce peak per-formances in four major races, a boxer to climb into the ring for four title fights, or a racehorse run four Classics.

WORKLOAD

In previous years there has been some elbow room after the end of the season. But not this time, and I firmly believe that by beating Leeds United in the FA Cup and Rumbelows Cup we reduced their workload and helped them to win the championship for the first time since 1974. Leeds United seem to have been cruising while we have been battling to cram games in, and they have seized their chance and congratulations to them. I can only hope that this season sees the end of the crazy fixture chaos that punishes the successful and handicaps the teams struggling for survival in the relegation zones. We have been in the driving seat until the last two games of the season. We threw the title away, but we gave our best and in the end we have to admit that our best wasn't good enough. But in our crushing disappointment the season must not be written off as failure. We won the Rumbelows Cup and the Super Cup. We have been in the top two every month of the season and made considerable improvement on the sixth place we achieved last season. Football is going to miss the exciting talents of Gary Lineker and Gazza Gascoigne next season. I sincerely hope Gary has a successful time in Japan and that his son George continues to improve in health, and that Gazza is able to prove his fitness in Italy.

SPECULATION

I want to end unwelcome speculation about my own situation at Old Trafford. I have a contract for next season and have no intention of quitting just because a prize I have coveted during a long career has eluded me. The team can only get better.

In an interview with Derek Potter

UNITED REVIEW

The Captain

It has been a funny old summer for the players and supporters of Manchester United. The sun may not have been shining but we have been basking - in the glory of having won the Premier League title. For too many years we have watched others begin the season as championship defenders.

This season will tell us much more about our ability as individuals, as a team and about our mental fibre. More than ever, Manchester United will be THE team to beat; the team others will use as a measuring stick of their own qualities. You can take it that the management and players know the pitfalls and consequences of being defenders rather than contenders. It is still hard to comprehend the struggle Leeds United faced all last season after their brave title snatch from under our noses.

I have already been an unhappy victim of the Old Trafford regime I expect and respect. After working hard - in our game you work hard to prepare yourself for work! - I hoped to be in the team at the start of the Charity Shield showpiece. So before a ball had been kicked in anger, I had to face a reality that will test the resilience of every player at Old Trafford before the Carling Premiership is resolved. Players who believe they have a right to be automatic selections in any team are half way to destroying what they have created by their skill and effort. It is a dream world for a manager. He will not always be right in his selections, especially if the options are numerous. But just having them is a measure of a boss's strength. It is a wand and a baton I would like to hold.

Roy Keane made a wise decision to join United. He has grasped the nettle by realising that Old Trafford is a stadium of a thousand dreams. Roy has skill, he is strong and has a rapidly maturing football brain, and at just 22 he is still short of his physical peak.

I have already seen enough of Roy to know that he has a grasp of the problems that could face a player with such a wide range of assets. I hope Roy adds to his "roundness" by learning from the players of high quality who share the same dressing room.

"I have never taken anything for granted in football"

We finished with the flourish I hoped for last season, equalling the record of the previous champions in 1967. We won it in style. It is not difficult to predict which teams will be the dangers this season. The main threat could come from any of the seven teams in the slipstream of our ten-point advantage. You can't write off Liverpool, Arsenal, Leeds and, of course, the newcomers Newcastle, West Ham and Swindon. Of the 'new boys' Newcastle look to have the biggest punch with considerable playing strength, an imposing stadium and hungry fans. But I fancy the main threat will come from any one of half a dozen wary old campaigners. Which one? I'm hedging my bets. I have never taken anything for granted in football.

Bryan Robson

United9Review

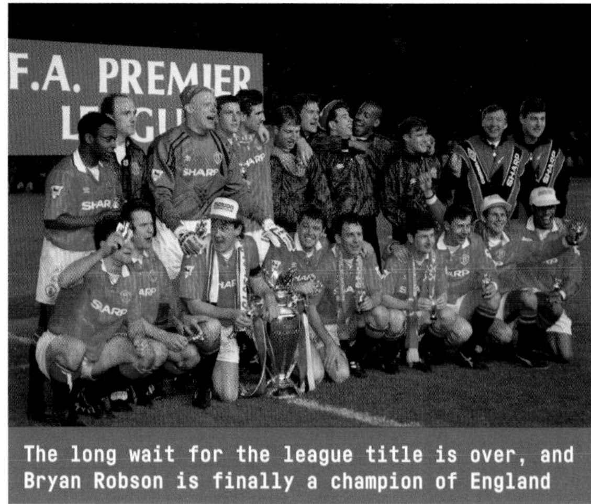

The long wait for the league title is over, and Bryan Robson is finally a champion of England

18 AUGUST 1993, v SHEFFIELD UNITED
Robbo uses his captain's column to warn his team-mates of the difficulties ahead in retaining the league title, and has words of advice, plus plenty of praise, for his new colleague Roy Keane.

REDleader

Atmosphere

Wembley is beginning to feel like a second home....two FA Cup Finals and two semis, and four League Cups and Charity Shields. There's still no place like it, no matter how long a player has been in the game or how many times he has played there. Now, at the end of a long, hard season, I can't wait to get back there to tackle Everton. It's great for the supporters and a great occasion for the players whose families will have been caught up in the atmosphere long before setting out to Wembley. I recall my old room mate and pal from Norwich City, John Deehan, advising me before I first played there: "Do your best to take it all in - if you don't it will be a blur." He was absolutely right. It becomes easier after the first game there not to be distracted by all that goes on around you in the build-up and in the dressing room.

Drama

Everton will battle all the way and will be difficult to beat. Even though I expect it to be a hard-fought and classic Final. Finals involving Manchester United never fail to produce excitement and drama. But we are going to miss a number of

key players. It is amazing to note that the team that beat Chelsea 4-0 at Wembley last year has not played together since after being together for twenty-two games and winning them all. Yes, injuries and suspensions have cut a huge chunk out of our season and undoubtedly reduced our efficiency. A repeat of the 1-0 win over Everton ten years ago will suffice, but Joe Royle has proved he is an astute manager and motivator and will not miss any tricks to stop United winning the Cup for a record ninth time, one ahead of Tottenham Hotspur.

Faithful

I am delighted Southampton escaped relegation (and equally dismayed at the struggle Norwich City faced) and after the game against the Saints, managed by another ex-Everton "great", we can concentrate on Wembley where we hope to reward our masses of faithful fans for their support and encouragement during a hard and eventful season.

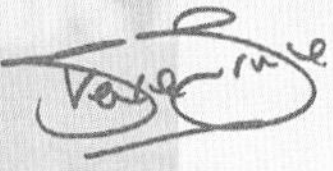

10 MAY 1995, v SOUTHAMPTON
United skipper Steve Bruce looks ahead to the Reds' trip to Wembley to face Everton in the FA Cup final. It would be the 11th and last time he'd visit the national stadium as a United player, but unfortunately it ended with a 0-1 defeat to Everton.

21 SEPTEMBER 2003, v ARSENAL

The rivalry between Sir Alex's United and Arsene Wenger's Gunners reached boiling point in this early-season league encounter, in which Ruud van Nistelrooy was jostled by Arsenal players after missing a late penalty.

HE BLEEDS RED. HE SEES RED. HE WRITES RED

PAT CRERAND

JUST TWO GAMES IN, SAHA'S ALREADY THREATENING TO BECOME A RED LEGEND

Oh dear me, what a match at Goodison. The first half saw one of the best United performances I've seen in a long, long time. If it had been 7-0 at half-time it wouldn't have been a shock. Then, in the second half, nobody could cope with the aerial threat of Duncan Ferguson, someone who's always posed problems for United through the years. But I can't understand whatsoever all the complaints about the United players' celebrations when the fourth goal went in.

United came back to score a winner right at the death, so of course they were going to celebrate. Nobody made any gestures as far as I could see. But it makes me laugh when fans these days complain to the police about players. How often do you see fans abuse players during a match, call them names that aren't repeatable and then if something is said back they're straight to the police? I'm not talking specifically about Everton fans, it happens everywhere and it's an absolute joke. A waste of police time.

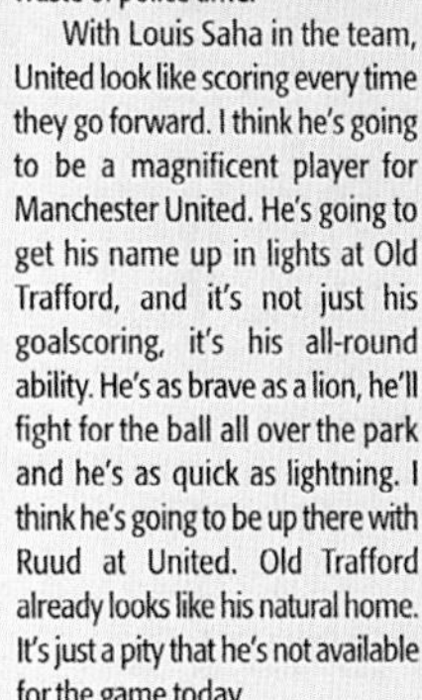

"I THINK THE FA CUP HAS LOST A LITTLE BIT OF MAGIC BECAUSE THE FINAL HASN'T BEEN STAGED AT WEMBLEY RECENTLY"

With Louis Saha in the team, United look like scoring every time they go forward. I think he's going to be a magnificent player for Manchester United. He's going to get his name up in lights at Old Trafford, and it's not just his goalscoring, it's his all-round ability. He's as brave as a lion, he'll fight for the ball all over the park and he's as quick as lightning. I think he's going to be up there with Ruud at United. Old Trafford already looks like his natural home. It's just a pity that he's not available for the game today.

We've all been looking forward to another derby, especially after that amazing match against Spurs. City have been better away from home than they have been at the City Of Manchester Stadium where they've really struggled. In that new ground the crowd are a fair bit away from the pitch and I would imagine it's like an away match for City to a certain degree. But this is what the FA Cup is all about. There'll be 9,000 City fans here and they'll all be up for it.

The FA Cup has died a little bit over the years, but with Arsenal playing Chelsea and United playing City, it'll give the tournament a big, big lift. The competition has been devalued because the bigger clubs are more interested in the European Cup than the FA Cup. I think the FA Cup has also lost a bit of magic because the final hasn't been staged at Wembley recently. I know Cardiff is a lovely stadium and for a lot of people it's easier to get to, but it's just not Wembley; it doesn't have that same history and magic. It was every player's dream to play in an FA Cup final at Wembley and it was no different for me. When we won it in 1963 it was a day I'll never forget – and I'm sure Sir Alex will be thinking five years is far too long for United not to have won the tournament.

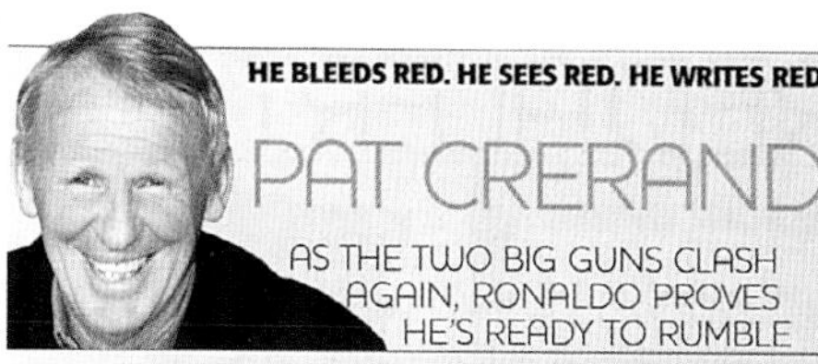

HE BLEEDS RED. HE SEES RED. HE WRITES RED

PAT CRERAND

AS THE TWO BIG GUNS CLASH AGAIN, RONALDO PROVES HE'S READY TO RUMBLE

Ruud didn't have one of his better days against Charlton last Saturday but he still did the business. When you need three points, he's always there to put it in the back of the net. No matter how well you play, managers like good defensive displays and it was pleasing to see how strong the back four and the keeper looked. Ferdinand was exceptional. Against a big, strong fella like Jason Euell, you're going to get knocked all over the place, but he didn't let that happen. In my opinion the best back four for United at the moment are John O'Shea at left back, Mikael and Rio as centre backs, and Gary Neville at right back.

It was Ronaldo's first full game against Charlton and he was tremendous. In the papers some said he dives – he definitely does not. How the Charlton right back stayed on the pitch was unbelievable, he could have been sent off after 10 or 15 minutes! To be fair to him, though, if you're faced with someone taking the mickey out of you all the time, what do you do? If you can't stop him by fair means you try foul, and if you're fortunate enough to get away with it, you keep at it. But I think Mike Riley gave him too much rope, he should have been off.

"ARSENAL'S MAIN MAN IS PATRICK VIEIRA. I THINK MOST UNITED FANS WOULD ADMIT HE'S THE ONE THEY'D WANT TOO"

What I like about Ronaldo is that if he gets whacked, he doesn't say anything, he just gets on with it. The bone of contention among the fans is who plays through the middle if something happens to Ruud, but I think the kid could play there. It'd be interesting to see him play just behind Ruud, especially with his pace. If he starts against Arsenal there'll be more pace on the pitch than ever in the history of football!

I know there's always been this war of words between Alex and Arsène Wenger but there's no doubt he's been a great manager for Arsenal. Obviously they try to wind each other up, that's part and parcel of football, but I'm not sure there's a great depth to their animosity. That sort of relationship between managers didn't go on in my day, but I think Alex is excellent at it. He's a typical Glaswegian and loves a mickey-take, and that's it.

One thing's certain, after last season, Arsenal will have the raving needle. They may have won the Cup but that meant nothing to them. I don't doubt for one minute that the players will have been thinking, "This is the wrong trophy." The championship's the big one. Try to pick out the Arsenal danger man and you'd probably have half-a-dozen names, but their main man is Patrick Vieira, no doubt about it. I think most United fans would admit he's the one they'd want, too.

If you had to face Vieira and Roy Keane in the middle of the park together, would you bother turning up? I hope the result goes well for United but there's so much at stake, it could easily end up a draw.

14 FEBRUARY 2004, v MANCHESTER CITY

Paddy was certainly impressed with new signing Louis Saha, although the striker is cup-tied for this quarter-final clash with the Blues.

Unitedfront

The Pat Crerand Column

SO MANY MEMORIES – ON AND OFF THE PITCH – OF A MAN WHO CAPTURED THE IMAGINATION LIKE NO OTHER...

Putting the Reds on the map: Bestie's European Cup-winning exploits are the stuff of legend...

It's been an emotional week. I've spent a lot of my time talking about George, but that's not been a problem – George is easy to talk about. He was such a great lad, and the fun we had with him down through the years...

One occasion I remembered this week was celebrating his 21st birthday in San Francisco in 1967. United were on tour and we all had a night out to celebrate his birthday and, well... if I told you what had happened you wouldn't be able to print it in the programme!

So many things have made me laugh over the last few days – like thinking about the Brown Bull pub in Salford. George used to be driven mad by fans in most places he went to. He was looking for somewhere quiet to go and he found this little pub round the corner. So after a match on a Saturday we used to start off in the Brown Bull. Within a fortnight the place was heaving, all because George and the players were there. An American lad owned it and he must have made an absolute fortune.

George moved in with me and my family at the height of his fame, but he only lasted four days. My kids were four and five at the time and they drove him mad. If he climbed out the window to escape it wouldn't have been the first time!

"PEOPLE WANTED TO WATCH GEORGE PLAYING NO MATTER WHO THEY SUPPORTED"

He was such a shy lad but he came to the fore just as televised football was taking off. And because of his ability people wanted to watch him playing when he was in their town, no matter who they supported. George was one of the players who put United on the map – the Busby Babes, Bobby and Denis, George... people couldn't get enough of them. Nowadays of course every kick is televised, but there were so many of George's greatest moments that weren't seen. Even European football was hardly televised in those days but fortunately George's great performance in Benfica in 1966 is there for posterity.

I remember we played Chelsea one night at Stamford Bridge. They were top of the league and we were second, and we beat them 2-0. There were 60-odd thousand at the game and George got a standing ovation, I'm talking about the Chelsea fans as well as United fans, saluting a performance that was just incredible.

I thought West Ham, the club and the fans, were absolutely magnificent last Sunday. What they organised with the speeches and the minute's applause was something special. I think the applause is the way to go because you don't hear the morons then, but when George Best was on a football pitch, nobody kept quiet when he was on the ball. Don't forget, it wasn't so long ago that West Ham lost their greatest player in Bobby Moore, a great friend of mine as well. He was very much like George. People got the wrong impression of Bobby because he was tall and blond and some thought he was a bit haughty. That was the last thing in the world he was. He liked a laugh and giggle as well. But in the end footballers are just like football fans – it's only that players are in the public eye. But players do get respect for their ability. I heard there was a big flag in the Barcelona end at their game at the weekend which said, "God bless George Best." That's respect.

I last saw George in Manchester not that long ago, in Harpers restaurant. He always went there because it's run by little Felix, a good mate of George's who worked for him when he had Slack Alice's. I heard George was in town so I went down there one Tuesday afternoon. There he was, sat on his own, but he was on great form as usual.

He'll never be forgotten. They'll put a statue up or do something similar at Old Trafford, maybe name a stand after him. But anybody who's ever seen him play will never forget him. The parents tell the sons, the sons tell their sons, it's an ongoing thing. People will know what a great player George was 100 years from now.

3 DECEMBER 2005, v PORTSMOUTH

In an emotional week for Paddy, he regales readers with tales of his good friend George Best following the sad passing of our former no.7 at the age of just 59, including the time the Northern Irishman lived with his family for four days.

Fans pay their respects to George Best following his sad passing in November 2005

United beat Celtic 3-2 in the first-ever competitive meeting between the clubs

THE**LAST**WORD

Divided loyalties

As a Glasgow lad, Paddy once cheered on Celtic against United, but not tonight...

I just knew we were going to draw Celtic this time. MUTV's Steve Bower and I were on our way back from commentating on the match against Charlton, the day before the Champions League draw, and I said, "There's no doubt, we're going to draw Celtic." After the long years that both teams have been in Europe, somewhere along the way they were going to draw one another. I was at the Coronation Cup game in 1953 when Celtic beat United 2-1. And let me tell you something, as a little kid in Glasgow I wasn't supporting Manchester United that night, but obviously it'll be different for this game!

It's a great draw and another bonus is that United don't have to travel far for the return match. And I'm sure that somewhere along the line United will want to do Celtic a favour by beating Benfica twice and hope that Celtic can get through to the next round. But they'll be looking at the group and feel confident they can qualify on their own efforts – if they can beat Copenhagen home and away and beat Benfica at Celtic Park, that will probably get them through. But you never know!

United had a convincing win against Rangers at Old Trafford a few seasons ago and at the end of the day, English football is a higher standard than Scottish football. A lot of money is spent compared to over the border, and the television deals have a lot to do with that. But that stands for nothing on the night – just look at the games United have had against Exeter and Burton Albion over the last few seasons. Football can be crazy sometimes and anything can happen.

It'll be a difficult game for United because with the support they'll have behind them, Celtic will battle from the first minute to the last. They'll be up for it, no doubt about that.

Celtic's fanatical followers...

Celtic have got 6,500 tickets for the game but you can bet there will be a lot more of their fans in the ground somehow – the chase for tickets for this game has been crazy! At all the testimonial matches the fans have mixed well with no problems. Although there won't be the same mix this time, I hope this game has the same friendly spirit, even though there's a lot more at stake. Celtic fans have a great reputation all over the world and I'm sure it'll be the same story tonight.

13 SEPTEMBER 2006, v CELTIC

A born-and-bred Celt but when his boyhood club came to Old Trafford for a European tie, Paddy was very much backing the club of his heart.

THE LAST WORD

Keep the Red flag flying to see United over the line

PAT CRERAND

We're still buzzing after the ecstasy of Tuesday's semi-final success, but United will need the fans' support again today for that last push

"WHAT A NIGHT it was on Tuesday. I hope you've recovered your voices, because United will need your support today.

We have a golden opportunity to win the Premier League and Champions League this season, and this game is critical to that. But if you all get behind the team like you did four days ago, it will frighten the life out of West Ham. I have to admit, Tuesday was excruciating. The pressure was on and the second half seemed really long. But we got through it. Defensively, United were magnificent while the support was the best I've ever known. It took me back to the 3-0 win over Barcelona here in 1984.

The result gives everyone at the club and the fans a big boost for today. But I hope nobody here has a casual attitude and thinks: 'United will win this one, easy.' You must realise that when a player's on the pitch and the crowd is behind them, it gives a real lift. On Tuesday, a few players looked dead on their feet. But they kept going because of the fans.

It's easy for supporters to make noise when the team is winning 3-0. But when players struggle fans can really play a part. Nobody could deny the role the supporters had against Barcelona, and that effect could be similar today.

MESMERIC MESSI

I have to mention Lionel Messi's performance on Tuesday – what a wonderful footballer he is. I love watching great players, even if he did make watching the game uncomfortable at times. For United, Rio Ferdinand and Wes Brown were pillars of strength, while Carlos Tevez and Ji-sung Park never stopped running. Park is an unsung hero. He put everything into the 90 minutes. It's that mixture of characteristics in this squad that gives United a great shot at a double.

DELIGHTED FOR SCHOLESY

I'm glad Paul Scholes scored the winner on Tuesday – and what a goal. He's done that many times, but scoring the goal that takes United to the final after missing out nine years ago was poignant. Roy Keane said to me after the final in 1999 that he didn't want his medal. Denis Law was the same in '68. They battled to get the team there, but because they miss a game they think they don't deserve a medal – they do. I'm delighted Paul will play on that stage.

BRING THE CUP HOME

On 29 May, Old Trafford is holding a dinner to celebrate the 40th anniversary of United's 1968 European Cup final win and Sir Alex is guest of honour. A replica trophy will be on hand and some recently won silverware would be great, too! For meal details and more info on the event, email wendyveevers@hotmail.co.uk."

You can speak to Paddy on his MUTV phone-in on Monday nights.

3 MAY 2008,
v WEST HAM UNITED

Paddy was buzzing after the Reds had reached Moscow and outlined the part fans had played in making it such an incredible evening. He picked out United's heroes on the night but also had words of caution ahead of a tricky fixture with the Hammers.

United followed up victory over Barcelona with a 4-1 thrashing of West Ham, with Ronaldo scoring twice

Gary Neville

Sir Bobby Charlton

Andy Cole

Denis Law

Gary Neville

Bryan Robson

Peter Schmeichel

THE AMBASSADOR'S COLUMN

IT'S FITTING THAT THE GREATEST MANAGER OF ALL TIME SHOULD DEPART ON HIS TERMS, SAYS GARY NEVILLE, AND HE LEAVES BEHIND A TEAM ON AN UPWARD CURVE...

It's a day we all knew would come sooner or later, but that doesn't lessen the shock. It's hard to imagine Manchester United without Sir Alex Ferguson in charge. Working in the media, the question I've been asked more than any other is when I thought he would stop managing United, and I honestly never thought I'd see the day that he'd be sat up in the directors' box, watching somebody else in charge of the team.

But here we are; while I'm shocked I'm nevertheless so relieved and grateful he's taken the decision on his own terms. There are no issues over his health or anything like that, it's a decision he's made when he wanted to.

As you'll have heard from so many who've played under him, I consider myself privileged and fortunate to have worked with Sir Alex – a father figure to so many of us and an inspiration to work with. Growing up as a United fan, I was gutted as this club was the butt of all the jokes while Liverpool were dominating the league. Then the manager came along; he changed everything, inspiring an even greater era of dominance with this club. Yes, he's had a vast list of fantastic players doing the business for him on the pitch, but he's been the difference. He has made every player carry his mentality, his dedication to the cause and it has been 11 versions of himself taking to the field in every game. Even with the sheer size of Manchester United now, that inspiration has applied to employees all over the club as well; his influence is everywhere around us, in every single individual.

He's everything you'd hope for in a boss. He inspires you. Just watching him during games, seemingly fighting a war from the touchline; always going, always battling to the death – that's why his teams have developed such an incredible knack of retrieving lost causes and winning against all odds.

That spirit's filtered into his current team, and while there was never going to be an easy time to hand it over to a new manager, the man coming in to replace Sir Alex is inheriting a club that is on an upward curve again. There is a lot of experience in key positions, but there are so many good young players in there who have all sampled highs and lows. David De Gea, Rafael, Phil Jones, Jonny Evans, Chris Smalling, Tom Cleverley, Anderson, Danny Welbeck, Javier Hernandez and Shinji Kagawa are all young players who know what it takes to be champions because they learned under the man who knew it better than anyone.

I said recently, the incredible thing about Sir Alex is that with him the battle is never complete, but now it is. The war has been fought and won, and today provides every Manchester United fan with the chance to pay a proper tribute to an unbelievable man.

Winners! Gary Neville and Sir Alex in 2008; (right) Welbeck and Kagawa

12 MAY 2013, v SWANSEA CITY

Gary Neville was part of a rotation of club ambassadors who spoke to *United Review* in each issue, and as Sir Alex took charge of an Old Trafford fixture for the last time, the former full-back shared a few heartfelt words on his old boss.

CHAPTER 6

The opposition

The match programme has always been a valuable source of information for fans on the players in the away dressing room – with a changing job down the years when it comes to profiling those we often love to hate...

Over 110 years have passed since Liverpool were the first visitors to Archibald Leitch's latest architectural football marvel: Manchester United's Old Trafford stadium. The great North West rivals started as they meant to go on in M16, slugging out a seven-goal thriller to enthral the expectant crowd.

Sadly, Liverpool spoiled the party that day, winning 4-3. But, back then, contests with the other Reds from the opposite end of the East Lancs Road were nothing like the vitriolic, tense encounters that have become so familiar to us since the 1970s.

Then, in a world where the car and even the bicycle were still new, emerging technologies, Liverpool was a relatively distant city. Their players were almost as mysterious as the European visitors that would arrive at Old Trafford (or Maine Road) in the 1950s, during United's first wave of continental football. Unless you read match reports in the national papers, or had perhaps caught them playing Manchester City across town, the arrival of every team was something novel.

Above: United and City players walk out on to the pitch prior to the 145th Manchester derby in September 2005

That gave the matchday programme a very important job. As thousands descended on Old Trafford for each game, the offering of information and insight on the opposition was key.

In the 1920s, spectators might, for example, have known a bit about the great Huddersfield Town side that became the first club to win three top-flight titles on the bounce. But fans craved background knowledge, so as to recognise and relate to the stars out on the pitch – or maybe throw a joke or some light ribbing their way!

But what would fans know of Plymouth Argyle, who visited six times in Division Two during the 1930s? Or Bradford Park Avenue? For most fans,

Mark Hughes gets stuck in during a typically feisty clash with Leeds – just one side guaranteed to set the pulses racing for Reds

Victory over Liverpool in 1977 was the perfect example of a rivalry in action

attending a game on a Saturday was the *nonpareil* entertainment highlight of the week, and they wanted to make the most of it. Picking up a match programme was vital to help you extract the maximum richness out of your afternoon.

Over the decades, *United Review*'s role changed, as football's media presence grew, first via radio and then through television. Supporters knew more about players like Stanley Matthews or, later, Jimmy Greaves. They might even have seen them play an FA Cup final from their very own front rooms! So the programme's job became about building excitement and detailing the context of the game.

In the modern era, that has developed even further. Few Reds relished a reminder of how dangerous Steven Gerrard might be, or what damage Thierry Henry might do to our hopes of a perfect weekend. We're now familiar with so many teams and players – even European opposition.

So *United Review*'s job is to deliver something bespoke: an interview with an opposition player that fans cannot find anywhere else, tactical details, or even basic information like squad numbers or this season's appearance and goal statistics. In the digital age, where information is constantly swamping us, accurate figures can be surprisingly elusive.

But looking back through the archives, you primarily remember the great rivalries; the great teams that have flooded through Old Trafford.

Our battles with Liverpool, City, Leeds, Arsenal and many others have given euphoria at times, and pain at others. But they've always been afforded respect in *UR*. And when you glance back through the programme's history, there's a clear reason for that: their contribution to our great story is crystal clear, and has made for some epic, indelible stories...

West and Turnbull take a break from football to enjoy a spot of cricket

2 APRIL 1915: THE GOOD FRIDAY SCANDAL

George Anderson got both of our goals in this Easter win against Liverpool, but United's Sandy Turnbull, Arthur Whalley and Enoch West, as well as Liverpool's Jackie Sheldon, Tom Miller, Bob Pursell and Thomas Fairfoul, are the names this league clash is remembered for (even if a few are missing from the predicted team sheet here). Following an FA investigation, all seven were found guilty of match-fixing, having placed large sums of money on the correct 2-0 scoreline.

4 MANCHESTER UNITED PROGRAMME.

MANCHESTER UNITED

1 BEALE Goal

2 HODGE Right Back — 3 SPRATT Left Back

4 MONTGOMERY Right Half — 5 O'CONNELL Centre Half — 6 HAYWOOD Left Half

7 MEREDITH Outside Right — 8 POTTS Inside Right — 9 ANDERSON Centre — 10 WEST Inside Left — 11 NORTON Outside Left

Referee : Mr. J. G. A. SHARPE — KICK-OFF, 3-30.

12 NICHOLL Outside Left — 13 MILLER Inside Left — 14 PAGNAM Centre — 15 BANKS Inside Right — 16 SHELDON Outside Right

17 M'KINLAY Left Half — 18 BRATLEY Centre Half — 19 LACEY Right Half

20 PURSELL Left Back — 21 LONGWORTH Right Back

22 SCOTT Goal

LIVERPOOL

Any change in the Teams will be notified by number on the board which will be sent round the enclosure.

6 Manchester United Programme.

TO-DAY'S VISITORS.

ASTON VILLA'S WONDERFUL RECORD OVER A LONG PERIOD.

SIX times winners of both the English Cup and the First League championship, records which no side have even approached, Aston Villa will be welcomed by a big crowd at Old Trafford to-day.

The name of Aston Villa is known throughout the world wherever football is read, spoken of, or played. No club, it can truthfully be said, has done more to popularise football.

Space does not permit me referring to the "stars" who have worn the Villa colours during the past thirty years or more. Many of them are still an household word. Their memory is cherished

F. BARSON (Aston Villa).

not merely for what they accomplished in their day and generation, but for the inspiring example which they have handed down to their successors in the Villa team in particular and players in general.

Like every other club, the Villa have had their "bad times," but the finest qualities of sportsmanship have always characterised their play. And indicating their popularity with Manchester enthusiasts it may be mentioned that the two largest crowds ever accommodated at Old Trafford assembled when the "Villains" were the visitors.

ONE OF THE ORIGINALS.

Aston Villa were one of the original founders of the League, and in the first season, 1888-89, they finished second to Preston North End. Since then they have reached the top position six times. At two distinct periods they have secured the championship trophy in successive seasons. In the season 1896-7 they equalled Preston North End's record of winning both the Cup and the League. That feat has not since been repeated. Their last League honours were gained in 1909-10. Six times also they have been runners-up. Last season they finished tenth with 43 points, or two points better than our record.

CUP WARRIORS.

As Cup warriors the Villa figured just as prominently in football history. When they defeated Huddersfield Town the season before last in the final they set up a new record of six successes. Blackburn Rovers and the Wanderers had each won five final ties.

And the remarkable thing about that success is that for over two months of the season they were firmly established at the bottom of the League and in danger of losing their place in the "charmed circle" for the first time in their career. But the Villa have a reputation for team building. The advent of Frank Barson from Barnsley marked a great difference, and many others they secured virtually on their own doorstep and at little cost.

With such a man as Barson behind them these men developed rapidly. During the close season the Villa "parted company" with such fine players as Sam Hardy, Charlie Wallace, Andy Ducat, and at the end of last season Clem Stephenson and James Harrop. The "youngsters" left have taken their chance, and are undoubtedly playing good sound football.

Villa's first Cup success was in 1886-7, when they beat their neighbours, West Bromwich Albion, 2—0. In 1891-2 the Albion took revenge with a 3—0 victory. On all five subsequent occasions on which the Villa have reached the final they have taken the Cup back to Birmingham, where in 1895 the original trophy was stolen from a shop window. They were the finalists when 120,028 spectators watched the match with Sunderland—the biggest crowd that has ever assembled at a football match in England. The players at the disposal of the Villa this season are:—

Player. Birthplace. Position.	Height. ft. in.	Weight. st. lb.
T. Jackson, Newcastle (G.)	6 0	12 0
C. H. Spiers, Birmingham (G.)	6 0	12 0
T. Smart, Blackheath (Staffs.) (R.B.)	5 10	12 7
T. Weston, Halesowen (L.B.)	5 10	11 7
E. Blackburn, Crawshawbooth (Lancs.) (L.B.)	5 9	12 0
H. Humphries, Aston (L.B.)	5 10	11 0
H. Maxted, Sutton Jnc. (Notts.) (L.B.)	5 9	12 0
T. Ball, Usworth (Durham) (R.H.B.)	5 10	12 7
F. Moss, Aston (R.H.B.)	5 11	11 4
F. Barson, Sheffield (C.H.B.)	5 11½	12 0
J. J. Pendleton, Liverpool (C.H.B.)	5 9½	12 0
G. F. Blackburn, London (L.H.B.)	5 10½	12 0
J. Leach, Newcastle (L.H.B.)	5 10½	11 8
J. Humphreys, Burton (L.H.B.)	5 7½	11 0
R. E. York, Birmingham (O.R.)	5 9½	11 0
W. J. Kirton, Newcastle (I.R.)	5 7	11 4
H. Bourne, Bromsgrove (I.R.)	5 7½	10 2
H. J. Barnes, Walsall Wood (I.R.)	5 8½	11 8
J. J. Brooks, Brierley Hill (I.R.)	5 9	11 10
W. H. Walker, Wednesbury (I.L.)	5 11½	12 0
A. Young, Darlington (C.F.)	5 10	12 10
T. J. Bridges, Burton (I.L.)	5 10½	11 7
A. G. Davis, Birmingham (I.L.)	5 9	10 12
J. W. Dickson, Dumfries (I.L.)	5 9	11 10
G. Stephenson, Newcastle (I.L.)	5 9½	10 10
M. Taylor, Newcastle (I.L.)	5 9	11 0
H. Stott, North Shields (I.L.)	5 6½	11 10
M. M. Lyon, Nottingham (O.L.)	5 9	12 0
L. P. Price, Caersws (Mont.) (O.L.)	5 9½	11 7
A. R. Dorrell, Small Heath (O.L.)	5 6½	10 2

After becoming a Red, Barson was featured on this vintage trade card from *Boys' Magazine*, circa 1926

26 NOVEMBER 1921: PANTOMIME VILLAN

Hard man Frank Barson would be a United player come 1922, but the previous year he was still terrifying opponents for Aston Villa. Brutal in the tackle (he was once banned for seven months), Barson is named here as one of Villa's key players – but even he couldn't stop the Reds winning 1-0.

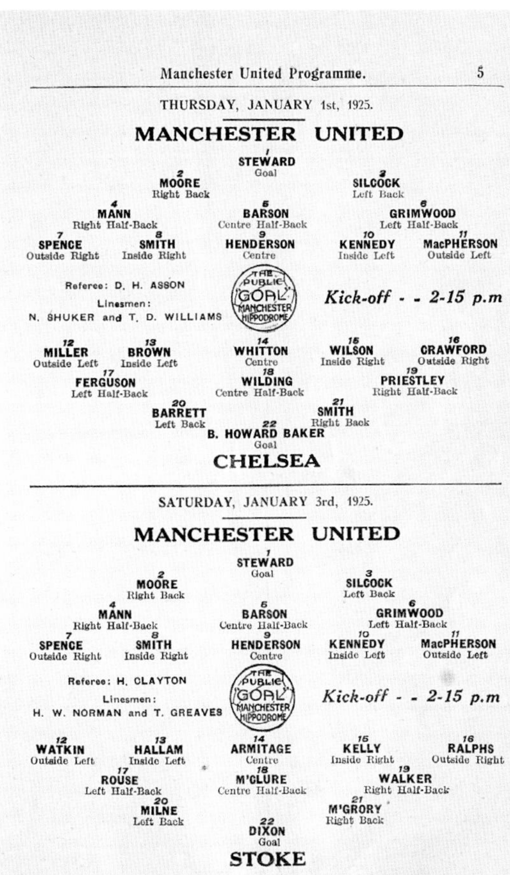

Manchester United Programme. 5

THURSDAY, JANUARY 1st, 1925.

MANCHESTER UNITED

1 **STEWARD** Goal

2 **MOORE** Right Back — 3 **SILCOCK** Left Back

4 **MANN** Right Half-Back — 5 **BARSON** Centre Half-Back — 6 **GRIMWOOD** Left Half-Back

7 **SPENCE** Outside Right — 8 **SMITH** Inside Right — 9 **HENDERSON** Centre — 10 **KENNEDY** Inside Left — 11 **MacPHERSON** Outside Left

Referee: D. H. ASSON

Linesmen: N. SHUKER and T. D. WILLIAMS

THE PUBLIC "GOAL" MANCHESTER HIPPODROME

Kick-off - - 2-15 p.m

12 **MILLER** Outside Left — 13 **BROWN** Inside Left — 14 **WHITTON** Centre — 15 **WILSON** Inside Right — 16 **CRAWFORD** Outside Right

17 **FERGUSON** Left Half-Back — 18 **WILDING** Centre Half-Back — 19 **PRIESTLEY** Right Half-Back

20 **BARRETT** Left Back — 21 **SMITH** Right Back

22 **B. HOWARD BAKER** Goal

CHELSEA

SATURDAY, JANUARY 3rd, 1925.

MANCHESTER UNITED

1 **STEWARD** Goal

2 **MOORE** Right Back — 3 **SILCOCK** Left Back

4 **MANN** Right Half-Back — 5 **BARSON** Centre Half-Back — 6 **GRIMWOOD** Left Half-Back

7 **SPENCE** Outside Right — 8 **SMITH** Inside Right — 9 **HENDERSON** Centre — 10 **KENNEDY** Inside Left — 11 **MacPHERSON** Outside Left

Referee: H. CLAYTON

Linesmen: H. W. NORMAN and T. GREAVES

THE PUBLIC "GOAL" MANCHESTER HIPPODROME

Kick-off - - 2-15 p.m

12 **WATKIN** Outside Left — 13 **HALLAM** Inside Left — 14 **ARMITAGE** Centre — 15 **KELLY** Inside Right — 16 **RALPHS** Outside Right

17 **ROUSE** Left Half-Back — 18 **M'CLURE** Centre Half-Back — 19 **WALKER** Right Half-Back

20 **MILNE** Left Back — 21 **M'GRORY** Right Back

22 **DIXON** Goal

STOKE

1/3 JANUARY 1925: DOUBLING UP FOR NEW YEAR

Here's an rare occurrence for the programme: a joint issue, covering two home games – in this case against Chelsea and Stoke in the opening three days of 1925. Such a publication would most likely have been as a result of Christmas closures at the printers, and on the pitch United proved just as efficient as the programme editor, the Reds winning both of these Second Division encounters without conceding a goal, as John Chapman's side chased (and ultimately succeeded) in sealing promotion.

Dean on England duty in 1928. Incredibly, he only won 16 caps - scoring 18 goals!

20 NOVEMBER 1926: DEVASTATING DEAN

When Everton arrived in M16 for this league match, the Toffees' teenage striker Dixie Dean had recently returned to action, following a motorcycling accident that left doctors unsure if he'd ever play again. Dean found the target at Old Trafford – although United won the game 2-1 – and after finishing 1926/27 with 36 club goals, the following term he would score 67.

6 Manchester United Programme.

OUR VISITORS.

EVERTON'S EXPENSIVE EXPERI ENCE — A RECENT REVIVAL — "DIXIE" DEAN.

EVERTON last season provided us with three points. We beat them at Goodison Park 3—1 and the return match at Old Trafford was a goalless draw. Prior to that we had not, of course, met since 1921 when, after losing 0—5 at Everton we won the return match 2—1.

In post-war football Everton have not been the power of old. Always an attractive side the common impression in recent seasons has been that effectiveness has been sacrificed for effect.

W. R. DEAN.

R. IRVINE.

It was a big blow to them that "Dixie" Dean should get badly injured in a motor smash during the summer. William Ralph Dean is one of the most talked-of players in the country.

He was secured by Everton at the back-end of season 1924-25 from Tranmere Rovers and he proved his worth last season by scoring 32 goals in 38 matches. His value to the side has again been demonstrated as since his return a month ago Everton have not scored fewer than three goals in each of their four matches and have greatly improved their position in the table.

CANDIDATE FOR HONOURS.

Dean, on Monday, played for the F.A. team at Wolverhampton and did so well that, barring accidents, he seems certain to get a further chance of proving his right to lead England's forwards in international matches.

It is doubtful if any club has found team blending a more expensive business than Everton have done. They rank as one of the wealthiest clubs in the League yet success has eluded them for a long time; though recent events suggest that they have "turned the corner."

Everton were one of the founders of the League, and like Aston Villa and Blackburn Rovers have never been relegated.

They were champions in 1890-91 and 1914-15. Twice they have won the F.A. Cup and eight times they have reached the semi-final. Everton's list of players includes:—

Player. Birthplace. Position	Height. ft.	in.	Weight. st.	lb.
H. Hardy, Stockport (G.)	5	9	11	8
J. Kendall, Broughton (G.)	5	11	12	0
A. L. Davies, Wallasey	6	½	12	0
C. G. C. Menham, Liverpool (G.)	6	1	13	0
D. Raitt Buckhaven (R.B.)	5	7½	11	6
H. Hamilton, Wallasey (R.B.)	5	10	11	10
J. M'Donald, Dykehead (L.B.)	5	10½	12	7
J. Kerr, Burnbank (L.B.)	5	8½	11	8
W. Brown, Cambuslang (R.H.B.)	5	8	11	6
J. Peacock, Ince (R.H.B.)	5	8½	11	2
D. Reid, Kilmarnock (C.H.B.)	5	8	11	8
D. Bain, Rutherglen (C.H.B.)	5	9	11	4
C. R. Butterfield, Darlington (C.H.B.)	5	9	11	0
H. Hart, Glasgow (L.H.B.)	5	9½	11	6
A. Virr, Liverpool (L.H.B.)	6	0	11	9
V. F. Romey, Liverp'l (R. or L.H.B.)	5	8	11	4
S. Edwards, Wrexham (L.H.B.)	5	8	11	7
H. Moffat, Camerton (O.R.)	5	5	10	4
T. Millington, Wrexham (O.R.)	5	8½	11	10
T. R. Parker, Bolton (O.R.)	5	6	10	0
R. Irvine, Lisburn (I.R.)	5	9	11	6
A. Dominy, Southampton (I.R.)	5	8	11	0
R. T. Woodhouse, Leyland (I.R.)	5	6¼	10	10
W. R. Dean Birkenhead (C.F.)	5	10½	12	7
D. J. Murray, Sth Africa (C.F.)	5	9½	12	0
J. O'Donnell, Gateshead (C. or I.F.)	5	8½	11	8
F. Kennedy Bury (I.L.)	5	6½	11	0
H. Houghton, Liverpool (I.L.)	5	8½	10	10
A. Troup, Forfar (O.L.)	5	5	10	7

CENTRAL LEAGUE.

	Pld.	Won	Lost	Drn.	Goals For	Goals Agst.	Pts.
Manchester Utd.	**15**	**10**	**3**	**2**	**35**	**18**	**22**
Huddersfield T.	16	9	5	2	38	22	20
Blackpool	15	9	4	2	36	35	20
Oldham Athletic	15	8	4	3	26	15	19
Derby County	14	9	4	1	40	24	19
Liverpool	15	8	4	3	33	24	19
Sheffield United	15	9	5	1	27	21	19
West Brom. Alb.	15	9	5	1	38	32	19
Wolverh'pton W.	15	9	5	1	31	27	19
The Wednesday	15	8	6	1	33	29	17
Leeds United	13	6	4	3	32	27	15
Everton	15	6	7	2	34	29	14
Blackburn Rov.	14	7	7	0	33	32	14
Bolton Wandrs.	15	5	6	4	24	34	14
Burnley	14	5	7	2	24	29	12
Stoke City	16	6	10	0	27	37	12
Manchester City	15	4	8	3	37	40	11
Bury	15	4	8	3	28	32	11
Birmingham	15	4	8	3	21	29	11
Preston N. End.	16	3	9	4	14	30	10
Aston Villa	14	1	9	4	21	45	6
Bradford City	13	1	11	1	12	32	3

4 DECEMBER 1926: TERRIERS ON TOP

Champions in each of the three previous seasons, Huddersfield were feared opponents for this one, making the 0-0 draw a respectable outcome for United, temporarily led by player-boss Lal Hilditch.

OUR VISITORS.

HUDDERSFIELD TOWN'S REMARKABLE ACHIEVEMENTS—MAKERS OF FOOTBALL HISTORY—UNIQUE AND ENVIOUS RECORD.

IN a few short years Huddersfield Town have achieved the seemingly impossible. Threateneed with extinction in the early days of the 1919-20 season they have advanced to a pinnacle of football fame, and established a record which is not likely to be equalled in our day and generation.

Not even in the early days of League football, when the level of equality among clubs was nothing like so marked as it is at present, and when the campaign was not so long and strenuous as it is now, did any club carry off the championship for three years in succession.

Huddersfield Town completed that history making "hat trick" last season, and he would be a bold man who would say that a fourth successive championship is beyond their capacity. Folk may talk about "Old Invincibles," and the "Team of all the talents," but no club past or present can present such a record as that held by our visitors to-day who, I am sure, will be warmly welcomed.

Town have gained every honour save one, and that they have no ambition of securing. I refer to the Second Division championship, as when they won promotion they were runners-up. That was season 1919-20 when they also reached the final of the F.A. Cup, and were beaten by Aston Villa in extra time.

From that time onward Town have never looked back. In 1921-22 they won the Cup by defeating Preston North End in the final by a penalty kick scored by W. H. Smith. Of the team that won the Cup only five are at present with the club, viz., Wadsworth, Wilson, Watson, Stephenson, and Smith.

But the Town have been eminently successful in team building, and are about the soundest and most consistent side in the country. They have a trio of international defenders, a splendid half-back line, and a forward division containing four internationals.

What is more they are splendidly endowed with Reserve talent having carried off the Central League championship for the past two seasons. Huddersfield's first League Championship success was obtained in 1923-24 when they headed Cardiff City on goal average only.

The following season they had a two points lead over West Bromwich, and last season were five points better than their nearest rivals, Arsenal. In the three seasons they gained a total of 172 points.

At present they occupy third position in the table, and are obviously again out for honours. Their away record is a curious and remarkable one. Of the eight matches played away they have drawn seven and won one, and are the only club in the League that has avoided defeat away.

Altogether they have figured in ten drawn games. Last season we drew 1—1 at Old Trafford, but lost at Huddersfield by five clear goals. Prior to that Town had only once beaten us. This was in a Cup-tie at Old Trafford in 1924. Of the five previous meetings we had won three and drawn two. Particulars of the champions array of talent are appended.

Player. Birthplace. Position.	Height. ft. in.	Weight. st. lb.
E. Taylor, Liverpool (G.)	5 8½	11 10
W. Mercer, Prescot (G.)	5 10½	11 8
H. Turner, Gateshead (G.)	5 10½	11 9
A. B. Sharman, Leeds (G.)	6 0	12 0
F. R. Goodall, Dronfield (R.B.)	5 11	11 11
E Barkas, Shields (R.B.)	5 7¾	12 0
S. G. Wadsworth, Darwin (L.B.)	5 9	11 7
H. Cawthorne, Handsworth (R.H.B.)	5 9½	11 13
D. Steele, Carluke (R.H.B.)	5 8½	11 4
G. Hobson, Leeds (R.H.B.)	5 10	11 7
T. Wilson, Seaham Har. (C.H.B.)	5 10½	12 7
M B Spence, Ferry Hill (C.H.B.)	5 10	11 7
W Watson, Bolton-on-D. (L.H.B.)	5 8½	11 7
N Smith, Newburn (L.H.B.)	5 7½	11 0
W. Carr, Horden (L.H.B.)	5 9	10 9
T. Langham, Hapton (H.B.)	5 10½	10 9
A. Grey Spennymoor (H.B.)	5 8½	10 2
A Jackson, Renton (O.R.)	5 9½	10 0
R. Cameron, Dumbarton (O.R.)	5 7	10 4
G Brown, Mickley (I.R.)	5 10½	11 2
H Raw, Tow Law (I.R.)	5 8	10 0
W Cook, Bishop Auckland (I.R.)	5 7	10 4
W. Devlin, Glasgow (C.F.)	5 9	11 1
J G. Dent, Spennymoor (C.F.)	5 10	13 0
C Stephenson, Seaton Delavel (I.L.)	5 7½	11 3
A W. Smith, London (I.L.)	5 8¾	11 11
W. H. Smith, Tantobie (O.L.)	5 10	11 4
J. Slicer, Leeds (O.L.)	5 7¾	9 9

OUR VISITORS

To-day we welcome Chesterfield to Old Trafford, and wish them a happy time and a good game. It was on November 26 that we played them on their ground. (The previous week we had beaten Fulham 4-3 !) Mr. Gibson was there, and Stewart played his first game for us—he had travelled from Scotland overnight. It was not a jolly game—the ground was in a shocking condition, there was a nasty wind, and regrettable incidents centreing around the referee. The game was drawn. Ridding scored a goal from a neat pass from Brown.

Since then Chesterfield have had their ups and downs. On November 26 they had gained 11 points out of 15 games, and Charlton Athletic had gained 10 out of 16. To-day they stand at 27 points out of 35 games, and Charlton Athletic stand at 25 points out of 34. Thus they lie at the bottom of the table, with West Ham United and Burnley in hardly better case. It follows that a point or two would be most valuable to our visitors to-day, while after Bury and Fulham our team must be longing to do something. It is a marvel the way Chesterfield supporters cheer on their boys on their own ground. Our supporters should do the same for our lads to-day. But, win or lose, give our visitors a welcome cheer also.

8 APRIL 1933: CHEERS FOR BOTH TEAMS!

Chesterfield are wished 'a happy time', with fans urged to give them 'a welcome cheer' – words you wouldn't read about many opponents these days!

OUR VISITORS—Barnsley

WE extend a cordial welcome to our visitors to-day. Barnsley are a club of outstanding traditions; famous players of the past have seen service with the Oakwell team, and that the club is fully prepared for the Second Division, to which they return this season, has been evidenced in their fine start. During the week they journeyed to Nottingham to play the County and secured a smashing 4-1 success, so the United will have to watch their step to-day.

It has been stated that Barnsley's promotion-winning team of last season cost only £19 in transfer fees, and in the main, the side which took them to the top of the Third Division (Northern Section) last season, is being relied upon to represent the club in the strenuous Second Division battle.

Everyone is pleased that Mr. Brough Fletcher has decided to continue his associations with the club with which he became connected 20 years ago.

Barnsley's manager is certainly a fine judge of a player, and his name and that of Barnsley are synonymous terms.

NEWCOMERS.

Barnsley's success of last season was reflected in increased attendances at the Oakwell grounds, and during the close season the club paid transfer fees for R. Pedwell and N. Beedles, the latter from Stockport County.

Other newcomers include Tom Sampy, formerly of Sheffield United, whose principal job, however, is to coach the young players; W. Adey, full back, also from Bramall Lane; A. Greaves from Crewe Alexandra; R. McLauchlan, who was with Gateshead for four seasons; T. Finnigan, a young centre forward from the Durham district, and M. Brannan, a goalkeeper who has seen service with Arsenal, Hull City and Denaby United.

For our second home match of the season we also have a Spence opposed to us, and, curiously enough, an outside right, although no relation of the Bradford City and former Manchester United player.—CASUAL.

9 SEPTEMBER 1934: CASUAL ANALYSIS

Having just avoided relegation to the third tier three months previously, Scott Duncan's United would have been pleased to start our 1934/35 home campaign with back-to-back wins, including a 4-1 beating of Barnsley. While the recognised writers at the time would include their byline at the end of each story, the freelance reporter for this particular opposition preview wasn't afforded such a privilege!

OUR VISITORS—MANCHESTER CITY

THERE is no match which produces greater interest in Manchester than the clash of the City and United. I have gone more fully into the past meetings of the clubs on another page, but I should be remiss in my duty if I did not extend to the City people to-day, a very warm and cordial reception.

We are glad to be back in the senior League, if only to renew acquaintances with our neighbours, and although the United, for to-day's match, may be considerably weakened owing to the abnormal number of injuries we have received, it does not detract one iota from the extraordinary interest in to-day's game.

All we—and the public—hope, is to see a game contested in the true sporting spirit ; may the best team win and may it be a game upon which we may all look back with pride and satisfaction.

The City have been very much in the public eye in recent years, with their Cup-tie exploits, and this season they are hoping to have their name inscribed on the Championship trophy for the first time in their career. In this respect they are still one down on the United, for we have secured every possible honour there is to be gained in football circles.

BILLY DALE.

In the City ranks to-day is one, Billy Dale, right or left full-back. Our old player! He has been a magnificent servant to the Maine Road club since circumstances compelled his transfer some five years ago. The present United board of directors did not wish to transfer him ; it was a deal (involving also Rowley, now back at Old Trafford, and Ridding), which our present board honoured when they took over control. The old board had made a bargain, and although Mr. J. W. Gibson and his fellow directors were under no obligation, they stood by the agreement. Our loss, City's gain !

WHO'S WHO.

Here are details of a number of the City playing staff from whom to-day's team is likely to be chosen :—

Player and Position	Birthplace	Height ft.	Height in.	Weight st.	Weight lbs.
Swift, F. .. .. (Goalkeeper).	Blackpool	6	2¼	13	13
Dale, W. .. .. (Right-back).	Manchester	5	9	11	1
Clark, G. .. .. (Right-back).	Gainsboro	5	7½	11	10
Barkas, S. .. .. (Left-back).	Wardley, Col. Durham	5	9	13	7
Percival, J. .. (Right-half-back).	Low Petting-ton, Durham	5	8½	11	12
Donnelly, R. .. (Centre-half-back).	Craignuk, Lanark	5	10½	11	10½
Marshall, R. .. (Centre-half-back).	Hucknall, Notts.	5	10½	12	12
Neilson, D. .. (Centre-half-back).	Blackhall, Durham.	5	9½	11	5½
Toseland, E. .. (Outside-right).	Northampton	5	6	10	3
Herd, A. .. .. (Inside-right).	Bowhill, Fife	5	8	10	10½
Heale, J. .. .. (Inside-forward).	Bristol ..	5	11½	11	9
Tilson, F. .. .. (Centre-forward)	Barnsley ..	5	9½	12	2
Doherty, P. .. (Inside-left). ..	Magherafelt, Derry.	5	10	11	6
Brook, E. .. .. (Outside-left).	Mexborough	5	9	11	13

CASUAL.

WARM

'MECCA PASTILLES' keep you warm, chill-proof, cough-free on the coldest day. Not a glorified sweet but the best Cough Pastille ever made. From chemists **1/3** per tin.

GIBSON'S BARLEY SUGAR STICKS are wholesome, energising. Athletes train on Barley Sugar and the best is definitely Gibson's.

ROBERT GIBSON & SONS LTD.
HULME MANCHESTER

Page 6

12 SEPTEMBER 1936: TALE OF TWO WILLIAMS

A first Manchester derby in five-and-a-half years grabbed the attention of the whole city, with former Red turned Blue William 'Billy' Dale the man in the spotlight. It was another William who would steal the headlines, though, outside forward William Bryant netting United's late winner in a 3-2 thriller.

The Reds toast promotion in 1936, with City being early-season opponents upon our top-flight return

31 AUGUST 1946: POST-WAR RETURN

In a game mirroring our season-opener from the previous competitive campaign, 1939/40, Grimsby were our first post-war opponents. New boss Matt Busby led us to a 4-0 win at Maine Road, with Old Trafford closed down due to bomb damage.

I SELDOM think about Chelsea, to-day's visitors to Old Trafford, without recalling the name of the late Tommy Meehan. Remember him ? One of the smallest footballers who ever played in League football, yet one of the greatest-hearted men I have ever watched. A native of Collyhurst, Tommy started football with his school team, St. Patrick's, Livesey Street, Rochdale Road. Afterwards he went to Woodhouses, then to Berry's (who played on the old Manchester North End ground), and then to Walkden Central. He was signed on amateur forms by Mr. Louis Rocca, the present United " scout " for nothing. When War broke out Meehan played for Rochdale, but on the cessation of hostilities he signed professional forms for United for whom he played nearly five seasons. He was transferred to Chelsea for £3,300, and secured an England " cap " against Ireland in 1924. He was then, of course, a member of the Chelsea club.

* * *

24 SEPTEMBER 1938: TRIBUTE TO TOMMY

With Chelsea in town, programme editor Sidney Wicks fondly remembers former Reds wing-half Tommy Meehan, who went on to join Chelsea in 1920 before his tragically young death from 'sleeping sickness' (encephalitis lethargica) four years later, aged just 28.

By TOM JACKSON of the "MANCHESTER EVENING NEWS"

IT seems much less than five months ago since Grimsby Town, hard-luck team of last season's cup tournament, were here at Old Trafford fighting out that dramatic semi-final tie with the Wolves. But so it is, almost to the day.

To-day they come to Manchester to inaugurate the 1939-1940 season, and they can be sure of a rousing welcome. It is on the cards that 10 members of their gallant cup team will appear in their colours in this opening league game.

The exception is goalkeeper George Moulson. Remember him ? He was the young man who blazed into the headlines when he was called upon to deputise for international Tweedy on the eve of Grimsby's departure for Old Trafford.

With what tragic results we all know. Twenty minutes had ticked by of Moulson's big debut . . . then disaster in diving at the feet of a raiding opponent. Grimsby, with 10 men, slided from a well-knit, confident side to defeat which, incidentally, robbed them of reaching Wembley for the first time in their career.

Judged on their close-season activities which have been mainly centred on adding young local players to their ranks, Grimsby are relying this season on the men who earned them such a distinguished run in the cup. Their only addition of note is Wardle, the former Southport and Manchester City winger.

Grimsby were well satisfied by the team's all-round showing last season. They finished half-way in the league table, and the strengthening of the attack by the acquisition of Boyd (Dundee) and Jones, T. W. (Blackpool) made a vital difference.

Defence and half-back talent has always been a strong point with the Mariners. That grand trio of Hall, Betmead and Buck is rightly classed as one of the best club half-back lines in the league. At full-back there is the former Stockport stalwart, Vincent, and the six-footer Hodgson again at call, while goalkeeper Tweedy is back in his old position between the posts.

Former United player, Mr. Charles Spencer, the Grimsby manager, has also helped to mould the club's attack into a live-wire combination. Howe, ex-Manchester City and Liverpool leader, proved a big success last season, while a local youth, Crack, reached the heights as the club's best wing discovery for a long time.

Perhaps Grimsby's best-known forward in recent years is missing from their ranks. I refer to Pat Glover, Welsh international centre-forward, whose departure a few months ago broke the last link of the famous Bestall-Glover-Craven inside forward trio that delighted countless soccer crowds by its artistry.

Until last season when United beat them 3-0 in the corresponding league fixture, Grimsby had a record of five visits to Old Trafford without defeat.

The teams which appeared here on January 14th, 1939, were:

United : Tapken ; Redwood, Griffiths ; Warner, Vose, McKay ; Bryant, Wassall, Hanlon, Carey, Rowley.

Grimsby: Tweedy; Vincent, Hodgson; Hall, Betmead, Buck; Boyd, Beattie, Howe, Jones, Lewis.

MUSIC PROGRAMME

L.N.E.R. (M'c. District) SILVER PRIZE BAND

March	" The Tiger's Tail " ...	*T. W. Thurban*
Entracte	" Shy Serenade " ...	*G. S. Wood*
Scotch Patrol ...	" The Wee Macgregor " ...	*H. J. Amers*
Euphonium Solo ...	" My Old Kentucky Home " ... *Soloist*, J. R. Donbavand.	*W. Rimmer*
March Medley ...	" Sousa on Parade ...	arr. *King Palmer* Score by *Dennis Wright*
	W. Paxton & Co., London, W.1.	
Half-time	" Beer Barrel Polka " ...	*L. B. Wladimir, T. J. Vejoda*

Conductor, Mr. G. T. Benson.

Secretary : H. Potter, L.N.E.R. Works, Cornwall Street, Openshaw.

6

Welcome to BLACKPOOL

Blackpool, popular visitors to Maine Road this evening, hardly need introduction to United followers.

Since the Wembley Cup Final last April, the teams have met twice in League fixtures, both matches being decided at Bloomfield Road.

United were defeated 1—0 there at the end of last season, but had their "revenge" a week last Monday by scoring a 3—0 victory. Mitten (2) and Pearson were the marksmen.

Blackpool, managed by Mr. Joe Smith, the famous Bolton Wanderer and England star, are undoubtedly one of the most attractive teams in the division. The Matthews-Mortenson combination is a grand main-spring in attack, while their defence has few equals.

It is likely that nine of their Wembley team will be on duty to-night, with Wardle, their close-season signing from Grimsby, and McCall completing the side.

BLACKPOOL PROBABLES

J. Robinson (goalkeeper). Succeeded "Jock" Wallace (now with Derby) as regular 'keeper last season. Hails from Pegswood, near Morpeth in the North-East, and was formerly with Hartlepools.

E. Shimwell (right full-back). Moved to Blackpool from Sheffield United two seasons ago. Strong, sure-footed and a grand link in the seasiders' defence. Derbyshire-born and first noted with a local amateur side.

R. Suart (left full-back). Dour and experienced, signed before the war from a Barrow-in-Furness junior club, and has proved an outstanding discovery. Has a keen positional sense and is a strong tackler.

H. Johnston (right half-back). English international, and Blackpool's captain. A Droylsden (Manchester) product regarded as one of the most constructive wing-halves in the game. Plays equally well in any half-back position.

L. E. Hayward (centre half-back). Tall and dominant in the middle. Previously with Port Vale, though he learned his football in the Gateshead district. A stalwart in defence for several seasons.

H. T. Kelly (left half-back). Signed in 1943 from Jeanfield Swifts, a Scots junior team. Proved a useful utility player in either wing-half positions before winning a regular place in the side two seasons ago.

S. Matthews (outside right). The one and only Stan Matthews, known the world over. Won a special award as the game's outstanding player last season. First capped in 1934 and has more than fifty to his credit.

A. Munro (inside right). Only 5 ft. 5 in. in height but capable of proving a big puzzle to defences. A Scots international signed from Hearts in 1931, and still going as strong as ever. Switches effectively to the wing when required.

S. Mortensen (centre forward). The other Stanley in Blackpool's rapid attacking scheme. Has been called the "human dynamo" for his lightning speed off the mark. A junior product from South Shields, and an England "regular".

A. McCall (inside left). Signed from Blantyre Celtic, a Scots junior team, on demob from the Army last year. Small and tricky, he has made a favourable impression in the opening matches.

W. Rickett (outside left). Another ex-Sheffield United player, signed this year. Made his debut in the sixth round cup-tie against Fulham. Is Sheffield-born, and a former schoolboy international.

W. Wardle (outside left). A newcomer to Blackpool's ranks, who may play at inside forward. Is the former City player who was transferred to Southport, and who joined Grimsby in 1939. Is experienced and resourceful.

TOM JACKSON

PAGE FIVE

1 SEPTEMBER 1948: STAN BY FOR A CLASSIC
Five months after we beat Blackpool in the FA Cup final, Stanley Matthews & co came to M16. Another classic ensued, but this time the 'Pool edged it 4-3.

24 SEPTEMBER 1952: BLACK-AND-WHITE PHOTO
What's this... the opposition on the cover? Well, it was the Charity Shield, v Cup winners Newcastle. The generosity ended there as the Reds won 4-2.

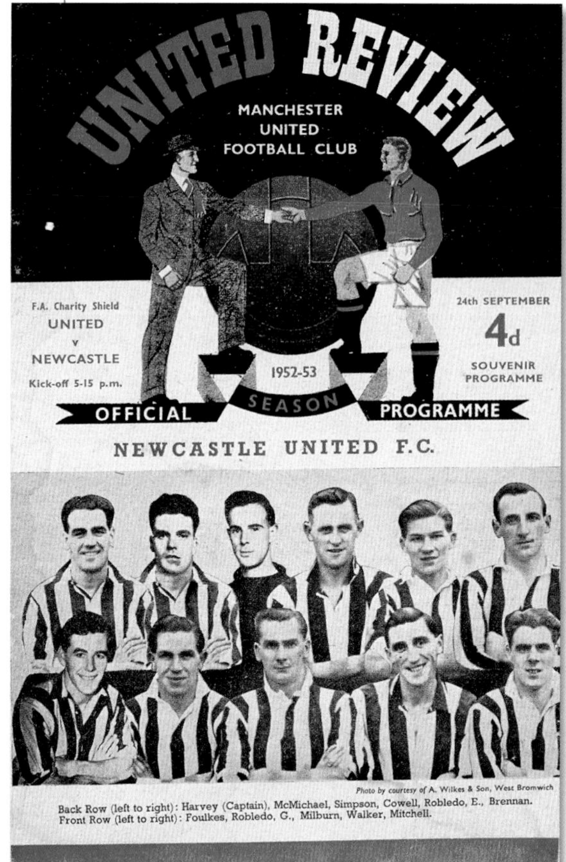

We are indebted to "Gilzean", sports cartoonist of the "Edinburgh Evening News" and the Hibernian F.C. Official Programme, for these entertaining and instructive close-ups. All these players have worn the dark blue jersey of Scotland.

29 MARCH 1952: SKETCHES FROM SCOTLAND
When Scottish side Hibernian headed south of the border for this springtime friendly, an *Edinburgh Evening News* cartoonist by the name of Gilzean kindly offered to provide this original take on the afternoon's visitors to Old Trafford. With a 'first-class ball juggler', 'wee Bobby Johnstone – a real cheeky chappie' and 'another wee chap' within their ranks, Hibs held Matt Busby's men to a 1-1 draw in front of just over 20,000 fans.

INTRODUCING...

OUR GUESTS by TOM JACKSON
of the "Manchester Evening News"

JOHNNY CAREY
A player whose name revives great memories of United's post-war League and Cup successes. John ended a brilliant career as captain of Ireland and United when he became manager of Blackburn Rovers three years ago after 17 years at Old Trafford.

JOHN CHARLES
This Welsh international and Leeds United giant ranks as the world's most versatile player. He's made such an impact on the game in most positions on the field that his present value is assessed at £40,000.

HENRY COCKBURN
Another of the old 1948 United brigade who made his way to the top of the international tree. Won a string of England honours as a crafty, dynamic little left-half before moving to Bury last season.

JIMMY DELANEY
The "Flying Scot" who just goes on and on in football. Since winning Cup-medals with Glasgow Celtic and then United has added Irish honours to his name. And he's still as superbly fit as the day he first turned out for Scotland.

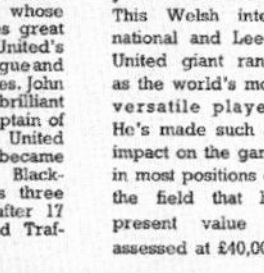

BILL ECKERSLEY
Ever since he became a professional with Blackburn Rovers in 1948, this compactly-built player has been recognised as one of the best and most stylish full-backs in the country. He has been an England choice on numerous occasions, as well as a great favourite at Blackburn.
(Photo by courtesy Fox Photos).

TOM FINNEY
Pride of Preston and a player whose wing prowess has brought England honours galore — both on the extreme right and the left. A master plumber — and a top tactician on the field who is still high on the international list.

NAT LOFTHOUSE
Top of the bill as a marksman and a centre forward who wears England's and Bolton Wanderers' colours with great enthusiasm and skill. Nat's speed off the mark and his eye for goals have made him an outstanding post-war international.

JOHNNY MORRIS
Derby County and now Leicester City have utilised his scheming abilities as an inside forward since he left Old Trafford with a Cup medal in 1949. Another England "cap", dark-haired Johnny was a real United local find.

PAGE FOUR

JOHNNY ASTON thanks the players and match officials for so generously offering their services
— and also the "Manchester Evening News" for the kind loan of all these pictures

STAN PEARSON
Now he's captain of Bury, but it was as a United local discovery that he first hit the headlines. One of the most polished inside-men who ever pulled on an England shirt, Stan's rise from the schoolboy ranks will always be remembered at Old Trafford.

DON REVIE
Footballer of the Year last season and the master link in Manchester City's famous deep centre forward plan. Has also played for Leicester and Hull City, but it was his move to Manchester which put him in the England limelight.

JACK ROWLEY
When he left United last season to become player-manager at Plymouth, the "Gunner" had earned a prominent place in the club's history book. His goal-punch for England and his scoring achievements in United's post-war run will never be forgotten.

LEN SHACKLETON
England and Sunderland star renowned as soccer's "Clown Prince" because of his uncanny artistry and ball-play. Won his caps at inside forward, but really plays anywhere to the delight of the crowds. A personality-plus.

FRANK SWIFT
Thirty-three times England's goalkeeper, "Big Frank" served Manchester City with great distinction from 1934 until his retirement in 1949. Now he makes a welcome return in the role in which he proved such a fine craftsman and personality.

JOE WALTON
This Preston North End full-back learned his football as a junior in Manchester. He served his "apprenticeship" at Old Trafford and since he left United in 1948 he has maintained a high place in the game.

BILLY WRIGHT
More times capped than any other Englishman — with a record of 72 to date. An outstanding personality as captain and centre half of England and Wolves, Billy has earned a place all to himself in the soccer hall of fame.

REFEREE
W. H. E. (BILL) EVANS
When W. H. E. (Bill) Evans of Liverpool went on the retired list in 1953, League football lost one of its ablest and fastest referees. He has officiated with great distinction at home and abroad and we take this opportunity of welcoming him back in the role in which he won the admiration of spectators and players alike. He will have two other well-known referees as his linesmen — Ken Collinge, of Sale, and Gordon Gibson, of Urmston, who make up a fine trio of match officials.

PAGE FIVE

24 APRIL 1956: AN ALL-STAR OCCASION

After John Aston Snr called time in on his career in the mid-'50s, the full-back (and occasional forward) was invited back to Old Trafford for a testimonial, with United's opponents being an 'All-Star XI', boasting some serious talent from across England's top flight. Sadly John wasn't able to play in the game himself, but this stellar group of visitors was an indicator of just how popular Aston was with his peers.

TOTTENHAM v UNITED
SATURDAY 24th NOVEMBER
LONDON 27/6
MANCHESTER London Road depart 7-25 am
Return at 5-50 pm

ASTON VILLA v UNITED
SATURDAY 8th DECEMBER
WITTON 10/9
MANCHESTER Mayfield depart 10-55 am
Return 4-15 pm

BRITISH RAILWAYS

football fans read

expert reports

Next Home Match
1st DIVISION
United v.
LUTON TOWN
1st Dec. kick-off 2 15 pm

Shirts Red — MANCHESTER UNITED — Knickers White

WOOD
FOULKES 2 — BYRNE 3
COLMAN 4 — JONES 5 — EDWARDS 6
R — BERRY 7 — WHELAN 8 — TAYLOR 9 — CHARLTON 10 — PEGG 11 — L

Next Home Match
CENTRAL LEAGUE
United v.
Wolverhampton Wanderers
24th Nov kick-off 2 15pm

Referee:
R. H. Windle (Chesterfield),

Kick-off 2-30 pm

FOOTBALL GREEN TONIGHT

Linesmen:
F. R. Bate, Stourbridge
(Red Flag)
S. C. Southern, Birmingham
(Yellow Flag)

L — OVERFIELD 11 — FORREST 10 — McKENNA 9 — CHARLES 8 — MEEK 7 — R
KERFOOT 6 — CHARLTON 5 — GIBSON 4
HAIR 3 — DUNN 2
WOOD

Shirts Old Gold — LEEDS UNITED — Knickers Black

Team changes will be indicated by loudspeaker

Team changes will be indicated by loudspeaker

MORE PAGES
MORE FEATURES
Don't miss to-night's
16-PAGE ISSUE

* MATT BUSBY & LES McDOWALL
Make sure you read their straight-from-the-shoulder articles
* BEHIND THE SOCCER SCENES with ALF CLARKE
* Most results and best reports in Saturday's Best — The Football Pink

PAGE SIX

PAGE SEVEN

17 NOVEMBER 1956: BOUNCING BUSBY BABES

What a United team this is, with Matt Busby's Babes spread across the pitch. Of those listed here, Duncan Edwards was the only one to miss the game against Leeds, with Wilf McGuinness taking his place in the XI. It's a pretty formidable opposition side as well, with Jack Charlton going up against brother Bobby for the first time in a senior game. Bobby was the smiling sibling at full-time, however, finding the Leeds net in a 3-2 home victory.

WELCOME TO

TOTTENHAM HOTSPUR

by DAVID MEEK

Tottenham are the season's most eagerly awaited visitors. They come 10 points in front of their nearest rivals in the League championship race and quite clearly they are one of the outstanding teams of post-war football.

United have been anxiously waiting for a return tilt at the League leaders after going down 4-1 at White Hart Lane in September.

United were one of the victims of the Londoners' record run of 11 wins to the start of their season.

Spurs also gained a double over the Reds last season with 5-1 at Old Trafford and 2-1 at White Hart Lane.

The teams for the match at Old Trafford last season were:

United: Gregg; Cope, Carolan; Goodwin, Foulkes, McGuinness; Bradley, Giles, Viollet, Charlton, Scanlon.

Spurs: Brown; Baker, Hopkins; Blanchflower, Norman, Mackay; Medwin, Harmer, Smith, Dunmore, Jones.

Spurs' playing personalities include:

Bill Brown (goalkeeper).
Born in Arbroath and joined the Dundee club in 1949. Won his first representative honour in 1956 when he played for Scotland "B" against England "B". Made his first appearance in the full international side in 1958 against France in the World Cup. Joined Spurs July 1959 for about £15,000.

Peter Baker (full-back).
Recruited from local club Enfield Town. Came seven years ago as a junior right-back. He made the League side first in 1954–55 season and has been a regular for the past three seasons.

Ron Henry (full-back).
Born Redbourne, Herts., and played for his local club until spotted by Spurs and signed in January, 1955. Got his first chance through injury to Welsh international Mel Hopkins, and now succeeded him as the regular left-back.

Danny Blanchflower (half-back).
One of football's most colourful characters, a great stylist and irreproachable sportsman on the field. Won fame as Ireland's captain and did a fine job leading the Irish to success in the last World Cup series. He is the elder brother of United's Jackie Blanchflower. Cost Spurs £30,000 when signed from Aston Villa in 1954. Born in Belfast.

Dave Mackay (half-back).
Born in Edinburgh and came to Tottenham from Heart of Midlothian in March 1959. Made his debut against Manchester City. Went to Hearts in 1952 after winning international schoolboy honours. First capped for Scotland in 1957. Spurs paid about £30,000 to Hearts for him.

Maurice Norman (centre-half).
A big signing from Norwich five seasons ago. A player who has won England under-23 honours, and although he did not play, was in England's last World Cup party. Plays anywhere in defence though has settled at centre-half. Makes full use of his 6 ft. 2 in. height. Born at Mullbarton, Norfolk.

Terry Medwin (outside-right).
Former Welsh schoolboy international who also involved Spurs in a big fee when he was signed from Swansea. Is now a full Welsh international who has been consistently among the goal scorers. Born at Swansea.

Bobby Smith (centre-forward).
Big Bobby has worried many centre-halves with his bustling play and is outstandingly nimble for such a powerful man. A former Chelsea player, he was signed five seasons ago. He was 17 when he made his league debut for Chelsea in 1950. Born at Lingdale, Durham. Is England's current success at centre-forward.

John White (inside-forward).
Signed by Spurs at the beginning of the 1959–60 season from Falkirk for about £20,000. Born Musselburgh and capped for both Scotland under-23 and the full international team. Immediate success in English football.

Les Allen (inside-forward).
Reached amateur Cup semi-final with Briggs Sports in 1954. Had trials with West Ham and Spurs before joining Chelsea in August, 1955. Made his League debut at 18. Transferred from Chelsea to Spurs in 1960 in exchange deal for Johnny Brooks.

Terry Dyson (outside-left).
Joined Tottenham after completing his National Service and being spotted in Army football. Born in Yorkshire where his father is a trainer and former jockey. Jockey-size himself, Terry has built a big reputation in the First Division.

Cliff Jones (outside-left).
Born in Swansea and joined his local club straight from school. Joined Spurs in February, 1958, near the end of his National Service. Welsh international, first capped in 1954. Plays equally well at outside-right.

14 JANUARY 1961: SPURS' TOP TERM

Long-time *UR* contributor David Meek runs the rule over Bill Nicholson's Tottenham. Bill's men lost this game 2-0, but Spurs would end '60/61 as the century's first Double winners.

16 OCTOBER 1968: INTERCONTINENTAL AGONY

A season-high crowd of over 63,000 attended our Intercontinental Cup second leg against Estudiantes. Unfortunately a goal from Juan Ramon Veron (front row, far right; father of future Red Juan Sebastian) proved decisive in a 2-1 aggregate win for the Argentinians, in what was a very physical encounter.

ESTUDIANTES DE LA PLATA F.C., 1968

Back row: (L. to R.) G. Flores, Poletti, Malbernat (Captain), Togneri, E. Flores, Madero, Medina.
Front row: (L. to R.) Pachame, Echecopar, Bilardo, Conigliaro, Veron.

Photograph, copyright by Estudiantes de la Plata

Manager Matt Busby with new signings Bobby Noble and David Herd ahead of the 1960/61 campaign

3 APRIL 1972: BUSBY'S FRIENDLY FOE

He may have managed our biggest rivals, but Bill Shankly was a dear friend to many at United throughout his 15 years with Liverpool, including Matt Busby, Bobby Charlton and Paddy Crerand. Here, two years before Bill's retirement, *UR* takes a closer look at the Scot's huge success on Merseyside.

Meet the Club

LIVERPOOL

by

PETER SLINGSBY

of the "News of the World"

MENTION THE NAME LIVERPOOL TO ANY FOOTBALL FAN ANYWHERE IN BRITAIN AND IT IS ODDS ON YOU'LL GET A RAPID REACTION. HE IS BOUND TO WANT TO TALK ABOUT BILL SHANKLY, THE MAN WHO HAS BECOME A LEGEND ON MERSEYSIDE AND WHO HAS BEEN DUBBED "MR. LIVERPOOL F.C." ESPECIALLY IN THE ANFIELD AREA.

The two go together like bread and cheese – or should that be steak and kidney? – for Mr. Shankly, having broken up the side that had given so much so often in the last decade has successfully re-shaped the team in the last couple of years.

Last season, when the pruning began, he led his side to the F.A. Cup Final and to the last-four stage of the European Cup Winners' Cup competition. Those were achievements to be proud of and if things have not gone exactly to plan this time round who would argue that in **Kevin Keegan** he has made a truly brilliant "discovery"?

Keegan, in so many ways, personifies the Shankly approach to football, for he never stops working, is hungry for success and at £30,000 represents a fine bargain as he has proved in his first campaign in the top flight. No wonder he is such a big favourite with the famous Kopites!

This famous section of an equally famous stadium is known all over Europe for the quality of its "choir" as much as its unstinting support of Tommy Smith and company who, for the sixth season in succession, look like finishing in the top five in the First Division. It is a magnificent record even if the trophies have eluded the side in recent years . . .

Liverpool, of course, have long been famous for finding their own "stars of tomorrow". We should see some of them on duty here today and, as usual, there are more waiting in the wings, and just itching for a crack at soccer at the top. That's proved by the fact that last season Liverpool completed a hat-trick of Central League Championship success at a time when first team calls were exceptionally heavy on their reserves.

Mr. Shankly himself began the hard way. A member of a big family, he began his football career as a professional with Carlisle after a spell in the pits and his dedication as a player was slavish to say the least. His approach to management follows a similar hard line . . .

He loves talking football; he loves watching the game and, even now, playing during training sessions. He still hates losing – whether it is a First Division fixture or just an every day five-a-side with his own boys in practice games.

That's **Shankly,** an extraordinary man who has never lost his appetite for soccer either as a spectator or a player. Somehow, his teams are just like him – Keegan, **Brian Hall,** Smith, **Emlyn Hughes, Ian Callighan** are names that spring to mind in this context

BILL SHANKLY, Manager. *Photo by Daily Express*

for they are fit, forthright, formidable and always full of running.

There is certainly no doubt at all that his arrival on Merseyside coincided with his club's golden years. Liverpool had spent some worrying seasons in the Second Division when **Mr. Shankly** was given the job of reviving their fortunes.

He had held managerial posts at Carlisle, Grimsby, Workington and Huddersfield when he took on the challenge in December, 1959, leading them to promotion in 1961–62 and, on either side of a triumph in the F.A. Cup, to two First Division Championships (in 1963-64 and 1965-66). They were runners-up three years ago, and reached the final of the European Cup Winners' Cup in 1966.

Now Mr. Shankly has an interesting blend of youth and experience. He has trimmed the size of his senior squad – **Ian Ross (Aston Villa)** and **Bobby Graham (Coventry City)** are the most recent departures – but the "pool" is still a good one and the envy of most of Liverpool's rivals.

That, in itself pays its own rich tribute to Bill Shankly and his backroom staff who have made it possible through their foresight, constant encouragement and seemingly endless enthusiasm.

NEXT HOME GAME
DIVISION TWO
MANCHESTER UNITED
v.
BOLTON WANDERERS
WEDNESDAY 25th SEPTEMBER
KICK-OFF 7.30 p.m.

NEXT HOME GAME
CENTRAL LEAGUE
UNITED RESERVES
v.
WEST BROM. RESERVES
SATURDAY, 28th SEPTEMBER
KICK-OFF 3.00 p.m.

Manchester Utd. v Bristol R.

Shirts: Red Shorts: White — Shirts: Blue & White Shorts: White

Manchester Utd.			Bristol R.
STEPNEY	1	1	EADIE
FORSYTH	2	2	JACABS
HOUSTON	3	3	PARSONS
GREENHOFF	4	4	AITKEN
HOLTON	5	5	TAYLOR
BUCHAN	6	6	PRINCE
MORGAN	7	7	STEPHENS
McILROY	8	8	STANTON
PEARSON	9	9	WARBOYS
McCALLIOG	10	10	BANNISTER
DALY	11	11	FEARNLEY
	S	S	RUDGE

Referee:
R. CAPEY
Crewe

Linesmen:
L. J. ENSON
Bebbington, Cheshire
Yellow Flag

C. J. RILEY
Stafford
Red Flag

Half-time Scoreboard Key September 21st

A	Aston Villa v. Millwall	....	N	Carlisle Utd. v. Birmingham City	....
B	Blackpool v. York City	....	O	Coventry City v. Everton	....
C	Bristol City v. Southampton	....	P	Derby County v. Burnley	....
D	Fulham v. Norwich City	....	Q	Ipswich Town v. Chelsea	....
E	Hull City v. Oldham Athletic	....	R	Leeds United v. Sheffield Utd.	....
F	Notts County v. West Brom. A.	....	S	Liverpool v. Stoke City	....
G	Oxford United v. Orient	....	T	Q.P.R. v. Newcastle United	....
H	Portsmouth v. Cardiff City	....	V	West Ham Utd. v. Leicester City	....
J	Sheffield Wed. v. Nott'm. Forest	....	W	Wolves v. Tottenham H.	....
K	Sunderland v. Bolton W.	....	X	Bury v. Huddersfield Town	....
L	Middlesbrough v. Man. City	....	Y	Rochdale v. Workington	....
M	Arsenal v. Luton Town	....	Z	West Brom. Res v. United Res.	....

21 SEPTEMBER 1974: BOLD PERFORMERS
With the Reds down in the second tier for the first time in 36 years, Tommy Docherty's side encountered many rare opponents in '74/75, including a maiden league meeting with Bristol Rovers, which United won 2-0. Recent improvements in technology saw the match programme begin to embrace the bold typography that was so popular at the time, with this line-ups list giving off some '70s disco vibes!

20 SEPTEMBER 1975: ROBSON ON THE RISE
Six years into his time as Ipswich boss, Bobby Robson had made such an impact, they'd become top-six regulars. Indeed, the future Sir Bobby would soon bring the FA Cup and UEFA Cup to Portman Road – although thankfully Stewart Houston won this game for United.

THE MANAGER

Bobby Robson

by Tony Pullein

Ipswich Town's championship-chasing performances in recent seasons are the culmination of years of blood, toil and sweat—and not a little bitterness—on the part of manager Bobby Robson.

Every manager has his own methods for achieving success and Mr. Robson knew he had a long and hard job ahead of him when he took over in 1969.

Bickering among players was rife at times and an exasperated Robson declared: "I've got to do some clearing out". There were times, during the Ipswich build-up, when "supporters" rallied with "Robson Must Go" posters. The board could well have taken the easy way out, sacked their manager and issued some statement to the effect that it was in the best interests of the club, etc. etc.

That chairman John Cobbold steadfastly refused to be bullied is to his eternal credit. Today he—and his board—can justifiably bask in the reflected glory of their success. They, too, have contributed towards it.

They have contributed in so far as, by giving the manager their backing and a certain security, they have enabled him to experiment without risking the sack if things had gone wrong.

Consequently, Bobby Robson has been given the time to build his team largely from the pool of young players he has nurtured since his arrival at Portman Road. The Ipswich team today will contain no more than three or four players who have played League football for rival clubs—Bryan Hamilton, Allan Hunter, David Johnson and possibly, Paul Cooper. And their total cost was only some £200,000!

Mr. Robson has insisted upon his team playing entertaining football and, in addition to delighting many thousands of fans up and down the country, Ipswich have met with considerable success.

In 1973/74 and 1972/73 they finished fourth in the table. Last season, when they came third, they were only pipped by Derby for the Championship by two points. They also reached the semi-final of the F.A. Cup and the quarter-final of the League Cup—both club records.

Though they have made a disappointing start this season, we can expect to see results improve once the team has scored one or two victories to repair confidence.

Mr. Robson's playing career began with Fulham in 1950. He first came to the fore as a goalscoring inside-forward and it was in this role he was chosen for the first of his 20 England caps in 1957, a couple of years after he had transferred to West Bromwich Albion.

After playing in the 1958 World Cup, Bobby Robson switched positions to wing-half and it was here that he really excelled. He regained his place in the England team, only to be replaced by Bobby Moore just before the 1962 World Cup.

He returned to finish his playing career with Fulham, then took a coaching appointment abroad before becoming Fulham's manager. He stayed only eleven months and took over at Ipswich in 1969.

He has undoubtedly achieved his best work at Ipswich and one must hope that he—and his excellent team—will shortly be rewarded with a trophy to show for all their endeavours.

County's Cavaliers

Left to Right: Ken Fogarty, Allan Thompson, Carl Halford, Derek Loadwick, Jimmy Goodfellow, Stuart Lee, Mike Rogan, Terry Carr, John Rutter, Eddie Prudham, Graham Smith, Andy Th[illegible], Les Bradd.

18

30 AUGUST 1978: TAKING STOCK OF THE OPPOSITION
A first meeting with local club Stockport County stirred up so much interest, the tie was switched from Edgeley Park to Old Trafford, with County's profile pics given an artistic treatment. United won the League Cup tie 3-2, with 41,761 in attendance.

16 SEPTEMBER 1978: STRONG WORDS FOR CLOUGHIE

With Nottingham Forest in town, *Daily Express* writer Peter Thomas penned this fascinating, sometimes ferocious, profile of their double-act in the dugout, Brian Clough and his assistant Peter Taylor. 'Sometimes a pain in the neck, but [Clough is] always, always, always honest,' he writes.

Profile on BRIAN CLOUGH

By PETER THOMAS of *The Daily Express*

Brian Clough, *Manager*.

In my mind's eye Brian Clough is always captured in a moment of honest anger. Middlesbrough, or rather Cloughie, had scored five goals at Charlton Athletic and Boro had lost 6—5.

The scene—Boro's dressing room at The Valley. Enter Clough. His shirt flies across the room.

"Maybe", he says in that unplaceable accent, "maybe, if I get six next week we might just get a point."

That was Clough when young; it is still Clough in the anxious, exciting forties. Time has not mellowed him. He has not changed, but, thank God, he has changed much about him for the better.

Define his shortcomings: pugnacity, over-defiance. Respect his outspoken condemnation of things other managers care to keep silent about. Sometimes a pain in the neck. But always, always, always honest.

He has, I suspect, always been a little bewildered by the fact that many of the qualities of human behaviour do not apply within the moralities that rule the game he loves.

For he is a political animal, a socialist from a town where steel was king, and more times than not, a cruel one. He is hard like steel, but as straight and strong as the girders of the Forth Bridge.

But there is also a vulnerability behind the brashness. A lot of the little boy, afraid of being alone.

Wherever he goes, The Family goes, too. It is a touching little group, fearlessly loyal to each other. Clough keeps close to the men who nurtured his 'coming of age' at Ayresome Park.

There is Jimmy Gordon, a greying, smiling hobbit of a man. We knew him well as kids in Middlesbrough, because he travelled to the ground by bus, and he knew our christian names, although we called him Mr. Gordon.

And there is Peter Taylor, a shrewd, sometimes ominously brooding 'protector'. A man of shadows. Clough is the substance of those shadows.

Peter Taylor, *Assistant Manager*.

Their partnerships have been touched by controversy and exhalted with glory. Stir the family nest, and you risk the treble bite of the deadly snake. No one can divide and conquer.

The Footballing Family Clough is forever dominant. But, you ask yourself, who dominates who?

Sure, the voice of Clough is clear and true and honest; yet still there are questions to be asked. Like who is the singer and who writes the songs?

4 OCTOBER 1978: ELTON FEELS THE LOVE

It was 1976 when Elton John – still in his twenties – took over as Watford chairman, with the third-tier Hornets our League Cup opponents two years later. The pop legend's ambitions for the club are highlighted here, as is the story of his footballing uncle Roy Dwight.

The chairman—with a World-wide fan club!

By Tom Tyrrell

It took Elton John and his football club just 29 months to keep a promise. That vow was made in May 1976, on the night that the pop star made football history, by becoming chairman of the club he had supported since boyhood.

"It's the greatest day of my life," Elton said, as he left the Watford board room. "I am now chairman of the club I love, and my first priority is to see us in the Third Division."

He had replaced Jim Bonser as chairman at the meeting on May 11th, 1976, three years after being elected to the board. Mr. Bonser stood down to make way for the younger man, and became life-president of Watford.

For 29-year old Elton the role of chairman was perfect. He had supported Watford as a schoolboy in Pinner, but through showbusiness had become known all over the World, now he could use his talents in another way, to help his football club.

After first being made a director, he had injected £20,000 into the club, then two pop concerts brought the total quickly to £75,000. The "Honky Cat" of pop music created another image, away from that of glittering suits and fantasy glasses. He showed everyone he was a level-headed businessman who could help to run a football club, and run it successfully.

As a pop millionaire, with his own record company Rocket Records, Elton has nowadays "retired" from the world of live performances, but his records are instant chart successes whenever they are released.

And record success is an apt phrase because as a singer-writer he broke the pop earnings chart by hitting the £60,000 a week mark in 1975.

How much of this actually found itself in Elton's bank account is something only he and the taxman know the answer to, but it was obvious that the Superstar would have financial security for the rest of his life, long before his 30th birthday.

So football can be thankful that Elton John decided that he would turn his attention to the game. But this can have been no surprise to those who knew him before his pop days.

With professional football in the family, Elton——real name Reg Dwight——was probably a Nottingham Forest supporter at one time. Well, he should have been in 1959 when Forest met Luton Town in the F.A. Cup Final.

Young Reg's uncle, Roy Dwight, opened the scoring for Forest who went on to win 2—1, but the celebrations in the Dwight household were somewhat subdued, because Uncle Roy broke his leg and was carried-off, before the final ended.

Fame and fortune certainly have not spoiled young Reg Dwight, one of football's super-fans, who often watches The Cosmos when he's in New York. When he took over the chairmanship from Jim Bonser, the retiring head of the Watford board said: "I could not think of a better young man to take over the helm. He's a friendly, polite, charming person with his heart fully in Watford football club."

Now ask anyone in Watford who is number one in their pop charts, and they will tell you it's the chairman of Watford Football Club! The man who kept his promise.

Elton John, chairman. *Photo by Harry Goodwin*

6

30 SEPTEMBER 1981: THE ROSES RIVALRY

The late '70s and '80s was a difficult time for fierce rivals Leeds, with a number of managers failing to come close to matching their previous success under Don Revie. The club's former striker Allan Clarke was in the hotseat for this 1981/82 league game (the Reds winning 1-0, courtesy of Frank Stapleton) in what proved to be Leeds' last Old Trafford outing of the decade.

LEEDS

The most daunting challenge that can be thrown at any manager, taking over a once-successful club, is: FOLLOW THAT!

Particularly where the club is Leeds United and where the man they all have to try and top is Don Revie. More particularly when such well respected characters as Brian Clough, Jimmy Armfield, Jock Stein and Jimmy Adamson have all tried . . . and failed.

Yet Allan Clarke is under no illusions as to his task at Elland Road. Indeed, he was himself part of the Revie era which saw the club appear in three European Finals, five Wembley Cup Finals and win two League Championships. Revie's team also finished runners-up in the First Division on five occasions.

Just how does any manager go about following that?

There is no point in trying to copy the old Maestro himself for it was largely his own personal chemistry that created so much success – and suffered so many near-misses.

Any club that has enjoyed a degree of major success must necessarily face the same problem. We have gone through a similar period at Old Trafford. Others, like Wolves, Everton, Arsenal, Tottenham, Portsmouth, Blackpool and Burnley have during the post-war era experienced depths of despair following triumphs.

Some, like Arsenal and Spurs, have recovered to take another crack at the top prizes. Others, as Blackpool, Burnley and Pompey, have faded into the distant light never to return; or, at least, not just yet.

So Leeds' present predicament is not at all unusual. It's just that those who have attempted to emulate Revie have had so much more difficult a task than, in many senses, Revie had himself in plotting success.

Because every time Leeds lose a game today there is always someone around to remind the team and staff that 'it's not like the old days'. 'Even moderate successes are compared, critically, with greater ones in the past.

The only thing to do is to do what Mr Clarke has done – to forget the past and take a positive approach to the future. It's almost exactly a year since he took charge at Elland Road and, during that time, he has been working towards getting a settled line-up.

His signing of England left-winger Peter Barnes has given the attacking formation a more balanced look though the manager is still having trouble finding a consistent goalscorer at centre-forward. Derek Parlane and Terry Connor have so far been used.

The midfield has been operating reasonably well but it is in defence where the Leeds' manager has had his deepest problems. Newly-promoted Swansea City slammed five goals into their net then, in their next away game, they were trounced 0-4 at Coventry.

If he can sort these things out he may not be so far away from the winning team he has been seeking. And that will leave him two more years – of the three he promised himself – to set the club back on the trophy-winning road again.

Back row (left to right): Derek Parlane, Brian Greenhoff, John Lukic, David Seaman, Paul Hart, Neil Firm
Middle row: Geoff Ladley *(Physio)*, Carl Harris, Kevin Hird, Arthur Graham, Terry Connor, Alex Sabella, Eddie Gray, Bob English *(Kit Manager)*, Peter Gunby *(Coach)*
Front row: Martin Wilkinson *(Deputy Manager)*, Peter Barnes, Byron Stevenson, Allan Clarke *(Manager)*, Trevor Cherry, Brian Flynn, Barry Murphy *(Coach)*

19 AUGUST 1987: GRAHAM'S GUNNERS
Long-standing *United Review* editor Cliff Butler recognises a team on the rise for our 1987/88 opener, Arsenal having finished fourth the previous term, as well as winning the League Cup. With former Red George Graham in charge the Londoners would lift the title in 1989 and 1991. This particular contest was a cagey one, which finished goalless.

Welcome to Old Trafford

Cliff Butler previews tonight's game

Welcome to Old Trafford, and to another season of League football. This, of course, is a very special season with the Footbll League celebrating its 100th year, and we could scarcely have entertained more illustrious visitors at the opening of this important milestone in football history.

United and Arsenal go back a long way, but there's been few more dramatic clashes than the one which was played out here last January.

It was the 136th meeting of the clubs and most definitely one of the most keenly contested.

Arsenal were riding high atop the League table and looking a sound bet to end the Merseyside domination of the premier prize.

A fiery ninety minutes ensued in which United ended Arsenal's unbeaten run of 22 League and Cup games. So intense was the heat of the battle that Arsenal's David Rocastle found himself leaving the fray early following one of the game's many rule infringements.

Arsenal's title challenge tailed off following that game, but at least they finished the season with the Littlewoods Cup shining brightly on the sideboard.

Gordon Strachan and Terry Gibson were United's scorers in that titanic battle.

The teams that day were: Manchester United: Turner, Sivebaek, Duxbury (sub. McGrath), Whiteside, Garton, Moran, Blackmore, Strachan, Stapleton, Gibson T., Olsen.
Arsenal: Lukic, Anderson, Sansom, Williams, O'Leary, Adams, Rocastle, Davis, Quinn, Nicholas (sub. Caesar), Hayes.

HALF-TIME SCORES

A	Norwich City v Southampton	...	...
B	Nottingham Forest v Watford	...	...
C	Queens Park Rangers v Derby County*	...	...
D	Tottenham Hotspur v Newcastle United*	...	...
E	Leeds United v Leicester City	...	...

*Kick-off 7.45 pm

OUR FOOTBALL LEAGUE RECORD AGAINST ARSENAL

	P	W	D	L	F	A	Pts
Home	68	40	17	11	137	66	100
Away	68	17	10	41	79	143	47
Total	136	57	27	52	216	209	147

Previous League Meetings — Manchester United v Arsenal

Season	*Home*	*Away*	*Season*	*Home*	*Away*	*Season*	*Home*	*Away*
1894-95	3-3	2-3	1928-29	4-1	1-3	1964-65	2-1	3-2
1895-96	5-1	1-2	1929-30	1-0	2-4	1965-66	2-1	2-4
1896-97	1-1	2-0	1930-31	1-2	1-4	1966-67	1-0	1-1
1897-98	5-1	1-5	1936-37	2-0	1-1	1967-68	1-0	2-0
1898-99	2-2	1-5	1938-39	1-0	1-2	1968-69	0-0	0-3
1899-1900	2-0	1-2	1946-47	5-2	2-6	1969-70	2-1	2-2
1900-01	1-0	1-2	1947-48	1-1	1-2	1970-71	1-3	0-4
1901-02	0-1	0-2	1948-49	2-0	1-0	1971-72	3-1	0-3
1902-03	3-0	1-0	1949-50	2-0	0-0	1972-73	0-0	1-3
1903-04	1-0	0-4	1950-51	3-1	0-3	1973-74	1-1	0-3
1906-07	1-0	0-4	1951-52	6-1	3-1	1975-76	3-1	1-3
1907-08	4-2	0-1	1952-53	0-0	1-2	1976-77	3-2	1-3
1908-09	1-4	1-0	1953-54	2-2	1-3	1977-78	1-2	1-3
1909-10	1-0	0-0	1954-55	2-1	3-2	1978-79	0-2	1-1
1910-11	5-0	2-1	1955-56	1-1	1-1	1979-80	3-0	0-0
1911-12	2-0	1-2	1956-57	6-2	2-1	1980-81	0-0	1-2
1912-13	2-0	0-0	1957-58	4-2	5-4	1981-82	0-0	0-0
1919-20	0-1	3-0	1958-59	1-1	2-3	1982-83	0-0	0-3
1920-21	1-1	0-2	1959-60	4-2	2-5	1983-84	4-0	3-2
1921-22	1-0	1-3	1960-61	1-1	3-2	1984-85	4-2	1-0
1925-26	0-1	2-3	1961-62	2-3	1-5	1985-86	0-1	2-1
1926-27	2-2	0-1	1962-63	2-3	3-1	1986-87	2-0	0-1
1927-28	4-1	1-0	1963-64	3-1	1-2			

UNITED v ARSENAL LEAGUE ATTENDANCES

(at Old Trafford)	
1977-78	53,055
1978-79	45,460
1979-80	54,295
1980-81	49,036
1981-82	43,833
1982-83	43,198
1983-84	48,942
1984-85	*32,279
1985-86	44,386
1986-87	51,367
(at Highbury)	
1977-78	40,829
1978-79	45,393
1979-80	44,380
1980-81	33,730
1981-82	39,795
1982-83	23,602
1983-84	42,703
1984-85	48,612
1985-86	37,145
1986-87	41,382

*Live television

Sunday 15th November 1987

TODAY'S TEAMS

UNITED *Red Shirts, White Shorts*		**LIVERPOOL** *Silver Shirts, Silver Shorts*
Gary Walsh	1	Bruce Grobbelaar
Viv Anderson	2	Gary Gillespie
Colin Gibson	3	Mark Lawrenson
Mike Duxbury	4	Steve Nicol
Billy Garton	5	Ronnie Whelan
Kevin Moran	6	Alan Hansen
Bryan Robson	7	Peter Beardsley
Peter Davenport	8	John Aldridge
Brian McClair	9	Craig Johnston
Norman Whiteside	10	John Barnes
Jesper Olsen	11	Steve McMahon
	12	
	14	

TODAY'S OFFICIALS *Referee:* Mr D. Scott (Burnley)
Linesmen: Mr J. Caulkin *(Red Trim)*, Mr K. Hughes *(Yellow Trim)*
Standby: Mr D. Hudson

15 NOVEMBER 1987: REDS v REDS
Liverpool were hard to stop throughout the '80s, but United had more success than most. This autumnal league game saw Norman Whiteside and John Aldridge share the goals in a 1-1 draw.

Back row (left to right): Pier Angelo Pagani, Giulio Nuciari, Marco Van Basten, Angelo Colombo, Filippo Galli, Giovanni Galli, Paolo Maldini, Ruud Gullit, Antonio Virdis, Daniele Limonta, Franco Pagani.
Middle row: Roberto Mussi, Alessandro Costacurta, Mauro Tassotti, Vincenzo Pincolini, Arrigo Sacchi, Italo Galbiati, Franco Baresi, Carlo Ancelotti, Francesco Zanoncelli.
Front row: Walter Bianchi, Mario Bortolazzi, Alberigo Evani, Roberto Donadoni, Giovanni Stroppa, Daniele Massaro.

17 MAY 1988: *ROSSONERI* FRIENDLY
With no European football for the Old Trafford faithful to enjoy in 1987/88, AC Milan were invited to Manchester for a high-profile 'European challenge match' played in front of over 37,000 fans. The Italian giants had just won their 11th *Serie A* championship that season, and they got the better of Alex Ferguson's Reds with a 3-2 victory.

UNITED REVIEW

A.C. MILAN By Cliff Butler

Could you imagine City sharing Old Trafford with your beloved United or Rangers appearing on alternate weekends at Parkhead? Unthinkable! Not so in the soccer-mad city of Milan. For there, A.C. and Internazionale, are the co-residents of the giant Guiseppe Meazza Stadium.

Better known by the district of its location (San Siro) it has a capacity in excess of 80,000 and is regularly packed to the seams with fanatical Milanese supporters of both persuasions. A.C. (Associazione Calcio) were founded in 1899.

Their great rivals (Inter) were formed by a group of Milan dissenters nine years later. A record showing them as European Cup winners in 1963 and 1969, World Club Champions in 1969, and winners of the Cup Winners' Cup in 1968 and 1973 illustrates Milan's present standing as one of the premier clubs in Europe.

The northern cities of Milan and Turin have long dominated the football scene in Italy with Juventus, Torino, Inter and Milan continuously amongst the honours.

Our visitors tonight have been successful since the earliest days of their existence.

Founded as Milan Cricket and Football Club (shades of Newton Heath?) by mainly English residents, the embryo club was also lucky to have the Pirelli rubber manufacturing family as one of their backers. Their first Italian Championship arrived in 1901, and they were again crowned in 1906 and 1907.

A long break followed before they were again amongst the major prize winners, but re-emergence in 1951 as League Champions heralded in a period of enduring greatness for the 'Red Devils' – heard that nickname somewhere before!

The early 50s team was built around a threesome of Swedish forwards: Gunnar Gren, Gunnar Nordahl and Nils Liedholm, who became known collectively as the 'Grenoli'.

Milan headed the League a further three times during the 1950s and of course their success was rewarded with a place in the European Cup.

They were included in the first, and only, invited entry competition in 1955-56 and they reached the semi-final before being eliminated by the all conquering Real Madrid.

Two seasons later they were again on the Champions' Cup trail and went one better by reaching the final, only to lose 3-2 to Real Madrid, after extra time in Brussels.

They finally won the premier trophy in 1963, when they clipped the wings of Benfica 'The Eagles of Lisbon' with a 2-1 win at Wembley. Their subsequent success at that level was six years later when an ascending, but inexperienced, Ajax were thrashed 4-1 in Madrid. Milan had beaten United, the reigning champions in the semi-final.

Later that year (1969) they succeeded where we had failed twelve months before, in defeating the notorious Estudiantes of Argentina to win the World Club Championship. The home leg was won comfortably (3-0) but Milan lost the return in Burnos Aires, 2-1.

On the European front they have also won the European Cup Winners' Cup on two occasions: 1968 (Hamburg S.V., 2-0 in Rotterdam) and 1973 (Leeds United, 1-0 in Salonika).

They again reached the final the following year but surprisingly failed to retain the trophy after losing 2-0 against East Germans F.C. Magdeburg in Rotterdam.

Champions of Italy ten times, a total likely to have been increased to eleven by the time of their arrival in Manchester, they have also won the Italian Cup on four occasions.

Throughout their illustrious history they have been fortunate in having the services of some truly great players from all parts of the globe.

The aforementioned 'Grenoli' trio, fellow Swede Kurt Hamrin, Uruguay-born Juan Schiaffino, Brazilian Jose Altafini, master German defender Karl-Heinz Schnellinger and one of the geatest Italian stars of all time, Gianni Rivera.

Jimmy Greaves, later of 'Saints and Greavsie' fame was on Milan's books for a brief period in the early 60s and more recently, both Joe Jordan and Ray Wilkins left Old Trafford for the cauldron of San Siro. Mark Hateley (now at Monaco with Glenn Hoddle) is another ex-A.C. player.

A.C. Milan are indeed a club with a rich heritage and they rightly occupy a place amongst the game's top bracket.

Tonight we will be privileged to see the most expensive footballer on earth, Ruud Gullit, and any player who can wrest that burden from the shoulders of Diego Maradona must alone be worth the entrance money.

30

UNITED REVIEW

TONIGHT'S VISITORS

PIETRO VIRDIS

GIOVANNI GALLI

PAELO MALDINI

MARCO VAN BASTEN

31

17 MAY 1988: MILAN'S MEN TO MARC
1988 *Ballon d'Or* winner Marco van Basten was understandably given the biggest photo in the AC Milan opposition section for the friendly fixture, although a teenage full-back by the name of 'Paelo' (oops!) Maldini also pops up in a headshot. One to watch, that kid...

ERIC CANTONA

Forward. Eric was the first player to score two hat-tricks this season. Following his trio against Liverpool at Wembley in the FA Charity Shield with another three in Leeds' recent 5-0 victory over Spurs. Eric originally joined the club on loan from Nimes in January 1992 but the transfer was completed for £900,000 this summer. Eric, a France international, started with Auxerre, then spent a loan period with Martigues. Marseille paid £2.2-million for him in 1988 and he later spent loan periods with Bordeaux and Montepellier. He was transferred to Nimes for £1-million in the summer of 1991.

6 SEPTEMBER 1992: CANTONA'S PROFILE
Ooh (aah), who's this Leeds player featured in the opposition pages? Just two months later, Eric was on his way to Old Trafford for £1.2m.

27 JANUARY 1993: FERGIE'S MIDFIELD TARGET
One midfielder to join Alex Ferguson's team in the early '90s was Roy Keane, who had made a real name for himself at Nottingham Forest when they visited in 1992/93 – his final season at the East Midlands club.

ROY KEANE

Midfield. Roy's performances this season have been attracting envious eyes from some of Europe's top clubs. Now a fixture in the Republic of Ireland side. Roy won his 10th cap against Spain in November. Roy, who scored 14 times last term, joined Forest from Cobh Ramblers in the summer 1990 and has since been a regular member of the side.

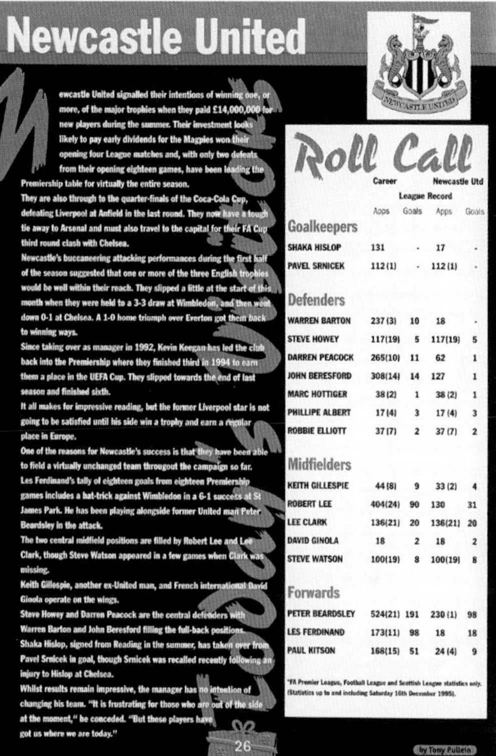

Newcastle United

Newcastle United signalled their intentions of winning one, or more, of the major trophies when they paid £14,000,000 for new players during the summer. Their investment looks likely to pay early dividends for the Magpies won their opening four League matches and, with only two defeats from their opening eighteen games, have been leading the Premiership table for virtually the entire season.

They are also through to the quarter-finals of the Coca-Cola Cup, defeating Liverpool at Anfield in the last round. They now have a tough tie away to Arsenal and must also travel to the capital for their FA Cup third round clash with Chelsea.

Newcastle's buccaneering attacking performances during the first half of the season suggested that one or more of the three English trophies would be well within their reach. They slipped a little at the start of this month when they were held to a 3-3 draw at Wimbledon, and then went down 0-1 at Chelsea. A 1-0 home triumph over Everton got them back to winning ways.

Since taking over as manager in 1992, Kevin Keegan has led the club back into the Premiership where they finished third in 1994 to earn them a place in the UEFA Cup. They slipped towards the end of last season and finished sixth.

It all makes for impressive reading, but the former Liverpool star is not going to be satisfied until his side win a trophy and earn a regular place in Europe.

One of the reasons for Newcastle's success is that they have been able to field a virtually unchanged team througout the campaign so far.

Les Ferdinand's tally of eighteen goals from eighteen Premiership games includes a hat-trick against Wimbledon in a 6-1 success at St James Park. He has been playing alongside former United man Peter Beardsley in the attack.

The two central midfield positions are filled by Robert Lee and Lee Clark, though Steve Watson appeared in a few games when Clark was missing.

Keith Gillespie, another ex-United man, and French international David Ginola operate on the wings.

Steve Howey and Darren Peacock are the central defenders with Warren Barton and John Beresford filling the full-back positions.

Shaka Hislop, signed from Reading in the summer, has taken over from Pavel Srnicek in goal, though Srnicek was recalled recently following an injury to Hislop at Chelsea.

Whilst results remain impressive, the manager has no intention of changing his team. "It is frustrating for those who are out of the side at the moment," he conceded. "But these players have got us where we are today."

Today's Visitors

Roll Call

	Career League Record		Newcastle Utd	
	Apps	Goals	Apps	Goals
Goalkeepers				
SHAKA HISLOP	131	-	17	-
PAVEL SRNICEK	112(1)	-	112(1)	-
Defenders				
WARREN BARTON	237(3)	10	18	-
STEVE HOWEY	117(19)	5	117(19)	5
DARREN PEACOCK	265(10)	11	62	1
JOHN BERESFORD	308(14)	14	127	1
MARC HOTTIGER	38(2)	1	38(2)	1
PHILLIPE ALBERT	17(4)	3	17(4)	3
ROBBIE ELLIOTT	37(7)	2	37(7)	2
Midfielders				
KEITH GILLESPIE	44(8)	9	33(2)	4
ROBERT LEE	404(24)	90	130	31
LEE CLARK	136(21)	20	136(21)	20
DAVID GINOLA	18	2	18	2
STEVE WATSON	100(19)	8	100(19)	8
Forwards				
PETER BEARDSLEY	524(21)	191	230(1)	98
LES FERDINAND	173(11)	98	18	18
PAUL KITSON	168(15)	51	24(4)	9

*FA Premier League, Football League and Scottish League statistics only. (Statistics up to and including Saturday 16th December 1995).

26

by Tony Pullein

27 DECEMBER 1995: WINNING WITH KIDS
Kevin Keegan's Newcastle were 10 points clear of Alex Ferguson's bright young things going into this tasty festive fixture – a 2-0 home win narrowed the gap... and you might recall how the season ended!

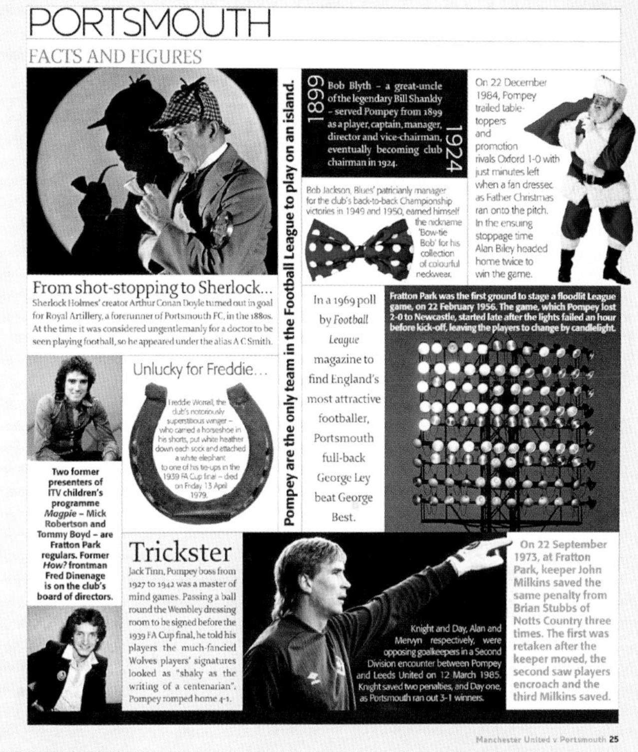

PORTSMOUTH

FACTS AND FIGURES

From shot-stopping to Sherlock...
Sherlock Holmes' creator Arthur Conan Doyle turned out in goal for Royal Artillery, a forerunner of Portsmouth FC, in the 1880s. At the time it was considered ungentlemanly for a doctor to be seen playing football, so he appeared under the alias A C Smith.

Pompey are the only team in the Football League to play on an island.

1899 Bob Blyth – a great-uncle of the legendary Bill Shankly – served Pompey from 1899 as a player, captain, manager, director and vice-chairman, eventually becoming club chairman in 1924. 1924

Bob Jackson, Blues' patricianly manager for the club's back-to-back Championship victories in 1949 and 1950, earned himself the nickname 'Bow-tie Bob' for his collection of colourful neckwear.

On 22 December 1984, Pompey trailed table-toppers and promotion rivals Oxford 1-0 with just minutes left when a fan dressed as Father Christmas ran onto the pitch. In the ensuing stoppage time Alan Biley headed home twice to win the game.

Unlucky for Freddie...
Freddie Worrall, the club's notoriously superstitious winger – who carried a horseshoe in his shorts, put white heather down each sock and attached a white elephant to one of his tie-ups in the 1939 FA Cup final – died on Friday 13 April 1979.

In a 1969 poll by *Football League* magazine to find England's most attractive footballer, Portsmouth full-back George Ley beat George Best.

Fratton Park was the first ground to stage a floodlit League game, on 22 February 1956. The game, which Pompey lost 2-0 to Newcastle, started late after the lights failed an hour before kick-off, leaving the players to change by candlelight.

Two former presenters of ITV children's programme *Magpie* – Mick Robertson and Tommy Boyd – are Fratton Park regulars. Former *How?* frontman Fred Dinenage is on the club's board of directors.

Trickster
Jack Tinn, Pompey boss from 1927 to 1942 was a master of mind games. Passing a ball round the Wembley dressing room to be signed before the 1939 FA Cup final, he told his players the much-fancied Wolves players' signatures looked as "shaky as the writing of a centenarian". Pompey romped home 4-1.

Knight and Day, Alan and Mervyn respectively, were opposing goalkeepers in a Second Division encounter between Pompey and Leeds United on 12 March 1985. Knight saved two penalties, and Day one, as Portsmouth ran out 3-1 winners.

On 22 September 1973, at Fratton Park, keeper John Milkins saved the same penalty from Brian Stubbs of Notts Country three times. The first was retaken after the keeper moved, the second saw players encroach and the third Milkins saved.

Manchester United v Portsmouth 25

1 NOVEMBER 2003: NEW CENTURY, NEW LOOK
The turn of the century saw *UR* change to a squarer format, giving the designers a bit more space to get creative – as they did for this visit of Portsmouth, when Cristiano Ronaldo scored his first Reds goal in a 3-0 win.

ARSENAL

DAVID SEAMAN

David Seaman
(Goalkeeper)
Age: 35
England international who had spells at Leeds, Peterborough, Birmingham and QPR before joining Arsenal for £1.3 million in May 1990. He played in all four of England's France 98 games and has won League, cup and European honours at Highbury.

Alex Manninger
(Goalkeeper)
Age: 21
Impressed when he deputised for Seaman in 16 appearances last season and is a promising talent. Signed from Austrian side Cazino Salzburg for £500,000 in June 1997.

Tony Adams
(Defender)
Age: 32
Club captain and influential Arsenal stalwart who played in England's four World Cup France 98 fixtures. He has recently returned to the first team after a troublesome back injury during the early part of the campaign.

Martin Keown
(Defender)
Age: 32
A non-playing member of England's squad at France '98, this renowned man-marker began his career at Arsenal before spells at Aston Villa and Everton. Signed for £2 million from the Goodison Park outfit in February 1993.

Lee Dixon
(Defender)
Age: 34
A player who has made more than 350 appearances for the club since joining from Stoke in January 1988 for £400,000. A combative and threatening presence on the right, he used to be regular in the England international set-up and was called up for England's recent friendly with France.

Nigel Winterburn
(Defender)
Age: 35
Signed for over £400,000 from fellow Londoners Wimbledon in May 1987, this left-back has proved a valuable servant to Arsenal by making more than 500 appearances. Proved that age is not a barrier to him by making more league appearances than any Highbury player last term.

Matthew Upson
(Defender)
Age: 19
Made one substitute league appearance for Luton before being snapped up by Arsenal for £1 million in May 1997. A former England youth international, it is hoped he can continue the high quality of defenders at Highbury.

Steve Bould
(Defender)
Age: 36
Former England international, he made more than 200 appearances for his hometown club Stoke City before switching to Arsenal for £390,000 in June 1988. Strong, reliable and committed central defender.

Gilles Grimandi
(Defender)
Age: 28
Signed from Monaco in June 1997 for £1.5 million, he is a versatile player who can play in central defence or at right-back. Striving for more consistency to aid him in his challenge for a regular first team berth.

Nelson Vivas
(Defender)
Age: 29
Another who may not be a first team regular at Highbury but exemplifies the squad strength at the club. A member of Argentina's squad for France '98, he was brought to Arsenal at the start of the season from Swiss side Lugano.

Remi Garde
(Defender/Midfielder)
Age: 32
Frenchman who signed a new contract, despite announcing his retirement at the end of last season. A former Olympique Lyon and Racing Strasbourg player, he signed from the latter in August 1996.

Ray Parlour
(Midfielder)
Age: 25
A major influence in Arsenal's double-winning campaign last season. A graduate of the club's youth scheme, he blends hard-work and tough-tackling with powerful and dangerous forward runs.

Emmanuel Petit
(Midfielder)
Age: 28
A member of France's World Cup winning squad, he scored the final goal in his country's 3-0 win againt Brazil in the final last summer. After a slow start in English football following a move from French club Monaco, he has risen to become one of the most complete midfielders in the Premiership.

Patrick Vieira
(Midfielder)
Age: 22
Figured in France's World Cup winning squad as well, but not as prominently as Petit. However, developed into an equal presence in their midfield partnership for Arsenal since signing for £3.5 million from AC Milan in August 1996.

Fredrik Ljungberg
(Midfielder)
Age: 31
Swedish international who joined the club not long after impressing in his country's 2-1 win against England in a European Championships qualifier. Signed from Halmstads BK in September and scored against Manchester United later that month after appearing as a substitute.

Marc Overmars
(Midfielder)
Age: 25
A £7 million buy from Dutch club Ajax in July 1997, he possesses pace, control and finishing prowess - qualities which helped him score 16 goals last season. He is another of Arsenal's international brigade and was in Holland's World Cup squad last summer.

Stephen Hughes
(Midfielder)
Age: 22
A graduate of the club's youth policy, this 1994 FA Youth Cup winner has been capped at England under-21, youth and schoolboy level. A calm and confident player who is pressing hard for a more regular first team place.

Nwankwo Kanu
(Midfielder)
Age: 22
Captain of the 1996 Nigerian Olympic gold medal winning team, the former African Player of the Year also played for his country in last summer's World Cup outing. Made his name at Ajax before a move to Inter Milan.

Dennis Bergkamp
(Striker)
Age: 29
The PFA and Football Writers' Player of the Year winner last season after scoring 22 goals from 40 starts. Scored a last gasp winner against Argentina in the World Cup which showed his skill and ice-cool persona.

Nicolas Anelka
(Striker)
Age: 19
Signed for £500,000 from Paris Saint Germain in March 1997, this Frenchman harasses opposition defences with his enthusiasm and pace. Maturing into a regular goalscorer, he is a constant threat in attack.

Luis Boa Morte
(Striker)
Age: 21
Capped at Portuguese under-21 level, this signing from Sporting Lisbon in July 1997 has found his first team opportunities limited. A developing talent, he has pace and skill and could be one to watch.

Kaba Diawara
(Striker)
Age: 23
Former French under-21 international who began his career at Toulon before a move to Bordeaux where he scored five goals in seven starts.

17 FEBRUARY 1999: CHASING TROPHIES
United and Arsenal were neck-and-neck at the league's summit for most of 1998/99, with the Reds pipping Arsene Wenger's side to the trophy, as well as edging an incredible FA Cup semi-final. Nicolas Anelka gave the Gunners the lead in this league contest, before Andy Cole levelled in a 1-1 draw.

20 AUGUST 2006: ELECTRIC VOLZ

Opposition interviews often make for an enjoyable read (especially when the players are United fans!), but this chat with Fulham defender Moritz Volz is something else completely, as the German recalls his antics in his 'Motherland' during that summer's World Cup.

TODAY'S MATCH

PLAYER INTERVIEW: **FULHAM'S**

Moritz Volz

Germans might not be famous for their sense of humour, but the Fulham defender's website shows he is an exception to that rule

It's no secret that many of today's Premiership stars have their own websites. While the details may differ, the majority are pretty similar in terms of their content, offering stats, pictures and biogs along with formal and messages to fans. However, the website of Fulham defender Moritz Volz is certainly an exception to the norm.

Check out www.volzy.com and you'll find yourself face to face with a highly original, amusing and honest website, which, not surprisingly, has been the subject of a bit of attention of late!

It's his regularly updated diary that makes the best reading. The site was launched to coincide with the World Cup. But more importantly for Volz, it marked the start of a two-week jaunt around "the Motherland", taking in games and soaking up the carnival atmosphere.

"Headed to the Portugal hotel to try and catch up with Boa," reads the entry after the Portugal-Angola game. "Met a load of Angolans on the train. Had a sing-song and ended up losing my brand new Angola shirt in a bet about pull-ups on those metal bars you get on train carriages!" That's what happens when you take on Angolans at train carriage pull-ups…

"Orange was definitely the colour for the Holland-Ivory Coast game," reads another entry. "Made sure I got hold of a big orange wig for the occasion! Was hard to choose who to support with Kolo in the Ivory Coast side and Ed (United keeper Edwin van der Sar) as Holland captain… In the end I ended up wearing both team's shirts – Holland in the first half and Ivory Coast in the second! Was sat in amongst all the Dutch fans – the only one wearing an Ivory Coast shirt, and when they scored I was the only one who jumped up cheering. But I'd also gone mental earlier when Holland had scored so they must have thought I was some kind of schizophrenic orange-wigged weirdo!"

As well as the diary, the site also features a section called "Where It's At" in which Volz lists his latest musical leanings, along with things that Germans are really good at but that nobody knows about. For example, did you know that his countrymen excel at cherry stone spitting? Or that a man from Cologne holds the world record at 19.56m?

It's not all comedy, however – there's also much genuine insight into the life of a Premiership footballer. This week we found out his thoughts on the build-up to today's game and the 2006/07 campaign.

"Man Utd is a massive game to start off with," he says. "They'll be favourites, but it's the first game of the season and they'll be under huge pressure to win which is something we can hopefully make use of. So we've just got to be confident, fresh and positive.

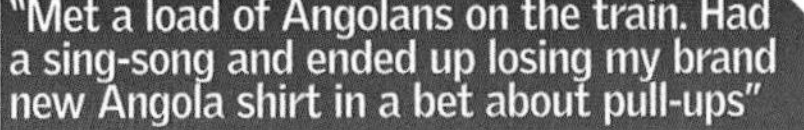

"A lot of eyes will naturally be on Rooney after the World Cup. People criticise him, but he's the kind of player who has that fire in his belly, and that's part of what makes him stand out. I'm sure he'll be keen to keep his cool this season, because he'll know more than anyone that if he misses games, it really hurts the team."

Okay, enough of the serious stuff. If Volz is playing today, try and get a look at his boots. Why? Let him tell you. "Headed to Nike Town on Oxford Street. Using a computer you can put your own identity on football boots, so I ordered two pairs – one with 'The Hoff' embroidered on them and the other with 'Volzy.com'. Should be fun in close-up TV shots next season!"

Who said Germans don't have a sense of humour?!

Volz's World Cup

Going Dutch: can you spot the orange-wigged weirdo?

Beware of taking on the Angolans at a pull-up competition!

Cameroon's Roger Milla meets his favourite German comedian

THE MATCH

PLAYER PROFILES

Chelsea

The title race could be a run-off between Chelsea and United, so these men know today's clash will be pivotal...

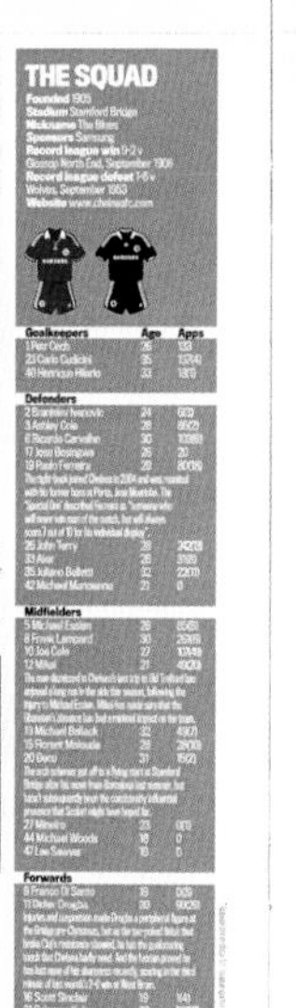

"He has taken to heart the degree of frailty that has crept into the defence this season – particularly at home"

BRAZILIAN AT THE BRIDGE

26 Manchester United v Chelsea

Manchester United v Chelsea 27

11 JANUARY 2009: BLUES BATTLE

The 'noughties' saw Chelsea take over the mantle as United's main trophy rivals, the two clubs winning eight of the 10 league titles throughout the decade. Blues captain John Terry featured most heavily in this preview, with this being his first trip to Old Trafford since his very costly slip in the 2008 Champions League final.

STOKE CITY

THE POTTERS ARE EYEING A SUCCESSFUL TRIP TO M16

>> p22-23 STOKE PLAYER PROFILES p24 MICHAEL OWEN INTERVIEW p25 LOCAL REPORT

TOP DOLLAR
Stoke's current record signing is Peter Crouch, a £10m capture from Spurs. Ex-Reds Jimmy Greenhoff (£100,000 in 1969), Sammy McIlroy (£350,000 in 1982) and Ryan Shawcross (£1m in 2006) all broke the club's transfer record on joining the Potters.

Old Vic
Stoke City's former home, the Victoria Ground was the oldest operational stadium in Football League history when it was pulled down in 1997. Stoke had played there for 119 years.

592
Eric Skeels holds the record for most appearances for Stoke City. The Eccles-born defender played full-back and left-half between 1959 and 1976.

Near miss
In 1946/47 Stoke needed to beat Sheffield United in their final game to win the league for the first time. But with unsettled star Stanley Matthews departing to Blackpool only weeks earlier, the Potters lost 2-1.

RETURNING HERO
This is boss Tony Pulis's second spell as manager of Stoke. He was sacked in June 2005 after falling out with the previous owners, but shrewdly brought back by new chairman Peter Coates (also back for a second spell) a year later.

Manchester United v Stoke City 21

20 OCTOBER 2012: POTTED HISTORY

A tough 90 minutes was guaranteed whenever Tony Pulis brought his Stoke City side to United's home, and it didn't look good after Wayne Rooney scored an early own goal when the teams met it 2012. Thankfully Wayne and the Reds battled back to win 4-2, with goals either side of the interval – the perfect time to absorb this succinct 60-second guide to the Staffordshire club.

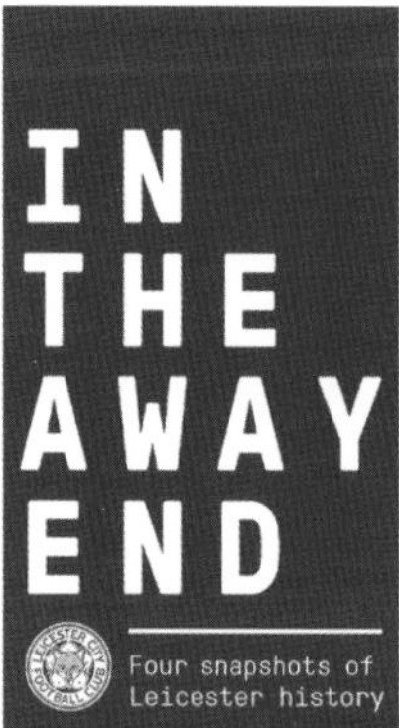

LONGEST SERVING BOSS △

MATT GILLIES
A defender with the club in the 1950s, the Scot went on to boss the Foxes for 508 games between 1958-68, and he nearly won the Double along the way. His 1962/63 side, known as 'the Ice Kings' for their imperious form in the long, cold winter, saw their winning momentum thaw out when spring finally arrived, and they finished 4th, before losing the FA Cup final to United a week later (above). Leicester did win the League Cup the following year, though – the Foxes' first major trophy.

△ CLASSIC KIT

1976-78
Leicester-based underwear-turned-sportswear company Admiral was the leading name in Britain's replica kit market at this time – also producing United's kit – but nothing screams '70s quite like the sight of flamboyant forward Frank Worthington in this stylish number (above). From the shoulder bars to the large circular badge (and no shirt sponsor), to that vast open collar (perfect to show off that gold chain), it's a shirt with cult status these days (even if the Foxes were relegated in it in 1978).

△ ICONIC IMAGE

The greatest underdog triumph in the history of the English game had been confirmed five days earlier, but even still, the sight of boss Claudio Ranieri and his charges lifting the Premier League trophy on 7 May 2016 was a surreal moment. For all the home fans crammed into the King Power that day, it was an occasion they'll never forget: Italian tenor Andrea Bocelli got the goosebumps going with his pre-match performance, ahead of the Foxes beating Everton 3-1. Then, the crowning moment (above): lifting the league trophy for the first time in the club's 132-year history.

SECOND-TIER SPECIALISTS ▽

While Leicester's recent league title triumph was a first for the Foxes, no club has won more second-tier titles (seven, a record they share with Manchester City). The first of Leicester's successes came in 1924/25, when they were promoted alongside United, with the most recent title at this level coming in 2013/14. It was Nigel Pearson (below) who led them to the top flight with a club-record 102 points – and while his time at the club would end acrimoniously, for many of that squad, far greater glory would lie ahead in the Premier League.

26 AUGUST 2017: PICTORIAL MEMORIES

'In the away end', which ran throughout 2017/18, picked out some nuggets of trivia, as well as a classic kit and iconic photo – which in Leicester City's case was snapped just over a year earlier.

MANCHESTER CITY 1894

STATE OF PLAY

Latest talking points from the blue side of Manchester...

City claimed the first major trophy of the English season at Wembley last Sunday

FORM GUIDE
Recent results (not including Wednesday's FA Cup fixture)

W - **Aston Villa**
2-1 · Carabao Cup · 01.03.20 · Neutral

W - **Real Madrid**
2-1 · Champions League · 26.02.20 · Away

W - **Leicester City**
1-0 · Premier League · 22.02.20 · Away

W - **West Ham United**
2-0 · Premier League · 19.02.20 · Home

L - **Tottenham Hotspur**
0-2 · Premier League · 02.02.20 · Away

Midfielder De Bruyne on Guardiola's team selection:

"In our four years with Pep we've had some surprises – even the players don't really know until the game starts what we need to do"

Guardiola's possession obsession
Fresh from beating Real Madrid at the Bernabeu in the Champions League last 16 and Aston Villa to lift the season's first piece of silverware in the Carabao Cup final, Manchester City come into the derby with confidence high. Though he has come to disown the phrase 'tiki-taka', manager Pep Guardiola demands that his team dominates possession. Midfield fulcrum Rodri helps, but it's at full-back where the Catalan tactician's masterplan comes into full effect. Whoever plays there – usually Kyle Walker and Benjamin Mendy – they overlap, as has become the norm in elite football, but also occupy half-spaces between the touchline in the middle third of the pitch, acting as extra midfielders alongside schemers such as Kevin De Bruyne, David Silva and Bernardo Silva. The relentlessness this provides means goals, and lots of them. For all the table-topping form of Liverpool, Manchester City remain the Premier League's highest scorers, as they were last season and the season before that.

Springing a tactical switch
Having come unstuck against United's counterattacking in the second leg of the Carabao Cup semi-final in January, as well as in the reverse Premier League fixture, don't be surprised to see Guardiola pull another tactical surprise today. He has a history of doing so in big fixtures. Against Real Madrid last month, he swapped his standard 4-3-3 for an unexpected 4-4-2 hybrid system, with Gabriel Jesus on the left of a midfield four and De Bruyne and Bernardo Silva as a pair of false nines, the idea being to draw the Spaniards' defence out of their comfort zone. "In our four years with Pep we've had some surprises and even the players, they don't really know until the game starts what we need to do," said De Bruyne at full-time in the Spanish capital. Having a player of the Belgian's prodigious gifts is vital. He has 16 assists in the Premier League alone this season and is so technically gifted he can seemingly play anywhere.

Centre-back decisions
With Guardiola's defensive talisman Aymeric Laporte facing another spell on the sidelines in a season dogged by injuries, the manager will again have to shuffle his rearguard pack today. Fernandinho will most likely drop into the back four alongside Nicolas Otamendi, who has been unable to form a successful partnership with John Stones at the heart of the City defence in Laporte's absence. The Blues have won five and drawn one of the six games Frenchman Laporte has started this season, and their campaign could have looked vastly different without his injury problems. "We've missed him a lot," said Guardiola recently. "He's fast, strong in the air – he has all the attributes."

8 MARCH 2020: UNLOCKING CITY'S SYSTEMS

Away from the player profiles, tactical analysis of the opposition has been given a greater focus in recent years. In what was United's final home fixture before the coronavirus lockdown, *UR* takes a look at Pep Guardiola's deployment of different formations depending on Manchester City's opponents. United went on to win this Premier League derby 2-0... who knows, maybe the programme's extensive research played a very small role in that!

see

your sport

It's better to see a goal than read about it. Why be content merely to read your Sport in the papers? Nobody has time to see all the big matches; all the races; all the fights. But at the Tatler News Theatre you can see them at your own time . . . . in perfect comfort and at negligible cost. All the News; all the Sports; the best short films and the crispest cartoons. A seventy-five minute programme includes: 30 minutes **News** and **Sport, Interest, Travel, Colour Cartoons.** All the Latest Disneys.

NEXT WEEK

EAST MEETS WEST (Part I)

Two colour Cartoons together with interest films and 30 minutes news

ADMISSION SIXPENCE AND SHILLING

● TO-NIGHT

THE IMMORTAL SWAN

A Film of Pavlova and her Art

tatler

OXFORD RD. STATION

CHAPTER 7

Adverts

Where once local firms would promote themselves in the hallowed pages of *United Review*, the adverts are very different nowadays, with big businesses from across the globe proudly showing off their connection to the club...

The relationship between Manchester United and advertising has not changed in some respects. The club, and football in general, is still a hugely powerful tool to help promote and share ideas and products.

But in another sense, everything has shifted. Back in the early 20th century, mass media was limited to only print, so a football match and its captive audience of thousands was a huge opportunity for local businesses to get their wares and events into the popular consciousness. And, for the club itself, advertising could bring in important revenue.

The earliest adverts in the programme were for shows at venues like the Palace Theatre on Oxford Street, or local cinemas and music halls.

Saturday afternoon's entertainment might have been taken care of, but what would fans do of an evening? Those in showbusiness knew United could help put bums on seats. Then there were, of course, the football-related advertisements, like cheap rail fares for away matches.

And what would fans do while in the stadium? They might smoke – could their brand of choice be influenced by a witty advert? They may have a celebratory beer in the pub after watching United earn a late win – might their euphoric mood encourage them to try a different pint of bitter, promoted in the programme?

These types of desired transactions dominated the programme for many years, with adverts for all kinds of products. But the emphasis was on the local, whether it was circuses or ties being promoted.

But this changed with the times. In some cases for obvious reasons: cigarette advertising was

Above: Back in the 1930s, the programme provided vital promotion for local theatres, with many fans looking for somewhere to go after the game

The programme gives club sponsors the opportunity to connect directly with matchgoing fans

Huge brands now pay for the exclusivity of their relationship with United, with LED perimeter boards complementing the programme adverts

phased out, as the UK's health authorities pushed towards a smoking ban in stadiums.

But the biggest change came when the club began to expand its own remit. As sponsors like Sharp Electronics came on board, they received the privilege of having their products displayed ahead of other brands. Now, companies were paying for the exclusivity of a relationship with United, rather than purely the advertising space.

As the make-up of football crowds diversified, more and more companies saw the value of linking up with the club to reach their intended audience. Cigarettes might have been out of the question, but souvenirs, clothing and soft drinks could replace them.

And then came the club's other platforms, as the thirst for football 'content' exploded throughout the 1990s and 2000s. *Inside United* magazine, MUTV and, latterly, the club's official app have all been featured in the pages of *UR*, further enriching the relationship between United and its fans.

UR's adverts map how society has changed in the last 100 years, with global brands across a multitude of sectors recognising the strength and power of communicating directly to the most loyal and connected group of fans – those regular matchgoing supporters.

But what our modern-day adverts do show is how football and United have grown. Whereas once advertising space was a simple commodity used to bring in extra revenue, now the same spaces in *UR* benefit our chosen sponsors, Manchester United Foundation or the services we provide for fans. Advertising is now the carefully curated preserve of the club itself – a long way from the days of woodwork firms and Woodbines!

THE MANCHESTER UNITED OFFICIAL PROGRAMME
League Champions 1908 1911 — Winners English Cup 1909 — Season 1914 1915

Vol. 5. No. 19. Friday, April 2, 1915. One Penny.

THE NEW PALACE
Oxford Street, Manchester.
Proprietors: THE MANCHESTER PALACE OF VARIETIES, LTD.
Managing Director: Walter de Frece. General Manager: Alan Young.

TO-MORROW (Saturday) at 6-30 and 8-55
ELLA RETFORD **CHARLOTTE PARRY**
Wilson Hallet. Sam Barton.
Heeley and Meeley, Lily Leonhard, Jackley and le Sine, Guest and Newlyn

Next Week (Matinees Monday and Wednesday at 2-15),
First Appearance in Manchester
SHIRLEY KELLOGG
LONDON'S REVUE IDOL (Creator of the Famous "Wedding Glide," in America and England).
Alice Hollander. Ernest H. Mills. O'Hana San.
Con Conrad's Novelty Minstrels.
Clown BARKER and his Comic Circus.
HORACE MILLS and Co., including Miss Violet Gould and James Prior, in "MAN—THE BRUTE."

PRICES OF ADMISSION:
Boxes, 15/- and 10/6; Grand Stalls, 2/-; Grand Circle 1/6 and 1/-; Orchestra Stalls, 1/6; Stalls, 1/-; Balcony, 6d.
Every seat reservable in advance. No Extra Charge. Box office open 10 a.m. to 9 p.m. Telephone 1077 City.
Seats ordered by telephone and not paid for by the rise of the curtain will be sold

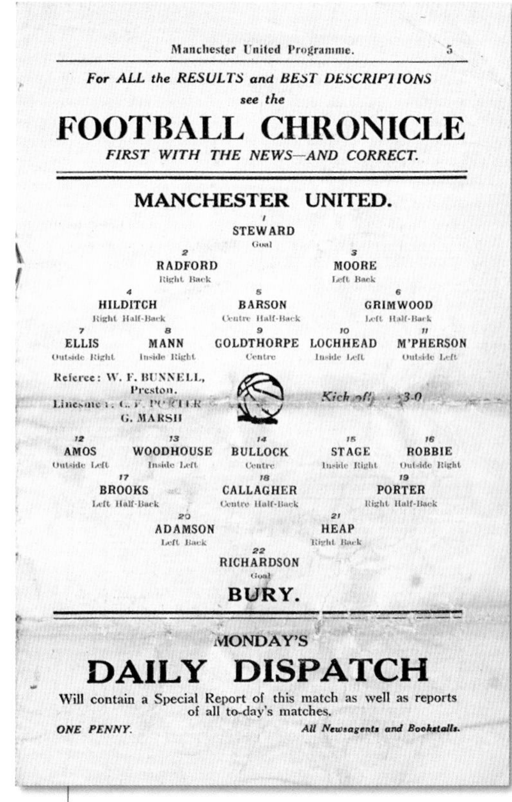
Manchester United Programme. 5

For ALL the RESULTS and BEST DESCRIPTIONS see the
FOOTBALL CHRONICLE
FIRST WITH THE NEWS—AND CORRECT.

MANCHESTER UNITED.
1 STEWARD Goal
2 RADFORD Right Back — 3 MOORE Left Back
4 HILDITCH Right Half-Back — 5 BARSON Centre Half-Back — 6 GRIMWOOD Left Half-Back
7 ELLIS Outside Right — 8 MANN Inside Right — 9 GOLDTHORPE Centre — 10 LOCHHEAD Inside Left — 11 M'PHERSON Outside Left

Referee: W. F. BUNNELL, Preston.
Linesmen: C. F. PORTER, G. MARSH
Kick off 3-0

12 AMOS Outside Left — 13 WOODHOUSE Inside Left — 14 BULLOCK Centre — 15 STAGE Inside Right — 16 ROBBIE Outside Right
17 BROOKS Left Half-Back — 18 CALLAGHER Centre Half-Back — 19 PORTER Right Half-Back
20 ADAMSON Left Back — 21 HEAP Right Back
22 RICHARDSON Goal
BURY.

MONDAY'S
DAILY DISPATCH
Will contain a Special Report of this match as well as reports of all to-day's matches.
ONE PENNY. *All Newsagents and Bookstalls.*

2 APRIL 1915, v LIVERPOOL
Shirley Kellogg (an American actress, and nothing to do with breakfast cereal) was the big draw at Manchester's Palace Theatre in 1915, with this front-page promotion.

15 SEPTEMBER 1923, v BURY
Read the *Daily Dispatch*'s report on our local clash with the Shakers, as well as details on all the other games, for a penny (61p in today's money).

CHESHIRE LINES RAILWAY.

UNITED v. LIVERPOOL

December 24th, 1927.

Special Half-Day Excursion will run as under:—

		a.m.
Manchester (Central) - - -	dep.	11.50
Trafford Park & Stretford- -	,,	11.55
Urmston - - - - -	,,	12. 0
Liverpool (Central) - - - -	arr.	12.40

Third Class Return Fare **2/6**

Return from Liverpool (Cen.) at 6.0 p.m.

A. P. ROSS,
Manager and Engineer.

17 DECEMBER 1927, v ARSENAL
Useful travel information ahead of a big Christmas Eve trip to Anfield back in 1927, scheduled for a week after this home meeting with Arsenal. While Christmas Day was usually a matchday back in the 1920s, people often had other priorities the day before, with only 14,971 fans in attendance at the Merseyside fixture.

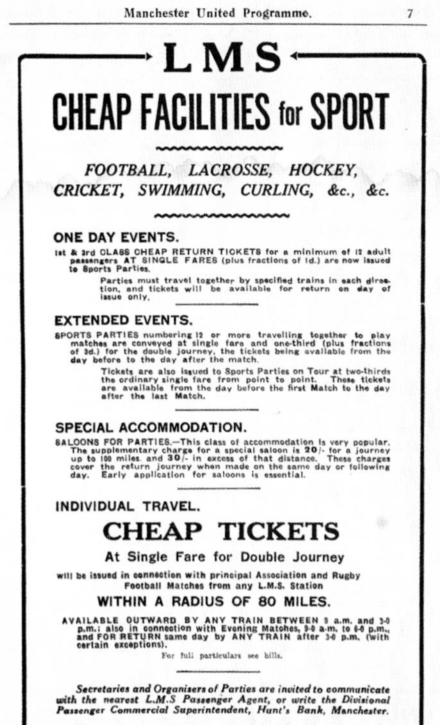

YOUNG MAN!

Why not spend your 1930 holiday at

GOVERNMENT EXPENSE?

If you are between 18 and 38 years of age join one of the undermentioned Territorial Army Units. ALL drills outside the camp period can be done in spare time.

THE TRAINING IN CAMP ALLOWS LEISURE FOR SPORTS, RECREATION AND LEAVE.

PAY IN CAMP AS FOR REGULAR SOLDIERS, MARRIAGE ALLOWANCE DURING CAMP FOR MARRIED MEN OVER 26 YEARS OLD.

APPLY AT THE HEADQUARTERS FOR FURTHER PARTICULARS.

52nd (M/c.) Field Brigade R.A., Headquarters, Hyde-road, Manchester

42nd (E. Lancs.) Divnl. Royal Engineers, Headquarters, Seymour-grove, Old Trafford.

52nd (E. Lancs.) Divnl. Royal Signals, Burlington-street, Manchester.

7th Bn. The Lancashire Fusiliers, Cross-lane, Salford.

8th Bn. The Lancashire Fusiliers, Great Clowes-street, Salford; also Patricroft.

6th/7th Bn. The Manchester Regiment, Stretford-road, Manchester.

8th (A.) Bn. The Manchester Regiment, Ardwick Green, Manchester.

R.A.M.C. (T.A.), Upper Chorlton-road, Manchester.

MEN OF THE FOLLOWING TRADES ESPECIALLY REQUIRED FOR THE

42nd (E. Lancs.) Divnl. Royal Engineers.
Blacksmiths (for training as farriers), Bricklayers, Carpenters and Joiners, Electricians, Fitters, Masons, Painters and Decorators, Plumbers and Gas Fitters Stokers (stationary engines).

42nd (E. Lancs.) Divnl. Signals, Royal Corps of Signals.
Motor Drivers, Motor-cyclists, Electricians, Fitters, Instrument Repairers, Linemen, Telegraphists, &c.

28 DECEMBER 1929, v NEWCASTLE UNITED

A call for new recruits to the Territorial Army, nowadays known as the Army Reserve. Aimed at men aged 18-30, football was the ideal recruiting ground.

26 DECEMBER 1927, v BLACKBURN ROVERS

This rail company's 'Cheap Facilities for Sport' campaign offers special discounts for passengers travelling to take part in popular sporting activities – including football, cricket and, erm, curling.

12 Manchester United Programme.

LMS

SPECIAL

CHEAP TRIPS

From MANCHESTER on SUNDAYS to From MANCHESTER

	s.	d.		s.	d.
Derby	4	0	Birmingham	5	0
Loughborough	4	6	Stafford	4	0
Hope	2	6	Batley	3	0
Sheffield	3	6	Sowerby Bridge	2	6
Dudley Port	5	0	Nottingham	4	6
Stoke	3	0	Edale	2	0
Dewsbury	3	0	Grindleford	3	0
Leeds	3	6	Wolverhampton	5	0
Bradford	3	0	Coventry	5	6
Matlock	3	0	Huddersfield	2	6
Chinley	1	6	Morley	3	6
Hathersage	3	0	Halifax	3	0
Liverpool	3	0	Etc., Etc.		

Ask for the "Monthly Cheap Trip Programme." It's worth looking into.

LMS

17 FEBRUARY 1932, v BURNLEY

More LMS (London, Midland and Scottish Railway) offers here – this one focusing on family day-trips, with some bargain Sunday train fares available.

Billy Meredith

Stretford Road Hotel

(Adjoining Pauldens). MANCHESTER.

Telephone 1822 Moss Side.

ROBINSON'S, STOCKPORT NOTED ALES.

DRAUGHT BASS.

Wines and Spirits of the Finest Quality.

Select Concerts

EVERY WEEK.

SPECIAL CLUB ROOMS TO LET.

PARTIES CATERED FOR.

In the same programme, a listing for rooms in the Stretford Road Hotel, where owner and retired ex-Red Billy Meredith would relive former glories with guests. The Welsh wizard – or 'Old Skinny' as he was otherwise known – would certainly have had a story or two...

H. Wright Greaves

Large and Up-to-date Stock of

MUSIC

Including the latest Songs, and Dances, Operas, Libretti, Miniature Scores, Text-books, Anthems, Part Songs, Festival and Examination Music.

Music Carriers, Metronomes, Batons, Busts and Portraits of Musicians. Strings and Accessories.

INSPECTION IS INVITED, AND COPIES MAY BE TAKEN ON :: APPROVAL. ::

11 Royal Exchange Arcade,

MANCHESTER.

TELEPHONE — BLACKFRIARS 6957

Sticking with the Wolves programme, check out these musical offerings from H Wright Greaves, situated in a prime location at the Royal Exchange theatre arcade. 'Inspection is invited' of 'the latest songs'.

Cigarette ads used to be commonplace (and were only banned from print in 2003). This gift listing for Trawler's 'bigger and better' smokes also appeared in the Wolves issue from Christmas Day 1931.

GIFTS!

BETTER GIFTS with BIGGER CIGARETTES.

TRAWLER CIGARETTES

ARE BIGGER AND BETTER THAN OTHER BRANDS AT

10 for 4D.

START SMOKING TRAWLER CIGARETTES TO-DAY AND OBTAIN THESE BETTER GIFTS

ASK YOUR TOBACCONIST for GIFT BOOK with Particulars of 150 GIFTS for TRAWLER SMOKERS.

N.B. Speedway Issue of Coupons are accepted for all TRAWLER GIFTS.

MANCHESTER

HIPPODROME

OXFORD STREET

Chairman and Managing Director - SIR OSWALD STOLL
Manager - - - - FRED C. BROOKS

6.30 TWICE NIGHTLY 8.45

MATINEES WEDNESDAY and SATURDAY at 2.30

TO-NIGHT

A Feast of Spectacle, Song and Dance.
OUR CABARET
with BILLY CHILDS and his PLAYBOYS
Jack Stanford. The Kemmys.
12 Hippodrome Girls and Chas. Windsor's Orchestra.

NEXT WEEK, MONDAY, OCT. 17th.

The most-discussed Variety Artiste of the Year.
The sensational
LOUIS ARMSTRONG,
King of the Trumpet,
And full Variety Programme.

POPULAR PRICES 3/6 to 9d. (Including Tax)
EVERY SEAT BOOKABLE IN ADVANCE WITHOUT EXTRA CHARGE
BOOKING OFFICE open 10 to 9 'PHONE: CITY 7778

KAYS Surgical Appliances, etc.

FOOTBALLERS–Anklets 2/6, Knee Caps 2/6

SPECIAL TEAM RATES

—RUPTURE—

KAYS SUPER TRUSS

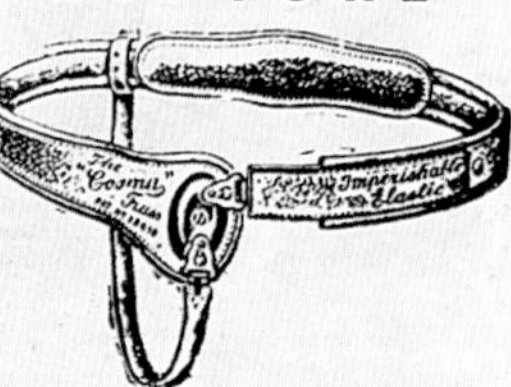

10/6 Single
17/6 Double

Catalogue Free

Ko-lastic PADS any shape

"TRUST KAYS TRUSS"

H. KAY & Co. (City Medical Co.)

Cromford Court, Corporation Street, MANCHESTER

BRITAIN'S BEST

Walker & Homfrays'

BEER IS THE DRINK OF THE BRITON. THE ATHLETIC MAN WHO USES UP HIS ENERGY IN FEATS OF ENDURANCE NEEDS A DRINK WHICH IS HEALTHFUL AND REFRESHING AND

BEER is brewed from the finest materials and is sold at a reasonable price. Why take tablets for your digestion?

● THERE IS NOTHING LIKE BITTER BEER TO ADD TO HIS PLEASURE

IT'S MUCH PLEASANTER TO DRINK ●

WOODSIDE BITTER BEER

15 OCTOBER 1932, v BRADFORD PARK AVENUE (both left); 22 OCTOBER 1932, v MILLWALL (above)
An eclectic mix of promotions here, pushing a performance from the great 'King of the trumpet' Louis Armstrong at the Manchester Hippodrome, as well as strange surgical appliances and beer – which according to this particular brewery is the perfect cure for indigestion. 'Why take tablets?', indeed...

12 SEPTEMBER 1934, v BOLTON WANDERERS
A programme isn't where you'd look now for a new home, but that wasn't the case in 1934. They are 'the "goal" of every keen house buyer'. Yes, very clever.

...and why not add some home improvements with a free-standing garage, among other options? Would you like wood or asbestos? We'll take the wood, thanks.

14 SEPTEMBER 1935, v WOLVES RESERVES
The iconic Mae West has a star on the Hollywood Walk of Fame and was voted the 15th greatest female screen legend of classic cinema by the American Film Institute. And in autumn 1935 she was starring in Manchester cinemas.

3 OCTOBER 1936, v ARSENAL
Horrockses, Crewdson & Co was a fashion firm from Lancashire that regularly appeared in the pages of the programme. This advert is for a 'washable, uncrushable' tie – making it ideal for wearing to the football, apparently.

WAKE UP YOUR LIVER BILE

without Calomel—and you'll jump out of bed in the morning full of vim and vigour.

THE LIVER should pour out two pints of liquid bile into your bowels daily. If this bile is not flowing freely, your food doesn't digest. It just decays in the bowels. Gas bloats up your stomach. You get constipated. Your whole system is poisoned and you feel sour, sunk, and the world looks punk.

Laxatives help a little, but a mere bowel movement doesn't get at the cause. It takes those good old CARTERS Brand LITTLE LIVER PILLS to get these two pints of bile flowing freely and make you feel "up and up." Harmless, gentle, yet amazing in making bile flow freely. Ask for CARTERS LITTLE LIVER PILLS. Stubbornly refuse anything else. 1/3 and 3/- or trial packages for 1d.

TUNE IN *to Radio Luxembourg, Sundays at 11-15 a.m.; Radio Normandy* Sundays at 2-45 p.m.*

*Transmission arranged through the International Broadcasting Company Limited.

26 JANUARY 1938, v BARNSLEY

Any advert that begins with the words 'The liver should pour out two pints of liquid bile into your bowels daily,' is certain to grab any reader's attention. And according to this ad, Calomel is the number one answer to making sure that happens.

Also against Barnsley, a promotion for something a little more family-friendly (well, unless clowns give your kids nightmares, that is) – roll on up for a menagerie of exotic animals from around the globe, coming to Manchester in 1938.

24 SEPTEMBER 1938, v CHELSEA

Know your audience! This advert is definitely aimed at the youngsters, fronted by a host of Disney's biggest characters of the time urging locals to come and see them on the big screen, (alongside some boring stuff for Mum and Dad to watch).

WHAT ABOUT IT, DAD?

You like Football . . . The Kiddies love the Circus

TREAT THEM TO THIS GREAT SHOW

BELLE VUE

MAMMOTH XMAS

CIRCUS

Now in Full Swing!

TWICE DAILY

2.30 & 7.30

GIGANTIC PROGRAMME OF

18 INTERNATIONAL ALL-STAR ACTS

with SENSATIONAL WILD ANIMAL ACT "THE JUNGLE"

LIONS, TIGER, JAGUAR, HYENAS, BEARS, DOGS . . . PETTOLITTI'S

21 LIBERTY HORSES

A Host of Fun-making Clowns, and World-famous Circus Artistes.

ADMISSION (Including Tax)

ADULTS -	1/3	2/-	2/6
CHILDREN -	9d.	1/-	1/3

Reserved Seats

ADULTS 3/6 CHILDREN 2/-

NOTE: No Reduced Prices for Saturday Evening Performances.

Seats Bookable Belle Vue (East 1331) Cooks', Lewis's and Midland Hotel.

FREE PONY RIDES FOR KIDDIES IN THE RING BEFORE EACH PERFORMANCE

Featuring in the same 1938 Chelsea issue, readers are told that a good coat to keep you warm and dry is an essential piece of the matchday inventory. No furry hoods and chunky zips back in those days, though – that bowler hat wouldn't even keep your ears warm standing on the Stretford End!

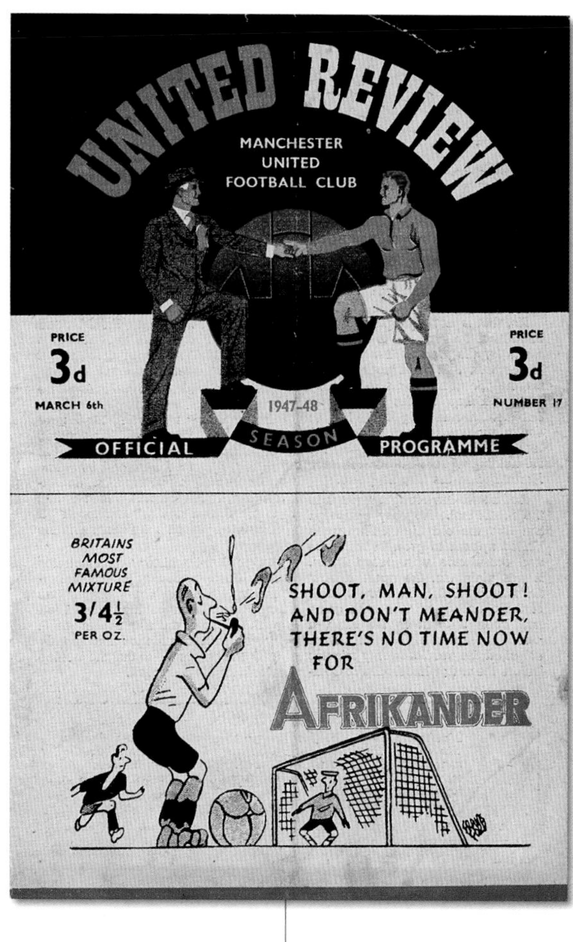

6 MARCH 1948, v SUNDERLAND

A sign of the times as radios begin to become more prominent in advertising, with the medium going on to become greatly associated with football – especially at 5pm on a Saturday afternoon.

In the same programme, Afrikander gets creative on the *United Review* cover to promote its popular tobacco products. In the 1940s, nearly two-thirds of males over the age of 16 enjoyed a puff, making for some very hazy terraces at the football.

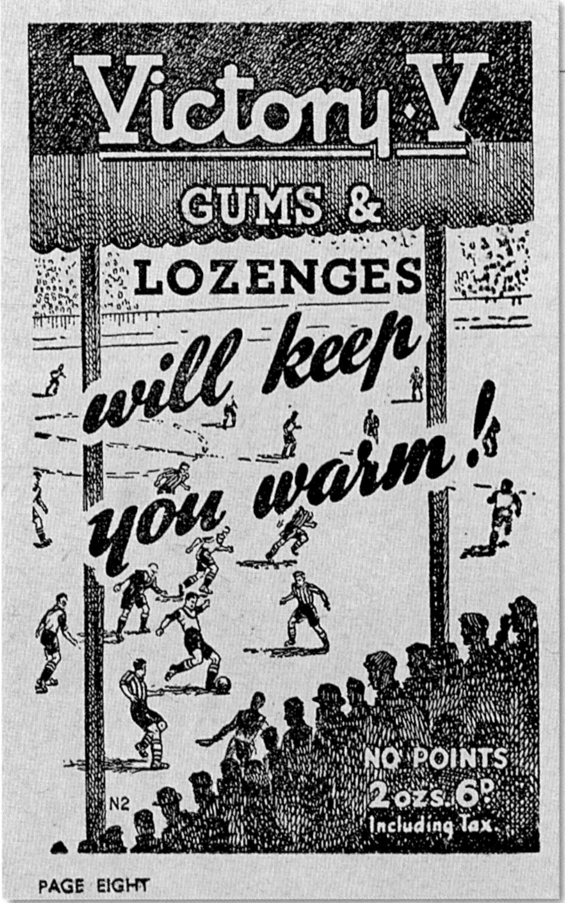

When fans weren't smoking, they'd often enjoy a throat sweet to warm the cockles. This advert – also from the Sunderland issue in 1948 – appeared at a time when fans were packing out football stadiums following the end of the Second World War.

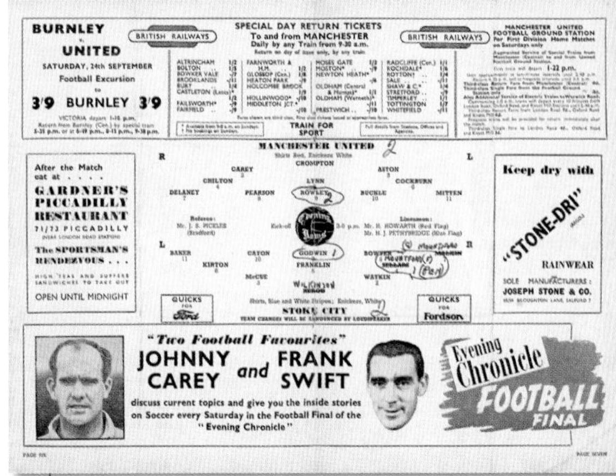

17 SEPTEMBER 1949, v STOKE CITY
More train travel promotions, as well as pushing the writing talents of former Red Johnny Carey and Frank Swift, a legendary goalkeeper-turned-journalist who would tragically die in the Munich Air Disaster.

20 MARCH 1948, v WOLVES
Herbs and Honey sounds pleasant enough for half-time, but we're not sure it would beat a meat pie and a Bovril...

In the same issue, news of an exclusive inside-track from United's chief scout Louis Rocca, who had sat down with the *Evening Chronicle* to share some first-hand insights.

Secrets of MANCHESTER UNITED

GRAND FOOTBALL SERIES
By LOUIS ROCCA

Fifty-five years with Manchester United, and now the club's chief scout, Louis Rocca reveals "behind the scenes" stories of the famous "Reds". Every United supporter will want to read this fascinating series now appearing every Saturday exclusively in the

Evening Chronicle

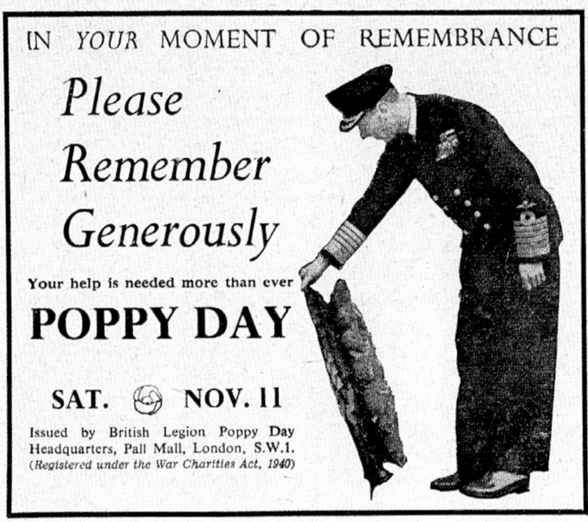

4 NOVEMBER 1950, v BURNLEY
In the week before Remembrance Day, a tribute to those who made the ultimate sacrifice – this box-out appearing just five years after the end of the Second World War.

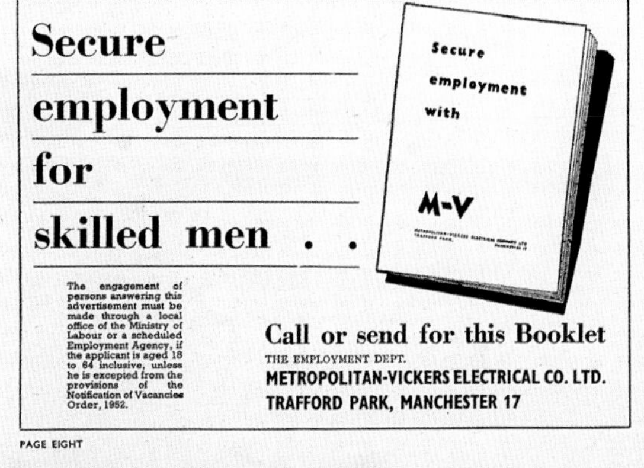

26 AUGUST 1953, v WEST BROMWICH ALBION
The post-war economic boom led to job adverts aplenty. Here, a chance to spark off a new career at Metropolitan-Vickers Electrical, based at nearby Trafford Park.

9 SEPTEMBER 1953, v MIDDLESBROUGH
A story not to miss as legendary United boss Matt Busby opens up on his eye for a player and how he identifies new signings – exclusively in *The People*.

Don't miss your . . .

Charles Buchan's

FOOTBALL

MONTHLY

★

The world's greatest soccer magazine

Packed with pictures and exciting articles

Ask at the paper-shop for YOUR copy without delay

17 SEPTEMBER 1955, v PRESTON NORTH END
Considered Britain's first true football magazine, *Charles Buchan's Football Monthly* ran for just under 23 years before its final edition in June 1974. Buchan himself was a former professional, capped six times by England and who was prolific for Sunderland and Arsenal before becoming a magazine editor.

21 NOVEMBER 1959, v LUTON TOWN
The chance to hire a company who helped build part of Old Trafford – Edward Wood. The future executive vice-chairman would surely approve...

INTERNATIONAL MATCH

ENGLAND v SCOTLAND

Saturday, 15th April

WEMBLEY 57/-

Piccadilly depart 10-30 . . . . Return Wembley Central 17-40

(LIGHT REFRESHMENTS AVAILABLE)

FARE - Inclusive of Luncheon on outward journey - Dinner on return and Coffee - 103/-

Bookings strictly Regulated | **British Rail** | **Reserve your seat in advance**

28 MARCH 1967, v FULHAM
This game would be England's first defeat since winning the World Cup the previous summer, with British Rail offering seat reservations and light refreshments for the Wembley day-trip.

25 FEBRUARY 1970, v MIDDLESBROUGH
Car dealership chain Lookers were previously very closely linked with the Austin Motor brand... almost as much as United are linked with football! Nah, doesn't really roll off the tongue, does it?

13 AUGUST 1969, v EVERTON
A glimpse into the Manchester nightlife courtesy of Mecca Ltd. Mecca is best known for its bingo halls, but it's doubtful that anyone got their dauber marker out at any of these three establishments.

Good luck to United!

from the

all stars team

you can be sure of them!

Edited by SIDNEY F. WICKS LTD., Manchester M1 1HJ
Printed by DIRECT PRINTING LTD., Manchester M14 5TF

15 AUGUST 1970, v LEEDS UNITED
Wilf McGuinness's Reds get the backing of Shell Oil for a big game against our fierce rivals from Yorkshire. Did it work? Unfortunately not, as we lost this Old Trafford season-opener by a single goal.

4 SEPTEMBER 1971, v IPSWICH TOWN
Plenty of bargains to be had at the club's souvenir shop. In the years before the vast, shiny Megastore first opened its doors, it could be an almighty squeeze to get to the tills on a matchday.

THE RED DEVILS SOUVENIR SHOP
OLD TRAFFORD • MANCHESTER 16

JUST ARRIVED ! ! !

M.U.F.C. FOOTBALL DIARY 71/72 25p. (30p post paid)

UNITED'S OWN STICK GAS LIGHTER
(Club Crest Engraved) 75p. (80p. post paid)

NEW SEASON 71/72 HAND POLISHED GOLD PLATE METAL BADGE 25p. (30p. post paid)

UNITED PLAYER BADGE,
Hand Polished Gold Plate 25p. (30p. post paid)

SPECIAL LARGE STRETFORD ENDER HAND POLISHED GOLD PLATE BADGE 30p. (35p. post paid)

F.A. OFFICIAL YEAR BOOK, 1971/72 35p. (40p. post paid)

FOOTBALL LEAGUE YEAR BOOK, 1971/72 90p. (£1·00 post paid)

Send s.a.e. for latest lists.

PAGE TEN

MANCHESTER UNITED DEVELOPMENT ASSOCIATION

Office: FOOTBALL GROUND, OLD TRAFFORD, MANCHESTER, 16
Telephone: 061-872 4676 and 5208

Committee: Mr. L. C. EDWARDS *(Chairman)*, Mr. J. A. GIBSON, Mr. W. A. YOUNG, Mr. D. D. HAROUN, J.P. Sir MATT BUSBY, C.B.E.

Secretary: Mr. W. D. BURKE
Organiser: Mr. F. E. DIXON *Admin. and Ticket Manager:* Mr. W. HOWELL

NEW AGENTS 1977-78

- **MONTHLY DRAW FOR A NEW SALOON CAR**
- **DRAW for 10 PORTABLE RADIOS EACH WEEK**
- **10% EXPENSES ON ALL STAKE MONEY**
- **10% BONUS ON ALL OUTRIGHT WINNERS**

We are accepting applications for Agents for 1977-78 Season. It is only necessary for you to complete the application form below in order that full details may be sent to you. Only 10 Members are required to commence an Agency. No obligation is incurred upon enquiry.

To the Organiser, Manchester United Development Association,
Manchester United Football Ground, Old Trafford, Manchester 16.

I am interested in becoming an Agent for the Manchester United Development Association for the Season 1977-78, and would be pleased if you would send me full particulars as soon as possible (I am over 18 years of age). No obligation is incurred.

NAME *(Block letters)* ....

ADDRESS ....

....

THIS DOES NOT APPLY TO EXISTING AGENTS

14 MAY 1977, v ARSENAL
The Manchester United Development Association was set up to help generate funds for work on Old Trafford. There were some good prizes on offer, too...

Also against Arsenal, a definite conversation starter here! There are plenty of photo combinations, too, with the ability to rearrange the slides.

RED DEVILS SOUVENIR PHOTOBELT OFFER!

It's unique—it's United!

Individual photo-slides of all your first team players on a fabulous black belt with chromium buckle.

Each slide shows player in coloured team strip with an individually printed autograph.

Slides can be arranged in any order and the belt fits any waist size.

HURRY WHILE STOCKS LAST!

Red Devils Souvenir Belt Offer!

Send £2.00 Cheque/Postal Order made payable to Seekgrove Limited. Allow 7 - 14 days for delivery.

Post to:- Seekgrove Limited, Arrowscroft Mill, Hollingworth, Via Hyde. Tameside.

Name ....

Address ....

....

Get a pair of hard wearing, well fitting jeans with the club name embroidered for all to see. Made in top quality denim by Banner.

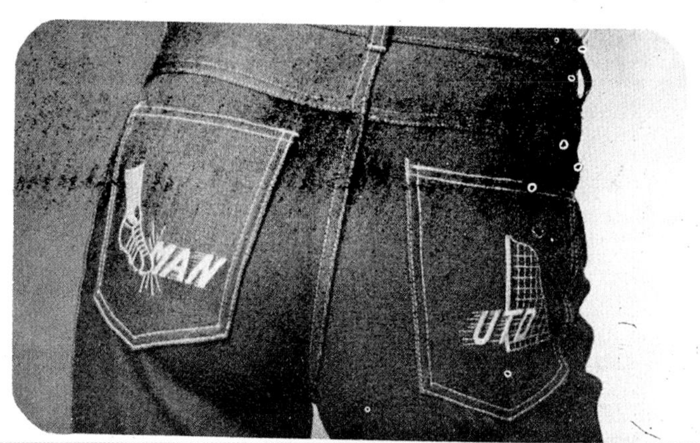

TAYLOR + CROSS
31/33 STAMFORD NEW ROAD
ALTRINCHAM
PRESTWICH CO-OP SOCIETY
TOWN BUILDINGS PRESTWICH
AMIN STORES
81/83 BANK STREET
RAWTENSTALL ROSSENDALE
K + A MENS + BOYS WEAR
163 LANGWORTHY ROAD SALFORD
MR CUPPELLO
1152 ROCHDALE ROAD
HIGHER BLACKLEY MANCHESTER
JAMES STEWART
3 BRUNSWICK STREET
ARDWICK GREEN MANCHESTER
HAZEL GROVE CO-OP SOCIETY
104 LONDON ROAD HAZEL GROVE
STOCKPORT
MOTLERS
113 LIVERPOOL ROAD PATRICROFT

2 SEPTEMBER 1978, v EVERTON
Show your support for the Reds in style – and comfort – with these United-branded jeans. It would have been nice to have seen a bit more than just someone's backside, though – are these tight-fit or a flared finish?

3 NOVEMBER 1979, v SOUTHAMPTON
The year 1978 signalled a full century of Manchester United Football Club. You can't go wrong with an ornamental plate to mark such an occasion, which the club were still promoting the following season.

4 SEPTEMBER 1985, v NEWCASTLE UNITED
Make the big game that little bit more special with a VIP executive package – a unique experience that after starting small has since become a major part of matchday at Old Trafford.

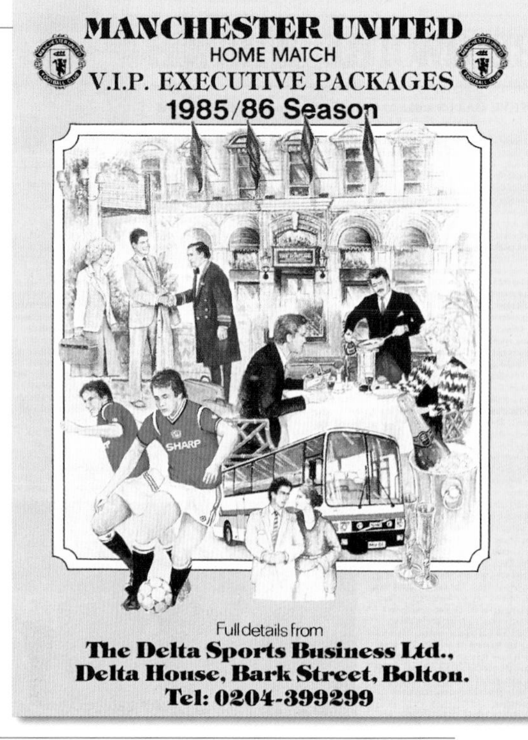

SOUVENIR SHOP

Visit the official souvenir shop, now situated in brand new premises alongside the Development Association Office.
Hundreds of gifts and souvenirs available, including . . .
. . . 'Touch and Go' Steve Coppell's autobiography.
Also in stock, FA Cup Final sweatshirts 18″ (£5) to ex-large £9.
Personal callers are welcome and the shop is open weekdays from 9.30 am to 4.30 pm.
A comprehensive Mail Order Service is also offered and out-of-town supporters should send a stamped addressed envelope for a full list of items available.

Telephone enquiries, please ring (061) 872 3398.

29 OCTOBER 1985, v WEST HAM UNITED
Another plug for the souvenir shop, including a visit from former winger Steve Coppell to sign copies of his autobiography, *Touch and Go*.

26 SEPTEMBER 1987, v TOTTENHAM HOTSPUR
Sharp had its name emblazoned across the chest of the United players for close to two decades, with the electronics firm becoming synonymous with the Reds until the turn of the century.

9 MAY 1988, v WIMBLEDON

The perfect way to deck out your bedroom, where you can dream of leading MUFC to glory. We like to think there are still a few grown-up Reds out there sleeping under these fine covers each night...

26 FEBRUARY 1992, v CHELSEA

Our 1991 Cup Winners' Cup triumph was one to savour, particularly if you could get your hands on a limited print of the final's two-goal hero, Mark Hughes.

19 AUGUST 1989, v ARSENAL

Before social media, one way to keep up-to-date on all the latest news and rumours was Clubcall. The one drawback was its price – 38p per minute equates to a half-pint of lager every 60 seconds in 1989, and there's not even a reminder here to 'get permission from whoever pays the phone bill'!

28 OCTOBER 1995, v MIDDLESBROUGH
Proof that United were really starting to pop, both on and off the pitch in the '90s. We're not too sure the ad designers got the colours right, however – and what do the three stars represent: average reviews for the 'premier' fizzy drink?

3 JANUARY 1999, v MIDDLESBROUGH
As every Red knows, 'Yip Jaap Stam is a big Dutchman'... so we had to make sure the club's Megastore was big enough, too.

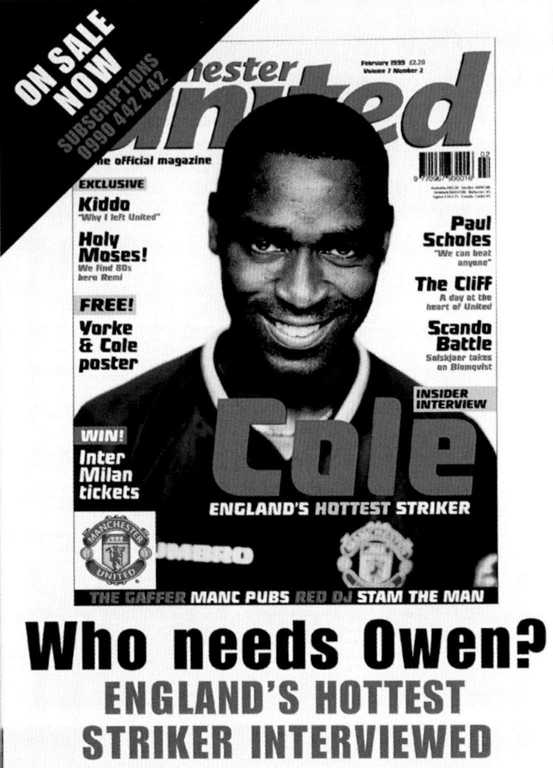

3 FEBRUARY 1999, v DERBY COUNTY
A cheeky dig at a certain rival frontman in a '90s edition of the club's official magazine (not that it put the Liverpool striker off joining us years later!)

11 AUGUST 1999, v SHEFFIELD WEDNESDAY
A new way to follow the Reds around the world arrived in the late '90s, with the launch of the club's own TV channel, MUTV. The first broadcast came in September 1998, with the Treble success leading to a spike in sign-ups.

13 SEPTEMBER 2000, v ANDERLECHT
As technology continued to develop, new shirt sponsors Vodafone helped give fans the chance to stay updated on the go through their mobile phones.

29 SEPTEMBER 1999, v MARSEILLE
Fans flocked from far and wide to see our Treble collection up close in person with a special exhibition in the Old Trafford Museum.

GET SCORES ON YOUR MOBILE
SCHOLES 18
WAP!
REGISTER AT manUmobile.com
vodafone

11 NOVEMBER 2000, v MIDDLESBROUGH
The 1999/2000 campaign provided the basis for the club's first official feature-length film, *Beyond the Promised Land*. Although the DVD format was starting to gain momentum, the trusted VHS cassette still proved very popular.

ACCEPT NO SUBSTITUTES!

THE OFFICIAL MANCHESTER UNITED MOVIE
Manchester United Beyond The Promised Land

OFFICIAL MOVIE
NO FAN SHOULD BE WITHOUT IT!

excite. OWN IT ON VIDEO AND DVD FROM 27th NOVEMBER AT WOOLWORTHS

2 NOVEMBER 2002, v SOUTHAMPTON
The Red Cafe, located in the Sir Alex Ferguson Stand, remains a popular place to grab a bite to eat at Old Trafford, and it has celebrated some iconic United no.7s over the years.

THE ULTIMATE EXPERIENCE

THE NEW QUADRANTS

• Tickets to ALL Home Matches
• Luxurious Facilities

CALL: 0870 442 1994
(Option 1)

26 MARCH 2006, v BIRMINGHAM CITY
Fans are offered an all-new experience at the Theatre of Dreams, with expansions to the north-west and north-east quadrants increasing the stadium's overall capacity by around 8,000 seats.

8 MARCH 2008, v PORTSMOUTH
Supporters can get even closer to their beloved United by becoming an official club member – with more Reds now choosing to sign up over the internet, rather than ring up the ticket office.

31 JANUARY 2009, v EVERTON
United were crowned world champions at the end of 2008, with plenty more big games to look forward to upon our return from Yokohama, en route to a third straight Premier League title.

Elsewhere in the Everton programme, Manchester United Foundation – which was founded three years earlier in 2006 – shows how it had already helped countless youngsters from across the region. The club's associated charity has to continued to grow and inspire people to build a better life for themselves.

CHAPTER 8

Match action

Before the days of rolling sports news channels, satellite television and the never-ending internet experience, the matchday programme was *the* place to get the lowdown on how United had performed last time out...

For the modern fan, football is an intravenous experience. Through the advent of online coverage and social media plus the evolution of live broadcasting, a supporter would now have to entirely disconnect themselves from their daily routine to avoid discovering their team's results – and all others from around the grounds – within moments of the final whistle, regardless of their location and time zone.

It was in light of those advancements that *United Review* scaled back its reports from the Reds' previous matches in the late 2010s. Why tell people what they've already learned, digested and departed days or weeks earlier? Until that point, however, the programme's devotion to detailing the team's every single outing had been on the rise for a century.

Back in the 1910s and 1920s, the programme's editor would cover off United's most recent fixture with an account in his latest column. Initially this was purely a text article where the author's words were the sole clue as to what had unfolded on the pitch. Images were restricted to pen pics illustrating players named within articles. Moving into the 1930s, however, readers' imaginations were bolstered by occasional match images, which would appear courtesy of a local newspaper – usually the *Manchester Chronicle* or *Manchester Evening News*. The presence of this editorial crutch gave the programme an altogether classier feel.

The increase in imagery became a staple part of the match action round-up over time, with a steady rise throughout the 1940s. By the end of the 1960s, these action shots had taken centre-stage, replacing adverts on *United Review*'s front cover to further increase the match-centric feel within the whole programme.

Above: Alex Stepney gathers the ball as photographers watch on during a pre-season friendly at Craven Cottage in August 1971

REDS HIT BURNLEY FOR SEVEN
United skipper, Bryan Robson, sets our stall out early on as he opens the scoring with goal number one after just 12 seconds.
Young Mark Hughes then turned the match into a personal triumph with a super hat-trick – see goals two, three and four.
With a solid 4-0 lead from the first leg, United journeyed to Turf Moor two weeks later and promptly took up where they left off!
Alan Brazil made his mark on the tie with his first 'brace' and then 'stands back in amazement' as Jesper Olsen scores arguably the pick of the seven from what seemed an impossible angle.

16

17

United's derby-day victory in 2019/20 was watched by more than 73,000 people inside Old Trafford, as well as millions more around the world

A picture special with a difference following our aggregate cup win against Burnley in 1984/85

Entire pages – mostly photo-led – were soon devoted to the action from the Reds' recent games, providing readers with shots from encounters which had taken place between home programmes; an intriguing insight at a time when TV coverage was still virtually non-existent.

While families could count on the annual event of watching the FA Cup final live from Wembley, the BBC didn't screen a live league match until 1983 – coincidentally United v Tottenham – and until the Premier League era began in August 1992, the *Review*'s match images were the only visual alternative to attending every single game and hoping that United featured on *Match of the Day*'s highlights package.

In the mid-1990s, then-editor Cliff Butler began writing full match reports for each game; accounts which would later be repurposed and published in the club's official Yearbook as a chronicle of the entire season's work. This coverage continued to grow as of 2003, when recent matches were allocated two or three pages in each edition of *United Review*. As well as reflecting on the Reds' displays, the articles would also act as scene-setters for that day's fixture, taking on more of a holistic approach rather than a blow-by-blow account of events.

With a sense of completionism in mind, each issue of *United Review* across the course of a season would collectively contain reports from every single fixture, until the end of the 2010s when the unavoidability of action prompted the editorial decision to scale back coverage of previous matches. Big fixtures and key results still tend to get a more detailed post-mortem, however, as the *Review* retains a keen eye on events on the field.

Play and Players

A SET-BACK AT FULHAM, BUT PROMOTION STRUGGLE STILL VERY OPEN—NEW FORWARD FROM LEICESTER—NEXT SATURDAY'S CUP-TIE.

MOST of us expected at least one point from Fulham last Saturday, but the "Cottagers" played the more convincing football and merited their success. It can rain "some" in Manchester, as most of my readers well know, but that rainstorm in London on Saturday has got us whacked to a frazzle.

"Sunny South," indeed! The ground at Craven Cottage is well covered with grass, and had the weather been at all propitious, it might have suited our play. But the rain rendered the ground tremendously heavy and Fulham adapted themselves to the conditions admirably.

Therein lies the fundamental cause of their success, and by their failure to realise that the conditions called for something different to "pretty pretty" football our men contributed to their own defeat. Full credit must be given to the Londoners for their victory.

They were a well-balanced side, strong in defence and virile in attack; a side that certainly belied their lowly position in the table. It is a remarkable fact that whereas in the First Division of the League a margin of 22 points separates the top and bottom clubs, the corresponding difference in the Second Division only amounts to 14 points.

fascination. Fulham, at the time of writing, are second from bottom in the League, but their home record is not at all bad.

They certainly played well on Saturday. The recent acquisition of Edmonds from Wolverhampton Wanderers has been eminently successful, for he has already scored nine goals for his new club. In getting three against us he proved a very smart opportunist.

There was not much to choose between us for the first 25 minutes or so. Indeed, we might easily have gone ahead.

Then Edmonds got two goals in as many minutes, an experience which naturally took a lot of "fight" out of our men. Still, there was a chance when, soon after resuming, Lochhead reduced the lead, but Edmonds clinched matters with a third goal.

AN OFF DAY.

There can be no disguising the fact that the team had an off day and that the points went to the better side. Andy Ducat, the Surrey cricketer and international half-back, played a sterling game in his new position as full back.

26 JANUARY 1924, v FULHAM
The *United Review* editor had plenty to say about the team's defeat away to Fulham the week before, and was forthright in his views regarding the Reds' inability to get stuck in and deal with a west London downpour. The return match between the sides at Old Trafford ended 0-0.

12 SEPTEMBER 1934, v BOLTON WANDERERS
This early action shot sees United goalkeeper Jack Hacking diving to keep out Barnsley striker Andrews. The Reds won this Second Division home clash 4-1, before losing to Bolton.

HACKING SAVES FROM ANDREWS (Barnsley)

"Photo by courtesy of Allied Newspapers, Manchester."

FIRST DIVISION SHOVE! Bamford and Laking (Wolverhampton Wanderers) racing for possession in the United v. Wanderers Match. We are indebted to the "Evening Chronicle" Football Edition for this photograph.

9 SEPTEMBER 1936,
v HUDDERSFIELD TOWN

The match photographer captured a full-blooded moment in the 1936/37 Division One opener between United and Wolves at Old Trafford, printed in the next issue for the visit of Huddersfield. A good old-fashioned shoulder challenge!

19 SEPTEMBER 1936,
v SHEFFIELD WEDNESDAY

The Manchester derby has always been a huge draw, and this image was taken at United's 3-2 win over City at Old Trafford in front of 68,796 fans... and a few more perched on the roof of the stand.

REDWOOD KEEPS 'EM OUT! Our right back checks a City raid last Saturday. Note the supporters obtaining a bird's eye view of the Game. Photo by courtesy of the "Evening Chrônicle," Football Edition.

20 MARCH 1948, v WOLVERHAMPTON WANDERERS

United's first-ever trip to Wembley had been secured thanks to a 3-1 semi-final win over Derby at Hillsborough in March, which was given the pictorial treatment for the next programme, against Wolves.

THE SEMI-FINAL
UNITED v. DERBY
Saturday, March 13th, 1948

Photos by Courtesy of: The Manchester Evening News

(Left). Pearson (on extreme right) scores the first of the three goals for United. The other players (left to right) are Morris, Howe, Leuty, Mitten, Mozley and Wallace.

(Right). Howe runs across to intercept a centre from Pearson during a United attack on the Derby goal. Mitten is on extreme left.

(Left). Howe, of Derby County, clears as Rowley runs up to challenge.

(Right). United supporters ringed by Derby supporters prior to the kick-off.

PAGE NINE

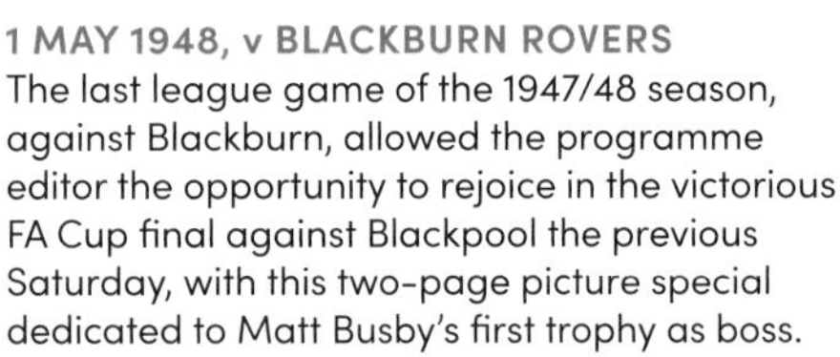

1 MAY 1948, v BLACKBURN ROVERS

The last league game of the 1947/48 season, against Blackburn, allowed the programme editor the opportunity to rejoice in the victorious FA Cup final against Blackpool the previous Saturday, with this two-page picture special dedicated to Matt Busby's first trophy as boss.

Right: H.M. The King shakes hands with Chilton before the match.

Above: Matt Busby leads the team on to the field.

Left: Johnston shakes hands with Carey before C. J. Barrick, the referee.

Below: Rowley scores United's first equaliser.

Above: Carey is carried off the field by Cockburn, Mitten and Crompton after the presentation by H.M. The King at Wembley Stadium, April 24th, 1948.

Left: H.M. The King presents the F.A. Cup to Carey.

Delaney and Hayward in a tackle for the ball.

Above: Robinson fails to save from Pearson, giving United the third goal at 4.31 p.m.

Right: Anderson and Chilton sandwich Mortensen in heading duel.

Below: A header by Mitten beats Robinson but goes over the bar whilst Shimwell (extreme right) watches.

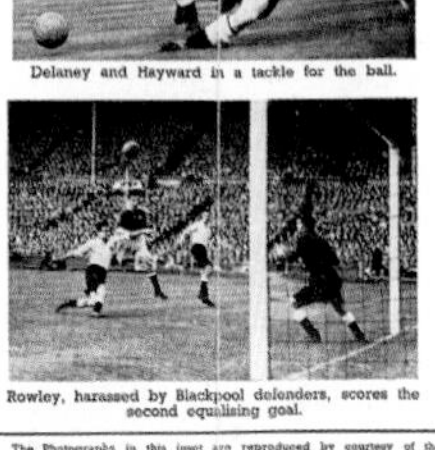

Rowley, harassed by Blackpool defenders, scores the second equalising goal.

The Photographs in this issue are reproduced by courtesy of the Daily Graphic, Manchester Evening Chronicle and Manchester Evening News.

ATTACK versus DEFENCE by Stanley Pearson

Again the courtesy of the "Daily Mail" has enabled us to reproduce these splendid pictures—this time Stan Pearson shows us a short cut to goal. Cameraman Peter Howard was responsible for the photographs and Eric Thompson writes:—

(Top left): Ball is bouncing across Pearson to his opponent, and the situation could lead to a clashing of bodies and a tangle of disputing legs. Pearson's left foot hooks the ball—"you're coming my way." (Lower left): Full-back's left-foot attempt to intercept this move comes too late, and Pearson is running on to the ball, eyes fixed on it. Note that a Pearson infield touch would have been thankfully received by covering defender in the background. (Top right): Defender, quick to follow, also gives a reminder about keeping eyes on the ball, but he has to turn, and Pearson wins the lead he needs. Still no time for dallying. (Lower right): From the nicely balanced action of that opening left hook, Pearson is now poised to bring the right foot into action for a quick centre—rest depends on anticipation of team-mates.

29 APRIL 1950, v FULHAM
This detailed set of four images perfectly captured United forward's Stan Pearson's personal duel with an unnamed Portsmouth full-back, with in-depth captions by writer Eric Thompson describing the scene...

26 DECEMBER 1952, v BLACKPOOL
Who doesn't love a win over Liverpool at Anfield? The programme editor made sure the Boxing Day issue versus Blackpool carried pics from our 2-1 win from the previous fortnight...

Photo by courtesy of Kemsley Newspapers Ltd.

Liverpool v. United at Anfield, 13th December, 1952. All heads up in the Liverpool goalmouth, as centre-half Jones just reaches the ball before United players Doherty (No. 8) and Pearson (No. 10). Interested onlooker is centre-forward Aston.

EUROPEAN CUP COMPETITION · UNITED v. BILBAO · February 6th, 1957

Left.
United's first goal after 42 minutes . . . centre we see Viollet's shot beating Spanish goalie Carmelo to his knees.

Right.
United's second goal after 60 minutes . . . Viollet acclaims the shot from Tommy Taylor that left Carmelo on the ground.

Left.
This time Carmelo has things his own way and leaps above Viollet to punch away the ball that could have made the winning goal.

So there it is. Another match passes into history. But a match that will be remembered by 65,000 spectators in Manchester as the match of the decade. A match that hoisted Britain's soccer prestige . . . and a match that won us the whole-hearted admiration of our worthy opponents . . . Atletico de Bilbao of Spain.

We acknowledge the courtesy of the "Daily Mail" for allowing us to print these splendid pictures.

PAGE TEN

16 FEBRUARY 1957, v EVERTON

United fans were loving the club's first foray into European competition in 1956/57, watching 10 goals sail in at home (Maine Road, not Old Trafford) against Anderlecht, three against Borussia Dortmund in the next round and another three in the European Cup quarter-final at home to Athletic Bilbao, as showcased in this programme for a Division One clash with Everton.

UNITED REVIEW

MANCHESTER UNITED FOOTBALL CLUB

MANCHESTER UNITED v CHARLTON ATHLETIC

Kick-off 3-0 pm

6th October

4d.

NUMBER 6

1956-57

OFFICIAL SEASON PROGRAMME

UNITED v. ANDERLECHT

Maine Road, September 26th, 1956.

We thank the "Daily Mail" and cameraman John Smart for permission to reproduce these "under the floodlights" incidents of the return match with the Belgian champions in the preliminary round of the European Cup Competition.

Left, we see Taylor running in to score goal number six, with De Koster and Week on the deck. Bottom left shows Viollet netting number eight with Week prostrate before his goal. Bottom right was the scene as Berry scored our ninth. Final score: United 10 Anderlecht 0.

16 FEBRUARY 1959, v MANCHESTER CITY

This programme was produced for a derby that enjoyed five goals – thankfully four for United – but the issue highlighted a recent eight-goal thriller with Newcastle that saw the spoils shared between the Reds and the Magpies.

VINTAGE FOOTBALL — United v. Newcastle, 31st January, 1959.

When vintage football is played memories alone can become inaccurate. Fortunately a photographer recorded the eight great goals which made this match a classic draw. Through the courtesy of the "**Sunday Express**" United's pictures are printed — doubtless our Newcastle friends have similar intentions!

1 No mistake about this penalty by Charlton — Harvey is virtually helpless.
2 Quixall dribbles round Harvey — to score a fine goal from an acute angle.
3 Scanlon shoots past Newcastle full-back McMichael.
4 The impetus of Viollet's shot makes him join Newcastle's full-back Keith and keeper Harvey already prostrate in the penalty area!

PAGE THREE

22 OCTOBER 1960, v NEWCASTLE UNITED

As United continued to rebuild post-Munich, the club's friendship with Real Madrid led to a series of high-profile friendlies between the two European giants. The third of five ties, held at Old Trafford in the autumn of 1960 and covered in this Newcastle programme, ended 3-2 to Real.

18 NOVEMBER 1967, v SOUTHAMPTON

George Best – ever the man for the big occasion – was the hero of the hour for United in this trip to Anfield, with his double in our 2-1 win commemorated in the next issue of *United Review.*

GREGG

VIDAL BRENNAN

THAT GAME!

United v. Real Madrid

October 13th, 1960

United 2 — Real Madrid 3

Top left

Vidal of Madrid secures Real's second goal from a pass by Puskas.

Daily Express picture

Centre

Real Madrid's Marquitos pushes a long shot towards the United goal. Bobby Charlton (extreme left). Gregg extreme right.

Daily Mail picture

Bottom left

Di Stefano puts Real Madrid one up.

Daily Express picture

Bottom right

Gregg collects a high corner from Gento as Canario jumps high for the ball.

Manchester Evening News picture

PAGE FIVE

LIVERPOOL v. MANCHESTER UNITED, November 11th, 1967.

United's splendid victory at Anfield brought us to the top of the table and ended Liverpool's unbeaten home record. Best scored both United's goals – here's the first flashing over the head of Liverpool 'keeper Lawrence with Byrne (No. 3) a helpless spectator. Hunt scored for the home side.

Photo by courtesy of the Sunday Express

1

2

5

THE GREATEST OF THEM ALL?

3

May 29th, 1968. The night of the European Cup Final at Wembley. The night United beat Benfica of Lisbon by four goals to one. We thank the Manchester Evening News for allowing us to reproduce these memorable pictures of what has been acclaimed as United's greatest ever game of football. United 4 – Benfica 1.

1. United's first goal – a header from Charlton.
2. Best puts United 2-1 up in extra time.
3. Fourth for United – the second from Charlton.
4. Birthday celebration for Kidd – No. 3 for United.
5. At last! Skipper Charlton receives the coveted cup.
6. "The Boss" gets a victory hug from Foulkes and Crerand.

6

4

10 AUGUST 1968, v EVERTON

United entered the 1968/69 season as England's first European champions and naturally took the opportunity in that season's opening programme against Everton to celebrate that glorious May night at Wembley. And aptly, the 2-1 win over the Toffees came courtesy of goals from two of the Wembley heroes, George Best and Bobby Charlton.

F.A. CUP 5th ROUND, NORTHAMPTON v. UNITED

Best's back . . . with a vengeance!

At the Northampton v. United 5th round cup tie, Best scored a record-equalling 6 goals with Kidd adding another two against Northampton's 2-goal reply. The picture below shows Best after scoring his first and right a picture that sums it all up – a smile of admiration from Northampton 'keeper Kim Book after Best's 6th.

Photographs by the Sunday Express.

14 FEBRUARY 1970, v CRYSTAL PALACE

The headline says it all! The Reds enjoyed a league date with Palace a week after Georgie had torn Northampton to shreds in the Cup with six goals in a remarkable 8-2 fifth-round victory.

MANCHESTER UNITED 3, MANCHESTER CITY 3, November 6th, 1971.
Despite a six-goal battle of the giants the match was made the more memorable by the debut of 17-year-old Sammy McIlroy who was hoisted from the reserves a few hours before kick-off. McIlroy opens the scoring with his first League goal *(Above)*. Alex Stepney foils them again – with yet another superb save from the Maine Road attack *(Left)*.
Both pictures by the "Sunday Express".

Steve James, Brian Kidd, Alan Gowling and Bobby Charlton effectively neutralise an attack by City's Wyn Davies.
Photograph by "Manchester Evening News".

PAGE FIVE

13 NOVEMBER 1971, v TOTTENHAM HOTSPUR

Young Sammy McIlroy enjoyed a debut to remember against Manchester City, the 17-year-old scoring in the 3-3 draw at Maine Road. A week later he made it two goals in three games, bagging one in this 3-1 win over Spurs at Old Trafford.

LEEDS UNITED 1, MANCHESTER UNITED 2, 11th October, 1975.
A shot from Sammy McIlroy beats the Leeds 'keeper for United's second goal.
Photo courtesy of Mirror Group Newspapers Ltd.

LEEDS UNITED 1, MANCHESTER UNITED 2, 11th October, 1975.
Leeds substitute, Harris, is stopped by Tommy Jackson after making a great break down the wing
Photo by courtesy of "Sunday Express"

112

18 OCTOBER 1975, v ARSENAL

The programme for this match with the Gunners (which ended 3-1 to United) carried a couple of stirring images from the Reds' 2-1 win away at Elland Road in our previous league match, with Docherty's side settling straight back into life in Division One following our year away.

CUP FINAL ACTION

F.A. CUP FINAL
Saturday 12th May 1979
Manchester United 2 Arsenal 3

Left: Brian Talbot scores the opening goal for Arsenal

Below: Stapleton heads Arsenal's second

Right: Gordon McQueen slams in United's first from Joe Jordan's cross

Below Right: Sammy McIlroy shoots past the diving Jennings for United's equaliser

16 MAY 1979, v CHELSEA
There was plenty of Cup final action to digest when United hosted Chelsea in our final game of 1978/79, coming just a few days after the breathless FA Cup showdown at Wembley, with Chelsea's London rivals Arsenal ultimately triumphant.

Will history repeat itself? Last season Spurs lost in the final of the then Football League Cup to you-know-who, but went back to Wembley a few months later to win the FA Cup.

Semi-finals have a reputation for being tense affairs, but fortunately no-one told the players, the result was a match which showed the very best of all that is good about the English game.

Not even the disappontment of Remi Moses' early goal being disallowed and first blood being drawn by Arsenal was enough to shake the conviction that it was to be our day and it was only a matter of time before United struck back. Skipper Bryan Robson led from the front as he beat Brian Talbot to a ball played forward by Arthur Albiston, he turned quickly and gave keeper George Wood no chance as he struck the ball home.

United were now in full flight and Norman Whiteside, the youngest player on the field, had the distinction of scoring a winning goal worthy of the great occasion. He hit a screaming left foot shot that the Arsenal keeper didn't see, let alone get to!

The determination in the United camp was epitomised by the picture of Kevin Moran as he was stretchered off the field late in the game as United moved closer to their sixth Wembley appearance in seven years.

4 5

9 MAY 1983, v LUTON TOWN
Que sera, sera indeed! The Reds had given up hope of catching Liverpool at the top of the table by the time we faced Luton in our last home game of 1982/83, but Big Ron's boys had an FA Cup final against Brighton to look forward to, following this exhilarating semi-final victory over Arsenal at Villa Park.

United travelled to Turin for the second leg of the Cup Winners' Cup semi-final knowing that they faced an uphill battle to reach the final, after drawing the first leg 1-1.
A capacity crowd at the Stadium Comunale provided a 'warm' welcome for the Reds with an incredible pre-match show of colours (above). The scene facing the players as they emerged from the tunnel was both colourful and noisy as the fans let off fire-crackers and smokebombs, (main pic).
Undaunted by the fervour and hysteria of the Italian support, United set about their task with confidence and set the scene for a memorable match by refusing to adopt a defensive approach and Juventus' opening goal came, in fact, from a breakaway as Zbigniew Boniek raced almost half the length of the pitch to put the home side into the lead after 13 minutes (below). Half-time arrived with Juventus still leading and United still attacking.

The pattern in the second half remained unchanged and it seemed only a matter of time before the equaliser came. Norman Whiteside, who replaced the injured Frank Stapleton midway through the second half, was to be the man who put United back on level terms as he swivelled to smash the ball home from close range (top centre), after good work by Paul McGrath (above).
As the match progressed, it seemed more and more likely that if anyone were to grab the winner it would be United. Certainly the feeling in the United camp was one of optimism as extra time became a real possibility with the visitors looking much the stronger of the two sides, in fact United could have gone in front but a fine header by Paul McGrath, deputising for the injured Brian Robson, went narrowly wide. With just 30 seconds remaining our hopes of a trip to Switzerland for the final lay in ruins as Italian World Cup hero, Paulo Rossie, hit the winner after a scramble in the United goalmouth.

SEMI-FINAL
SECOND LEG
JUVENTUS 2
Boniek Rossi
UNITED 1
Whiteside

16 17

7 MAY 1984, v IPSWICH TOWN
United's trip to the Stadio Comunale to face Juventus in the Cup Winners' Cup semi-final was a colourful and dramatic affair, with the Italians squeaking through 2-1 on the night, and 3-2 on aggregate, to book a final date with Porto in Basel. The other losing semi-finalists? Alex Ferguson's Aberdeen.

1-0 2-0 3-0 4-0

REDS HIT BURNLEY FOR SEVEN
United skipper, Bryan Robson, sets our stall out early on as he opens the scoring with goal number one after just 12 seconds.
Young Mark Hughes then turned the match into a personal triumph with a super hat-trick — see goals two, three and four.
With a solid 4-0 lead from the first leg, United journeyed to Turf Moor two weeks later and promptly took up where they left off!
Alan Brazil made his mark on the tie with his first 'brace' and then 'stands back in amazement' as Jesper Olsen scores arguably the pick of the seven from what seemed an impossible angle.

5-0 6-0 7-0

UNITED ACTION

16 17

30 OCTOBER 1984, v EVERTON
When United scored seven against Burnley home and away within a matter of weeks, it inspired the *United Review* designer to get creative with the page layout for the subsequent programme against Everton. Top work!

30 APRIL 1988, v QUEENS PARK RANGERS
The 100th anniversary of the Football League was marked by a rather curious tournament where 16 sides faced off over one knockout weekend at Wembley. United made it to the last four thanks to wins over Luton and Everton, but lost to Sheffield Wednesday at the semi-final stage.

UNITED REVIEW

ONE HUNDREDTH BIRTHDAY PARTY

FOOTBALL LEAGUE MERCANTILE CENTENARY CLASSIC

Saturday 16th April — First Round.
UNITED 2 LUTON TOWN 0
McClair, Davenport

Quarter Final
UNITED 1 EVERTON 0
Bruce

Sunday 17th April — Semi Final
UNITED 1 SHEFFIELD WEDNESDAY 2
Davenport (pen).

Steve Bruce clears his lines.

Liam O'Brien wins the ball easily.

Acrobatics from Chris Turner.

The parade gets under way.

Don't fence us in — or, what it's like to be a fan!

After progressing through to the final stages of the Football League Centenary celebrations at Wembley two weeks ago as one of the few sides who hadn't needed the aid of a penalty shoot-out, we began to fancy our chances of success. Luck wasn't on our side however for a fiercely struck free-kick from just outside the penalty area was ajudged to have struck Bryan Robson on the arm. The resulting penalty helped to see Sheffield Wednesday through to the final against Nottingham Forest and send a dejected United party back home on Sunday tea-time. Better luck next time lads!

8 9

UNITED REVIEW

SPECTACULAR

A packed house, the reigning League Champions as visitors and a 4-1 win to celebrate at the end of ninety-minutes. We couldn't have dreamt of a better opening to the new season.
It was a first-day of spectacular proportions in many ways and it left most of the 47,245 breathless.
Arsenal suffered the setback of having Tony Adams, their skipper and influential defender, substituted in the first few minutes as he felt unwell. But, nevertheless, it is debateable whether even his presence would have made any difference with United in such stunning form.

Main picture: Celebrations all round following Brian McClair's goal.

Above: Mark Hughes crashes home United's second.

Below: Not to be outdone, Neil Webb hits a similar shot as United go 3-1 up.

6 7

30 AUGUST 1989, v NORWICH CITY
The 1989/90 season had got off to a flyer at Old Trafford with United sweeping aside champions Arsenal with a thrilling 4-1 victory. The glorious afternoon was recapped in technicolour inside the next programme, against Norwich.

COLOUR ACTION
FROM PÉCS

Laszlo Bodnar, the Pecsi Munkas goalkeeper, is rooted to the spot as Brian McClair acclaims his 77th minute winner in Pecs.

24 Picture by club photographer Cliff Butler 25

23 OCTOBER 1990, v WREXHAM
'COLOUR ACTION FROM PECS' was not a sentence the *United Review* editor had cause to write before (or indeed since), but so it was as the programme covered our Cup Winners' Cup first-round win in the Hungarian city, setting the Reds on the road to glory.

20 MAY 1991, v TOTTENHAM HOTSPUR
Five days before the Reds rounded off the 1990/91 season at home to Spurs, we enjoyed a dream night in Rotterdam as Alex Ferguson delivered the second trophy of his reign with a Cup Winners' Cup final triumph over Barcelona.

COLOUR ACTION
FROM ROTTERDAM

VICTORY IN EUROPE
Main picture: Steve Bruce heads the ball towards goal for Mark Hughes (not in picture) to apply the final touch. United 1, Barcelona 0.
Above: Hughes again as he cracks our second goal from the tightest of angles.

6 Pictures by Club Photographer Cliff Butler 7

UNITED
PICTURE NEWS

Main picture: Four minutes to go and skipper Steve Bruce puts United on level terms against The Owls.

Inset: Paul Ince is launched into the air by Owls' captain and former United star Viv Anderson.

17 APRIL 1993, v CHELSEA
United's hunt for a long-awaited championship title was still on track when Chelsea came to town, mainly thanks to Steve Bruce's late, late double in the previous home game against Sheffield Wednesday. It was a much more straightforward afternoon against the Blues, with Ferguson's men winning 3-0.

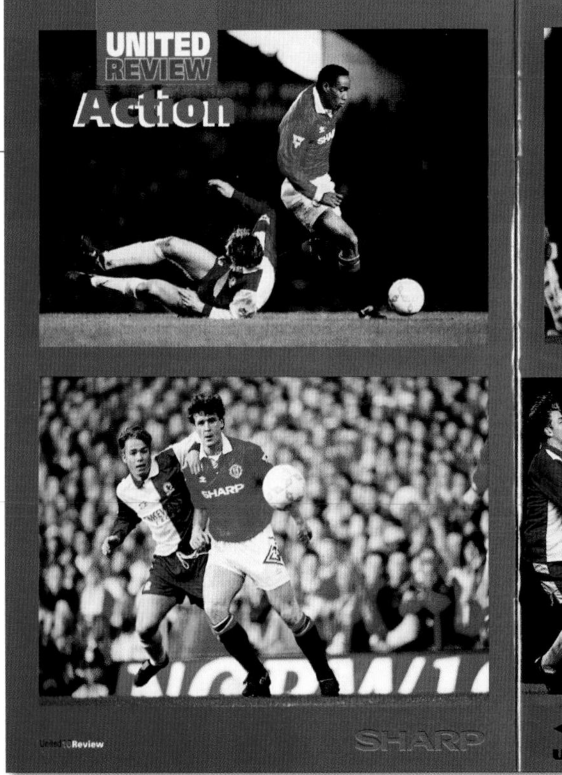

31 JULY 1993, v BENFICA
After the tension, the glorious coronation. The title-winning party against Blackburn saw the champions shake off their celebratory hangovers to put on a show, and images from that memorable night ran in the programme for the pre-season friendly against Benfica two months later.

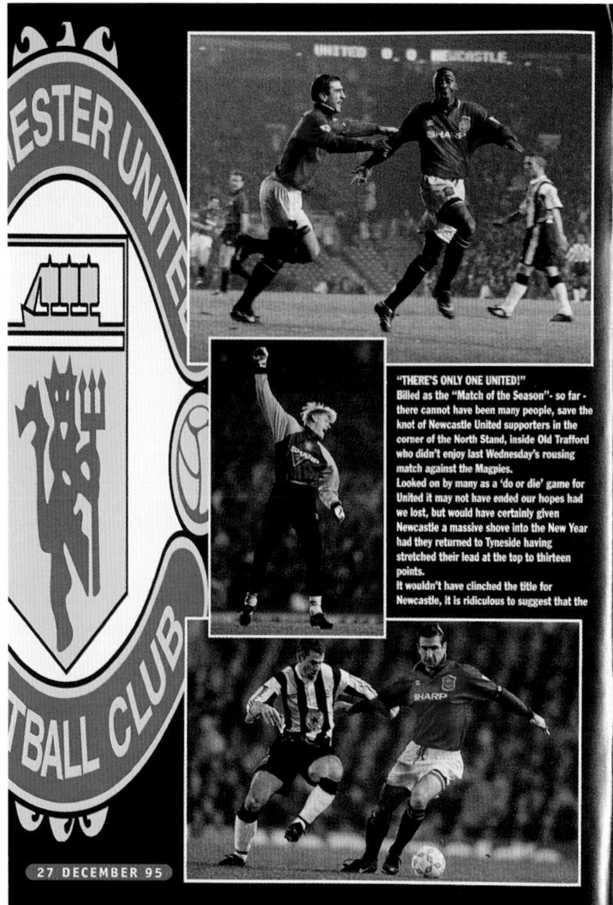

"THERE'S ONLY ONE UNITED!"

Billed as the "Match of the Season"- so far - there cannot have been many people, save the knot of Newcastle United supporters in the corner of the North Stand, inside Old Trafford who didn't enjoy last Wednesday's rousing match against the Magpies.

Looked on by many as a 'do or die' game for United it may not have ended our hopes had we lost, but would have certainly given Newcastle a massive shove into the New Year had they returned to Tyneside having stretched their lead at the top to thirteen points.

It wouldn't have clinched the title for Newcastle, it is ridiculous to suggest that the

27 DECEMBER 95

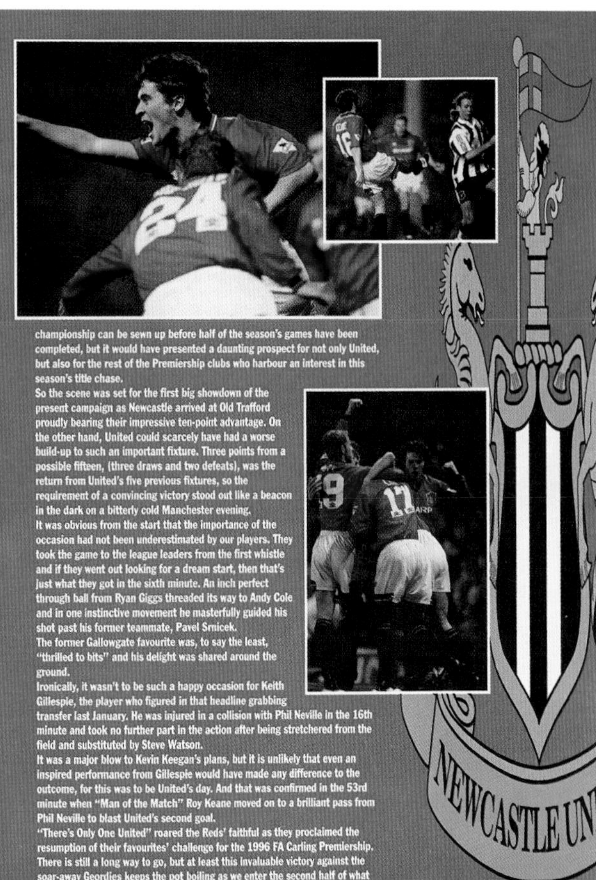

championship can be sewn up before half of the season's games have been completed, but it would have presented a daunting prospect for not only United, but also for the rest of the Premiership clubs who harbour an interest in this season's title chase.

So the scene was set for the first big showdown of the present campaign as Newcastle arrived at Old Trafford proudly bearing their impressive ten-point advantage. On the other hand, United could scarcely have had a worse build-up to such an important fixture. Three points from a possible fifteen, (three draws and two defeats), was the return from United's five previous fixtures, so the requirement of a convincing victory stood out like a beacon in the dark on a bitterly cold Manchester evening.

It was obvious from the start that the importance of the occasion had not been underestimated by our players. They took the game to the league leaders from the first whistle and if they went out looking for a dream start, then that's just what they got in the sixth minute. An inch perfect through ball from Ryan Giggs threaded its way to Andy Cole and in one instinctive movement he masterfully guided his shot past his former teammate, Pavel Srnicek.

The former Gallowgate favourite was, to say the least, "thrilled to bits" and his delight was shared around the ground.

Ironically, it wasn't to be such a happy occasion for Keith Gillespie, the player who figured in that headline grabbing transfer last January. He was injured in a collision with Phil Neville in the 16th minute and took no further part in the action after being stretchered from the field and substituted by Steve Watson.

It was a major blow to Kevin Keegan's plans, but it is unlikely that even an inspired performance from Gillespie would have made any difference to the outcome, for this was to be United's day. And that was confirmed in the 53rd minute when "Man of the Match" Roy Keane moved on to a brilliant pass from Phil Neville to blast United's second goal.

"There's Only One United" roared the Reds' faithful as they proclaimed the resumption of their favourites' challenge for the 1996 FA Carling Premiership. There is still a long way to go, but at least this invaluable victory against the soar-away Geordies keeps the pot boiling as we enter the second half of what promises to be another thrilling race for glory.

Pictures: Action Images

30 DECEMBER 1995, v QUEENS PARK RANGERS

The Reds shook off a Christmas Eve defeat to Leeds United in December '95 to record a vital win over title rivals Newcastle – covered in the programme for the visit of QPR three days later – a match that delivered three more important points.

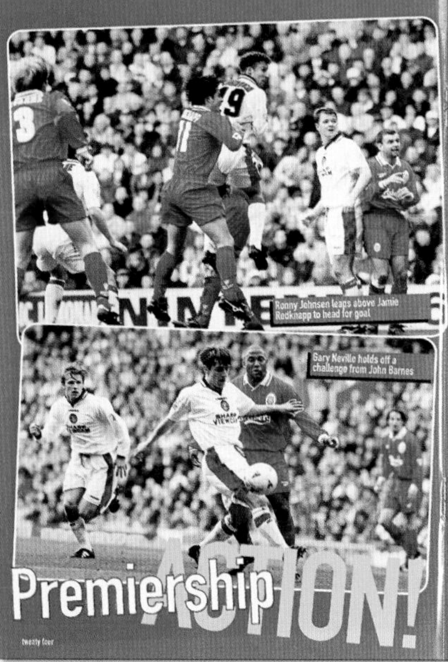

Ronny Johnsen leaps above Jamie Redknapp to head for goal

Gary Neville holds off a challenge from John Barnes

Premiership ACTION!

twenty four

Andy Cole heads United into a 3-1 lead

v. Liverpool

twenty five

8 MAY 1997, v NEWCASTLE UNITED

Gary Pallister is an interested onlooker in this gallery of images from a famous 3-1 win over Liverpool that printed in the programme for the visit of Newcastle, but in truth Pally took centre-stage at Anfield with two rare goals for the Reds.

14 SEPTEMBER 1999, v CROATIA ZAGREB

Oh what a night! Our first match of the 1999/00 Champions League campaign as reigning champions was against visitors from Croatia, so of course the programme took a look back at that magical night late in May...

DAVID BECKHAM AND DWIGHT YORKE

OLE GUNNAR SOLSKJAER

50 MANCHESTER UNITED

TEDDY SHERINGHAM

Nou Camp, Barcelona

MANCHESTER UNITED 2	1 BAYERN MUNICH
(Red shirts, white shorts)	(Grey shirts, grey shorts)

RAIMOND VAN DER GOUW AND NICKY BUTT

THE TRIPLE COMPLETED

UNITED REVIEW 51

The Dell

SOUTHAMPTON 1	MANCHESTER UNITED 3
(Red & White Shirts, Black Shorts)	(Blue Shirts, White Shorts)
Pahars	Beckham, Benali o.g., Solskjaer

22 MANCHESTER UNITED

FA CARLING PREMIERSHIP CHAMPIONS 1999-2000

CHAMPIONS AGAIN! THIS TIME AT SOUTHAMPTON

UNITED REVIEW 23

6 MAY 2000, v TOTTENHAM HOTSPUR

The Reds secured title no.13 in 1999/00 with four games to spare away to Southampton, and yet more championship celebration pics lit up the pages of *United Review* for our final home game against Tottenham – albeit a much less stressful occasion than the match with Spurs 12 months earlier!

ACTIONREPLAY

Tottenham Hotspur 0

Manchester United 2

Scholes 69, van Nistelrooy 90

Barclaycard Premiership **Sunday 27 April** White Hart Lane **Attendance 36,073**

When United completed the league leg of the Treble four years ago against Tottenham, the Spurs fans had banners saying "Let Them Win." And if the mood in the stands was the same this time, the sentiment failed to filter to Kasey Keller, who made it his day's mission to hand the impetus back to rivals Arsenal. But good things come to those who wait, and United's relentless attacks were rewarded with late goals from two Reds in unstoppable form.

With Roy Carroll in for Fabien Barthez and Paul Scholes and David Beckham restored to the side, United charged at the Spurs goal with just 15 seconds gone, only for van Nistelrooy to be thwarted by Keller – not for the last time. In fact, van Nistelrooy could have broken his 40-goal mark for the season on at least five first-half occasions.

At the other end of the park Carroll was rarely threatened, save for a brave block at the feet of Robbie Keane. Keane's namesake and former international captain worked tirelessly in the centre of the pitch, driving his team-mates on and launching a few well-timed verbal rockets whenever concentration and work-rate dropped below what he considered acceptable standards. It did the trick... despite the efforts of Keller.

The second half started where the first left off, with the Spurs keeper immediately tipping a fierce Solskjaer drive over the bar. Teddy Sheringham had the travelling fans cheering when he almost turned into his own net, forcing a rueful grin from the former Red.

With 18 goals in the last five league games it seemed impossible that such continuous pressure would go unrewarded, and with 21 minutes remaining United made the breakthrough. Beckham supplied a pinpoint pass which was cleverly flicked by Scholes into the path of Giggs. Scholes continued into the box just in time to meet Giggs' perfect cross. The win looked inevitable but these days no United victory is complete without a goal from Ruud, which the Dutchman duly delivered in the dying seconds after a wonderful break from substitute Quinton Fortune.

So, the day after Arsenal slipped up just 17 miles from Old Trafford, United collected what could be a vital win four miles up the road from Highbury.

MAN OF THE MATCH
ROY KEANE
If Mark Twain had been watching the Spurs match, no doubt he would have said: "Reports of Keane's demise have been greatly exaggerated." United's inspirational captain was at his hurrying, hustling best and made sure this latest hurdle was safely negotiated.

Tottenham Hotspur: Keller; Carr, Taricco, King, Richards (Gardner 31); Davies, Poyet, Toda (Iversen 78), Etherington (Bunjevcevic 79); Sheringham, Keane
Subs not used: Sullivan, Acimovic

Manchester United: Carroll; Brown (G Neville 54), O'Shea, Ferdinand, Silvestre; Beckham, Keane, Scholes, Giggs; van Nistelrooy, Solskjaer (Fortune 72)
Subs not used: Blanc, Ricardo, Forlan

MANCHESTER UNITED v CHARLTON ATHLETIC 7

3 MAY 2003, v CHARLTON ATHLETIC
As a double-act, Scholes and van Nistelrooy were unstoppable throughout the 2002/03 season and both shot the Reds to victory away to Spurs, as reported on in this issue for the final home game against Charlton. A 4-1 win over the Addicks edged us ever-closer to another title...

ACTION REPLAY

Everton 2

Stubbs 12, Fernandes 50

Manchester United 4

O'Shea 61, P Neville o.g. 68, Rooney 79, Eagles 90

Barclays Premiership **28 April 2007** Goodison Park **Attendance: 39,682**

Amazing comeback gives the Reds victory at Everton, as Chelsea drop points on a potentially decisive day in the Premiership race

Agony for Phil as the former Red levels the scores

Substitute Chris Eagles scored on his Premiership debut to cap a remarkable comeback that saw United score four times in 32 minutes and snatch all three Premiership points at a gobsmacked Goodison.

The result, significant enough when you consider the Reds trailed 2-0 with an hour gone, tasted even sweeter when news of Chelsea's 2-2 draw with Bolton Wanderers filtered through at the final whistle.

But on a day when football fans around the country honoured former Everton great Alan Ball, the current generation of Toffeemen were always going to prove difficult opponents. Indeed, the home side started much the brighter and took the lead on 11 minutes when a long-range Alan Stubbs free kick caught enough of Michael Carrick's boot to deflect it over the diving Edwin van der Sar.

The Reds prodded and probed in search of an equaliser but failed to test stand-in goalkeeper Iain Turner until Wayne Rooney blasted a shot towards the near post in the 20th minute. Shortly afterwards, Alan Smith wasted a glorious chance when he dragged his shot wide of Turner's right-hand post.

Wayne wheels away after putting ahead in the 79th minute

"Rooney, booed all afternoon by his former fans, eased the ball past Turner to send the Reds into raptures with 12 minutes to go"

The Reds may have begun to create openings but still appeared jaded and, without Cristiano Ronaldo, who was nursing a minor injury on the bench, lacked invention going forward. It took a second Everton goal – a brilliant strike just after the interval from on-loan midfielder Manuel Fernandes – to jolt United into life. John O'Shea sparked the revival when he was first on the scene as Turner dropped a routine corner on 61 minutes. Seven minutes later, it was another defensive error that gifted United an equaliser.

Ronaldo, sent on immediately after O'Shea's strike, rose well at the back post to head goalwards. His header was saved on the line by Turner but, in the ensuing scramble, former Reds favourite – and current Everton captain – Phil Neville turned the ball into his own net.

More drama was to follow and, as is often the case when United are concerned, the script seemed more like fantasy than anything within the realms of possibility. Wayne Rooney, who'd been loudly booed all afternoon by his former fans, beat Tony Hibbert before easing the ball past Turner and into the far corner to send the Reds into the raptures with 12 minutes to go. It was an astoundingly assured finish under the circumstances, as the England striker registered his 23rd goal of the season.

Eagles completed the scoring in injury time but by that stage Reds fans were already celebrating. United, it seemed, were going to win the league.

THE TEAMS

EVERTON
Turner; Hibbert, Yobo, Stubbs, Lescott; Arteta, Neville, Carsley (Van der Meyde 83), Fernandes, Osman (McFadden 72); Vaughan (Beattie 71)
Subs not used: Wright, Naysmith
Booked: Vaughan

MANCHESTER UNITED
Van der Sar; O'Shea, Brown, Heinze, Evra (Richardson 56); Solskjaer (Eagles 86), Scholes, Carrick, Giggs; Rooney, Smith (Ronaldo 63)
Subs not used: Kuszczak, Lee
Booked: Heinze

MAN OF THE MATCH

WAYNE ROONEY
Rooney returned to Goodison Park to sink his former club with a superbly taken 78th minute strike. His badge-kissing celebration and the way he toyed with the Toffees' defence during injury time just reinforced his position as a fans' favourite.

STATISTICS opta index

EVERTON		MANCHESTER UNITED
43%	POSSESSION	57%
3	SHOTS ON TARGET	10
6	SHOTS OFF TARGET	6
4	CORNERS	9
18	FOULS	13
3	OFFSIDES	2

Manchester United v West Ham United 15

13 MAY 2007, v WEST HAM UNITED
Tales of another significant away win in the hunt for the Premier League crown. The title race took a big twist at Goodison and by the time West Ham came to M16, rivals Chelsea had blinked and the Reds were champions once more.

ACTION REPLAY

Rooney's precise, curled effort finally unlocks the resolute Ecuadorian defence

It's official: United are the best on the planet

14 Manchester United v Chelsea

ACTION REPLAY

LIGA DE QUITO 0
MANCHESTER UNITED 1

ROONEY 73

FIFA CLUB WORLD CUP FINAL 21 DECEMBER 2008 YOKOHAMA STADIUM ATTENDANCE: 68,682

Thanks to a fine Wayne Rooney strike, the 10-man Reds overcome stern Ecuadorian resistance to be crowned the world's finest football club

"Obla-di, obla-da, Man United, champions of Planet Earth." Has a nice ring, doesn't it? And for all the pre-match pondering over how detrimental the taxing trip to Japan would prove in the Reds' season, the delight that greeted victory over Ecuador's LDU – secured by Wayne Rooney's clinical finish – showed just how much the competition meant to Sir Alex Ferguson and his players, not to mention the 800 delirious fans who had made the arduous trip.

Some would argue that the title of 'world's greatest' was essentially secured by overcoming Barcelona and Chelsea en route to winning last season's UEFA Champions League, but the manner of this victory over the Copa Libertadores winners made success even sweeter. The Reds had to play almost the entire second half with 10 men after the dismissal of Nemanja Vidic – a straight red card for an off-the-ball skirmish with LDU's Claudio Bieler. Moreover, United were repeatedly frustrated by opposing goalkeeper Jose Cevallos.

The veteran stopper was called into action early on by Rooney, fielding two powerful efforts from the in-form striker (scorer of two goals in his semi-final cameo against Gamba Osaka) as the Ecuadorians set out to sit back and try to contain United, fielding Bieler as a lone striker. They did, however, manage to create the clearest opening of the half, only for unmarked defender Jairo Campos to blaze his close-range shot wide of Edwin van der Sar's post. But that scare aside, the half – at least in terms of pressure – belonged to United. Carlos Tevez's stinging 20-yard effort was spectacularly palmed away by Cevallos, while Ji-sung Park, Cristiano Ronaldo and Michael Carrick all came close to a telling breakthrough.

Rio rises highest to celebrate Rooney's moment of magic

That dominance continued after the interval, but was brought to a temporary halt when Vidic, battling for the ball with Bieler, swung an arm at the Argentinian striker. The Serbian was immediately red-carded, prompting the introduction of Jonny Evans for Tevez and leaving Rooney as a lone striker.

Argentinian playmaker Damian Manso, the Ecuadorians' outstanding threat throughout, sought to take advantage with a superb swerving shot which drew the best out of van der Sar. The game then drifted into such a cagey affair that extra time seemed inevitable. But with 13 minutes remaining, Rooney struck the decisive blow. Carrick and Ronaldo combined to tee up the striker just inside the area, and he calmly steered an effort inside Cevallos' far post.

LDU made an attempt to get back into the game, but, as the clock ticked down, the Reds remained largely untroubled bar another Manso effort that came close. That, however, proved the final scare on United's successful Japanese jaunt. And having gained the title of the best club side in existence – and subsequently learnt that Chelsea, Liverpool and Arsenal had all dropped points – the new world champions could reflect on a very worthwhile trip.

The Reds' no.10 proves big in Japan...

LIGA DE QUITO Cevallos; N Araujo, Calle, (Ambrossi 77), Campos, Calderon; Reasco (Larrea 82), Urrutia, W Araujo, Manso, Luis Bolanos (Navia 87); Bieler
Subs not used: Dominguez, Viteri, Obregon, Delgado, E Vaca, D Vaca, Chango

MANCHESTER UNITED Van der Sar; Rafael (Neville 85), Ferdinand, Vidic, Evra; Ronaldo, Carrick, Anderson (Fletcher 88), Park; Tevez (Evans 51), Rooney
Subs not used: Kuszczak, Amos, Berbatov, Giggs, Nani, Scholes, Welbeck, O'Shea, Gibson

"This has always been a big trophy for us ... and now we've got our hands on it" *Rio Ferdinand*

MAN OF THE MATCH
WAYNE ROONEY
Having won his one-man war with keeper Cevallos, firing United to the title, Rooney was rightly named Player of the Tournament.

Manchester United v Chelsea 15

11 JANUARY 2009, v CHELSEA
It's not every week you get to celebrate becoming world champions, and it was apt that it featured in a Chelsea programme, our Moscow final opponents.

23 SEPTEMBER 2009, v WOLVES
UR readers had just three days to digest the most dramatic derby of all time before reading all about it in this programme for the League Cup visit of Wolves.

MATCH REPORT

Michael Owen seals it, long after two clinical first-half finishes (below)

6 Manchester United v Wolverhampton Wanderers

MANCHESTER UNITED 4
ROONEY (2), FLETCHER (49, 80), OWEN (90)
MANCHESTER CITY 3
BARRY (16), BELLAMY (52, 90)

The most eagerly anticipated derby in decades exceeds expectations, as Michael Owen swings a seven-goal thriller in the 96th minute

The hype was justified after all. A kaleidoscope of mistakes, clinical finishes and subplots conspired to generate perhaps the most dramatic Manchester derby in history.

An epic encounter ebbed, flowed and finally swung in United's favour as Michael Owen struck in the sixth added minute to end the resistance of a Manchester City side who had thrice come from behind to level.

Victory was all United deserved. While City bossed matters for a 25-minute spell to end the first half, the Reds' magnificent second-half display should have buried the visitors hopes long before Owen's dramatic intervention.

Pre-match, neutrals lapped up the concept that the long-term threat to United's dominance of English football could principally come from our near neighbours. City's unblemished start to the season merely fanned the flames, as did the return of former United striker Carlos Tevez.

The Argentinian's 'welcome' back to M16, four months after winning his second title with United, made for a crackling pre-match atmosphere, and it wasn't long after kick-off that the stadium was really bouncing.

In the second minute, Ryan Giggs caught City napping with a quick throw to Patrice Evra, whose pull-back allowed Wayne Rooney to shimmy his way past two challenges and slot home from close range.

Within long, however, and despite United's dominance, City were level. Joleon Lescott's errant punt put Ben Foster in two minds and the keeper allowed Tevez – as ever chasing lost causes – to steal the ball and tee up Gareth Barry for a cool finish.

The nature of the goal deflated United, while a geed-up City almost went into the interval ahead – only for Tevez to fire wastefully against the post after a Stephen Ireland dummy.

That sobering moment preceded a storming second half from United. Giggs threatened constantly, defying the years with 45 minutes of brilliance that left heads shaking in wonder.

The Welshman crossed for Darren Fletcher to sneak a header inside Shay Given's post, only for Craig Bellamy to quickly level matters with a scorching 25-yard drive.

Fletch nods the Reds 2-1 up, then (below) 3-2 ahead

"We could have won 6-0 or 7-0, but the fact we made those mistakes made it probably the best derby game of all time" Sir Alex Ferguson

BARCLAYS PREMIER LEAGUE
MATCH STATS
20 September 2009
Old Trafford
Attendance: 75,066

MANCHESTER UNITED
Subs not used

MANCHESTER CITY
Subs not used

MAN OF THE MATCH
RYAN GIGGS
Back on the wing, the veteran had a hand in all four goals, and gave Micah Richards a hellish afternoon. Utterly ageless.

Manchester United v Wolverhampton Wanderers 7

Previous matches

A quickfire strike, and RvP is all too aware of its importance

1-0

Cool as you like, van Persie makes perfect contact with Rooney's superb lofted pass – majestic!

2-0

Man of the match

ROBIN VAN PERSIE
The Dutchman netted his first Old Trafford hat-trick and arguably the goal of the season with a stunning volleyed finish to help seal the title. Viva van Persie.

3-0

Giggs to van Persie... control, a shimmy and unerring finish

8 Manchester United v Chelsea

Previous matches

22 April 2013 // Old Trafford // Kick-off 8pm // Attendance: 75,591

Manchester United 3
Van Persie 2, 13, 33

Aston Villa 0

Van Persie hat-trick fires Reds to title no.20 – and includes one of the best goals seen at OT

Job done – let the celebrations begin!

On a memorable night for the Red half of Manchester it was fitting that United's no.20 sealed title no.20... and how! Following Tottenham's come-from-behind victory over Manchester City in north London just over 24 hours earlier, the Reds knew three points would be enough to claim a 13th Barclays Premier League crown. Within 13 minutes Sir Alex's men were well on the way to title glory, with the Old Trafford faithful also witnessing a goal of the highest order from Robin van Persie, who completed a superb first half hat-trick. And the champagne flowed long into the night as Sir Alex and his men reflected on a memorable campaign...

"I think it was a big job to do. The way we lost it helped us really and with the fact it was City, it gave us an incentive and you've got to admire the focus we've shown this season. Our resilience and the consistency have been good. Like all previous teams, they never give in and that's a fact."
Sir Alex Ferguson

"I want to win it again. I want to win more stuff. I want to win the FA Cup, the Champions League, the Capital One Cup. I want to win it all. This is a trophy for all of us – the management, staff, all the players and the fans have been brilliant too. They've been absolutely amazing, cheering us on every single game, home and away, so credit to them as well."
Robin van Persie

"Everyone is really happy. We deserve the title. I remember, last year when we lost the title, everyone was laughing and saying Manchester City would take control of the Premier League. I said we didn't play well, I admit it, but, if Manchester United get the consistency back, we will win the title by 10 points. I was wrong as now we're winning it by more, but I was not too far away! I believed it. I just trust when Manchester has that consistency, we will be the best team in the Premier League and we showed that we deserved it."
Patrice Evra

"It was a marvellous hit by Robin. Head down, over the ball, perfect timing – a magnificent strike"
Sir Alex Ferguson

"Last season has been in the back of our minds and perhaps subconsciously it gave us an extra motivation. But we're always determined to succeed here no matter what – you can't keep thinking about last season going into every game. You have to look forward. We've got a lot of experience and players who are maturing at the right time – there is a great mix in the team."
Jonny Evans

"Congratulations to United. The best team always win the league and they have been the best team all season. They work really hard, they work for each other and have a mentality that has been here for years and years."
Paul Lambert, Aston Villa manager

MANCHESTER UNITED
De Gea; Rafael, Evans, Jones, Evra; Valencia, Carrick, Rooney (Welbeck 72), Giggs; Kagawa; van Persie
Subs not used: Lindegaard, Ferdinand, Büttner, Nani, Cleverley, Hernandez

ASTON VILLA
Guzan; Lowton, Vlaar, Baker, Bennett (Clark 80); Westwood, Delph; Weimann, N'Zogbia (El Ahmadi 46); Agbonlahor; Benteke
Subs not used: Given, Holman, Sylla, Bent, Bowery

SHOTS ON TARGET
UNITED 5 VILLA 5

SHOTS OFF TARGET
UNITED 5 VILLA 3

POSSESSION
UNITED 52% VILLA 48%

Manchester United v Chelsea 9

5 MAY 2013, v CHELSEA

The title had been wrapped up with four games to spare in the past, but never with such style as the time Robin van Persie stole the show in April 2013.

25 MARCH 2014, v MANCHESTER CITY

Wayne Rooney's rocket from the Upton Park halfway line is a goal for the ages, and this image in *United Review* captured the moment he sent it on its way...

LAST MATCH

WEST HAM UNITED 0

MANCHESTER UNITED 2
Rooney 8, 33

22 March 2014 · Barclays Premier League · Upton Park · Attendance: 34,237

A double from captain for the day Wayne Rooney – including an all-time classic – seals the points for United

Wayne Rooney scored two goals of contrasting quality to secure a comfortable 2-0 win over West Ham, building on the momentum gathered by Wednesday's victory over Olympiacos.

David Moyes made seven changes to the XI that started that Champions League triumph over the Greek champions and fielded a whole new midfield, with Michael Carrick also filling in at centre-back with Nemanja Vidic suspended and Rio Ferdinand, Chris Smalling and Jonny Evans all injured.

United started brightly and almost took the lead in the third minute through Marouane Fellaini, whose downward header from Ashley Young's cross was cleared from danger by Andy Carroll. Juan Mata then went close moments later when his left-footed shot was comfortably saved.

The deadlock was then broken – and in spectacular fashion – as captain Rooney beat Jack Collison to the ball before lobbing Adrian from just inside the Hammers' half. The goal was reminiscent of David Beckham's famous effort against Wimbledon in 1996 and, ironically, the Reds legend was in attendance to applaud his former England team-mate at the Boleyn Ground.

Shinji Kagawa should have doubled the advantage in the 24th minute when sent clear on the left flank, though the Japanese international could not beat the goalkeeper at the near post. Moments later, Mata forced another decent save from Adrian following a neat pirouette inside the area.

A swift counter attack in the 32nd minute led to Rooney scoring his second of the game, this time from close range after Mark Noble's failed clearance teed up a tidy six-yard finish. The goal notably moved the no.10 above Jack Rowley and up to third in the list of United's all-time scorers, closing the gap on record holder Sir Bobby Charlton to 37.

Neither manager made changes at the break, though Sam Allardyce's words of encouragement were effective in the opening exchanges of the second half as the Hammers pressed forward, pumping several crosses into the area and winning three corners that placed United on the back foot.

Having resisted the early pressure, the Reds regained a foothold on proceedings and could have put the result beyond doubt when Mata's 57th-minute shot ricocheted off a defender before Young's left-footed volley missed the target from inside the box just moments later. Alex Büttner, playing at left-back in place of Patrice Evra, also fired high and wide with 70 minutes on the clock.

With the match approaching its final act, Danny Welbeck and Javier Hernandez were both sent on for Rooney and Mata as Moyes cast an eye to this evening's Manchester derby. West Ham also made a change as Carlton Cole replaced Kevin Nolan to join Carroll up front, though the Hammers did little to trouble the largely untested David De Gea.

United could have won a penalty in the 89th minute when the impressive Fellaini clashed with Antonio Nocerino, though Lee Mason waved play on before calling time on a fine victory that leaves the Reds with the best away record in the Premier League, but still 11 points shy of the top four.

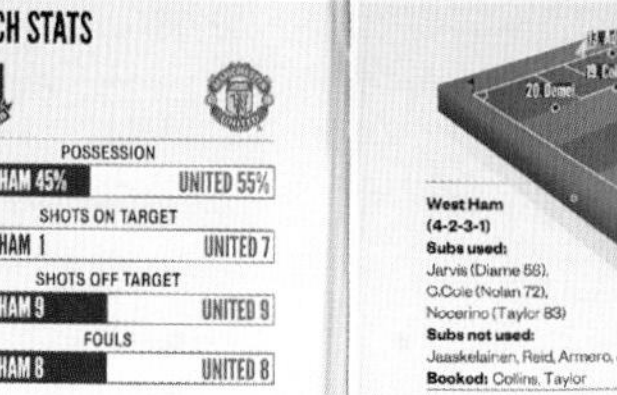

Wayne doubles United's lead inside the first half

MATCH STATS

	POSSESSION	
WEST HAM 45%		UNITED 55%
	SHOTS ON TARGET	
WEST HAM 1		UNITED 7
	SHOTS OFF TARGET	
WEST HAM 9		UNITED 9
	FOULS	
WEST HAM 8		UNITED 8

08 Manchester United v Manchester City

Rooney sets himself to let fly with the goal of the season

LINE-UPS

West Ham (4-2-3-1)
Subs used: Jarvis (Diame 56), C.Cole (Nolan 72), Nocerino (Taylor 83)
Subs not used: Jaaskelainen, Reid, Armero, J.Cole
Booked: Collins, Taylor

Manchester United (4-2-3-1)
Subs used: Hernandez (Rooney 77), Welbeck (Mata 78)
Subs not used: Lindegaard, Evra, Cleverley, Nani, Januzaj
Booked: Rafael

MAN OF THE MATCH
WAYNE ROONEY

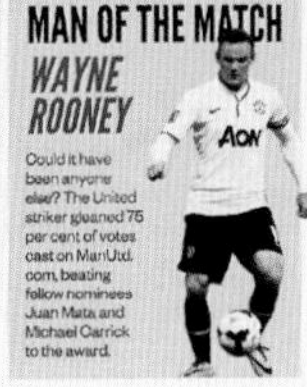

Could it have been anyone else? The United striker gleaned 75 per cent of votes cast on ManUtd.com, beating fellow nominees Juan Mata and Michael Carrick to the award.

Manchester United v Manchester City 09

MATCH HUB

ROUND-UP FROM... WEMBLEY JOY, PLUS FURTHER EUROPEAN AND FA CUP PROGRESS

SINCE LAST TIME

Reds lift the League Cup for a fifth time after a classic final, overcoming Saints' fightback thanks to late Zlatan winner

The champagne corks are popped as the celebrations begin in north London

Lingard doubles United's lead with a well-placed shot

Gabbiadini runs off in delight following his equaliser for Saints

Ibrahimovic celebrates after powering home the winner with just three minutes left

United fans had a day to remember

Rooney lifts our fifth League Cup

The season's first silverware (or the second if you include the Community Shield) was brought back to Old Trafford last Sunday after a dramatic victory over Southampton in the EFL Cup final.

Zlatan Ibrahimovic took his goals total for the season to 26 with two excellent finishes as the Reds built up a two-goal lead, had it wiped out, then rallied for a late winner to land the trophy and send United fans wild inside Wembley.

Our leading scorer has proven himself to be the man for the big occasion countless times in his career, so it was little surprise when he broke the deadlock in the 19th minute. After a foul on Ander Herrera just outside the Saints' box, the Swede stepped up to strike a dipping 25-yard free-kick beyond Fraser Forster. It was United's first goal direct from a free-kick at Wembley and a stunning start for the Reds. When Jesse Lingard added another 19 minutes later, calmly stroking a Marcos Rojo pass into the corner of the net, the tie appeared all but over – but Claude Puel's men had other ideas.

The Saints had looked the more fluent side in the first half and were left to rue Manolo Gabbiadini having an effort ruled out for offside after 11 minutes. But their reward came in injury time at the end of the first half, when the Italian striker pounced on a James Ward-Prowse cross to half the deficit.

When Gabbiadini struck again three minutes after the break, this time spinning in a crowded Reds' box to fire past David De Gea, United fans were stunned. For a while it appeared the team were, too, with our Spanish stopper called into one fine stop, then thankful that an Oriol Romeu header found only his woodwork and not his net.

It's said that good teams find a way of winning even when not at the top of their game, and the Reds once again dug deep to plunder a decisive goal. In a quick breakaway, Anthony Martial shifted the ball to the unmarked Herrera and the Spaniard duly floated a pinpoint cross to the head of United's unmarked no.9. Cue pandemonium behind the Saints' goal as the brilliant Ibrahimovic powerfully headed beyond Forster. The celebrations were renewed moments later at the final whistle, then again when the trophy was held aloft by club captain Wayne Rooney.

"He [Zlatan] won the game for us, he was outstanding," said Jose Mourinho. "Paul Pogba was at a similar level, but Zlatan was outstanding in a match where our opponent was better than us for large periods of the game. They deserved to go to extra-time, they didn't deserve to lose, but Zlatan made the difference and won us the cup."

As for the man of the hour, Ibrahimovic was also a happy man. "It feels amazing because we won the game," he said. "Southampton played very well and we didn't play like we normally do, but we did what we needed to do and that's the most important thing.

"Before coming to England I could have settled down and been happy with what I'd achieved," added the 35-year-old striker. "But that's not me. I'm not satisfied. I want more and I'm still hungry, even at this age."

EUROPA LEAGUE AND FA CUP MATCH ROUND-UP

JESSE'S HAT-TRICK

The EFL Cup final saw Jesse Lingard bag his third goal in three Wembley visits, adding his first-half strike to his winner against Crystal Palace in last year's FA Cup final and his opener against Leicester City in the Community Shield.

32 AND RISING...

United's Wembley hero added yet another trophy to his career haul, with the League Cup success seeing him claim his 32nd winner's medal (although Juventus's 2004/05 and 2005/06 *Serie A* titles were later revoked). Incredibly, he's won a trophy every season since 2001.

REACTION v SOUTHAMPTON

"UNITED HAVE A HISTORY OF WINNING TROPHIES. WE WON ONE LAST YEAR [THE FA CUP] AND ONE AT THE START OF THE SEASON [COMMUNITY SHIELD], SO WE'VE GOT A KNACK FOR WINNING AND AS SOON AS YOU GET THAT WINNING FEELING, YOU ALWAYS WANT MORE" – JESSE LINGARD

MATCH HUB

MATCH CENTRE

MANCHESTER UNITED	SOUTHAMPTON
3	2
IBRAHIMOVIC 19, 87, LINGARD 38	GABBIADINI 45+1, 48

26 FEBRUARY 2017, EFL CUP FINAL, WEMBLEY

LINE-UPS

Manchester United	Southampton
DE GEA	FORSTER
VALENCIA	CEDRIC
BAILLY	YOSHIDA
SMALLING	STEPHENS
ROJO	BERTRAND
HERRERA	ROMEU
POGBA	DAVIS (90)
(77) ⚽ LINGARD	WARD-PROWSE
(45) MATA	TADIC (77)
(90) MARTIAL	REDMOND
⚽⚽ IBRAHIMOVIC	GABBIADINI (83) ⚽⚽

SUBSTITUTES USED

Manchester United	Southampton
(45) CARRICK	BOUFAL (77)
(77) RASHFORD	LONG (83)
(90) FELLAINI	RODRIGUEZ (90)

UNUSED SUBSTITUTES

Manchester United	Southampton
ROMERO	HASSEN
BLIND	CACERES
YOUNG	McQUEEN
ROONEY	HOJBJERG

STATISTICS

Manchester United		Southampton
48%	POSSESSION	52%
6	SHOTS ON TARGET	5
2	SHOTS OFF TARGET	1
3	CORNERS	12
11	FOULS	13

10 • Manchester United v AFC Bournemouth

Manchester United v AFC Bournemouth • 11

4 MARCH 2017, v BOURNEMOUTH
For a league visit from Bournemouth, *United Review* reported on our League Cup final win over their south coast rivals Southampton, and some Zlatan magic.

12 DECEMBER 2019, v AZ ALKMAAR
The Reds completed a league double over Man City in the 2019/20 season, with the programme covering the brilliant away win with these euphoric images.

BIG PICTURE

MANCHESTER IS RED!

2

IT'S A SUPER SATURDAY!

Get in there! These images, taken by club photographers Ashley Donelan and John Peters, capture the joy and emotion experienced in Saturday's dramatic, delirious derby. Ole's men flew out of the traps and never looked back on the way to a big, big win over Pep Guardiola's Blues, with Anthony Martial's strike putting us 2-0 ahead on the night (main image). The final whistle sparked equally epic scenes in front of a buzzing away end (far left pictures), as players, fans and the manager rejoiced in the victory. On the back of the win over Spurs in our last home game, there's no greater boost to confidence as we work our way through the busiest spell of the season, with matches across three competitions over the next seven days. UNITED!

BIG PICTURE

06

07

CHAPTER 9

Europe

When Matt Busby led his pioneering Reds into the unknown in the 1950s, *United Review* was an invaluable guide to fans, while it's continued to chronicle every challenge posed by the cream of the continent ever since...

"The only way to become the best team in Europe is by winning the European Cup," stressed Matt Busby, upon taking United into the continental game in 1956 – dragging English football, initially kicking and screaming, along for the ride.

The Football League had forbidden Chelsea from entering the competition's inaugural edition in 1955, but Busby's ambition ensured that United would not be blocked so readily. And so, the Reds' long and undulating relationship with European football began; a tale laced with glory and tragedy penned over the ensuing decades.

All along the way, *United Review* has been there to document the journey. Even when the absence of floodlights at Old Trafford meant home ties initially had to be staged at Maine Road, the *Review* captured the mystique of this new competition, immediately revelling as a guidebook for the unknown. The first-ever continental edition of the *Review* opened with what was, for almost every single supporter picking up a copy, the first glimpse of European opposition: RSC Anderlecht's team photo. The Reds led 2-0 from the first leg over in Belgium, and ensured that the matchday programme would become one of the ultimate collector's editions by registering a 10-0 club record victory at Maine Road.

Above: As United brushed aside Anderlecht in our first European 'home' game, *UR* was there to inform fans about the new frontier

With that, the special air of a European night was born, and the excitement only continued to build as United journeyed through the competition. When Real Madrid arrived in the semi-final stage – by now hosted at Old Trafford, its lighting issue resolved – the front cover comprised a welcome note for the visitors penned entirely in Spanish, and a translation contained within.

'The European Cup competition has opened up a new era in soccer,' beamed Busby's programme

Juventus come to town in the Cup Winners' Cup in 1984 - another titanic Euro clash

Busby felt winning the European Cup in 1968 lifted a huge psychological weight

column. 'When Manchester United joined this wonderful competition this season I never dreamed that we should enjoy ourselves so much.'

The Reds' obsession with lifting the European Cup was under way. The following term, those ambitions were seemingly shattered by the Munich Air Disaster but, thanks to the incomprehensible rebuilding work of Busby and Jimmy Murphy, the Reds were only out of European competition for five seasons.

A maiden appearance in the European Cup Winners' Cup in 1963/64 preceded a return to the top table in 1965/66 and 1967/68, the latter providing the stage for United's first European Cup triumph just a decade on from Munich. "It cleansed me," said Busby, after his side overcame Benfica in the final. "It eased the pain of the guilt of going into Europe. It was my justification."

While United's European fortunes duly waned for much of the interim between knights Busby and Ferguson, a smattering of European giants still visited Old Trafford. AC Milan, Barcelona, Juventus and Ajax were welcomed by the *Review*, which often laid on special-designed covers for the occasion.

Following the Reds' return to continental prominence from the early 1990s onwards, those covers were often reproduced and repurposed as retro frontings for modern ties to celebrate the club's storied continental past.

Between 1990 and 2020, United were without European football in just one season (2014/15), providing a stampede of new opponents. The sense of unknown is largely a thing of the past, given the widespread coverage of leagues worldwide, but the excitement of a European night at Old Trafford still pulsates within the pages of *United Review*.

26 September 1956

United v Anderlecht

European Cup

THIS IS THE OFFICIAL PROGRAMME OF

MANCHESTER UNITED

FOOTBALL CLUB LIMITED

OLD TRAFFORD - MANCHESTER

Chairman: H. P. HARDMAN, Esq.
Directors: Dr. W. MACLEAN, G. E. WHITTAKER, Esq., J. ALAN GIBSON, Esq., W. H. PETHERBRIDGE, Esq.
Manager: MATT BUSBY Secretary: W. R. CRICKMER
Editor: DAVID W. WICKS
Advertisement and editorial enquiries should be addressed to the "United Review", Sidney F. Wicks Ltd., Cheetwood House, 21 Newton Street, Manchester 1. Telephone: CENtral 9047/8

VOLUME XVIII (Special Edition) 26th SEPTEMBER, 1956

welcome!

Ce soir, des milliers d'enthousiastes britanniques du football se joignent au Club de Manchester United pour offrir aux célébres champions du Royal Sporting Club Anderlecht de Belgique un accueil des plus chaleureux.

Bien que ce match de nocturne ne compte encore que pour le tournoi préliminaire du championnat d'Europe, c'est pour nous une véritable aubaine d'assister à un match qui réunit les meilleurs footballeurs de deux pays dont l'esprit sportif autant sur le terrain que partout ailleurs est une des plus hautes traditions du sport.

Bonne chance Anderlecht! Nous espérons que votre visite en Angleterre vous sera aussi agréable qu'a été pour nous le séjour que nous avons fait chez vous en Belgique.

To-night, many thousands of British football enthusiasts join with Manchester United Football Club in extending the heartiest of welcomes to the celebrated champions of Belgium — Royal Sporting Club, Anderlecht.

Although this match under floodlights is still in the preliminary round of the European Football Championship we are indeed fortunate to witness a contest between football champions of two countries whose reputation for good sportsmanship on and off the field is in the very highest traditions of the game.

Good luck Anderlecht! We hope you enjoy your visit to England as much as we enjoyed our stay with you in Belgium!

OUR COVER PICTURE

R.S.C. ANDERLECHTOIS

(Champion de Belgique 1955-6)

Standing, left to right
P. Gettemans, H. Matthys, F. Week, J. Culot, F. Longin, A. DeRaeymaeker (assistant-trainer).

Seated (centre), left to right
Bill Gormlie (trainer and ex-Blackburn Rovers), F. Degelas, W. Dekoster, P. Hanon, M. Lippens.

Seated (first rank), left to right
J. DeDryver, R. VanderWilt, H. Vandenbosch, J. Mermans, G. Dewael, J. Jurion, P. Vandenbosch.

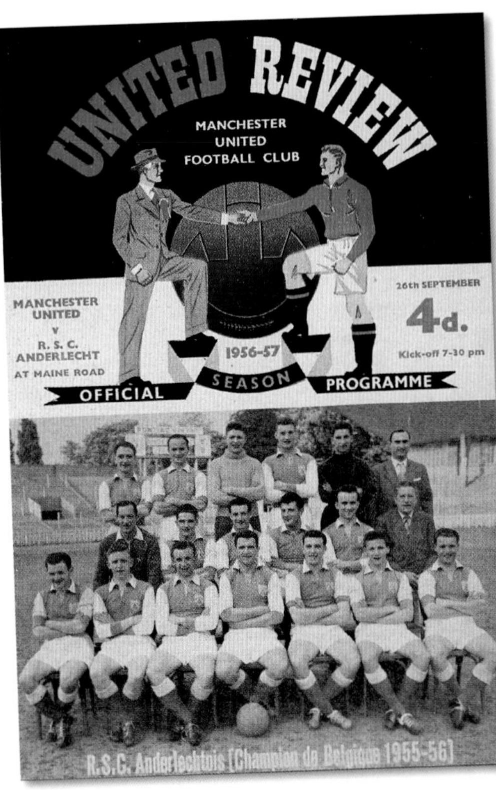

HOW THE EUROPEAN CUP WAS BORN

Although the European Cup — or to give it its full name, the European Champion Clubs' Cup — was initiated only last year the possibility of some kind of European Championship competition has been talked about for many years. Indeed, in 1927 a proposal was laid before the F.I.F.A. (Federation of International Football Associations).

A keen promoter of the idea was the late Henri Delauney, secretary of the French Football Federation and the Union of European F.A.s. Unfortunately nothing resulted from these proposals. It was said that clubs had too many fixtures to make it practicable.

It was in December, 1954 that a French sporting newspaper "L'Equipe" revived the idea. The paper suggested that the champion clubs of each of the European F.A.s should participate.

Four months later in April, 1955 representatives from sixteen different nations met in Paris to discuss the first round. Still further discussion took place at the congress of the European Union in Vienna, at which the French paper's representatives again put forward their proposals. Eventually sixteen clubs, all winners of their respective national championships were entered. They included Rapid, of Vienna, R.S.C. Anderlecht (Belgium), Stade de Rheims (France), A.C. Milan (Italy), Partizan of Belgrade (Yugoslavia), Gwardia (Poland), Real Madrid (Spain), Hibernian (Scotland), Sporting Club (Portugal) and teams from Germany, Denmark, Hungary, the Saar, Switzerland, Sweden and Holland.

Originally England was represented by Chelsea (League champions 1954-5) but unfortunately at the last moment they were compelled to withdraw, the Polish club Gwardia taking their place.

Because of the bad weather attendances at the initial matches averaged 20,000. In the semi-finals, Rheims beat Hibernian and Real Madrid beat Milan.

In a thrilling final in Paris in June last year Real Madrid of Spain beat Rheims to become the first holders of the European Cup.

Competition is bound to be very keen and if United get through this round it could lead to quite a few trips through Europe and — which is much more exciting — it would give us the chance to see some of the crack European teams here in Manchester. It is going to be tough. Some idea of how tough is given by the fact that Real Madrid gave a bonus of £400 to each player after their success.

Matt Busby fought tooth and nail with the English football establishment to allow United entry into the European Cup and so it was a proud moment when he welcomed the Belgian side Anderlecht to Manchester for our first home tie. Our continental adventure got off to a flyer and a 10-0 win in the first round second leg provided a remarkable opening chapter to the tale

Shirts Red — MANCHESTER UNITED — Knickers White

WOOD

FOULKES 2 — BYRNE 3

COLMAN 4 — BLANCHFLOWER 5 — EDWARDS 6

BERRY 7 — WHELAN 8 — TAYLOR 9 — VIOLLET 10 — PEGG 11

R — L

Referee: M. Lequesne, France
Kick-off 7-15 pm

EVENING NEWS FOR RESULTS

Linesmen: C. Le Men, France (Red Flag)
E. Harzic, France (Yellow Flag)

L — R

GENTO 11 — RIAL 10 — DI STEFANO 9 — MATEOS 8 — KOPA 7

ZARRAGA 6 — MARQUITOS 5 — MUNOZ 4

LESMES 3 — BECERRIL 2

ALONSO

Team changes will be indicated by loudspeaker — Shirts White — REAL MADRID — Knickers White — Team changes will be indicated by loudspeaker

MANCHESTER UNITED WELCOME REAL MADRID *(Translation of Cover Greeting).*

To-night, Manchester United Football Club join with football lovers throughout the United Kingdom to offer Real Madrid the heartiest of sporting welcomes. To-night, two of the most celebrated football teams in Europe duel for the privilege of meeting the final contender for the silver cup awarded to the winner of the European Champion Club Competition. Although Real Madrid are formidable opponents with their unmatched sporting record we too hold honours which the Spanish Champions have found worthy of respect. But whatever the outcome of this memorable game let us thank the farsighted organizers of this international contest not only for bringing together football's finest exponents but for promoting genuine friendship amongst the sportsmen of Europe.

MANCHESTER UNITED WELCOME REAL MADRID

Esta noche, el Manchester United Football Club se unirá a los aficionados al fútbol de todo el Reino Unido para ofrecer al Real Madrid la más cordial y sincera bienvenida deportiva.

Esta noche, dos de los equipos de fútbol más celebrados en Europa lucharán por el privilegio del encuentro competidor final en el que se adjudicará la copa de plata al vencedor en el European Champion Club Competition.

Aunque el Real Madrid es un formidable oponente con su record deportivo sin igual, nosotros también poseemos titulos honorificos que los Campeones Espanoles hallan dignos de respeto. Pero cualquiera que sea el resultado de este partido memorable, démos las gracias a los perspicaces organizadores de este encuentro, no sólo por haber reunido los más finos exponentes del fútbol, sino también por aumentar la amistad sincera entre los deportistas de Europa.

United's welcome message to Real Madrid for our semi-final second leg – presented in Spanish on the cover – summed up the warmth and respect shared by both clubs

A handshake from United's Manager . . . MATT BUSBY

It is with very great pleasure that I extend to our opponents to-night my sincere wish that we have a very pleasant game of football and that Real Madrid take back with them happy memories of this trip to Old Trafford. My directors join with me in this tribute to their wonderful achievements over the years in Spanish football circles. The European Cup competition has opened up a new era in soccer. I am convinced that nothing but good can come from the clashes of clubs from all over the world. When Manchester United decided to join in this wonderful competition this season I never dreamed that we should enjoy ourselves so much. All over the Continent we have experienced wonderful hospitality, and my team has been received magnificently by the peoples of the various centres in which we have had to play. The European Cup has brought us all nearer to the reality that here is a competition which has at least provided Manchester United supporters with the opportunity of seeing some of the greatest soccer sides in the world. The game is the thing and I am certain we, in Manchester, shall always recall with pleasure, the memories of the thrilling games in which we have participated this season.

Busby's joy at his side's debut showing in Europe was palpable in his programme notes

25 April 1957
United v Real Madrid
European Cup

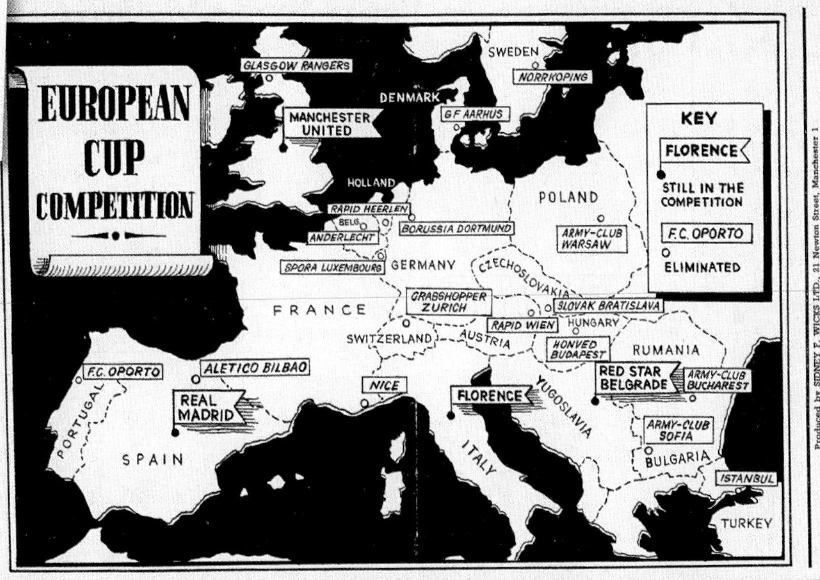

An at-a-glance guide to the champions taking part in the 1956/57 European Cup

14 January 1958

United v Red Star Belgrade

European Cup

WELCOME TO . . .

RED STAR, BELGRADE

by TOM JACKSON

of the MANCHESTER EVENING NEWS

Here are brief sketches of the players in the Red Star team of all-internationals who are likely to be on view to-night:

BEARA, Vladimir (goalkeeper).
Aged 29 and a former ballet dancer of the Yugoslav Opera. Rated one of the best goalkeepers in Europe because of his amazing agility and daring. Has a host of international caps and has also played for the Rest of Europe.

STANKOVIC, Branko (full-back).
Aged 33 and a Yugoslav international on sixty-two occasions. Is a great favourite with the Belgrade public and regarded as one of the best all-rounders in the game. Has also played against England.

ZEKOVIC, Miljan (full-back).
Aged 28 and sixteen times an international. Last season played in the Yugoslav national team in all their matches — a sturdy and energetic full-back who is very difficult to beat.

POPOVIC, Vladimir (wing half-back).
Aged 24, gained his first honour at right-half for the Yugoslav "B" team against England at Maine Road in October, 1955. Has since shot to the top as a full international, noted for his fine constructive ability.

SPAJIC, Ljubisa (centre half-back).
Also many-times capped in recent seasons. A cool pivot and an all-round athlete who excels in his covering in the goalmouth.

TASIC, Lazar (wing half-back).
Was right-half at Wembley in November, 1956, but at home anywhere in the middle line. Has made big strides in club and international football in the last two seasons. Aged 29.

MITIC, Rajko (outside-right).
Probably the best-known player in Yugoslavia and the hero of many internationals. Has captained the international team on numerous occasions and is the schemer of the attack. Joined Red Star when he was a student in Belgrade and has won every honour in the game.

SEKULARAC, Dragoslav (inside-forward).
A young international who has shot to the top by his powerful shooting. A fine link on the right-wing with Mitic and a big scoring success on Red Star's recent trip to Morocco. Aged 19.

TOPLAC, Ivan (centre-forward).
Aged 24 and leader of the Yugoslav attack at Wembley two years ago. Now has six caps and has won a reputation for his powerful play and goal snatching.

KOSTIC, Borovoje (inside-forward).
Was a young reserve when Red Star played at Old Trafford in 1951. Has been developed into a striking force at inside left. Former Belgrade University student. Aged 26.

DURKOVIC, Vladimir (outside-left).
Under-study to the famous Zebec in the Yugoslav international team and a young player destined for more honours.

Dobrodoslica Crvenoj Zvezdi Iz Beograda!

Mi oduvek tvrdimo da nema boljih ambasadora od sportista jedne zemlje, a zaista nema ambasadora koji bi bili vise dobrodosli nego prvaci Crvene Zvezde iz Beograda. Mozda ce biti neobicno Jugoslovenskim prvacima da igraju protiv jednog tima koji govori drugi jezik, ali cim oni istrce na igraliste osvetljeno reflektorima i cuju nasu mancestersku dobrodoslicu, oni ce odmah da osete da je jezik sporta podjednako razumljiv i Jugoslovenima i Britancima.

Mi, u Manchesteru, divimo se kontinentalnom stilu igre — brilijantnoj kontroli lopte povezanoj sa silovitim napadima i strastvenom odbranom. Reputacija beogradskog tima je takva, da cemo mi morati da upremo sve nase moci, da bi mogli da dostignemo njihovu brilijantnost. Mi necemo zaboraviti da nas susret sa Crvenom Zvezdom nece biti zavrsen, pre nego sto se sa njima susretnemo na njihovom terenu. Neka pobeda bude nagrada boljem timu, a neka ucesce u ovim nezaboravnim igrama bude uteha pobedjenima.

Fudbalski klub Manchester United, prvak engleske lige, pozdravlja prvaka Jugoslavije Crvenu Zvezdu iz Beograda.

WELCOME TO RED STAR, BELGRADE!

We have long contended that there are no finer ambassadors than a country's sportsmen and no ambassadors to England could be more welcome than the Red Stars of Belgrade! It will be strange for the Yugoslav Champions to play against a team unable to speak their language but when they run out under the floodlights and hear our Manchester welcome they will know at once that the language of sportsmanship is understood by Yugloslav and Briton alike.

We in Manchester admire the continental style of play—brilliant ball control wedded to fierce attack and impassioned defence. The reputation of the Belgrade team is such that we must strive our utmost to match their brilliance. We shall remember also that our contest with the Red Stars is not complete until we too have played on foreign soil. May victory reward the better team and may the losers find consolation in their contribution to these memorable games.

Manchester United Football Club, champions of the English League, salute the champions from Yugoslavia — Red Star Belgrade!

MANCHESTER UNITED F.C.
(ENGLISH LEAGUE CHAMPIONS)

Photo by courtesy of the Provincial Press Agency Southport

Insets of Scanlon, Gregg and Morgans by the Manchester Evening News

Back row, left to right: FOULKES, COLMAN, WHELAN, WOOD, JONES, EDWARDS
Front row, left to right: BERRY, VIOLLET, BYRNE (Captain), TAYLOR, PEGG
Insets: BLANCHFLOWER, SCANLON, GREGG, MORGANS, McGUINNESS

VOLUME XIX. No. 17 EUROPEAN CUP COMPETITION 14th JANUARY 1958

MATT BUSBY talking

I would like to take this opportunity of wishing our Red Star visitors from Belgrade, a warm welcome to Old Trafford. I recall their visit to our city in the year 1951, when they gave such a splendid exhibition. I feel, however, that United now have a stronger side — as records prove — and, of course, they are now much better equipped, after their many other European Cup games to challenge the best teams of Europe.

But the game is the thing and I feel certain we shall again see another thrilling match. No greater incentive is afforded the peoples of Europe of "getting together" than our great game of football. We of Manchester United have made many new friendships since we were fortunate enough to participate in the European Cup series. Without exception all the United party have proved fine ambassadors on their travels abroad and we can certainly say that our several visitors to Manchester have also set a splendid example by their deportment on and off the field.

A hearty welcome to our friends from Belgrade!

Photograph by Douglas Glass
Reproduced by courtesy of the Sunday Times

LANCASHIRE SCHOOLS CUP
3rd Round
THE CLIFF, BROUGHTON
Wednesday, 15th January, 7.30 pm
(Under floodlights)
SALFORD BOYS
v
BOLTON BOYS

A matchday programme filled with tragic significance, as United faced Red Star Belgrade in the European Cup quarter-final first leg at Old Trafford in January 1958

Sport Lisboa E BENFICA
(See photo on opposite page)
Top row (l. to r.): (A) Eusébio, (B) Costa Pereira, (C) Cavem, (D) Simões, (E) Cruz.
Middle row (l. to r.): (F) Serafim, (G) Coluna, (H) Pedras, (J) Ferreira Pinto, (K) Augusto Silva.
Bottom row (l. to r.): (L) Germano, (M) Raul, (N) Torres, (O) Jacinto, (P) José Augusto.

Benfica of Portugal had proved to be one of the giants of the continental scene, winning the European Cup twice and finishing runners-up three times before this inaugural match with United in February 1966

2 February 1966
United v Benfica
European Cup

position and has emerged as a leading goal scorer.

Eusébio (inside-forward)
European Footballer of the Year in succession to Denis Law. A remarkable player often called the "Black Panther" because of his lithe movement and powerful shooting. Born Mozambique, he is another brilliant discovery from Portuguese East Africa, joining Benfica in 1960–61 season. Made his international debut against England at Wembley in October, 1961, and now the big hope of Portugal in the World Cup.

Torres (centre-forward)
Exceptionally tall and strong centre-forward who specializes in heading goals from the

Profiling Benfica's star man and the reigning European Footballer of the Year - Eusebio

EUROPEAN CUP
UNITED v BENFICA
at Lisbon, March 9th, 1966
SPECIAL FLIGHT
29½ gns.
(Includes: Flight - Hotel - Grandstand Ticket - Transfers, etc.)
CREDIT FACILITIES AVAILABLE
ECCLESIA
TRAVEL LIMITED
37a, Oxford St., Manchester 1
CEntral 3657

Fans were given the chance to follow the Reds to Lisbon for the second leg

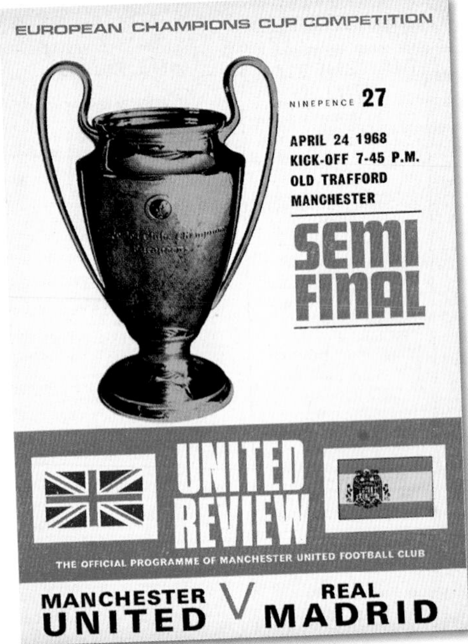

Greetings to

REAL MADRID

from LOUIS C. EDWARDS
Chairman M.U.F.C.

Manchester United and Real Madrid share a very special relationship.

The famous Spanish club have come to stand for all that is best in international football and they are also something of a symbol for our own entry into European football.

Old Trafford will never forget the European Cup of 11 years ago when we were drawn with Real in the semi-final.

Real Madrid won that tie, indeed they went on to win the Cup, and of course, it meant the end of our own ambitions in that season's competition.

But a friendship and understanding was born which went on to see Real and United meet over the years in five friendly matches in Manchester and Madrid.

Now we meet again in serious competition.

Should we win, we know we can go very proudly indeed into the final. Should we lose, we know we shall have lost to one of the finest teams and clubs in the world.

We also know that whatever the outcome, there will still be a mutual respect and friendship that will be even more richly endowed as a result of these semi-final matches.

On behalf of Manchester United, I offer a most sincere welcome to the officials, players and supporters who are our guests at Old Trafford this evening.

Creo que le Manchester United y el Real Madrid tienen una afinidad muy especial.

El famoso club español representa todo lo mejor que existe en el fútbol internacional y es también algo asi como un símbolo de nuestro propio ingreso en el fútbol internacional.

Old Trafford no se olvidará nunca de la Copa Europea de hace 11 años cuando jugamos con el Real Madrid en los semifinales.

Real Madrid ganó ese partido, realmente ganó la copa, y naturalmente eso representó el fin de muestras propias ambiciones en el concurso de aquella estación.

Pero nació una amistad y armonía que ocasionó el encuentro del Real Madrid y del United durante años, en cinco partidos amistodos en Manchester y en Madrid.

Ahora, volvemos a encontrarnos en seria oposición.

Si ganamos, sabemos que podemos ir, con orgullo, para el final. Si permedos, sabemos que hemos perdido porque uno de los mejores equipos y clubs del mundo ha ganado.

También sabemos que pase lo que pase, todavía queda un respeto mutuo y una amistad sincera que serán más altamente fundados como resultado de estos partidos semi-finales.

En nombre de Manchester United, doy la más sincera bienvenida a las personalidades, jugadores y aficionados que son invitados nuestros, esta noche, en Old Trafford.

We had met Real Madrid at the semi-final stage of the European Cup in 1957, with the Spanish kings proving too good for the young Reds on that occasion. But 1968 would prove to be a different story...

24 April 1968

United v Real Madrid

European Cup

REAL MADRID Playing Personalities

by DAVID MEEK
of the Manchester Evening News & Chronicle

Antonio Betancort (goalkeeper)
Experienced goalkeeper aged 30, with Spanish League and European Cup medals. Has played twice for Spain earlier in his career, of stocky-build, he has a reputation for steadiness rather than spectacular play and did extremely well in the last round against Sparta Prague.

Andres Junquera (goalkeeper)
Aged 21, he is Real's goalkeeper of the future. Tall and athletic, he kept Betancort out of the team earlier this season. Is likely to be named substitute tonight.

Vincente Miera (full-back)
A 28-year-old full-back, he has all Real's honours of League, Cup and European Cup. A solid type of experienced player, he has two international caps.

Manuel Sanchis (full-back)
Another extremely experienced defender, aged 29, who has shared in a great many of Real's successes including the last European Cup win two years ago. Has played in 11 internationals.

Fernando Zunzunegui (centre-half)
Came into the team when Pedro de Felipe was injured. He is aged 23 and a comparative newcomer but is rated a solid, tough centre-back.

Eduardo Gonzalez (half-back)
Plays in the back four, sometimes at right back or as the defensive wing-half. Is still an amateur with nearly 20 caps and played against the British Olympic team recently. Is aged 23.

Ignacia Zoco (half-back)
A midfield wing-half aged 28 and one of Real's current internationals with over 20 caps. Has played against Manchester United in friendly matches and for Spain against England recently and against Scotland. Tall and well-built, he has shared in Real's honours of recent years.

Jose Veloso (outside-right)
Is a thrusting forward with experience at centre-forward as well as on the wing. He is 29, a fast mover with the ball and has a strong shot. Was in Real's last European Cup winning team and has four international caps.

Jose Pirri (inside-forward)
Is 22-years-old and rated one of Spain's most promising players. He is a junior international who also won full amateur honours and is now a current international with nine caps who played against England earlier this month. Has a European Cup medal and plays a midfield game, though always likely to come into the attack.

Amancio Amaro (centre-forward)
Is under suspension and so won't play tonight, but mention must be made of him because he is probably Real's best player. Strong and stocky, he is their leading scorer with great ability. He is 27 and has played for Spain on 17 occasions including the match against England this month.

Ramon Grosso (centre-forward)
A deep-lying player more in the mould of the great Di Stefano. He is 23 and won nine amateur caps before becoming a current Spanish international. He was in the team against England, his fourth cap, and also in Real's European Cup winning side of 1966.

Manuel Velazquez (inside-forward)
One of the team's midfield schemers, he is 24 with Spanish League and European Cup honours. Gained 12 amateur caps and has also played for the full international team. He is in Spain's international squad though he didn't play at Wembley against England three weeks ago.

Francisco Gento (outside-left)
Now 33, he is Real's captain and the only survivor of their great side which won five successive European Cups. He played against Manchester United 11 years ago in the European semi-finals, and is still a winger of electric speed. He holds 42 international caps and has played in 80 European Cup games.

PAGE EIGHT

Longtime *United Review* contributor David Meek profiled the visiting *Madrilenos*, while Peter Slingsby told the story of the esteemed visitors from the Spanish capital

THE STORY OF THE "OLD"

REAL MADRID

by **PETER SLINGSBY**
of the "News of the World"

If you eavesdrop on any conversation between football fans the name of this club or that player crops up within a few seconds. It must happen, for everyone has their favourite team or star and, anyway, that's what soccer is all about . . . names.

And one club always mentioned with favour is Real Madrid. The prefix "Real" in fact means "Royal" and, in view of their glittering run of success throughout Europe, is highly appropriate even though the title was bestowed as long ago as 1920 by King Alfonso XIII.

The incredible thing about a club, now a household name the world over, is that in 1955 when the European Champion Clubs' Cup first became a reality Real were hardly known north of the Pyrenees but a great team had been gathered in Madrid and a beggarly £24,000 had bought the key forward, Alfredo Di Stefano from River Plate.

Just how much Real owe him for their subsequent success it is impossible to calculate; suffice it to say he was twice European Footballer of Year (1957 and 1959), won 38 caps for Argentina and Spain, and scored a record 49 goals in European ties.

But the story of the "old" Real Madrid will be linked forever with Don Santiago Bernabeu, the man after whom their ground is named. He played for them for 14 years before joining their directorate.

He was the inspiration behind the building of their stadium and the teams that have graced it ever since. Remember the names? The flying Gento, fifteen years with the club and lone survivor from the halcyon days, Di Stefano of course, Puskas, that deadly finisher, and those sterling defenders Santamaria, Munoz (now the manager), Marquitos, Rial, Zarraga and so many more.

The performance most British fans recall best in the glorious history of Real was that in 1959-60 at Hampden Park when, in a ten goal final, the Spaniards beat Eintracht (Germany) 7-3 . . . and inspired is hardly the word to describe the football played by Real in the "home" of soccer that day.

Puskas and his lethal left foot produced four goals and Di Stefano the other three against a tip-top side on the day. That display was rightly compared with those of the Hungarians a few years earlier.

However, look at Real's record in the European Cup – and remember they have taken part every season since its inception in Paris thirteen years ago . . . winners in 1955-56, 1956-57, 1957-58, 1958-59, 1959-60, 1965-66 and finalists in 1961-62 and 1963-64.

Manchester United's links with Real go back as far as 1956-57 and, in all the clubs have met seven times. The results show that United have won twice, drawn once and lost the other four matches.

One distinction that belongs to United is that in September, 1962 they became the first English side to beat the Real "giants" on their own pitch since the war.

The occasion was the testimonial match for the Spanish side's veteran skipper, Jose Zarrage and 80,000 spectators saw David Herd and Mark Pearson score the goals which gave the visitors a 2-0 victory.

As a point of interest, these were the line-ups – Real Madrid: Vincente; Rivilla, Miera (sub. Casado); Muller, Santamaria, Zarraga (Zoco); Amancio, Evaristo (Ruiz), Di Stefano, Mendoza (Yanko), Gento.

United: Gaskell; Brennan, Dunne; Stiles, Foulkes, Lawton; Giles, Law, Herd, Pearson, Moir.

In European Cup matches, Real beat United 5-3 (on aggregate) in 1956-57; at the semi-final stage and went on to defeat Fiorentina in the Final by 2-0. The team in those days read Alonso; Torres, Lesmes; Munoz, Marquitos, Zarraga; Kopa, Mateos, Di Stefano, Rial, Gento.

Certainly United fans of yesteryear will remember the names of the greats who shaped the glittering run of success in Europe, in the 1960 World Club Cup, the "Little World Cup" in 1956 and of course the players who have dominated the Spanish League since the mid-50's.

We will remember them tonight with affection as we watch the "new" Real Madrid in action.

PAGE FIVE

Dave Sexton manager

We meet in peculiar circumstances tonight.

This is the "home" leg of our European Cup Winners' Cup first round with St. Etienne, yet we find ourselves playing at Plymouth.

I am not complaining because there could so easily not have been any game at all; it was only through the tremendous efforts of my board of directors and secretary Les Olive that the injustice of U.E.F.A.'s original ruling was reversed in Zurich by the Board of Appeal.

THANKS TO PLYMOUTH

We also have cause to be grateful to Plymouth who have undertaken to act as our hosts and entertain our visitors from France.

So I write in a spirit of appreciation for all the people who have helped us back into the competition and enabled us to complete our tie with St. Etienne.

It remains to be seen just how big a penalty playing our home leg on someone's else's ground proves to be. It was intended as a punishment of course and there is no escaping the fact that the U.E.F.A appeal commission, while granting us a reprieve on the one hand, have made our chances more difficult.

My job as manager has been to try and isolate the players from all the controversy and tension involved in first the expulsion and then the appeal.

None of the trouble has been any of their doing. The facts of winning the Fair Play League for the past two seasons make it quite clear that on the field the record of Manchester United is unblemished.

So we have gone about our normal business of training and playing while the great debate has gone on in Zurich and probably every pub and club in the country!

This evening though there is no escaping the problem for the players. This is where the U.E.F.A. punishment bites home as the team come out at Plymouth instead of in the familiar surroundings of Old Trafford.

I hope that the players will be professional enough to try and put the strange circumstances out of their minds. But it won't be easy to achieve the result we all want.

The tie is most delicately balanced after our 1–1 draw in France, particularly when we remember that St. Etienne have a reputation for being just as dangerous away from home as on their own ground.

SPIRITED ATTACK

So we must put to one side all feeling about the merit or injustice of playing on a neutral ground and concentrate on the job in hand. The boys played splendidly at St. Etienne. They showed composure allied to spirited attack.

I know they will give a good account of themselves. We welcome St. Etienne to England; we thank Plymouth our host club and now let's hope that we shall see a great game of football, because when all the fuss and furore has died down about the fans . . . it's the football that really counts.

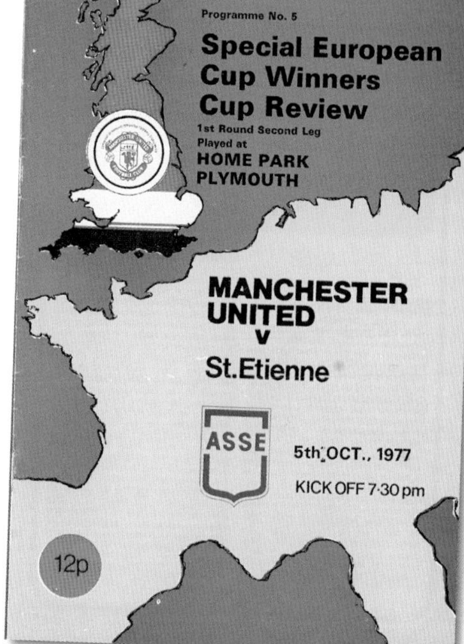

5 October 1977

United v Saint-Etienne

European Cup Winners' Cup

United had played a few European 'home' games at Maine Road in the 1950s, but in 1977 the Reds were made to host Saint-Etienne at Home Park, Plymouth, as a punishment for crowd disturbances. 'Peculiar circumstances' was manager Dave Sexton's astute summary...

Manchester United Squad

STEPNEY
ROCHE
NICHOLL
HOUSTON
ALBISTON
McILROY
GREENHOFF (B)
BUCHAN
COPPELL
McGRATH
GREENHOFF (J)
McCREERY
MACARI
HILL
PEARSON
GRIMES

Team Check

St. Etienne Squad

CURKOVIC
JANVION
FARISON
MERCHADIER
PIAZZA
LOPEZ
SANTINI
SYNAEGHEL
BATHENAY
REVELLI (P)
REVELLI (H)
SARRAMAGNA
ROCHETEAU
BARTHELEMY
ZIMAKO
REPELLINI

Printed by Direct Printing Ltd., Piercy Street, Ancoats, Manchester M4 6FB

United's Team

by MIKE DEMPSEY

It would be a shame if the events on the pitch before the first leg at St Etienne were allowed to overshadow what happened when the game got under way. To many observers, it was the night when this United team demonstrated that they can become just as illustrious as any of the great sides that Old Trafford has given to Europe in the past. The names and faces may have changed since the glory days of the sixties, but the old excitement is back.

Alex Stepney is the last playing link with those times and gets better as he gets older. Tony Waiters said of him just before last year's F.A. Cup Final that he is the most composed goalkeeper in the country. But what about the rest? Can they be as good as the team that boasted three European Footballers of the Year in the same line-up?

Full backs Jimmy Nicholl and Stewart Houston have already made names for themselves here—the one as a prodigiously talented ex-Belfast schoolboy and now Northern Ireland international with a knack of scoring the most spectacular and unexpected goals; the other first as the Brentford bargain, then as the man who missed out on Wembley through injury.

Together with Brian Greenhoff and Martin Buchan, they form a back four that play football, pioneers of a new trend in England. Greenhoff is a United junior who rose through the ranks to make his debut in 1973 and ultimately win international recognition. Buchan has already tasted life in the Cup Winners' Cup. Before his £125,000 move to Old Trafford at the start of 1972, he played for the Aberdeen side that reached the quarter finals where Juventus knocked them out.

Lou Macari is another big signing from Scotland who knows what European football is all about. His campaigns with Celtic make him United's most experienced European player, with five seasons of continental competition and more than 30 ties under his belt. One of his biggest admirers is Frank Blunstone, who reckons him to be one of the best headers of a ball in the game for his size.

Sammy McIlroy, the last of Sir Matt Busby's Irish signings, made his debut for United six years ago at the age of 17. He is the youngest player ever to win a Northern Ireland cap. The man he was inevitably compared with, George Best, said: "He just oozes talent. He's got the skill to play anywhere in the forward line. He's a delight to play alongside."

The front four is unusual for United in that it's all English. The two wingers are about as dissimilar as you can get. Steve Coppell, who is said to have perfected his dribble by using a row of clothes props in the back garden, is a tireless worker and patient attacker. United bought not just a winger, but a thinking winger.

Gordon Hill, a £70,000 snip from Millwall two seasons ago, is the classic, natural winger—a left foot that was born to kick a ball. Cheek, confidence, brilliance and lethal finishing mark him out from every other left winger.

The spearhead of Stuart Pearson and Jimmy Greenhoff is amazing when you consider that one was in the second division with Hull and the other seemingly playing out his career at Stoke. The story of Greenhoff's signing and his Wembley appearance with the winning goal is straight out of the comics. Pearson has come on in leaps and bounds since the £200,000 transfer in 1974, helped enormously by his international experience. He's probably the most mobile centre forward Old Trafford's ever seen.

Last season's brief appearance in the U.E.F.A. Cup hardly gave the team chance to show what they might be capable of abroad. It's unfortunate that in the first two seasons back in Europe they should be drawn against arguably three of the continent's top five teams in the opening rounds. But if they get past St. Etienne, the trail could be blazing again.

OUR THANKS TO PLYMOUTH ARGYLE F.C.

I would firstly like to say a very sincere "Thank You" to Mr. Gillan and his Board of Directors for so kindly agreeing to our request to stage tonight's match at Home Park. We very much appreciate your ready response to our approach and we are greatful to have the use of your facilities this evening. We would also like to thank the public of Plymouth and surrounding area for the interest you have shown in attending here tonight and we hope you will be well rewarded by seeing an excellent game.

L. C. Edwards, Chairman M.U.F.C.

10

MUFC chairman Louis Edwards took the opportunity to thank the Plymouth board for allowing his side to use their ground for a unique tie which the Reds won 2-0

BACK ROW: JOSÉ CARRETE, KURT WELZL, MANUAL-ANGEL BOTUBOT, FRANK ARNESEN, ANGEL CASTELLANOS, JOSÉ-MANUEL SEMPERE. FRONT ROW: ENRIQUE SAURA, DANIEL SOLSONA, MIGUEL TENDILLO, JAVIER SUBIRATS, RODRIGUEZ PABLO.

Ron Atkinson booked United's place in the 1982/83 UEFA Cup thanks to a third-place finish in the league, but the Reds were handed a tough first-round tie against Valencia

15 September 1982

United v Valencia

UEFA Cup

The Spanish side included the legendary Argentinian Mario Kempes among their ranks and the visitors proved too strong for Big Ron's developing side, winning 2-1 on aggregate

TONIGHT'S TEAMS

UNITED v VALENCIA C. de F.

Red Shirts, Black Shorts — *White Shirts, White Shorts*

BRYAN ROBSON

FRANK STAPLETON

UNITED		VALENCIA
Gary Bailey		Sempere
Mike Duxbury		Carrete
Arthur Albiston		Botubot
(Captain) Ray Wilkins		Arias
Kevin Moran		Tendillo
Gordon McQueen		Castellanos
Bryan Robson		Saura (Captain)
Arnold Muhren		Solsona
Frank Stapleton		Subirates
Norman Whiteside		Kempes
Steve Coppell		Moreno
Stephen Pears		Bermell
Ashley Grimes		Roberto
Scott McGarvey		Pablo
Remi Moses		Weltzl
Lou Macari		Rebes

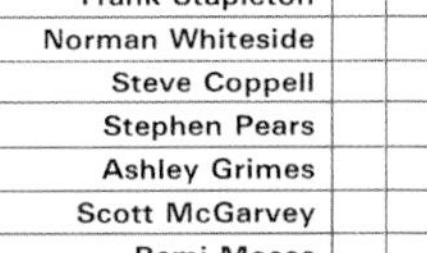

REBES

ROBERTO

Referee: Mr D. KRCHNAK. Linesmen: Dr. J. FOUSEK (Red Flag) Mr I. GREGR (Yellow Flag) Tonight's Match Officials are all from Czechoslovakia.

Team changes will be announced before the match. The player's numbers will also be announced and should be marked in the appropriate box alongside each player's name.

The full draw for the 1st Round of the UEFA Cup is as follows:

Manchester United v Valencia CF
Glentoran FC v Banik Ostrava
FC Utrecht v FC Porto
Progrès Niederkorn v Servette FC
SL Benfica v Real Betis Sevilla
Haarlem v KAA Gent
AS St-Etienne v Tatabanyai Banyasz
Bohemians Prag v FC Admira Wacker
AEK Athènes v IFC Köln
AS Roma v Ipswich Town
Ferencvaros v Atletico Bilbao
Hajduk Split v Zurrieq FC
RSC Anderlechtois v Kuopion Pallotoverit
Slask Wroclwa v Dinamo Moscou
Lyngby BK v IK Brage
FC Vorwärts
Frankfurt/Oder v SV Werder Bremen
Dundee United v PSV Eindhoven
Spartak Moscou v Arsenal FC
Stal Mielec v KSC Lokeren
Viking Stavänger v IFC Lok. Leipzig
FC Carl Zeiss Jena v Girondins de Bordeaux
Shamrock Rovers v Fram Reykjavik
Southampton FC v IFK Norrköping
Borussia Dortmund v Glasgow Rangers
POAK Saloniki v FC Sochaux
Universitatea Craiocva v AC Fiorentina
Sevilla FC v Levki Spartak Sofia
Pezoporikos Larnaca v FC Zürich
Dinamo Tbilsi v Calcio Napoli
IFC Kaiserslautern v Trabzonspor
FK Sarajevo v Slavia Sofia
Graz ASK v Corvinul Hunedoara

The dates for the remaining rounds of the competition are;
2nd Round: October 20th & November 3rd.
3rd Round: November 24th & December 8th.
Quater-final: 2nd & 16th March.
Semi-final: 6th & 20th April.
Final: 4th & 18th May.

12 13

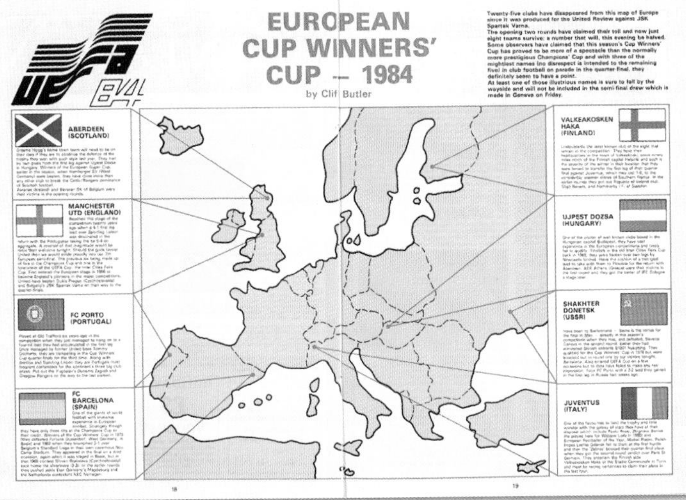
EUROPEAN CUP WINNERS' CUP – 1984

by Clif Butler

Twenty-five clubs have disappeared from this map of Europe since it was produced for the United Review against JSK Spartak Varna.
The opening two rounds have claimed their toll and now just eight teams survive: a number that will, this evening be halved.
Some observers have claimed that this season's Cup Winners' Cup has proved to be more of a spectacle than the normally more prestigious Champions' Cup and with three of the mightiest names (no disrespect is intended to the remaining five) in club football on parade in the quarter final, they definitely seem to have a point.
At least one of those illustrious names is sure to fall by the wayside and will not be included in the semi-final draw which is made in Geneva on Friday.

ABERDEEN (SCOTLAND)

MANCHESTER UTD (ENGLAND)

FC PORTO (PORTUGAL)

FC BARCELONA (SPAIN)

VALKEAKOSKEN HAKA (FINLAND)

UJPEST DOZSA (HUNGARY)

SHAKHTER DONETSK (USSR)

JUVENTUS (ITALY)

The runners and riders in the 1983/84 European Cup Winners' Cup last eight included some giants of the European game, with United paired with Barcelona

Another Argentinian genius was in town in the shape of Diego Armando Maradona. But unlike Kempes, Diego wouldn't enjoy his night in Manchester, with United winning 3-0 on a glorious Old Trafford occasion

21 March 1984

United v Barcelona

European Cup Winners' Cup

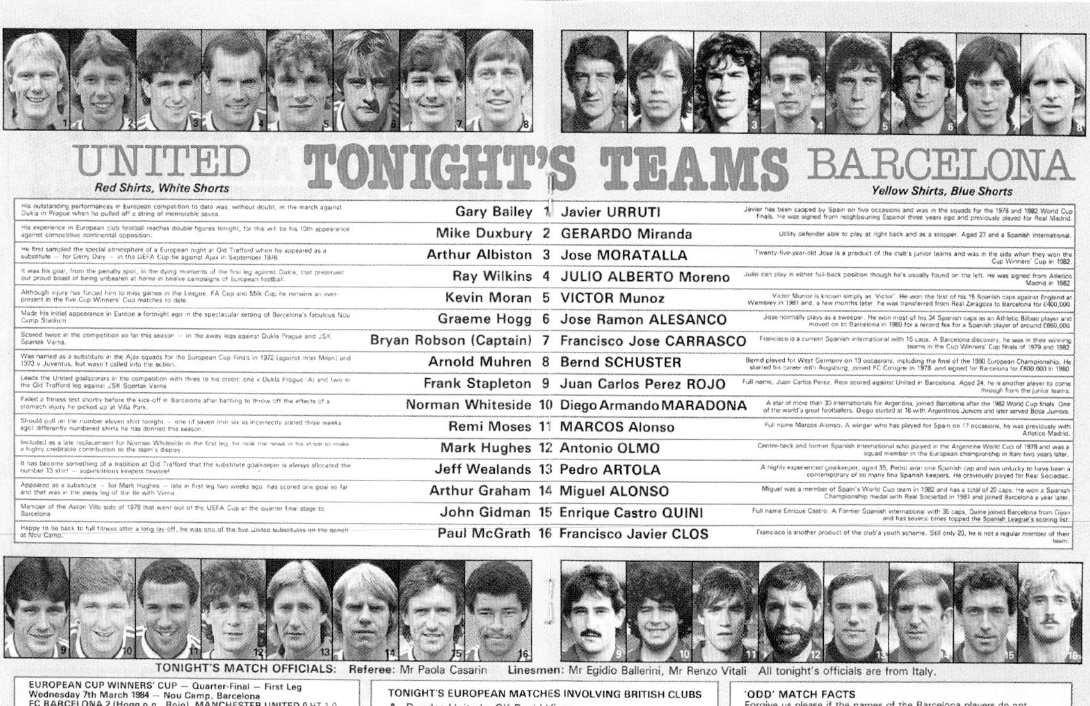

UNITED — TONIGHT'S TEAMS — BARCELONA

Red Shirts, White Shorts | *Yellow Shirts, Blue Shorts*

United note	United	No.	Barcelona	Barcelona note
His outstanding performances in European competition to date was, without doubt, in the match against Dukla in Prague when he pulled off a string of memorable saves.	Gary Bailey	1	Javier URRUTI	Javier has been capped by Spain on five occasions and was in the squads for the 1978 and 1982 World Cup Finals. He was signed from neighbouring Espanol three years ago and previously played for Real Madrid.
His experience in European club football reaches double figures tonight, for this will be his 10th appearance against competitive continental opposition.	Mike Duxbury	2	GERARDO Miranda	Utility defender able to play at right back and as a stopper. Aged 27 and a Spanish international.
He first sampled the special atmosphere of a European night at Old Trafford when he appeared as a substitute — for Gerry Daly — in the UEFA Cup-tie against Ajax in September 1976.	Arthur Albiston	3	Jose MORATALLA	Twenty-five-year-old Jose is a product of the club's junior teams and was in the side when they won the Cup Winners' Cup in 1982.
It was his goal, from the penalty spot, in the dying moments of the first leg against Dukla, that preserved our proud boast of being unbeaten at home in twelve campaigns of European football.	Ray Wilkins	4	JULIO ALBERTO Moreno	Julio can play in either full-back position though he's usually found on the left. He was signed from Atletico Madrid in 1982.
Although injury has forced him to miss games in the League, FA Cup and Milk Cup he remains an ever-present in the five Cup Winners' Cup matches to date.	Kevin Moran	5	VICTOR Munoz	Victor Munoz is known simply as 'Victor'. He won the first of his 15 Spanish caps against England at Wembley in 1981 and, a few months later, he was transferred from Real Zaragoza to Barcelona for £400,000.
Made his initial appearance in Europe a fortnight ago in the spectacular setting of Barcelona's fabulous Nou Camp Stadium.	Graeme Hogg	6	Jose Ramon ALESANCO	Jose normally plays as a sweeper. He won most of his 34 Spanish caps as an Athletic Bilbao player and moved on to Barcelona in 1980 for a record fee for a Spanish player of around £860,000.
Scored twice in the competition so far this season — in the away legs against Dukla Prague and JSK Spartak Varna.	Bryan Robson (Captain)	7	Francisco Jose CARRASCO	Francisco is a current Spanish international with 16 caps. A Barcelona discovery, he was in their winning teams in the Cup Winners' Cup finals of 1979 and 1982.
Was named as a substitute in the Ajax squads for the European Cup Finals in 1972 (against Inter Milan) and 1973 v Juventus, but wasn't called into the action.	Arnold Muhren	8	Bernd SCHUSTER	Bernd played for West Germany on 19 occasions, including the final of the 1980 European Championship. He started his career with Augsburg, joined FC Cologne in 1978 and signed for Barcelona for £900,000 in 1980.
Leads the United goalscorers in the competition with three to his credit: one v Dukla Prague (A) and two in the Old Trafford leg against JSK Spartak Varna.	Frank Stapleton	9	Juan Carlos Perez ROJO	Full name, Juan Carlos Perez. Rojo scored against United in Barcelona. Aged 24, he is another player to come through from the junior teams.
Failed a fitness test shortly before the kick-off in Barcelona after battling to throw off the effects of a stomach injury he picked up at Villa Park.	Norman Whiteside	10	Diego Armando MARADONA	A star of more than 30 internationals for Argentina, joined Barcelona after the 1982 World Cup finals. One of the world's great footballers, Diego started at 16 with Argentinos Juniors and later served Boca Juniors.
Should pull on the number eleven shirt tonight — one of seven (not six as incorrectly stated three weeks ago) differently numbered shirts he has donned this season.	Remi Moses	11	MARCOS Alonso	Full name Marcos Alonso. A winger who has played for Spain on 17 occasions, he was previously with Atletico Madrid.
Included as a late replacement for Norman Whiteside in the first leg, he took the news in his stride to make a highly creditable contribution to the team's display.	Mark Hughes	12	Antonio OLMO	Centre-back and former Spanish international who played in the Argentine World Cup of 1978 and was a squad member in the European championship in Italy two years later.
It has become something of a tradition at Old Trafford that the substitute goalkeeper is always allocated the number 13 shirt — superstitious keepers beware!	Jeff Wealands	13	Pedro ARTOLA	A highly experienced goalkeeper, aged 35, Pedro won one Spanish cap and was unlucky to have been a contemporary of so many fine Spanish keepers. He previously played for Real Sociedad.
Appeared as a substitute — for Mark Hughes — late in first leg two weeks ago, has scored one goal so far and that was in the away leg of the tie with Varna.	Arthur Graham	14	Miguel ALONSO	Miguel was a member of Spain's World Cup team in 1982 and has a total of 20 caps. He won a Spanish Championship medal with Real Sociedad in 1981 and joined Barcelona a year later.
Member of the Aston Villa side of 1978 that went out of the UEFA Cup at the quarter-final stage to Barcelona.	John Gidman	15	Enrique Castro QUINI	Full name Enrique Castro. A former Spanish international with 35 caps, Quini joined Barcelona from Gijon and has several times topped the Spanish League's scoring list.
Happy to be back to full fitness after a long lay-off, he was one of the five United substitutes on the bench at Nou Camp.	Paul McGrath	16	Francisco Javier CLOS	Francisco is another product of the club's youth scheme. Still only 23, he is not a regular member of their team.

TONIGHT'S MATCH OFFICIALS: Referee: Mr Paola Casarin Linesmen: Mr Egidio Ballerini, Mr Renzo Vitali All tonight's officials are from Italy.

EUROPEAN CUP WINNERS' CUP — Quarter-Final — First Leg
Wednesday 7th March 1984 — Nou Camp, Barcelona
FC BARCELONA 2 (Hogg o.g., Rojo). MANCHESTER UNITED 0 HT 1-0
FC BARCELONA: Urruti, Gerardo, Moratalla, Julio Alberto, Victor, Alesanco, Carrasco (sub: Alonso), Schuster, Rojo, Maradona (sub: Clos), Marcos.
Substitutes: Olmo, Artola, Quini.
MANCHESTER UNITED: Bailey, Duxbury, Albiston, Wilkins, Moran, Hogg, Robson, Muhren, Stapleton, Hughes (sub: Graham), Moses.
Substitutes: Wealands, Gidman, Macari, McGrath.
Referee: Michel Vautrot (France) Attendance: 70,000 (to be confirmed).

TONIGHT'S EUROPEAN MATCHES INVOLVING BRITISH CLUBS
A Dundee United v SK Rapid Vienna
B SL Benfica v Liverpool
C Aberdeen v Ujpest Dozsa
D FK Austria Memphis Vienna v Tottenham Hotspur
E SK Raika Sturm Graz v Nottingham Forest
Latest scores will be announced over the Public Address system during this evening's match.

'ODD' MATCH FACTS
Forgive us please if the names of the Barcelona players do not appear quite straightforward. There is however, a tendancy on the continent for certain players to be either known by their nickname or even by a name which seems to bear no resemblence to their own. Therefore, the part shown in capitals on the Barcelona squad is the name by which the player is generally known.
That's simple enough isn't it!

12 13

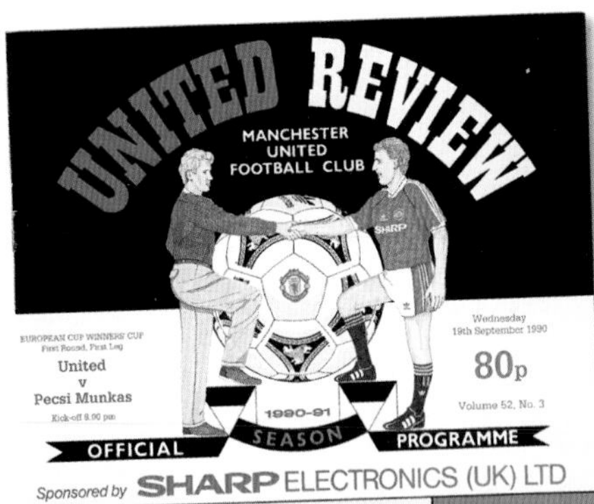

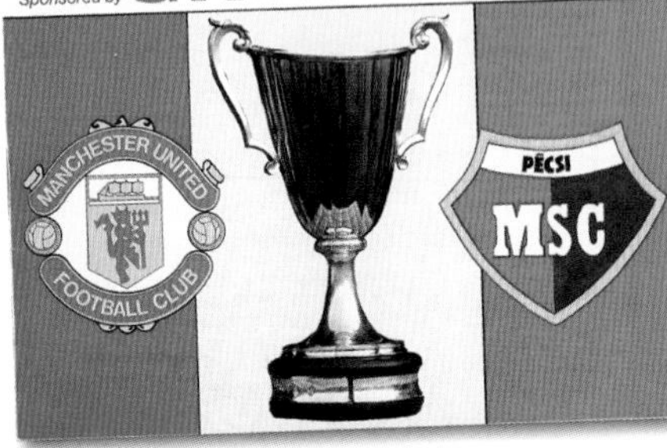

19 September 1990

United v Pecsi Munkas

European Cup Winners' Cup

EUROPEAN CUP WINNERS' CUP
FIRST ROUND 1990-91

SWIFT HESPERANGE (Luxembourg) (18)	v	LEGIA WARSAW (Poland) (23)
TRABSONSPOR (Turkey) (30)	v	BARCELONA (Spain) (27)
VIKING STAVANGER (Norway) (22)	v	RFC LIEGE (Belgium) (3)
SLIVEN (Bulgaria) (4)	v	JUVENTUS (Italy) (17)
MANCHESTER UNITED (England) (10)	v	PECSI MUNKAS (Hungary) (15)
DYNAMO KIEV (Soviet Union) (31)	v	KUOPION PALLOSEURA (Finland) (11)
PSV SCHWERIN (East Germany) (8)	v	AUSTRIA MEMPHIS (Austria) (2)
DUKLA PRAGUE (Czechoslovakia) (6)	v	SLIEMA WANDERERS (Malta) (19)
FAMAGUSTA (Cyprus) (5)	v	ABERDEEN (Scotland) (26)
MONTPELLIER (France) (12)	v	PSV EINDHOVEN (Netherlands) (20)
FLAMURTARI VLORA (Albania) (1)	v	OLYMPIAKOS (Greece) (14)
GLENTORAN (Northern Ireland) (21)	v	STEAUA BUCHAREST (Romania) (25)
WREXHAM (Wales) (32)	v	LYNGBY BK (Denmark) (7)
ESTRELA DA AMADORA (Portugal) (24)	v	NEUCHATEL XAMAX (Switzerland) (29)
REYKJAVIK (Iceland) (16)	v	DJURGARDENS (Sweden) (28)
KAISERSLAUTERN (West Germany) (13)	v	SAMPDORIA (Italy) (17)

● Numbers denote map reference

5

ALEX FERGUSON

I offer you a particularly warm welcome this evening as the curtain goes up on European football again.

It's an auspicious occasion after five years in the soccer wilderness serving the ban imposed by UEFA following the terrible tragedy at Heysel.

Everyone at Manchester United is proud that it has fallen on this club along with Aston Villa to lead the way back. It's a big responsibility of course because the eyes of the world will be scrutinising this match and the behaviour of spectators, both inside and outside the ground, very closely.

But I must add that I think it very fitting that it should be United showing not just the way back, but the way forward. For it was this club of course who pioneered the way into Europe for English football.

Looking back it was an incredibly daring and adventurous decision because it involved incurring the wrath of the Football League who thought that it would lead to a congestion of fixtures and somehow undermine the importance of the domestic League game.

The magical success since of European football showed that they lacked the vision of Sir Matt Busby and that their thinking was insular.

The European Cup and the other competitions which followed like the Cup Winners Cup have provided some thrilling nights for fans, and even supporters with no direct commitment have enjoyed the extra dimension.

I know that the peak of my career as manager of Aberdeen was the glorious evening we beat Real Madrid of all people to win the European Cup Winners Cup.

I know also how much United supporters will welcome the return of European football to Old Trafford, for in addition to blazing a trail for others to follow the club has established a tradition which is highly valued and rightly so.

We have all missed Europe, supporters, players and management alike. Some of our younger fans may never have seen it first hand, and the same goes for our young players of course.

Indeed we might well have only a couple of players in the side against Pecsi Munkas tonight who have had experience of the game at this level. It will be a big step up for everyone but useful in the learning process.

We shall have to make sure that no-one gets carried away by the occasion, but at the same time I shall be looking for us to reveal typical British assets and play with passion.

Our opponents looked a useful side when I saw them play in a tournament soon after the draw was made. They are young and one of them, Balazs Berczy, was in the Hungarian team which played against England at Wembley last week.

If you give them time, Pecsi display typical Hungarian skills, though how they will react to the atmosphere of Old Trafford remains to be seen. Certainly I hope our fans are in good vocal mood, because they can help us considerably to secure the two or three goal lead I would like to take as a cushion to Hungary for the second leg next month.

I want our players to keep cool, and let the crowd do the rest!

At the same time I would like to extend the warmest of welcomes to our Hungarian guests. They are a very friendly club and I am sure we are going to see a fine game worthy of this historic occasion as we pick up the European challenge once more.

Welcome to Manchester

A Manchester United Football Club szívélyes udvözletét küldi a Pécsi Munkás Sport Club igazgatóságának, személyzetének és játékosainak remélik, hogy szép emlékkel térnek viboza Manchesterból

AF

CLUB TELEPHONE NUMBERS

Main Switchboard (General Enquiries) 872 1661

Ticket & Match Information Service 872 0199

Commercial Department 872 3488

Development Association 872 4676

Membership & Supporters Office 872 5208

(Information Line) 873 8303

Executive Suite 872 3331

Red Devils Souvenir Shop 872 3398

Please Note: Callers from outside of Manchester should first dial 061

UNITED REVIEW

The official programme of Manchester United Football Club plc.

Edited by Cliff Butler.

Printed by Hemmings & Capey (Leicester) Ltd

The visit of Hungarian side Pecsi Munkas in September 1990 not only marked the first European tie of the Alex Ferguson era at United; it kicked off a thrilling campaign that reached a dramatic conclusion in Rotterdam eight months later

There were 32 teams from across Europe who had designs on the trophy when the tournament began, including fellow UK representatives Aberdeen, Wrexham and Glentoran. The 1990/91 season was the first time English teams had been able to take part in European competition for five years, due to the ban imposed in the aftermath of the Heysel Stadium disaster in 1985

EUROPEAN CUP WINNERS' CUP 1991

EUROPEAN CHAMPION CLUBS' CUP 1991

FIRST ROUND

v. PECSI MUNKAS (Hungary)
First Leg (Manchester)
MANCHESTER UNITED 2, PECSI MUNKAS 0
Second Leg (Pecs)
PECSI MUNKAS 0, MANCHESTER UNITED 1

v. GRASSHOPPERS ZURICH (Switzerland)
First Leg (Belgrade)
RED STAR BELGRADE 1, GRASSHOPPERS ZURICH 1
Second Leg (Zurich)
GRASSHOPPERS ZURICH 1, RED STAR BELGRADE 4

SECOND ROUND

v. WREXHAM (Wales)
First Leg (Manchester)
MANCHESTER UNITED 3, WREXHAM 0
Second Leg (Wrexham)
WREXHAM 0, MANCHESTER UNITED 2

v. GLASGOW RANGERS (Scotland)
First Leg (Belgrade)
RED STAR BELGRADE 3, GLASGOW RANGERS 0
Second Leg (Glasgow)
GLASGOW RANGERS 1, RED STAR BELGRADE 1

QUARTER FINAL

v. MONTEPELLIER HERAULT (France)
First Leg (Manchester)
MANCHESTER UNITED 1, MONTPELLIER HERAULT 1
Second Leg (Montpellier)
MONTPELLIER HERAULT 0, MANCHESTER UNITED 2

v. DYNAMO DRESDEN (Germany)
First Leg (Belgrade)
RED STAR BELGRADE 3, DYNAMO DRESDEN 0
Second Leg (Dresden)
DYNAMO DRESDEN 1, RED STAR BELGRADE 2

SEMI FINAL

v. LEGIA WARSAW (Poland)
First Leg (Warsaw)
LEGIA WARSAW 1, MANCHESTER UNITED 3
Second Leg (Manchester)
MANCHESTER UNITED 1, LEGIA WARSAW 1

v. BAYERN MUNICH (Germany)
First Leg (Munich)
BAYERN MUNICH 1, RED STAR BELGRADE 2
Second Leg (Belgrade)
RED STAR BELGRADE 2, BAYERN MUNICH 2

FINAL

v. BARCELONA (Spain)
in Rotterdam
MANCHESTER UNITED 2
BARCELONA 1

v. OLYMPIQUE MARSEILLE (France)
in Bari
RED STAR BELGRADE 0
OLYMPIQUE MARSEILLE 0
After Extra Time Red Star
won 5-3 on penalties.

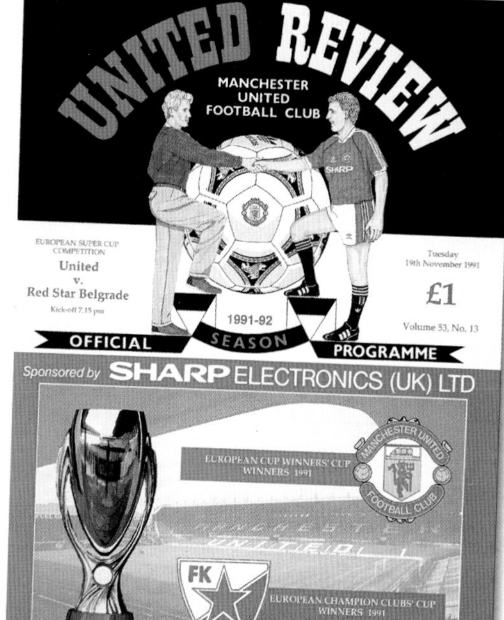

19 November 1991

United v Red Star Belgrade

European Super Cup

As Cup Winners' Cup champions, United faced European Cup holders Red Star Belgrade in the Super Cup at Old Trafford in November '91. It was the first time we'd met the Yugoslavs since February 1958 and a solitary Brian McClair goal was enough to win another trophy for Ferguson and co

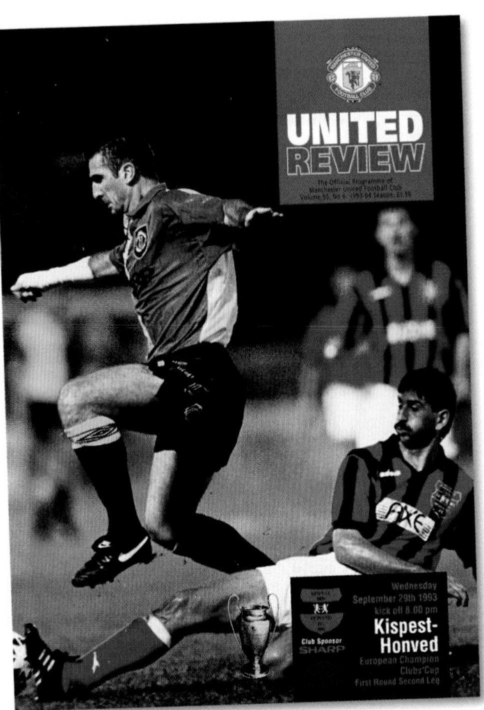

29 September 1993
United v Kispest Honved
UEFA Champions League

Welcome to Old Trafford

It is with great pleasure that we welcome officials, players and supporters of Kispest-Honved, the champions of Hungary.
Whilst the first leg resulted in a victory for our team, we must take nothing for granted tonight.
Indeed, we have a very proud record to protect for wb have never lost a home European Cup-tie.
This evening will evoke many happy memories for those of us old enough to remember previous occasions when we played in the Champions Cup. For those too young to indulge in such nostalgia, remember that every team in this tournament (with the exception of Monaco) are the champions of their country. This truly is the most prestigious club competition in Europe.
It can be seen that the perimeter fences are at their lower height this evening and not the full 2.2m as has been the case at previous matches in Europe. During the summer a FA/UEFA delegation visited Old Trafford to discuss arrangements for the European Championships in 1996. During that visit we raised the question of perimeter fences and were delighted to learn they now feel that full fences may not be necessary. I think this can be seen as a just reward for our club following the scenes after the F.A. Premier Trophy was presented last May.
The discipline of our supporters that night was incredible. The whole affair could have so easily ended in a shambles of supporters had come on to the pitch. Instead we all enjoyed a wonderful occasion to the full. If this is seen as a 'thank you' to our supporters then it is thoroughly well deserved.

C. Martin Edwards. Chairman

WELCOME
Üdvözöljük a Kispesti Honvéd csapatát.
A Manchester United vezetői, játékosai és a csapat támogatói nevében fogadják meleg üdvözleyünket. Romélyük, hogy látogatásuk Manchesterben kellemesen telik el és városunkból szép emlékekkel térnek haza. Szeretnénk be legjobb sport bagyomágyinkboz bivn együtt élvezbetnénk egy olyan labdarugo mérközést melyben a jobbik fél lesz a gyöztes.

UNITED REVIEW

Chairman Martin Edwards wrote the welcome note in the programme for Old Trafford's first European Cup tie in 24 years, a tournament now rebranded as the UEFA Champions League

European Legend

FERENC PUSKAS, captain of Honved in their greatest days, remains one of the greatest players of all time.
He learned his football in a country which had built up the game on the firmest of foundations. Football had been brought to Hungary by English students in the 1870s and was refined after the First World War by the legendary coach, Jimmy Hogan.
Puskas's father was a player and later coach with the local club, Kispest. Everyone there soon knew his son could play. At 16, young Ferenc was a regular at inside left, terrorising opposing goalkeepers with the power of his shooting. He never used his right foot - his left was so lethal he never needed it.
At 18 he was in the national team. His brilliance had much to do with the decision to convert Kispest into a new army sports club named Honved. That team formed the basis of a national side which swept all before it.
For four years the team built around Puskas, lifelong friend and righthalf Jozsef Bozsik and fellow forwards Sandor Kocsis and Nandor Hidegkuti crushed all opposition. Hungary won the 1952 Olympic title before ending England's record of invincibility against continental opposition with a stunning 6-3 triumph at Wembley.
Hidegkuti scored after a minute, Jackie Sewell hit back and then Puskas took over. He was flat on his back when he laid off a pass for Hidegkuti to restore Hungary's lead. Next, in a moment of technical magic, he collected a short cross, outplayed Billy Wright on a sixpence and fired home himself. When Bozsik shot for goal it was again Puskas who provided the touch which deceived goalkeeper Gil Merrick.
No wonder Hungary were overwhelming favourites to win the 1954 World Cup in Switzerland.
But Puskas presented a problem. He had been injured in an early round game against West Germany and was a hobbling spectator at training before the Final, against these same West Germans, in Berne. Could his great left foot withstand the strain? Puskas thought so and decided to play.
After six minutes the gamble appeared to be paying off when Puskas shot Hungary in front. Two more minutes and Zoltan Czibor scored Hungary's second.
It should have been all over but the Germans were undaunted. Inside right Max Morlock pulled one goal back and right winger Helmut Rahn equalised. Time, and Hungary's luck, were running out. Winger Jozsef Toth saw a shot blocked on the goal-line; a header by Kocsis scraped the face of the bar; Puskas shot home only to be flagged offside....and Rahn struck the Germans' winning goal.
Puskas would return to the World Cup finals in Chile in 1962, his trusty left foot was doing duty for Spain because Puskas had, in the meantime, joined Real Madrid.
Honved had been abroad when the Hungarian Revolution of 1956 erupted. Puskas and several team-mates decide to stay in the West. He tried to sign for several Italian clubs, but they thought him too old. How wrong they were was underlined when Puskas developed, at Madrid, a new career to emulate his first in brilliance.
Four times he was the Spanish league's top scorer and his partnership with the Argentine centre-forward, Alfredo Di Stefano, was one of the greatest of all time. They hit perfection when Madrid thrashed Eintracht Frankfurt 7-3 in the European Champions' Cup Final before a 135,000 crowd at Hampden.
In 1966 he retired taking his coaching know-how around the world. Last year he returned home to Budapest to be feted once again as a national hero. Hardly surprising. After all, how many players can boast 83 goals in 84 games for their country?

FACTFILE
Ferenc Puskas. Forward.
Born : Budapest, April 2, 1927.
Clubs : Honved (1943-56)
Real Madrid (1958-66)
84 Caps for Hungary; 4 for Spain.
Honours : 1960 World Club Cup; 1960 European Champions' Cup; 6 Hungarian championships; 5 Spanish championships.

United19Review

The visitors were Hungarian side Kispest Honved, who we'd beaten 3-2 in the first leg in Budapest. Two goals from Steve Bruce at Old Trafford helped United to a 2-1 win in the return game

Kispest-Honved

Manager Martti Kuusela brings his side to Old Trafford this evening still believing they can recover from that 2-3 first-leg defeat and go through to the second round of the European Champions Cup for what would be the fifth time.
The late goal from Istvan Stefanov gave the men from Budapest a lifeline after they had been in danger of being outplayed at one stage of the game.
But it was Jozsef Szabados who had the distinction of scoring Honved's first-ever goal against English opposition in a European tie.
Mr Kuusela said that he was pleased how his side held out when under pressure against United in the first game. "As soon as the draw was made I knew it would be difficult for us," he said. "I have a good team but it has yet to reach its peak. It would have been better for us to have played a smaller club at this stage. It was exciting to be drawn against Manchester United because they are one of the most famous clubs in the world.
"But the present United team is one of the best in Europe and I know we had ab big job. Yet my players learned a lot from the first game and, being only one goal down, who knows what might happen at Old Trafford?"
This is the second time Honved have played a European tie in Manchester. When they previously journeyed here in November 1970 their destination was Maine Road. The first-leg of their Cup-Winners' Cup tie in Budapest had swong City's way, a goal from Francis Lee giving them a 1-0 win.
So, on that occasion, Honved were in a similar position to today. They were a goal down with everything to do. The task was too much for them. Colin Bell opened the scoring for City and Lee got another as City won 2-0 on the night and 3-0 on aggregate.

Martti Kuusela

United28Review

The return leg

Until now Honved had met only one other English club in European competitions - Liverpool. In 1966 Honved smashed a club record by reaching the quarter-final stage of the Cup-Winners'-Cup.
Drawn against Liverpool in that quarter-final, the first game in Budapest ended goalless. Goals from Chris Lawler and Ian St John gave Liverpool a 2-0 win at Anfield.
Only on one other occasion have Honved survived to the last eight in Europe. In 1979 they went through to the quarter-finals of the UEFA Cup.
It is two years since Honved enjoyed their last European venture. In the first round of the Champions' Cup in 1991/92 they were held to 1-1 at home by the Irish club Dundalk but they recovered to win the return game 2-0 in Ireland.
They then produced one of their finest performances in defeating Sampdoria 2-1 in Budapest. The Italians, who went on to lose 0-1 to Barcelona in the final, won the second-leg 3-1.
The Honved club was formed from the remnants of the old Kispest Athletic Club in 1949. Financed by the state, Honved was Hungary's Army club covering all sports but the football section quickly established itself as a force in Hungarian football.
They won the Hungarian Championship in the short 1949/50 season and again, later that year, when they also lifted the Mitropa Cup, a competition for the top clubs of central Europe.
Honved were among V.I.P. visitors invited by Wolves to feature in many exciting televised friendly games in the 'fifties. Ferenc Puskas, Josef Bozsik and Zoltan Czibor were the stars of the side that went to Molineux in December 1954.
That trio had engraved their names indelibly upon the minds of all England fans after master-minding Hungary's famous 6-3 victory at Wembley in 1953.
At Molineux Honved swept into a 2-0 lead but Wolves hit back with a penalty. Two late goals from Roy Swinbourne gave the English side a 3-2 victory.
Whereas Wolves were then beginning to fade - and made little impact when the European Champions Cup was introduced - Honved were a maturing side.
Coincidentally, they made their European debut at the same time as United in 1956/57. Honved received a bye in to the First Round and went in at the deep end against Atletico Madrid. After losing 2-3 in Spain they were forced by political requirements to play the return leg in Brussels. A 3-3 draw meant an early exit from the competition.
The club's name was changed to Kispest-Honved in 1991 and they won the Hungarian Championship for the 13th time last season.
Whilst participating in the European Champions' Cup for the ninth time this season, they have never survived beyond the second round.
Since state aid for football ended in the 'eighties, Hungarian clubs have undergone considerable change. The Honved club was split up in 1991, the footballing interest re-forming as Kispest-Honved, which is now a limited company owned by the Belgian Louis de Vries.

United29Review

Alex Ferguson

There were perhaps a few Manchester United supporters who groaned when we were drawn again in the same group as Juventus for this season's UEFA Champions League.

Their misgivings are based of course on the fact that we lost both our group games against the Italian champions last season.

My reaction, though, was more one of elation because we now have the opportunity to set the record straight. Life doesn't always give people a second chance; but here in European competition at least, that is exactly what this year's draw has given us.

This is our opportunity to make up for the mistakes that saw us beaten, albeit on both occasions by the narrow margin of 1-0, and make it plain that we consider we have gone up a gear since then.

Our aim now is twofold, obviously to do well, but perhaps even more importantly make it clear that we have the ability to learn.

This is not just a matter of whistling in the wind because I think there was evidence even last year as the competition progressed that out players are prepared to absorb experience and use it to emerge a better team.

As the first game against Juventus in Turin wore on, we were better in the second half than we had been in the first, and by the time we were playing them at Old Trafford, I thought we had nothing to fear.

We lost, but that sometimes happens in football, and I think it would be fair to say that Juventus felt that on the night they had the touch of luck that makes all the difference.

So I certainly welcome this opportunity to play then again and I extend the warmest of welcomes to their players and Marcello Lippi, a coach for whom I have the greatest respect.

We cannot at the moment put up a record in Europe to compare with Juventus, but he knows we are an emerging team and I think he will know that he will be taking on a slightly harder task this year.

Juventus will be feeling pretty confident themselves of course after opening with a 5-1 win at home to Feyenoord, but I was certainly happy enough to open our own account with an away win to the tune of 3-0 against Kosice in Slovakia.

We were good in the first half, perhaps a little patchy in the second, but you cannot control a game all the time. It was a very good result for us and hopefully tonight we will have one or two of our injured players back in action to give me more options.

So, on to this evening's game and it's great to have Juventus again with the chance to measure ourselves against the best. This is what the game is all about, especially in Europe, and I am really looking forward to it.

Alex Ferguson

1 October 1997

United v Juventus

UEFA Champions League

This thrilling tie ended 3-2 to United, with goals from Teddy Sheringham, Paul Scholes and Giggs cancelling out strikes from Alessandro Del Piero and Zinedine Zidane

Manchester United

Stadium
Old Trafford (56,387)

Club Honours
National Championships (11)
1908, 1911, 1952, 1956, 1957, 1965, 1967, 1993, 1994, 1996, 1997
Cups (9)
1909, 1948, 1963, 1977, 1983, 1985, 1990, 1994, 1996
National League Cup (1)
1991
European Champion Clubs' Cup (1)
1968
European Cup Winners' Cup (1)
1991
European Super Competition (1)
1991

Manager	
Alex Ferguson	
Goalkeepers	
van der Gouw, Raimond	17
Pilkington, Kevin	25
Schmeichel, Peter	1
Defence	
Berg, Henning	21
Clegg, Michael	19
Irwin, Denis	3
Johnsen, Ronny	5
May, David	4
Neville, Gary	2
Neville, Phil	12
Pallister, Gary	6
Midfield	
Beckham, David	7
Butt, Nicky	8
Keane, Roy	16
McClair, Brian	13
Forwards	
Cole, Andy	9
Cooke, Terry	22
Cruyff, Jordi	14
Giggs, Ryan	11
Mulryne, Philip	28
Nevland, Erik	24
Poborsky, Karel	15
Scholes, Paul	18
Sheringham, Teddy	10
Solskjaer, Ole Gunnar	20
Thornley, Ben	23

Referee: A.J. Lopez Nieto (Spain)

Juventus FC

Head Coach	
Lippi, Marcello	
Goalkeepers	
De Sanctis, Morgan	17
Peruzzi, Angelo	1
Rampulla, Michelangelo	12
Defence	
Birindelli, Alessandro	15
Dimas, Manuel Marques	6
Ferrara, Ciro	2
Iuliano, Mark	13
Montero, Paolo	4
Pessotto, Gianluca	22
Torricelli, Moreno	3
Zamboni, Marco	23
Midfield	
Ametrano, Raffaele	24
Conte, Antonio	8
Deschamps, Didier	14
Di Livio, Angelo	7
Pecchia, Fabio	5
Tacchinardi, Alessio	20
Zidane, Zinedine	21
Forwards	
Amoruso, Nicola	16
Del Piero, Alessandro	10
Fonseca, Daniel	18
Inzaghi, Filippo	9
Padovano, Michele	11

Assistant Referees: V. Giraldes Carrasco (Spain)
S. Chinito Rivera (Spain)
Fourth Official: C. Garcia Redondo (Spain)
UEFA Delegate: D. Casey (Ireland)
Referee's Observer: E. Halle (Norway)

Stadium
Nuovo Stadio Delle Alpi (69,041)

Club Honours
National Championships (24)
1905, 1926, 1931, 1932, 1933, 1934, 1935, 1950, 1952, 1958, 1960, 1961, 1967, 1972, 1973, 1975, 1977, 1978, 1981, 1982, 1984, 1986, 1995, 1997
National Cups (9)
1938, 1942, 1959, 1960, 1965, 1979, 1983, 1990, 1995
European Champion Clubs' Cup (2)
1985, 1996
European Cup Winners' Cup (1)
1984
UEFA Cup (3)
1977, 1990, 1993
European Super Cup (2)
1985, 1996
European/South American Cup (2)
1985, 1996

Record in UEFA Champions League
Feyenoord (Netherlands) home 5-1

25

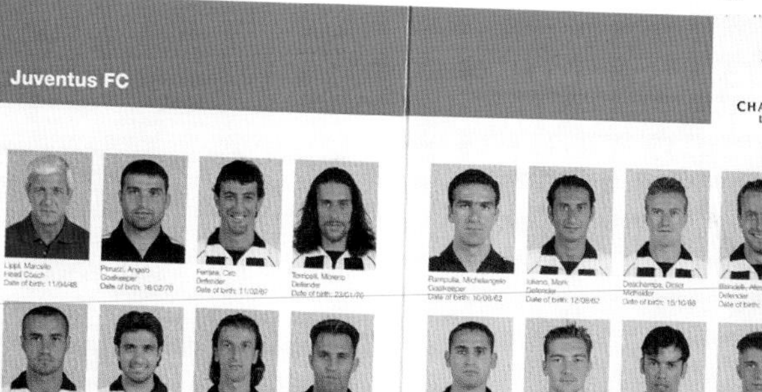

Marcello Lippi's superstars had beaten United home and away the previous year, so this result marked an important staging post in the development of Ferguson's side

3 March 1999
United v Internazionale
UEFA Champions League

At the quarter-final stage of the 1998/99 Champions League, the programme mapped out our route to the Nou Camp final

UEFA CHAMPIONS LEAGUE

Group	03.03 1999 17.03 1999	07.04 1999 23.04 1999	26.05 1999
Group A: Olympiakos FC, NK Croatia Zagreb, FC Porto, AFC Ajax			
	Juventus FC – Olympiakos FC		
Group B: Juventus FC, Galatasaray SK, Rosenborg BK, Athletic Club Bilbao		Semi-finals	
	Manchester United FC – Internazionale FC		
Group C: Internazionale FC, Real Madrid CF, Spartak Moscow, SK Sturm Graz			Final
Group D: FC Bayern Munich, Manchester United FC, FC Barcelona, Brondby IF			
	FC Bayern Munich – 1. FC Kaiserslautern		
Group E: Dynamo Kiev, RC Lens, Arsenal FC, Panathinaikos FC		Semi-finals	
	Real Madrid CF – Dynamo Kiev		
Group F: 1. FC Kaiserslautern, SL Benfica, PSV Eindhoven, HJK Helsinki			
	03.03 1999 17.03 1999	07.04 1999 23.04 1999	26.05 1999

The six group-winners and the two best runners-up shall play the Quarter-final matches.
The two best runners-up have been determined with the criteria listed below, from left to right, in decreasing order of importance.

		Points	Goal difference	Goals scored	Goals scored away
1	Real Madrid CF	12	+9	17	7
2	Manchester United FC	10	+9	20	11
3	Galatasaray SK	8	0	8	2
4	SL Benfica	8	-1	8	2
5	RC Lens	8	-1	5	2
6	NK Croatia Zagreb	8	-2	5	1

The semi-final pairings shall be drawn by lot.

53

The game reunited old foes David Beckham and Diego Simeone, of Inter and Argentina

Manchester United

CHAMPIONS LEAGUE

      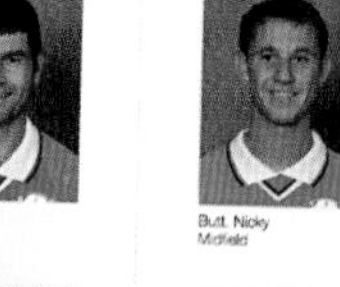      

Schmeichel, Peter
Goalkeeper

van der Gouw, Raimond
Goalkeeper

Neville, Gary
Defender

Irwin, Denis
Defender

Butt, Nicky
Midfield

Keane, Roy
Midfield

Scholes, Paul
Midfield

Mulryne, Philip
Midfield

May, David
Defender

Johnsen, Ronny
Defender

Stam, Jaap
Defender

Neville, Phil
Defender

Cole, Andy
Forward

Sheringham, Teddy
Forward

Giggs, Ryan
Forward

Blomqvist, Jesper
Forward

 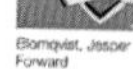         

Berg, Henning
Defender

Clegg, Michael
Defender

Brown, Wesley
Defender

Beckham, David
Midfield

Yorke, Dwight
Forward

Solskjaer, Ole Gunnar
Forward

Nevland, Erik
Forward

Jonathan Greening
Forward

30

31

Simeone, Diego
Midfield

MANCHESTER UNITED

1	Fabien **BARTHEZ**
2	Gary **NEVILLE**
3	Phil **NEVILLE**
4	Juan Sebastian **VERON**
5	Laurent **BLANC**
6	Rio **FERDINAND**
7	David **BECKHAM**
8	Nicky **BUTT**
10	Ruud **VAN NISTELROOY**
11	Ryan **GIGGS**
13	Roy **CARROLL**
14	David **MAY**
15	Luke **CHADWICK**
16	Roy **KEANE**
17	Michael **STEWART**
18	Paul **SCHOLES**
19	**RICARDO**
20	Ole Gunnar **SOLSKJAER**
21	Diego **FORLAN**
22	John **O'SHEA**
24	Wes **BROWN**
25	Quinton **FORTUNE**
26	Danny **PUGH**
27	Mikael **SILVESTRE**
30	Ben **WILLIAMS**
31	Darren **FLETCHER**
34	Lee **ROCHE**
36	Jimmy **DAVIS**
37	Danny **WEBBER**
38	Mark **LYNCH**
39	Paul **TIERNEY**
40	Daniel **NARDIELLO**
41	Alan **TATE**
42	Kieran **RICHARDSON**
43	Mads **TIMM**
44	Luke **STEELE**
45	Christopher **EAGLES**

REAL MADRID

1	Iker **CASILLAS**
2	Michel **SALGADO**
3	Roberto **CARLOS**
4	Fernando **HIERRO**
5	Zinedine **ZIDANE**
6	Iván **HELGUERA**
7	**RAÚL**
8	Steve **McMANAMAN**
9	Fernando **MORIENTES**
10	Luis **FIGO**
11	**RONALDO**
12	**TOTE**
13	**CÉSAR**
14	**GUTI**
16	Flavio **CONCEIÇÃO**
17	Oscar **MIÑAMBRES**
18	Javier **PORTILLO**
19	Esteban **CAMBIASSO**
20	Albert **CELADES**
21	Santiago **SOLARI**
22	Francisco **PAVÓN**
25	Carlos **SÁNCHEZ**
24	Claude **MAKELELE**
27	**NÚÑEZ**
28	José Luis **CABRERA**
29	**RUBÉN**
30	Jordi **CODINA**
31	Enrique **CORRALES**
32	**BORJA**
33	Luis **GARCIA**
35	José Angel **ANGELO**
36	Juan Carlos **DUQUE**

EMERGENCY PROCEDURES

Manchester United and the Greater Manchester Police have a very detailed evacuation procedure in place should the need arise. Regular supporters will know we frequently test our emergency tone. In the event that the tone should be sounded in a real situation:

Please remain in position and listen carefully to the announcement. Loud speakers are located not only in the stands but in all concourse areas, toilets and outside the stadium. Whole stands, part stands or the entire stadium may be evacuated. Depending on the nature of the incident, this may take place onto the playing area and out of the stadium. Our PA system operates on a zone-to-zone basis. It may be, therefore, that certain zones are affected but not others.

In such an event our main attention will be focused on the zone concerned. If you hear an announcement broadcast in an area other than your own you should ignore it and respond only to messages directed at your section. All spectators are asked to respond calmly but as quickly as possible. Part of our emergency evacuation policy is to make spectators aware of what is happening and to update this information as frequently as necessary.

23 April 2003

United v Real Madrid

UEFA Champions League

Unitedvoices

The Reds and Real launch a mutual appreciation society

"IF WE SCORE AT OLD TRAFFORD, IT WILL SET THE PLACE ALIGHT"

SIR ALEX FERGUSON LOOKS FOR AN EARLY BREAKTHROUGH

"MANCHESTER UNITED ARE A GREAT TEAM AND THE GOAL GAVE THEM MORE FOR THE SECOND LEG. BUT IT'S NOT A BAD RESULT FOR US"

REAL MADRID CAPTAIN FERNANDO HIERRO SOUNDS A WARNING

"I STILL THINK MANCHESTER UNITED CAN BEAT THEM [REAL MADRID] AT HOME BECAUSE THEY LOOKED VERY VULNERABLE DEFENSIVELY"

AN UNLIKELY ALLY: ARSÈNE WENGER SHARES HIS OPINION

"THEY HAVE TAKEN PART IN A FANTASTIC GAME OF FOOTBALL. YOU WON'T GET ANOTHER GAME AS GOOD OR AS INTENSE AS THAT. ALL THE REAL MADRID PLAYERS SAID AFTERWARDS THEY HAD NOT HAD AS HARD A EUROPEAN GAME"

SIR ALEX WITH YET MORE TO SAY ON THAT MESMERIC MATCH

"THE FIRST HALF WAS VERY DIFFICULT. WE GAVE THEM FAR TOO MUCH RESPECT AND THEY WERE ABLE TO DO WHAT THEY WANTED"

DAVID BECKHAM BELIEVES THERE IS ROOM FOR IMPROVEMENT

"PEOPLE SAY WE GAVE THEM TOO MUCH RESPECT, WE WERE NERVOUS, BUT SOMETIMES YOU HAVE TO ADMIRE A TEAM LIKE REAL. THEY PLAYED SUCH WONDERFUL FOOTBALL. AT TIMES IT WAS LIKE THE HARLEM GLOBETROTTERS"

GARY NEVILLE RECOGNISES GREATNESS

"RYAN GIGGS CAN OPEN UP THE GAME. HE IS VERY FAST, VERY DIRECT. I LIKE ALL THE MANCHESTER TEAM, BUT IF I HAD TO CHOOSE ONE IT WOULD BE RYAN GIGGS"

RAÚL LIKES THE LOOK OF THE WELSH WIZARD

Real fans in a *liga* their own

75,000 regularly rock up at the Bernabéu – and they expect to be entertained

Rightly acclaimed as one of the finest sights in world football, surely only the hardest of hearts could fail to be lifted by the majestic Bernabéu stadium. Towering steeply into the Iberian sky, it's full to its 75,000 capacity for most matches, has staged a World Cup final, three European Cup finals and countless Spanish internationals. That said, there is an argument that visitors seeking a cauldron of passion would be better off watching Madrid's less illustrious neighbours Atlético.

For Real (Royal) Madrid, with their aristocratic connections (King of Spain, Juan Carlos, is a fan) and powerful establishment allies (General Franco was also a Madrid acolyte) are seen by many as the team of the middle classes. True, they may also number thousands of impoverished Andalusian farmers and Raúl-loving Japanese teenagers in their huge fan base, but their match-going fans tend to be middle-aged, middle class and are met with regular accusations of arrogance from rival fans. Indeed, it's perceived as something of a crisis if Real are in second spot in *La Liga*, an 'only the best is good enough' attitude more than backed up by Jupp Heynckes' sacking just a month after guiding the Whites to victory in the 1997/98 Champions League.

Even the ground – Real's home since lawyer Santiago Bernabéu raised money through public subscriptions to build what was originally known as the Chamartín Stadium in 1947 – sits on the wealthy Paseo de la Castellana (formerly the Avenida del Generalíssimo Franco). On a wide, leafy thoroughfare, lined by skyscrapers in the heart of commercial Madrid, the Bernabéu nestles among Spanish banking and business institutions – some consider it the ideal location.

Then there's the radical *Ultra Sur* fan group. These are the young right-wing fanatics who stand (usually on their seats) behind the south-facing goal and orchestrate the giant banners and chants heard on television. They revel in a notorious reputation but their bark is worse than their bite. Founded in 1982, a couple of hundred often provide Madrid's only genuine travelling support.

Like United, Real lay claim to being the biggest club in the world, using different barometers to back their point. Madrid are undeniably more successful, but United have a bigger turnover. Madrid boast many more *penyos* (supporters' clubs), but the depth of their individual memberships makes the matter a moot point. What is indisputable is that like United, Madrid have a vast nation-wide and international following. They even have strong support in the Barça stronghold of Catalonia and when Madrid played at Espanyol recently, half the 51,000 crowd were *madrileños* – mainly internal immigrants living in Barcelona. The scenario, if you could imagine it here, is akin to United playing at Everton in front of a Goodison Park half-full of Merseyside-based United fans.

RONALDO

FORWARD

Born 22 September 1976, Rio de Janeiro, Brazil

Wrote one of the game's great comeback tales, returning from four years' injury torment to help Brazil to World Cup glory last year with eight goals. Current World and European footballer of the year, he is every inch the complete striker.

What a match – 4-3 to United on the night, 6-5 to Real on aggregate, with the show stolen by Brazilian genius Ronaldo

13 September 2006

United v Celtic

UEFA Champions League

TONIGHT'S **MATCH**

PLAYER INTERVIEW

Darren Fletcher

United's only Scotland international will be putting club loyalty firmly in front of national pride tonight and expects the Reds to put in a strong team performance

After last season's premature European exit, Darren Fletcher says United are determined to make amends. And the perfect start would be even sweeter for the Scot with victory over Celtic.

Is there greater determination to do well in Europe after last year?
You always look forward to the Champions League, but this season there's a different attitude. The disappointment of last year means we want to show people we're good enough in Europe. We had so many injuries and suspensions last time. It was a nightmare. We didn't show what we're capable of at all, but we're determined to rectify that, starting tonight.

What do you make of the group?
We know from experience that, particularly away from home, Benfica are tough opponents. They're your classic Portuguese team and technically very good. We've played Celtic many times in friendlies, but this will be totally different. The only thing we know about Copenhagen is they knocked Ajax out in the qualifiers, so they can't be a bad side. It's not an easy group because each team is very different, and everyone will think they have a chance of progressing.

Does this game hold more significance for you?
Definitely. It's the whole England-Scotland rivalry, so that will make the game more intense. For me, if I play I want to give a good account of myself against a Scottish team. The atmosphere should be amazing, both sets of supporters will be right up for it.

Are you expecting a completely different kind of European tie?
It will almost be like a Premiership match, with both teams playing at high tempo. I imagine it will be like a local derby, which is unusual in the Champions League. But that makes you want to experience it even more. It's a game I'm really looking forward to.

Presumably you've been inundated with ticket requests?
[Laughs] It feels like everyone in Scotland has asked me for a ticket! I've had to scrounge for tickets from the rest of the lads. I'll have about 50 friends and family at the match. Most of my mates in Scotland are Celtic fans, so they have split loyalties because they want me to do well and want their team to win. In most cases I think they'd settle for a draw, but I don't want anything other than a United win.

You must know a few of the Celtic players from playing for Scotland...
Yeah. I spoke with Kenny Miller about the game and we mentioned the two friendly results earlier this year, but we won't take those matches into account. It's a clean slate and this will be a totally different kind of game.

Do you keep up to date with Scottish football?
I watch a lot of the games on TV. I like to keep an eye on things back home, mainly to see how my Scottish team-mates are doing, but I also like to follow the SPL.

"Most of my mates in Scotland are Celtic fans, so they have split loyalties. They want me to do well and want their team to win"

Fletcher scored a cracker in the 3-0 win over Charlton

Which players do United need to watch out for tonight?
Kenny Miller is definitely one to keep an eye on. He's not scored for Celtic yet, but he scored two in two games in the recent Euro 2008 qualifiers, so we'll need to be careful. He's quick, works really hard outside the box and he's selfless for the team. He'll run all night and will be full of confidence after his recent performances for Scotland. He's not the only player… we know a lot about Thomas Gravesen, he's top quality. But the one everyone is talking about is the Japanese lad Shunsuke Nakamura, he's a special player. He's got good feet and can split defences open with a pass.

Wayne Rooney and Paul Scholes return tonight, how important is it they are in the team?
It's great to have them back after the injustice of their suspensions. You're talking about two world class players that any team would miss. Scholesy has been brilliant since coming back from his eye injury, and everyone knows what Wayne can do. They've both been restless in training. You prepare all summer and then to only have one league game is frustrating. They're itching to get back into it.

Finally, are you confident the team can produce a good display tonight and a better showing in Europe this season?
We are confident. The team has started the season well and we're playing good, attacking football. We want to continue that. If we perform to our capabilities, I'm sure we'll get three points, which would be the perfect start for us in Europe.

United Review spoke to boyhood Celtic fan Darren Fletcher when United first met the Bhoys in European competition

There won't be any room for niceties on this occasion - both teams are out to win

Time to make amends

United seeking a perfect start in order to banish last season's Champions League woes

Premiership matters are put aside tonight as all eyes turn to the Champions League and a first competitive encounter with Celtic. United have only ever met the Hoops in friendlies before (see our feature on page 34), but seriousness rather than sociability is the order of this evening.

For Sir Alex's men, it is the first opportunity to bury the memory of last season's below-par European campaign, which saw United finish bottom of Group D with just one win and three goals scored. The early exit was a dent to the Reds' prestige in the tournament, ending a proud United record of reaching the knockout stages for nine consecutive seasons.

However, a stumble won't make United fall, and there is a fierce determination to make amends in a group that also contains Benfica and FC Copenhagen. "We have to repay our fans and the club for a disappointing campaign," said Sir Alex recently. "We won't let them down this time. I feel there's a maturity in this team, and that could take us a long way."

"With 6,500 Celtic fans expected in Manchester, a full house could be in for one of Old Trafford's classic European encounters"

Wayne Rooney will be vital to the manager's plans; he returns after a three-match domestic suspension tonight and could face his former Everton team-mate, Thomas Gravesen, who joined Celtic from Real Madrid over the summer. The feisty Dane could be charged with denying Rooney space to weave his creative magic. Surprisingly, the 20-year-old Reds striker is still searching for his first goal in the competition proper since his incredible debut hat-trick against Fenerbahce two years ago. Few would back against that drought ending tonight.

Rooney is one of many problems for Celtic boss Gordon Strachan to contend with, although the absence of Cristiano Ronaldo due to suspension may ease matters. Strachan was none too pleased to be drawn in the same group as United. Aside from two friendly defeats this year, his competitive record against the Reds reads 14 defeats and two victories from 16 meetings. "I'm fed up with the sight of United," he said. "I'd rather play Real Madrid or Barcelona."

With 6,500 Celtic fans expected in Manchester, a full house could be in for one of Old Trafford's classic European encounters.

Group F fixtures

Celtic (home) 13.9.06
SL Benfica (away) 26.9.06
FC Copenhagen (home) 17.10.06
FC Copenhagen (away) 1.11.06
Celtic (away) 21.11.06
SL Benfica (home) 6.12.06

This match preview appeared in the news section of the programme, with both managers looking forward a competitive group that also included Benfica and Copenhagen

Ronaldo has vowed to score and help United get to the final in Russia

Moscow calling

Reds focused on sealing a berth in the Champions League final

THE OLD TRAFFORD stage is set, the fans are ready, now it's the moment of truth. Having left Camp Nou with a goalless draw last Wednesday, Sir Alex Ferguson believes that the Reds have a "marvellous chance" of reaching the Champions League final.

Cristiano Ronaldo has echoed that sentiment and, after missing an early penalty in the first leg, is on a personal crusade to fire the team to Moscow.

"Sometimes you score, sometimes you don't. Yes, I missed a penalty, but it's no problem. Now I'm going to score at Old Trafford," declared the winger.

"Tonight's game will be totally different [to the first leg]. Barcelona won't keep the ball like they did over there. I think we'll create more chances and play better. We are at home, we'll have 76,000 people behind us. We will try to play good football and win."

HOME AND AWAY (2007/08)	P	W	D	L	F	A
United (H)	5	5	0	0	9	1
Barcelona (A)	5	3	2	0	8	4

Getting over the last-four hurdle in Europe's elite club competition has proved a tricky task for the Reds over the years. United have reached the semi-final stage on nine previous occasions, including last season. But 1968 and 1999 aside, it's an obstacle that has been a step too far.

Barcelona will be intent on making sure the Reds fall short once again and striker Samuel Eto'o (below) reckons a repeat display of the Spaniards' first leg showing – where they enjoyed plenty of possession – tonight will see Barça through.

"If we play like that then there's no reason why we shouldn't reach the final," he insisted. "We are capable of scoring and if we play at our true level there are very few sides who can live with us."

The same could be said of United. Just ask Roma. Barça may feel confident, but they face a side who have been unstoppable on home turf this term – winning all five of the Champions League clashes there. The Reds will be desperate to make it six out of six and, with ardent support, the scene is set for a classic European night at Old Trafford. And if the fans can help roar the Reds to Moscow, it could be the best ever.

29 April 2008

United v Barcelona

UEFA Champions League

▲ 19 **Lionel Messi** FORWARD
Age 20 **Nationality** Argentinian
League appearances 53(20) **Goals** 30

The few hundred who watched Messi as a 14-year-old playing for Barcelona's youth teams will not be surprised at his progression to football's 'A' list. Most best world XIs would now include the 5ft 4in Argentinian, which is a staggering achievement for a 20-year-old.

Messi has never let physical deficiencies or age prevent him from performing ahead of his years. At 14, he was so small that his legs didn't touch the floor when he sat on the bench – a fact that earned him the nickname 'the flea'. Still, he rose through the ranks at Barcelona, and shattered youth team scoring records on the way, before making his first-team debut at 16 in a friendly against Juventus which left a watching Fabio Capello wondering who "the little devil" was.

Statistics can't quantify Messi's brilliance, though. There will be more prolific goalscorers and better free-kick specialists, but the Rosario-born attacker is the most enduring challenger to the 'new Maradona' tag. While shy off the field – he prefers home cooking and computer games – on it, he's a creative livewire who regularly produces moments of jaw-dropping skill with a deftness of which Barça legend Johan Cruyff would be proud. Messi can play as an attacking midfielder, on either wing or even as a centre-forward. Quick, cool-headed, two-footed (although he favours his left), he has risen from an emerging star barely two years ago to Barça's most important player.

❝ He's a creative livewire who produces moments of jaw-dropping skill with a deftness of which Barça legend Johan Cruyff would be proud ❞

A semi-final finely poised following a 0-0 draw in the Nou Camp's first leg that saw Ronaldo and Messi pitted together for the first time, United and Barça faced off at Old Trafford in the return. But the star of the evening was to be our homegrown legend Paul Scholes...

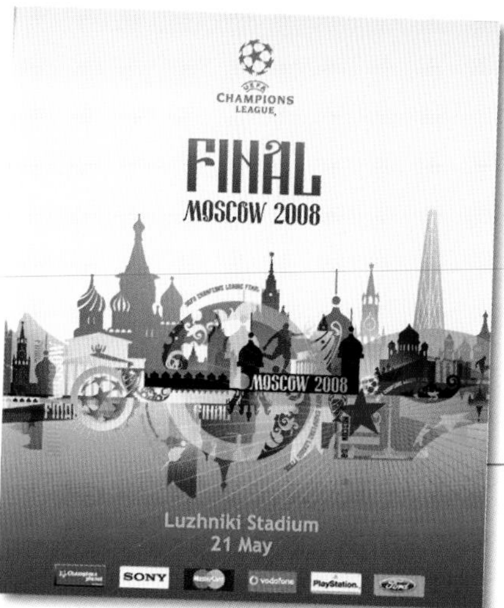

The *United Review* cover paid homage to the semi-final programme from 1968 and the issue gave a taste of things to come with this ad

Talking point

We welcome Rangers tonight, but do you think the Old Firm should join the Premier League?

"It is a debatable one. I'd say no, they shouldn't be in the Premier League. They're at the top of their league but I don't think they would be in England. I can see the appeal of moving them, but it's not for me."
Gary Bowman, Stretford

"I don't know if they have the quality to be capable of competing in the Premier League – maybe in the lower divisions, but not at the top. They have some good players but not good enough to compete with the best."
Graeme Morris, Dublin

"I can see why a lot of people think they should because of the big crowds they get. I'm sure a club like Celtic, with the big gates they attract, would be of benefit to the Premier League, but it just wouldn't seem right to let them in."
Nigel Williams, Chichester

"It is a good idea because Rangers and Celtic are the top teams in the Scottish leagues and are too good for their domestic competition. Maybe you could put them in the English Premier League and see how they do."
Hasan, Manchester

"I don't think that Rangers and Celtic should join because they do not belong to the Premier League. The Scottish League is Scottish and English league is English, they should not be mixed up! It is much better that they remain separate."
Luis Milanez, Brazil

"My brother-in-law is a Rangers fan but I still think they should stay where they are. They're just not good enough. The top six clubs in England could join in a European league, but Celtic and Rangers wouldn't get in that, either."
Stewart Sorrie, Driffield

The ex-player
Lou Macari says...
"I can see a major problem with the idea. Every English club outside the Premier League is striving to reach the top, so it's unfair to give Celtic and Rangers a free pass. The only fair way would be to make the Scottish sides start in the fourth tier, and they'd never agree to that. Also, the SPL need Celtic and Rangers (and the revenue they create) much more than the Premier League does. Just forget the idea."

The pundit
Steve Wyeth, BBC broadcaster says...
"I'd welcome the Old Firm into the Premier League... if they work their way through the pyramid like everyone else who covets a share of the riches. They won't fancy that, though. Wigan and Blackpool have proved it's possible to come through the divisions to earn a chance, and others deserve the same dream. There would be financial benefits to welcoming Scotland's big two, but membership should be down to on-field exploits, not outgrowing your own league."

Manchester United v Rangers 15

The opposition

Rangers

In this section: Player and manager profiles; United v Scotland

Despite financial restrictions limiting Walter Smith's ability to dip into the transfer market last season, the Gers still won the Scottish Premier League with room to spare, finishing six points above second-placed Old Firm rivals Celtic.

This term, however, thanks to that second successive title win (53rd in all), Smith does have funds to spend as he embarks on a Champions League campaign and looks to go out in style in his last season in football. To that end Nikica Jelavic was brought in from Rapid Vienna for £4 million, becoming the most expensive player the club had signed in eight years. And more reinforcements arrived in the shape of loan midfielder Vladimir Weiss from Manchester City, Stoke striker James Beattie, and defender Richard Foster from Aberdeen.

The Scots will, though, have to go some to do their boss proud this season – the Gers have got past the Champions League group phase only once since almost reaching the semi-final in 1993. That campaign included Smith's last 'Battle of Britain' clash, when he was in charge of a Rangers team that beat English champions Leeds home and away, but few people will be banking on the Gers to pull off that kind of result this time round. A positive result tonight would be deemed a bonus, with Smith looking to the games against Bursaspor and Valencia as his best hope for points.

Despite the summer signings, arguably Smith's biggest achievement during the transfer window was to hold on to Kenny Miller who – following the departure of last season's top scorer Kris Boyd to Middlesbrough – was said to be attracting interest from English Premier League clubs. Miller (second to Boyd in Rangers' 2009/10 goalscoring stakes) stayed put, however, and had to be at his predatory best in a recent 2-1 win over St Johnstone to get Rangers out of a hole. With Smith's side failing to impose themselves as they had done throughout last season, they were looking at two points dropped until Miller popped up with his fifth goal in three games with minutes to spare.

It's that kind of never-die-spirit that Rangers will need if they're to make Smith's last season one to remember.

The club

Founded: 1873
Nickname: The Gers
Honours: Scottish League champions in 1891, 1899–1902, 1911–1913, 1918, 1920, 1921, 1923–1925, 1927–1931, 1933–1935, 1937, 1939, 1947, 1949, 1950, 1953, 1956, 1957, 1959, 1961, 1963, 1964, 1975, 1976, 1978, 1987, 1989–1997, 1999, 2000, 2003, 2005, 2009, 2010; Scottish Cup winners in 1894, 1897, 1898, 1903, 1928, 1930, 1932, 1934–1936, 1948–1950, 1953, 1960, 1962–64, 1966, 1973, 1976, 1978, 1979, 1981, 1992, 1993, 1996, 1999, 2000, 2002, 2003, 2008, 2009; Scottish League Cup winners in 1946, 1948, 1960, 1961, 1963, 1964, 1970, 1975, 1977, 1978, 1981, 1983, 1984, 1986–1988, 1990, 1992, 1993, 1996, 1998, 2001, 2002, 2004, 2007, 2009; European Cup Winners' Cup winners in 1972
Record league victory: 10–0 v Hibernian, December 1898
Record league defeat: 0–6 v Dumbarton, May 1892
Sponsors: Tennent's
Website: www.rangers.co.uk

Local report

Inside Ibrox with Rangers reporter Richard Wilson of Glasgow's *The Herald*

What was the key to being Scottish champions last season?
Mostly, a miserly defence and a refusal to be overcome – by circumstances or opponents. With finances preventing signings for two years, a profound team spirit developed, which enhanced the qualities of defiance and self-respect that shaped the side's nature.

What are Rangers fans' expectations going into the 2010/11 Champions League?
Not to suffer as uncomfortable a time as last season, when they lost 4-1 to Unirea Urziceni at Ibrox and finished bottom of their group, with two points and no wins.

What will it take for Scottish club teams to be a force in Europe?
Rangers and Celtic would become significant competitors if they could play in the Premier League and tap into the vast broadcasting riches available. Otherwise, a miracle, or decades of patience while the country rethinks its youth development.

Which United players will Walter Smith's side have to keep a particular eye on?
Rangers will likely line up in a 4-5-1 shape, so the first concern will be who picks up Wayne Rooney when he drifts off the front. The powerful overlaps of Patrice Evra will also be a threat down the left.

Are fans pleased with the new players that the manager has brought in this summer?
They are relieved that there are any new arrivals at all, since they are the first signings in a while. Vladimir Weiss is a favourite – partly because Celtic missed out on him. Fans are also looking forward to seeing more of striker Nikica Jelavic.

How do you see tonight's game panning out?
Rangers will be organised and disciplined, with the intention of limiting United's attack. Walter Smith would relish a result over his old friend, Sir Alex Ferguson, but the visitors will be cautious and United are too strong in comparison. A home win.

Manchester United v Rangers 19

Old Trafford hosted Scottish champions Rangers in 2010, with the programme cover celebrating all of United's European Cup winners, while the issue carried a topical debate widely discussed at the time

The *United Review* profile of the visitors highlighted their lengthy honours list, including 53 titles. The Glasgow side held United to a 0-0 draw in this tie, but a late Wayne Rooney penalty gave United victory in the return at Ibrox two months later

MEET THE VISITORS

OLYMPIACOS

ΟΛΥΜΠΙΑΚΟΣ ΣΥΝΔΕΣΜΟΣ ΦΙΛΑΘΛΩΝ ΠΕΙΡΑΙΩΣ 1925

PLAYER PROFILES

Buoyed by first-leg victory, the Greek champions are aiming to see out the tie at Old Trafford and reach the quarter-finals of the UEFA Champions League for the first time p28-30

ROY CARROLL

Former Reds goalkeeper recalls his time at United, talks life in Greece and reveals the visitors' confidence ahead of tonight's return leg p32-33

ON A MISSION

Having pulled off a shock 2-0 victory in the first installment of this Round of 16 tie, the attention of the *Erythrolefkoi* (the Red and Whites) shifts to finishing the job. Michel's team are ready and confident...

Manchester United v Olympiacos 27

19 March 2014

United v Olympiacos

UEFA Champions League

The Greeks came to Manchester carrying a 2-0 lead, with the cover sounding a rallying cry. Robin van Persie heeded the call and delivered the goods with a brilliant hat-trick

This infographic celebrated United's 250 games in the European Cup/Champions League, a milestone passed in the first leg

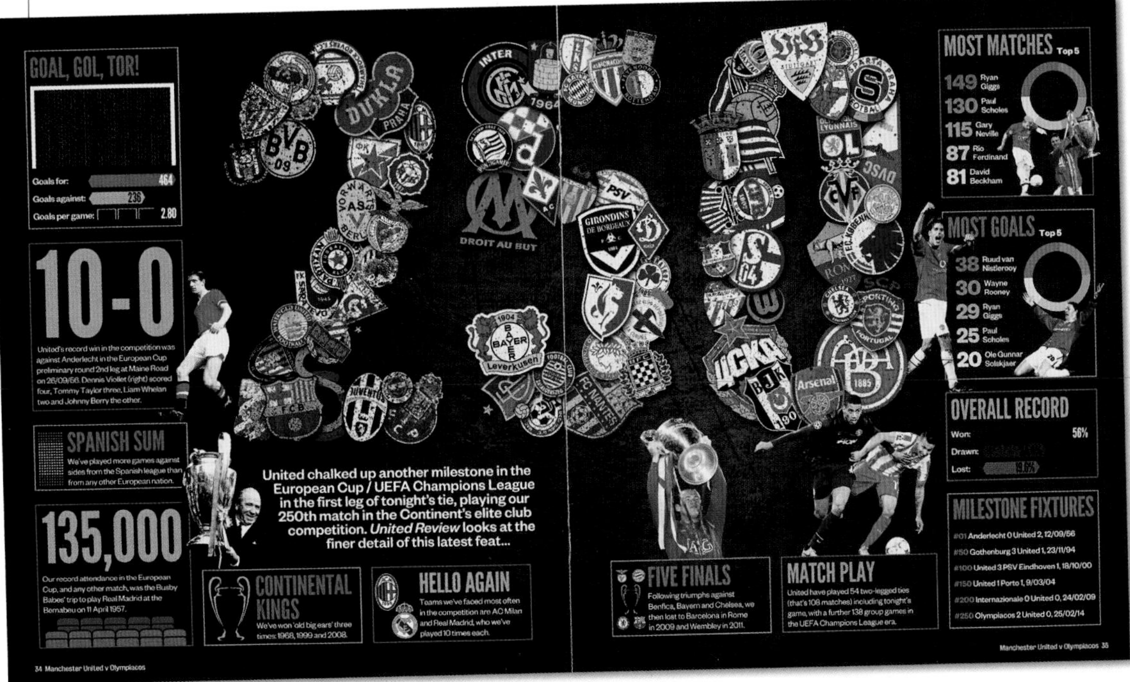

GOAL, GOL, TOR!

Goals for: 464

Goals against: 236

Goals per game: 2.80

10-0

United's record win in the competition was against Anderlecht in the European Cup preliminary round 2nd leg at Maine Road on 26/09/56. Dennis Viollet (right) scored four, Tommy Taylor three, Liam Whelan two and Johnny Berry the other.

SPANISH SUM

We've played more games against sides from the Spanish league than from any other European nation.

135,000

Our record attendance in the European Cup, and any other match, was the Busby Babes' trip to play Real Madrid at the Bernabeu on 11 April 1957.

United chalked up another milestone in the European Cup / UEFA Champions League in the first leg of tonight's tie, playing our 250th match in the Continent's elite club competition. *United Review* looks at the finer detail of this latest feat...

CONTINENTAL KINGS

We've won 'old big ears' three times: 1968, 1999 and 2008.

HELLO AGAIN

Teams we've faced most often in the competition are AC Milan and Real Madrid, who we've played 10 times each.

FIVE FINALS

Following triumphs against Benfica, Bayern and Chelsea, we then lost to Barcelona in Rome in 2009 and Wembley in 2011.

MATCH PLAY

United have played 54 two-legged ties (that's 108 matches) including tonight's game, with a further 138 group games in the UEFA Champions League era.

MOST MATCHES Top 5

149 Ryan Giggs
130 Paul Scholes
115 Gary Neville
87 Rio Ferdinand
81 David Beckham

MOST GOALS Top 5

38 Ruud van Nistelrooy
30 Wayne Rooney
29 Ryan Giggs
25 Paul Scholes
20 Ole Gunnar Solskjaer

OVERALL RECORD

Won: 56%
Drawn:
Lost: 19.6%

MILESTONE FIXTURES

#01 Anderlecht 0 United 2, 12/09/56
#50 Gothenburg 3 United 1, 23/11/94
#100 United 3 PSV Eindhoven 1, 18/10/00
#150 United 1 Porto 1, 9/03/04
#200 Internazionale 0 United 0, 24/02/09
#250 Olympiacos 2 United 0, 25/02/14

34 Manchester United v Olympiacos

Manchester United v Olympiacos 35

11 May 2017

United v Celta Vigo

Europa League

OPPOSITION

IN THE AWAY END

BACK IN THE BIG TIME

Founded in 1923, *Os Celestes* (the Sky Blues) created few headlines throughout their first half-century of existence, bar the odd promotion and relegation to and from *La Liga*, as well as UEFA Cup qualification in 1970/71. It was in the late '90s when they started to make a real impact, finishing between 4th and 7th in Spain's top flight every season between 1997/98 and 2002/03, with Alexander Mostovoi (above), Valery Karpin and Haim Revivo among the stars. Financial woes saw the club plummet as low as 17th in the second tier in 2009, but they've been on an upward trajectory ever since, which this year has taken them to new ground in Europe...

BREAKING DOWN THE BADGE

Celta's full name is Real Club Celta de Vigo – with Real meaning royal, after the club was granted patronage by the Spanish crown in 1923. So, much like Real Madrid, they have one of these shiny things on the badge...

Like many clubs in this corner of Spain, the crest features the red cross of Saint James – the patron saint of Galicia (and all of Spain, for that matter)

While this graphic on the blue shield doesn't immediately resemble two 'Cs', that's what it says – and it stands for 'Club Celta'

IN SEARCH OF SILVERWARE

It was 2003/04 when Celta reached the last 16 of the Champions League (where they lost to Arsenal, above), while they've reached the last eight of the UEFA Cup/Europa League on four occasions, including this season. So not only is tonight's tie a first ever European semi-final for Celta, but it's put them within touching distance of winning a major trophy for the first time in their 93-year history. The closest the Galicians have come is in the *Copa del Rey*, where they've lost in three finals (1943, 1994 and 2001), but a trip to Stockholm for this month's Europa League final would be the biggest night in the club's history by some margin.

BRITISH OPPOSITION

Celta's first game in Europe was against Aberdeen (a 3-0 aggregate loss in the '71/72 UEFA Cup), and they've since had mixed results against British teams. Their next UEFA Cup campaign ('98/99) saw them eliminate Aston Villa (above) and Liverpool – the 3-1 home win over the Merseyside club entering club folklore. They were then knocked out of Europe by Celtic (2002/03) and Arsenal (see top right), while they lost to Newcastle in 2006/07.

RECORD BREAKERS

MOST LEAGUE GOALS
Hermidita, 110 goals in 170 appearances, 1944-56

HIGHEST TRANSFER FEE RECEIVED
€14m, Claude Makelele (right) to Real Madrid, 2000

GALICIAN RIVALS

With Vigo nestled up in the north west of Spain, fans can take their pick of some top away-days in the nearby regions of Castile and León, Cantabria, Asturias and the Basque Country. But when it comes to local duels, only one fixture stands out: *O derbi galego* against Deportivo La Coruna. For the second time in three seasons, Celta have done the double over Depor, with October's 4-1 win an ear-splitting encounter at Balaidos, as Iago Aspas (above) scored two. Celta lead the rivalry 49-45, with 30 draws.

22 ● Manchester United v Celta de Vigo

MATCH HUB

ONE GOAL UP FROM THE FIRST LEG IN SPAIN, MOURINHO'S MEN SET SIGHTS ON STOCKHOLM

The Reds are focused on tonight's task and the prize of a European final

TONIGHT'S MATCH

MANCHESTER UNITED v CELTA DE VIGO

Rashford's stunning free-kick in Vigo puts us ahead in the tie

There will be no let-up from the Reds as they seek a first Europa League final appearance

Reds hold slender advantage after the first leg in Spain, but are taking nothing for granted as the tie resumes on home turf

"It was good for us [in Vigo] but now we have to focus again and make sure we do another good job." That's the message from United midfielder Paul Pogba as United and Celta resume our Europa League semi-final tie at Old Trafford this evening.

The Frenchman was the Reds' outstanding performer a week ago, as Jose Mourinho's side left Balaidos stadium with a 1-0 victory thanks to Marcus Rashford's stunning second-half free-kick. And while some are suggesting the task of reaching the Stockholm final on 24 May is all but done after that first-leg result, Pogba insists such thoughts are far from the minds of the United players.

"It was a good result for us with a very important goal," says the Reds' no.6. "Now we have to focus on the second leg and get ourselves ready for the result we need. I feel good that we can do that but we have to be careful as well because it's not finished and we won only 1-0 in the first leg."

In order to turn the first-leg result into an aggregate success and a trip to Sweden, the Reds boss and players have been united in their message that the supporters can play a very important part. It's a message Pogba was keen to reinforce.

"The crowd at Old Trafford has to be as good as the crowd was at Celta Vigo," he says. "Even when they were losing the game they kept up their energy. Our fans, they always help us – maybe they don't know how much it helps us – but we know. When you hear supporters shouting our names it pushes us to the limit. We need the fans and we want to win the game for them."

Marouane Fellaini provided able assistance to Pogba in the Reds midfield a week ago, and outlined the threat that Celta – a side who have reached this stage on the back of strong away displays – will pose tonight. The Belgian said: "Now we have a second game and we have to be ready because it will be a big game for us. It will be tough, we know that. They are a good team, they can play, they have good players. Also, we play at Old Trafford, in front of 75,000 people, so we have to give everything."

While the Reds have not given up hope of clinching a Champions League place via a top-four finish in the Premier League, the chance to win a third trophy of the season – after the Community Shield and EFL Cup – is now the priority for the team.

Ajax hold a clear advantage in tonight's other semi-final, while United are looking to capitalise on a strong away leg at Old Trafford. It promises to be another nervy, thrilling and hopefully glorious European night under the floodlights at the Theatre of Dreams.

Pogba applauds the away support in Vigo and expects more of the same at Old Trafford

Tonight's game is our 49th meeting with a Spanish side, having previously taken on (in the order we first played them): Athletic Club, Real Madrid, Valencia, Barcelona, Atletico Madrid, Deportivo La Coruna, Villarreal, Real Sociedad and now Celta Vigo.

United have experienced mixed fortunes against Spanish sides at Old Trafford, as these last half-dozen matches show...

1-0 WON (23.10.13) · 1-2 LOST (05.03.13) · 2-3 LOST (08.03.12) · 1-1 DREW (07.12.10) · 0-0 DREW (17.09.08) · 1-0 WON (29.04.08)

TONIGHT'S OFFICIALS

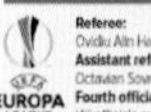

Referee: Ovidiu Alin Hategan
Assistant referees: Octavian Sovre, Sebastian Eugen Gheorghe
Fourth official: Radu Adrian Stefan Ghinguleac
(All officials are from Romania)

AWAY FINALISTS: The winner of tonight's tie will be the designated 'away' team in the final at Stockholm's Friends Arena.

FINAL COUNTDOWN: Should United make it to Stockholm, it will be our first Europa League final and our seventh final overall in UEFA competition. For Celta it would be a first European final.

08 ● Manchester United v Celta de Vigo

The programme cover for this Europa League semi-final vividly illustrated that this competition was the only one to have eluded United in our history

The Reds carried a slim 1-0 lead from the first leg in Spain thanks to Marcus Rashford's winner, which meant a 1-1 draw in the return was enough to book our place in the Stockholm final

Salvio

Benfica's Argentinian winger **Eduardo Salvio** says tonight's visitors are relishing their visit to Manchester and have only one thing on their minds... to win!

How is the mood at Benfica ahead of this game at Old Trafford?
Old Trafford is a venue with great history and prestige, as is Estadio da Luz. Playing in stadiums like these is always stimulating for any football player, but our biggest motivation is to win the match. That is what we work for, every day, and we've prepared for the game with that in mind. We are very confident in our work and preparation, and we know what we have to do. We're going to fight for a win.

What did you make of the recent game at Estadio da Luz?
It was competitive, with brilliant moments of football and fair play that should be present in every European fixture. We tried our hardest to score, with the fans' support. I'm sure that the Manchester United players and the supporters who flew to Lisbon enjoyed the environment of our stadium, too.

"You can tell that Matic and Lindelof are grateful for the experience and knowledge they got at the club"

Some of the United players approached young goalkeeper Mile Svilar after the game, offering some words of encouragement. Was that good to see?
Players from both Benfica and Manchester United approached Mile at the end of the match. He is a young, talented goalkeeper, and it was wonderful to see that after the final whistle. The rivalry was gone and everyone wanted to give him a word of encouragement. Moments like that only add value to European football.

You were up against Nemanja Matic and Victor Lindelof in that game. Was it good to play against two old team-mates?
Matic and Lindelof are two of many quality players who have thrived at Benfica and moved on to other European clubs. Throughout the years, we have had excellent rosters, and it's only natural that Benfica players are highly regarded in Europe. It is always a pleasure to see these fellow footballers, with whom we conquered many trophies.

It would seem that both players still hold much affection for Benfica...
Of course. Everyone who plays for Benfica becomes passionate about them. We have a united team, amazing supporters, and a spectacular training centre. It is impossible to remain indifferent. Matic and Lindelof were here when they were young, and now that they have left, you can tell they are grateful for the experience and knowledge that they got at the club.

Salvio goes up against Lukaku in Lisbon

You've played against English teams before – famously against Fulham (for Atletico Madrid) and Chelsea in Europa League finals. Do you have good memories of such games?
Every game has its history. Throughout my career, I have played European fixtures against a number of English teams, and their value is clear. I have good memories of some games, not so good memories of others, but none of that influences the next one, which is always the most important. Of course, everyone enjoys seeing how passionate the English are about football, but it is also wonderful to see so many Benfica fans on the streets and in the stands.

What are Benfica's aims in the remaining Champions League group games?
Benfica's aim is always to win. We have not managed to do that in the previous matches, but we know we are good enough, and we will play every game with the three points as a goal. We are working to get the most possible points out of the remaining group games.

31 October 2017
United v Benfica
UEFA Champions League

EUSEBIO

The emblem of tonight's visitors Benfica frequently crossed paths with United during his epic career, building a relationship of mutual admiration that endures to this day...

A reunion with our old friends Benfica was celebrated by *United Review*, and their winger Eduardo Salvio (top, left) welcomed facing current Reds Nemanja Matic and Victor Lindelof, who used to play for the Lisbon side

In the 50th-anniversary season of United defeating Benfica in the European Cup final, the programme paid homage to two club legends

CHAPTER 10

Munich

The events of 6 February 1958, when eight United players were among those to die on a Bavarian runway, will never be forgotten. The aftermath of the crash saw *UR* play an important role in honouring those lost – which it continues to do to this day...

Over 60 years on from the Munich Air Disaster, sadness still aches within the hearts of Manchester United fans. Even for those who did not live through 6 February 1958, that arguably the club's greatest ever side was all but destroyed in just a few minutes of carnage still seems unfathomable, unfair, unspeakable.

To suggest that the team history remembers as 'the Busby Babes' was maybe United's greatest is no exaggeration: this was a side that was romping to league titles by 11 and eight points – at a time when a win earned just two points! When you factor in that the average age of the eight great players who perished was just 23 and a half years, you can only dream of what heights they might have gone on to reach.

The disaster and the Busby Babes is indisputably at the heart of what Manchester United is about as a football club, and always will be. The events on that cold, snowy, merciless runway could have broken the club, yet somehow fuelled it with the reason and the strength to carry on. Now, whenever United step on to a field, whenever they go into Europe, it is always to honour the Babes and their memory.

Above: a plaque outside Old Trafford offers a permanent reminder of the young lives lost on that fateful day in Munich

Fans that endured the grief of February 1958 still live with the joy of seeing the Babes deep within their soul. And their mission is to tell other Reds about the great Duncan Edwards; about the heroism of Harry Gregg; about the steel and resolve of Jimmy Murphy.

At the 60th anniversary commemorations in 2018, there were more people at Old Trafford to pay tribute than ever before. Over two thousand more travelled to the crash site in Trudering, Germany. There is no danger that one of football's great teams is about to fade into the footnotes of the sport's history.

United Review has been a big part of preserving their memory and that of the other 15 people who

A month on from the crash and *United Review* still retained a defiant message on its front cover, as the Reds made steady programme in the FA Cup

Harrowing press photos showed the tail of the squad's Airspeed AS-57 plane engulfed in flames

died, including many journalists who had served the programme so loyally for years and who died alongside the players they wrote about.

'United will go on' read the headline on the front cover of the first post-Munich issue (for an FA Cup tie with Sheffield Wednesday), above an emotional, defiant message from the club's chairman Harold Hardman. Inside there were heartbreaking blank spaces where the team line-up should have been positioned, and poignant messages of encouragement to those still being treated in Rechts der Isar Hospital in Bavaria. One of those mentioned, Duncan Edwards, would not make it.

It's the little things within that programme which break your heart – like the note about the obviously devastated regular cartoonists asking to be excused from duties. Stained across every page are similar indications of how deeply this loss was felt.

Every year since, the club's programme has remembered Munich. For landmark anniversaries, special covers have been designed. In 2018, a commemorative book entitled *The Flowers of Manchester* was given away with each copy.

Barely a month goes by without a feature article covering the Babes in some way; their legacy is the cornerstone of Manchester United. And *United Review* too.

That we must keep their flame burning goes without saying. But maybe that instruction misleadingly implies some kind of burden – on the club, its staff and its fans. Nothing could be further from the truth.

The truth is simpler: the Babes were magnificent, they were ours, they are loved. And as long as Manchester United stands, their beauty as footballers and humans will be forever celebrated.

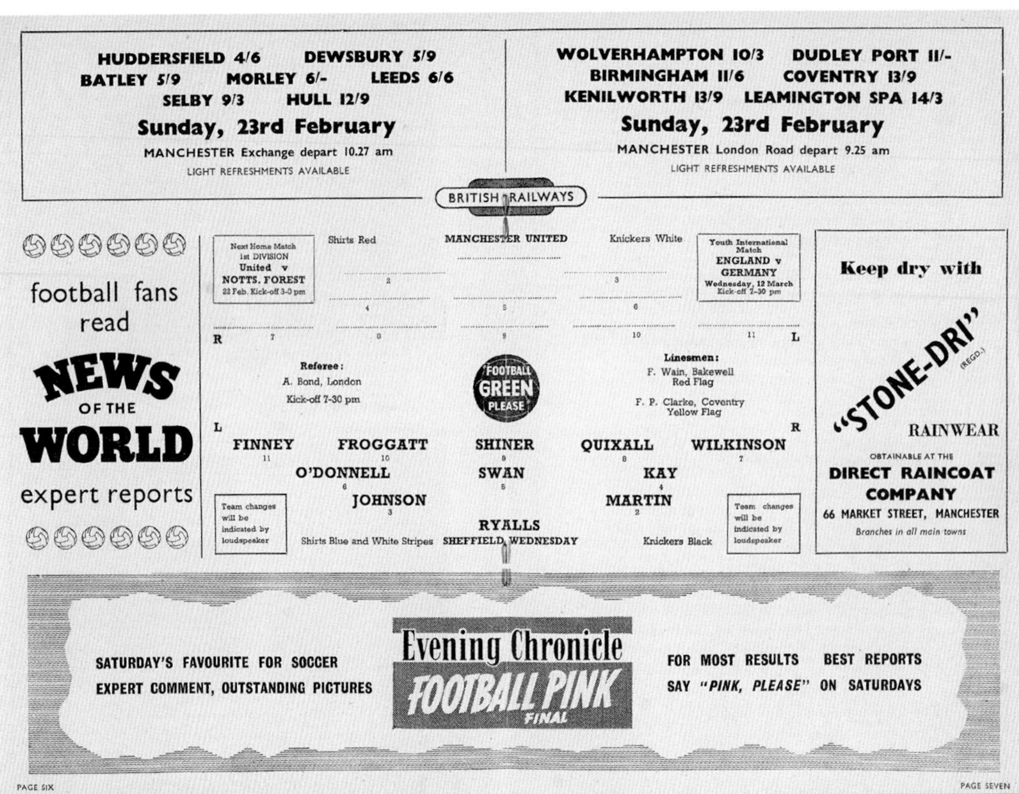
HUDDERSFIELD 4/6 DEWSBURY 5/9
BATLEY 5/9 MORLEY 6/- LEEDS 6/6
SELBY 9/3 HULL 12/9
Sunday, 23rd February
MANCHESTER Exchange depart 10.27 am
LIGHT REFRESHMENTS AVAILABLE

WOLVERHAMPTON 10/3 DUDLEY PORT 11/-
BIRMINGHAM 11/6 COVENTRY 13/9
KENILWORTH 13/9 LEAMINGTON SPA 14/3
Sunday, 23rd February
MANCHESTER London Road depart 9.25 am
LIGHT REFRESHMENTS AVAILABLE

BRITISH RAILWAYS

football fans read
NEWS OF THE WORLD
expert reports

Next Home Match
1st DIVISION
United v
NOTTS. FOREST
22 Feb. Kick-off 3-0 pm

Shirts Red
MANCHESTER UNITED
Knickers White

Youth International Match
ENGLAND v
GERMANY
Wednesday, 12 March
Kick-off 7-30 pm

1 2 3 4 5 6
R 7 8 9 10 11 L

Referee:
A. Bond, London
Kick-off 7-30 pm

FOOTBALL GREEN PLEASE

Linesmen:
F. Wain, Bakewell
Red Flag
F. P. Clarke, Coventry
Yellow Flag

L R
FINNEY 11 FROGGATT 10 SHINER 9 QUIXALL 8 WILKINSON 7
O'DONNELL 6 SWAN 5 KAY 4
JOHNSON 3 MARTIN 2
RYALLS

Team changes will be indicated by loudspeaker

Shirts Blue and White Stripes
SHEFFIELD WEDNESDAY
Knickers Black

Team changes will be indicated by loudspeaker

Keep dry with
"STONE-DRI" (REGD.)
RAINWEAR
OBTAINABLE AT THE
DIRECT RAINCOAT COMPANY
66 MARKET STREET, MANCHESTER
Branches in all main towns

SATURDAY'S FAVOURITE FOR SOCCER
EXPERT COMMENT, OUTSTANDING PICTURES
Evening Chronicle
FOOTBALL PINK
FINAL
FOR MOST RESULTS BEST REPORTS
SAY "PINK, PLEASE" ON SATURDAYS

PAGE SIX
PAGE SEVEN

A MESSAGE TO MUNICH

from OLD TRAFFORD

Our thoughts are constantly with those who still lie in the Rechts der Isar Hospital, Munich. All of them have been through a terrible ordeal and now face a long period of convalescence during which they will need the prayers of everyone.

Amongst them is our dear manager Matt Busby, and we know that his first concern is always for his players. Even in the first moment after regaining conciousness we recall his words to Jimmy Murphy. "Glad to see you, Jimmy, how are the lads? Look after them for me."

We will certainly do that for you Matt and wait eagerly for the day when we can welcome you back to the helm at Old Trafford.

To the lads still with you — Ray Wood, Albert Scanlon, Ken Morgans, Dennis Viollet, Johnny Berry, Jackie Blanchflower and Duncan Edwards we say "Get well soon — United needs you."

Mercifully a few of our players escaped serious injury. These were Harry Gregg and Bill Foulkes who have since arrived safely home. We hope to welcome Bobby Charlton within the next few days and look forward to the time when they will be able to take their place in the team once more.

PAGE EIGHT

19 FEBRUARY 1958: AN EMPTY FEELING

With the makeshift United line-up still unconfirmed until close to the kick-off of the club's first competitive fixture since Munich, this edition of *United Review* left the home side blank, for readers to fill in themselves.

A MESSAGE FROM M16

Elsewhere in the programme, thoughts were sent via the match programme to Matt Busby and other members of the travelling party still fighting for their lives in a German hospital.

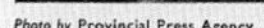
Photo by Provincial Press Agency.

Photo by Manchester Evening News.

TOM CURRY and BERT WHALLEY

Amongst those who died at Munich were two of United's most celebrated back-room boys — trainer Tom Curry and assistant coach Bert Whalley. Between them they had served the club for forty-four years and were known throughout the British Isles. Genial Tom Curry, whose words of wisdom and encouragement have helped so many players, was beloved for his fatherly supervision of their activities, both on and off the field. Bert was known and respected especially by the young players for his character and code of living which was a great example to them all.

Theirs was a tragic end — but they were not alone. They died as they had lived — amongst the lads . . . their lads.

Our sincere condolences are extended to the relatives of Mr. William Satinoff, Mr. B. P. Miklos and Mr. W. T. Cable who were also killed in the disaster.

NOT FORGOTTEN

Among the United coaching staff that lost their lives in Munich were trainers Tom Curry and Bert Whalley, who were commemorated before the Sheffield Wednesday FA Cup fixture that would be the first Old Trafford fixture to take place since the disaster.

AGELESS REDS

On pages four and five, the United first-team players that had been confirmed dead at this point were remembered in lines of poignant verse. They shall grow not old...

They shall grow not old . . .

as we that are left grow old,
Age shall not weary them,
nor the years condemn.
At the going down of the sun,
and in the morning
We will remember them.

LAURENCE BINYON

ROGER BYRNE

MARK JONES

GEOFF BENT

PAGE FOUR

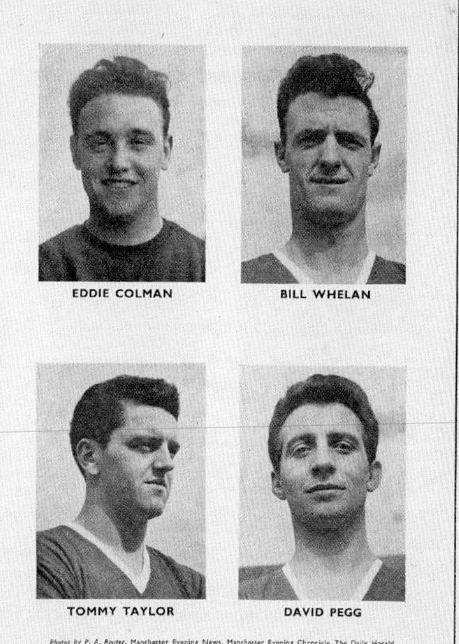
EDDIE COLMAN

BILL WHELAN

TOMMY TAYLOR

DAVID PEGG

Photos by P. A. Reuter, Manchester Evening News, Manchester Evening Chronicle, The Daily Herald, The Daily Mirror.

REMEMBERING WALTER

Among the dead in the air crash were long-serving club secretary Walter Crickmer, who helped establish United's renowned youth policy before the war.

THESE WERE OUR FRIENDS...

Some of the other individuals who died in Munich were also remembered in this Sheffield Wednesday issue, among them local sports reporters Alf Clarke and Tom Jackson, as well as former City goalkeeper-turned-journalist Frank Swift.

Photo by P. A. Reuter.

FAREWELL TO WALTER CRICKMER

When an aircraft carrying players and officials of Manchester United Football Club crashed at Munich Airport on 6th February, 1958, Walter Crickmer, Club Secretary, was amongst the twenty-one who died.

How to write an epitaph for Walter? He was more than our Secretary — he was a part of Manchester United. He had served the club for thirty-eight years and was known and respected wherever football was played. He was a religious man, modest and quietly spoken yet with a ready wit and a cheery word for all. A lifetime spent in football made his advice valued by players, managers and directors alike. He'd a hand for everything, from helping with the *United Review* to building the floodlighting pylons, but was never there to claim the credit. He preferred to praise others. How richly he deserved the gold medal presented to him by the Football League for service to the game.

Walter once claimed that he'd never watched a game of football — half a game sometimes — because he was always too busy seeing that things ran smoothly behind the scenes!

He was an indefatigable worker and a man of great integrity and personal charm — a friend to all. We thank him from the bottom of our hearts for his wonderful service and devotion to the Club. Walter, we salute you.

Photos by: Manchester Evening Chronicle *and* Manchester Evening News

ALF CLARKE and TOM JACKSON

On 6th February, 1958, Alf Clarke of the Evening Chronicle *and Tom Jackson of the* Evening News *died when their aircraft crashed at Munich. So ended a lifetime's service to the club they loved as much as any of their player friends who died with them. So ended a lifetime's association with the* United Review.

Although they worked for different newspapers Alf and Tom were inseparable. "Casual Comments" and "United Topics" were not only the result of teamwork but of mutual respect and affection. Throughout the twenty-five years they wrote for this Programme never once did they fail to send their copy in time for the printers . . . They took a pride in their work. Their articles were accurate, imaginative, detailed and concise. And that's how they were for nigh on a quarter of a century.

Alf was a serious-minded sportswriter. Slow smiling and slow speaking but quick to praise talent when he saw it which was often when watching his beloved team. On the other hand Tom bubbled with joyful enthusiasm for United assignments but was as coldly efficient as Alf whenever the occasion demanded. Once when preparing a programme for a European Cup fixture, press morning arrived without a shred of information about the visitors — not even a photograph. But somehow, Alf and Tom performed their usual miracle and a programme that was fresh and informative was ready for the supporters.

In bidding farewell to Alf and Tom we send our heartfelt sympathy to Mrs. Clarke and her son and daughter and Mrs. Jackson and her son. Throughout their association with the club many good friendships have been formed and they have been deeply respected by everyone. Whenever and wherever United play football we shall remember . . . Alf Clarke and Tom Jackson — Master Reporters.

PAGE TEN

THESE WERE OUR FRIENDS . . .

Amongst the celebrated sportswriters aboard that ill-fated aircraft on 6th February, 1958, were many contributors to the *United Review*. In addition to our own Alf Clarke and Tom Jackson these were our friends who died at Munich.

ERIC THOMPSON of the *Daily Mail*

HENRY ROSE of the *Daily Express*

DON DAVIES of the *Manchester Guardian*

ARCHIE LEDBROOKE of the *Daily Mirror*

GEORGE FOLLOWS of the *Daily Herald*

FRANK SWIFT of the *News of the World*

Both the Newspaper and the Soccer worlds mourn the loss of these fine writers. Their reports had become a part of the soccer scene, brilliant word pictures come only when the heart guides the pen.

We offer our deepest sympathy to those who were dear to them.

Amongst the survivors were *Daily Mail* cameramen Peter Howard and Edward Ellyard who miraculously escaped injury.

To Frank Taylor of the *News Chronicle-Dispatch*, who still lies injured at Munich, we send our best wishes for a speedy return home.

PAGE ELEVEN

The EDITOR'S notebook

For reasons known to all of us it will be some little time before Matt Busby can continue his usual article. "Editor's Notebook" must replace "Matt Busby Talking" but none will be better pleased than I when Matt is ready to write once again for the Programme. In the meantime we send Matt and all the boys still with him in Munich our affectionate greetings.

It is with mixed feelings that I welcome Eric Thornton of the "Manchester Evening News" and Keith Dewhurst of the "Manchester Evening Chronicle" to the United Review. I say with mixed feelings because it is a very real pleasure to have such fine writers join our team but at the same time it is a sorrow to realize they must fill the gap left by the tragic loss of Alf Clarke and Tom Jackson. I shall, however, never forget their willingness to help me in a time of need and for this I owe them my deep gratitude. Although the United Review has lost two wonderful friends I feel sure we have gained two new ones.

Our cartoonists George Butterworth and Frank Smart have asked to be excused from their contributions for the time being. I feel sure that all of us will understand and appreciate their reasons and look forward to their joining us again in happier times.

I must thank all those who sent poems and tributes to commemorate the air disaster but as our programme space is so extremely limited it is with regret that these contributions must be returned.

We are glad to welcome to Old Trafford, England international Ernie Taylor from Blackpool. The hopes of many are with you Ernie — good luck to you!

Last, but not least, I welcome back my old friend Jack Crompton just appointed trainer-coach. Memories of that wonderful 1948 Wembley come flooding back . . . and of that wonderful 4-2 victory over Blackpool. Let's hope that Jack's return is a good omen for United.

22 FEBRUARY 1958: NO WORD FROM MATT
As the United manager fought for his life in hospital, it was left to the *United Review* editor to make the usual introductions to Old Trafford before the Reds' first league game since the tragedy, against Nottingham Forest.

CLUB COMMENTS

by

KEITH DEWHURST

of the "Evening Chronicle", Manchester

The damage done to English football as a whole by the Manchester United air disaster is much deeper than it seems, and extends far beyond the loss to the international team of Byrne, Edwards and Taylor.

This in itself is bad enough. England, drawn in the same group as Russia and Brazil, has a very tough task in the World Cup, and there is very little time now to find a new blend. But even though many of the reserves in the England World Cup party would have come from United, the blow is not so crippling to our country as that suffered by Italy when the Turin team was wiped out in 1949. Turin provided more than half the national team, which has not recovered to this day.

It is none the less tragic because it has destroyed the team which was the spearhead of the revival of English football. In the past the curse of English football has been its insularity, its refusal to recognize the importance of what was happening beyond these shores.

United were great not only because they played great football, but also because they looked beyond domestic supremacy to European and even world horizons. If they had beaten Real Madrid in this year's European Cup they really would have been the greatest team in the world.

Who can take their place? Wolves and West Brom are the only candidates. Frankly, their performance in friendly games are no guide. It is a different matter when the chips are down, as Real Madrid showed when they hammered Seville 8-0 recently.

I think that Wolves, West Brom or Preston (one of them must surely be our European Cup candidate next season) will fight hard, and I wish them luck. But none of them look quite good enough to go far.

This, together with the fact that United were crippled by an air accident, is bound to have its effect. I hope and pray that it will not cause a swing back to the old insularity.

Ultimately the future of football lies in more international competitions. The vast crowds who have watched United in the European Cup at Old Trafford and on television prove that the public is ready for it.

We have lost a superb team and a great example. But the inspiration that created United is still there, and I do not think it will be very long before it is felt again.

PAGE FIVE

A TOUGH ASSIGNMENT
Manchester sports writer Keith Dewhurst had the unenviable task of writing a column in the Forest programme, in the same month as the death in Munich of his *Evening Chronicle* colleague Tom Jackson and several other press contemporaries. His sentiments about the future of European football would be proved prescient in the years that followed.

THE MANCHESTER UNITED SUPPORTERS CLUB

AIR DISASTER FUND

Chairman:
MAJOR HARRY RAWCLIFFE
57 Port Street, Manchester, I. Central 4094.

Bankers:
MARTINS BANK LTD.,
88 Great Ancoats Street, Manchester, I.

OBJECTS

To raise and collect funds for the relief of all who suffered in the Munich Air Disaster.

DONATIONS

Donations may be handed to the Chairman of the M.U.S.C. at his address above or to any branch of Martins Bank Ltd.

The Chairman of the M.U.S.C. offers his warmest thanks to the Chairman of Manchester City F.C., Alan Douglas, Esq., and his Directors, for allowing a collection at Maine Road on Saturday 15th February. Despite appalling weather conditions the collection realized the magnificent sum of £489 5s. 0d.

FUNDRAISING EFFORTS
The Manchester United Supporters Club Disaster Fund used the pages of the Forest programme to appeal for donations.

5 MARCH 1958: THE LAST OF THE BABES

The programme for the FA Cup replay hosting West Brom was the first issue since the awful news that Duncan Edwards had lost his battle for survival.

Photo by the Evening Chronicle, Manchester

DUNCAN
EDWARDS

Still the pages of tragedy turn for us and the death of Duncan Edwards on 21st February made the sadness we have shared the more pointed. Despite a fifteen-day struggle to save his life by a group of dedicated surgeons and nurses, Duncan Edwards joined his seven team-mates at whose funerals we paid homage so recently.

We who thrilled to his awe-inspiring demonstrations of seeming invincibility, coupled with a joy-of-living that infected his comrades whenever and wherever the going was tough, will always remember Duncan. Let the words of Robert Browning be his epitaph.

One who never turned his back but marched breast forward,
Never doubted clouds would break,
Never dreamed, though right were worsted, wrong would triumph,
Held we fall to rise, are baffled to fight better,
Sleep to wake.

PAGE THREE

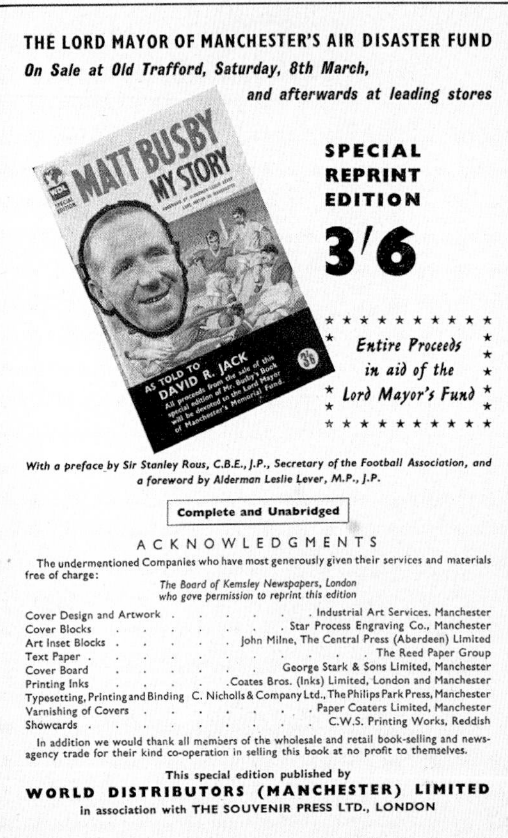

THE LORD MAYOR OF MANCHESTER'S AIR DISASTER FUND

On Sale at Old Trafford, Saturday, 8th March,
and afterwards at leading stores

SPECIAL REPRINT EDITION

3/6

★ *Entire Proceeds in aid of the Lord Mayor's Fund* ★

With a preface by Sir Stanley Rous, C.B.E., J.P., Secretary of the Football Association, and a foreword by Alderman Leslie Lever, M.P., J.P.

Complete and Unabridged

ACKNOWLEDGMENTS

The undermentioned Companies who have most generously given their services and materials free of charge:

The Board of Kemsley Newspapers, London who gave permission to reprint this edition

Cover Design and Artwork	Industrial Art Services, Manchester
Cover Blocks	Star Process Engraving Co., Manchester
Art Inset Blocks	John Milne, The Central Press (Aberdeen) Limited
Text Paper	The Reed Paper Group
Cover Board	George Stark & Sons Limited, Manchester
Printing Inks	Coates Bros. (Inks) Limited, London and Manchester
Typesetting, Printing and Binding	C. Nicholls & Company Ltd., The Philips Park Press, Manchester
Varnishing of Covers	Paper Coaters Limited, Manchester
Showcards	C.W.S. Printing Works, Reddish

In addition we would thank all members of the wholesale and retail book-selling and news-agency trade for their kind co-operation in selling this book at no profit to themselves.

This special edition published by
WORLD DISTRIBUTORS (MANCHESTER) LIMITED
in association with THE SOUVENIR PRESS LTD., LONDON

MATT'S MEMOIRS

To raise money for the Lord Mayor's charity appeal, a special reprinted edition of Matt Busby's 1957 autobiography was released.

The EDITOR'S notebook

It was inevitable of course. When disaster befell United the people of Manchester became a family in their efforts to raise relief for the wives and children and dependants of those who died. For such is the love amongst sportsmen. There was the spontaneous gesture of Alderman Leslie Lever, M.P., The Lord Mayor of Manchester, who immediately opened an Air Disaster Fund. Closely following came the announcement by Major Harry Rawcliffe of the United Supporters Club Fund whose helpers collected nearly five hundred pounds at Maine Road alone. And now a group of Manchester industrialists have combined together to print a 3/6d. edition of Matt Busby's book "My Story". Everyone concerned in its publication is making a donation of material or service. This means that every penny of the 3/6d. you give for a copy of this splendid book will be handed to the Lord Mayor's Manchester United Disaster Fund. I believe such an effort is unique in charitable history. The artwork, blocks, paper, inks, printing, binding, varnishing, showcards etc., are all being executed without charge as are the services of the wholesale and retail bookselling and newsagency trade — without which its distribution would be impossible. I understand that the first copies will be on sale at United's ground this Saturday, 8th March and thereafter it will be on sale at all leading Manchester stores — Lewis's, Kendal Milnes, Affleck & Brown, Boot's Chemists, Woolworths etc. Should you experience difficulty in obtaining your special edition of "My Story" I suggest you contact the publishers. They are World Distributors (Manchester) Ltd., P.O. Box 111, Grosvenor House, All Saints, Manchester, 1. Lastly, but by no means least, our thanks are due to the Board of Kemsley Newspapers, London who so kindly gave permission for the reprinting of this special edition. I was privileged to receive advance information of the book. There is a moving tribute by the Lord Mayor and Sir Stanley Rous, C.B.E., J.P. He points out that the Football Association, The Football League, Manchester United Football Club and their Supporters Club, The National Union of Journalists and possibly the Air Pilots Association are all anxious to help and administer the Fund and to ensure that the bereaved may receive the maximum monetary compensation.

One day a sequel will be written to this book. I believe it will tell a story even more inspiring than "My Story".

PAGE TWO

MANCHESTER UNITES

The programme editorial for the West Brom game noted how local businesses had come together to raise funds for the bereaved through the reprint of Busby's autobiography.

The EDITOR'S notebook

After the wonderful treatment afforded to those who suffered so deeply at Munich it was fitting to invite Professor Georg Maurer and his surgeons and nurses to Old Trafford to receive a personal thank you. Our cover picture shows Doctor Erika Maurer, wife of Professor Georg Maurer (extreme left) receiving a bouquet of red and white carnations from skipper Bill Foulkes. On his left is our Chairman H. P. Hardman and facing him is the Lord Mayor of Manchester, Alderman Leslie Lever, M.P. To the rear stands the Senior Nursing Sister of the Rechts der Isar Hospital, Munich. And the photographer? Who else but Peter Howard of the "Daily Mail" who with Bill Foulkes and Harry Gregg miraculously escaped injury. Peter was 'phoning his Manchester office within forty-five minutes of the tragedy — the first, I think, to reveal the terrible news. Few noticed Peter amongst the adulation. We did though. Here's a photograph of a master photographer.

It is now clear that the United Disaster Fund is fast approaching a total whereby the dependants of those who suffered so grievously can expect a very real measure of financial assistance. Heartening too is the fact that contributions show no sign of dwindling. A few days ago the Refuge Assurance Company Table Tennis Club sold 1,000 tickets for a Charity Match and a cheque for the magnificent sum of £25 was handed to Mr. Nash, a member of the United Supporters Club Disaster Fund Committee. On 19th April next at 7.15 p.m., there is to be a concert at the Levenshulme Town Hall, Stockport Road and proceeds are to be donated to the Lord Mayor's Disaster Fund. The Lord Mayor of Manchester and his Lady Mayoress have kindly promised to attend together with several members of the City Council. Ticket enquiries should be addressed to Mr. W. R. Platt, at the Town Hall, Levenshulme. Tel. RUSholme 4118.

Cameraman
Peter Howard in action

—continued on page four

4 APRIL 1958: CHARITY FUNDS KEEP COMING

United's league game against Sunderland was our first home fixture for nearly a month, so there was much to update on the progress of the charitable causes campaigning to raise money for the victims' families.

CLUB COMMENTS

by

KEITH DEWHURST

of the "Evening Chronicle", Manchester

The whole outlook for United has suddenly become much brighter, and the brightest thing by far is that by a masterly shuffle of the forward line Jimmy Murphy has virtually solved the problem of finding a forward balance for Wembley.

The Portsmouth game experiment of playing Ken Morgans at outside left and Alex Dawson at outside right was a great success. Morgans found his real form for the first time since Munich, and made all United's goals, and young Alex showed touches of true greatness to come. The whole line moved well, and with Dennis Viollet now available Jimmy Murphy really has a hand to play with. Once again, however, inexperience and some slack play in defence lost a point.

Portsmouth roared into the attack in a desperately exciting second half, and it says much for United that they came back into the game again with some fine football.

The return of Gregg and Goodwin should bring more confidence to the defence in moments of crisis, although it is only fair to say that young Gaskell had a fine game in goal. He needs only experience in dealing with high crosses.

The second great event is the return of "The Boss", Matt Busby. What can be said about him that has not been written already? Except that it took Munich to reveal the true greatness of the youth system and the team spirit that he had built up, and that he chose well when he made his best signing — Jimmy Murphy.

I would like to take this opportunity of welcoming him back on behalf of all the pressmen who follow United.

There is now only one of the Munich party left in hospital — sports writer Frank Taylor. The players have made remarkable recoveries.

Gregg, Foulkes, Charlton, Morgans and Viollet are all playing again. Albert Scanlon is doing energetic exercises and is sure to play at the start of next season. Ray Wood awaits medical clearance.

Jackie Blanchflower, although he has yet to have another operation on his arm, is happily with us in Manchester. Johnny Berry, who made the most miraculous recovery of all, is doing nicely in Manchester Royal Infirmary.

WITH THE JUNIORS

Continued from page eleven

16th April, 1958.

United "B" 1 v. Rochdale "A" 2.

United were well on top in the early stages and after good efforts by Gillespie and Sutton had been just off target the latter gave us the lead with a well taken goal. Only good work by Torrance enabled Rochdale to hold United to a narrow interval lead.

Rochdale came more into the game on the resumption but their lack of punch near goal enabled Ronan to have a quiet time. At the other end, however, Torrance made a number of excellent saves. This and the missing of several easy chances by the home forwards kept Rochdale in the game with a chance.

Some slack defensive play in the home penalty area conceded a corner. From the flag kick the ball came loose to Duff who smashed it into the net to level the scores.

The home forwards continued to fluff easy chances and Smith in particular was remiss in this respect.

In the 89th minute, in a desperate tackle on Orwin, Haydock conceded a penalty. Newell gave Ronan no chance with the spot kick to settle the issue.

Team: Ronan; Maddison, Yeomans; Stiles (N), Haydock, Elms; Smith (G), Gillespie, Meachin, Sutton, Stiles (C).

PAGE FIVE

UNITED JOTTINGS

by

DAVID MEEK

of the "Manchester Evening News"

Bobby Charlton
A Daily Mail Photo

Only ten weeks ago 20-year-old Bobby Charlton was hurled out of Manchester United's crashing plane as it shuddered and broke in two at the end of a Munich runway.

Many died and others were seriously injured. Bobby himself was cut about the head and taken to hospital suffering from concussion and shock.

Then came the miracle of Munich — the struggle back to health of players like Albert Scanlon, Jackie Blanchflower and Johnny Berry, and as far as football is concerned the amazing recovery and soccer upsurge of Bobby Charlton.

It is quite true that before the crash, Charlton was making steady improvement but few people saw him as an England player at that stage.

But what a tremendous transformation since Munich. Bobby has developed poise and confidence. Perhaps it was the realization that no longer was he just one of the youngsters but an old hand on whom rested a great deal of responsibility for United's recovery.

Just how brilliantly he faced up to that responsibility we know to our delight.

Deservedly his fast-swerving, hard-shooting performances for the new-born Reds caught the eyes of the England selectors.

Congratulations on your first international Cap Bobby — may it be the first of many. Apart from admiring your personal success, Old Trafford supporters are delighted that you will be able to keep alive United's close association with the England team.

I doubt if few people watched the game against Scotland at Hampden Park or on television on Saturday without seeing the images of Roger Byrne, Tommy Taylor and Duncan Edwards. But at least these fine players now have an old clubmate to keep the United flag flying with England.

While congratulating Bobby Charlton let's not forget Manchester United's other international Cap last week — Harry Gregg who again played for Ireland last Wednesday.

I'm glad the United Board agreed to release him, even though Gregg is one of the most reliable men in the side.

When the English Football Association select a player all clubs must toe the line and release him.

But when outside associations like the Scots, Welsh and Irish want someone playing with an English league club they must seek permission.

In the old days many clubs used to jib at releasing key players and the number of Caps lost by exiles in this way must be legion. Happily, times have changed so that now even Manchester United although hard hit by the deaths of so many of their top players did not hesitate to release Harry.

So I say well done Bobby, well done Harry . . . and well done Manchester United Board!

PAGE EIGHT

23 APRIL 1958: DAVID MEEK STEPS UP...

As the Reds prepared to face Newcastle, an England cap for Bobby Charlton was hailed by a man also on the up: David Meek would go on to cover United in the *Manchester Evening News* for 38 years. Soon after (see above and below), the Reds would be Wembley-bound in the FA Cup.

PAGE SIX PAGE SEVEN

8 MAY 1958: WEMBLEY SETBACK

The *Evening Chronicle*'s Keith Dewhurst had strong words after defeat to Bolton in the FA Cup final: United had not performed. But in this edition of *UR*, as the Reds hosted AC Milan in the European Cup semi-final first leg, five days after Wembley, he still saw some positives.

WEMBLEY COMMENTS

by

KEITH DEWHURST

of the "Evening Chronicle", Manchester

What a disappointment! What a sad end to such a brave dream. United never at any time in the game touched their best form, and Bolton were worthy Cup winners.

United's Wembley plan was to beat Bolton centre-half John Higgins down the middle. Bolton's plan was to use Edwards to blot out Ernie Taylor, and to cover Higgins with their full-backs. Everything went according to plan — for Bolton! Ernie Taylor has had far better games. United's wingers Alex Dawson and Colin Webster rarely threatened enough to pull the Bolton backs away from Higgins. The ball just didn't run for United's wing halves Goodwin and Crowther as it did at West Bromwich and Highbury.

Viollet played wonderfully well and this was only his fourth game since Munich. Bobby Charlton always looked likely to turn the game with his prodigious shooting.

What would have happened if that great second-half shot of his had gone into the net instead of bouncing off the post straight into Hopkinson's arms?

Was Lofthouse's second and decisive goal in the very next minute in fact a foul on Harry Gregg?

These are the questions that will be discussed for as long as this final is remembered. Perhaps if Charlton had scored United would have played better and Bolton would have lost the edge of confidence. But Charlton did not score, and the referee gave Lofthouse a goal; and there is perhaps little point in arguing more because on the day and on the run of play Bolton were the better team. They were crisper, and they invariably dictated the play.

As a spectacle it was not so good as most finals — there was too little good constructive play and Bolton, although they were well on top, never did enough shooting to add the final dramatic punch to their moves.

Perhaps from United's point of view one of the best things was the display of centre-half Ronnie Cope. Here is a player who has steadily matured and improved since Munich. He has a classic style and an ideal temperament and who soon will be deserving of international honours. He played Lofthouse, the hero of the game, extremely well.

A word, too, for captain Bill Foulkes. Week in and week out he has given solid and consistent displays. He played Holden out of the game at Wembley. If he plays in both the European Cup-ties Bill will establish a record for the number of competitive club appearances in a season — sixty-four. A fine record, and richly deserved.

PAGE FIVE

Photo by the Daily Mail

A MESSAGE FROM THE CHAIRMAN

My dear Friends,

To-day United stands at the crossroads.

Many of our finest players together with some of the most experienced members of our staff are no longer with us. Matt Busby regains his strength, but the team you cheer to-day is about to start one of the most testing seasons in the history of the club.

What has the future in store for us? From last season's tragedy there sprang the realization that great team work can bring success. Supported by only two first team players and two fine new club men, a team of reserves and juniors began the road to Wembley and the Semi-Final stages of the European Cup Competition.

Were these boys inspired? Inspired yes, not only by the memory of their comrades but by the inspiration they derived from our supporters. In asking once more for your cheers in victory we ask also for your tolerance in defeat. Give us your loyalty and United will be great again.

Yours sincerely,

H. P. Hardman,
Chairman,
MANCHESTER UNITED FOOTBALL CLUB LTD.

PAGE THREE

23 AUGUST 1958: HARDMAN... BUT FAIR

The opening league game of the 1958/59 season, at home to Chelsea with the returning Matt Busby back in the dugout, was the occasion for a rallying cry from the club chairman, Harold Hardman. His promise that 'United will be great again' would be borne out in the years to come.

6th FEBRUARY 1958

For as long as football is played by Manchester United 6th February 1958 will be remembered as the date of the Air Disaster at Munich. On that sad day we lost our Secretary, Trainer, Assistant Coach and eight players — one dying on the 21st February. Eight of our newspaper friends also perished including Alf Clarke and Tom Jackson.

To commemorate the anniversary of Munich a one minute silence will be observed before the match at Old Trafford next Saturday, 7th February.

ROLL OF HONOUR

Walter Crickmer — Tom Curry — Bert Whalley

Roger Byrne — Geoff Bent — Eddie Colman

Duncan Edwards — Mark Jones — David Pegg

Tommy Taylor — Liam Whelan

*"At the going down of the sun,
and in the morning
We will remember them."*

PAGE THREE

31 JANUARY 1959: A MINUTE'S SILENCE

A traditional moment of reflection was in order as the Reds prepared to face Newcastle United with the first anniversary of Munich looming large.

5 MARCH 1960: MUNICH CLOCK

Two years after the disaster, a clock was erected on the stadium wall in tribute to those who died. This featured in the Wolves programme that season.

OUR MUNICH MEMORIALS

Following the Munich air disaster our Directors gave considerable thought to a Memorial which would be a fitting and lasting tribute, worthy of the Club.

It was finally decided to proceed with a design submitted by a local Architect, Mr. J. Vipond, L.R.I.B.A., and the construction was entrusted to Messrs. Jaconello (Manchester) Limited. The firm's representative, Mr. A. E. Sheppard was responsible for the setting out and production of the completed memorial.

The design of the memorial is, in effect, a complete plan of the ground, and the size, excluding figures and canopy measures 7 ft. 9 in. by 6 ft.

The green slabs of Faience marked out as a football pitch are incised to receive the black and gold glass letters forming the inscription and names of those who lost their lives. The terraces, gangways and steps are also carried out in Faience to scale and are of a memorial colour in mauve and grey. The stand roofs and perimeter path are worked from solid Quartzite, these being enclosed by Red Balmoral Granite forming the boundary walling of the ground. The carving of the Teak figure group represents players, officials and spectators standing with bowed heads and outstretched hands over a laurel wreath and ball inscribed "1958".

The Directors wish to express their appreciation to Mr. J. Vipond, Mr. A. E. Sheppard, and the following firms for their interest and part they played in the work involved:

Main Contractors: Messrs. Jaconello (Manchester) Ltd., Pendleton. Sub Contractors: H. Rowlinson, Manchester 21. Faience Work: Shaw's Glazed Brick Co. Ltd., Darwen. Quartzite: John Stubbs & Son Ltd., Liverpool. Glass Lettering: L. Oppenheimer Ltd., Manchester. Granite: W. Kay & Son Ltd., Aberdeen. Teak Figure Group: Bond & Hall, Manchester. Copper Canopy: A. Cheetham & Co. Ltd., Failsworth, Manchester. Side Torches: General Electric Co. Ltd., Manchester.

Above: This handsome bronze plaque has been erected in the Press Box by the Football Writers' Association. The inscription includes the names of Alf Clarke, Donny Davies, Archie Ledbrooke, George Follows, Henry Rose, Tom Jackson, Frank Swift and Eric Thompson — all of whom were contributors to the "United Review".

Left: An illuminated clock erected by the Ground Committee on the wall at the Old Trafford end of the ground.

4 FEBRUARY 1961: BUSBY LOOKS BACK

In the programme for the Aston Villa home game, two days before the third anniversary of Munich, Matt Busby urged us never to forget the victims.

MATT BUSBY *talking...*

Monday, 6th February, marks the third anniversary of the Munich air disaster which resulted in the loss of so many well-loved officials, players and friends of Manchester United.

It is inevitable that this period of the year must open up deep wounds of grief which time can only partially heal. Yet it would be wrong on that account to let this sad anniversary day pass without acknowledgement to or remembrance of those who lost their lives in the service of football.

Indeed, it is the sole purpose of this sincere acknowledgement to ensure that they are not forgotten rather than to re-open those wounds and revive the grief which must still be felt by United supporters, in general, and by those with closer ties to the victims, in particular.

It only remains for me to add that the achievements of those we lost will always be an inspiration to those of us left to carry on and to those who will follow in our footsteps.

* * *

OUR VISITORS

This afternoon we welcome Aston Villa to Old Trafford. This famous club, now managed by Mr. Joe Mercer, has made a fine return to the First Division, establishing an excellent reputation for good football. I feel sure today's clash will provide an exciting game in every way.

10 FEBRUARY 1968: TEN YEARS AFTER

A decade on from the tragedy, United were English champions. In this Manchester City issue (match postponed), *The Sun*'s sports writer considered how the fallen Babes might have gone on to even greater glory.

MUNICH

Ten years afterwards

by Arthur Walmsley

(Sports writer for the Sun)

Ten years ago this week – 6th February, 1958 – there was Munich. No signal, this, for maudlin reminiscence or the hurtful probing of time-healed wounds.

Yet it is a special time. A decade is a convention in the life-span; a marker on the endless tides of time; so in this week ten years on from Munich it would be unseemly not to remember.

In remembering there can be no total escape from a lingering sadness – but it is not my wish to engender melancholy here. Rather would I draw on the rich storehouse of unclouded memory for recall of the golden days when those whose time was short were writing their imperishable chapter of Manchester United history.

Such is the fleeting passage of time that already there is a generation of young Old Trafford devotees among us who know them only as legends – names in the folklore of football to be uttered with uncomprehending awe.

There is not space here for detailed enlightenment of the individual talents of those who died at Munich – but each one, in his own way, is inextricably interwoven in the fabric of success spun during Matt Busby's brilliant Old Trafford reign.

But some measure of their total meaning to Manchester United can be indicated here. The players among them inherited an awesome task. Most were little more than schoolboys – the Busby Babes – when on to their shoulders passed the burden of sustaining the greatness achieved by Johnny Carey and his men.

Where Carey's men left off – they had to carry on. How brilliantly they bore the load. Blending with the more mature ones they confirmed and consolidated the club name as a by-word in Europe for all that was best in football.

At home they were fast becoming an irrestible force, as illustrated by their winning of the League championship twice in the two years immediately preceding Munich.

Each one, to a greater or lesser degree, was a star in his own right – yet their power lay in collective strength. Flamboyance was scorned in the cause of the greater good for the greater number – a discipline which came as much from within as without.

What Olympian heights would they have scaled had fate allowed them their full span? There lies a whole realm of fascinating speculation. Those of us who saw them flowering would put no limit on their potential. At home they were already undisputed masters – only the time that was denied prevented them extending that dominance to Europe and the world.

But United then, as now, were more than a team on the field. They were a team right through from the backroom – and here again Munich took its toll.

For those "backroom boys" were not just men doing a job – but loyal servants dedicated to a cause. The cause was "Manchester United" and they, as much as any player, played their own parts in building the mystique which now surrounds the club's name wherever Soccer is played.

So with the ten-year cushion between Munich and emotion we can remember them not in sorrow but in appreciation for their services to football and their club.

Let us remember then, players Geoff Bent, Roger Byrne, Eddie Coleman, Duncan Edwards, Mark Jones, David Pegg, Tommy Taylor and Billy Whelan; secretary Walter Crickmer; trainer Tom Curry and coach Bert Whalley; and United Review writers Alf Clarke and Tom Jackson.

Indeed, those who knew and saw them will never forget.

The Wolves programme from the 1959/60 season showed another lasting memorial to be erected at the stadium – a scale model of Old Trafford listing the names of the victims.

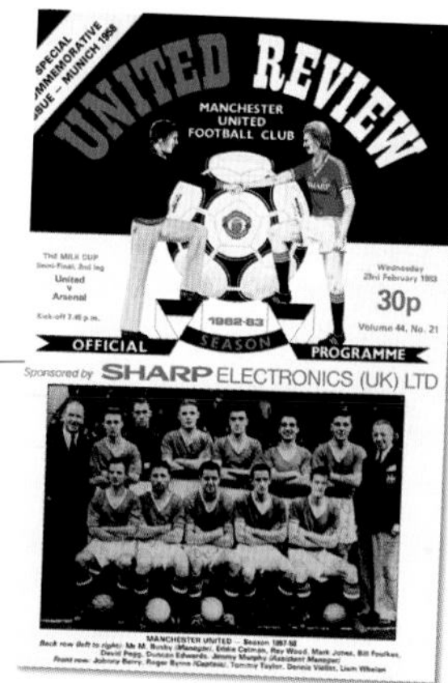

23 FEBRUARY 1983: *UNITED REVIEW* PAYS TRIBUTE
Twenty-five years after that fateful day, the programme for this League Cup clash with Arsenal included a tribute pull-out.

HOW THE WORLD EXPRESSED ITS SYMPATHIES
In the same midweek programme, we looked back at the many kind gestures offered to the club and the bereaved.

EXPRESSIONS of sympathy flooded into Manchester from all corners of the world. Nearer home, the Lord Mayor of Manchester immediately set up a Disaster Fund which was to top £50,000; an equivalent sum in today's terms would probably be in the region of £750,000.

A moving tribute of a different type was received from the men of Pentonville Prison. Another scroll was from much nearer home, from the members of the Ex-Servicemen's Club in Stretford and was received on United's behalf by Bert Trautmann — for those too young to know, Bert was a German ex-prisoner of war who won a special place in the hearts of Mancunians with his wonderful goalkeeping skills with Manchester City.

A poem, 'The Flowers of Manchester' was also written and again gives some indication of the feelings of the time.

Our great friends from Spain, Real Madrid, responded to manager Busby's plea for a friendly fixture — so that United could continue to play against the very best. They came to Manchester in October 1959, in order that Matt Busby might gauge the progress of his task of restoring United to greatness again.

Whilst in Manchester, Senor Bernabeu, president of Real Madrid, took his players to Weaste Cemetery in Salford, to lay flowers on the grave of Eddie Colman.

The people of Dudley in Worcestershire spearheaded a fund set up to install a stained glass window dedicated to the memory of Duncan Edwards at the church of St Francis's in the Priory, Duncan's Parish Church.

It is impossible to show fully the extent to which the nation, and the world, joined in our sadness. We hope that the few examples shown give some idea of the depth and the range of the feeling.

PROFILE
Jackie Blanchflower
By David Meek

Manchester United remember Munich today and the evidence of their respect is all around us as the club mark the 30th anniversary of the horrific accident.

The crash has been the most significant experience in the history of Old Trafford.

As Bobby Charlton, himself one of the survivors, said the other day: "There is a little bit of all those who didn't come back built into the club we see around us today."

Those who lost their lives will be especially remembered at this time by those who escaped. Fate ranged widely among the survivors.

There were those who walked away with hardly a scratch, some had to fight for their lives, and then there were those who had to come to terms with a different kind of situation.

They survived, but their playing careers were over.

Such a survivor is Jackie Blanchflower who was in hospital a long time recovering from crippling injuries to his pelvis, ribs and arm.

I suspect that in the first few years he didn't know whether to give thanks for his life or curse the blows which had robbed him of his football.

Jack still has mixed emotions about Munich and its remembrance.

"I have one set of feelings I keep to myself and another when I am asked. My truth probably lies somewhere in between.

"The thing is that Munich has become a legend and I must admit that I have tired of the pathos of it. My memories now 30 years later are of all those fit, young men so full of life.

"As a team we were unbelievably close and happy and those are the times I like to remember now.

"When we had the 25th anniversary I was interviewed by television and recalled some of the humorous experiences we had shared. But they were all cut out. They wanted only the sadness.

"I don't want to forget, especially the happy times we all shared. We will never see them grow old of course. They will never be fat and balding like I'm going to be.

"All the survivors have their different memories and ideas. Most of us have come to accept things. Some people think I am bitter but I'm not really."

What Jack does have is a mischevious sense of humour which at times in the early days could suggest he was a touch cynical, but he has mellowed now.

His sense of fun and humour is most in evidence when he steps into the role of after-dinner speaker, an art in which he excels.

His wife, Jean, is a professional entertainer and singer who has become a popular comedienne in recent years. They live at Stalybridge.

Jack who is now 54 has worked in a variety of jobs ranging from pub to betting shop and describes himself as a bookkeeper.

He says: "I'm overweight and unfit, but I'm all right. There are the odd twinges and pains, but I'm not complaining."

He joined United straight from school in Belfast, the younger brother of Danny, the Spurs and Northern Ireland captain.

Jack made his League debut in 1951 and made 105 League appearances. He also won 12 international caps for Ireland before the crash called a halt to a talented career and makes today such a poignant anniversary.

6 FEBRUARY 1988: BLANCHFLOWER'S SADNESS
On the 30th anniversary of the crash, our columnist focused on an individual who survived but would never play again – Northern Irish international Jackie Blanchflower.

MUNICH REMEMBERED

MUNICH REMEMBERED

By Frank Taylor, OBE., President International Sports Writers' Association

February 6th: For me (and I have no doubt for all the other survivors) is a day for quiet reflection.

A day to thank God for being alive. A day to remember all our comrades who were lost on that sad day, at the end of the runway at Munich Reim airport.

After 30 years, I can well understand there may be people who believe it is time to forget. After all, anybody younger than 40 will not know just what the Busby Babes meant to British soccer.

Forget? We who are left can never forget. Last summer I went to the World Student Games in Zagreb, Yugoslavia, as President of the International Sports Writers' Association. I was interviewed by the press, radio and on television. And what do you think they wanted to know?

"How is Matt Busby? How is Bobby Charlton? How is Harry Gregg and Bill Foulkes? What are they doing? How is the team doing? We want to see Manchester United back in Europe."

The Babes played their last match in Belgrade, and you can take it from me, the true Yugoslav soccer fans, many of them learning the story from their fathers, have this feeling of kinship with Old Trafford. They have this link with the past. They want success for the Reds.

In Moscow, Mexico, even Peking, where I went in 1978 with Bryan Robson when he was a player with West Brom, I have been asked the same kind of questions by colleagues in newspapers, radio or television: "How are Manchester United doing these days? Will they be champions?"

The truth is Manchester United cannot escape their destiny. They were, after the end of World War II, always one of England's most attractive and successful sides. What happened on February 6th 1958 turned them into a Living Legend.

I can well imagine some United players may feel that this places an unnecessary burden upon them. It shouldn't. The Babes belonged to one era. They belong to another. What is important, they do not forget the tradition. It is not just enough to win, but to win with style.

That's a tall order, but when I was a young reporter in 1947, until 1953, Manchester United with Jack Rowley, Jimmy Delaney, Johnny Carey, Stan Pearson, Charlie Mitten and the rest made their style enjoyable to watch. They didn't win the League as often as they might, because they were dedicated to playing attacking football which pulled in the fans.

The Babes were the same, only more so. Consider that last match in Belgrade when they scored three goals in the first half. How many English teams do you know who could score three goals away from home against one of Europe's top teams?

That Wednesday afternoon I asked myself: "Are the Babes now mature enough to take over from Real Madrid as Europe's undisputed master team?"

That question was stilled 24 hours later along with so many great young players, and left those of us who survived with our own personal memories.

In my case so may of them are unforgettable:

THE BLAZING COURAGE of Harry Gregg and Peter Howard *(Daily Mail photographer)* in risking their own lives to save others in the wreckage. In wartime they would have had George Medals.

THE DEDICATED LOYALTY of Jimmy Murphy who promised Matt Busby he would keep the flag flying at Old Trafford until he got back to Old Trafford. Jimmy did just that. No club has had a more loyal servant.

THE DETERMINATION and COURAGE of survivors Bill Foulkes and Bobby Charlton. Bill scored the vital goal which took United to the European Cup Final in 1968 and Bobby Charlton was the goalscoring hero for England in the World Cup and United in the European Cup.

THE MASTERMIND of MATT BUSBY: His three sides of 1948 . . . 1958 . . . and 1968 have left a glittering heritage of how soccer should be played, with panache, with style, and with a firm but unwritten policy of entertaining the fans. Only a superman would have pulled himself together after the tragedy of Munich to create his great team of Best, Law, Crerand, Charlton and Stiles to become the first English club to win the European Cup and thus keep faith with the Babes.

They were unforgettable, and for me, so were my friends the sports writers who died. Remember them? "Old International" (Donny Davies of the *Guardian*), Henry Rose *(Daily Express)*, George Follows *(Daily Herald)*, Eric Thompson *(Daily Mail)*, Archie Ledbrooke *(Daily Mirror)*, Alf Clarke *(Manchester Evening Chronicle)*, Tom Jackson *(Manchester Evening News)* and Frank Swift *(News of the World)*. They all played a great part in popularising the game of soccer. They were characters, with style, flair, and a passion for soccer. They too are a part of the Manchester United story, and we should never forget it.

I am sorry that I am not able to accept the invitation to meet all my friends and fellow survivors today.

I have to go to Kuwait, to conduct a seminar for Asian Sports Writers. I will of course tell them of the great days reporting Manchester United in Europe, and of the club that rose again from the ashes of tragedy. I will urge them to try to recapture the best of the English style of prose writing, best epitomised by Donny Davies "Old International of the *Guardian*". He was a model for any young journalist, I only wished I had his talent. Although I will be 2,000 miles away my heart will still be at Old Trafford.

Good luck boys. Do the old club proud!

13

6 FEBRUARY 1988: 30 YEARS OF HURT

In the *UR* published on the 30th anniversary of Munich, as the Reds faced Coventry, veteran sports writer and Munich survivor Frank Taylor reflected.

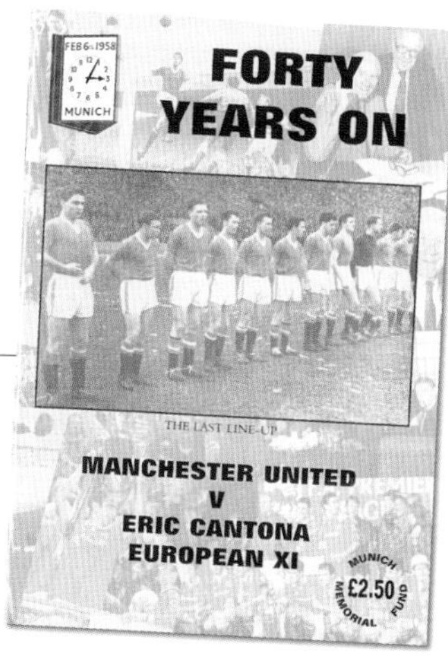

18 AUGUST 1998: TRIBUTE TO OLD FRIENDS

At the start of a momentous season for United, the team faced an old team-mate and friends for a charity match for the Munich Memorial Fund.

Bobby Charlton lays a wreath ahead of our 1998 game against Bolton Wanderers

7 FEBRUARY 1998: 40 YEARS ON

The day after the 40th anniversary of the Munich tragedy, as United faced Bolton in the Premier League in a very different footballing landscape from that of 1958, *United Review* was determined not to allow future generations to forget.

Forty years on and the tragic events which occurred on the snowy wastes of Munich Reim airport are still vivid in the minds of those old enough to remember.

Sir Matt Busby

In a few fateful seconds, twenty-two people lost their lives as the chartered BEA Elizabethan aircraft failed, on its third attempt, to take off from a snow-covered runway in the Bavarian city. Duncan Edwards, who later died of his injuries, became the disaster's 23rd victim.

The party, which included club officials, players, press and travel representatives, was returning from a European Cup quarter-final tie with Red Star in Belgrade.

The game ended in a 3-3 draw, enough to take United through to the competition's last-four after winning the home leg 2-1. So it was a happy group which set off on the return journey from Yugoslavia the following morning.

The flight to Manchester involved a brief stop at Munich to refuel. Everyone disembarked and made their way to the terminal building for a warming cup of coffee.

Soon after they were called to re-board the plane for the final leg of their journey to Ringway. Twice they tried to take off and both times the attempt was aborted. The party was again requested to leave the aircraft and return to the airport building.

A short time later the flight was called again and they made their way back to the airliner.

The plane's crew, once again, went through the usual procedures in readiness for take-off, unaware that disaster was a few fleeting minutes away.

Frank Taylor OBE, the only writer to survive the tragedy, and author of the acclaimed and definitive account of the accident, 'The Day A Team Died', shares his thoughts and emotions in an evocative look back to the day which stunned the football world.

Munich 6th February 1958

10 FEBRUARY 2008: A CITY UNITED
To commemorate the 50th anniversary of Munich, United commissioned a special 1958-style kit for the team to wear in this league derby. We also took the opportunity to remember a City great, Frank Swift, who also died in the crash (see opposite page).

MANCHESTER UNITED

Edwin VAN DER SAR
Ben FOSTER
Tomasz KUSZCZAK
Tom HEATON

Gary NEVILLE
Patrice EVRA
Rio FERDINAND
Wes BROWN
Nemanja VIDIC
Gerard PIQUÉ
John O'SHEA
Danny SIMPSON
Mikaël SILVESTRE
Craig CATHCART
Jonny EVANS

Owen HARGREAVES
Cristiano RONALDO
ANDERSON
Ryan GIGGS
Ji-sung PARK
Michael CARRICK
NANI
Paul SCHOLES
Darren FLETCHER
Chris EAGLES
Rodrigo POSSEBON

Louis SAHA
Wayne ROONEY
DONG Fangzhuo
Carlos TEVEZ
Danny WELBECK

MANCHESTER CITY

1	Andreas ISAKSSON
19	Kasper SCHMEICHEL
25	Joe HART
2	Micah RICHARDS
3	Michael BALL
4	Nedum ONUOHA
16	Vedran CORLUKA
17	Sun JIHAI
22	Richard DUNNE
24	Javier GARRIDO
34	Sam WILLIAMSON
37	Malcolm LOGAN
6	Michael JOHNSON
7	Stephen IRELAND
8	GEOVANNI
13	ELANO
15	Martin PETROV
21	Dietmar HAMANN
28	Gelson FERNANDES
30	Nery CASTILLO
36	Kelvin ETUHU
41	Ashley GRIMES
9	Emile MPENZA
12	Darius VASSELL
29	Valeri BOJINOV
35	Daniel STURRIDGE

TODAY'S FIXTURES

NEXT HOME MATCH

CLUB CHARTER

EMERGENCY PROCEDURE

SMOKING

A fitting tribute

Reds aim to pay respect to the lost Busby Babes with derby-day victory

TODAY'S MATCH WILL be laced with emotion for everyone inside Old Trafford. In the game closest to the 50th anniversary of the Munich air disaster, United's stand-in skipper Ryan Giggs believes his team-mates can keep their feelings in check and honour the memories of those who perished with a performance and result of which they would be proud.

It was the Welshman who scored the winner in the 1-0 victory over Everton that marked the passing of Sir Matt Busby in January 1994. A lone piper led the teams out that day as Old Trafford fell silent. Giggs admits it was a surreal experience, but uppermost in the players' minds was the need to focus on the 90 minutes ahead. And that will again be the intention today.

"You know there's going to be a lot of emotion surrounding the game," said Giggs. "However, you've just got to try and be professional. Our job is to go out and win the game for ourselves, the fans and those who died.

"It's difficult to put into words what it was like walking out at a silent stadium with a bagpipe leading you out after Sir Matt died. It was very emotional. But I felt ready to play and was looking forward to the match once the build-up was over. I just wanted to get on with the game. I'm sure all the players will feel the same way this afternoon."

The major focus of today's game has been the 50th anniversary commemorations, but three points and local pride are still at stake.

“Our job is to go out and win the game for ourselves, the supporters and those who died”

Triumph for the Reds would give the team 13 Premier League victories against the Blues, who have won just four of the 21 top-flight clashes – all on their own patch. City's last derby scalp at Old Trafford came in the old Division One on 27 April 1974.

Sven-Goran Eriksson's men have found goals hard to come by of late and they face a United side that not only possesses the meanest defence in the Premier League, but is also determined to ensure today, of all days, ends victoriously for the Red half of Manchester.

TOP SCORERS

Player	Team	Goals
Ronaldo	United	19
Benjani*	City	12*
Tevez	United	11
Rooney	United	6
Elano	City	5

LAST FIVE LEAGUE MEETINGS AT OT

9 DECEMBER 2006
United 3-1 City
10 SEPTEMBER 2005
United 1-1 City
7 NOVEMBER 2004
United 0-0 City
13 DECEMBER 2003
United 3-1 City
9 FEBRUARY 2003
United 1-1 City

LEAGUE FORM H&A

	P	W	D	L	F	A
United (H)	13	12	1	0	31	3
City (A)	12	2	5	5	11	17

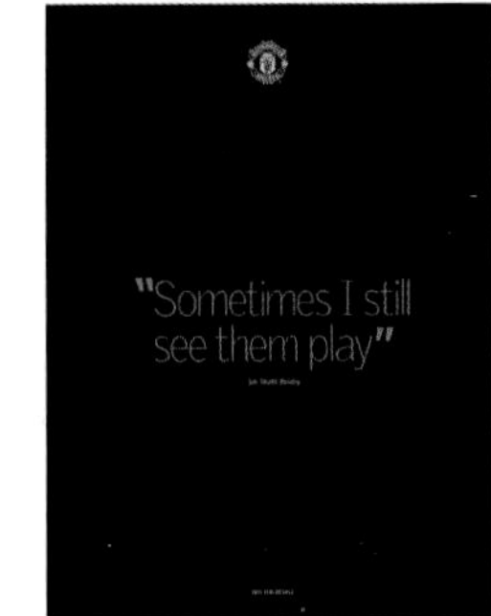

GIGGS'S AIM TO DO THE BABES PROUD
As United's longest-serving player at that point, Ryan Giggs felt the importance of the 50th anniversary as keenly as anyone, and he told *United Review* of the team's resolve to honour the memory of those who died at Munich. Our old friends in blue weren't about to let sentiment get in the way of results, though, the visitors winning the game 2-1.

FRANK SWIFT (1914–1958)

Frank Swift was a goalkeeping great. An imposing figure, he was a favourite at City before and after the Second World War. Swift won Division One and Division Two title medals and an FA Cup winner's medal alongside Matt Busby in 1934. Regularly throwing, rather than kicking the ball out – and often heading it away – he helped to revolutionise goalkeeping. A close friend of Busby, Swift was working for the *News of the World* when he accompanied United to Belgrade. His successor at City was Bert Trautmann (pictured below left, with Swift), now 84, who recalls him clearly.

"I was concerned for everyone on the plane, but Frank especially," says Bert. "It was human nature, I knew him. He was my predecessor.

"Frank was a legend and the former captain of England. And he was good to me. I first saw him play in 1948 and Matt Busby tried to sign him then, that's what United thought of Frank. He came into the dressing room at Burnden Park in 1949 before my debut and sat beside me. 'Now listen son,' he said. As a German, I wasn't sure what to make of him calling me 'son', but the other players told me he called everyone 'son'. It was his term of endearment. 'There will be 40-50,000 spectators,' he said. 'Ignore them.'

"I was naturally very nervous as I'd only been playing for St Helens Town in front of 2,000, but Frank's words made me relax. He had a big personality, but never tried to impose his views on me or talk down to me. When I was established, people made comparisons between us. I obviously

felt flattered. I vividly remember the night the bodies came home from Ringway airport. It was one of those awful Mancunian winter nights that I don't miss now I live in Valencia. I wanted to pay my respects and intended going alone, but my wife wanted to come. So did my friends, and people who had no interest in football. The disaster touched us all."

3 FEBRUARY 2018: 60 YEARS SINCE '58

United's Premier League clash against Huddersfield Town fell three days before the 60th anniversary of Munich, and *United Review* produced a striking souvenir cover.

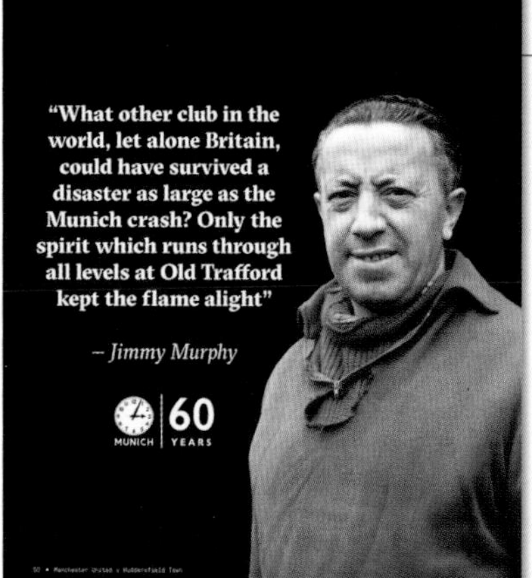

WORDS FROM THE WISE

The issue featured reflections from a number of key United figures from past and present, including Jimmy Murphy, one of the relatively unsung heroes of the Munich era who not only played a pivotal role in nurturing the Babes, but also took control of first-team affairs during Matt Busby's lengthy recovery period in hospital.

THEIR SPIRIT LIVES ON

The poignant back-cover photo (above, right) of our pre-Munich side – proud champions of England and looking forward to taking on Europe – was one of many haunting images in this 60th anniversary programme, a copy for which was placed on every seat in the stadium, along with a book telling the full story of the disaster. As the years roll past and Manchester United's name continues to gain renown, *UR* will help ensure that these young men who captured the hearts of football fans around the world will remain an indelible part of the club's history.

CHAPTER 11

Supporters

As recent times have shown us, home fixtures aren't the same without fans cheering the lads on. The flat caps and trilbies have gone, but the modern-day Red still loves a bar scarf, as well as singing about our heroes, past and present...

Usually, it's a particular player or a specific game that first attracts someone to Manchester United. Maybe family and friends provide a helpful nudge in the right direction at an early age, but you still need that lightning-rod moment to draw you into the magic of United.

But once you're in, you soon come to realise that it's not just the club, the team and its triumphs that make being a Red so wondrous – it's being part of a supporting community that is like no other. Dedicated, diverse and encompassing the whole world, there really are few passions that compare with the love United continues to inspire in millions.

In 1910, when Old Trafford first opened, the club had been named 'Manchester United' for just eight years. Supporters might go to watch United one week and then City the next, while the Reds were contesting an away fixture. These were the days of the flat-cap fan, when it was still customary even to wear a suit and tie to the game.

Above: United fans rattle into London's Euston Station, 1937; The Reds are back in the capital for the 1968 European Cup final

Football was one of the few forms of mass entertainment on offer to the average person in those days, and a glance at the match programme from that era shows that maintaining the link between club and paying customer was paramount. The programme was often the only source for information about matches: kick-off times, ticket sales, season tickets and the rest.

If you fancied taking an exotic trip to watch United play away in Yorkshire, your away match travel information could be found in the programme: how to get your special offer train ticket, for example.

Back then, United was a local concern. But after the war, as Matt Busby's Babes became a national phenomenon and gates rose, that began to change.

Eye-catching banners became a more common sight in the '70s, such as these at our 1977 FA Cup final triumph against Liverpool

These days the club's vast all-seater stadium attracts Reds from all over the globe

Supporters started to follow the team away more regularly. Fans from further afield flocked to M16 to watch this new, young and exciting side that was the pride of Manchester. Colours and scarves became more keenly adopted, as supporters sought to more strongly identify themselves with United.

That tendency revealed a darker side in the 1970s, as football hooliganism took hold in Britain. Inside *UR* there were ever more desperate pleas for fans to behave themselves, particularly away from Old Trafford. Violence was a big problem, an embarrassment, for the club and football in general, but it was also a sign that football fan bases were diversifying. Crowds were no longer simply filled with local workers looking for something to do on a Saturday afternoon. Many different types of supporters were emerging, all attracted to different aspects of what being a United fan might mean.

But for every young Red who fancied a scrap, there were 10 who just loved to turn up and take part in the matchday rituals of singing and roaring the team on at Old Trafford.

As the 1980s and 1990s hoved into view, more families could be seen attending matches, particularly following the move to all-seater stadiums in the wake of the Hillsborough disaster and the subsequent Taylor Report. Tourists from abroad rushed in on once-in-a-lifetime trips, as the Premier League began to draw an increasingly global audience.

But while these fluctuating cultural shifts may have brought changes, they have not dampened the passion of support for United. If anything, they have only revealed how deep, rich and vast our fan base is; and how many different multitudes 'the Red Army' can contain.

Our New Headquarters.

The history of the Manchester United Football Club is an interesting one, and the opening of the new ground at Old Trafford is certainly one of the most important events in its career, it is a striking testimony of what the club management have done, and what they intend to do, not only for Manchester enthusiasts, but football generally. Those who have followed United since the days of the old Newton Heath Club know full well what Mr. Davies and his colleagues have accomplished since the day they took over the "ashes" of the old concern. At that time there was precious little to cheer them on in their efforts to build up a famous team in Manchester.

19 FEBRUARY 1910, v LIVERPOOL
United's programme for the inaugural match at Old Trafford was printed on a paper with a slight blue/green tint to it and included this welcome note praising the vision and generosity of owner John Henry Davies and the club directors.

Football's first superstar, Welshman Billy Meredith

CROWD ESTIMATE COMPETITION.

PRIZE: £2 Cash or Season Ticket

CONDITIONS.

Fill up coupon in ink, cut it out, and address as under:—

CROWD ESTIMATE (No. 2),
MANCHESTER UNITED F.C.,
OLD TRAFFORD,
MANCHESTER.

Coupons must be posted or delivered so as to reach the office of the club not later than 10 a.m. on the morning of the match.

The Competition Editor's decision on all matters relating to the Competition is final and legally binding, and acceptance of this rule is an express condition of entry. Any number of Coupons may be enclosed in one envelope, but each coupon must be signed.

.... CUT HERE ....

I estimate that the attendance at the match with **SOUTH SHIELDS** on September 29 will be:—

....

Name ....

Address ....

....

....

(2)

15 SEPTEMBER 1923, v BURY
There was the generous prize of a season ticket (or £2, the equivalent of £120 today) up for grabs during the 1923/24 season. All you had to do was have the closest guess to the attendance for the next home match – in this case, 9,750 v South Shields.

10 APRIL 1925, v STOCKPORT COUNTY
United's first superstar Billy Meredith had recently retired at the age of 49, having returned for a second spell at Manchester City. Such was the affection for him, though, that the United programme promoted his forthcoming testimonial match.

MEREDITH'S TESTIMONIAL.

Grand Football Match at Maine Road

WEDNESDAY, APRIL 29, 1925. *Kick-off, 6-30 p.m.*

GLASGOW RANGERS & CELTIC *v.* MEREDITH'S PICKED XI.

(COMBINED TEAMS).

APPEAL TO SPECTATORS.

I am now going to tread on what I know is very delicate ground, but in addressing the spectators as I propose doing they will, it is hoped, accept my remarks in the best possible spirit, and endeavour to act up to them.

No football club can, of course, exist without spectators. Their patronage is essential, but I do submit—and it can hardly be controverted—that no spectator, or group of spectators, can be allowed to become a nuisance to those around them.

Let me make it clear that I consider Old Trafford spectators in the main as good and as well behaved as any other in the country. But a football crowd is made up of all sorts and conditions of men and in these days, women also.

Personally, I welcome the interest women take in football. I don't think it is a game for women to play, but it can afford them a vast amount of pleasure and recreation to watch, and their presence should exercise a restraining influence on men, who are not merely the stronger sex physically, but also in their language.

You won't need to be a Sherlock Holmes to detect what I am getting at. I regret to say that last season complaints were lodged about the objectionable language heard in some parts of the ground. I have used the word objectionable; some of the complainants have described it as disgraceful.

The complaints refer not merely to language. The conduct of some of the spectators has been anything but that of gentlemen and sportsmen. We all know that there is a rush at half-time and at the close of the game for the retiring rooms and lavatories. When the Old Trafford ground was constructed ample and adequate provision was made for this demand, and I don't think any reasonable person can contend otherwise.

Yet men have been seen behaving in a way that can only be described as disgusting. Perhaps it is better to write plainly on this matter, because every effort is going to be made to stop it and the people who can assist most in this direction are those spectators who retain their sense of sportsmanship and gentlemanly behaviour and detest the lack of it in others.

A Grounds Committee is to be appointed to look after the comfort of spectators and to endeavour to suppress the nuisances referred to. Spectators who have any complaints can lodge them with members of this committee, and I think I can promise that drastic action will be taken against habitual offenders. We want all our spectators to enjoy their sport. Almost everything the directors can do to that end has been done.

We have one of the finest grounds in the country with accommodation second to none, and for the sake of their own reputation, as well as that of our club, we hope those spectators who know how to conduct themselves will assist us to eliminate the "pests."

2 SEPTEMBER 1925, v ASTON VILLA
The programme editor addresses concerns at the poor behaviour of supporters at recent home matches, requesting fans to cease the use of bad language and to use the toilet facilities provided.

EVIL OF BARRACKING.

The victory at Leicester once again calls attention to the fact that our team has given by far its best displays away from home, for the eight away games have yielded eight points, including three wins.

To beat Cardiff, Bury, and Leicester on their own grounds must strike everybody as performances of merit. There must be a reason for such good form away contrasted with some poor displays at home.

I ask our spectators to give very serious consideration to this matter, and to ask themselves whether they—or a section of them—are not to a very large extent responsible. Spectators may be within their rights to criticise, but when it oversteps reasonable bounds and develops into barracking a certain player or players, it becomes not only a nuisance, but a real menace.

Many a good player has been ruined because of the "dead set" made against him. A player who goes on the field with the "barracking nightmare" before him cannot do himself justice. Barracking is mean, despicable, and cowardly. Those responsible are not supporters; they are the worst enemies a club can have.

It is generally useless to appeal to the "barracker." He belongs to the type who will not listen to reason. I therefore appeal to those who have the best interests of the club and team at heart to do everything they can to suppress any around them who give vent to their feelings in this offensive manner.

We would much prefer the room to the support and company of the spectator who "barracks." Such men would be doing themselves and everybody else a kindness by staying away.

THE EDITOR.

20 NOVEMBER 1926, v EVERTON
Two months on and the editor again feels it necessary to request fans to alter their behaviour. 'The worst enemies a club could have,' he says, describing how singling out scapegoats within your own team is negatively impacting United's home form. Did his plea work? Possibly, Clarence Hilditch's Reds beat Everton 2-1.

Home sweet home. An aerial view of Old Trafford, taken in 1930

1 JANUARY 1927, v SHEFFIELD UNITED
Old Trafford's giant scoreboard kept the crowd updated on scorelines from around the country – as long as you had the programme showing which letters referred to which match. Scores would be phoned in and the numbers changed accordingly.

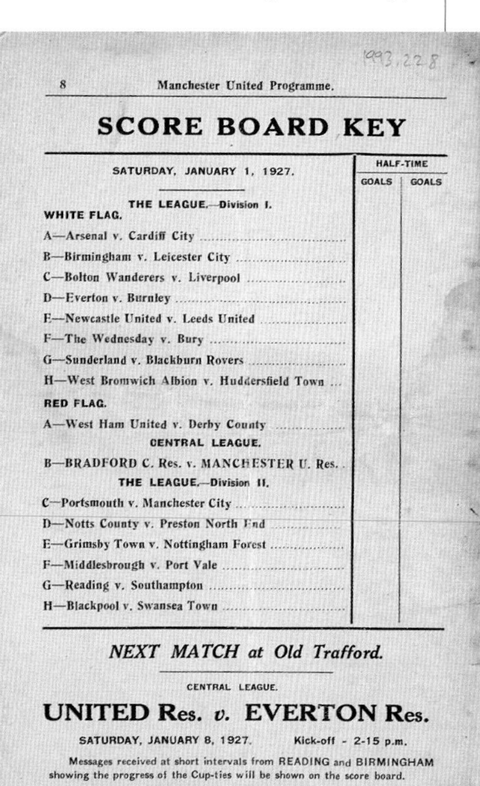

1993.22.8

8 Manchester United Programme.

SCORE BOARD KEY

SATURDAY, JANUARY 1, 1927.

	HALF-TIME GOALS	GOALS
THE LEAGUE.—Division I.		
WHITE FLAG.		
A—Arsenal v. Cardiff City		
B—Birmingham v. Leicester City		
C—Bolton Wanderers v. Liverpool		
D—Everton v. Burnley		
E—Newcastle United v. Leeds United		
F—The Wednesday v. Bury		
G—Sunderland v. Blackburn Rovers		
H—West Bromwich Albion v. Huddersfield Town		
RED FLAG.		
A—West Ham United v. Derby County		
CENTRAL LEAGUE.		
B—BRADFORD C. Res. v. MANCHESTER U. Res.		
THE LEAGUE.—Division II.		
C—Portsmouth v. Manchester City		
D—Notts County v. Preston North End		
E—Grimsby Town v. Nottingham Forest		
F—Middlesbrough v. Port Vale		
G—Reading v. Southampton		
H—Blackpool v. Swansea Town		

NEXT MATCH at Old Trafford.

CENTRAL LEAGUE.

UNITED Res. *v.* EVERTON Res.

SATURDAY, JANUARY 8, 1927. Kick-off - 2-15 p.m.

Messages received at short intervals from READING and BIRMINGHAM showing the progress of the Cup-ties will be shown on the score board.

THE BARRACKER.

Some time ago I commented on the "barracking" nuisance and urged supporters to aid in suppressing it. The following letter from "Supporter" (Stretford) embodies sound practical commonsense and deserves attention.

"Just a line to ask if anything can be done to take in hand the "barracker." We can always see in the Press, "United require new forwards." Have the supporters ever thought that our players are short of support? They often got plenty of abuse, which has a tendency to make them hesitant in front of goal, when, if encouraged, no doubt they would take some of the chances that are missed.

"If every supporter who has the welfare of the club at heart was to remonstrate with these barrackers they would be doing a kindness to the player and also the club.

"I think it would stop, as most of these barrackers are cowards at heart, and if tackled would soon be silenced, for when all is said and done we must admit we always have eleven triers whoever is selected to play for the team, and as it is the player's bread and butter we should be tolerant and not blame the player, for, poor devil, his lot is not a happy one, and his wages are restricted and his playing life with ordinary luck is only short.

"We should at the least encourage him to give of his best and blame not him, but those responsible for putting him there."

I hope those spectators guilty of barracking will take this letter to heart. Give our players more encouragement and less criticism and we shall get better results. THE EDITOR.

12 FEBRUARY 1927, v CARDIFF CITY

One United fan from Stretford wrote in giving his backing to the programme editor's call for supporters to stop barracking their own players, asking others in the crowd to shout down those damaging the confidence of Hilditch's team.

REGRETS.

I am asked by the United management to offer their regrets to those people who attended Old Trafford ground last Saturday under the impression that there was a Central League match. Originally the Reserves should have played Sheffield United Reserves on that date, but it will be recalled that, on January 28 we had a vacant date owing to the seniors being engaged with Bury in the English Cup at Gigg-lane. Therefore, the Sheffield United Reserves match was brought forward to that date, and the consequence was a blank day last Saturday. The misunderstanding seems to have arisen owing to the fact that a few posters which had been put out were not afterwards covered over as they should have been.

I am told that the Sunderland match, which should have been played at Old Trafford on March 24 has been provisionally fixed to take place at Old Trafford on the 24th inst.

7 APRIL 1928, v BURNLEY

The club is forced to apologise after confusion over the rearrangement of a Reserves game leads to fans turning up at Old Trafford for a match that had been played a week earlier. Oops!

ANNUAL DANCE.

The second annual dance of the Manchester United Ground Committee will be held on December 10 at the Old Trafford Technical Institute. Tickets are limited, and can be had at the offices of the United club or from any member of the Ground Committee. The charge, including refreshments, is 2s. 6d. Get your tickets now !

17 NOVEMBER 1928, v DERBY COUNTY

Tickets for a fundraising dance are advertised in the programme, with proceeds going towards the upkeep of the stadium.

25 AUGUST 1928, v LEICESTER CITY

United's crowds are struggling, with the attendance for this opening-day fixture with the Foxes only 20,129 – worryingly down on the previous season's average of 25,218. Hence this reminder to supporters that season ticket were still available 'for disposal'.

Season Tickets

There are still a few Season Tickets for disposal.

INQUIRE at the OFFICE after the MATCH.

Should Women Support Football?

The very question will arouse the scorn of the modern woman. Why, indeed, shouldn't she do anything? It was because she was told not to do something that she got Adam into trouble in the Garden of Eden. If she can fly to Australia and swim the Channel, and be a Cabinet Minister, or a doctor, or a lawyer, why shouldn't she share the joys of sport, side by side with her comrade man?

In any case we are glad that so many girls and women support the Manchester United. A woman wields the greatest influence, whether she be sweetheart, wife or mother, when she shares the life of those around. Sport keeps men good-humoured any way, and since men need the lesson that to be a sportsman is not to be too proud in victory, and not too downcast in defeat, but to love the game for the sake of the game—then perhaps women can profit by this ideal, too!

27 AUGUST 1932, v STOKE CITY
Despite the rather misleading headline, the programme editor expresses the club's pleasure that more females are attending matches at Old Trafford.

15 OCTOBER 1932, v BRADFORD PARK AVENUE
John Glover-Kind's music-hall hit, *I Do Like to Be Beside the Seaside*, is given a football makeover – although it remains to be seen whether it ever caught on!

THE Daily Herald
FOOTBALL SONG

"I do like to see a game of football."

1. When you wake and see the sun a-shining,
Even if the clouds are cold and grey,
You know ev'ry son of a gun is pining,
Pining to be out and shout hoo-ray!

Chorus:

Oh, I do like to see a game of football,
When Saturday afternoon comes round,
Hip-hooray! when they break away
The cheers roll round the ground,
Oh, I do like to see a game of football,
It's great, upon my soul,
The best team wins, but all the fun begins,
When "our side" scores a goal.

2. Buck up all you "forwards" and you "half backs,"
Hear the crowd as happy as can be,
When they've finished making their little wise cracks,
Hear them cheer the good old referee.

(Chorus):

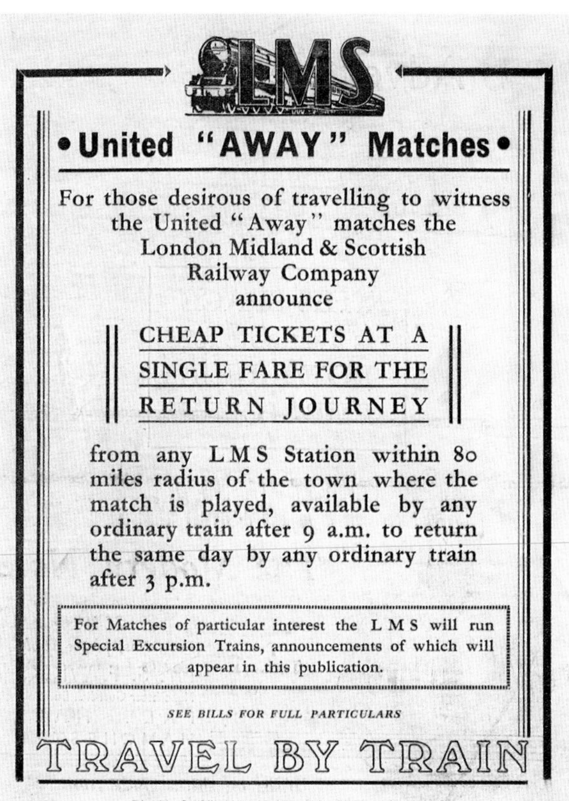

Train travel meant that fans were able to attend United matches away from Old Trafford. Special offers such as this one, which also appeared in the Bradford Park Avenue programme, made such day trips more affordable.

Manchester United
Football Supporters' Club
MEMBERS OF THE NATIONAL FEDERATION OF SUPPORTERS' CLUBS

Chairman: H. MINSHULL, Esq. Vice-Chairman: J. WARMISHAM, Esq.
Founder and Secretary: G. H. GREENHOUGH, Esq. Treasurer: R. COY, Esq.

All communications to the Secretary, 47 Birch Lane, Longsight

Telephone RUSholme 1273.

Open Letter to All Supporters

Dear Sir or Madam,

During the last fortnight, I am sure, as a supporter of the dear old club, you have had plenty of thrills to enthuse over. What a wonderful victory it was over Millwall—it is many years ago since we witnessed a 7-1 victory in a league match at Old Trafford. May it not be the last is my earnest wish.

Then I would like to express my personal and the directors' thanks to all who travelled to Port Vale last Saturday in such atrocious weather to cheer our lads on again, and in my opinion the referee was not kind to United, the lads **did** play extra time, and the sending off of Frame was in no way justified. I am not afraid to say the referee made a big mistake in this action. The same opinion was expressed by many of the Port Vale supporters that were round about me on the stands. I do hope that the referee will have the courage of his convictions and acknowledge his mistake.

As a Supporters' Club I am sure you will agree that it was our game right up to this incident, but never mind—let us to-day cheer our boys on to victory. I am sure the directors must feel they have now a loyal band of supporters when you think that it took six motor coaches and ten private cars to convey members of the Club to Port Vale, and considering the weather that it was. It is only by such organised trips that encouragement can be given to our team when playing away, and it is my intention to prove to the Bury people next Saturday that Manchester United Supporters' Club is a very live body. I have engaged six 'buses already for this trip, leaving the "Haunch of Venison" Hotel, Dale Street, at 1.30 p.m., tickets **1/6** each which must be obtained before Friday evening next, November 11. Therefore, if you do intend being one of the merry party, I would advise you to book a seat as soon as possible.

I should like to tender my heartfelt thanks to the different branches for the loyal manner in which they are helping the Supporters' Club, and it was a welcome surprise to me to be invited to the private residence of one of the Salford members to partake of supper. I found about 30 more loyal members of the branch present. The proceeds of this supper were given to the branch funds. The majority of members of the Supporters' Club have no idea what enjoyment they are missing by not attending the branches. It has been a great joy to me to hear the appreciation expressed by the supporters who stayed at home last Saturday with regard to the small portion of the covered stand already completed. A very long-felt want will soon be completely provided.

I appeal once again to all you supporters to get your friends to purchase the programmes which members of the Supporters' Club sell on the ground.

I am,
Yours faithfully,
G. H. GREENHOUGH.

SUPPORTERS—ATTENTION !

TO-NIGHT.—A Concert for members and friends only will be held in the "Haunch of Venison" Hotel, Dale Street, at 7.30 p.m.

TO-MORROW, SUNDAY.—A Members' Whist Drive at 7.30 p.m. in the "Haunch of Venison" Hotel, Dale Street. Special prizes. Tickets **6d.** each.

MONDAY, NOV. 7.—A Select Dance will be held in the Old Trafford Technical Institute from 7.30 p.m. to 11.30 p.m., tickets **1/6** each, including refreshments. Come and spend a merry night with the players !

FORTHCOMING EVENTS—

TUESDAY, NOV. 8.—Mr. Greenhough will speak to the Harpurhey and District Branch members in the Derby Inn, Barnes Green, Blackley, at 8 p.m.

WEDNESDAY, NOV. 9.—Executive Council Meeting, where complaints and suggestions are attended to—so if you have any suggestion to make, please let us have it in writing to be discussed at this meeting. No visitors allowed on this occasion.

SPECIAL NOTICE.—Members of the Supporters' Club, ladies or gentlemen, desirous of looking round the ground and training quarters are invited to attend at the Supporters' Club Refreshment Room at 11.30 a.m. to-morrow morning, Sunday, November 6th, 1932.

Page 13

5 NOVEMBER 1932, v NOTTS COUNTY
The supporters' club were given a page in the United programme for the 1932/33 season, with their founder and secretary clearly proud of the club's following: a 'loyal band of supporters' in 10 coaches and six cars making the trip to the Reds' recent away game at Port Vale.

A Tip to Motorists

Going to the Fulham game, the Editor was reminded of the days when he was a lad at Epsom on Derby Day. It was a sweet sight to see such a traffic jam. And all on their way to United. We want to tell motorists that Manchester United is the ideal Club for them to support. We are surrounded by first-class garages and car parks (and you can buy a Ford next door), but we just want to say a word for ourselves. We have a fine car park of our own, where for the nimble shilling, you can leave your car, at the door as it were and go in and see United accelerating along the road to victory.

3 DECEMBER 1932, v BRADFORD CITY
There were over a million cars on UK roads by 1930, and ample provision was provided at Old Trafford for those choosing to drive to matches.

Lancashire
County Cricket Club

Park your Car
at the County Cricket Ground Motor Park
Cars 1/-
Motor Cycles and Cycles 6d.

Parking Season Tickets
are now available for Manchester United First Eleven Matches :
Cars 10/6
Motor Cycles and Cycles 5/-

To be OBTAINED AT THE COUNTY CRICKET GROUND, OLD TRAFFORD

24 DECEMBER 1932, RESERVES v BIRMINGHAM CITY
There was also parking available at the other Old Trafford, with this advert showing the options available to fans when attending games – be it in a car, motorbike or bicycle. Many supporters still use the cricket ground for matchday parking.

There were plenty of parking options around Old Trafford, including at the cricket ground - pictured here in 1934

"FLOOD-HEATING"

Our Directors forget nothing—now they are experimenting with " Flood heating " of the Stands, so that the cockles of our heart shall be warmed. The team, of course, are taking their own special measures against " cold feet." A great authority on football says, that nothing warms up a crowd of supporters quite so much as seeing a few goals scored. Inspiration as well as perspiration is a fine thing. Still we thank the Directors for the warm glow of friendship which they always provide.

The same Reserves programme takes a witty approach to revealing that the board of directors are investigating the potential installation of heaters in the Grand Stand. However, after a short trial the club decided the system was not yet advanced enough to justify the expense.

Manchester United Football Supporters' Club

MEMBERS OF THE NATIONAL FEDERATION OF SUPPORTERS' CLUBS

Chairman: H. MINSHULL, Esq. Vice-Chairman: J. WARMISHAM, Esq.
Founder and Secretary: G. H. GREENHOUGH, Esq. Treasurer: R. COY, Esq.

All communications to the Secretary, 47 Birch Lane, Longsight

Telephone RUSholme 1273.

Dear Sir or Madam,

I have been requested by the Editor to write a cheery Christmas article in this programme and the brightest thing my pen can do at this time is to thank all loyal supporters for standing by our Board of Directors, Manager, Secretary and Players in the way they have done since Mr. Gibson took over the Club.

No doubt you recollect twelve months ago it was touch and go whether we had a team or not in 1932—and who is there amongst us who could forsee that by standing loyally by the true sportsman which Mr. Gibson has proved himself to be, we are now a power in the league to be reckoned with ?

3,000 MEMBERS.

Also take the Supporters' Club—who is there at Old Trafford who would believe that our membership would, in the first twelve months of its re-organisation, reach the wonderful figure of nearly 3,000 ? If the powers that be at Old Trafford will pause and think of the work that has been done on the ground at Old Trafford by members of the Supporters' Club, and will refresh their memories of the support that has been given to our Team when they have played away from home, they will be bound to agree that far from our Supporters' Club being a hindrance, it has been a blessing. This, ladies and gentlemen, is the object of the Club, that a body of truly loyal supporters of Manchester United might be banded together in one organisation, always to be ready and willing when called upon by the powers that be—to help and not to hinder !

HEADQUARTERS.

I have been asked by a great many well-wishers of the Supporters' Club, if it is not possible to remove the Club's headquarters out of licensed premises. As you all know that there are many things in any organisation that require alteration as time goes on, for your information, I may say that I am doing my best to obtain suitable accomodation to form a **SOCIAL CLUB** which every supporter of our team will be proud to visit.

We were all pleased to see that the innovation of having a branch meeting on Sunday evening in the Sherwood Hotel, Temple Street, C-on-M, turned out a great success. These meetings will continue every Sunday evening at 7.30 p.m.

BRAVO SALFORD !

I cannot close without mentioning the wonderful work that has been carried on by the different branches. The City of Salford Branch, which meets every Monday in the Clowes Hotel, Trafford Road, Salford at 7.30 p.m., has been a most wonderful branch and under the guidance of Mr. Gatley, Mr. Hill, Mr. Wall, Mrs. Wall and Mrs. Houghton, this branch has more than doubled its membership. You will never believe what you are missing until you drop in to see this branch at work.

I have no space to write more now, but I shall tell you of the work of other branches in subsequent issues.

Wishing you all the compliments of the season,

I am,

Yours faithfully,

G. H. GREENHOUGH.

EVENTS TO THE END OF THE YEAR.

TUESDAY.—The following meetings will be held at 7.30 p.m. City of Salford Branch Meeting in the Clowes Hotel, Trafford Road, Salford.

also

Hulme and District Meeting in the Sherwood Hotel, Temple Street, Rusholme Road, C.-on-M.

also

City of Manchester Branch Meeting in the " Haunch of Venison " Hotel, 24 Dale Street, Manchester.

WEDNESDAY.—A special extraordinary executive Council Meeting to be held on Wednesday at **7.30 p.m. prompt** in the " Haunch of Venison " Hotel, 24 Dale Street, Manchester.

THURSDAY.—Moss Side Branch Meeting at 7.30 p.m. in the Marlborough Hotel, Upper Moss Lane, Moss Side.

SATURDAY.—December 31st, 1932, at 7.30 p.m. a great jovial evening will be held in the " Haunch of Venison " Hotel, 24 Dale Street, Manchester, to " send out " the old year. Come and spend a merry evening.

Page 15

Elsewhere in this Christmas Eve 1932 issue, there's much gratitude towards club owner James W Gibson in a festive update from the supporters' club, which now boasts 3,000 members. And it seems there was quite a social scene for fans to enjoy, such as the New Year's Eve party.

The Directors Appeal to Supporters

Will You Play Your Part ?

MANCHESTER United is now assured of a great future in the football world of the North; and that is entirely due to the valiant efforts and public spirit of the Chairman and his fellow-directors. They undertook an uphill task, and have not flinched from shouldering a heavy burden of financial responsibility.

All the way through they have been cheered by the loyalty of supporters like yourself. A conviction has deepened that many supporters would welcome a suggestion as to the most practical method of helping the Club. The Directors have thought of such a method. It is simply this: book your Season Tickets for 1933–1934 *immediately*, and thus give the Club a pledge of continued loyalty which would be of material assistance during the close season.

In order to facilitate this plan the Directors have agreed to accept payments in instalments to be made in *May, June* and *July*. Details of this plan are given below.

The Chairman would be immensely heartened by your prompt response. He and his colleagues have cheerfully undertaken heavy responsibilities—here is an opportunity which we believe you will welcome, of playing your part in the progress of the Club.

May we have an answer without delay ?

In order to help the Club during the close season and to make it easier for our supporters to obtain their Season Tickets for next season, the Directors have decided to accept payment in instalments as follows :—

		Amount payable end of	*May*	*June*	*July*, 1933
Reserved Chairs,	Gent's ..	at £3 : 3 : 0 ..	£1 : 1 : 0	£1 : 1 : 0	£1 : 1 : 0
,, ,,	Ladies' ...	at £2 : 2 : 0 ..	10 : 6	10 : 6	£1 : 1 : 0
Stand " D "	Gent's ...	at £2 : 2 : 0 ..	10 : 6	10 : 6	£1 : 1 : 0
,,	Ladies' ..	at £1 : 1 : 0 ..	5 : 0	5 : 0	11 : 0
Ground Side	Gent's ..	at £1 : 0 : 0 ..	5 : 0	5 : 0	10 : 0
,,	Ladies' & Boys' at	10 : 0 ..	2 : 6	2 : 6	5 : 0

Fill in this slip NOW and post to the Secretary, or hand to a Steward, Gateman or any official.

N.B.—*If you do not wish to cut the page please copy the form on your notepaper.*

CUT ALONG THIS LINE

To the Secretary,
Manchester United F.C.,
Old Trafford, Manchester.

SEASON 1933-34

No. .... *Class* ....
FOR OFFICIAL USE ONLY.

Please book me a Season Ticket for (state Stand or Ground) ....

at a cost of £ .... *, payable in three instalments, as above.*

Signed ....
(Mr., Mrs. or Miss).

Address ....

Date ....

Page 5

8 APRIL 1933, v CHESTERFIELD

With the north of England still suffering the effects of the Great Depression of the early 1930s, the club announces new payment plans for season tickets. The scheme means tickets can be paid for in three monthly instalments across the close season.

Make UNITED
Famous for Big Gates!

NEXT GAMES
AT OLD TRAFFORD

Wednesday, September 12th

Return Game with BOLTON WANDERERS
THIS SHOULD BE A GREAT FIGHT!

Central League

SECOND TEAM versus DERBY COUNTY

EVERY CHEER HELPS!

8 SEPTEMBER 1934, v BARNSLEY
There's a call to arms early in the 1934/35 season, with Second Division football evidently not appealing to some United fans. Despite the pleas, the Bolton game still only attracts a crowd of 24,760.

12 SEPTEMBER 1934, v BOLTON WANDERERS
The supporters' club goes on a recruitment drive in the match programme.

MEN

STAND TO YOUR COLOURS

Make yourself a Manchester United Man and join the . . . . .

MANCHESTER UNITED **NEW** (Official) SUPPORTERS' CLUB

Enjoy the warm friendship of Sportsmen and do your bit to

HELP THE CLUB ALONG!

HOW TO JOIN

Call at the "New Supporters' Refreshment Bar" on the Popular Side, or (from 7.30 p.m. on Mondays) at Headquarters, The Clowes Hotel, Salford. Or send an application to the Head Office at 176 Hulton Street, Salford, 5

MEMBERSHIP FEE

GENTLEMEN **1/-** LADIES **6d.**

Chairman H. GATLEY *Secretary* B. WALL

THE ONLY **RECOGNISED** SUPPORTERS' CLUB

18 SEPTEMBER 1935, v HULL CITY
The Reds might be in the second tier but the club continues to think big, with owner Gibson paying for a platform to be built at the stadium.

IMPORTANT NEWS!!

New Football Ground Station adjacent to the Manchester United F.C.

SUPPORTERS and visitors to the Manchester United Football Club matches at Old Trafford will in future be able to visit their favourite team expeditiously and in comfort. The Cheshire Lines Committee is providing a new station which will be named the "United Football Ground Station," exactly opposite to the entrances to the Ground, to and from which there will be a frequent service of trains from Manchester (Central) Station for 1st Team League matches and other special occasions. The journey will occupy approximately five minutes and the return fare from Manchester (C.) will be 4d. Single tickets will not be issued from Manchester (C.) to the new station, but people visiting the ground by other means on the outward journey will be able to return by the special trains on payment of 2d. at the Turnstiles.

The drive to increase attendances goes on and on this page of the Hull programme the call is for a bumper crowd for our next home game: a first meeting with Spurs since the 1932/33 season.

AN APPEAL TO OUR SUPPORTERS

FOOTBALL GROUND STATION

DO'S and DONT'S

Travel from Manchester Central Station by the early trains so as to ensure comfort to all. Don't delay. First come—first served.

Don't crush—it doesn't help. Play the game—don't foul.

Don't alight before the train stops—there are no football matches "up above."

When returning don't concentrate at one turnstile—there are five others.

Again don't crush—it's easier, besides you won't get your corns trodden on.

Remember—tickets LEFT, pay RIGHT.

It's your station—use it—don't abuse it.

At present 4,000 return by rail—don't all expect to get on the same train.

Let's be UNITED and make OUR station a success, en route to the First Division.

For those looking to use the new train service to and from the ground, details of the etiquette for travel are outlined for supporters in the Hull City issue – and all with a bit of humour thrown in.

WHAT ABOUT SATURDAY?

It's a long time since we met the 'Spurs—but as someone said to us only this morning

"Does absence make the 'eart grow fonder?
Not on your blinkin' life!"

That's the spirit! We've beaten London at Old Trafford once this season, and lifted a point in the enemy's country.

Now let's show them again!

TRY TO MAKE IT A 50,000 GATE!

MANCHESTER UNITED
versus
TOTTENHAM HOTSPUR
SATURDAY, SEPTEMBER 21st

A VERY OLD SUPPORTER'S THANKS.

The following letter addressed to the Supporters' Club gave great pleasure. :—

11 Melford Avenue,
Stretford,
April 20, 1936.

I along with other pensioners and others who could not stand through physical inability, have been able to attend and enjoy matches, wish to express the thanks of those on the Stand for these privileges gained for us by the kindness of the Supporters' Club.

Many of the elderly men have followed the fortunes of the club ever since the days of the Newton Heath L.Y.R. Club. Myself since 1882.

And so I thank you on behalf of the above.

Yours faithfully,
C. DRYLAND.

25 APRIL 1936, v BURY
The supporters' club makes a section of the Grand Stand available to elderly and physically impaired fans, and receive this letter of thanks from a long-serving Red.

ON SATURDAY

MANCHESTER UNITED

VERSUS

MANCHESTER CITY

MAKE IT THE GREATEST GATE IN OUR HISTORY

9 SEPTEMBER 1936, v HUDDERSFIELD TOWN
Gates are up after United's return to the top flight and the club is keen to fill Old Trafford for this first Manchester derby in five years. A bumper crowd of 68,796 watch the Reds beat the Blues 3-2.

31 AUGUST 1946, v GRIMSBY TOWN
League football resumes after the war and with Old Trafford out of use, the club explains why fans must pay for each match individually at Maine Road.

WHY SEASON TICKETS CANNOT BE ISSUED

One of the many inconveniences incidental to the continued closing of the ground at Old Trafford is that it is impossible to issue season tickets unless it has full control of its own ground and all the games. Manchester City has done a lot for us at Maine Road, but this is one of the things that must wait until we fly the flag once more over the old ground.

4 OCTOBER 1947, v STOKE CITY
With the programme now rebranded as *United Review*, there's a raft of new features for readers to enjoy – like this one calling on fans to send in their tales from the terraces.

CAN YOU BEAT IT ? No. 1.

"I was on the Popular Side last season when United played the Wolves at Maine Road. Nearby was a little man with a parcel under his arm. Ten minutes before the kick-off he opened this parcel and took out a pair of home-made wooden shoes with soles at least nine inches thick. He slipped these on his boots and saw the match with ease !"

Half-a-guinea goes to James Royle, of 59 Aston Avenue, Fallowfield, Manchester 14. Now supporters, can you beat this story ? Make it short and remember it MUST be about a United game. Ten shillings and six-pence for all stories published. Address your contribution to The Editor United Review, c/o Sidney F. Wicks Ltd., 14 Ridgefield, Manchester 2.

THE UNITED v. CITY "DERBY"
February 7th, 1948

Walter Crickmer tells us that plans are well under way for the great all-ticket match next February. There are 78,000 tickets available—68,000 for the popular side! This means an enormous amount of extra work for the staff and we would appreciate supporters sending early application to help spread the pressure.

To assist those unable to reach the ground on working days we now accept block ticket application from Secretaries of Welfare and Social organisations connected with large industries. Applications for any reasonable number of popular-side tickets will be considered. So you see, supporters, it's up to you to fix up with your Works Club Secretary to get your name on his list to enable him to apply quickly. Secretaries should remember that ticket requests should be covered by a remittance and Postal applications require a stamped addressed envelope for the return of the tickets.

We remind supporters that applications must be made to the Old Trafford ground between 9 a.m. and 5.30 p.m. Tickets are also on sale during the United Central League home matches.

Prices remain the same: Juniors 9d., Popular Side 1/3. The Stand tickets at 5/-, 4/- and 2/6 are in the course of printing and will be available shortly.

In the event of the match being postponed through Cup-ties or other circumstances beyond control the tickets will be valid for the re-arranged date.

6 DECEMBER 1947, v BLACKPOOL
A crowd of 71,364 had attended the first Maine Road meeting of United and City in 1946/47, and with the return match designated our 'home' fixture, ticket sales began early. A good job, too – a crowd of 71,690 watched the game.

20 MARCH 1948, v WOLVERHAMPTON WANDERERS
Cup final fever hits Old Trafford as the Reds reach Wembley for the first time, and with a month to go until the big game with Blackpool, *United Review* gives an update on the plans for applying for tickets.

TICKETS FOR WEMBLEY!

Tickets for the Cup Final will be sent to successful applicants at the earliest possible moment and an announcement will be made in the Press when the last ticket has been posted. The unlucky ones will then have their remittances returned. Season ticket holders will shortly be advised through the Press when to apply for their tickets and as usual, personal application will be necessary. Don't forget to bring your book of vouchers for franking.

20 OCTOBER 1951, v SUNDERLAND
The club react to increased interest from fans wanting to attend away matches and print this message requesting that supporters stop sending in enquiries for tickets.

TICKETS FOR AWAY MATCHES

Much as we would like to accommodate our supporters with tickets for away matches we regret it is not possible to do so as we do not get a quota. We hope this notice will save our supporters a lot of trouble and expense in applying, and ourselves a lot of work in returning applications!

UNITED REVIEW TO COST 4d.

For a long time the cost of paper and wages has gone higher and higher and on no occasion has the increase been passed on to the public. Although the "United Review" is not a profit-making organisation it stands to reason that no standards could be maintained were there to be a loss on production, and so, after very careful thought and with great reluctance we announce that as from November 3rd, when we play Huddersfield Town, the cost of the "United Review" will be 4d. per copy.

Should at any time the cost of materials decrease supporters are assured that the Club will pass on any economy to the readers of our Programme.

Worth every penny! In the same issue, *United Review* reveals plans to increase the price of the programme, revealing that the cost of overheads had left them no other choice.

SEASON TICKETS 1952-3

If you wish to renew your Season Ticket please tear out Voucher No. 15 from your current book. Forward it with your application (stating row and seat number) and cheque or P.O. for £6 10s. You have until 31st June, 1952, to reclaim your seat — but please don't delay!

The uplift in cost is regretted but is necessary through the increase in Entertainment Tax Duty.

All applications to The Secretary, Manchester United F.C. Ltd., Old Trafford, Manchester 16.

26 APRIL 1952, v ARSENAL
It's season ticket renewal time and fans are urged to send in their applications promptly, with an apology for the slight increase in cost due to a rise in Entertainment Tax Duty.

THIS IS THE OFFICIAL PROGRAMME OF

MANCHESTER UNITED

FOOTBALL CLUB LIMITED

OLD TRAFFORD - MANCHESTER

Chairman: H. P. HARDMAN, Esq.

Directors: Dr. W. MACLEAN, G. E. WHITTAKER, Esq., J. ALAN GIBSON, Esq., W. H. PETHERBRIDGE, Esq.

Manager: MATT BUSBY Secretary: W. R. CRICKMER

Editor and Advertisement Manager: DAVID W. WICKS

Please address all matters concerning the programme to the "United Review": Sidney F. Wicks Ltd. · 21 Newton Street, Manchester 1 · CENtral 9047/8

VOLUME XVII, No. 21 21st APRIL, 1956

Photo by courtesy of the "Provincial Press Agency"

The Chairman, Directors, Executives, Players and staff wish to acknowledge with grateful thanks your kind messages of congratulation on the team's success in winning the League Championship.

The host of communications is significant that we are in the thoughts of our countless friends, and has created added warmth to the happy atmosphere which abounds the Club in it's hour of triumph.

PAGE TWO

The Babes are the champions of England for 1955/56 and proudly show off the First Division trophy

21 APRIL 1956, v PORTSMOUTH

The club thanks supporters who sent in letters or telegrams of congratulations to Old Trafford following Busby's thrilling young side's title triumph.

1 SEPTEMBER 1956, v PORTSMOUTH

Tokens were issued in each home programme, and affixed to this token sheet, in order that the most loyal fans were given ticket priority for cup finals and other big cup ties.

MANCHESTER UNITED FOOTBALL CLUB LTD.

Name ....

Address ....

.... *(Please write in Block Capitals)*

LEAGUE MATCH (1st Division)		1	TOKEN SHEET SEASON 1956–1957	
2	3	4	5	6
7	8	9	10	11
12	13	14	15	16
17	18	19	20	21

IMPORTANT

With this League Match Token Sheet and the Central League Token Sheet we hope to offer our supporters the fairest possible chance of obtaining admission to those special matches where demands for tickets invariably exceed the supply. The procedure is simple and the following notes are printed for your guidance.

1 Cut out and keep this Token Sheet together with the Central League Match Token Sheet published on August 29th.

2 Cut out and paste in the numbered square the Ball Token printed in this programme and subsequent League programmes. Do the same with the red Central League Tokens printed in the Central League Programmes, but be sure they are pasted on the Central League Token Sheet. It is important that the number on the Token corresponds with the number on the Token Sheet.

3 If you watch both first and reserve team home games you should, in due course, have two sheets each carrying the tokens representing the games you have actually attended.

4 If you follow the first team's away fixtures please keep the front pages of the programmes as evidence of your support. The appropriate numbered space should be cancelled on the Central League Token Sheet with an X.

5 Another Central League Token Sheet will be printed in the "United Review" on 18th September.

PAGE ELEVEN

ADVANCE BOOKING FOR HOME MATCHES

In view of the great demand in previous seasons it has been decided to make the whole of the seating accommodation bookable in advance.

Reserved seats can be obtained for Football League matches price 7/6 and 6/- each. These are on sale at the Club offices 12 days before the match, postal applications should include correct remittance and stamped addressed envelope.

Any tickets still unsold on the day of the match will be on sale at the Ticket Sales Office alongside the railway.

9 SEPTEMBER 1959, v LEEDS UNITED

Such was the demand to see the Reds play by the end of the decade, all seats were put on sale in advance of matchday, although standing sections for most fixtures remained pay at the gate.

A Special Notice for Juniors

In view of the increasing number of juniors who are now attending our matches more entrances have been made available for their use.

In addition to Nos. 21 to 24 inclusive, turnstiles 24A and 25 at the Stretford End of the ground can now be used.

We would especially recommend these for juniors who are accompanied by adults as they will be able to enter the ground by adjoining turnstiles.

Old Trafford's new turnstiles, specifically for youngsters, are promoted in the September 1959 Leeds issue, as football continues to attract new converts.

IMPORTANT NOTICE

It has come to our notice that at a recent match a small boy suffered a serious eye injury through another boy firing an air pistol or rifle into the crowd. This youngster was detained in hospital for more than a week, and was very lucky not to lose the sight of one of his eyes.

The Directors are most concerned that this should happen and wish to call upon the assistance of all older spectators to prevent anything of this nature being repeated. It would be appreciated if you would keep your eye on the boys around you and check them if they are misbehaving. If you have any difficulty please do not hesitate to call a steward or the nearest policeman.

5 MARCH 1960, v WOLVERHAMPTON WANDERERS

The club calls for help in controlling unruly behaviour from young fans.

NEW...THE UNITED RECORD REQUEST PROGRAMME!

Manchester United have decided to run a record request programme this season instead of having music played by the Beswick Prize Band.

Supporters are invited to take part by requesting a record to be played for a friend or relative or member of the staff and are asked to include a short message stating the reason for their request.

United will have their own special Disc Jockey who will be ex-player Harry McShane. Requests (post-cards only), should be addressed to Mr. H. McShane, c/o Old Trafford Ground, 14 days in advance and stating the match at which it should be played.

Those who have been supporting the Club for a few years will remember Harry as our outside-left from 1950 to 1954. He joined the club from Bolton Wanderers in exchange for Johnny Ball. To the younger generations Harry's son is Ian McShane – film and T.V. actor who has already, at the age of 22, starred in a number of films and T.V. plays.

The club's aim is to make this a personal programme for the fans and between records Harry will give items of information about the club and players and also pass on the messages requested.

Anyone wishing to have a record played should write without delay in order to have their messages included in the opening programmes. It will not be possible for Harry to enter into any correspondence but every endeavour will be made to meet all requests.

MUSIC

Manchester's leading record specialists, Hime & Addison, 37 John Dalton Street, supply all the records played at Old Trafford.

22 AUGUST 1964, v WEST BROMWICH ALBION

More changes inside Old Trafford – with the brass band replaced by music played over the public address system. Well, it was the swinging sixties!

15 DECEMBER 1965, v EVERTON

World Cup Willie featured often in *United Review* in the months leading up to the 1966 tournament, along with ticket details for the matches to be played at Old Trafford.

WORLD CUP CHAMPIONSHIPS

The list of countries qualifying for the Finals is now almost complete and the following will play in England next July.

England, the host nation, and Brazil, the holders, lead the 15. The full list is:

From Europe: England, West Germany, France, Portugal, Switzerland, Hungary, Russia, Spain, Italy.

From South America: Uruguay, Brazil, Chile, Argentina.

From North America: Mexico.

From Asia: North Korea.

One group has yet to be decided. Belgium and Bulgaria are due to meet in a play-off to decide the winners of Group 1.

Sale of Tickets

Three-match season tickets are available for the games at Old Trafford. Applications must be made on the OFFICIAL FORM which can be obtained from the Club Offices after today's match or by post enclosing s.a.e.

Prices are as follows:

Grade 1 Seating	Grade 2 Seating	Grade 3 Standing	Grade 4 Standing
£6 6 0	**£3 0 0**	**£1 17 6**	**£1 2 6**

Applications for seven- and ten-match season tickets should be made on the OFFICIAL FORM but this should be sent with remittance DIRECT to the World Cup Organisation, White City Stadium, London, W.12.

CALLING ALL MANCHESTER UNITED SUPPORTERS!

- There is a thriving Supporters' Club in London with nearly 1,000 Members but plenty of room for new Members!
- If you would like to become a Member and gain new friends, write to the Secretary for full details.
- The Secretary is Mr. J. Brooke of 63 Hurst Avenue, London E.4.
- As a Club Member you will be entitled to travel on coach trips organised by the Club and receive the monthly newsletter.
- Write to Mr. Brooke right away!

19 MARCH 1966, v ARSENAL
United's appeal had long stretched beyond the North West of England, as demonstrated by this advert for the London supporters' club, which had 1,000 members and rising.

TICKETS FOR AWAY MATCHES

For guidance and assistance we publish details for obtaining tickets for United's next four away matches.

Supporters are advised to enclose the appropriate remittance and a self-addressed stamped envelope when making applications for tickets.

Stoke City—Victoria Ground, Stoke-on-Trent.
Price of Tickets : 8/-, 10/-, 12/6
Apply : 2 weeks in advance.

Tottenham Hotspur—High Road, London, N.7.
Price of Tickets : 10/-
Apply : 3 weeks in advance.

Nottingham Forest—City Ground, Nottingham.
Price of Tickets : 8/-, 9/-, 10/-
Apply : 2 weeks in advance.

Blackpool—Bloomfield Road, Blackpool.
Price of Tickets : 7/6, 8/-, 10/-
Apply : 4 weeks in advance.

3 SEPTEMBER 1966, v NEWCASTLE UNITED
The Reds' away following was the biggest in the country in the late 1960s and into the 1970s, with allocations now set aside for visiting fans in order to avoid crowd disorder between rival sets of fans.

24 SEPTEMBER 1966, v BURNLEY
Sunday Mirror journalist Peter Slingsby does not mince his words when tackling the subject of what he calls 'the scourge of soccer'. Matt Busby had called for supporters to behave themselves at matches, but hooliganism was an increasing phenomenon at games.

CLUB COMMENTS

BY PETER SLINGSBY
THE SUNDAY MIRROR

Fanatics! That, in a word, describes the current scourge of soccer, an evil epedemic which in the last few days caused the most even tempered manager in the game to comment forcefully and in somewhat uncharacteristic terms:

"WE MUST RID THE GAME OF HOOLIGANS WHO MASQUERADE AS SOCCER SUPPORTERS".

The speaker was Matt Busby and the manager who has become a legend in his own lifetime undoubtedly was angry about the antics of a small minority of fans whose outrageous conduct has regularly hit the headlines, and damaged the reputations of the clubs they purport to support.

Mr. Busby feels that the time has come for a much sterner approach to the problem, a problem that clubs have done the best they can to remedy through programme appeals and even by banning those guilty of unruly behaviour from attending matches.

But still hooliganism continues. It seems to be linked with success . . . and the more successful the club, the greater the number of unsavoury incidents by an unruly handful who – worst of all – interfere with the comfort and enjoyment of the true supporter.

It is this point which upsets the clubs. Thousands and thousands of pounds have and are being spent on improving ground amenities in an effort to attract wives, mothers, sweethearts and the youngsters who are tomorrow's fans.

But because of the thugs – and I do not think that is too harsh a description – soccer's present-day image is at a low ebb.

Certainly, I would not take a woman relative or a child on to the terraces at a football match. In some ways, I would not even think of providing them with a stand seat when certain teams are the visitors because of the fear that they might be insulted – or worse!

The clubs themselves are well aware of the fears which yours truly, as a football fan, has expressed here. Now there is another way of looking at the problem – in terms of hard cash.

The game needs more finance. But these are hard days for the country as a whole and the economic situation is such that smaller rather than larger pay packets are the order of the day.

Clubs in the Midlands already are feeling the pinch with short-time working and redundancy in the motor car industry. This, allied to the obscene chanting, the stupid song paradies and the like, will continue to hit the box office hard unless the problem is attacked by all of us who have any affection for this great game of ours.

The courts have an effective answer. But the true supporter can also play his part – by drawing the attention of the police or club officials to those who, so it seems, are determined to "enjoy" themselves by embarrasing the clubs they support and their fellow fans.

In this way, we can all hit back at those who, as Mr. Busby rightly said, merely masquerade as supporters and whose behaviour on and off the terraces is becoming a disgrace and a match-by-match scourge which soccer cannot afford to tolerate.

Although Manchester United has always welcomed free comment by contributors to the United Review we must point out however that their views are not necessarily those of the Club Management.

PAGE NINE

MESSAGE FROM J. BATTERSBY,
(Secretary, Chelsea F. C.)

We would remind spectators NOT to bring fireworks to Stamford Bridge next Saturday, 5th November. These can be particularly dangerous in the crowd and we intend to ask the police authorities to take stringent action against anyone using fire-works inside the ground.

Please leave the players to provide the fireworks (football-wise) on the field!

29 OCTOBER 1966, v ARSENAL
Ahead of United's Bonfire Night trip to Stamford Bridge, the programme includes a message aimed at the Reds' boisterous travelling support.

THE OFFICIAL PROGRAMME OF
Manchester UNITED
FOOTBALL CLUB LTD

Chairman: LOUIS C. EDWARDS
Vice Chairman: J. ALAN GIBSON
Directors: W. A. YOUNG, D. D. HAROUN, J.P. C. M. EDWARDS SIR MATT BUSBY, C.B.E.
Manager: TOMMY DOCHERTY
Secretary: LESLIE OLIVE
Programme Editor: DAVID W. WICKS

OLD TRAFFORD · MANCHESTER M16 0RA. VOL. XXXIV No 21 · 17 MAR 1973
Advertisement enquiries should be addressed to the Editor, Sidney F. Wicks Ltd., 21 Newton Street, Manchester M1 1HJ.

a message to
MANCHESTER UNITED
supporters . . .

V.A.T. AND PRICES OF ADMISSION

"In the last programme I referred to the excellent support we have received this season and how much this is appreciated by everyone at Old Trafford. I am pleased to tell you that the Board and I have decided to show our appreciation in a practical way by absorbing the cost of Value Added Tax on admission prices for the five home games after the 1st April until the end of the season.

"Although we have a very large adverse bank balance after our transfer activity this season we feel we must do this to show that we are not just using words when we say how grateful we are for the magnificent support you have given us. We still have a hard struggle ahead of us but we are confident that given a reasonable run of the ball we shall avoid relegation and have the opportunity of continuing our progress next season. We wish you all good health and good sport."

from
LOUIS C. EDWARDS
chairman

Honours

European Cup Winners 1968

European Cup Semi-Finalists 1957 1958 1966 1969

First Division League Champions 1908 1911 1952 1956 1957 1965 1967
Runners-up 1947 1948 1949 1951 1959 1964 1968

Second Division League Champions 1936 Runners-up 1897 1906 1925 1938

F.A. Cup Winners 1909 1948 1963
Finalists: 1957 1958
Semi-Finalists: 1926 1949 1962 1964 1965 1966 1970

F.A. Charity Shield Winners 1908 1911 1952 1957 1956
Joint Winners 1965 1967
Finalists 1948 1963

F.A. Youth Cup Winners 1953 1954 1955 1956 1957 1964

Inter Cities Fairs Cup Semi-Finalists 1965

World Club Championship Finalists 1968

League Cup Semi-Finalists 1969 1970

17 MARCH 1973, v NEWCASTLE UNITED
In what was a tough term on the field, chairman Louis Edwards shows appreciation to the fans by lowering ticket prices for our last five home outings.

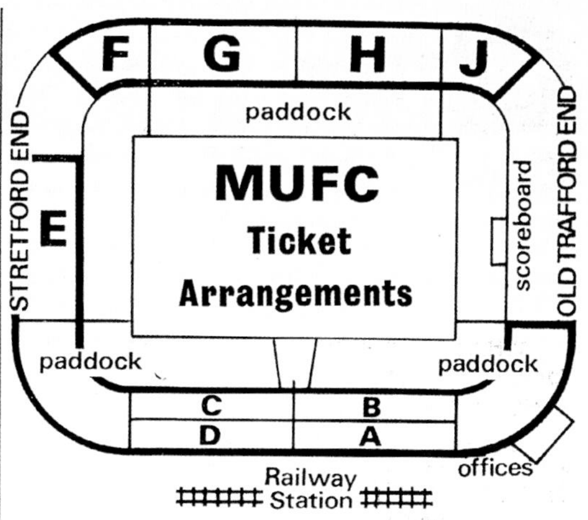

UNITED v. EVERTON

Wednesday, 2nd September, 7-30 p.m.

ADMISSION BY TICKET ONLY! Season Ticket Holders and League Match Ticket Book Holders should use the ticket from their book on entering the Ground as usual.

Reserved seats priced **10/-** and **13/-** and unreserved seats priced **8/-** in Stand "E" (Jnrs. and O.A.P.'s **5/-**), together with Goundside and Paddocks will be on open sale at the Ground from Sunday, 23rd August, 9-30 a.m. to 1-00 p.m. and weekdays from 10-00 a.m. to 6-00 p.m. Seats will be limited in accordance with the demand.

Postal applications will be accepted for Groundside and Paddock tickets ONLY, and should include correct remittance and s.a.e.

19 AUGUST 1970, v CHELSEA
In order to try and avoid crowd trouble at matches there were an increasing number of all-ticket matches played, like this one against Everton in September 1970.

UNITED
v.
ESTUDIANTES

IN THE EVENT OF A PLAY-OFF
IN AMSTERDAM

SPECIAL FLIGHT
Sat. 19th Oct. 8 pm
16½ gns
INCLUDING MATCH TICKET

MANCUNIA TRAVEL LIMITED
THE SPORTSFLIGHT SPECIALISTS
120 PORTLAND ST. MANCHESTER 1
061 CENtral 3657

PAGE NINE

2 OCTOBER 1968, v WATERFORD
Had United and South American champions Estudiantes drawn 1968's Intercontinental Cup final, a play-off was pencilled in for three days after the second leg at Old Trafford – and there were even flight options available, as advertised in the programme for our European Cup meeting with Irish side Waterford.

7 AUGUST 1978, v REAL MADRID

David Smith of the official supporters' club thanks United officials for the backing given to its members in the programme for the match marking the Reds' centenary year.

A time for celebration

By David Smith

On the occasion of Manchester United Football Club celebrating their Centenary it is with immense pride that the present supporters club finds itself involved in providing supporters of the club with an organisation to which they can become affiliated by way of membership and reap the many benefits which have been acquired over the past ten years.

Benefits which have, themselves, resulted from the assistance and co-operation of Manchester United Football Club.

Through the good offices of the Directors of Manchester United an office has been provided at Old Trafford in order that we might continue to offer what is felt to be an invaluable and worthwhile service to those supporters who comprise the present membership of the club.

An exclusive 15% discount facility on souvenir purchases is available to all members of the club as a result of such generous offer being made by the Red Devils Souvenir Shop situated at the ground.

The information and photographs contained in the supporters club publications have only been possible as a result of such material being so kindly provided by Manchester United and the attendance of Directors, Players and Staff at social functions has been the direct result of the co-operation from the management and playing staff of the club.

Over the years, club branches have been formed throughout the U.K. and the match ticket restrictions imposed in recent years has led to special considerations

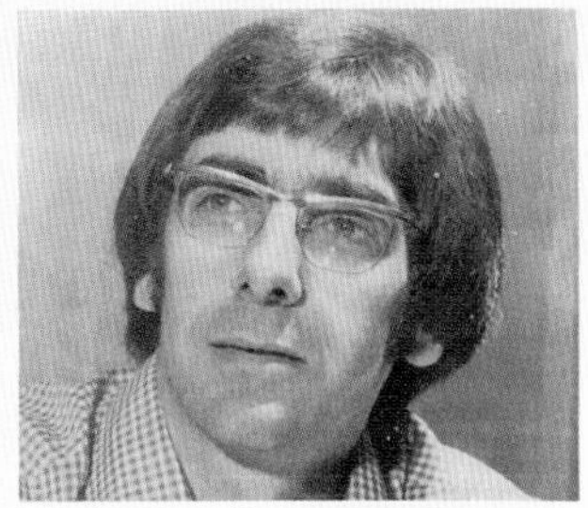

being offered by the Manchester United Ticket Office to responsible organisations within the supporters club movement.

Those are but a few of the instances involving the assistance of Manchester United Football Club towards the present supporters club and whilst it is often said that supporters are the life-blood of soccer, without whom no club could hope to survive, it is only fair to acknowledge that without the help of Manchester United this supporters club would never achieved its present standing as a bona-fide organisation worthy of the club we all support.

In congratulating Manchester United Football Club on their 100th Anniversary, we take this opportunity, on behalf of all supporters, to thank them for their generosity and encouragement at all times.

It is, indeed, a time for celebration.

27 AUGUST 1975, v COVENTRY CITY

United fans earned a reputation for being the worst behaved in the country, and the club was determined to root out the trouble-makers and alter the perception of its supporters.

MANCHESTER UNITED OFFICIAL OPEN DAY

We hope that all supporters who attended enjoyed the rather unique pre-season Open Day at Old Trafford on Sunday 12th August and that the various activities and displays, some of which are pictured below, catered for supporters of all ages.

We would like to express our grateful thanks to all those involved — not least the Greater Manchester Police and their Gymnastic and Dog Display Teams, Barratts 'free-fall' Parachute Team, Green Howards Military Band, Warner Brothers Incorporated (America), Lancashire Hussars Hot-Air Balloon Team, Variety Club of Great Britain (Manchester Committee), Roger Day (Piccadilly Radio) and Maybank Press (who supplied the Open Day programmes free of charge).

Extra special thanks are due to the Directors, players and staff of Manchester United Football Club for their involvement, the Club gatemen, stewards and catering staff for their voluntary assistance and all those supporters who attended and donated so generously to such a worthy cause in aid of underprivileged children.

Further pictures from the Manchester United Open Day will appear in the next issue of the United Review.

Greater Manchester police highly professional gymnastic display team entertains the crowd.

22 AUGUST 1979, v WEST BROMWICH ALBION

The Reds warmed up for the 1979/80 season with an open training session that also included other light entertainment for fans to enjoy. There was even a programme on sale (left).

Dear Mr Olive,
As you are aware the Malta Branch of the Manchester United Supporters Club hold an annual dinner and dance in Malta, to which several of the players are invited as guests.

In 1980 the event is being held on the 5th July, and we have arranged a 14 day holiday in Malta departing from London on the 30th June.

Our club have enjoyed many social occasions with our friends from Malta both in London and in Manchester, and we are sure this will be a holiday to remember.

There are a limited number of tickets available to other supporters and their friends, and we are wondering, therefore, if you could kindly arrange for details of the trip to be published in the United programme. For further information please telephone Gerrards Cross 83339.

May I take this opportunity of thanking you and your staff for the kind assistance you have always given us.
Yours sincerely,
Brian Roake, Chairman,
Manchester United (London & District) Supporters' Club.

5 APRIL 1980, v LIVERPOOL
The social scene of following the Reds even extended to organised holidays to United hotbeds like Malta, with an invitation to all.

30 AUGUST 1980, v SUNDERLAND
The emergence of the Solidarity movement in Poland had caused what the programme called 'troubles' in the country, and there was important advice for fans wanting to attend our UEFA Cup tie at Widzew Lodz.

UEFA CUP FIRST ROUND

All supporters interested in attending the away leg of the game versus Widzew Lodz should note that whilst the political situation in Poland is some-what unstable at the present moment, bookings are still being accepted for travel to the match on Wednesday 1st October. Naturally, we are keeping a close eye on the current situation and will cater where possible with any subsequent developments as they occur. However, of utmost importance, is the fact that in the event of the troubles being ended, which we expect before the date of the game, it might very well be that any supporters who have not yet booked (as a result of waiting a little longer to see what happened) will have left it too late for their Visa applications (in particular) to be processed in good time for the trip. All supporters are advised, therefore, to ensure that their booking form and visa application (available from the supporters club office) are completed and forwarded to the office, together with deposit by the final date for applications.

Dear Editor
During our home match against Crystal Palace, Steve Coppell was wearing an odd pair of boots and all the other player's were wearing the same. Why was it?

I think that any letters that are published in the programme, the person who sent it should get something like a Manchester United Pen.
Yours Sincerely
Mark Hamilton (age 13)
20, Atherton-Gt.
Peel Green
Eccles
M30 8PZ

'Hawk-eye' must be your middle name young man. During the early part of the match, the laces on one of Steve's boots was ripped by a Palace defender. Rather than spend a great deal of time re-lacing the boot, Ray Wilkins (United's substitute) threw on one of his own boots whilst Steve's boot was re-laced. Fortunately they both take the same size.
Editor

25 APRIL 1981, v NORWICH CITY
Fans would occasionally write in with questions about things they'd spotted on their trips to Old Trafford, and sometimes they'd get a reply.

Also in the Norwich programme from April 1981 is a plea for help from an exiled United fan who had recently (reluctantly?) emigrated to Colombia with his wife.

Sir,
As a loyal United fan for many years it seems now as though a part of me is missing.

You see last August 1980, I married a Colombian girl and in March this year we came to live in Colombia.

I would be most grateful if any of the Reds fans would send me results and cuttings from March 1st onwards. I will in return send South American Programmes.
Thanks a lot
Geoff Beaumont
PS. If this can be done by any Red it will make my wifes life a bit easier as I am unbearable to live with on a Saturday not knowing a thing.
Keep going United & Dave Sexton
Almacen Orianna 109
Pasaje Junin Maracaibo
Medellin Colombia
South America
Wednesday 25th March 81

Modern day Old Trafford has huge provision for disabled supporters, but back in the 1980s it wasn't quite so easy to attend matches. So hats off to these two visually impaired supporters who followed games via radio feed, as featured in the April 1981 Norwich issue.

SUPER REDS

Two of Manchester United's staunchest fans attend Old Trafford each week and whilst there will be others who might claim to be even more staunch in their support, it should be pointed out that these particular supporters follow the fortunes of their No. 1 Club despite severe handicap. Graham Ward from Knutsford is totally blind and his friend, Nigel Taylor of Cambridge is partially sighted and unable to identify individual players from his seat in the stands.

Both supporters follow the game thanks to the provision at Old Trafford of a special allocation of seats behind the Press Box where they are able to 'plug in' to the hospital commentary service provided each week and relayed to hospitals in Manchester, Salford and District. Nigel, in fact, is a member of the Peterborough Branch MUSC and travels to away games as well as homes and our photograph shows Nigel (centre) and Graham being interviewed by Eric Purnell of Radio Manchester for the half-hour weekly programme for the blind and partially-sighted, TORCHLIGHT.

11 SEPTEMBER 1982, v IPSWICH TOWN

Another season, another token sheet – this one proving to be extremely important come the season's end. Not only was there the scramble for League Cup final tickets (if you'd collected enough tokens, that is) but there was also an FA Cup semi-final, final and a final replay to apply for.

MANCHESTER UNITED

Football Club Ltd

Old Trafford, Manchester M16 0RA

OFFICIAL TOKEN SHEET SEASON 1982-83

COVERING FIRST TEAM AND SELECTED ADDITIONAL MATCHES PLAYED BY THE M.U.F.C. AT OLD TRAFFORD

Please write in block capitals

Name

Address

FOOTBALL LEAGUE MATCHES
RESERVED SEATS

Application can be made by POST ONLY for reserved seats in Stand A priced £3.00 (OAPs and accompanied Juniors £1.50) and Stands B, C and D priced £3.80. Tickets are bookable one calendar month in advance. Applications should include the correct remittance and sae. No tickets will be retained for personal callers at the ground unless tickets are still available after postal applications have been dealt with. If this is the case the tickets will then be on sale at the ground on the Monday prior to the match, from 9.30 a.m. to 5 p.m. daily. In the event of seats being over-applied for on the first day of sale, a ballot will be held to determine the successful applicants. 3,500 unreserved seats are available by payment at the turnstiles, in the following sections, for all home League matches, except when otherwise stated.

STAND E £2.40
STAND E (Juniors and OAPs – Stile 49) £1.20
STAND K (Cantilever) £3.20

STANDING ACCOMMODATION

Admission to standing accommodation for approximately 34,000 spectators is by payment at the turnstiles as usual at the following prices:

Groundside .... £1.80 Juniors 90p
Covered Paddocks.................. £2.00 Juniors (at Stretford End only) £1
OAPs £1 at the United Road Paddock (Stile 30) or through the Junior turnstiles in the Stretford End Paddock.

In the event of all-ticket matches, details may vary from those above and special arrangements will be announced in the club programme (if time permits) and in the Manchester Evening News.

Up to the minute ticket and match information

Telephone (061) 872 7771 — 24 hour service

1	2	3	4
5	6	7	8
9	10	11	12
13	14	15	16
17	18	19	20
21	22	23	24
25	26	27	28
29	30	31	32

SPECIAL TOKEN A	SPECIAL TOKEN B	SPECIAL TOKEN C
SPECIAL TOKEN D	SPECIAL TOKEN E	SPECIAL TOKEN F
SPECIAL TOKEN G	SPECIAL TOKEN H	SPECIAL TOKEN J
SPECIAL TOKEN K	SPECIAL TOKEN L	SPECIAL TOKEN M
SPECIAL TOKEN N	SPECIAL TOKEN P	SPECIAL TOKEN R

IMPORTANT: Please read these notes carefully before completing your token sheet

With the experience gained over past seasons, it is felt that the M.U.F.C. token scheme offers our regular supporters the fairest chance of obtaining admission to those special matches where demand for tickets invariably exceeds the supply. The instructions below should be read carefully. The Directors reserve the right to vary the method of using the scheme from time to time and to withdraw it or any individual sheet if it is felt that it is being abused. At all times every effort will be made to ensure a fair distribution of tickets when these are in short supply.

1 Tokens will be printed in First Team HOME MATCH programmes and in any programmes FOR MIDWEEK games played at NIGHT by M.U.F.C. teams playing at Old Trafford when the First Team are not playing away in a League or Cup match on any evening during the same week. (This is subject to alteration without notice).
2 Carefully detach this token sheet from the programme by lifting up the binding wires.
3 Away match programmes will NOT be accepted.
4 Cut out and paste the tokens collected in the appropriate numbered squares. Please ensure that the numbers on the tokens correspond with the numbers on the token sheet. GUM ONLY. TOKENS COVERED WITH SELLOTAPE OR SIMILAR. WILL NOT BE ACCEPTED.
5 Only the OFFICIAL TOKEN SHEET together with tokens properly affixed on the correct squares will be considered when the token scheme is put into use. Mutilated tokens on token sheets cannot be accepted.
6 The possession of the required number of tokens does NOT ensure that an application will be successful. NO GUARANTEE can be given that all requests will be met and in the event of the demand exceeding the supply it is inevitable that some disappointment may be caused. Every effort will be made to keep them to a minimum.
7 Any sheet containing mutilated, defaced, forged or altered tokens will not be accepted irrespective of the number of genuine tokens presented.

FOR SALE . . . WANTED . . . PEN-PALS . . . SWAPS . . .

FOR SALE Mrs P. Taylor of 20 Selkirk Road, Ipswich, has a complete set of United autographs, obtained following a match versus Luton Town, in December 1957. Offers invited.

PEN-PALS Audvzej Marchwat is a 17 year old Polish boy who would like to correspond with United supporters. His address is: 93-129 Kodz, Lubelska 12 m 35, Poland.

PEN-PALS James Barrie of 1 Southampton Drive, Kelvindale, Glasgow, is 15 years of age and a Partick Thistle fan. He would like to swop programmes and information about United.

PEN-PALS Gino de Reland lives at Malartic II, Rose Hill, Mauritius and is 27 years of age. He would like to correspond with Manchester United fans, male or female.

HELP Lloyd Fatmote lives in the Bishop Stortford area and would like a lift to Old Trafford, he is willing to share expenses and can be contacted at 82 Manor Road, Stansted, Essex.

FOR SALE Mr P. Fealey from 2 Mildenhall Road, Woolton, Liverpool, has for sale United home and away programmes from the last two seasons.

FOR SALE Patrick Harrison, 29 Quarry Way, Southwater, Horsham, West Sussex, has approximately 600 duplicate United programmes, mainly from 1968 onwards. Any offers or enquiries should include SAE.

WANTED Two programmes, United v Southampton (4.11.78) and United v Birmingham City (2.1.78) are required by Mr R. C. Maule, of 25 Third Avenue, Bradford Moor, Bradford, West Yorkshire. Mr Maule also seeks old photographs of United and can be contacted on Bradford 662428.

27 NOVEMBER 1982, v NORWICH CITY
Swapping programmes, sharing lifts and selling memorabilia was a normal part of following the Reds in the early 1980s, and the *Review* was happy to help out.

HILLSBOROUGH TRAGEDY

A great deal has already been said, and written, about the disaster in which 95 football supporters lost their lives at the F.A. Cup semi-final tie between Liverpool and Nottingham Forest recently.

Martin Edwards writes elsewhere in today's 'Review' about the tragedy and the possible implications for football. Our comments therefore are brief at this point and cover more practical aspects.

We know that many fans have made their way to Anfield to pay their tribute personally and because we believe it to be your wish, we have opened a Book of Remembrance so that United fans can identify with those who have lost family or friends. The book is situated in the Sir Matt Busby Suite and is available for signature Sunday to Friday, 10.00am to 4.00pm.

We have also been moved by the letters and telephone calls from Liverpool fans. In the main they cover two particular points; firstly they are full of appreciation for the messages of sympathy, from football in general but from Manchester United fans in particular. Secondly, a number have made the comment that they now understand what Munich means to United and how painful taunts about the aircrash must have been. Not all letters were signed and there have been too many to reproduce. One constant theme running through them all however was the thought that out of their loss should emerge a new beginning of friendship and mutual respect. The heart, and the strength of English football lies in this region. Perhaps we can show to the rest of football a United front which, more than anything, will do much to overcome all that is unacceptable and unsavoury in the game.

29 APRIL 1989, v COVENTRY CITY
United Review shares the club's thoughts two weeks on from the horrific scenes of the Hillsborough disaster, which took the lives of 96 Liverpool supporters.

1 JANUARY 1986, v BIRMINGHAM CITY
Fans are urged to join the official supporters' club, with plenty of goodies on offer.

UNITED REVIEW

FAN FARE

BACK HOME — ALMOST!
The Supporters Club has now moved back into its main office at Old Trafford and all enquiries should now be made to the new office, which is situated under Stand K at the scoreboard end of the ground opposite Car Park No. 1. Unfortunately, with moving the week prior to the Christmas period it has not been possible for our direct phone line to be re-installed and it will now be early in the New Year before this can be dealt with. In the meanwhile, supporters should note that our information tape (061-872 6000) will continue to operate from our temporary accommodation of the past 12 months, with up-to-date details continuing to be available 24 hours a day. Our apologies for any inconvenience this has caused and trusting the arrangements made have proved satisfactory under the circumstances.

BACK ON THE BOX
Supporters should note that the recent agreement between the Football and Television authorities in respect of live coverage of forthcoming League fixtures will mean that United's away matches at West Ham and Liverpool in February will now be played on Sunday 2nd and 9th respectively.

Travel and ticket information will be announced in due course.

SUPPORTERS CLUB PACK 1985-86
This season's Club Pack is still available and comprises: Supporters Yearbook, Club Information Guide, Souvenir Shop List, Official Club Discount and Travel and Identity Car, Christmas Newsletter and exclusive Poster-Calendar for 1986. The Easter Newsletter, which will be posted in April 1986, will complete this season's Club Pack and the official application form can be obtained only from the Supporters Club Office here at Old Trafford. All postal enquiries must include sae in order that application form can be returned at the earliest opportunity.

SUPPORTERS CLUB OFFICE HOURS 1985-86

Weekdays	Morning	Afternoon
Monday	Closed	1.30 - 5.00
Tuesday	10.00 - 1.00	1.30 - 5.00
Wednesday	10.00 - 1.00	1.30 - 5.00
Thursday	10.00 - 1.00	1.30 - 5.00
Friday	10.00 - 1.00	Closed
Matchdays	**Before**	**After**
Saturday	12.00 - 2.45	4.45 - 5.00
Midweek	5.00 - 7.15	9.15 - 9.30

SUPPORTERS CLUB TRAVEL

Saturday 11th January OXFORD
Coach: £8.00
Depart: 9.00 am
Bookings available from Saturday 4th January

9

Lock-out
For the first time since the introduction of our membership scheme, we were unable to cater for all our members, when we opened the new season against Coventry City at Old Trafford recently. Our configuration has, of course, changed since the installation of additional seats and it is becoming increasingly important for members to arrive early, in order to gain entry.
Members would also assist themselves greatly if, as they approach the turnstiles, they have the appropriate voucher(s) and correct remittance ready to hand to the gateman. The turnstile entrance is not the place to fumble for a pen so that members guest details can be written on the appropriate voucher!!

8 SEPTEMBER 1990, v QUEENS PARK RANGERS
The official membership scheme gave priority to 'members' attending home matches, but evidently some were still adjusting to the new process at the turnstiles – cue this helpful reminder from the club.

ANFIELD SUPER SHOW
Whilst Alex Ferguson can rightly congratulate the team for their magnificent performance at Anfield just before Christmas, we, as a club, are equally as proud of our supporters who behaved so well that day. There is no point denying that, over the years, a great deal of animosity has built up between United and Liverpool fans and our tragedy at Munich together with the loss of Liverpool's legendary Bill Shankly, have both proved to be distasteful focal points for abuse. The disaster at Hillsborough last April gave the genuine United supporters a chance to show their true colours and the gestures of reconciliation at that time, were greatly appreciated by Liverpool Football Club and their fans. Perhaps, after all, a new era has dawned and we look for it's continuation when Kenny Dalglish and his team visit Old Trafford in March.
There was some embarrassment in the United camp when it was announced, during the half-time interval on the 23rd December, that Rod Stewart's son had been chosen as the United mascot for the day. It was something that had been done in good faith by Liverpool but was an arrangement which Club Secretary, Ken Merrett, was completely unaware of until he arrived at the ground with the United team. The whole question of mascots is a very difficult one, particularly with a club such as ours which enjoys a huge following nationwide. In general terms, we do not encourage mascots. On rare occasions, however, we do apply a very special criteria, one being that junior members are offered the chance as part of a prize in one of our competitions, another being a special case usually involving a very sick child.

Incidentally, during the interview which took place, at half-time the singer was asked whether he would like to perform a concert at Anfield. Perhaps Denis Law's greatest fan is not aware that Old Trafford has been given a licence to stage a concert during the summer of 1990. Have you checked your diary Rod?

13 JANUARY 1990, v DERBY COUNTY
The programme praises United fans who'd recently attended the Reds' game at Anfield, and gives musician Rod Stewart a nudge about the availability of Old Trafford as a concert venue.

Caught Out!
A number of supporters, particularly from out-of-town, were caught out by our announcement immediately after the conclusion of the 5th Round 2nd Replay between Barnsley and Sheffield United, that tickets would go on sale for 6th Round tie the following day. Clearly, the short amount of time available to sell tickets was far from ideal and we regret the inconvenience caused, particularly to those who live some considerable distance from Old Trafford who find personal application at best, extremely difficult and at worst, well-nigh impossible. There is no ready solution to the problem but fans with a particular difficulty should always telephone the club in advance to seek guidance. We cannot put away tickets for postal applicants and we cannot promise miracles. We will do, however, everything in our power to assist, wherever possible.

Lucky Mascot

Ten-year-old Daniel Beirne really came up trumps for the Reds when he led his favourites out before our match against Luton Town. It was a special day for the youngster and a well-deserved treat, for Daniel was involved in a very serious road accident and spent some considerable time in a coma. Whilst on a hospital visit, Bryan Robson, Steve Bruce and Brian McClair called in to see Daniel but unfortunately, were not able to get any response from the lad. Steve did return, however, when Daniel recovered consciousness and as part of an incentive to get well, invited him along to watch a training session. Alex Ferguson added another incentive when he invited Daniel to be our mascot and he clearly had the time of his life during the pre-match kick-about.

14 MARCH 1990, v EVERTON
There's an apology to fans for the short notice ahead of tickets going on sale for our FA Cup tie at Sheffield United, and one young fan is given a dream day out.

5 MAY 1990, v CHARLTON ATHLETIC
There's no gala dinner at Old Trafford to announce United's 1990 Player of the Year, just this brief article and a quick presentation on the pitch. Well done, Pally!

Members' Player of the Year

Gary Pallister has done it! He is this Season's Members' Player of the Year. After the first voting stage Pally was in third position behind Bryan Robson and Mark Hughes but such has been the consistency of the big man throughout the Season that he has finished way in front of Sparky in second place with third place honours going to Robbo even though he missed a number of games through injury.
All credit must to to Gary after receiving criticism on arrival to United he has settled in well and deserves this coveted award which he will receive just prior to kick-off from Christopher Brown from Longwell Green, Bristol who was one of the members who voted for him.

Alf's Bar
We recently received a letter from a J A Dickinson which reads as follows:
"Whilst most clubs are spending their money on improvements and renovations to the grounds a certain life long supporter of Manchester United is doing the same to his house.
What's unusual about that you may ask, well the difference is that 'Alf' has spent a lot of time and money converting his cellar into a bar. Not just any old bar, but the 'United Arms'.
'Alf' or as he is correctly known, Brian Drake, has decorated his bar from top to bottom with every piece of United memorabilia available to him, however, his crowning glory is the slightly amended mural resembling the cover of the United Review."
We take this opportunity of showing Alf's, sorry Brian's, mural and hope he won't mind if any fellow United supporters pop in to sample his stock - he lives at 33 Malsis Road, Keighley, West Yorkshire. Cheers!

23 JANUARY 1991, v SOUTHAMPTON
One fan creates his own bar at home and themes it on his beloved club, complete with a reproduction of the *United Review* handshake on the wall. Nice!

21 DECEMBER 1991, v ASTON VILLA
The authorities were winning the battle against hooliganism, but there were still reminders within match programmes – including this postponed game against Villa – that the problem had not totally gone away.

NATIONAL FOOTBALL
INTELLIGENCE UNIT
HOOLIGAN HOTLINE
PLEASE RING
071 230 5340
IN STRICT
CONFIDENCE

Also in the pre-Christmas Villa programme, thoughts were on three – yes, three! – trips to Elland Road in the space of 10 days (eventually 18 days due to the postponement of the FA Cup tie).

LONG ARM OF COINCIDENCE

What odds on the recent cup draws resulting in three matches against championship contenders Leeds United, all at Elland Road, within the space of ten days?
We were delighted to learn that the Yorkshire Club moved speedily, and decisively, to defuse any ticket problems. In order to accommodate our supporters, Leeds have re-located their Family Stand for both cup ties, thus giving us the complete end of the ground which contains excellent facilities.
Leeds must also be applauded for the very positive steps they have taken, and continue to take, to identify and isolate the minority amongst their supporters who, to the embarrassment of their club, taunt Manchester fans with "Munich".
The forthcoming matches offer supporters of both clubs an ideal opportunity to demonstrate their support in a proper manner. What a chance to show the watching millions that we can enjoy competition without confrontation.

PLAYER OF THE YEAR
MID-SEASON VOTE

The votes have really flooded in this time, with 13 players each receiving a number of votes. Coming out on top at this stage with 30% of the total votes, is Ryan Giggs, who is clearly becoming a firm favourite with the fans. Ryan is closely followed by Brian McClair, who only received 6 votes less. In third place is Andrei Kanchelskis, closely followed by Neil Webb, Bryan Robson, Steve Bruce and Gary Pallister.

Details of how to make your second and final vote will be published in the magazine which is distributed to all our members before the end of the season. In the meantime, well done Ryan!

5 FEBRUARY 1992, v SOUTHAMPTON
United Review gives an update on voting for the 1991/92 Player of the Year, with Ryan Giggs leading the way with three months to go of his breakthrough season. He's eventually pipped to the award by Brian McClair.

European Cup Travel

BARCELONA VERSUS MANCHESTER UNITED
Nou Camp Stadium,
Wednesday 2nd November, Kick-off 8.30pm (local time)

The Membership and Supporters' Travel Club are pleased to advise that booking forms are now available from the Membership Office to personal callers, or by post by sending a 10" x 7" stamped addressed envelope marking your preference ie: air or coach travel in the top left hand corner of your incoming envelope. Write to:
MEMBERSHIP AND SUPPORTERS TRAVEL CLUB
BARCELONA AWAY MATCH
MANCHESTER UNITED FOOTBALL CLUB
OLD TRAFFORD
MANCHESTER
M16 0RA
Telephone enquiries: **061 872 8208**
Fax: **061 877 9711.**

By Coach

Departs Manchester on Monday 31st October. Pick up en-route. Return to Manchester early morning Friday 3rd November.
***£90.00.**
Price includes executive coach travel and 1 night half-board accommodation (sharing twin room). Insurance is offered as an optional extra.

Match Tickets

All members travelling with us will be guaranteed a match ticket. At the time of going to print, the cost of the ticket has yet to be confirmed, although it is anticipated to be around £52.00.

Early demand for places on our trips has been overwhelming. Therefore, if it is of interest to you, you are advised to act quickly in order to avoid any disappointment.

By Air
One Day Trip

Flights from Manchester, Birmingham and Gatwick (subject to demand)
***£170.00** from Manchester and Gatwick
***£178.00** from Birmingham (due to higher airport taxes)
Price includes flight on chartered aircraft, airport taxes, travel insurance and coach transfers.
Flights depart Wednesday, approx 12.30pm and return to UK on Thursday, approx 2.30am

Two Day Trip

Flights from Manchester and Gatwick (subject to demand). Travel Wednesday, return Thursday evening - *£265.00. Price includes flight on chartered aircraft, airport taxes, travel insurance, coach transfers and 4-star hotel accommodation in Central Barcelona (1 night B&B sharing twin room - single room supplement £35.00).
Fly Wednesday morning - return to UK Thursday evening

Away Travel Club

Details of our coach travel arrangements from Old Trafford to Hillsborough for our forthcoming away fixture are as follows:

***SHEFFIELD WEDNESDAY** Saturday 8th October*

Executive coach	£8.00
Luxury coach	£5.00
Depart Old Trafford	12.30pm
Estimated return	7.15pm

Please note that these arrangements are for official Club members only and are subject to demand. Bookings can be made at the Membership Office.

1 OCTOBER 1994, v EVERTON

Excitement builds ahead of United's first trip to the Nou Camp in 20 years, with details revealed for travel options and how to apply for tickets a month ahead of the clash in Catalonia.

3 JANUARY 1995, v COVENTRY CITY

Another season, another chance for fans to have their say on the campaign's star performer – now known as the Sir Matt Busby award. The phone vote is eventually won by Andrei Kanchelskis.

Sir Matt Busby Player of the Year

Squad No	PLAYER	TEL.NUMBER
1	Peter Schmeichel	0891 2345 **01**
2	Paul Parker	0891 2345 **02**
3	Denis Irwin	0891 2345 **03**
4	Steve Bruce	0891 2345 **04**
5	Lee Sharpe	0891 2345 **05**
6	Gary Pallister	0891 2345 **06**
7	Eric Cantona	0891 2345 **07**
8	Paul Ince	0891 2345 **08**
9	Brian McClair	0891 2345 **09**
10	Mark Hughes	0891 2345 **10**
11	Ryan Giggs	0891 2345 **11**
12	David May	0891 2345 **12**
13	Gary Walsh	0891 2345 **13**
14	Andrei Kanchelskis	0891 2345 **14**
15	Graeme Tomlinson	0891 2345 **15**
16	Roy Keane	0891 2345 **16**
18	Simon Davies	0891 2345 **18**
19	Nicky Butt	0891 2345 **19**
24	Paul Scholes	0891 2345 **24**
25	Kevin Pilkington	0891 2345 **25**
27	Gary Neville	0891 2345 **27**
31	Keith Gillespie	0891 2345 **31**

VOTE NOW BY SIMPLY TELEPHONING 0891 2345 FOLLOWED BY THE PLAYER'S SQUAD NUMBER

The cost of a call has been limited to less than the price of a first class stamp, but juniors wishing to vote should seek permission before using the telephone.

1 MAY 1999, v ASTON VILLA

This visit to the Nou Camp was even more eagerly anticipated than the one five years earlier, with all the details of how to be there on the big night announced here.

UEFA CHAMPIONS LEAGUE FINAL
MANCHESTER UNITED v BAYERN MUNICH
Nou Camp Stadium, Barcelona
Wednesday 26th May 1999, kick off 8.45pm

UEFA have agreed to supply the finalists with 30,000 match tickets, mainly priced £12.00 and £28.00 and Manchester United's allocation is primarily situated behind the north goal of the stadium.

Initially tickets will be sold to the following categories.

1. Private Box and Executive members (who will receive by post a letter of invitation to apply, together with a list of the required documentation).

2. Those supporters who either purchased a match ticket from the club or who travelled on one of the club's official trips to this season's quarter-final versus Inter Milan will receive by post a letter of invitation to apply, together with a list of the required documentation).

3. Season Ticket holders and Members in possession of voucher 60/ZZ and the maximum of 12 special match vouchers listed properly affixed to the official voucher sheet.

Special Match Vouchers:
31 (LKS Lodz); 32 (Barcelona); 33 (Brondby); 34 (Bayern Munich); 35 (Bury); 36 (Nottingham Forest); 37 (Middlesbrough); 38 (Liverpool); 39 (Inter Milan); 40 (Fulham); 41 (Chelsea), 42 (Juventus).

Season Ticket holders successfully applying for FA Cup Final tickets will receive a letter of invitation to apply together with a list of the documentation required when they receive their Cup Final tickets.

Members who are in possession of the 12 special match vouchers stated should contact the Membership Office for a travel/ticket order form.

Everyone applying MUST produce a photocopy of that page in their passport which shows their photograph. Also required is a photocopy of the page in your passport showing your passport number should this not be displayed on the same page as your photograph.

THOSE WISHING TO PURCHASE MATCH TICKETS ONLY will be able to apply to the Ticket Office on Saturday/Sunday 8th/9th May, 1999 from 9am - 4pm. THOSE APPLYING FOR CLUB TRAVEL PACKAGES, WHICH INCLUDES A MATCH TICKET, SHOULD APPLY TO THE MEMBERSHIP OFFICE in its new location on the United Trading Estate behind the North Stand at the same times.
Those wishing to apply by post should include the following:

1. Completed travel/ticket order form
2. Voucher 60/ZZ (duly completed)
3. The 12 special match vouchers properly affixed to the official voucher sheet
4. Photocopy of passport (page bearing photograph) and if necessary a photocopy of the page showing passport number
5. Relevant payment (cheque/credit card details)
6. Registered sae

In the event of tickets and club travel packages remaining, a further announcement will be made via the usual channels.

THE CLUB HAVE THE FOLLOWING TRAVEL OPTIONS AVAILABLE

OPTION 1
3 Day Trip from Manchester. £475.00 plus match ticket. Includes two nights 4 star hotel accommodation in Tarragona.
Departs Tuesday 25th May
Returns Thursday 27th May.
OPTION 2
Day Trip from Manchester* £275.00 plus match ticket
OPTION 3
Coach Trip from Old Trafford. £245.00 plus match ticket (Pick-ups en route to Dover)
Departs Monday 24th May
Returns to Old Trafford Friday 28th May.
Includes two nights accommodation in 2/3 star coastal tourist hotels.
* Subject to demand, flight also available from Gatwick

Miss Ellies World Travel (Manchester) will be given a small allocation of tickets in order to cater for those supporters who travelled with them to Milan. Furthermore, additional travel packages are available to those Season Ticket holders/Members who have purchased a match ticket from the club. Please contact Miss Ellies on 0161 228 7363 or send a fax to 0161 228 7453 for details of their arrangements.

N.B. We are to receive a number of Day Travel Passes from the Barcelona Travel Authorities, priced £1.20 each. These will be available upon request when sales commence.

GENERAL INFORMATION

The Civil Aviation Authority (CAA) has issued the following message in respect of supporters planning to make their own travel arrangements to the UEFA Champions League final in Barcelona:

1. There may be a number of advertisements in newspapers and magazines offering flights to our matches abroad. You should, however, be careful as some adverts may be placed by unlicensed organisers and agents, and if you book with them your money could be at risk.

2. Check that the organiser with whom you intend to book has an ATOL number. An ATOL is a license issued by the Civil Aviation Authority (CAA). If a licensed organiser goes out of business your money will be refunded (less insurance) or you will be flown home.

3. Call the CAA on 0171 832 6600 to check that the operator you are thinking of booking with holds an ATOL before you pay any money.

4. If you book through a travel agent they must provide you with a receipt which names the ATOL organiser responsible for you. Always make sure you get a confirm which will show what you have purchased, how much you have paid, the flight details and the operator's name, address and ATOL number.

IN THE MEANTIME...
...Supporters are urged not to make their own travel arrangements on the basis that you may not be able to purchase a match ticket from the Club.

United News

Today will not be an occasion for the faint hearted as our final home fixture of the season brings down the curtain another fabulously exciting season of FA Carling Premiership football. Whatever the outcome, no one can deny that the Alex Ferguson, his players and staff have done us proud this season....and there is still the small matter of the FA Cup final and UEFA Champions League final to follow!

In keeping with end-of-season tradition we will be making two presentations before this afternoon's match, both of which acknowledge the achievements and progress of two of the club's younger players.

The Denzil Haroun Award is presented annually to the player who, in the opinion of the club's coaches, has contributed most to our reserve team and this year's winner is striker Jonathan Greening.

The Jimmy Murphy Award recognises the talent and potential of our younger players and this year's recipient is the club's latest full international Wesley Brown.

As is customary, The Jimmy Murphy Award will be presented by members of the Murphy family and the Denzil Haroun Award will be presented by Denzil's daughter, Magi Haroun.

These presentations are scheduled to take place towards the end of the players' warm up period at approximately 3.50pm.

Prior to the presentations we will be delighted to welcome on to the field locally-born tenor, Russell Watson.

Russell, a life-long United fan, who still lives in Irlam, became a professional opera singer three years ago and has already received critical acclaim from national and local press.

He recently sang the National Anthem before the London v. Leeds Rugby League Cup final at Wembley and later this year he is to perform a series of duets with Sir Cliff Richard in Hyde Park. He has also appeared regularly on Granada tv.

Russell, a South Stand regular at United's home games, sees today's performances - he will also sing at the end of the game - as an ambition fulfilled.

He will perform the 1982 World Cup anthem 'Nessun Dorma' before the kick-off and sign off with another classic at the close of this afternoon's proceedings.

Irrespective of your particular taste in music, we strongly advise you not to miss Russell Watson's first appearance at the 'Theatre of Dreams'.

Whatever the outcome of this afternoon's matches, both here and elsewhere, the players will return to the field at the end of the game to thank you all for another season of incomparable support.

16 MAY 1999, v TOTTENHAM HOTSPUR

Ahead of our decisive, final-day league game against Spurs, there's no tempting fate by mentioning the possibility of any post-game presentations. Instead, the pre-game running order is included in the programme, with United fan and tenor Russell Watson singing *Nessun Dorma* on the pitch. Well, it was the '90s... just!

United Members

Members' Treble Photo Session

A limited number of places are still available for the Treble Photo Session organised by the Membership Office to be held in the Premier Lounge on Sunday 16th January 2000. The sessions scheduled for Sunday 21st November and Sunday 28th November are now full. This is a unique opportunity for you as a club member together with your family and friends to have your photograph taken with the UEFA Champions League trophy, FA Carling Premiership trophy and the F.A. Cup.

The cost of a 10" x 8" mounted photograph is £15.00 which is inclusive of postage and packing.

Advance reservations are necessary and as places will be sold on a first come first served basis, anyone who is interested are advised to place a booking immediately in order to save any disappointment. Booking forms are available upon request from the Membership Office.

Please note these sessions are in addition to those organised by the Museum and Tour Department.

Stop Press all sessions now sold out

Toyota Cup Information

UEFA CHAMPIONS LEAGUE Winnres v. COPA LIBERTADORES DE AMERICA Winners

Manchester United v. S.E. Palmeiras
Tuesday 30th November

As we have now been oversubscribed with applications for match tickets for the allocation we are to receive for this game, regrettably, no further applications can be considered.

United Man Was a Prisoner in Graz!

Jimmy Hardman has worked in the Manchester United Development Association offices for well over 20 years, and when he heard that one of the teams we would meet in the UEFA Champions League was Sturm Graz, it brought back many memories for him.

Jimmy is an old soldier, and was unfortunate enough to be taken prisoner in the Western Desert during the Second World War. One of the Desert Rats, he was captured after the second battle of Tobruk and shipped to a prisoner of war camp near Rome via Bari.

After 11 months there, during which he escaped for a while before being recaptured, he was moved to another camp in Yugoslavia at Marburg. After almost a year there, he and the other British prisoners were moved over the Austrian border to a camp near Graz.

Just like prisoners of war held in Britain, they were given the opportunity to work on farms, and Jimmy was placed on one in Gossendorf, just south of the city. This was the brightest spell during his time as a prisoner of war.

"Credit where it is due," says Jimmy, "they were very nice people and looked after us well. The only other workers on the farm were the family, and everybody had their duties. I wasn't treated any differently."

"Herr Lugert was the farmer, and he had three children: a girl in her late teens; a boy a little younger; and another girl. The boy may have been Karl and one of the girls Peppi, I think. It was over 50 years ago and it's hard for me to remember."

"The farmer asked if I could handle a horse and I said yes even though I'd never touched one before. I soon sorted out how everything worked, and before long I was regularly driving a waggon full of produce into Graz market with the son. After unloading we would go to a café for a cup of coffee. There were always a few people there who could speak English, and we all got on well together."

Altogether Jimmy was there for another 11 month stay which he remembers warmly. "You could never forget there was a war on with all the road blocks and checks," he says, "but we had a fair amount of freedom and were quite comfortable, really."

Not long before Jimmy left, he remembers the consternation among the Lugert family when the boy had to go into the army at the age of 16. "They were very short of men in their armed forces towards the end, and had to draft everybody they could. I always hoped he came through it all right."

When the Americans arrived, Jimmy's group were marched over the Alps to a transit camp, then by lorry to Salzburg whence they were flown home in a Dakota via Rheims to Worthing.

Jimmy hopes that tonight's game is a memorable one, and that both sets of supporters get on together. "The people of Graz were very good to us P.O.W.s," he said. "That is why I have the fondest memories of the city."

2 NOVEMBER 1999, v STURM GRAZ

This fascinating wartime tale from a club staff member, and former 'Desert Rat', provided an unusual take on a European tie.

6 NOVEMBER 1999, v LEICESTER CITY

There's bad news for some fans here: photo sessions with the Treble trophies are sold out, and ticket applications for our Intercontinental Cup tie in Tokyo are oversubscribed.

On top of the world: United were 1-0 winners against Palmeiras in the Inter-continental Cup

FANSPOTTING

Know your neighbour

Among the 67,000 who file into Old Trafford week in, week out, you get all sorts, from the Old Timers, who have been backing the Reds since the dawn of time, to the Pessimists (you know who you are...)

MAN UNITED

Vodafone

The Believer
The Believer has 100 per cent faith in the Reds, 100 per cent of the time. They won't hear a word of criticism about any player and are never anything less than certain that their team will turn things round, even if United should happen to be 4–0 down with a minute to go. Away at Highbury. Forget rose-tinted spectacles, the Believer has rose-tinted contact lenses surgically attached to the retina. Should you find yourself in their vicinity they will waste little time in telling you that Garry Birtles would have come good if only he'd been given a bit more time, and that Eric Cantona will come back and partner van Nistelrooy next season. But before you dismiss the Believer's attitude as being wholly unrealistic, cast your mind back to the Nou Camp on 26 May 1999 with United a goal down to Bayern Munich and the 90 minutes up.

Most likely to say: "Keep the faith and your loyalty will be rewarded."
Least likely to say: "I think we're due a change of manager."

The Old Timer
Never question the Old Timer's memory. They can recall travelling to games in Newton Heath on a horse and cart, with Billy Meredith cadging a lift to get to the game in time. They can remember Old Trafford being built, Leeds not having a football club and Manchester City being the best team in Manchester. Like it was yesterday. Still, they're among United's greatest supporters, and when an Old Timer actually applauds something that's happened on the pitch, you can be sure that you're watching quality football.

Most likely to say: "He's not a patch on Billy Meredith/Johnny Carey/Duncan Edwards/Best – Law – Charlton*."
[*Delete according to age.]
Least likely to say: "They don't get paid enough, the players of today."

The Singer
Largely young, passionate and loud, the singer's dream would be to see the whole stadium in full voice, just like those magical, mythical days of yore when Old Trafford held 200,000 and every single fan got behind the team for 90 minutes. The Singer feels their efforts are all worthwhile when they receive a text message from a friend watching at home telling them that the atmosphere sounds loud "on the box".

Most likely to say (while gesticulating wildly): "Come on! Get behind the lads!"
Least likely to say: "Quiet please, all that racket is undermining my ability to appreciate the subtle nuances of this intriguing contest."

The Pessimist
Thinks that there's an ongoing, worldwide conspiracy against United by every authority, journalist, referee, opposition player and manager. During the game, the Pessimist can be relied upon to see the absolute worst in any situation. If the other team should happen to venture into the United box, the Pessimist will cry "There it is!" in a "told-you-so-they've-scored-and-it's-the-first-of-six" voice. Or if a player goes down injured: "He's out for the season. Mark my words." And if United are a goal up after 90 minutes, the Pessimist is always convinced there'll be at least seven minutes' injury time; "It's this ref. He's being paid off by South American secret agents to fix a draw. I read it on the Internet." Fortunately for those seated nearby, repeated exposure to the Pessimist breeds immunity.

Most Likely to say: "Alan Green/David Ellery/Tony Blair – they're all closet Liverpool fans you know."
Least likely to say: "The opposition were the better side today and that alone was the reason for their hard-fought victory."

The Tactician
Mr Tactician (it's almost always a bloke) wears an expression of pensive concern sporadically interspersed by furious, and for the most part unfathomable, arm movements when something goes wrong on the pitch. He bellows convoluted instructions to players who can't hear him from the comfort of a quilted coach's jacket, an approximation to the one worn by Sir Alex, which he is considering having embroidered with the initials KIA (Know-It-all). A household name in his own household, the Tactician manages a Sunday league team and likes to ring local radio phone-ins on a frequent basis. There, he is afforded the oxygen of publicity to tell like-minded individuals where United are going wrong, even if they are doing well.

Most likely to say: "Keep it tight, Giggs. Watch the double overlap."
Least likely to say: "I'm wrong. How stupid of me."

The Away Fan
It's the game they look forward to more than any other. Manchester United in the League. Away. In the face of adversity and with the odds stacked against a victory, they unite and get behind their team, working through a not-so-original repertoire of songs. "Stand Up If You Hate Man U"; "60,000 muppets"; "We support our local team"; "You don't come from Manchester". European fans are different, especially those from the Balkans, Greece and Turkey. They create more noise than an F1 car at full throttle, get louder with every goal their team concedes, and can usually be relied upon to belt out some mad, wonderful anthem which involves lots of sabre rattling and carefully choreographed, swaying arms.

Most likely to say (domestic): "Of course. I knew we wouldn't get a result here."
Most likely to say (European): "Just wait till we get you back to the [insert name of appropriate, intimidating European stadium]."
Least likely to say (both): "Credit where it's due. United are a cracking team."

52 MANCHESTER UNITED v MANCHESTER CITY

MANCHESTER UNITED v MANCHESTER CITY 53

9 FEBRUARY 2003, v MANCHESTER CITY
United Review takes a satirical look at the types of fan making up the Old Trafford crowd. Which one are you?

31 DECEMBER 2005, v BOLTON WANDERERS
It's only midway through 2005/06 but such is the demand for season tickets that the club are already prompting fans to get their names on the waiting list.

SEASON TICKETS

EXCLUSIVELY AVAILABLE TO ONE UNITED MEMBERS NEXT SEASON!

To become a ONE UNITED member just call: 0870 442 1994 or visit www.manutd.com

ONE UNITED

The Official Manchester United Membership Scheme

BRANCH NEWS

REDS ON THE ROCK

Boss officially opens new home for Gibraltar branch

Gibraltar branch members welcome Sir Alex

Sir Alex made a special visit to Gibraltar this summer for the official opening of the local branch's new premises.

The manager was on hand to open the supporters' club's new home, situated in the Wellington Front area, and was joined on the trip by United legend Bryan Robson and the team's assistant manager Mike Phelan. The inauguration ceremony was attended by more than 500 branch members, together with chief minister of Gibraltar and branch patron, the Hon Peter Caruana (left), and branch chairman Clive Moberley (right in far left picture). A gala dinner to mark the occasion was later held in the magnificent setting of St Michael's Cave.

"It was a truly memorable occasion for all United supporters on the Rock," said Clive. "We were honoured to have Sir Alex, Mike and Bryan as our guests and we're delighted with our new home."

The branch was founded in 1993 and organises regular trips to Old Trafford so that members can see their heroes in action up close. As well as this, members get together to watch televised games, which they can now do in their new home.

For more detailed information on the branch, its committee members, special events and how to join, visit the website **www.manutd-gibraltar.com**

20 SEPTEMBER 2009, v MANCHESTER CITY

These days United's support is truly global with many international branches becoming extremely slick operations – much like the Gibraltar branch, who were delighted to receive a visit from Sir Alex Ferguson for the official opening of their new club house.

This is the section that is dedicated to you, the fans.

Read interviews, tackle our half-time teasers and find out supporter-related news. And play your part, too... Send us your high-resolution photos, birthday messages, fans stories and tributes to: unitedfamily@manutd.co.uk

Send your fan pics from yesteryear to unitedfamily@manutd.co.uk

Classic fan pic

Hey, it's Eric Cantona giving us a wave! Maybe not, but one Red is happy with life in May 1996 – United winning the Double no doubt helped, with King Eric reigning supreme.

Q&A: USAIN BOLT

The fastest man on the planet graced the OT pitch, met the players and still found time to speak to *United Review* about all things Red...

Bolt shows his colours and the winning time

You were introduced to the crowd before the Fulham game, but how much did you want to be out there playing in a United shirt?
It would have been nice! I always love going out on the pitch – who wouldn't, it's Old Trafford. It's always such a great feeling to walk out there. I can only imagine what it would be like to play on the pitch – I'm sure it would be a wonderful feeling.

We hear the manager has invited you to train with the team...
Yes, we had a good chat about it. It'll be great to see how the guys prepare for games because it's very different to track and field. And, as I've said before, I definitely want to come and give it a try because I think I'm good enough to play.

Where would you fit in and what would you bring to the team?
I've played football for most of my life and been involved in a lot of charity matches in Jamaica so I've got good enough experience. I can see myself on the wing – I think the other players would have a tough time catching me out there!

What have you made of United's summer signings? Van Persie (left) and Kagawa have certainly made a big impact already...
I think we have a great squad now. We have a lot of guys who can pass the ball very well in midfield and Valencia, Young and Nani on the wings are very dangerous – van Persie, Rooney and the other strikers are going to get a lot of chances to score, without a doubt. I think it's going to be a really good season for van Persie, especially.

Do you see a similar winning mentality in the manager and players to the one you have?
Absolutely. The hunger and desire to win is fantastic at this club. All the players want to win and you can see that even in the new players. Sometimes it can take time for them to settle, but ultimately all these players are winners.

Finally, how would you sum up the last few weeks following your Olympic success?
It's been very exciting and a great experience. There's been a lot of attention but lots of support from the fans over here, which has been brilliant. I've really enjoyed myself.

Win a United Family badge

Fancy getting your hands a woven United Family badge, like this one? Simply email unitedfamily@manutd.co.uk with the word BADGE in the subject line, including your name and postal address in the email, and if you're one of the first 30 people we'll send your own embroidered patch.

Fan messages

Happy 50th birthday to **Robert Walker** – lots of love from Claire, Ryan, John and Abbie.

Hello to eight-year old OT first-timer **Morgan Bamford**, cheering for the Reds today with his father Alfred.

Happy 10th birthday to **Barnaby Lewis**, at the Theatre of Dreams for the first time with father Paul, from Mark and Norma.

Manchester United v Wigan Athletic 27

15 SEPTEMBER 2012, v WIGAN ATHLETIC

As celebrity Reds go, few are as famous as sprinter Usain Bolt, who happily shared his passion for United on a visit to watch Sir Alex's side take on Fulham just weeks after his incredible success at the London Olympics. Seems he has an astute eye for a player, too, predicting big things for new signing Robin van Persie.

10 AUGUST 2018, v LEICESTER CITY

This Salford Red appeared as the fan in the *United Review* handshake for the opening month of the 2018/19 season, and happily talked about her enduring passion for the club.

"I'd be here every night if there was a match on!"

Meet **Brenda**, one of the club's most long-standing, loyal fans, who still goes to every game...

It doesn't take long in Brenda Doyle's company to realise just how staunchly she supports Manchester United. At 80 years old, she's still travelling the length and breadth of not only this country, but across Europe, too.

But probably the best example is, when we meet her at Old Trafford a couple of weeks before the start of the season, she spends minutes chastising her daughter, Jackie, for once going to Maine Road to watch a fun-day five-a-side competition. This was decades ago, but Brenda's not laughing.

It's little wonder. She's lived her whole life in Irlam and Peel Green, Salford, where United is virtually the law of the land. Brenda and her seven children are no exception. Enemy lines must not be crossed – unless United are playing, of course.

The love affair started in 1953, Brenda estimates. "I'd come with friends, but having my first baby at 18 in '57 cut it back a bit."

She was pregnant with her second when tragedy struck at Munich – a day that remains vivid in the memory.

"I was changing nappies in front of the coal fire, so I won't forget that! My dad come in at six and said: 'There's been a crash.' My mum worked in a cotton mill, and she fetched the paper. We just knew about the crash; we didn't know who had died or any of the other details."

Brenda speaks fondly of the era that followed, but nothing beats here and now.

"The late '60s and '70s was a great time, with George Best. And I loved [Bryan] Robson and [Ole Gunnar] Solskjaer. But I like it a lot now. I always had tiddlers with me in the past! I've got more freedom now."

"We go to all the games, even if it's just for the trip. It might be raining in Manchester! I don't drink though, unless it's a shandy," she insists, though later, Jackie does tell one frankly unprintable tale about a New Year's Eve Jagermeister session that resulted in the disappearance of Brenda's beloved Stone Island winter coat.

"I'd come every night if there was a match," she confesses, and only a serious bingo addiction competes with United as her favourite hobby.

Attending at 80 isn't without challenges, though. Two years ago, Brenda was run over, breaking every bone down her right side. Undeterred, she got a trolley to help her balance. At away grounds, sympathetic stewards would sneak her into disabled sections.

"If our Mark [son] had his way, he'd stop me going," she admits. But despite his well-intentioned concerns, he has a battle on his hands. "I just ask him if he'll give his beer up!"

"I just like being here," Brenda explains, and the new season can't come quick enough for this match-going juggernaut. "It's boring without it!"

Brenda adorns the famous handshake logo as we kick off our 2018/19 campaign, and (above) the Reds' superfan alongside her daughter Jackie

SEASON 2018/19

#allredallequal

CHAPTER 12

News and features

In an ever-changing world, *United Review*'s core duties of chronicling the club's exploits and connecting with the fans remain the same – in this chapter we celebrate some of its most newsworthy highlights...

Like Manchester United the football club, *United Review* has changed immensely during the last couple of decades or so. Whereas once the match programme was a way for the club to deliver information and messages to supporters, *UR* has developed to become a glossy magazine in its own right, full of huge amounts of detail, insight and exclusive material.

A cursory glance at early issues shows squad pictures, news of potential transfers and background profiles on players who may well have been heroes to United's fan base, but of whom little might have been known.

That probably seems unfathomable to young fans of today, who receive a daily social media feed from many of their favourite stars of the 21st century. But that was where *UR* stepped in back then: filling in the blanks when it came to the career histories and statistics of the first-team's top players.

Above: The programme's relationship with modern stars like Marcus Rashford is inevitably different to the dynamic from days gone by

Those profiles still make for fascinating reading today. For while the internet might be able to tell us everything about Marcus Rashford, many anecdotes about players from bygone eras have only been preserved on the printed media of the period. If you want to learn more about Joe Spence or Jack Rowley, you could do far worse than trawling through a stack of old *UR*s.

The other content of the era is spellbinding too, though for different reasons. From fan poems to cartoon sketches, *UR* reflects the different types of entertainment that thrilled previous generations at the match.

Entertainment is still very much the name of the game today, even now that fans are

Despite being a Manchester United superstar, players like Jack Rowley would have been mysterious figures to most supporters at the time

A young Red tucks into *UR* ahead of our 2019/20 curtain-raiser against Chelsea

much more clued-up on details about the players, helped by every United match being televised across the world.

The programme's duty is two-fold. Firstly, there is a responsibility to chart and celebrate the progression of United's players and teams. As this book highlights powerfully, *United Review* is an important documentation of the different stages of the club's life, and it is essential that continues. Secondly, it must provide insight and enjoyment to those fans reading on the day of the game. After all, while every match becomes history the moment it finishes, that's of no concern to the supporters that crave something engaging to read and pore over while supping their mid-match Bovril.

Thankfully, *United Review* is studded with just the kind of exclusive content that cannot be found elsewhere: interviews with first-team stars, features on United's rich history, important news and all the statistics and analysis a fan could want.

Whether the supporters picking up a copy are season ticket holders or merely attending their first match, *United Review* will fully immerse them in both the team's current travails and United's deep and entrancing history.

There's still all the useful information required – who has been nominated for Player of the Month, announcements of fixture changes, how many appearances a certain first-teamer has made to date – but really that's only scratching the surface.

Pick up a copy of *United Review* from a programme booth today, and you'll find in-depth writing, visually arresting infographics and enough quality to chew on for the journey home and way beyond.

Clubs and Players

Out of the welter of discussion at the meetings of the Football Association and The League emerged the following interesting items: —

The continuance of the war may prevent the opening of the season next September. In the event of the military situation taking a turn unfavourable to the Allies, football will be out of the question. No arrangements have been made for the International matches or the F.A. Cup Competition. If a commencement is made next season, the F.A. are invested with the power to suspend the game summarily.

Only players with existing agreements will receive summer wages. The others cannot receive pay between May 1 and August 2, the earliest date fixed for training. Although close-season wages have been abolished, clubs at the end of April are entitled to retain the services of players who have been offered in April an engagement at £3 per week for the following season.

The maximum wage will be £3 per week for the term of engagement only—that is, August 2 to April 29 inclusive—with an increase of 10s. per week for each two seasons of continuous service.

Starting with Monday, August 2, 1915, and ending with Saturday, April 29, 1916, there are to be 39 weeks in the next football season, and the maximum amount receivable by any player will be £117. The present maximum is £250, including summer wages, and the leading professionals who depend exclusively upon football for a living will thus have their incomes more than halved.

On their way to Cup final, Sheffield United beat four Lancashire clubs and one from their own county. This will not prevent them being received with rousing cheers from a largely Lancashire crowd when they make their appearance at Old Trafford. Each of the Cup finalists possesses a spacious enclosure at home, and the sumptuous arena of the Manchester United Club is greatly to the liking of both Sheffield United and Chelsea.

THE LEAGUE—First Division.

RESULTS TO MONDAY, MARCH 29 (Inclusive)

	Pld.	Won	Lost	Drn.	Goals For	Goals Agst.	Pts.
Oldham Athletic	31	15	7	9	64	48	39
Manchester C.	32	14	7	11	44	32	39
Blackburn Rovers	32	16	10	7	71	50	39
Sheffield Wednesday	33	13	8	12	56	48	38
Everton	31	15	9	7	66	40	37
Sunderland	31	16	12	3	69	61	35
Sheffield United	30	12	7	11	39	29	35
Bradford City	31	11	8	12	50	39	34
West Bromwich A.	32	12	10	10	39	31	34
Bradford	30	14	10	6	50	52	34
Middlesbrough	32	11	11	10	52	62	32
Burnley	30	12	13	5	48	42	29
Liverpool	32	10	13	9	54	65	29
Aston Villa	30	10	12	8	47	61	28
Bolton Wanderers	32	9	17	6	60	76	24
Tottenham Hotspur	32	7	15	10	49	75	24
Newcastle United	30	8	14	8	38	42	24
Manchester U.	30	6	13	11	37	48	23
Notts County	32	6	15	11	33	52	23
Chelsea	29	5	12	12	36	49	22

2 APRIL 1915, v LIVERPOOL

Serious business was being discussed by the FA and reported on in the programme, as the developing 'military situation' took its toll on football.

Soldiers take in a match at Old Trafford in April 1915, before football was halted

15 SEPTEMBER 1923, v BURY

The programme editor had plenty to say about the ugly scenes that marred United's away game with local neighbours Bury...

2 Manchester United Programme.

Play and Players

A "NASTY" MATCH—UNPLEASANT SCENES AT BURY—OUR FIRST DEFEAT—A PROMISING RECRUIT.

We met with our first defeat at Bury and thereby lost a point compared with last season, when the result at Gigg-lane was a draw of two goals each. We all fervently hope that last week's result will be reversed to-day.

But all true sportsmen will hope that the unpleasant scenes witnessed at Bury will not be repeated. If they are I feel sure that some official action will be taken by those whose duty it is to purge the game from malpractices on the field just as they see that their regulations in club management are respected and strictly observed.

Old Trafford spectators have a splendid reputation, and I look with confidence to them retaining it. Maybe the spectators at Bury had something to do with the "bother," but to be perfectly candid the chief blame rests with the players, and no amount of "white-washing" can alter the fact.

It is not for me to try and apportion the blame for what happened at Bury as between our players and those of Bury. There were stupid indiscretions on both sides.

WILL NOT BE TOLERATED.

The plain fact is too much temper was shown. Footballers, we know, are only human, and the desire for revenge may be strong. But the desire to be good sportsmen should rise superior to this, and I hope that on both sides any bitterness of feeling will be left in the realms of things forgotten when the twenty-two players trip on to the field this afternoon.

I am perfectly certain that the F.A. and the League will not tolerate scenes calculated to bring the game into disrepute. They would be unworthy of their great trust if they did. A skilful, clean, and sportsmanlike game to-day will go a long way towards wiping out the memory of last week's happenings.

I hope, therefore, that the players of both sides will realise their responsibilities to the game, their club, and their own personal reputations. The spectators—our own and those of Bury—I urge to refrain from incitement to wrong-doing. By doing so they will enjoy the game all the better.

THE INNOCENT SUFFER.

In football, as in every other walk of life, the ill disposed can easily invent an excuse for his evil doing. Quarrelsome and tyrannical persons always have a ready plea for their misconduct. But it is a truth universally acknowledged that, sooner or later, punishment overtakes the wrong-doer.

It is true that the most quiet and timid natures may become exasperated into efforts of retaliation and revenge, and it often happens in connection with football that the innocent suffer for the wrong-doing of others. When players lose their tempers and roughness develops, the men chiefly responsible often escape at the expense of a colleague whose play has been above reproach.

I am writing, of course, of football generally and not of last Saturday's match in particular. Viewed from every standpoint rough play is unprofitable. Football can be fast and vigorous, but yet remain clean.

Our defeat at Bury was frankly disappointing, and so was the play, which suffered very badly by comparison with that at Southampton the previous Monday. We had chances early on to have gained what might easily have proved a winning advantage.

Opportunities neglected seldom return, and it may be that we have not yet struck our best forward line combination. The goal scored by Amos was a wonderful effort, and as it was close on time when Bullock got the second goal the even nature of the game is easily realised.

F. M'PHERSON, Manchester United.

FORWARD OF PROMISE.

The Central League team restored themselves to favour by defeating Bury Reserve 2—0 at Old Trafford, the goal-scorers being Whittle and David Bain. The former, an amateur from the Little Lever district, created a very favourable impression. In fact, I have heard him described as not far removed from the best inside forward on the club's books.

David Bain also scored two goals and Spence one at Barrow on Monday, when we paid the Furness club a visit in connection with the transfer of M'Pherson. With four goals Bain is thus "top-scorer" of both teams.

Next Wednesday there is an interesting cup-tie at Old Trafford. In the second round of the Lancashire Cup we entertain Stockport County. The kick-off is at 4-30, and as both of us will field strong sides the game should be a capital one.

3 Manchester United Programme.

SUPPORTERS' CLUB.

The Supporters' Club continues to make good progress, but the membership roll is a long way from being full. Those desirous of joining can obtain the necessary forms at the refreshment room behind the grand stand near the public bar after the match.

The general meeting of the Supporters' Club is to be held on **Thursday evening next, September 20,** at 7 p.m., in the Packers' Hall, Sorton-street, Charles-street, off Oxford-road, at which the balance-sheet will be read, and in addition to transacting the business usual on such occasion, opportunity will be given to all members to "air their opinions" on matters relating to the Club.

The Supporters' Club have a mascot, who is only four years old, but the umbrella is in need of attention from a dry cleaner.

A great charabanc outing to Oldham on October 6. The accommodation is rather limited, and those who intend going should book their seat without delay. The Supporters' Club again contemplate organising whist drives and dances, which proved a big success last season.

MISSED A TREAT.

The only disappointing part about the visit of the "Hearts" on Wednesday evening was the attendance, but those who did assemble felt well repaid for their visit.

If the game lacked the excitement incidental to a League match, it produced football of a very high standard. The result 2—2 is of little or no consequence, but the play was fascinating to all who like to see the real arts of football.

Lochhead's goal I heard described by an expert as "the finest I shall see this season." Lochhead, indeed, played a capital game, and Ellis has not been so conspicuous since he came to Old Trafford. Mann scored our other goal and Welsh the two for the "Hearts."

Our supporters are not to be congratulated on their lack of judgment in missing so delightful a game.

THE EDITOR.

FIRST TEAM—SEASON 1924-25

Top Row (left to right): J. PULLAR (*Trainer*), A. W. LOCHHEAD, J. SILCOCK, A. STEWARD, C. MOORE, J. B. GRIMWOOD, C. G. HILDITCH.
Bottom Row: F. D. MANN, J. W. SPENCE, T. SMITH, F. BARSON (*Captain*), W. HENDERSON, F. MACPHERSON.
Inset: Mr. J. A. CHAPMAN (*Secretary and Manager*).

Supplement to MANCHESTER UNITED PROGRAMME, *Jan. 1st*, 1925.

1 JANUARY 1925, v CHELSEA

A look at the United squad for the 1924/25 season, who were to gain promotion from Division Two.

FREE PHOTOS.

I am sure our supporters will welcome the photographic supplement to this issue of the programme. They are an excellent reproduction, as I think all will agree, and should be well worth framing.

This programme covers both New Year matches with Chelsea and Stoke, so that anyone unable to obtain a programme on Thursday will be able to do so on Saturday.

Many may have friends abroad or in other parts of the country who follow very closely the doings of United, and who would greatly appreciate the photographs if sent to them.

CENTRAL LEAGUE TEAM—SEASON 1924-25

Top Row (left to right): E. PARTRIDGE, J. ASTLEY, S. R. BENNION, F. JONES (*Asst. Trainer*), G. HASLAM, J. BAIN, Mr. G. H. DALE, and Mr. W. R. CRICKMER (*Asst. Secretary*).
Middle Row: S. EVANS, C. TAYLOR, J. W. MEW, J. HANSON, F. KENNEDY, H. THOMAS.
Bottom Row: S. H. DAVIES, T. JONES.

Supplement to MANCHESTER UNITED PROGRAMME, *Jan. 1st* 1925.

The first programme of 1925 also carried a picture of United's reserve squad, clad in their distinctive chevrons.

26 FEBRUARY 1927, v BOLTON WANDERERS

This programme for a visit of Bolton included an in-depth profile of United trainer John Pullar, as well as detailed analysis of the trainer's role at a club.

4 Manchester United Programme.

PORTRAIT GALLERY — JOHN PULLAR

A POSITION in connection with a football club that demands very high qualities is that occupied by JOHN PULLAR, our trainer. It does not need great scholastic attainments, but it is essential that the man holding it has a sound knowledge of the human body, and be a close student of human nature in all its aspects.

He must, too, possess a sound body himself, and set a high standard of physical fitness. A weakling could not do the "rubbing down" which players must receive both in their daily training and after matches.

The advice on physical fitness which a trainer gives to his men would fall on "stoney ground" unless the trainer himself "practiced what he preached," and

by personal example and conduct won the respect and confidence of those placed in his charge.

Football trainers do not figure very much in the public limelight. To many they are merely "men with the magic sponge," and it is indeed often surprising what "wonders" the application of this sponge performs.

Personally, I think there is no keener spectator than a trainer. He is always in a way "looking for trouble." No sooner a man goes down he is ready with his sponge. There are few better judges of a player than a trainer, especially one, who like Pullar, has a sound and thorough knowledge of the game from personal experience.

Another quality which the successful trainer must possess is tact. Without it, and an even temper, failure is as certain as night follows day. It may be far-fetched to assert that a first-class trainer can make a first-class team.

If that were so, I am satisfied we should be on top of the League and in the running for the Cup, for I doubt if any club is better served in this respect. It cannot, however, be doubted that a good trainer is a very valuable asset, and that a bad, or even an indifferent one, can go a long way towards wrecking a good team.

The successful trainer, whilst being a strict disciplinarian, must avoid any suggestion of "bullying." He must do all he can to make training a pleasure; to avoid his men getting stale. It can truly be said that a very good spirit prevails in our training camp, and John Pullar has proved himself a worthy successor to Fred Bacon, Harry Taylor, and Alfred Nelmes.

A trainer's life has more than a fair share of trials and troubles. There have been times, especially in our Second Division days, when Pullar has done real "hard labour" to get players fit. No one could have been keener than he to "get out" of Division II., and the achievement when it came about found him as happy as a schoolboy.

The acquisition of new players is not a trainer's business. Everybody will agree that Pullar has done well with the material provided him, and many of our players have benefitted from the advice he has given them.

Pullar, I think, has the confidence of the directors and the players. He came to Old Trafford during the war period as assistant trainer, and when Nelmes left for Brighton, was appointed to his present position. Few people who have met him would recognise in Jack Pullar a Scot.

Yet the fact remains that he was born at Edinburgh, but at the early age of 18 months he was brought to Lancashire, his place of residence being Salford. As a youth Pullar played full back for Springfield Athletic in the Manchester League, and for Eccles Caucasians in the Manchester Federation.

Later he assisted Eccles Borough and Eccles United, his partner being Peter Boyle, the old Sheffield United back. It was on Peter's advice that Pullar took up training, and for a time he was player-trainer at Eccles.

Among those who passed through his hands there was Peake, who went to Bury; Kay, who led West Ham to promotion and to the first Cup-final at Wembley; Tommy Lucas, of Liverpool; Eddie Connor, and Albert and Peter Fairclough. [Continued on Page 7.

TOPICS OF THE DAY.

"BILL" HOGG AS COACH: BRADFORD CITY DELIGHT: EVERTON'S RECORD ATTENDANCE: GIBSON OR DR. MILNE?: BLACKPOOL'S CAPTURE: FORMER CITY GOALKEEPER: BARNSLEY DENY A RUMOUR.

SUNDERLAND have appointed William Hogg as coach to the team, and he commences his duties this week. Hogg is a native of Sunderland, and when playing for the Wearsiders at outside right gained International honours.

⊙ ⊙ ⊙

Bradford City people are highly satisfied with W. Summers from St. Mirren.

⊙ ⊙ ⊙

At the Everton v. Liverpool match there was a record attendance of 64,000, the receipts being over £4,100.

⊙ ⊙ ⊙

It isn't generally known that Pat Hunt, one of Hamilton Academical's best players, is English-born.

⊙ ⊙ ⊙

J. M'Dougall, Airdrieonian's centre half-back, may go to Liverpool.

⊙ ⊙ ⊙

J. M'Nab, Dundee's right half-back, may be transferred shortly.

⊙ ⊙ ⊙

It is the opinion of Manager Maley, of the Celtic F.C., that greyhound racing will never harm football.

⊙ ⊙ ⊙

It is on the cards that Bradford City will make a request for the transfer of R. Skinner, centre-forward, of Dunfermline Athletic.

⊙ ⊙ ⊙

Jimmy Gibson tells his old manager in Glasgow that he likes Birmingham, but would be better pleased if Aston Villa would play him at centre half. But is Dr. Milne a wing half?

⊙ ⊙ ⊙

Mathieson is keeping goal finely for Middlesbrough. The Scottish selectors are not losing sight of the fact.

⊙ ⊙ ⊙

Cardiff City were charmed with the play of Tom M'Inally at Celtic Park last week. He would be welcomed at Ninian Park.

⊙ ⊙ ⊙

An expert has valued at £20,000 the forward line that played for the Scottish League against the Irish League at Belfast.

Dundee have secured the transfer of Gus Smith, an inside forward from Ebbw Vale, who has proved a prolific goal-scorer.

⊙ ⊙ ⊙

Nelson have transferred their centre-forward, James Hampson, to Blackpool for a substantial figure. The Nelson club were loth to part with this player, but owing to their gates dwindling to a low ebb they have been forced to transfer him. Hampson, who is a native of Little Hulton, came originally as an outside left.

⊙ ⊙ ⊙

Willie Harper has taken the place of Tom Blair as goalkeeper to the Fall River (U.S.A.) team. The latter has been transferred to Hartford F.C. Blair is the former Manchester City goalkeeper.

⊙ ⊙ ⊙

Both Sheffield League clubs—United and Wednesday—are out to strengthen their sides, and are on the look out for players.

⊙ ⊙ ⊙

Hearts are understood to be after a fine centre-forward named David Brown, a real Yank, who leads the attack of the New York Giants.

⊙ ⊙ ⊙

Harry Callaghan, Leicester City's new man from Scotland, isn't a Scot. He was born in India.

⊙ ⊙ ⊙

It is stated by the Barnsley Football Club that there is no truth in the rumour that they contemplate parting with Brook, their young outside left, for whom, it is said they have been offered £6,000.

MANCHESTER UNITED PRIZE BAND

PROGRAMME FOR TO-DAY

"GARLAND OF CLASSICS."

"SO BLUE."

"ROSES OF REMEMBRANCE."

"SIDE BY SIDE."

"SHALIMAR."

Conductor - - - - W. C. MATHER.

22 OCTOBER 1927, v DERBY COUNTY

Readers of the programme in 1927 were kept abreast of footballing matters in this fascinating 'Topics of the Day' column.

Nº 2238

At half-time a board will be sent round with six numbers on. If the number of your programme corresponds, you are entitled to Two Free Seats. Apply with programme at the office after the game.

25 DECEMBER 1931, v WOLVES

Was this Christmas Day programme a winner for this United fan, we wonder...

MUSICAL PROGRAMME, CHRISTMAS DAY—Dec. 26th.

Arranged by Audible Advertising Ltd., 7, Grosvenor Gardens, S.W.1.

1.—"The Way With Every Sailor." H.M.V. B.6100
Lewis Ruth's Band.
2.—"Minstrel Show of 1929." H.M.V. C.1739
Darktown Melody Makers.
3.—"Christmas Memories By The Fireside." Parlophone E.6234
Westfield's Orchestra.
4.—"Look In The Looking Glass." H.M.V. B.6099
Johnny Hamp's Orchestra.
5.—"Swastika March." H.M.V. B.3459
Coldstream Guards.
6.—"This Is The Day Of Days." H.M.V. B.6091
New Mayfair Orchestra.
7.—"Savoy Hunting Medley." H.M.V. B.6089
New Mayfair Orchestra.
8.—"The Mocking Bird Went Cuckoo." H.M.V. B.3968
Gracie Fields.
9.—"Poet And Peasant." H.M.V. B.3980
Arthur Meale and Organ.
10.—"Three Little Times." Decca E.2681
J. Hylton's Orchestra.

The musical playlist – as seen here in the same Wolves programme – is a part of matchday that still remains.

TOPICS OF THE DAY.

MIDDLESBROUGH SATISFIELD?: CARDIFF FAILING: PETER BELL RETURNS: FLETCHER'S NEW ROLE: A LITTLE WELSH VILLAGE.

Considering that they were the wooden spoonists of the First Division, and next season will have to play in the Second Division, it is surprising to find that Middlesbrough are the only first-class club who have not signed a new player during the close season!

* * *

Now that he has had a little experience, Portsmouth are expecting big things of young Weddle, the centre-forward who did so well towards the close of last season. Weddle is another product of the Durham playing fields, and must surely be one of Manager Jack Tinn's best finds.

* * *

English League clubs are scouring Wales again. Bradford City have signed Trevor Edmunds, a young Cardiff boy, who last season scored 57 goals for Aberdare Reserves. What were Cardiff City thinking of?

* * *

After a spell in England with Manchester City, outside-right Peter Bell has returned to Scotland to play for Falkirk. Bell first became known when he was with Willington Athletic. Oldham took him in hand, and after a while passed him on to Darlington. He later crossed the Border to join Raith Rovers, only to come over again to Manchester.

* * *

If Manchester Central had scoured up and down the country they could not have hit upon a better man to train and coach them than Eli Fletcher, the old Manchester City full-back. Eli is the hero of many an historic battle, in which Manchester City have been one of the chief participants, and a better tactician in defensive play never donned a football jersey.

* * *

Geo. Duckworth, the Lancashire wicket-keeper, did not share the optimism of his colleagues that he would be invited to go out to Australia with the M.C.C. team. So little did the little Warrington man fancy his chance that he now owes another member of the side £10.

* * *

It is stated that the Welsh village of Llanfairpwllgwyngyllgogerychwyrndrobwll-llan, etc., etc., is to have a football club next season. Bennion, Williams, Jones, or Thomas will pronounce it for you!

25 AUGUST 1928, v LEICESTER CITY

Transfer talk was a popular topic of conversation a century ago... no doubt Boro fans weren't happy with this state of affairs!

Manchester United Portrait Gallery

Bremner's Press Agency

No. 5. JOE SPENCE

The Editor asked, " Who shall go in this week ? " and echo answered, " Give it to Joe." Where did that slogan start ? It was in March, 1926 at Bramall Lane, Sheffield. Joe was playing for United against City. The game was going badly and the crowd yelled, " Give it to Joe."

His life story :

Went down the mine at 13 and played football in spare time. Professional career began with Scotswood club. Army 1917—helped to win the Battalion League Championship. On March 29th, 1919, Jack Robson brought him to Manchester. International honours 1927 (England v. Ireland). In League games, Joe has scored 140 goals for United.

Joe Spence is fearless and robust—believes that inside forwards are the pivot of the game—has faith in United. He says, " We're going to get to the top again."

15 JANUARY 1932, v BRADFORD PARK AVENUE
A profile of United legend Joe Spence, in which the writer riffed on the famous phrase oft-shouted by the fans of the time... 'Give it to Joe!'

Joe Spence is still no.10 in United's all-time appearance list

4 FEBRUARY 1933, v OLDHAM ATHLETIC
Plenty to digest in this column, with the editor dishing it out to the London press corps and their 'boastings' following a United victory over Spurs; and paying tribute to 'our friends the City'.

WHAT *WE* THINK!

RIDING WITH SPURS.

WHEN in our last issue I said that in spite of pessimistic prophecies by journalistic Jeremiahs, all things were possible, I had more faith than I fancied. Little did I think that my bold brave words would gain an immediate confirmation in a victory over the Spurs which was remarkable in its way as the historic victory of Walsall over Arsenal. I had been hypnotised by the boastings of the London Press and quite believed that the Spurs had got into the habit of picking up 6—0 victories, or as one boosting punster said—" they're tottin' 'em up." No criticism of the game can detract from the glory of the victory.

We are all glad that the Manchester Press gave an encouraging pat on the back to Manley. The strength of a Club must always be estimated by the strength of its reserves. The arrival of this promising recruit from the reserves is a very good sign.

A MIGHT AND " MAINE " GAME

I was privileged to be the guest of a Director at the Cup-tie last Saturday between our friends the City and Walsall the giant killers. On Friday night the Manchester press was confident of a win for City. And so it proved. In all that constitutes essential football, City was delightfully superior. Walsall was full of pluck and maintained a desperate defence well served by the goalkeeper ; but they were outplayed. The referee inexorably maintained the etiquette of First Division play and allowed no Cup manners. This gave the illusion of severity against Walsall and perhaps it was Spartan discipline to send Reed off the field. However, it must not be supposed that the game was played with bad spirit. Walsall were beaten, but not dishonoured. But their brief spurt of glory was ended . . . .*by Manchester!* Good Luck City.

GRIM WORK AT GRIMSBY.

I was sorry to learn that Mr. Stacey Lintott was prevented by 'flu from attending the game at Grimsby. One depends so much on his judgments. All sportsmen will be wishing him a speedy recovery. Judging from the morning papers it was a queer game with honours uneasy. The team that removed the spurs from Tottenham just managed to draw with a team struggling to avert relegation. United put the ball through twice, but one was deducted for offside. Stewart tasted the goal-scorer's joy for the first time. A queer game—witness these :—

" The game had been a very lethargic affair." (D.D.)

" Play in the first half was always exciting." (M.G.)

" Ridding was left to plough a lonely furrow . . . ." Grimsby stuck valiantly to their guns . . . ." (D.D.)

" Tweedy (the goalkeeper) received a kick on the jaw and was carried off like a knocked-out boxer. . . . Somebody on the Grimsby side thought that retaliation was necessary . ." (M.G.)

For the rest, McDonald played with great enthusiasm and collided with Tweedy ; and Ridding was seized (like Reid in a famous incident) with paralysis of the foot when a goal was dead certain. Both teams retired carrying away a rather bedraggled point.

ARSENAL AND UNITED !

Councillor Thomson lunched with the Chairman of the Arsenal on Wednesday last and went on to Bolton to see the victory over the Wanderers. The game made one realise that Arsenal is a great team.

PHYSICAL PLUCK—A FOOTBALL WRITER'S KNOCK

A Manchester football journalist honoured me last Saturday evening by extensive quotations from this page. He quoted it as " official." It is hardly that. The Directors are not to be committed by opinions expressed here.

Our friend (whose writings I always study) waxed gently sarcastic about my optimism, accusing me of achieving promotion—in print ! But it was clear that I was not imitating so much of football journalism by indulging in dogmatic prophecy. I merely maintained the obvious principle that since nothing is impossible to human nature, then it is *not impossible* to achieve promotion. As if to justify my words, a few hours after the publication of them, *United beat the Spurs*—in spite of the prophecies of the entire press. How's that, sir ?

Then this sportsman fell from grace. He went on to say, " the same writer tried to tell the truth." This is clumsy and offensive. Honest men do not *try* to tell the truth—*they tell it*. A mistaken opinion is not an untruth. Somehow I am reminded of the saying of a great judge :

" Paternity is a matter of opinion ; maternity is a fact."

Here are the exact words which appeared in this evening paper.

The same writer tried to tell the truth. He spoke of United's players going down dauntlessly, fighting until the light faded.

I say that that is not accurate criticism.

With more physical pluck on the part of some of the players, United would have been well on the way to promotion by now.

Well, well, as one who likes to sit in utmost comfort to watch players being knocked about by hefty athletes, I am not so eager to talk about physical pluck. But, of course, I admire the writer's pluck . . . . in print ! Perhaps he confuses disinclination to tackle and cowardice. Perhaps we know what he was awkwardly struggling to say. I notice that referees (foolish fellows) seem determined to curb exuberance in physical pluck. Personally I too feel disinclined to tackle our friend—I prefer to do a bit of passing . . . to Mr. A. Scott Duncan.

Apropos of nothing at all, is there not a famous poem by Walt Whitman which begins :

" O Captain ! My Captain ! our fearful trip is done."

S.F.W.

Page 7

Manchester United Football Club Ltd.

OLD TRAFFORD, MANCHESTER

1933 — 1932

Chairman: Mr. J. W. GIBSON

Directors: Colonel G. WESTCOTT — Mr. MATTHEW M. NEWTON

Councillor A. E. THOMSON — Mr. HUGH SHAW

Secretary: W. R. CRICKMER — *Manager:* A. SCOTT DUNCAN

TELEPHONE TRAFFORD PARK 0112 and 0113

MAY 6th, 1933
NUMBER 33

Official Programme

PRICE TWOPENCE

Editor: Sidney F. Wicks — *Manchester Guardian* Buildings, Pall Mall, Manchester

Mr. A. SCOTT DUNCAN says Au Revoir

To-day, you and I are reviewing the past and wondering about the future. On another page the Editor is analysing the season's record, so I need not comment on that. One fact alone I wish to stress—out of 21 games played *away*, the team was only beaten nine times—a curious record. The team has played rather better away than at home.

But I want to pay a tribute to the loyalty of the supporters. At the beginning of the season they were buoyed up with hopes which were far too optimistic, and the failure to achieve promotion might have damped the enthusiasm of less keen sportsmen. Yet the gates have been wonderfully maintained. This proves that you realised the earnestness of the directors, and that you were confident of the future.

Years ago I played in England, and to-day I notice one difference in the game. The off-side law has influenced England more than Scotland. The game is much faster in this country, and the Scottish players introduced to Old Trafford have had some difficulty in adapting themselves. But I hope that next season they will prove the success of a judicious blend of the Scottish and English game. Play is so unceasing that it is not easy to weld together a team when a new player is introduced.

Success lies ahead, and if you will maintain your loyalty, you will be prouder than ever of your Club. There will be no faltering on our part. I look forward to meeting you again at the end of August.

A. SCOTT DUNCAN.

Page 3

"Photo by courtesy of Allied Newspapers, Manchester."

Mrs. GIBSON UNFURLS THE FLAG

With the sun shining blandly and amidst the enthusiastic cheers of supporters, Mrs. J. W. Gibson unfurled the new flag presented by the Ground Committee. Thus the season most happily began and the spirit of the occasion was soon reflected in the way the team played to a fine victory. There is nobody who is more concerned to make United's flag a flag of victory than the wife of our chairman. Those who are privileged to know her, think of a gracious lady who is wholeheartedly devoted to Manchester United. Supporters have in her a true friend and fellow "sportsman." We even venture to say that in the dark days of last season her never-failing confidence was a source of strength to our chairman. In the photograph, taken by the Allied Press, we see Mr. Gibson gazing up at the flag and wondering if all his dreams will come true. With such leaders the team should feel inspired. We know that supporters will rally round the flag.

Page 5

6 MAY 1933, v SWANSEA CITY
Manager Scott Duncan used the last programme of the season to address the United fans.

8 SEPTEMBER 1934, v BARNSLEY
A happy occasion captured as chairman James Gibson proudly unfurled the new United club flag.

BERT and th' ETERNAL TRIANGLE

When chatting at the Golden Crown
I saw Bert Barker, looking glum.
"What's up," I sez, "art feelin' down?
Here, Bill, fetch us a drop of rum."

"Eh, lad," he said, and took a sup,
"Hast sin mi missis? Ee, ba gum,
She's bowt a hat, an' bowt some shoes,
While ah've no brass ter buy mi rum."

So then he started on his tale:
"Last Sat'd'y," he moaned and said
"I'd 'ad a pinter two of ale;
It must 'a gone up to mi 'ead."

"Now ah were goin' up to see
Bradford and t' United play;
But wife sez, 'Bert,' she sez ter me,
'Yer drunk—no match fer *you* to-day.'

"She locks me in an' meks me chop
Some sticks, an' mend the rockin' chair;
I tell thee, I felt fair ter drop,
So narked ah were; 'ee, did ah swear!"

"An' then when t'next game came around
(Them Barnsley lads was playin' then)
Ah felt ah must get on that ground
And see t' United play agen."

"And so ah sez, 'Ah'm wukkin' late
'A Sat'd'y, lass, up at the mill.'
'That's reet,' she sez, 'at any rate
Tha'll get more brass. Ah, That tha will.'

"And so ah goes to t' Trafford match,
An' sees us whack them Yorkshire gumps,
An' gets whoam late, an' lifts the latch,
An' out into t' back kitchen stumps."

"T' wife were theer. She sez, 'Eh, lad,
Tha' must 'a wukked quite 'ard to-day.'
Ah tells thee, ah felt really bad,
Deceivin' of 'er in that way."

"When Monday come ah thowt 'twas reet,
T' missis, ah thowt, 'ad never 'eard.
That neet ah whistles down our street,
As 'appy as a singin' bird."

"Ah starts to say 'ow tired I am,
An' feels quite 'ero-like, tha' knows.
Then t' missis snorts an' sez, 'Yer sham,
Yer lyin' hog; yer great rednose.'

"She points at *Chronicle* an' shouts,
'Tha' *does* wuk 'ard, mi pretty man;
You an' yer gang o' beery louts!
Now say tha's wukkin'—if tha can.'

"An' theer a football crowd gawped out
('Win a guinea,' t' headline said)
An' theer so plain tha couldna doubt—
Me wi a triangle round mi 'ead."

"Wull, that were that! The missis sends
And gets the brass beneath 'er thumb.
So 'ere I am, and 'ere's thee lends
Me fo'pence for a drop a' rum."

H. N. B.

Page 6

12 SEPTEMBER 1934, v BOLTON WANDERERS
A unique take on one fan's matchday experience (United beat Barnsley 4-1, by the way!)

18 SEPTEMBER 1935, v HULL CITY
The fan's obsession with statistics is by no means a modern-day invention...

FUN WITH FIGURES

Cynics say that "statistics can be made to prove anything." This may be so where the simpler types of mankind are concerned, but as far as football fans are concerned—no sir! No football fan has ever been hoodwinked by a "cooked" goal average—but on the other hand a true one is a copper-bottomed argument that may just be enough to convince the opposition.

Once you start keeping charts and tables, the habit grows on you, and may become almost an obsession. But no one can deny that the hobby is interesting.

At first, it is wisest to concentrate on one or two of one's favourites—say one team in each division. Later one's scope can be enlarged. (We know of one enthusiast who used to spend half his week-end plotting out a complicated position chart for every team in the First and Second Divisions).

Here are a few of the most interesting ways of carrying out this little hobby.

1. THE FIXTURE LIST.

This is a sheet containing a complete list of fixtures for the season for the team in question. After the date and the name of the opposing team come the following details. (a) Home or Away. (b) Goals for. (c) Total goals for season. (d) Goals against. (e) Total goals against for season. (f) Points. (g) Position. (h) Goal average. From these data can be plotted the following charts.

2. PROMOTION & RELEGATION CHART.

This chart was invented by Mr. S. F. Wicks, and is probably well-known to all United supporters by now. Briefly: the progress of the team is shown by a line plotted on a piece of squared paper according to points gained in each match. Two lines run across the chart (promotion line and relegation line), and the position of the "team line" in relation to these shows the prospect of the team, and the fortunes of the whole season. We shall start this chart again in Saturday's programme as a regular feature.

3. GOAL AVERAGE CHART.

In this, the goal average (in 20 divisions, numbered 0, .1, .2, etc., up to 2.0) is plotted against "games played," and provides an interesting commentary on the goal-scoring power of the forward line.

4. POSITION CHART.

Here, position is plotted against "games played."

It will be seen that all the charts mentioned must have as one of their essentials "games played." Thus, if a suitable scale can be evolved, all the activities of the club can be shown on one piece of squared paper. It goes without saying, that if one of these "hold-alls" is compiled every season, the enthusiastic supporter has at his finger-tips accurate and graphic evidence of his club's fortunes that will bring him out top-dog in the toughest football argument.

H.N.B.

PROMOTION CHART ONCE MORE!

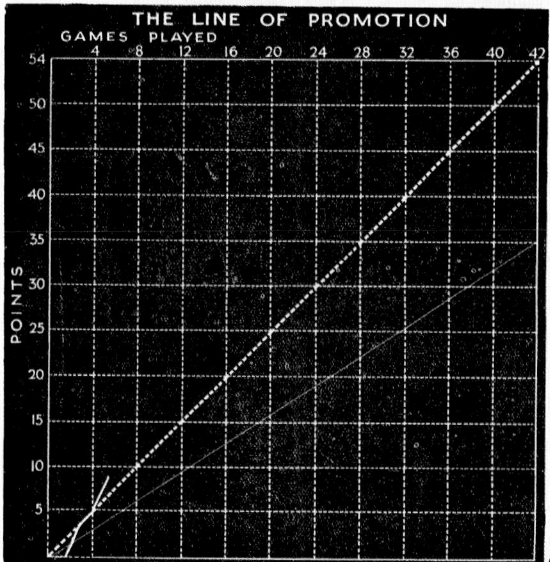

This is how it works: The figures along the top represent games; the figures vertically on the left hand represent points. The theory is that five points per four games represents promotion form. The diagonal line (in thick dots) shows the line of promotion; the lower thin line shows the line of relegation. The zig-zag line tells you the story of Manchester United's progress.

Page 13

21 SEPTEMBER 1935, v TOTTENHAM HOTSPUR
United fans were desperate to see the club get out of Division Two, so programme editor Sidney Wicks invented this chart to track our ongoing progress...

1 FEBRUARY 1936, v SOUTHAMPTON
Pity the poor policeman who's officiating a football match in the middle of a blizzard!

Here is a record of the snow that was for so long a part of football.

Supporters evidently took the policeman for the referee. It looks as if there are possible recruits for the forward line among the crowd—judging by the accuracy of the snowball shots registered in the goal of the bobby's back.

"This photograph is reproduced by courtesy of the 'Manchester Evening Chronicle' (Football Edition)."

A Supporter Caricatures Bamford

We have pleasure in publishing another clever caricature—by Alex. R. Wade, whose work as a commercial artist does not depress his enthusiasm as a United Supporter. He expresses the earnestness and hard work of Bamford and the cannon-ball shot when he really gets his foot to the ball. The fortunes of football are queer. It happens that this picture appears on the very day on which Bamford is not found in his usual place. The change is obviously made as an echo of the many changes. This we know—there is nobody who hopes Ferrier will do well more than that good sportsman—Bamford.

16 NOVEMBER 1935, v WEST HAM UNITED
A supporter's submission of a caricature of United's Tommy Bamford, complete with trademark cannonball shot.

LONDON FRIENDS

Congratulate SCOTT DUNCAN

Mr. Scott Duncan has been gratified by a whole bunch of letters from London friends who felt moved to such admiration for our team at West Ham that they had to write about it. We have been privileged to see these letters and are able to quote from a few of them. They all show that residence in the great city does not destroy the sportsmanship learned at Old Trafford.

Mr. R. W. Proctor, of Tonbridge, Kent (born in Macclesfield), wrote: "Manchester teams usually lose in London. I was glad to see the tables turned at last. What struck me was the machine-like working of your team. I am hoping to see Manchester United in the First Division."

Mr. G. White writes from Poplar: "I think Mutch is one of the best centre-forwards I have seen. I hope to see you at Highbury next season."

Mr. R. Booth (Greenford, Middlesex): "I used to attend United's home matches between 1920—1929, when I came to London. I had come to the conclusion the team was not worth watching. At West Ham I could hardly believe my eyes. The passing and combination was a revelation. I hope Mutch, Vose, McKay and Griffiths receive International Caps. I feel sure the United will carry off the Second Division Medal."

Mr. A. C. Hadley (Ilford): "Allow an Old United supporter to offer my heartiest congratulations on a great display. That defence will stop any team. Mutch—what a player, and Brown a great captain."

Mr. J. H. Wakeson (?) (Ilford): "I arrived home with my throat sore as it generally is when United is in London. Mutch and McKay played a great game. Now—no slips; we have a better chance than ever."

Mr. Scott Duncan and all the team are inspired by these letters. They show that United has friends everywhere. Our team simply must line up to their friend's expectations.

14 MARCH 1936, v SWANSEA CITY
A recent 2-1 win for United against West Ham at Upton Park inspired many fans from the south to write in...

CITY GREETS UNITED

Dear Mr. Chairman,

On behalf of all at Maine Road I desire to express to yourself and players our best wishes for a successful season, your last in all probability, at this ground.

On the eve of normal football after seven years in the wilderness you appear to have a team capable of bringing honour to our city despite your war-time trials. May this promise be fulfilled to the utmost and may we keep you company in the "upper circle" next year.

Yours cordially and sincerely,
Robt. Smith (*Chairman*),
Manchester City F.C.

31 AUGUST 1946, v GRIMSBY TOWN
City's chairman welcomed United to their new temporary post-war home for the first league game of 1946/47.

19 DECEMBER 1936, v WEST BROMWICH ALBION
King George VI's reign began on 11 December 1936 following the abdication of Edward VIII, a moment covered in the pages of the programme.

THE KING'S BIRTHDAY

The different volumes of Manchester United Programme may be valued in years to come, and it would seem strange to those who turned up to-day's number if they found no record of the crisis through which the nation has just passed. In this Programme our job is to "play the game" and not to venture outside football, but as good sportsmen it only seems right to register our loyalty to the new King—King George VI.

King George has a very big job; he is the one symbol which unites not only the United Kingdom, but also the great Dominions overseas. The King, if we may say so in our own language, is not only the chairman of one football club, but of a whole League. His task is to set every team playing to win, and playing the game. A nation is very much like a football club with its chairman and directors and manager and players—and the supporters who contribute the enthusiasm and the gates. When all work together for one end without distinction of class or creed, then you have a great club.

May King George be the leader of a Great People.
A well-known writer affirms that he is British to the back-bone in the possession of the following qualities:—

His shyness, His love of home, His love of sport,
His kindly friendship, His love of fair play.

Well, we say bluntly, if that is true (and it is true) then it suits us. God Save the King!

This is written on the King's birthday. We wish him many happy returns of the day, and the coming of peace, employment and prosperity to all his subjects.

Page 3

UNITED ROLL CALL

Photo by Manchester Evening News

Here is the playing staff, at the University Ground, Fallowfield, when they reported for training on July 24th. Manager Busby is offering a few well-chosen words of advice, and judging by the expressions he has time for a little joke, too.

Left to right, front row: Mr. Busby, Tom Curry (trainer), McGlen, Walton, Crompton, Anderson, Worrall, Hanlon, Warner, Mitten and J. Murphy (coach).

Back row: Bill Inglis (assistant trainer), Pearson, Whalley, Buckle, Delaney, Collinson, Wassall, Carey, Chilton, Rowley and Aston.

First day of pre-season training following the league's resumption and a big day for new boss Matt Busby and coach Jimmy Murphy, as they plan for our season-opener against Grimsby.

Walter Crickmer Still Smiling

It is indeed like old times to see Walter Crickmer, our genial secretary, in his usual office. The war years have not left the marks upon him which we might have expected He was on police duty during the blitz and the station received a direct hit by a high explosive bomb. Walter was a lucky one who escaped alive. Also he has been doing tremendously strenuous and important work during the war—of which storage of Government supplies was not the least. In spite of these troubles and trials he is bubbling over with enthusiasm for the old team. His great grudge against the universe is that it has proved impossible to rebuild the stands—thus the games at Maine Road.

Also in the Grimsby issue, the programme editor took the opportunity to pay a warm tribute to club servant Walter Crickmer, who kept the club going during the wartime trials and tribulations.

14 SEPTEMBER 1946, v MIDDLESBROUGH
Columnist Tom Jackson profiled striker Jack Rowley, who went on to carve a place in United history with a mammoth 211 goals for the club.

SPOTLIGHT ON THE PLAYERS. No. 1—ROWLEY

This is the first of a series of sketches of United players specially contributed by *Tom Jackson.*

Jack Rowley comes from a footballing family. He and his two brothers, one with Notts County and the other with West Bromwich, owe their early interest in the game to their father, who, many years ago, was a goalkeeper with Walsall.

Jack was first "spotted" when he was 15 years of age by Major Frank Buckley. He had played for his town team and was a reserve for England boys.

He joined the Wolves ground staff and got his introduction to senior football through the "A" and Central League sides. Eventually he went on loan to Bournemouth. After five months Rowley was signed by United, in November, 1937, and played the rest of that season at outside left.

Later he was developed as an inside-forward, a position in which he has found great scope for his quick goal-scoring thrusts.

Jack Rowley served for six years with the South Staffordshire Regiment, and gained several honours with service teams. He has appeared with F.A. and other representative elevens, and in one war-time international—against Wales in 1944.

Now he has been chosen for the Combined XI which meets the F.A. side at Nottingham on September 18 in aid of the Willie Hall Fund.

He is 5 ft. 9 ins. in height, and weighs 12 st. 3 lbs.

Photo: Manchester Evening News
ROWLEY IN ACTION

8 NOVEMBER 1947, v HUDDERSFIELD TOWN
The *Manchester Guardian*'s H.D. Davies – known to his friends as Donny – was a regular contributor to the programme , often writing under the alias 'An Old International'. Here he recalled a Cup Final goal described as 'the most farcical ever scored'.

OUR GUEST SPORTSWRITER—**No. 6**

H. D. DAVIES

OF "THE MANCHESTER GUARDIAN"

GOALS WE REMEMBER

Rowley has long been known as one of the best shots in contemporary football. His technique is worth study, for it embraces just those elements which make it a model for youngsters to copy—balance, timing, controlled swing and the application of pure instep. No one can middle a ball with greater ease or precision than Rowley: few, if any, can loose a deadlier missile at goal. His "block-buster" against Aston Villa a fortnight ago was worth travelling miles to see. Providentially, Rutherford, the Aston Villa goalkeeper, was not in the line of fire on that occasion, or help might have been needed for a goalkeeper suffering from staved-in ribs and the prospect of becoming permanently humpbacked.

Rowley's shooting set one thinking of memorable goals on other occasions. There have been others who could hit 'em hard and hit 'em often. Once at Burnden Park when Sunderland were playing Bolton Wanderers, Charles Buchan swung his illustrious boot (and a mighty long swing it was) behind a perfect rolling pass from Cuggy, and helped it along at such a rate that it seemed a meteor, and not a football had caused the bulge that appeared at the back of the Bolton net. There now, we thought, that is the last word in murderous projectiles. But was it ? Soon after half time, the Welsh artist, Vizard, tied the Sunderland defence in knots with a snake-like dribble which brought him wriggling along the dead-ball line to within six yards of the Sunderland post. Glancing up, he saw Joe Smith's mighty limbs pounding along and heard the familiar husky " With you, Ted!" Back came the ball, placed to a nicety, and Smith hit it with all he had. To say that there was a flash and a detonation would be a pardonable over-statement of what really happened. In any case, it was the nearest football equivalent to a shattering explosion I have ever seen and I'll swear to this day that the Sunderland goal-mouth was temporarily smothered in dust. For Joe Smith believed, like Napoleon before him, that there was nothing like a " whiff of grape-shot " to cow the opposition.

Perhaps the most appropriate conclusion to this light-hearted survey—the goal which has strong claims to be regarded as the most farcical ever scored. It occurred in the second leg of a war-time Cup Final between Blackpool and Aston Villa. Someone had tripped the Aston Villa centre forward as he was going through, and as he lay on the ground squirming with vexation, he took an angry swipe at the ball with his clenched fist (this from about the penalty spot) and in the view of water polo experts at least, netted beautifully. It occurred to one of the Villa players standing by to claim a goal, and to the stupefaction of all concerned, the referee, after consulting that linesman who was officiating on the blind side of the incident, graciously allowed it. This is a sober account of what took place at Villa Park in broad daylight in the year of grace 1942. To say that laughter rang round the terraces for fully five minutes is an understatement. In the ears of one spectator at least it is ringing yet.

PAGE NINE

1 MAY 1948, v BLACKBURN ROVERS
A pictorial tribute to the staff and players who had contributed to United's second FA Cup triumph the week before at Wembley.

WHAT'S HAPPENING TO JIMMY ?

Photo: Manchester Evening Chronicle

Don't worry—it's all in fun. Billy McGlen takes Jimmy Delaney for a ride during loosening-up exercises a few days ago!

PAGE NINE

21 AUGUST 1948, v DERBY COUNTY
A spot of high jinks during training between team-mates Billy McGlen and Jimmy Delaney.

25 SEPTEMBER 1948, v ASTON VILLA
Two United stalwarts, Allenby Chilton and Johnny Carey, are given the sketch treatment by United fan Leslie Scott. Fans were encouraged to collect the set.

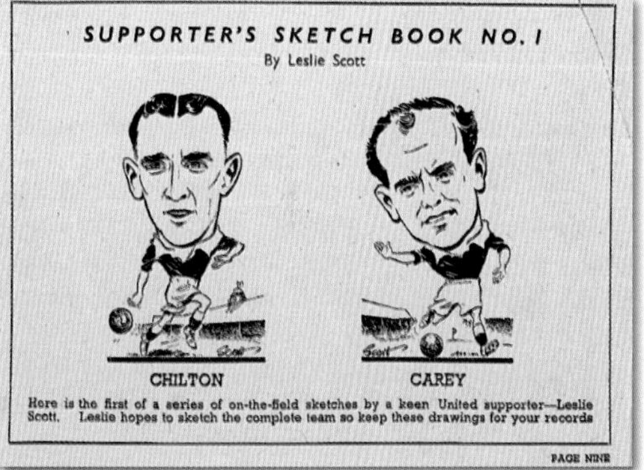

SUPPORTER'S SKETCH BOOK NO. I
By Leslie Scott

CHILTON CAREY

Here is the first of a series of on-the-field sketches by a keen United supporter—Leslie Scott. Leslie hopes to sketch the complete team so keep these drawings for your records

PAGE NINE

SPOTLIGHT ON THE PLAYERS—THIRD SERIES

By TOM JACKSON — *No. 6 MITTEN*

CHARLIE MITTEN, United's outside left, is proving the club's most consistent senior marksman so far this season—as well as an "expert" penalty-taker.

In recent games he has been at the peak of his form, notably against Everton a fortnight ago when he played a leading role in giving Ted Sagar one of his busiest afternoons!

Mitten, born in Rangoon, was discovered locally, and is one of many real Old Trafford products. At 16 he was on United's ground staff, helping in the office during the week and turning out for the "A" team at week-ends. In the R.A.F. during the war, he appeared in Services representative teams, and was also in demand as a coach in the Azores.

Last season he played in 38 League matches and all the Cup-rounds, and on one occasion showed possibilities as a goalkeeper when Crompton went off with an injury. Certainly he lacks nothing in enthusiasm, and can be equally as entertaining off the field, with his keen sense of humour.

Photo: Manchester Evening Chronicle

CHARLIE MITTEN

20 NOVEMBER 1948, v BIRMINGHAM CITY
For this programme against Birmingham, writer Tom Jackson turned his attention to Busby's wing wizard Charlie Mitten.

"UNITED THEY STAND"

Specially composed for the Review by Miss M. P. Wherrit— one of our loyal lady supporters.

A is for ASTON, he's first for the call,
B is for BOGAN for BIRCH and for BALL.
C stands for CROMPTON with COCKBURN so small,
with CAREY and CHILTON the biggest of all.
D for DELANEY and DOWNIE both clever,
E for their Energy lasting for ever.
F is for FEEHAN a player of note,
G is their ground which heavy bombs smote.
H is the Happiness in watching their play,
I for the inches they won't give away.
J is the jostle of crowds every week,
K is their keenness, just watch that technique!
L is for LOWRIE and LYNN just two more.
M for McGLEN and for MITTEN, fine score.
N is the noise of the rattles and cheers,
O their Opponents who go home in tears (?)
P is for PEARSON the one with nice hair,
Q for the Queues that wait for hours there.
R is for ROWLEY with thunderbolt shot,
S is the strength and the smoothness they've got.
T is for TIP-TOP, the best in the land,
U for UNITED, United they stand.
V is for Victory and Valour ne'er ceased,
W for WARNER, the last but not least.
X is for Xmas, three matches to play,
Y for the yells as they run the right way.
Z is for Zeal, they all show their worth.
Surely the grandest team here on the earth?

26 DECEMBER 1949, v ARSENAL
The programme has always carried fan submissions, as illustrated by this alphabetical guide to United from Boxing Day 1949, written by Miss M. P. Wherrit.

M.U.F.C. 1955-56 LEAGUE CHAMPIONS

Photo by courtesy of "The Provincial Press Agency"

Back row (left to right): E. Colman, W. Whelan, M. Jones, R. Wood, I. Greaves, D. Edwards.
Front row (left to right): J. Berry, R. Byrne, D. Viollet, T. Taylor, D. Pegg.

THE LEAGUE DIVISION I (As at 7th April)

	P.	W.	D.	L.	Goals F.	Goals A.	Pts.
MAN. UNITED	40	24	9	7	80	49	57
Blackpool ...	39	20	9	10	85	57	49
Birmingham C.	39	17	9	13	70	53	43
Manchester C.	38	16	10	12	72	60	42
Arsenal ...	39	16	10	13	56	58	42
Bolton Wand....	39	17	7	15	65	48	41
Wolves ...	37	16	8	13	74	58	40
Newcastle Utd.	40	17	6	17	82	66	40
Burnley ...	39	16	8	15	57	49	40
Luton Town ...	39	16	8	15	61	57	40
Portsmouth ...	39	16	8	15	75	79	40
Charlton Ath. ...	40	17	5	18	75	77	39
West Brom. A.	39	17	4	18	55	65	38
Everton ...	40	14	10	16	53	63	38
Sunderland ...	38	15	8	15	73	88	38
Preston N.E. ...	40	14	8	18	72	69	36
Cardiff City ...	38	14	7	17	52	67	35
Chelsea ...	39	12	10	17	55	74	34
Sheffield Utd. ...	37	12	8	17	54	62	32
Tottenham H. ...	37	13	6	18	54	63	32
Aston Villa ...	39	8	13	18	45	67	29
Huddersfield T.	39	11	7	21	45	81	29

Produced by SIDNEY F. WICKS LTD., 21 Newton Street, Manchester 1.
Printed at the Philips Park Press by C. NICHOLLS & COMPANY LTD.

25 APRIL 1956, v ALL STAR XI
This special programme for John Aston Snr's testimonial took the opportunity to pay tribute to Busby's recently crowned Division One champions.

23 AUGUST 1952, v CHELSEA
The season ahead for Matt Busby's reigning Division One champions, who kicked off their defence with a 2-0 win at home to Chelsea.

FIXTURES AND RESULTS

FOOTBALL LEAGUE
OLD TRAFFORD

1952			Results 1952-53 F	A	Results 1951-52 F	A
Aug. 23—Chelsea	H				3	0
,, 27—Arsenal	A				3	1
,, 30—Manchester City	A				2	1
Sept. 3—Arsenal	H				6	1
,, 6—Portsmouth	A				0	1
,, 10—Derby County	A				3	0
,, 13—Bolton Wanderers	H				1	0
,, 20—Aston Villa	A				5	2
,, 24—Newcastle Utd. (F.A. Charity Shield)	H				–	–
,, 27—Sunderland	H				0	1
Oct. 4—Wolverhampton W.	A				2	0
,, 11—Stoke City	H				4	0
,, 18—Preston North End	A				2	1
,, 25—Burnley	H				6	1
Nov. 1—Tottenham Hotspur	A				0	2
,, 8—Sheffield W.	H				–	–
,, 15—Cardiff City	A				–	–
,, 22—Newcastle United	H				2	1
,, 29—West Bromwich A.	A				3	3
Dec. 6—Middlesbrough	H				4	2
,, 13—Liverpool	A				0	0
,, 20—Chelsea	A				2	4
,, 25—Blackpool	A				2	2
,, 26—Blackpool	H				3	1
1953						
Jan. 1—Derby County	H				2	1
,, 3—Manchester City	H				1	1
,, 10—F.A. Cup 3rd Round.						
,, 17—Portsmouth	H				1	3
,, 24—Bolton Wanderers	A				0	1
,, 31—F.A. Cup 4th Round.						
Feb. 7—Aston Villa	H				1	1
,, 14—Sunderland (5th)	A				2	1
,, 21—Wolverhampton W.	H				2	0
,, 28—Stoke City (6th)	A				0	0
Mar. 7—Preston North End	H				0	2
,, 14—Burnley	A				1	1
,, 21—Tottenham Hotspur	H				2	0
,, 28—Sheffield W.	A				–	–
April 3—Charlton Athletic	A				2	2
,, 4—Cardiff City	H				–	–
,, 6—Charlton Ahtletic	H				3	2
,, 11—Newcastle United	A				2	2
,, 18—West Bromwich A.	H				5	1
,, 25—Middlesbrough	A				4	1
May 2—Liverpool	H				4	0

CENTRAL LEAGUE
OLD TRAFFORD

1952			Results 1952-53 F	A	Results 1951-52 F	A
Aug. 23—Blackburn Rovers	A				2	2
,, 27—Derby County	A				0	1
,, 30—Manchester City	H				2	2
Sept. 6—Everton	H				0	1
,, 10—Derby County	H				0	0
,, 13—Bolton Wanderers	A				0	1
,, 17—Barnsley	A				1	2
,, 20—Wolverhampton W.	H				1	3
,, 27—Huddersfield Town	A				1	2
Oct. 4—Aston Villa	H				3	1
,, 11—Liverpool	A				2	1
,, 18—Bury	H				2	0
,, 25—West Bromwich A.	A				0	3
Nov. 1—Leeds United	H				0	1
,, 8—Newcastle United	A				0	3
,, 15—Sheffield W.	H				1	1
,, 22—Chesterfield	A				0	1
,, 29—Stoke City	H				3	0
Dec. 6—Burnley	A				1	3
,, 13—Preston North End	H				4	0
,, 20—Blackburn Rovers	H				3	0
,, 26—Blackpool	A				2	4
,, 27—Blackpool	H				3	0
1953						
Jan. 3—Manchester City	A				1	3
,, 10—						
,, 17—Everton	A				0	1
,, 24—Bolton Wanderers	H				5	1
,, 31—Barnsley	H				0	0
Feb. 7—Wolverhampton W.	A				1	0
,, 14—Huddersfield Town	H				3	0
,, 21—Aston Villa	A				0	2
,, 28—Liverpool	H				6	1
Mar. 7—Bury	A				0	1
,, 14—West Bromwich A.	H				3	0
,, 21—Leeds United	A				2	1
,, 28—Newcastle United	H				1	1
April 3—Sheffield United	H				1	1
,, 4—Sheffield W.	A				0	2
,, 6—Sheffield United	A				0	1
,, 11—Chesterfield	H				4	0
,, 18—Stoke City	A				0	1
,, 25—Burnley	H				0	1
May 2—Preston North End	A				2	0

SCOREBOARD KEY, Saturday, 23rd August, 1952

LEAGUE DIVISION I		LEAGUE DIVISION II	
A	Aston V. v. Arsenal	N	Brentford v. Lincoln
B	Bolton v. Derby County	O	Doncaster v. Barnsley
C	Burnley v. Middlesbro'	P	Everton v. Hull City
D	Portsmouth v. Blackpool	Q	Fulham v. Bury
E	Preston N.E. v. Liverpool	R	Huddersfield v. Leeds Utd.
F	Sheff. Wed. v. Newcastle	S	Leicester City v. Notts C.
G	Stoke City v. Man. City	T	Notts. Forest v. Blackburn
H	Sunderland v. Charlton	V	Plymouth v. Luton
J	Tottenham v. West Brom.	W	Rotherham v. Birmingham
K	Wolves v. Cardiff City	X	Swansea v. Sheff. Utd.
		Y	West Ham v. Southampton

Edited by SIDNEY F. WICKS LTD., 14 Ridgefield, Manchester 2.
Printed at the Philips Park Press by C. NICHOLLS & COMPANY LTD

23 JANUARY 1954, v BOLTON WANDERERS
A focus on physio Ted Dalton, who at this point in the 1953/54 season had Allenby Chilton, Henry Cockburn and Colin Webster in his treatment room.

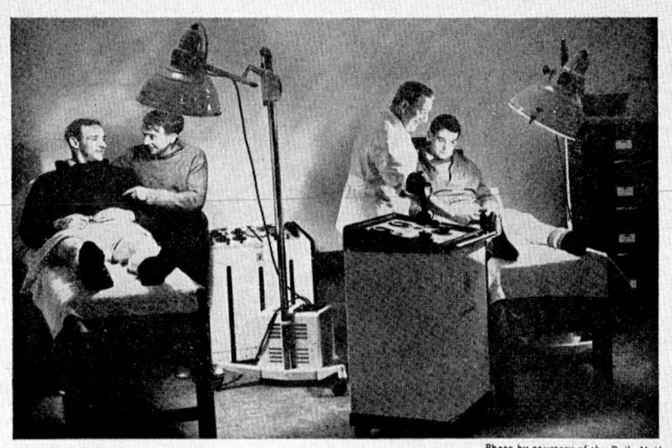

Photo by courtesy of the *Daily Mail*

All of us read about our soccer players and the knocks they get in the game. The phrase "So-and-so will have a fitness test next Friday" is all too familiar. But without in any sense minimizing the tumbles received, many a United player owes his speedy convalescence to our physiotherapist Ted Dalton. In the Old Trafford Medical Room pictured above we see Allenby Chilton talking to Henry Cockburn whilst receiving short wave dio-thermy treatment — note the pad across his thighs. On the right Ted Dalton administers heat treatment to "patient" Colin Webster.

FLOODLIGHTS AT OLD TRAFFORD . . . the first game

UNITED
v
BOLTON WANDERERS
25th March 1957

Here is the scene of the inaugural floodlit match at Old Trafford — Monday evening, 25th March, 1957. Although the lighting lived fully up to expectations, Bolton Wanderers had the privilege of performing the unexpected — inflicting our first home defeat under floodlights! The photograph was supplied by the General Electric Company Ltd., who were responsible for the installations.

22 APRIL 1957, v BURNLEY

A momentous occasion for Old Trafford as the newly installed stadium floodlights are switched on for the first time, for a match with Bolton.

FLOODLIGHTING

Although our new floodlighting installation is one of the most modern in Europe, there's always the million-to-one chance of a mains failure. In this unlikely event we ask for your co-operation **by keeping perfectly still** for about two seconds until the emergency lighting comes on automatically. As we are in direct communication with the Electricity Board an announcement will be made over the loudspeakers to tell you when full power will be restored. Thank you!

25 APRIL 1957, v REAL MADRID

The floodlights were installed in time for the European Cup semi-final with Real Madrid, with the programme carrying this warning!

Manchester United Calypso

Verse.

Now football is a pleasant game
Played in the sun,
Played in the rain,
And the team that gets me excited,
Manchester United.

Chorus.

Manchester, Manchester United
A bunch of bouncing Busby babes
They deserve to be knighted
If ever they're playing in your town,
You must get to that football ground
Take a lesson come to see
Football taught by Matt Busby
and Manchester, Manchester United.
A bunch of bouncing Busby babes
They deserve to be knighted.

Couplet 1.

They are the greatest team to-day
If you don't believe me go and see them play
A type of football second to none
Now they're at the top of Division One.

Couplet 2.

The greatest thrill you've ever seen
They are known as the soccer machine
They are the best there is no doubt,
So raise a cheer and give a shout.

Words and music by Eric Watterson and Ken Jones. Published by Robbins Music Corporation Ltd., 23 Denmark Street, London, W.C.2.

A popular chant which has stood the test of the time, the Manchester United Calypso was first recorded in 1957, with the lyrics printed in the Burnley programme.

THE MEN OF MANCHESTER UNITED . . .

TED DALTON and JIMMY MURPHY

Jimmy Murphy, assistant manager, has faded from the headlines slightly — and nothing could please Jimmy more! With the return of manager Matt Busby, Jimmy has been able to spend more time coaching the youngsters. He came to Old Trafford at the end of the war after Matt Busby had heard Sgt. Murphy giving a lecture on soccer to troops in Italy. When Matt came to Old Trafford he was not long sending for him. The wisdom of his choice was borne out for all to see when Jimmy stepped into the breach to reorganise the shattered Reds so magnificently that they finished up at Wembley.

Ted Dalton is United's physiotherapist. Ted came down to Old Trafford 22 years ago to buy a ticket for an international match against Ireland — and stayed to become the first qualified physiotherapist ever to be appointed to a football club. Walter Crickmer spotted him at the ground and asked him in to discuss a treatment machine that United had. The conversation finished with Mr. Gibson inviting Ted to be their physiotherapist. He accepted and has stayed to win the confidence of the hundreds of injured players who have passed through his hands.

Jack Crompton the trainer knows his way about Old Trafford. He joined United from local junior football and served as their goalkeeper for most of the 13 years he was here as a player. He left after captaining the Central League side at the end of his playing career to become trainer-coach with Luton. But within a week of the Munich crash, Jack was back with United. It was a grand gesture by Luton who thought highly of him and a lucky break for United.

Bill Inglis celebrates 31 seasons with United this year. For the first five years he was a player and for the last 26 the assistant trainer. There was a break of four years in between when he went to Northampton first as a player then as trainer — but Bill was another United man who could not resist the lure of Old Trafford. In his native Scotland, Bill captained his local team Raith Rovers when they had a £50,000 forward line including Alex James. Then came his move to England and his fine service for Manchester United.

Photos by courtesy of the Manchester Evening News

BILL INGLIS and JACK CROMPTON

20 SEPTEMBER 1958, v TOTTENHAM HOTSPUR

Here the cover of *United Review* pays tribute to four stalwarts – Jimmy Murphy, Jack Crompton, Ted Dalton and Bill Inglis.

Smart's CARICATURE-COMMENTARY

No 6

Dennis Viollet

Born within cheering distance of City's ground, Dennis Viollet became a Manchester Boys' star and eventually captained England Schoolboys against Wales at Maine Road in 1949. He's one of the best forwards in the game with a tricky line in ball play, the ability to snatch goals from the most unpromising situations and a powerful shot. Look at United's scorebook for the last few seasons and the name Viollet is there — either at the top or very near to it.

These days his experience (over 150 League games) is proving a great asset in moulding our still new forward combination together, and wherever he plays — centre-forward, inside or on the wing — it's "Dennis the Menace" as far as the opposition is concerned. This popular club man is married with a "hat trick" of children.

Birthplace Manchester. ✱

8 NOVEMBER 1958, v BURNLEY

The unmistakable features of United striker Dennis Viollet are perfectly captured in 'Smart's Caricature-Commentary' series.

MEET THE PLAYERS

A SERIES OF PEN PICTURES BY DAVID MEEK AND PETER SLINGSBY

Golf, watching TV and listening to records. These are the hobbies of Denis Law, a Mancunian by adoption and a player who anticipates spending the rest of his days in the city where his soccer services have endeared him to the fans of both senior clubs.

But it was with Huddersfield that Denis made his League bow as an amateur in December, 1956 against Notts. County at Meadow Lane. He was then 16 years and 303 days old and, of course, still an amateur.

He played at inside-right that day and created a record along with his partner, Kevin McHale (17 years, 84 days), for they formed the youngest right-wing pair to play in League football.

Denis made his international debut for Scotland in October, 1957, scoring the second goal in a 3–0 victory against Wales at Cardiff, and has since won a string of honours for his country.

He spent the 1961–62 season in Italy and, from what he has said since, enjoyed the experience of football in lire land. But he also welcomed the chance to come "home" to Manchester and was signed by United on 12th July, 1962 for a British record transfer fee. Now Denis and his wife, Diana, who also hails from Aberdeen, look forward to the birth of their first child in 1964.

Law's career figures with United to date are:

	League Apps.	League Goals	FA Cup Apps.	FA Cup Goals
1962–63	38	23	6	6
1963–64	16	17	-	-

A Manchester Evening News Photo

DENIS LAW

14 DECEMBER 1963, v SHEFFIELD WEDNESDAY

A insight into the life and career of adopted Mancunian and proud Scotsman Denis Law.

18 APRIL 1960, v WEST HAM UNITED

This photo of the United youth team of 1959/60 included future club legend Nobby Stiles, as well as Alan Atherton, the father of former England cricket captain Michael.

MANCHESTER UNITED F.C. YOUTH TEAM — 1959-60

Photo by courtesy of the Manchester Evening News

Left to right, back row: J. Nicholson, R. Smith, R. Briggs, A. Atherton, W. Donaldson, S. Ackerley.
Front: I. Moir, S. McMillan, N. Stiles, P. Chisnall, T. Spratt.

F.A. YOUTH CUP

—★—

Semi-Final

Manchester United Youth

versus

Preston North End Youth

—★—

Second Leg

Old Trafford

Thursday, 21st April

Kick-off 7-30 p.m.

JUNIOR LEAGUE TABLES

LANCASHIRE LEAGUE

DIVISION ONE

(Up to and including 2nd April)

	P.	W.	D.	L.	Goals F.	Goals A.	Pts.
Bolton 'A'	21	12	7	2	38	16	31
Manchester City 'A'	18	9	5	4	27	23	23
Preston North End 'A'	17	10	3	4	36	31	23
Blackburn Rovers 'A'	19	8	5	6	38	23	21
Liverpool 'A'	19	9	3	7	41	31	21
Bury 'A'	19	6	7	6	33	36	19
Everton 'A'	19	5	7	7	44	40	17
Burnley 'A'	19	4	9	6	19	23	17
Rochdale Reserves	16	5	6	5	19	17	16
Blackpool 'A'	18	5	6	7	27	25	16
UNITED 'A'	**20**	**6**	**4**	**10**	**27**	**30**	**16**
Stockport County 'A'	18	1	1	16	18	74	3

DIVISION TWO

(Up to and including 2nd April)

	P.	W.	D.	L.	Goals F.	Goals A.	Pts.
UNITED 'B'	**19**	**14**	**1**	**4**	**57**	**35**	**29**
Everton 'B'	17	12	2	3	51	20	26
Blackpool 'B'	18	8	2	8	33	40	18
Accrington Stanley 'A'	16	7	3	6	32	38	17
Manchester City 'B'	16	6	4	6	38	47	16
Blackburn Rovers 'B'	15	7	1	7	46	38	15
Bolton Wanderers 'B'	18	6	2	10	41	35	14
Preston North End 'B'	15	5	3	7	40	40	13
Burnley 'B'	17	5	2	10	41	35	12
Rochdale 'A'	13	5	1	7	25	31	6
Oldham Athletic 'A'	16	2	2	12	28	59	6

MEET THE PLAYERS

A SERIES OF PEN PICTURES BY DAVID MEEK AND PETER SLINGSBY

George Best is the babe of the side, and having said that, not even a stranger would have any difficulty picking him out.

For George weighs only eight stone and stands five feet, which must make him about the lightest player in League football. At one time he thought he would never be strong enough to become a professional player.

But after making his League debut last September and playing regularly in recent games, he is glad he took his father's advice . . . and stuck at it.

He went to Lisnasharragh School and played for Belfast Schools. He has won Irish youth honours and was spotted by Manchester United playing for Cregagh Youth Club.

United recruited him to their ground staff nearly three years ago and he signed professional for them soon after his 17th birthday last May.

He likes watching all sports, including snooker. His favourite position is inside forward and his hero is Jimmy Greaves . . . "because of all the goals he scores."

United are playing him on the wing, but George of the dark hair and good looks who has earned his chance early, is not complaining about that!

His father played amateur football and his mother played hockey for Ireland. Now this slimly built lad is helping to paint United's future bright.

A Manchester Evening News Photo

GEORGE BEST

19 FEBRUARY 1964, v BOLTON WANDERERS

A fascinating early profile of snooker-loving, Jimmy Greaves-admiring George Best, described as 'the lightest player in League football'!

REFEREE'S notebook
by ARTHUR ELLIS

Arthur Ellis calls on his experiences to illustrate the laws of the game.

No. 17. THE CASE OF THE DUMBFOUNDED 'KEEPER

To signify the award of an indirect free kick, referees now raise their arm above the head. They do so as a direct result of my experience in the Chamartin Stadium, Madrid.

The atmosphere at a Spain v. Argentina international can make other games seem like garden tea-parties. This one stands out vividly in my mind. It was in 1952 and over 110,000 spectators were packed into the Stadium. How the crowd would have "exploded" if they had known at the time the background to the only goal of the game – scored by Argentina.

With the crowd in constant eruption and both sides striving desperately hard to open the scoring as the second-half reached the midway point, I penalised a Spanish player for jumping high and almost kicking the ball off the head of an Argentina half-back.

There appeared little danger as a harmless-looking indirect free-kick sailed into the Spanish goalmouth. But the goalkeeper fisted the ball into the air and an on-rushing Argentina forward tapped it into the net.

At the banquet after the game the goalkeeper was dumbfounded when I told him that if he had let the ball go into the net without touching it, the goal would not have been allowed. But LAW 12 (Fouls and Misconduct) states that a player "playing in a manner considered by the referee to be dangerous . . . shall be penalised by the award of an indirect free-kick."

My word, there were some red Spanish faces! Pedro Escartin, Spanish representative on F.I.F.A., reported the incident to the Rules Revision Committee, and now referees throughout the world are instructed to raise their arm above their head to denote to the players when an indirect free-kick has been awarded.

27 FEBRUARY 1965, v WOLVES

In this regular series, legendary referee Arthur Ellis would cast his eye over the rules of the game and share experiences of his life as an official.

14 AUGUST 1965, v LIVERPOOL

The sad passing of club chairman – and Olympic gold medallist – Harold Hardman was marked with this warm tribute written by David Meek.

A TRIBUTE TO H. P. HARDMAN

1882-1965

by David Meek

Harold Hardman departed this world as quietly as he lived and worked.

His spirits and faculties were as lively as ever to the end, but he was 83 and over the last months he lost strength and did not get much further than the fireside of his home in Fownhope Road, Sale.

He faded quietly from the scene. He was that kind of man. He disliked the limelight, a lot of fuss, newspaper headlines.

There are other chairmen in football whose names are as well known as many of the players and managers. But though H. P. Hardman has been chairman of Manchester United throughout the post-war era of success and public acclaim, it was not often that you heard his name linked with the fame of the club.

This was the way Harold Hardman wanted it and so, again typically of the man, this is the way it worked out.

For though the United chairman may have shunned personal publicity, he had authority and a firm hand on the helm. Don't under-estimate his part in bringing more success to United than any other club in the country has experienced since the war.

For this was the man who set the atmosphere and conditions for Matt Busby to emerge as the outstanding manager in football, probably of all time.

The chairman saw himself as the means of giving his manager full opportunity to pursue his policies to the full. Mr. Hardman once summed it up to me just a few weeks before his death with a typical shaft of his sense of fun . . . "What's the use of keeping a dog and barking yourself," he said.

But there is more to it than that. How many other men could have resisted the quite natural urge to enjoy the limelight and power that his position as chairman gave him? Yet this is the man who, when he was travelling away with the team refused to allow the club coach to pick him up at his home and instead he used to catch the bus to the ground.

And this he did even when he had turned 80.

This was his modest approach to power. Yet I can think of no director in football more qualified to have thrust his way into the limelight, for Mr. Hardman was distinguished as both player and administrator.

He was an outstanding left-winger of his day. He won an Olympic gold medal in 1908 and in the previous two years he played as an amateur with Everton to reach two Cup finals. As a player with Northern Nomads and Manchester United, he won 10 amateur caps for England and four with the professional international team.

He was still playing with Stoke City in the Southern League when he was invited to become a director with Manchester United. Thus began over 50 years' service on the board, through bad times as well as good. He became an F.A. Councillor, President of Lancashire F.A. and also the Central League.

He served football with the same unassuming quiet approach that he brought to United. The game has lost a man as friendly as he was thoughtful and a fine example of all that is best in a chairman of a famous football club. Farewell H. P. Hardman — and thank you.

MANCHESTER UNITED football club

Top row – *left to right*
J. Aston, R. Charlton, D. Herd, D. Law, J. Connelly, D. Sadler.
Centre row – *left to right*
P. Crerand, G. Best, N. Cantwell, W. Foulkes.
Bottom row – *left to right*
D. Gaskell, N. Stiles, A. Dunne, S. Brennan, P. Dunne, J. Fitzpatrick

The Liverpool match to begin 1965/66 saw Matt Busby's league champions host Bill Shankly's FA Cup winners for a Charity Shield clash at Old Trafford. The programme carried this pictorial tribute to the Reds' first-team squad.

UNITED'S COVERED TRAINING GROUND TAKES SHAPE

At our practice ground at the Cliff, Broughton the framework of the new covered stadium takes shape behind the youngsters training under the expert eye of United Coach, John Aston.

Work has now been going on for nearly three months and Mr. Busby is hoping for the work to be completed by the start of the really bad weather. This means that United will have the biggest covered playing surface in Britain – a composite pitch measuring 250 ft. by 50 ft. Mr. Busby believes that it is during hard winters that the players get their worst injuries – because they are unable to train properly between matches. With this new pitch not only will the senior players maintain their suppleness in readiness for a hard fought game but United's youngsters will be developed well away from the mud and frost of winter.

Photograph by courtesy of the Daily Mirror.

12 NOVEMBER 1966, v SHEFFIELD WEDNESDAY
A significant moment for the club's future development as The Cliff training ground gets a major makeover, under the watchful eye of coach John Aston.

2 DECEMBER 1967, v WEST BROM
The manager used the programme to say thank you to well-wishers, having recently been awarded the Freedom of Manchester honour.

Volume XXIX No. 13 2nd December 1967

THIS IS THE OFFICIAL PROGRAMME OF

MANCHESTER UNITED

FOOTBALL CLUB LIMITED

OLD TRAFFORD · MANCHESTER 16

Telephone: Trafford Park 1661

Chairman: LOUIS C. EDWARDS

Directors:

ALAN GIBSON, *Vice-Chairman*

W. A. YOUNG, D. D. HAROUN, J.P.

Manager:

M. BUSBY, C.B.E.

Secretary:

R. L. OLIVE

Programme Editor: DAVID W. WICKS

Advertising enquiries only should be addressed to the Editor "United Review" Sidney F. Wicks Ltd., 21 Newton Street, Manchester 1. All other correspondence and enquiries must be addressed to the Club.

MATT BUSBY

SAYS

"THANK YOU"

It was with a great sense of pride and gratitude and considerable humility that I received the Freedom of Manchester some ten days ago and I wish to take this opportunity of expressing my sincere thanks to the many soccer supporters who have showered me with their congratulations.

No one appreciates more than I do that I have been a very fortunate man. Indeed, I have spent many happy years in this great city that I have come to love very dearly; I am deeply conscious that I have received the highest honour which Manchester can bestow.

But more than that, I have been greatly moved by the sentiments expressed in the letters, telegrams and messages I have received from you, the supporters of this wonderful game of ours.

In this respect, may I say here that I have always enjoyed maximum support from my directors, my colleagues on the staff and the players – without which none of what has been achieved on and off the field would have been possible.

I believe Manchester United to be the finest club in the world and your continued support and encouragement, as I have often stressed in the past, has been vital in shaping any success that has come our way.

For this and especially for those many and generous good wishes to me and the club, my grateful thanks to you all as we look forward together to a happy and successful future here at Old Trafford. Here we feel that what matters above all else is that the game should be played in the right spirit, with skill and courage and the result accepted without bitterness or conceit.

Now one must turn to the business of the day and I know you will all join me in welcoming West Bromwich Albion and their supporters to our ground this afternoon.

We have had many enjoyable meetings with Albion in the past, and I feel we can look forward to another exciting clash this afternoon against opponents who scored six goals against us last winter but over whom we achieved a "double", winning here and at The Hawthorns.

Left—Matt Busby, C.B.E., writes himself into Manchester history as he signs the Roll of Freemen.

Photograph by courtesy of the Manchester Evening News

PAGE TWO

Photograph by courtesy of the Daily Mirror

The Directors have very much pleasure in announcing that the Prime Minister, the Rt. Hon. Harold Wilson, O.B.E., M.P., has honoured us by his presence at this match. We desire to accord him and Mrs. Wilson a very warm welcome. This is a historic event for our Club inasmuch as it is the first occasion that a Prime Minister has visited Old Trafford to witness one of our matches and we are very proud to have him with us this afternoon.

2 DECEMBER 1967, v WEST BROMWICH ALBION
A big day at Old Trafford, with Prime Minister Harold Wilson in attendance. George Best put on a show, scoring both United goals in a 2-1 win over the Baggies.

Well Played George!

George Best, acclaimed Footballer of the Year by the Football Writers' Association, became the youngest player ever to receive this coveted award. He joins John Carey and Bobby Charlton in this list of "greats" making a magnificant hat-trick for United. Please turn to page nine for Peter Slingsby's personal tribute.

Photo by courtesy of the Daily Express

11 MAY 1968, v SUNDERLAND
The programme for the last league game of the 1967/68 season celebrated Bestie joining the ranks of United greats to be named Footballer of the Year.

19 APRIL 1969, v BURNLEY
Big news at the tail end of the 1968/69 season, as Wilf McGuinness is promoted to chief coach.

Photograph by courtesy of the Manchester Evening News

WILF McGUINNESS
CHIEF COACH

Wilf McGuinness, our Assistant Trainer, will become Chief Coach on June 1st next. The Chairman Mr. Louis Edwards issued the following statement on April 9th.

"The Board has given further consideration to the changes which will occur at the end of the season and has decided to appoint a Chief Coach who will be responsible for team selection, coaching, training and tactics.

"Mr. Wilf McGuinness has been selected for this position and will take up his duties as from the first of June and in these circumstances it is not necessary to advertise for applications as was first intended.

"Sir Matt will be responsible for all other matters affecting the Club and Players and will continue as Club Spokesman."

Today Wilf McGuinness is assistant trainer to Jack Crompton. He is in charge of the reserve team and has a special interest in United's Youth Team.

McGuinness is a one-club man, a Manchester and England schoolboy international who first played in the League team in 1955 and continued his international career with the England Youth Team, the Under-23 side and then won two full caps before breaking his leg playing for the Reserves against Stoke City at Old Trafford on December 12th, 1959.

It was a bad break, but though it virtually ended his playing career, it started his rise on the management side.

United appointed him Assistant Trainer with the Reserve team and it was not long before the Football Association had him as England's Youth Team Trainer.

In 1968 he was appointed Manager to the International Youth Team and was one of Sir Alf Ramsey's training assistants during the 1966 World Cup Series.

At 32 years of age Wilf will be one of the youngest coaches in charge of a First Division side. We wish him the best of luck – and that goes for every United supporter as well!

PAGE FOUR

This is Old Trafford

Photo by Aerofilms Ltd

Manchester United's Cantilever stand on the North side of the ground was completed 5 years ago - the distinctive roof pattern can be seen on the right-hand side of the photograph. The stand offers an uninterrupted view for over 10,000 spectators and a row of private boxes with a separate lift spans the width of the Stand. Old Trafford - with a capacity of 63,000 spectators was chosen as a venue for the World Cup games in 1966, an F.A. Cup Semi-Final in 1968, the England v. Russia Under-23 International in 1969 and for the F.A. Cup Final Replay in April, 1970 - the first to take place since 1912. (In that match Chelsea overcame Leeds by two goals to one.)

We at Old Trafford join in offering the Semi-Finalists from Everton and Liverpool a hearty welcome to Old Trafford.

27 MARCH 1971, EVERTON v LIVERPOOL
Old Trafford hosted the all-Merseyside FA Cup semi-final of 1971, with this image welcoming the visitors to Manchester.

MEET THE Management

A NEW SERIES FEATURING THE OLD TRAFFORD STAFF
BY DENIS LOWE

LESLIE OLIVE
SECRETARY

(Photo by County Press)

This month Leslie Olive, the club's secretary since May, 1958, completes 30 years, service with Manchester United, an eventful period in which he has carried out every job on the administrative side, and played in two First Division matches as an amateur goalkeeper. Les, who switched to goalkeeping after several years as a full-back or centre-half for the "A" and "B" teams, was the emergency choice in April, 1953, when Jack Crompton and the other professional 'keepers were injured. "After playing for the Central League side for a time, I was brought into the first team at Newcastle" he recalls. "Dennis Violett also made his League debut that day, and we won 2–1. Then came a 2–2 draw with West Bromwich at Old Trafford. I should have done better with their first goal, but I hope I managed to do a reasonable job and not let the team down." Grateful for the chance to play at top level, if only briefly, Les, who had joined United as a 14year-old office boy after seeking a trial as a player, decided to concentrate on a career on the admin. side after R.A.F service. Appointed assistant secretary in March, 1955, he took over from the late Walter Crickmer following the Munich disaster and was appointed secretary three months later after handling the arrangements for United's F.A. Cup Final against Bolton. While he will never forget that game and the exacting weeks after Munich, Les names the 1968 European Cup Final success as his outstanding United memory. "We set the pace in European football in England, and that Wembley victory against Benfica was the culmination of so much effort throughout the club," he says. "Looking back over the years, there have been so many big changes here, like the introduction of the token scheme and the huge increase in ticket sales. At times, it has been hard work, but I have enjoyed my job and have been delighted to work with so many wonderful people at United." Born in Salford, Les lives in Stretford with his wife, Betty and 18-year-old daughter, Susan. "Both are keen and regular United supporters," but Betty also follows the fortunes of Salford Rugby League Club with a lot of interest." Manchester United's representative on the Manchester County F.A. for the last 13 years, Les also serves as secretary of his church, Salford Central Congregational.

At Home with Jimmy Rimmer

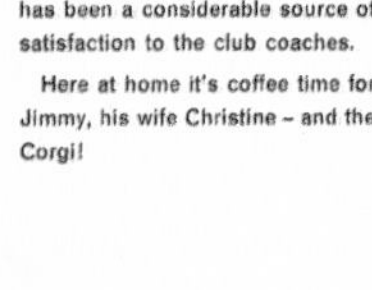

At a time when Alex Stepney was hampered by injury and lack of form, Jimmy Rimmer entered United's goal and deputised so ably he won a place in the England Under-23 squad. Jimmy, Southport-born, played for Lancashire Boys before joining United and his development into probably the best reserve goalkeeper in the country has been a considerable source of satisfaction to the club coaches.

Here at home it's coffee time for Jimmy, his wife Christine – and the Corgi!

An exclusive United Review picture by Philip Dunn.

19 APRIL 1971, v LIVERPOOL
An insight into the home life of United's Merseyside-born goalkeeper Jimmy Rimmer for the visit of Liverpool.

9 SEPTEMBER 1972, v COVENTRY CITY
Secretary Les Olive received a deserved profile on his 30th anniversary at MUFC.

A letter to the Board from George Best . . .

I had thought seriously of coming personally and asking for a chance to speak at the Board Meeting, but once again I am afraid when it comes to saying things face to face I might not have been completely honest.

I am afraid through my somewhat unorthodox ways of trying to sort my own problems out I have caused Manchester United even bigger problems.

I wanted you to read this letter before the Board Meeting commenced so as to let you know my feelings before any decision or statements are issued following the meeting.

When I said last Summer I was going to quit football, contrary to what many people said or thought, I seriously meant it because I had lost interest in the game for various reasons.

While in Spain I received a lot of letters from both friends and well-wishers quite a few asking me to reconsider. I did so and after weeks of thinking it over I decided to give it another try. It was an even harder decision to make than the original one. I came back hoping my appetite for the game would return and even though in every game I like to think I gave 100% there was something missing. Even now I am not quite sure what.

Therefore I have decided not to play football again and this time no one will change my mind.

In conclusion, I would like to wish the Club the best of luck for the remainder of the season and for the future. Because even though I personally have tarnished the Club's name in recent times, to me and thousands of others Manchester United still means something special.

Yours sincerely,

GEORGE BEST, 19th December 1972.

23 DECEMBER 1972, v LEEDS UNITED

Unorthodox as ever, Bestie used the pages of *United Review* to tell the board he had quit football. 'This time no one will change my mind,' he vowed.

Bobby Charlton makes his 758th and final United appearance, away to Chelsea in April 1973

● Before our game with Lazio in Rome (March 21st, 1973), the team was received in audience by Pope Paul VI in the Vatican, Rome. Sir Matt Busby afterwards presented a silver chalice to the Pontiff on behalf of Manchester United Football Club.

Farewell Bobby Charlton

By DAVID MEEK of the Manchester Evening News.

Manchester United has lost a football trinity . . . . Bobby Charlton, Denis Law and George Best – all now departed from Old Trafford.

These were the three names that invariably sprang to mind as the Reds swept to success in the European Cup and other honours. Each player had a completely different style but together they gave United attacking flair and panache that over the years marked them out from other teams as being so splendid to watch.

Many other players contributed to the club's success in that golden era of course – but not least Tony Dunne. It is unfortunate that Tony's free transfer and move to Bolton Wanderers has coincided with the departure of his celebrated colleagues at Old Trafford. His move has undoubtedly been overshadowed, but that is no reflection on the great work of the Eire international. It is just another indication of the tremendous impact made on football by that titanic Charlton, Law and Best trio.

As we all know, George Best finished prematurely in the game. We can still see Denis Law in action a few miles away at Maine Road. Like Tony Dunne, he will be back at Old Trafford for his Testimonial match.

Bobby Charlton though has severed his playing connections altogether and has made the step to the other side. Our former Skipper is now the Manager of Preston North End, and is facing the hazards and pitfalls that management entails.

Bobby's send-off last season was prolonged and extravagant, yet only in keeping with the respect and admiration he enjoyed from sportsmen of many codes and indeed many nationalities.

The reception given him at his Testimonial match against Glasgow Celtic was both nostalgic and rousing. From then on the presentations came thick and fast everywhere he went, with opponents as keen as anyone to mark the occasion of his retirement.

With typical modesty and understanding he accepted all the tributes with gentlemanly grace. Now he lives in a much tougher world, but well equipped to become a successful Manager. Toughness is not the only quality demanded. Respect, honesty and determination are also in the make-up of top Management men and Charlton is well equipped in this respect.

Meanwhile Manchester United must live without our beloved Bobby Charlton. It will not be easy as many a famous club has foundered through thinking too much of past glories and not enough of the future.

Fortunately our board of directors have their sights set firmly ahead. They have spared no expense in recruiting the right players to build fresh triumphs. The stage is now set for a new era of youngsters to follow in the historic footsteps of one of the greatest of them all – Bobby Charlton.

All of us wish him a well deserved success at Preston North End and eagerly await that memorable occasion in the perhaps non too distant future when Bobby Charlton will bring his own team to Old Trafford!

PAGE SIX

THE LAST GOAL . . . .
Bobby Charlton picks the ball out of the net after heading his last goal for United against Verona last May. *Photo: Daily Express.*

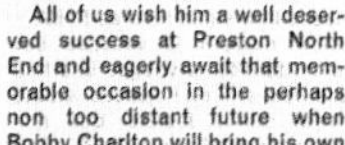

MAN in the MIDDLE

JOHN HUNTING (LEICESTER)

England's newest representative on the FIFA referees' list, succeeding Norman Burtenshaw this season, John Hunting is a lecturer in physical education at the City of Leicester Polytechnic. An all-round sportsman, he plays squash and badminton for the Polytechnic in the local county leagues. John's refereeing career began in the 1950's when he was on National Service with the Army in the Middle East, and he later progressed through the Leicestershire Senior League and Football Combination to the Football League line in 1966. Promotion to the middle followed two years later, and John has since had a number of top appointments at home and abroad. He was a linesman for the 1972 FA Cup Final between Leeds and Arsenal and refereed last season's second leg of the Texaco Cup final between Norwich and Ipswich.

29 AUGUST 1973, v STOKE CITY

End of an era. David Meek paid tribute to Bobby Charlton as United faced up to life without him in the squad.

24 AUGUST 1974, v MILLWALL

Introducing the Reds' new signing – the man once sent off for calling a linesman an onion!

11 APRIL 1973, v CRYSTAL PALACE

Sir Matt and United enjoyed an audience with the Pope while in Rome on Anglo-Italian Cup duty.

Stuart takes the "who" from Pearson

By Derek Hodgson (Daily Express)

Stuart Pearson has all the makings of becoming a 100% 24-carat scarlet-shirted Manchester United star. He has character, he has ability, he has enthusiasm and, above all, he has great pride in being a United player.

Character: If you are going to be sent off in a football match there is a certain amount of honour and a definite amount of humour in being despatched for calling a linesman "an onion".

Character: Stuart, an electricity lineman, dropped £9 a week to become a Hull City professional.

Enthusiasm: He began training a week earlier than all United's other players.

Ability: 47 goals in three seasons at Hull. Two goals in United's pre-season game in Ostend, the target of transfer offers from Manchester City, Everton and Birmingham.

Pride: "When I arrived in London on Cup Final eve I knew I was joining another club.

"But I didn't know which one so I was a little hesitant. Then, when I heard it was Manchester United, I didn't ask any more questions. I was ready to sign there and then."

I like his attitude when one newspaper greeted his arrival in Manchester with the headline "STUART WHO?" Far from offended he took the view that if someone had to ask the question then it was up to Stuart to make the name Pearson ring round football.

PRESENCE AND REPUTATION

There are always curious twists and turns to football history. Had Pearson been able to join United a year ago, I doubt very much if they would be kicking off in the Second Division today.

United were relegated simply because they did not score enough goals. Their defence was better than most, their standard of football was at least mid-table but the marksmanship deserted them.

It is Pearson's primary task to tuck the ball away and his presence and reputation alone should ensure much more space inside the opposing penalty area for Lou Macari and Sammy McIlroy.

We all wish him well and he should remember that at Old Trafford it is not good enough to refer to linesmen as fruit or vegetables. Please, Stuart, if you must, address him as "Mister Onion".

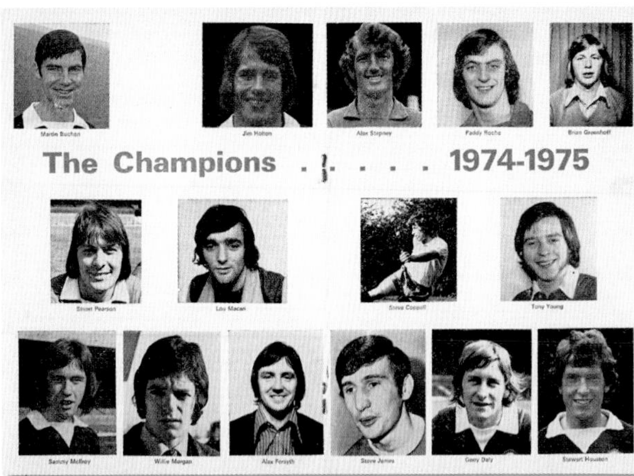

26 APRIL 1975, v BLACKPOOL
These are the Reds who made sure United's stay in Division Two was restricted to a single season, and who rounded it off in style with a 4-0 win over the Seasiders.

UNITED ON SONG

Record: Superstar Promotions No. F136 33

Manchester United aims to top another league—the pop charts with their new songs 'Manchester United'/'Old Trafford Blues' to be issued in early April.

United's captain Martin Buchan will be featured singing solo on one side of the single release. He will be singing his own composition, 'Old Trafford Blues'.

Martin wrote the humorous 12-bar blues when the team played in Denmark last summer.

"I have always enjoyed playing the guitar and learning new songs. On the beach in Denmark I decided to have a go at writing my own song. It pokes fun at the players and at myself, of course," he says.

On the other side, a song by Tony Hiller is featured called 'Manchester United'. Tony wrote the British entry in this year's Eurovision Song Contest. He also produced the recording session at Strawberry Studios, Stockport, where hit sounds from big names like 10cc and Neil Sedaka have been recorded.

27 MARCH 1976, v MIDDLESBROUGH
United captain Martin Buchan was a keen amateur songwriter and able to combine football with music when he wrote and recorded a single with his team-mates. It can still be found on YouTube if you want a listen.

PLAYERS PROFILE

By Tony Pullein

2. STEVE COPPELL

Though last season—when he played in the F.A. Cup final and gained his first England under-23 cap—was undoubtedly the most exciting in the young life of Steve Coppell, he's aiming for even better things this term.

He knows that anything's possible after his incredible experiences of the past three years. In 1973 he was playing for Liverpool University when a Tranmere scout spotted him. He joined the Third Division club as an amateur in June that year and by the following January he had made his League debut against Port Vale.

For many lads, such success might have represented the pinnacle of their ambitions. Not Steve!

He won a regular place the following season and, before the campaign was out, he was transferred to us for £30,000 just in time to help us make absolutely sure of promotion.

Then last season it all started to happen for him.

Here we analyse Steve's career to date, showing his season-by-season appearances record against each club. Figures in brackets show goals scored and 'S' indicates he played as substitute.

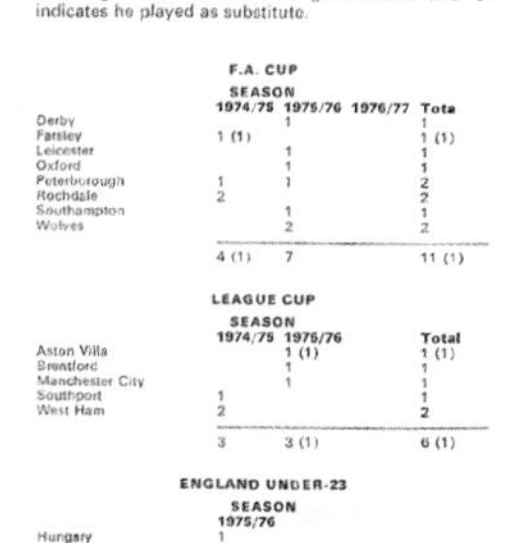

FOOTBALL LEAGUE

	SEASON 1973/74	1974/75	1975/76	1976/77	Total
Aldershot		1 (1)			1 (1)
Arsenal			2 (2)		2 (2)
Aston Villa			2 (1)		2 (1)
Birmingham			2		2
Blackburn	S	1			1+S
Blackpool		1			1
Bolton		1			1
Bournemouth	1				1
Brighton		2			2
Bristol Rovers		1			1
Burnley			1		1
Bury		1			1
Cambridge	1				1
Charlton		1 (1)			1 (1)
Chesterfield	S	1			1+S
Colchester		2 (1)			2 (1)
Coventry			2		2
Crystal Palace		1			1
Derby			2		2
Everton			2		2
Fulham		1			1
Gillingham		2 (1)			2 (1)
Grimsby		2 (2)			2 (2)
Halifax		1 (1)			1 (1)
Hereford		2 (1)			2 (1)
Huddersfield		1			1
Ipswich			2		2
Leeds			2		2
Leicester			1		1
Liverpool			2 (1)		2 (1)
Manchester City			2		2
Middlesbrough			2		2
Newcastle			2		2
Norwich		1	2		3
Nottingham For.		1			1
Notts. County		1			1
Oldham	1	1 (1)			2 (1)
Plymouth		1			1
Port Vale	1	2			3
Preston		2 (1)			2 (1)
Q.P.R.			2		2
Sheffield Utd.			2		2
Southampton		S			S
Southend		1			1
Southport	1				1
Stoke			1		1
Swindon		2 (1)			2 (1)
Tottenham			2		2
Walsall		1			1
Watford	1+S	1			2+S
West Ham			2		2
Wolves			2		2
Wrexham		1			1
York		1			1
	6+3S	38+1S (11)	39 (4)		83+4S (15)

F.A. CUP

	SEASON 1974/75	1975/76	1976/77	Tota
Derby		1		1
Farsley	1 (1)			1 (1)
Leicester		1		1
Oxford		1		1
Peterborough	1	1		2
Rochdale	2			2
Southampton		1		1
Wolves		2		2
	4 (1)	7		11 (1)

LEAGUE CUP

	SEASON 1974/75	1975/76	Total
Aston Villa		1 (1)	1 (1)
Brentford		1	1
Manchester City		1	1
Southport	1		1
West Ham	2		2
	3	3 (1)	6 (1)

ENGLAND UNDER-23

	SEASON 1975/76
Hungary	1

14

15

1 SEPTEMBER 1976, v TRANMERE ROVERS
United were drawn with Tranmere in the second round of the League Cup in 1976, so it was only natural that the programme decided to profile Coppell, who had signed from the Merseyside club the previous year.

27 DECEMBER 1977, v LEICESTER CITY
For the closest home match to 25 December in 1977, the programme contained a special Christmas card from the club inserted in the middle of the issue.

Left to Right: C. M. Edwards, Sir Matt Busby, C.B.E., L. C. Edwards (Chairman), J. A. Gibson (Vice-Chairman), W. A. Young, D. D. Haroun, J.P.

WINNERS OF THE DAILY MAIL/VERNONS POOLS FAIR PLAY TROPHY, 1976/77.

Back Row (Left to Right): D. J. Sexton (Manager), T. Cavanagh (Assistant Manager), D. McCreery, J. Nicholl, A. Stepney, B. Greenhoff, S. McIlroy, A. Albiston, G. Hill, L. Brown (Physio).
Front Row. (Left to Right): S. Coppell, J. Greenhoff, M. Buchan (Captain), S. Pearson, L. Macari.

F.A. CUP WINNERS 1976/77. JOINT HOLDERS OF F.A. CHARITY SHIELD.

The board of directors proudly presented our trophy haul from the previous year: the FA Cup, the Charity Shield and – the jewel in the crown – the Daily Mail/ Vernons Pools Fair Play Trophy. The original treble winners!

The Directors, Management, Players and Staff
hope that you and your family
have had a very Happy Christmas
and wish you
good health and prosperity
in the New Year.

from

OLD TRAFFORD MANCHESTER M16 ORA

CHRISTMAS 1977

The players certainly made it a very happy Christmas for the fans – they beat Everton 6-2 away on Boxing Day, then Leicester 3-1 at home a day later!

New Arrival

His latest was on his former home ground of Wrexham against Turkey.

He has a married sister and two brothers still at home in Colwyn Bay.

Mike Thomas

in action at Chelsea

Mike Thomas is a lively lad from Wales, aged 24, and a bachelor, but hardly likely to be tempted by the bright lights.

After football, his favourite hobby is music and his collection of records.

Born at Mochdre near Colwyn Bay he didn't move far when he decided to become a professional after winning representative honours with North Wales. His choice of club was Wrexham where he has spent the last nine years.

His £300,000 move to Manchester United threw his world upside down and he didn't sleep for two nights from when the deal was set up to actually signing at Old Trafford.

But he has packed a fair amount of travel into his football with two seasons of European football for Wrexham in the Cup Winners Cup and 12 caps for Wales.

7

16 DECEMBER 1978, v TOTTENHAM HOTSPUR

Readers of the programme enjoyed their first glimpse of a chirpy Welshman who went on to enjoy cult status at United in December 1978 – although the sobriquet 'Mike' was an uncommon one...

Football around the world at Christmas

by Tom Tyrrell

They reckon that the first soccer writer was a Greek chap called Antiphanes, who wrote about a Grecian ball game 600 years before the three wise men began their trek to Bethlehem.

It seems that whoever invented the first bouncing ball . . . probably some inflatable part of an animal . . . probably some inflatable part of an animal . . . started (if you'll forgive me) the ball rolling, towards the game as we know it today.

Mind you it's hard to think of what shape the first soccer match would have taken. Perhaps those tall Grecian pillars really were the first goal-posts, and those polished marble statues of muscular men in the altogether, were just scenes from the dressing room after the match.

OLYMPIAD

For one thing, they would not wear boots. Maybe they would not even wear those long flowing robes of Grecian days, or maybe, because there was no athletic competition in the true Olympiad sense, the men would have left the kicking of a ball to the children.

No one can really say how soccer developed, but one thing seems certain. If they were kicking a ball about in 600 B.C. then the youngsters for centuries after that, would have done the same thing.

A blown-up bladder would have found its way to the feet of young shepherd boys around Jerusalem, or perhaps a more solid type of ball made from grasses stuffed into a sewn-up skin.

The game would develop. Rules would be written, or at least argued out by the lads who were playing, and so the game we know today would be born.

There's a mythical tale that the first European game, played on a one-legged basis of course, was between Roman troops and the conquered British, back in 217 A.D. and although no evidence other than the written word of an ancient scribe, can be found, it appears that we won!

They had a name for the game in the years which came between the Roman occupation and its eventual title of Association Football (it isn't really footy you know). Did you know that you spend most Saturday afternoons watching Ludus Pilae? It sounds more like a Yugoslavian defender, but that's the Latin version of good old soccer.

BANNED

According to the historians football was banned in the 14th century, and one bloke who wished that they had put the ban on a few years earlier, was an unlikely character called John de Boddleworth (fancy chanting that!). He took part in a game in 1321 but didn't enjoy it. I can say that with authority because John lost his head over that game . . . in fact they used it as the ball!

Kicking somebody's head about a football field seemed to be a healthy pastime in ancient times, and many a battle would end with a kickabout.

But football had its good side as well. Healthy games like the one between Middleton and Oldham.

LONG PITCH

It was games like this which got the game a bad name in its early days. The reason was that the game was actually played between Middleton and Oldham, every able bodied man playing for his town, and the pitch stretching for about four miles. What the scores were no-one knows.

So soccer grew, from the barbaric to the polished thoroughbred we now know. From the days when the Greeks kicked a ball about, to the days of the World Cup, the multi-million pound stadia, and the Saturday afternoons we all love.

I don't really know whether that story about Antiphanes is true, but if he was the first sports writer, then on behalf of all his colleagues who've carried on since then, I'd like to say thanks. And of course Merry Christmas!

26 DECEMBER 1978, v LIVERPOOL

Another classic festive issue greeted fans arriving for the big match against our rivals on Boxing Day 1978, with long-time contributor Tom Tyrrell taking a historical look at the game we love.

22 AUGUST 1979, v WEST BROMWICH ALBION

The big summer signing in 1979 was Ray Wilkins, and he made his home debut in this 2-0 win over the Baggies.

The same issue – for the first home game of the 1979/80 season – contained two programme favourites: away directions and Face in the Crowd.

FACE IN THE CROWD

The first photograph in this new series was taken during the recent Open Day here at Old Trafford, if your face has been ringed, please contact the Ticket Office (tel: 061-872 1861) within the next three days to arrange collection of two free tickets for our next home match.

RAC GOING BY CAR?

Here is your RAC route to next week's away game at

ARSENAL

MANCHESTER

A56/A556 Princess Road (A5103)/ M56 to intersection 19, M6 at Tabley
15 miles

M6 southbound and via M6/M1 Midlands Link to intersection 2, Five Ways Corner, Hendon, North London junction A1/A41
189 miles

A1 (follow 'City' signs) joining North Circular Road (A406) for ¾ mile then fork right into Lyttleton Road and along Archway Road and Holloway Road. Turn left from A1 at Highbury, and Arsenal Football Ground.
196 miles

United win fair play trophy again!

Good football with better discipline is coming back into the game, says Ron Greenwood.

The England manager was at Old Trafford to present Manchester United with their trophy as winners of the Vernons Pools and Daily Mail Fair Play League.

And he reckons standards are improving throughout football.

"Manchester United are to be congratulated not just on winning last season's award but for their consistency in good behaviour. They have topped the League three times in the last four years and were runners-up on the other occasion. It's a tremendous effort."

1 SEPTEMBER 1979, v MIDDLESBROUGH

The Fair Play League mentioned in the previous pages was again won by the Reds in 1978/79, with the trophy presented to captain Martin Buchan by England manager Ron Greenwood.

5 SEPTEMBER 1979, v TOTTENHAM HOTSPUR

One of the most important backroom figures at the club in the 1970s was chief scout Joe Brown, who was profiled in this issue.

JOE BROWN

by Joe Lancaster

Chief scout Joe Brown has the benign appearance of a schoolmaster, youthful, kindly, and considerate and all the natural gifts for shepherding juniors into United's fold.

It is not only the young that Brown has to initiate. Besides the schoolboy players his responsibility is recruitment at all levels. A word from Dave Sexton and he takes up the scent.

Brown known as Joe throughout the club tests the scene. His judgement is not confined to playing ability. He states "Our club can stand or fall on a players character. United players are under pressure greater than at any other club.

"The ninety minutes in a match is not the only time the spotlight is on. It is never switched off for United's players. Everybody judges Manchester United all the time, the slightest mistakes are magnified. We cannot wriggle out, and indeed we never try to dodge issues. We have to be honest".

When Brown uses the word "Honesty" he says it with such conviction that I guarantee it is going to take over from "magic" in the sporting vocabulary. Joe a practising christian has let it be his dictum from his days of wing half with Middlesbrough, and Burnley as well as coach and manager of the East Lancashire club.

This and his schoolboy days at Newcastle on Tyne has given him a wide spectrum. Different environments produce different players but they must be adaptable. He admits "The club never wants to get into complicated situations with players. We want those who relish the privilege of playing before crowds of 50,000. Those who immediately feel they are part of the family.

"When some boys come here they are afraid of the club. They never sleep for a week before arriving and then we have to project our personality to break down the barriers. Nothing like a good laugh, and there is plenty of laughing going on here".

United's knack is to make the innocent schoolboy as well as a six figure star enjoy every session at the club. They are aware that first impressions are always best but want them to be lasting. That is like Brown who in the two years he has been at Old Trafford is still "Good old Joe" with all those he has helped through the Old Trafford portals.

Jimmy Murphy

Tips from the Top

by Joe Lancaster

Jimmy Murphy, coat open, hat at a jaunty angle beamed as he surveyed The Cliff, and with a touch of pride exclaimed "This is where it all happens".

Youngsters wanting to succeed might take note. "All happens" means the practice ground; that is where the homework should be done. Finding a place as superb as the Cliff could present problems, but in this day and age there are plenty of sports centres within reach of most people.

Rubbish tips and slag heaps for pitches are part of the past. The Cliff was once in that category but Murphy worked on the wasteland with Sir Matt Busby, and it is their everlasting contribution to United history. Murphy states "This is where we plant the little acorns and watch them grow into giant oaks".

Murphy is reticent about talking of the past. He said "Looking repeatedly over the shoulder is a sure way of dimming vision. A few cursory glances backwards are necessary, but you must always be looking towards the future".

He believes in the future. The man who was co-helmsman with Sir Matt and helped to make Manchester United the flag ship of British Soccer, believes the future for any youngster making the grade can only become better.

The former Manchester United Assistant Manager continued, "If the ability is there, what better choice can there be. It is difficult to make the grade but the rewards are great and will become greater. Remember, skill alone is not enough unless used properly. Have a belief in your ability, an aptitude to learn, determination to do well and the patience to wait for improvement. It does not come with every training session. It is when they are added together over a long period that the raw metal is burnished. Without going over my previous article, I would add a pennyworth of skill is worth a pound of theory any day. More rewards will come to players for success. That is the March of Time. Evolution has made everybody better off, and footballers will make even better progress.

There is no saying that the game itself will improve. A lack of personalities is not helping, and personalities are not only at a low ebb in soccer: it applies to all walks of life. Funny hats, gold chains on the wrist and neck and off-beat clothes, do not make personalities. It is what is under those clothes that makes a man different. That must start in boyhood. That is where it all starts no matter what profession or calling a boy goes for. All the pieces are placed before him by parents, teacher, friends, coaches, Clubs and environment. Pick up the wrong ones, and bad habits develop. That is why it is important for a youngster to think for himself and accept what is right, then he will make the grade.

Today, when the world is becoming smaller life moves faster and brings more spare time. We have to consider whether this should be devoted to training. It also brings along with it a lot of trappings and streamlining. In training grounds like the Cliff, kit is laid out, meals laid on and tuition in these soccer academies equals anything to public schools. There are no longer thirty boys to a class, all scrambling to dip into the wicker basket for the best kit.

Boys no longer have to run from work for training stints as they did two and three decades ago. If a boy had arrived in a car in those days they would have thought it was "Little Lord Fauntleroy". I remember Duncan Edwards turning up on a new bike he had bought to transport him more quickly to the training ground, and the rest of the lads inspecting it with admiration.

A lifetime of change has taught me that having and enjoying the comforts does not make a boy soft. A rider must be added . . . provided he gives off his best and mixes with the best.

Remember, in training and competition always try and match the best and don't be pulled down to the lower level."

22 MARCH 1980, v MANCHESTER CITY

A fascinating chat with the legendary Jimmy Murphy, who didn't want to spend too much time reminiscing. 'You must always be looking to the future...'

12 NOVEMBER 1980, v WOLVES

A touching vignette that captured life inside the Albiston family home in 1980. The photo also provides a vivid reminder of interior design styles of the late 1970s/early 1980s!

Away from it all

As our photograph shows, Arthur Albiston, United's Scottish under 21 international, really can get 'away from it all' with the help of his wife Elaine and baby Ross who came onto the scene just eight months ago. Arthur and Elaine met five years ago this month in a local discotheque when they were introduced by a mutual friend and they have been living in Sale since their wedding two years ago. Elaine will be at tonight's match (baby-sitter permitting!) and admits to being Arthur's most severe critic. Elaine was a regular visitor at Old Trafford until the baby arrived and thoroughly enjoys watching Arthur play.

29 NOVEMBER 1980, v SOUTHAMPTON

Club stalwart Jack Crompton made his first-team debut in 1946 – here we see him 34 years later, still working with the reserves.

THE CLIFF

In today's final look at the gymnasium at the Cliff training Ground, our top picture shows reserve team coach, Jack Crompton, supervising work on a piece of apparatus called "the leaper". The particular exercise shown here is used to develop the leg muscles. Jack tells us that the young players spend at least two afternoons each week in the gym', with emphasis placed on strengthening the legs and so help players with their running and jumping. The bottom photograph shows the youngsters going through some floor exercises.

11

Things have certainly changed for Remi Moses since he last stood on the Stretford End! Five or six years ago, Remi was a regular visitor to Old Trafford when he came with his pals from Miles Platting to watch the Reds. Whilst the young fan had no particular favourite amongst the players of the mid-seventies, he readily admits to becoming a United supporter because of the tremendous support we enjoy in that particular part of Manchester. As the 'stamping ground' of such favourites as Nobby Stiles and Brian Kidd, this is hardly surprising.

Although an avid Red at the time, Remi was quick to point out that he didn't attend the 1976 Cup Final – you've guessed it, he couldn't get a ticket!

Our photograph shows Remi back on the famous terracing, but this time with Granada TV's Elton Welsby and a film crew.

30 SEPTEMBER 1981, v LEEDS UNITED

Recent signing Remi Moses was the centre of attention in the autumn of 1981, and he was to make his first home start in this 1-0 win over Leeds.

28 NOVEMBER 1981, v BRIGHTON

The match programme always made an effort to highlight the contributions of Manchester United's unsung heroes, as we see here with this vital quartet.

FOCUS ON THE BACKROOM BOYS

This week we take the opportunity to look at the training and coaching staff who, with the exception of Jimmy Curran, have all joined United either just prior, or during the current season. The one man missing from this feature is our physiotherapist Jim McGregor, who, when the photographs were taken had a full treatment room to attend to – more about Jim a little later in the season.

MICK BROWN – Assistant Manager

Ron Atkinson's first signing. Mick was born in Walsall and was a more than useful club cricketer. Soccer always had the upper hand and he joined Hull City straight from school where he was to spend thirteen years playing at full back for the 'Tigers'. Mick was a member of the Hull side that won the Third Division Championship in 1966. From Hull he moved to Lincoln for a season and then spent the final eighteen months of his playing career at Cambridge (at that time members of the Southern League). In 1970 Mick left Cambridge to take up the post of reserve team coach with Oxford United (obviously a scholarly type). Mick was to hold this job for two years before promotion to assistant manager under Gerry Summers. In 1975 he took over as manager and during his spell at the Manor Ground faced up to United in both the FA and the FL Cup – losing narrowly on each occasion. 1979 saw Mick move to the Hawthorns to join Ron Atkinson as his assistant.

BRIAN WHITEHOUSE – Chief Coach

As well as managing the Central League side, Brian is the man with the overall responsibility for developing and coaching United's youngsters from apprentice to the fringe of the first team squad. As the man who guided the careers of such players as Bryan Robson, Derek Statham, Remi Moses, Ally Robertson, Cyrille Regis, Brendon Batson and John Trewick, it is easy to see why the manager moved quickly to bring Brian to Old Trafford. His own playing career began with West Bromwich where he was to spend eight years before moving on to Norwich City for three years. After helping the East Anglian club to promotion from the Third to the Second Division, there followed spells with Wrexham, Crystal Palace and Leyton Orient – where achilles tendon trouble forced his retirement from the game. Brian's coaching career began with a spell at Luton Town and from there he moved to Arsenal (where he was in charge of the team which won the FA Youth Cup in 1971) he later followed Don Howe back to the Hawthorns where he spent a further ten years before moving to Old Trafford last summer.

12

JIMMY CURRAN – Youth Team Coach

Joined United back in 1963 as a goalkeeper after being spotted by the legendary Joe Armstrong. This was the year in which United won the FA Youth Cup with Jimmy Rimmer (now with League Champions Aston Villa) keeping goal. Jimmy was to spend his first spell at Old Trafford mainly with the 'A' and 'B' teams in the Lancashire League, with just the odd appearance in the Central League side. In 1965 Jimmy left United for brief spells with Newcastle United and Oldham Athletic, before moving to Crewe Alexandra in 1968 where he was to stay for four years. Jimmy finally left the Football League for the Cheshire League in 1972 when he joined Rhyl on a part-time basis. After a spell with the Welsh club, Jimmy moved back to Manchester and took up the position of sports master at a school in Didsbury. It was in 1974 that, whilst showing a party of pupils around Old Trafford he was called into the office by Tommy Docherty and offered the job of youth team coach – a job he promptly accepted.

ERIC HARRISON – Youth Team Manager

Joined his local team (Halifax Town) from school in 1956 as a wing-half after playing for Yorkshire Schools. Eric was to spend nine years with Halifax before moving on to Hartlepool United (two years), Barrow (three years), Southport (two years) and then back to Barrow for a further year. The knowledgeable football fan will, by now, have noticed that, with the exception of Halifax Town, all Eric's previous clubs have gone out of the Football League! Is this just a coincidence we wonder? After a brief spell in non-League football with Scarborough, Eric joined Harry Catterick at Everton as youth team coach in 1971, after four years in this job, new manager Billy Bingham appointed him reserve team coach. 1977 saw a new manager, Gordon Lee, and a new job, first team coach – a position he was to hold for four years until last summer when both he and Gordon Lee both left Goodison. A keen student of the game, Eric gained his first FA coaching badge at the age of 21.

13

FANFARE

A 'DOUBLE' HONOUR

Martin Buchan was recently the recipient of a quite unique and rare statuette — or 'grog' as it is popularly known in Wales.

Welshman John Hughes specialises in making likenesses of Rugby stars and his latest masterpiece is only the second ever made of a footballer.

It was brought to Old Trafford by Welsh stars Tommy David and Steve Fenwick and presented to Martin by Jim Bentham, chairman of Moben Kitchens who organised a Sportsman's Evening for Martin Buchan's Testimonial Year at the Old Trafford Executive Suite towards the end of November.

In response to the surprise presentation, Martin said: 'I understand that Kevin Keegan is the only other footballer that John has 'tackled' and I am honoured.'

After a closer inspection, Martin added, 'I particularly like the way he has captured my broken nose.'

1 JANUARY 1983, v ASTON VILLA

An unusual presentation to Martin Buchan in his testimonial season, with the United legend wryly commenting: 'I particularly like the way he has captured my broken nose.'

Known as 'Sparky' to his friends, (although no one quite knows why), Mark joined United as an apprentice in May 1980 and signed professional forms in November the same year.
He played in all the FA Youth Cup matches during the successful runs of 1980-81 and 1981-82, scoring 11 goals in 18 matches.
Mark made his senior competitive debut when he came on for Norman Whiteside during the Milk Cup-tie versus Port Vale at Old Trafford earlier this season. He made his full first team debut, again in the Milk Cup at Oxford at the end of November, when he replaced the injured Arthur Graham and marked the occasion with a fine headed goal.

27 DECEMBER 1983, v NOTTS COUNTY

An early profile of 'Sparky', who had just turned 20. The striker had made three senior appearances for the Reds, but had to wait until the following month for his league debut.

UNITED REVIEW

BASKETBALL

NEXT HOME GAMES

SHARP
RED DEVILS
MANCHESTER UNITED
BASKETBALL

European Cup-Winners' Cup
UNITED v NEGNITA (Barcelona)
Tomorrow night 7.30 pm
Game Sponsors: **BRITISH AIRWAYS**
Raffle prizes: Air ticket for two to Jersey, Sharp Portable Sound System

'DOUBLE'-HEADER

See the soccer team take on Coventry on Saturday afternoon then come over to the Sports Centre to watch the basketball team in action against arch-rivals,
KINGSTON at 8.00 pm.
Game Sponsors: **7up/HORIZON**
Raffle prizes:
1. Horizon Holiday Getaway (value £500). 2. 7up Lounge Patio Set. 3. Sharp Portable Sound System

UNITED KEEP ON WINNING

The Red Devils continued their domination of the basketball scene when they outfought Murray Metals from Edinburgh in a re-match of the British Challenge Trophy.

Although billed as a friendly fixture, pride was very much at stake and in a nail-biting finish, United overhauled the Scottish outfit to win by 97-93 and maintain their unbeaten run.

Alas, all good things come to an end, and so it proved when we made the short journey down the A56 to face local rivals, Manchester Giants, at Altrincham. We had won our two earlier encounters this season but this time the Giants had their revenge beating United 80-74. There were no complaints from the United camp -- the best team won on the night. Our main concern now is to get our injured men back in action for tomorrow night's big game against NEGNITA. BBC cameras will be covering this important European game, but United really do need YOUR support. The Spanish side are one of the top three teams in their own country, and had three of their men in the basketball final of the Los Angeles Olympics.

We're entertaining our opponents at tonight's soccer match but you can be sure that friendship will be suspended when we meet on court at 7.30 , m tomorrow. United will need all the support they can get, so come on down to Stretford and get behind YOUR team.

WHAT, NO RICK! — We can only assume that the absence of General Manager Rick Taylor is something to do with the fact that Player of the Match Jeff Jones received a bottle of Scotch from Whitbread's Peter Wilson instead of the customary bottle of bubbly. Either that, or after so much champagne, Rick has finally lost his sparkle!

29 OCTOBER 1985, v WEST HAM UNITED

Like many football clubs across Europe, United's sporting footprint also extended to basketball in the 1980s, and the Manchester United Red Devils basketball side had a regular slot in the *Review*.

The Red Devils included three former NBA stars and won the 1985 national title

19 AUGUST 1987, v ARSENAL

A profile of United's new no.9 who arrived with a big reputation following his scoring exploits over the border. 'Choccy' made his home debut in this match against the Gunners, and scored his first goal three days later against Watford.

PROFILE BRIAN McCLAIR

By David Meek

Brian McClair spent two years at Glasgow University studying maths.

He gave up university life when Celtic made Motherwell an offer neither club nor player could refuse.

Going to Parkhead meant concentrating full-time on football and a degree had to take second place.

But Manchester United hope those couple of years dealing with figures won't be wasted. They want the 24-year-old Scot to work on a few scoring calculations in his new career at Old Trafford.

The player certainly proved himself a prolific marksman in Scotland. In his last season with Celtic he scored 41 goals in 57 games.

No wonder manager Alex Ferguson is licking his lips in anticipation. The Reds' boss does not need a maths degree to work out what kind of difference a scoring rate like that could make to Manchester United's chances of winning the championship!

He knows of course that scoring in England is not as easy as North of the border.

Charlie Nicholas, the striker McClair succeeded at Parkhead, scored 47 goals in 52 appearances in his final season for Celtic.

Yet at Arsenal in his first season he managed a meagre 13 in 46 matches. His best at Highbury has been 18 in 53 games . . . not quite the golden goal touch he had in Scotland.

Making a successful transition into English football may well be a test of temperament as well as ability.

Certainly the pressure at Manchester United is always tremendous, especially for strikers whose career corpses have littered Old Trafford over the years.

It's 20 years since anyone scored 20 League goals in a season at Old Trafford, which could be the most meaningful statistic behind the 20 year absence of the championship.

McClair knows the fans are looking to him to break the famine which cannot be a light burden.

But it seems to me that the player has the character to cope. He is a cool, laid-back customer with an undeserved reputation for being a typical dour Scot.

He may well be reserved with no particular relish for the razzmatazz of the media; but he is intelligent and has settled immediately into what is a new country as well as a new club.

He has set about the business of finding a house in Wilmslow in businesslike fashion, and he should soon have his wife, Maureen, and 14-month-old Siobhan down from Scotland.

He accepts the expectations of him without alarm.

"I know people are looking for goals from me. I'm a fan myself and it's only natural. I don't resent it and it doesn't bother me," he explains.

"Actually I think there is more to my game than just scoring. It's my performance which is important to me and I have been quite pleased with the way things have gone pre-season.

"I had a similar situation when I moved from Motherwell to Celtic. I was following Charlie Nicholas who had just scored nearly 50 goals.

"That didn't frighten me and I managed to get by. Hopefully I shall score goals for Manchester United as well, and then everyone will be happy.

"But even that doesn't really matter as long as we win the championship. It's winning that counts, not Brian McClair's goals".

It's a down-to-earth approach that could just make a hero out of the footballer his team-mates at Celtic dubbed "Choccy" McClair.

COLLECTORS

by Stuart Renshaw

Eight years ago this month a special commemorative postal cover was produced for the 25th Anniversary of European Football at Old Trafford. United were playing Widzew Lodz from Poland in the UEFA Cup. The covers were produced in red with silver embossing and a RED DEVIL appeared by the result since it was in Europe that they became widely known as The Red Devils.

The other cover features Middlesbrough having returned to the First Division, but in 1974 —

having won the Second Division Championship. Rather appropriate, as they've just returned to the top flight again. A feature with the design of these covers is that local items of interest appear at times and the Transporter Bridge is shown on this cover. All covers are limited editions and as stocks run short, their price rises. Current prices are: Manchester United (above) £2.00; Middlesbrough £4.00 from the Museum. Please add 30p for p&p if ordered through the post.

CORNER

10 SEPTEMBER 1988, v MIDDLESBROUGH

The popular Collectors Corner feature presented *United Review* rarities and allowed fans to purchase them from the Old Trafford Museum.

3 OCTOBER 1989, v PORTSMOUTH

This light-hearted snippet in a League Cup second-round tie's programme highlighted an advertising hoarding in Torquay that shared the same name of one of *United Review*'s longest-serving contributors, David Meek. The friendly on the south coast was arranged as part of the deal that took Lee Sharpe to United.

MOONLIGHTING

Those of us who have tried to reach ace United reporter David Meek by telephone, will no doubt know how difficult a task it is to find him in his office on any day with a 'y' in it. We, therefore assumed, wrongly, that he had the cushiest job in Manchester! Our photograph, taken when the "Reds" visited Torquay recently, suggests that Ol' Red Eyes is perhaps doing a spot of moonlighting on the English Riviera?

25 AUGUST 1990, v COVENTRY CITY

Bob Bishop, our legendary Northern Ireland scout, brought George Best and Norman Whiteside to United, and his death at the age of 90 was announced here.

Bob Bishop

Football talent scouts are, in the main, an anonymous breed. Week in, week out, they attend countless matches looking for that little extra something that sets one hopeful apart from the crowd.
Bob Bishop filled that role for United in Northern Ireland for many, many years, but he could never be called anonymous, for Bob Bishop who died in June, aged 90, was a legend. His captures for United read like a who's who of Northern Ireland football. Jimmy Nicholson, Sammy McMillan, Sammy McIlroy, Jimmy Nicholl and David McCreery were all spotted by the highly respected Belfast man. But without doubt his biggest successes were two youngsters who went on to make their name on the world stage. Two Belfast lads by the name of George Best and Norman Whiteside.
Bob Bishop played a major part in the United story. He will be sadly missed.

JIMMY MURPHY

Jimmy Murphy, a man who played such a vital role in United's post-war success, died suddenly on Wednesday 15th November. The 79-year-old Welshman was out walking in his local park when he collapsed.
Jimmy joined United in 1946 - though the invitation came a year earlier when Matt Busby, who had already been chosen to rebuild the club, came across Jimmy in South West Italy. Sir Matt was out there with an army football team whilst Jimmy was running the sporting activities at a forces' rest camp.
To say that theirs was an interesting partnership is something of an understatement. Sir Matt was known throughout football as a quietly spoken diplomat. Jimmy was the man who put the fire in the bellies of the United players. His role with United was clearly defined from day one. He was charged with the responsibility to seek out new talent to be groomed to United's methods and standards.
The young 15-year-olds who came to Old Trafford as awkward schoolboys, later to stride the world's soccer stages, are too numerous to mention. Let it be said, though, that our young men who first brought world recognition to the Manchester United name in those pre-Munich days were shaped largely by Murphy. They were his boys and he loved them like a father. He worked them hard though, for the standards he set were the very highest and anyone who knew him would quickly tell you that he did not suffer fools gladly. It has been suggested that after Busby had given his team talk, laying great stress on the importance of self-expression and skills, he would quietly return to his office, leaving the dressing room free for Murphy to make sure that the players were then left in no doubt that they had to make their presence felt out on the field - in every sense of the word!
One of the mysteries of Jimmy's career was that a man of such a pedigree and enormous ability should be happy to stay in the shadow of Matt Busby when he could have walked into the manager's office at almost any other club. There were, indeed, very many offers and Sir Matt, in fairness to his old pal, always told Jimmy when approaches were made. He did so, it must be said, with bated breath for he, more than anyone, knew Murphy's value to the club. Murphy's response was always an emphatic "no". His reason was simply that Manchester United was his club and no-one would entice him away.
Having said that, he was prepared to take on the part-time job as Welsh team manager, always ensuring that it did not conflict with his Old Trafford duties. That decision probably saved his life for on the day United were playing that ill-fated game in Belgrade, Jimmy was with the Welsh National side, his seat in the aircraft being taken by Bert Whalley. Had Murphy died in that crash, the chances are that United may never have recovered. For it was he who took over the managerial reins and somehow kept the team going. It seemed an odd collection of reserves and A team players, strengthened by just a couple of survivors and one or two imports from other clubs.
Such were the motivating skills of Jimmy that he harnessed an unlikely looking team, taking them on to Wembley within a few months of the crash. When Sir Matt returned to Old Trafford, Jimmy quietly stepped back into the role he much preferred, that of working with the raw material, shaping them into stars of the future.
Officially, Jimmy 'retired' in 1971, in actual fact, he last attended a match on our behalf just four days before his death. Jimmy Murphy never stopped working for Manchester United.
In a moving tribute to his friend, Sir Matt said, on learning of Jimmy's death: "The news has shattered me. We worked together to bring greatness to Manchester United and no-one outside the club will ever know how important he was to our success".
We began this tribute by saying that Jimmy died in his local park. It is not recorded whether or not there was a schoolboy game going on at the time - if there was, then rest assured that Jimmy died happy.
To his wife Winnie, two daughters, four sons, including Nick who was once on United's books, his grandchildren and very many friends we, on behalf of Manchester United supporters everywhere, extend sincere condolences.

Jimmy and Sir Matt.

25 NOVEMBER 1989, v CHELSEA

A sombre moment as the programme paid tribute to Jimmy Murphy, following the recent death of Sir Matt Busby's trusted lieutenant.

19 SEPTEMBER 1990, v PECSI MUNKAS

Gary Pallister was the latest player to get the caricature/profile treatment in the programme as United's Cup Winners' Cup adventure got under way.

MANCHESTER UNITED FOOTBALL CLUB

STARS OF OLD TRAFFORD

GARY PALLISTER

Even Alex Ferguson probably winced at times after paying a record £2.3 million for Gary Pallister.
The player himself would be the first to admit that his transfer from Middlesbrough to Manchester United did not meet with instant success.
Certainly there were moments when the huge fee looked a little inflated and Liverpool seemed to be on a better bet with their capture of international Glenn Hysen.
What made it harder for the fans to accept was that United had been on the point of signing Hysen from Fiorentina in Italy when they were pipped on the post by Anfield.
But those were early days; by the end of the season the tall commanding figure of Pallister was dominating matches and he came out on top in that most revealing of tests ... the voting by fans for their Player of the Year.
The manager's investment is making much more sense now. Indeed there are many who see the player as England's centre half of the future.
Mark Wright and Paul Parker are the current choice following the retirement of Terry Butcher and they played against Hungary at Wembley last week, but the United man is clearly in the thoughts of the new England manager Graham Taylor.
He had him in his squad and says "It wasn't his fault, but £2.3 million was a lot of money for a centre back and it put him under a great deal of pressure. "A club like Manchester United has such high expectations and this lad had not long been a professional.
"No-one offered that as an excuse, and the boy himself wouldn't make such an excuse, but as he got to the club all hell let loose.
"What impressed me was that he stuck at it and came through. He is a lot more comfortable on the ball and I would like to encourage him to be more confident in his own ability, more positive in his belief in himself.
"I hope that his inclusion in my first squad will go some way to give him that confidence."
Pallister made a late start in senior football, but he has learned quickly and also proved himself adaptable. In that sense he can play in an orthodox back four, or he is capable of making a sweeper system work.
This won't do his England prospects any harm because Taylor sees the game at international level going that way for England as well.
Ferguson has also used him in a three man defence and he has looked quite at home.
"Gary is quite capable of playing as an orthodox centre half for England and making that position his own, but he is equally effective operating as a sweeper", he explained.
He added: "Anyone joining this club goes under the spotlight and Gary was particularly under pressure because of the transfer money involved. But he has overcome his early problems and he is getting better all the time.
"At times last season he was quite magnificent."
Ferguson is a demanding boss and he also says that his centre half did not perform to his high standard often enough.
He has a point, but as far as the fans are concerned Gary Pallister is looking every inch a Manchester United player and that is the acid test!

Gary Pallister
Birthplace: Ramsgate
Birthdate: 30th June, 1963
Height: 6' 4" Weight: 13st 0lb
Previous Clubs: Middlesbrough., Darlington (loan)
Transfered from Middlesbrough to United 28th August 1989

FOOTBALL LEAGUE CAREER

Season	Apps.	Goals
(Middlesbrough)		
1985-86	28	0
1985-86*	7	0
1986-87	44	1
1987-88	44	3
1988-89	37	1
1989-90	3	0
(Manchester United)		
1989-90	35	3
1990-91	5	0
Total	203	8

* Darlington (on loan)

22 Gary Pallister was talking to David Meek (Manchester Evening News) 23

The 'King' in action.

'THE KING'

There may have been several pretenders to the throne, but there was only ever one 'King'.

Denis Law arrived here from Italian club, Torino, in the summer of 1962 and he immediately became a firm favourite with the Old Trafford crowd, and in particular the Stretford End. So much so that in no time he was crowned 'King'.

Undoubtedly one of all the time great players, Denis recently took time out to have a last look at the famous terrace. 'Running out to play in front of these fans was terrific, they really are the best in the business. It was like a shot of adrenalin when you heard the Stretford End roar. I was honoured and flattered when they adopted me as their 'King'.

I shall never forget them.'

20

21

2 MAY 1992, v TOTTENHAM HOTSPUR

This season-closer against Spurs was the end of the era – the final match in front of the Stretford End terracing. In this emotive photograph, the King of the Stretford End Denis Law admires the view from the famous old terrace.

STRETFORD *The* END *of an Era*

My long and lasting memory of the Stretford End was my very first United game versus Barcelona. I'd heard a lot of stories about the Stretford End but I didn't know if they were true, but I started to believe them all when the first goal went in, (Robson), but we were still 2-1 down, then Robbo scored again, and the noise was quite frightening, the cheers and songs carried on until Stapleton put the third in, that was it. Everybody men, women, grans, grandads, managers, players, no matter who you were if you were a Red you went mad, and again the noise was phenomenal, I'm positive I became slightly deaf that night.
PETER, Wythenshawe

On our fourth visit to Old Trafford, back in the early seventies, we decided to sell our stand tickets and go instead into the Stretford End. We were about 18 years of age at the time and remember asking the man next to us if we were stood in the best part of the Stretford End, i.e In the middle, right behind the goal. He, of course, answered "Yes".
Anyway United were playing Chelsea and trailing by two goals with something like five minutes to play. Feeling depressed with the way the match was going my friend, Jennie McCarthy and myself decided to leave early and make our way to the railway station. Imagine our horror when we bought the Football Pink to see that the final score was 2-2.
We'll certainly never forget our first match in the Stretford End.
ANDREW MONAGHAN & JENNIE McCARTHY, Co Cork

I would be about seven when I first started going to watch United at Old Trafford. My dad used to take me along with my older brother, he would see us both into the ground and take us to our place where he would leave us with a group of United fans who we got to know and who would keep an eye on us. My dad would then leave my brother and me on our own as he had to do some stewarding in the Stretford End. We were able to see my dad from where we stood. If there was any trouble there was always a steward of a police officer near by who we could count on for help. Second half of the match my dad would come and stand with us and keep us company, then after the final whistle had gone we would leave all together, talking about the match. Meanwhile eleven years on I am still supporting United in the Stretford End Paddock having had a short spell in the Scoreboard Paddock. This move was not through choice but the complementary section of the ground was transferred to this corner, but now having come full circle, I am back where I first started, supporting United in the Stretford End Paddock.
ALISON WILDE, Failsworth

My Stretford End memory was back in 1984 on Wednesday 21st March. There was a full house. The ground that night was unbelievable, United were 2-0 down from the first leg in Barcelona and had to score three goals. And that's just what they did. What a great night.
JOHN WARBURTON, Birmingham

The Spurs issue also saw *UR* editor Cliff Butler pen an emotional farewell to the terraces on which he spent so many hours.

Fans shared their personal tales of life on the Stretford End, where they had spent years cheering on the Reds.

It goes without saying that Old Trafford will never ever be quite the same again. I, for one, will see a very big part of my early life disappear from view. Something which meant so much to me in the days when I became a member of the United family.
In fourteen months time Old Trafford will be, without doubt, the best club stadium in England. The majestic sweep of the cantilever roof will be without comparison in these islands, but the gentle curves and the neat rows of seats could never replace the character that was Old Trafford.
United supporters are not alone in bidding farewell to a large and significant slice of their club's heritage. Because of the regulations which have been implemented in the aftermath of the Hillsborough disaster and the subsequent Taylor Report, every First and Second Division ground in the country will have to undertake similar changes to fall in line by the start of the 1993-94 season.
It's ironic that the demise of the Stretford End, and its like, has been brought about by the excesses of a minority of people who have their origins in the 1960s crowd revolution. In other words, we have come full circle. The 'Ends' and 'Kops' have self-destructed.
Sad as it is, progress is progress and we must look forward. Today's Stretford Enders - many have stood on the same spot for more years than they care to remember - will find it a heart-rending task to leave when the last ball of this season has been kicked. Knowing full well that within days the demolition men will be moving in.
Tears will flow unashamedly for it really is the 'End' of an era.

Cliff Butler, Editor

5 JANUARY 1993, v BURY

A list of players' hopes for the coming year were revealed in the first programme of 1993. Plenty of dreams came true in that first Premier League title-winning season....

Here's Hoping . . .

...for a return to full fitness as soon as possible. CLAYTON BLACKMORE

...that the World can start to resolve its problems. ERIC CANTONA

...for two weeks off at Christmas. PAUL INCE

...to stay healthy and happy. DENIS IRWIN

...to win a medal for the second successive season. PAUL PARKER

...to score more goals. DARREN FERGUSON

...to remain injury-free for the rest of my career. GARY WALSH

...to have a better April than last year. STEVE BRUCE

...to win back my first team place. LEE MARTIN

...to score my 100th League goal. MARK HUGHES

...to remain healthy and injury-free. GARY PALLISTER

...for a little run in the first team. DANNY WALLACE

...for continued health, happiness and the league title. PETER SCHMEICHEL

...for a League Championship and FA Cup double. BRIAN McCLAIR

...to get back into full training as soon as possible. DION DUBLIN

...for a return to the England squad. LEE SHARPE

...to get back into the first team reckoning. RUSSELL BEARDSMORE

...for a season free from injury for all my teammates. ANDREI KANCHELSKIS

...to increase my goalscoring output. RYAN GIGGS

...for a quick return to first team football. FRASER DIGBY

...to win a Premier League Championship medal. BRYAN ROBSON

...to score a goal for United at Old Trafford. MIKE PHELAN

A thought for '93

9 JANUARY 1993, v TOTTENHAM HOTSPUR

A classic player questionnaire, with our Geordie centre-back as its subject. Brucey wouldn't have been the first footballer to answer 'steak and chips, and a couple of pints of bitter' to the favourite meal question!

UNITED Review

Steve Bruce

ON THE SPOT

Q Which football club did you support as a boy and who were your favourite players?

A *That's an easy one for a start. Newcastle United were the team I supported and Jimmy Smith and Tony Green were my idols.*

Q What is your idea of a perfect meal?

A *Steak and chips with an onion and tomato side salad. Apple pie and custard to follow with a couple of pints of Boddington's Bitter.*

Q Which current player do you admire most, and why?

A *Paul Gascoigne. Not because he's a Geordie, but because of his brilliant all round ability. And for the magnificent way he's fought back from that terrible knee injury. It's great to have him back in the England set-up.*

Q When you get a rare Saturday off, how do you spend it?

A *Usually in one of two ways. Either I take my son, Alex, to watch a match at one of our local clubs, or I have a "flutter" on the horses then sit in front of the television and watch all my selections come in last.*

Q What is the worst injury you've ever had?

A *A broken leg whilst playing for my first club, Gillingham. I was out of action for six-and-a-half months, it was terrible.*

Q How do you spend the morning of a matchday?

A *Breakfast, then back to bed until it's time to leave for Old Trafford.*

Q How do you unwind after the game?

A *More often than not, I spend the evening by going out for a meal with my wife Janet, along with family and friends.*

Q What would you like to do if you were invisible?

A *I'd like to sit in on a Board Meeting and listen to what the manager and directors have to say about me.*

Q Who would be your Premier League "Player of the Season" so far?

A *I would have to say our own Paul Ince. I think he's been in brilliant form of late and thoroughly deserves his place in the England team.*

Q What were your best and worst subjects at school?

A *English and Games were my best subjects and I was absolutely useless at everything else.*

Q What is your favourite style of clothing?

A *I dress to suit the occasion. Casual clothes such as jeans and sweatshirts for informal moments. Suit, collar and tie when it's required.*

Q What are your main interests away from football?

A *I like watching most sports, and I enjoy playing golf and cricket.*

Q Which is the greatest match you've ever seen?

A *Malcolm Macdonald's first appearance for Newcastle United at St. James' Park after he'd joined them from Luton Town. It was in August 1971 against Liverpool. "Supermac" scored a hat-trick in a 3-2 win and was later carried from the field with a mouth injury. I remember 'cause I was there.*

Q How do you pass the time when travelling to an away match?

A *Predictable answer I'm afraid. I pass the hours by playing cards with some of the lads and the manager, who incidentally is the worst card player I have ever come across.*

Q If you had one wish, what would it be?

A *Health and happiness for my family and to steer clear of serious injuries for the remainder of my career.*

Q If there is one place in the world you could visit, where would it be?

A *Australia in the middle of our winter, watching England battle it out with the "Aussies" for The Ashes.*

Q Which is your favourite stadium outside of England?

A *Feyenoord Stadium, Rotterdam, because it brings back such great memories. It would be even better if it had a roof, our fans got a real soaking that night. Although I'm not sure they noticed.*

Q What is the best advice you've ever received?

A *My Dad, Joe, said to me when I was a kid: "Always go out and give 100 per cent and hope that it's enough." I've always tried to do just that.*

Q What has been the most amusing incident of your career to date?

A *That would have to be when I took short playing for Gillingham against Blackpool in 1979. The lads gave me stick about that after the game.*

Q Do you have a special routine or ritual during the moments up to the kick-off?

A *Because of what happened to me at Bloomfield Road (see last question) I am usually to be found in the toilet during the build-up to the kick-off.*

SEND YOUR QUESTIONS

Included in the questions above are those sent in by Ruth Mackie (South Bermondsey), Jonathan Brown (Royston, Herts), and Dorothy Granger (Keighley). What would you like to ask your favourite player?

Send in the question and we will do our best to have him answer it for you.

Questions to:

On The Spot (United Review),
Manchester United FC,
Old Trafford, Manchester M16 0RA.

20 UNITED REVIEW — UNITED REVIEW 21

22 JANUARY 1994, v EVERTON
As the opening line in this tribute stated, 'This is a terribly sad day for Manchester United,' as the club played its first game after Sir Matt's passing.

This is a terribly sad day for Manchester United but we are so grateful that we shared in Sir Matt's life and work.

When he joined the club in 1945 we had nothing and we were of no real consequence. Sir Matt, in his 25 years as manager, changed all that. He built a team which were champions on five occasions and runners-up seven times. Indeed, he only finished outside the top ten on two occasions. He brought FA Cup success to the club and managed the first English team to win the European Cup in 1968.

Perhaps the most fitting tribute to Sir Matt's life is the present side's success and playing style. He thoroughly enjoyed and approved of the type of football played by Alex Ferguson and the present team and we are all so pleased that he lived to share the joy of last season's Championship success. That was a fitting tribute to Matt.

C. M. Edwards, Chairman

Nobody lives forever. The sands of time run out for all of us eventually. But we all hoped that the man who became known as Mr Manchester United would live on forever.
To everyone connected with the club, Sir Matt Busby was immortal. A giant amongst men. A true gentleman who always had time for the ordinary man.

Sadly, however, even the great man himself couldn't cheat the clock and two days ago on Thursday, 20th January, at the Alexandra Hospital in Cheadle, he passed away peacefully in his sleep. He was 84.

No words can express the feeling of sadness which instantly swept not only football, but the world at large. Almost immediately supporters began to gather outside Old Trafford to pay silent homage to the man whose name will be legend as long as football is played.
A full tribute to the great man will be included in the next edition of the United Review.

SIR MATT BUSBY 1909 - 1994

UNITED REVIEW

1 OCTOBER 1995, v LIVERPOOL
This ongoing series profiling the greatest players to represent the club focused on one of our best ever strikers for the visit of Liverpool in autumn 1995.

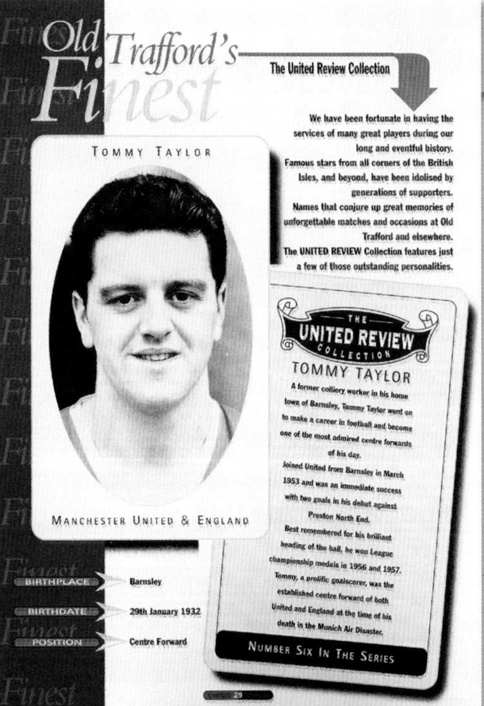

Old Trafford's Finest

The United Review Collection

We have been fortunate in having the services of many great players during our long and eventful history.
Famous stars from all corners of the British Isles, and beyond, have been idolised by generations of supporters.
Names that conjure up great memories of unforgettable matches and occasions at Old Trafford and elsewhere.
The UNITED REVIEW Collection features just a few of those outstanding personalities.

TOMMY TAYLOR

MANCHESTER UNITED & ENGLAND

THE UNITED REVIEW COLLECTION

TOMMY TAYLOR

A former colliery worker in his home town of Barnsley, Tommy Taylor went on to make a career in football and become one of the most admired centre forwards of his day.
Joined United from Barnsley in March 1953 and was an immediate success with two goals in his debut against Preston North End.
Best remembered for his brilliant heading of the ball, he won League championship medals in 1956 and 1957.
Tommy, a prolific goalscorer, was the established centre forward of both United and England at the time of his death in the Munich Air Disaster.

NUMBER SIX IN THE SERIES

BIRTHPLACE: Barnsley
BIRTHDATE: 29th January 1932
POSITION: Centre Forward

UNITED 29

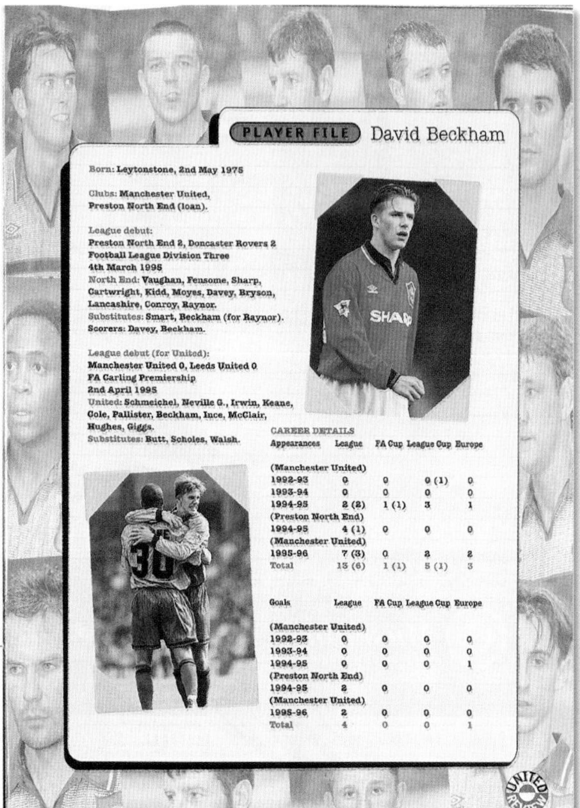

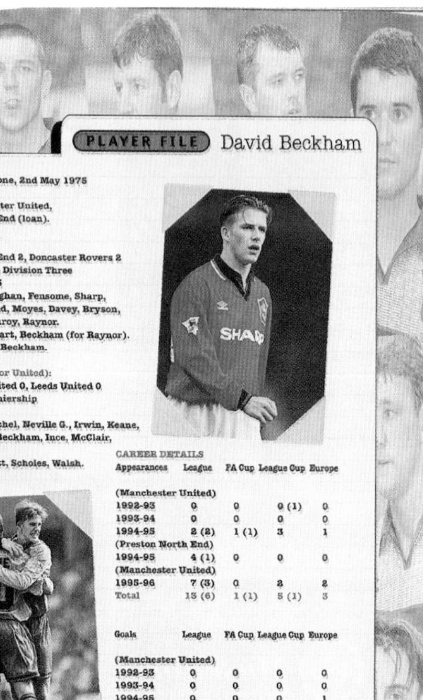

PLAYER FILE David Beckham

Born: Leytonstone, 2nd May 1975

Clubs: Manchester United,
Preston North End (loan).

League debut:
Preston North End 2, Doncaster Rovers 2
Football League Division Three
4th March 1995
North End: Vaughan, Fensome, Sharp, Cartwright, Kidd, Moyes, Davey, Bryson, Lancashire, Conroy, Raynor.
Substitutes: Smart, Beckham (for Raynor).
Scorers: Davey, Beckham.

League debut (for United):
Manchester United 0, Leeds United 0
FA Carling Premiership
2nd April 1995
United: Schmeichel, Neville G., Irwin, Keane, Cole, Pallister, Beckham, Ince, McClair, Hughes, Giggs.
Substitutes: Butt, Scholes, Walsh.

CAREER DETAILS

Appearances	League	FA Cup	League Cup	Europe
(Manchester United)				
1992-93	0	0	0 (1)	0
1993-94	0	0	0	0
1994-95	2 (2)	1 (1)	3	1
(Preston North End)				
1994-95	4 (1)	0	0	0
(Manchester United)				
1995-96	7 (3)	0	2	2
Total	13 (6)	1 (1)	5 (1)	3

Goals	League	FA Cup	League Cup	Europe
(Manchester United)				
1992-93	0	0	0	0
1993-94	0	0	0	0
1994-95	0	0	0	1
(Preston North End)				
1994-95	2	0	0	0
(Manchester United)				
1995-96	2	0	0	0
Total	4	0	0	1

UNITED 19 REVIEW

18 NOVEMBER 1995, v SOUTHAMPTON
United's emerging young right-sided midfielder was profiled in the programme for the visit of the Saints in 1995. The match – a 4-1 win for the Reds – was Beckham's 26th appearance in the first team.

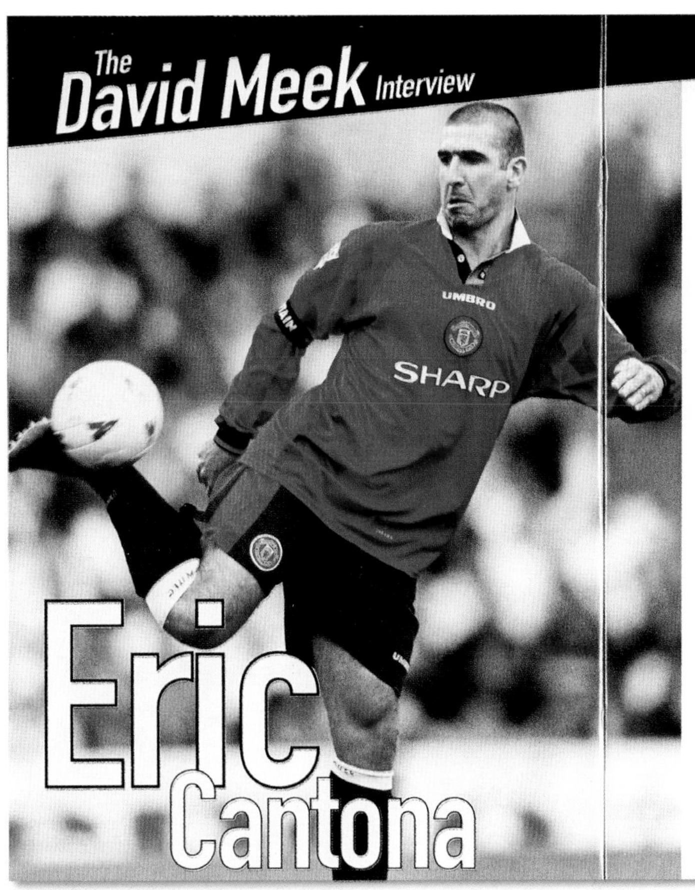

So what's happened to the happy wanderer, the restless spirit, the bete noir of French football?

Watching Eric Cantona these days, both on and off the field, is to see conformist man, a player who behaves in matches and has become so responsible away from the game that Alex Ferguson has made him captain.

But has he really changed? Has he got over the nomadic phase of his life and settled down? Can he now handle referees and opponents without losing his cool?

I put the points to him and found him still that much of a rebel to resist the idea that he is in danger of becoming just another boring old guy.

"I don't want to change but I also want to learn and not make the same mistakes twice. I still want to take risks and live a little dangerously.

"I am still a traveller in my head. I want to keep that feeling. If I am not happy I will live somewhere else. I don't stay in places if I am not happy. I think I still have a restless spirit.

"I have not really changed, it's just that I am staying longer in Manchester because I am happy here. In fact I think I will be with Manchester United for the rest of my career because I am at ease here. I didn't find this before.

Honoured

"It's something to do with the results and success of the team, the atmosphere and I think my wife has become a little weary of moving from city to city, house to house.

"We also have a baby daughter now and my son is eight. He is completely able to speak both French and English and an English education is very important.

"I am also very honoured to be captain. I was surprised to be offered it because there are a lot of players in the team with the responsibilities of a captain but I like to take responsibility.

"We have a young team and I think we have a good understanding. I try to help the young players but they help me because I can only play the way I do if there is a lot of movement. Maybe they have found in me something they needed but I have also found in them what I needed," he explained.

But though at Old Trafford Eric Cantona has become a king, or even a Dieu as the t-shirts proclaim, he continues to be ignored at international level for France.

"I have no burning ambition to play for France any more. I know all the reasons why I am not picked and that is important to me. I feel bigger than French football and regard them as smaller. There are as many big international games for me with Manchester United in the UEFA Champions League that I do not miss playing for France," he said.

And what chance have United got of success in Europe?

"If we play as we know we can we have got a very good chance. I think we have got the pace, the tactics and special qualities that we need not be scared of anyone. I know we were disappointing against Juventus in Turin but maybe we gave them too much credit. The way we played in the second half showed that there is no need to be frightened.

Toughest

"Some people say there is a gap in technique and understanding between football in England and in Europe but I don't think so. Manchester United and Arsenal have won the Cup Winners' Cup in recent years which is not so bad compared with other individual countries.

"The English League is the toughest in the world. In one game anyone can beat everyone but if you were to put a Spanish, German or Italian team playing forty games in the English League I don't think they would do very well."

12 OCTOBER 1996, v LIVERPOOL
A deep conversation between Eric Cantona and David Meek appeared in this programme, with the Frenchman discussing his happiness in Manchester and the sense of responsibility he felt in taking the captaincy at United.

United Review 50 Years On

The United Review is 50 years old this month. Our club's official programme was given its new title for the start of the 1946-47 season - the first complete league season following the end of the Second World War - and it has been synonymous with the club ever since. The famous front cover featuring the symbolic shaking hands of the player and supporter was first used for the Football League Division One match against Grimsby Town on Saturday 31st August 1946.

It has been the instantly recognisable front page of the club's official match publication in the time since, save for several seasons during the late 60s and 70s when various other designs were used.

The supporter's clothing may have changed over the years and the player's kit certainly has, but the basic image has remained unique to Manchester United.

To commemorate this milestone in the history of the United Review we have reprinted that original edition - twelve pages and two colour, except for a touch of red on the cover - and it is presented, with our compliments, as part of today's forty-eight page, full colour 1996-97 version.

We are also including a feature throughout the season, in which Iain McCartney, secretary of The United Review Collectors' Club, will present a brief history ....50 YEARS ON. It promises to be an interesting and informative series which will highlight the changing (or not) face of the United Review.

United Review News 1996 Season 1997

Allenby Chilton

Colorsport

Allenby Chilton, one of United's greatest ever stalwarts passed on in June. He was 77.

A strong, uncompromising and eminently dependable centre-half, he was the backbone of United's defence for many years during the late 40s and early 50s.

He made his league debut against Charlton Athletic on 2nd September 1939, but due to the outbreak of World War Two it wasn't until 31st August 1946 (v. Grimsby Town) that he made his next league appearance for the club.

He was member of the 1948 FA Cup winning team and also collected a League Championship medal four years later. He succeeded Johnny Carey as captain and went on to complete a marvellous career with the club which spanned almost 400 appearances. He also picked up two full caps for England. A North-Easterner from County Durham, he moved on to take up the position of player/manager at Grimsby Town in 1955.

It was with deep sadness that we learnt of his death and we take this opportunity to offer belated condolences, from everyone at the club, to his family and friends.

21 AUGUST 1996, v EVERTON
Two moments to note in this issue for the first home game of the 1996/97 season – the marking of 50 years of the programme as *United Review*, and a tribute to club legend Allenby Chilton, who passed away earlier that summer.

MEMORIES TO CHERISH

Certain events in life leave an indelible memory etched in the heart and mind. Moments so rare, you know instinctively that they will never ever be repeated.

Such a brief moment in time occurred in the Nou Camp Stadium on the evening of Wednesday 26th May this year.

Anyone who witnessed, either in the stadium or on television, the amazing closing stages of the 1999 European Cup final will never be able to erase from their mind the incredible scenes, which followed United's last-gasp goals.

Had they been under cover, the 60,000 or so United supporters who had gained access to the stadium, would have lifted the roof from its moorings. It was a supreme and unique occasion in the history of Manchester United and English football.

Those fortunate enough to have been at Wembley in 1968 when Bobby Charlton captained United to triumph over Benfica found it difficult to fight back

The pandemonium that greeted Teddy Sheringham's equalising goal, when all seemed lost, was simply unforgettable. The celebrations that followed Ole Gunnar Solskjaer's winner defy description.

Football would be nothing without passion and emotion, and can there ever have been such an explosion of collective relief and euphoria in the history of the European Cup, or any other competition for that matter.

All appeared lost. The dream of becoming the first ever English club to scoop the game's three most prestigious trophies in one season had all but faded. Many were consoling themselves: "Two out of three isn't bad!"

Even Alex Ferguson owned up to have been preparing himself to accept what seemed like inevitable defeat with dignity.

The moments, which followed are already firmly entrenched in football folklore.

the tears as Alex Ferguson and Peter Schmeichel hoisted aloft the huge gleaming trophy. And it wasn't easy either for those too young to have seen the first victory of 31 years before.

It was the perfect conclusion to a ten-day stint, which saw United claim a very special place in the pages of football history. The FA Carling Premiership, or simply 'the league' as many prefer to call it, and the FA Cup had already been snapped up in another history-making third domestic double. But the most glorious piece of icing a cake ever received, was supplied when the European Cup was added amid remarkable scenes in one of the world's truly great football arenas.

United's adoring supporters had travelled from all corners of the world, just to be there. Nobody wanted to miss this one and even those who held little hope of purchasing a ticket converged on the Catalan capital.

12 MANCHESTER UNITED

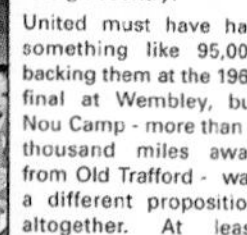

Can there ever have been a larger body of support assembled in a foreign country?

United must have had something like 95,000 backing them at the 1968 final at Wembley, but Nou Camp - more than a thousand miles away from Old Trafford - was a different proposition altogether. At least

The Club had made a request that the fans should "show their colours", and it wasn't ignored. Arguably, it was the greatest display of support that a Manchester United side has ever received. That evening in Barcelona stands

60,000 made it into the stadium, but how many had to content themselves with a place in front of a television screen in one of Barcelona's countless bars? We shall never know for certain, but there were one or two!

'Fergie's Army from Malta', proclaimed one banner. 'Sri Lanka Reds' was another. There was a Croatian flag, a Dutch flag and one from the Isle of Man. Everywhere from Hastings to Carrickfergus, and most places in between and beyond.

There was even a contingent from Glasgow, that most fervent centre of Scottish footballing passion where Green and Blue rules.

But, perhaps the most evocative of all the expressions of loyalty came in the resurrection of the 1968 classic, which simply boasted: 'Manchester United - The Religion'! Can it have been the same fans of 31 years earlier?

out as one of the truly great occasions in football history.

Alex Ferguson was right in demanding that United fans should enjoy to the full the closing days of the season, for it is hard to imagine that we will ever see the like again.

By Cliff Butler

UNITED REVIEW 13

11 AUGUST 1999, v SHEFFIELD WEDNESDAY
Editor Cliff Butler may have thought he'd seen it all in decades of following United... and then came 10 days in May 1999. In the first programme for the next season, he summed it all up.

Player of the Year

Reds' skipper receives his Sir Matt Busby Player of the Year Award from Sheena and Sandy Busby and fans' representative Fiona Milligan. Fiona, who lives locally, in turn was presented with a special club pennant to commemorate her very special day at Old Trafford

30 United Review

United Review 31

9 SEPTEMBER 2000, v SUNDERLAND
The recipient of the Sir Matt Busby Player of the Year award for the 1999/00 season was Roy Keane, and the smiling captain was presented with his trophy by Sir Matt's daughter and son – Sheena and Sandy – as well as one delighted fan.

13 SEPTEMBER 2000, v ANDERLECHT
Four friends, legends and former European Footballers of the Year were reunited on the Old Trafford pitch in August 2000, much to the delight of every single person inside the stadium.

GALAXY OF STARS

It isn't often that you get to see four European footballers of the year in any one place at the same time. But that was the case at Old Trafford on the opening day of the season when the great Eusebio, formerly of Benfica and Portugal, travelled to Manchester to present Bobby Charlton, Denis Law and George Best with life-time achievement awards ahead of the first National Football Awards event.

The crowd, including considerable numbers of Newcastle United supporters, gave the quartet of players a fantastic ovation as the ceremony was being conducted in the centre circle.

Denis Law was European Footballer of the Year in 1964, Eusebio (1965), Bobby Charlton (1966) and George Best (1968).

10 United Review

United Review

Obituary

They called him El Beatle, but George Best always danced to his own beat

George Best 1946-2005

Remembering the shy young lad from Belfast who became a footballing icon

The Belfast-born genius was, without a shadow of doubt, one of the greatest footballers the game has seen, and in the opinion of many, truly was the best. The great Pelé – perhaps the closest to contest his mantle – said George was incomparable. Loftier praise is hard to find.

It would be impossible to deny that Best possessed a singular talent laced with greatness. Some would suggest Stanley Matthews or Tom Finney were the greatest from these shores, Diego Maradona, Johan Cruyff and Alfredo Di Stefano would surely feature. It's a tricky exercise comparing players from different eras, but there can be no doubt George Best would always steal the show.

He was special in the world of football. He was destined to become the first genuine pop idol footballer, but his glittering career in the beautiful game almost didn't happen. Best arrived in Manchester as a youngster in 1961 with his friend Eric McMordie, who went on to play for Middlesbrough, but was so intimidated by the hustle and bustle of life in a big city that he was quickly back on the ferry to Belfast. Sir Matt Busby and Jimmy Murphy, Manchester United's legendary management duo, needed all their persuasive guile to tempt him back, but succeed they did. It was among the best day's work the pair ever did.

Originally tipped for stardom by Bob Bishop, United's hugely respected scout in Northern Ireland, Best fast-tracked his way to the top. He made his debut, aged 17, against West Bromwich Albion in September 1963, just a few months after helping United win the FA Youth Cup for a sixth time. The crowd took him to their hearts instantly: he was to be their darling for the next 10 years.

The club was still in the throes of re-building after Munich, and he proved to be the missing piece of the jigsaw alongside other great names like Bobby Charlton, Denis Law, Pat Crerand, Nobby Stiles and Bill Foulkes. United picked up a first post-Munich league title in 1965, Best's first season, and again two years later. Then in 1968 the European Cup, for so long the Holy Grail, was finally won, Best on target against Benfica in front of 100,000 ecstatic fans at Wembley.

It was a crowning moment, but an ageing team was ripe for another revamp. That would take time and Best was relied on to pull the team through. He was more than up to the task, and on occasion, won matches single-handedly.

His excesses away from the game invariably made headlines. More than once he announced he had played his last match for his beloved Manchester United.

He and United eventually reached the end of the road in January 1974 when, after yet another reconciliation, orchestrated by then-boss Tommy Docherty, he was left out of the team to play Plymouth Argyle in an FA Cup tie. Best knew it was the end and left Old Trafford on that dismal Manchester day never to return, at least not in a playing capacity.

At 27, he should have been reaching his peak when he played his last game for Manchester United. It wasn't his last outing as a player, as his travels took in Fulham, Stockport County and Hibernian as well as a mildly impressive career in America. But his personal demons never left him. His health suffered hugely and he became a shadow of the handsome, vital superstar.

Those lucky enough to see him in a Red shirt have an abiding memory; Best with a ball at his feet was a sight that transcended sport. Many have attempted to replicate his skills. None have come close to succeeding. Capped 37 times by Northern Ireland, he made more than 450 appearances for United, scoring 178 goals – including six in one match against Northampton Town. His passing will be mourned wherever football is played.

Manchester United v West Bromwich Albion **15**

30 NOVEMBER 2005, v WEST BROM

The tragic death of George Best – aged just 59 – happened a few days before United faced West Brom, the team George had made his debut against 42 years earlier. It proved to be a hugely emotional occasion at Old Trafford, with thousands of fans holding up this poster (left) before kick-off, in tribute to one of United's all-time greats.

TONIGHT'S MATCH

TEN MINUTES WITH...

Cristiano Ronaldo

The Reds winger has been in the form of his life this term but the goal-hungry Madeiran wants medals to cap his record-breaking season...

Heads up: Ronaldo soars highest to score his 36th goal of a prolific season

CRISTIANO RONALDO, STILL only 23, has been the star performer of 2007/08 so far. Top scorer in the Premier and Champions Leagues, the plaudits are being heaped on him weekly, his global fan club continues to grow and he's hotly tipped to sweep the board of individual awards for 2008. Last Tuesday, United's no.7 continued his brilliant European campaign with a vital opener in the Stadio Olimpico; tonight he aims to finish the job...

How pleasing was last week's result in the Stadio Olimpico?
The victory in Rome was very important and even better than we'd hoped for. A 1-0 win would have been a good result for us but 2-0 is magnificent. It definitely gives us an advantage going into tonight's game and you'd have to say we have a great chance of reaching the semi-final.

Some people are suggesting the tie is over already...
It's maybe natural the fans should think about the semi-final, but we still need to do the job tonight. If we think we're already through to the next stage then that's the wrong attitude. Like I said, 2-0 gives us the advantage but we need to respect Roma and we need to win. I can't tell you how much the players all want to win this trophy, so I'm confident there will be no slip-up.

As a team, do you feel you have the measure of Roma now?
Actually, the first leg was very difficult and Roma are a great team. They made it very hard for us but in the end I don't think you can argue with the result. We created some very good chances and I think we deserved to win.

It was a measured display in Rome last week, is that what is needed in the Champions League?
Well, playing in Europe is totally different to the Premier League. I think it's more difficult to win in the Champions League, especially away from home. Sometimes you can't attack for 90 minutes. Instead, you need to put in disciplined performances where you keep it tight and just break on the counterattack. In Italy last week we played like that – we were patient and compact and made the most of our opportunities. I think we showed we can play that game very well; tonight you'll see more attacking.

On a personal level, how happy are you with your current form?
I try to improve every season and I think this season has been even better than the last. Some people say I need to perform better in the big games; I respect that opinion but I don't feel I need to prove anything to anyone. I've been very pleased with my own progress and also the progress of the team. I believe this squad is the best I've been involved in since joining United. It's more consistent and more mature than any other side.

Your goal return has certainly improved. Not so long ago you were betting Sir Alex you'd score 15 goals; now you've scored 36...
That's true! Again, I'm happy with the improvement. I'm sure I'm a better player now than I was one year ago and definitely better than I was when I first came to Old Trafford. I really hope that trend continues. As for why I've scored more goals this season? Well, it's hard to say, but I think I've definitely had more chances. My team-mates help me – just look at Scholesy's cross in Rome...

You didn't even get to celebrate that goal!
[Laughs] Ha ha, I know! When I hit the ground I twisted my body a little bit and I was a little worried at first. But I was okay in the end and I was just happy to have given the team the lead.

Do you have a favourite goal from this season?
There have been a few I've really enjoyed. Last week's goal against Roma was very satisfying and I also like the free kicks against Portsmouth, Bolton and Sunderland. It's hard to pick just one. As long as the ball goes in the net I'm very happy. It's a real pleasure to score goals for United.

How proud were you to break George Best's record of 32 goals in a season from midfield?
I don't really want to break anybody's records – I feel a little bad – but it's certainly a wonderful record to now hold. George Best was an exciting player and I've had the opportunity to see a few tapes of his performances. He was fantastic. But my ambition is just to do my best and keep improving.

You're widely tipped to scoop the player of the year awards. How much would that please you?
It's nice to be recognised as an individual but if I had the choice of winning the Champions League or the Golden Boot I'd pick the Champions League every time.

> “Some people say I need to perform better in the big games; I respect that opinion but I don't feel I need to prove anything to anyone”

TONIGHT'S MATCH

THAT BOY RONALDO

After the Reds' no.7 found the net again during last week's first leg in Rome, team-mate John O'Shea admitted he was running out of superlatives to describe the Portuguese winger. Even the ever articulate Patrice Evra struggled to sum up Ronaldo's talent. "He's unbelievable," said Evra. "What else can you say?" Well, plenty it would seem. You see, United's stars haven't been the only ones raving about Ronaldo...

"You can't man-mark him because he starts off up front, drifts wide, comes into the hole. He's six foot two, brave as a lion, strong as an ox and quick as lightning. [Laughs] If he was good looking you'd say he has everything!"
Derby manager Paul Jewell

**"Even if you are a City fan, you want to see the tricks that Ronaldo performs because that is the art of football. He's an artist and maybe number one in the world at the moment."
City boss Sven-Goran Eriksson**

"Ronaldo right now is a 10 out of 10, the best in the world. For me, he's already better than Kaka."
Real Madrid boss Bernd Schuster

**"He makes the right decisions, taking the man on when he needs to and passing at the right time. He does everything – he takes free kicks and corners. He leaves goal kicks to Edwin van der Sar, but I expect him to start taking them soon!"
Ex-Red Ruud van Nistelrooy**

"I would love to have Cristiano Ronaldo in my fantasy league team; I doubt he would spend too much time on the bench."
Liverpool boss Rafa Benitez

**"The kid can't be human, can he? The trickery of Best, the technique of Zidane, the workrate of Bryan Robson, the heading ability of Nat Lofthouse. Ronaldo must be an android."
Ex-Chelsea star Tony Cascarino**

9 APRIL 2008, v ROMA

The programme for the Champions League quarter-final second leg versus Roma carried an interview with Cristiano Ronaldo, who had combined with Wayne Rooney to give United a 2-0 lead from the first leg in the Italian capital.

Rio was one of many players who gave their time to help the MU Foundation

A season of success

The first year of the MU Foundation has been one to remember

UNITED FANS HAVE had plenty to applaud this season, but off the pitch there's also cause for celebration, not least thanks to MU Foundation's sterling charity work.

The Foundation formed six new links with local and national charities on behalf of the club last August and since then has been tirelessly working with these partners to improve lives through the power of football.

United players have been at the forefront of many initiatives. In October, John O'Shea opened The Legacy, a Rainbow House centre for children with neurological disorders. Gary Neville fronted a DVD for Christie's aimed at encouraging young cancer sufferers to exercise, while Michael Carrick lent his time to raise awareness of life-limiting illnesses.

Rio Ferdinand and Edwin van der Sar went back to school to promote healthy eating and active lifestyles, and Ole Gunnar Solskjaer was a special guest at Old Trafford's inaugural Santa Run.

Reds' supporters have played their part too, with more than £20,000 raised via various matchday ground collections.

Of course, work doesn't stop when the season ends. In May, fans can abseil at Old Trafford to raise funds for Cystic Fibrosis and Francis House, and the New Children's Hospital and The Legacy will invite teams for a once-in-a-lifetime game on the pitch.

June will see each of United's charity partners enter a team, coached by an OT legend, into the Charity Challenge Cup, while a young Cystic Fibrosis sufferer will sit on as many Old Trafford seats as possible in an attempt to set a Guinness world record.

"It's been a fantastic season and things will get even better next term," Foundation Chief Executive John Shiels said. "We want to involve as many people as possible in our work to inspire the potential in young people."

For more information, visit **www.mufoundation.org** or email **enquiries@mufoundation.org**

3 MAY 2008, v WEST HAM UNITED

Ever since it was established in 2006, the MU Foundation has been supported by every first-team star – as well as the matchday programme, which covers its activities.

16 AUGUST 2010, v NEWCASTLE UNITED

This statistical snippet broke down the times United were at their most dangerous – and vulnerable – when it came to goals during the 2009/10 season...

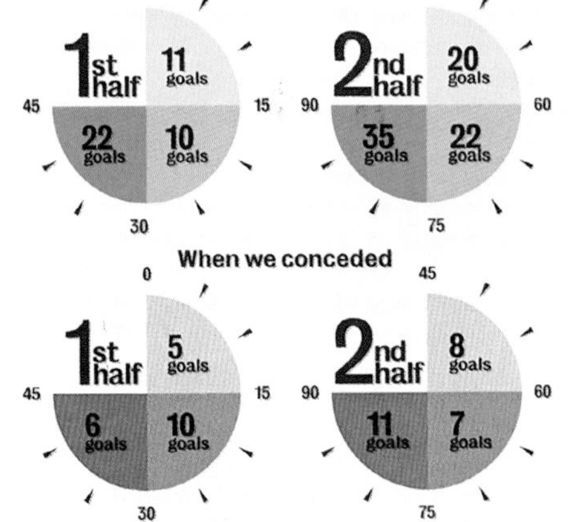

News

Reds want to continue home rule; Chicharito crowns stellar debut season...

News in numbers

Quick and quirky facts and figures

5 Today is the fifth time we have ended a Premier League season by lifting the trophy at OT. Previous opponents were Coventry (93/94), West Ham (96/97 and 06/07), Spurs (98/99).

10 English league titles won by Paul Scholes. The veteran midfielder has climbed to second in the all-time league winners' table. Ryan Giggs, of course, leads the way with 12.

22 Goals scored by United in the final 15 minutes of league games this term; almost a third of all the Reds' goals. Those strikes tacked on an extra 14 points to the Reds' haul.

33 Ryan Giggs' major honours total. Incredibly, Giggsy now has more major honours on his own than every club in England except United (59), Liverpool (59) and Arsenal (38).

1571 Points won by United since the Premier League began. In a cumulative table dating back to August 1992, the Reds lead – 193 points ahead of Arsenal, then Chelsea (-234) and Liverpool (-289).

For a review of another title-winning season turn to p40

Wayne tucks away the title-clinching penalty

Champions!

Reds delight in title, but intend to end league season on a winning note

United's Premier League season had been dogged by potentially costly away draws, so it was with no small hint of irony that a solitary travelling point proved enough last weekend to seal a historic 19th title.

Wayne Rooney ended the season on an upward swing after a trying term, hammering home a late penalty at Ewood Park to seal a draw with Blackburn before quickly dedicating his strike to United's supporters.

"It was terrifying," admitted the striker. "I just had to compose myself. I knew where I was going to put it, I'd been practising all week. It's a great feeling after the year I've had with the ups and downs, so this is for the fans."

The setting for United's triumph had added significance, coming a year after a point at Ewood Park effectively cost the Reds a fourth successive title, and Rio Ferdinand was pleased to bury the ghosts of 2010.

"It was here last year that we more or less lost the league, so it's nice to come back and make up for it," said the defender. "We put in hard graft and kept on persevering and got our rewards. You can't put into words what this means and it was great to celebrate with the fans at the end. They follow us all over the world and give us great support and they deserve this."

After embarking on richly-deserved celebrations of their own, the players have been back at Carrington this week, preparing to finish the domestic season against Blackpool. Victory today would round off a virtually flawless Old Trafford campaign from the champions, who have dropped two home points all term (turn to p67).

Ian Holloway's side have huge motivation to take points, as they currently occupy a spot in the relegation zone and are one of five teams who go into today's programme in danger of sinking into the Championship. Nevertheless, Michael Carrick insists United are intent on victory.

"We definitely want to end the season on a high," says the midfielder. "We've been brilliant at home all season, and we want to complete the job and pick up the Premier League trophy on the back of a win."

10 Manchester United v Blackpool

22 MAY 2011, v BLACKPOOL

The Reds had wrapped up the 2010/11 title – our record-breaking 19th – the week before at Ewood Park, which gave the programme cause for celebration in the closing game, against Blackpool at Old Trafford.

12 MAY 2013, v SWANSEA CITY

This infographic illustrated just how influential Michael Carrick had been throughout the 2012/13 campaign, when United secured our 20th top-flight title.

Focus on...

MICHAEL CARRICK

United's no.16 has proved pivotal this term

Carrick has made more accurate passes (2,290) in league fixtures this season than every other player in the Premier League, except Mikel Arteta (Arsenal).

Only one player – Robin van Persie – has made more appearances than Michael Carrick for the Reds this season.

Following the Reds' match at Swansea City on 19 November 2011, Carrick started every one of United's next 39 league fixtures.

70.5%

United's win percentage this season was 70.5 per cent when Carrick played and just 50 per cent when he didn't.

Since last season's game at the Liberty Stadium, he's featured in 59 of the Reds' 63 league matches.

The last time the Reds and Swansea met, Michael boasted a pass completion rate of 94 per cent – higher than any other United player on the pitch.

Man for the big occasion:

Opponents most faced

In Michael's 153 appearances at Old Trafford, he's only walked off the pitch a loser on 13 occasions.

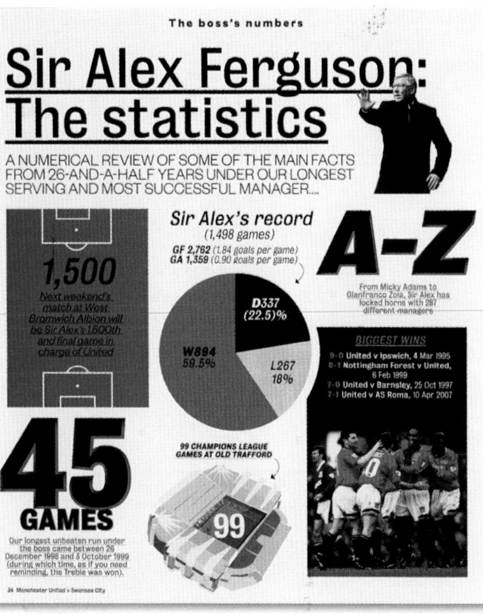

The boss's numbers

Sir Alex Ferguson: The statistics

A NUMERICAL REVIEW OF SOME OF THE MAIN FACTS FROM 26-AND-A-HALF YEARS UNDER OUR LONGEST SERVING AND MOST SUCCESSFUL MANAGER...

1,500

Next weekend's match at West Bromwich Albion will be Sir Alex's 1,500th and final game in charge of United

Sir Alex's record

(1,498 games)

GF 2,762 (1.84 goals per game)
GA 1,359 (0.90 goals per game)

A-Z

From Micky Adams to Gianfranco Zola, Sir Alex has locked horns with 287 different managers

BIGGEST WINS

9-0 United v Ipswich, 4 Mar 1995
8-1 Nottingham Forest v United, 6 Feb 1999
7-0 United v Barnsley, 25 Oct 1997
7-1 United v AS Roma, 10 Apr 2007

45 GAMES

Our longest unbeaten run under the boss came between 26 December 1998 and 3 October 1999 (during which time, as if you need reminding, the Treble was won).

99 CHAMPIONS LEAGUE GAMES AT OLD TRAFFORD

34 Manchester United v Swansea City

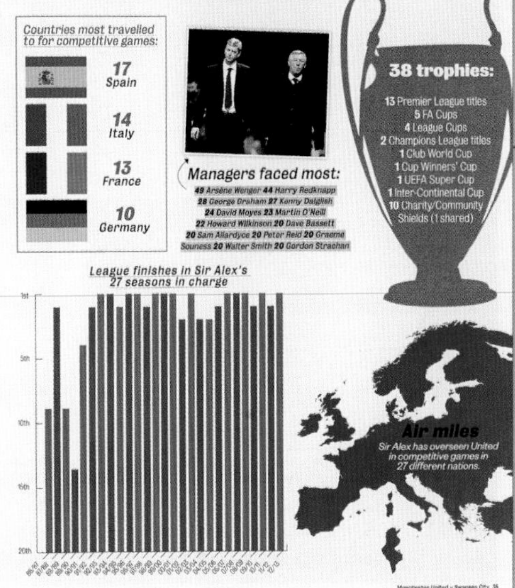

The boss's numbers

Countries most travelled to for competitive games:

17 Spain
14 Italy
13 France
10 Germany

Managers faced most:

49 Arsène Wenger 44 Harry Redknapp 28 George Graham 27 Kenny Dalglish 24 David Moyes 23 Martin O'Neill 22 Howard Wilkinson 20 Dave Bassett 20 Sam Allardyce 20 Peter Reid 20 Graeme Souness 20 Walter Smith 20 Gordon Strachan

38 trophies:

13 Premier League titles
5 FA Cups
4 League Cups
2 Champions League titles
1 Club World Cup
1 Cup Winners' Cup
1 UEFA Super Cup
1 Inter-Continental Cup
10 Charity/Community Shields (1 shared)

League finishes in Sir Alex's 27 seasons in charge

Air miles

Sir Alex has overseen United in competitive games in 27 different nations.

Manchester United v Swansea City 35

12 MAY 2013, v SWANSEA CITY

Sir Alex Ferguson was in charge of United for exactly 1,500 matches – 724 of them at Old Trafford – and the programme for his last home game detailed some of the stats behind his reign.

United's second-highest all-time goalscorer goes up against a double FA Cup winner with Tottenham to tackle six talking points ahead of today's meeting

DENIS LAW | GARTH CROOKS

WHAT HAVE YOU MADE OF YOUR CLUB'S PRE-SEASON?

We have brought in some good players and the pre-season tour of the United States was very successful. There were some fantastic games over there, particularly the 3-1 victory over European champions Barcelona.

Spurs tend to conclude their transfer business nearer the deadline so we'll have to wait and see! They will be keeping their fingers crossed that a club doesn't make an audacious attempt to try to lure Harry Kane away.

WHO DO YOU THINK WILL BE YOUR TEAM'S KEY PLAYER THIS SEASON?

Honestly speaking, I'm not too sure. It's always a bit difficult to say who is going to do this, or do that. You might expect a player to produce something and he doesn't, and then someone else might turn out to be really good.

I think it's imperative that Spurs retain Hugo Lloris in the squad if they have any ambitions of securing a Champions League spot, along with Christian Eriksen and the man with the golden feet, Kane.

HOW DOES YOUR TEAM GO ABOUT WINNING THE GAME TODAY?

They will need to play well to beat Spurs. I've got the answer – score more goals than them!

With difficulty. But the first game can be unpredictable, so United would do well to be cautious.

HOW WILL YOUR TEAM FARE THIS SEASON?

Extremely well. We're not looking to merely finish in the top four, like last season. We want more than that.

That depends on who Spurs buy to support Lloris, Eriksen and Kane before the window shuts.

HOW WILL TODAY'S GAME PAN OUT?

The beauty about the beginning of the season is we don't know what's going to happen in the months ahead, but to put it simply, we have to win today.

Having played for both clubs [he played seven times for United in 1983/84] I won't predict a score! They are great clubs but, sadly, only one wins anything on a regular basis.

WHAT'S YOUR STRONGEST PERSONAL MEMORY OF THIS FIXTURE?

It was a fixture I always enjoyed and all of us at United were all good friends with them. Spurs were always a team that played exciting football and Jimmy Greaves [right] was one of my heroes.

I wasn't on the pitch for it but Spurs 3 United 5 [in 2001] was one of the most extraordinary matches I've seen. It was arguably Juan Sebastian Veron's [left] best game for the Reds as they came back from 3-0 down.

Manchester United v Tottenham Hotspur 55

8 AUGUST 2015, v TOTTENHAM

For the 2015/16 curtain-raiser against Spurs, United legend Denis Law and Garth Crooks – who played for both clubs – discussed some pre-match hot topics and shared some personal recollections.

29 JANUARY 2017, v WIGAN ATHLETIC

When Rooney scored his record-breaking 250th goal for the Reds, it inspired the programme to present an illustrated guide to some of his all-time classic strikes in the colours of United...

History in the making. In the Wigan issue, this is how *United Review* covered the moment Wayne Rooney (partially obscured) became United's all-time leading goalscorer with this strike away to Stoke City, overtaking Sir Bobby Charlton's long-held record.

ROONEY'S 250

THE MOMENT ARRIVES...

Wayne Rooney looks on as his sublime free-kick sails into the corner of the Stoke City net. He may not have celebrated the 94th-minute equaliser like it was a historic moment as he still wanted to win the game, but he's received plenty of accolades since scoring what was his 250th United goal last Saturday. Our new all-time leading goalscorer was visited in the Reds' dressing room after the game by Sir Bobby Charlton, the man who had held the record for 43 years, and afterwards our current skipper said: "I don't really want to stand here and talk about myself, to be honest, but I think it's fitting that the player who got the two records off Sir Bobby is a Manchester United player." The record may be in the bag but Rooney is far from done, adding: "It's a huge honour to get that record, just a bit dampened by the result. It's about a career and I still feel there's a lot more to come, but overall it's a really proud moment for me."

Manchester United v Wigan Athletic • 35

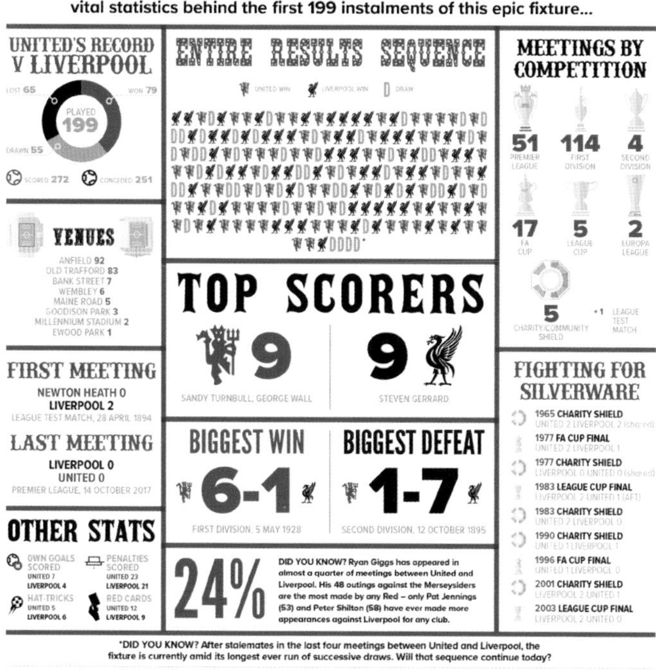
200 GAMES: THE STATS

RIVALRY IN NUMBERS

On the day of United's 200th meeting with Liverpool, here are the vital statistics behind the first 199 instalments of this epic fixture...

UNITED'S RECORD V LIVERPOOL

LOST 65 · WON 79 · DRAWN 55 · PLAYED 199

SCORED 272 · CONCEDED 251

ENTIRE RESULTS SEQUENCE

UNITED WIN · LIVERPOOL WIN · D DRAW

MEETINGS BY COMPETITION

51 PREMIER LEAGUE · 114 FIRST DIVISION · 4 SECOND DIVISION · 17 FA CUP · 5 LEAGUE CUP · 2 EUROPA LEAGUE · 5 CHARITY/COMMUNITY SHIELD · +1 LEAGUE TEST MATCH

VENUES

ANFIELD 92
OLD TRAFFORD 83
BANK STREET 7
WEMBLEY 6
MAINE ROAD 5
GOODISON PARK 3
MILLENNIUM STADIUM 2
EWOOD PARK 1

TOP SCORERS

9 SANDY TURNBULL, GEORGE WALL

9 STEVEN GERRARD

FIRST MEETING

NEWTON HEATH 0
LIVERPOOL 2
LEAGUE TEST MATCH, 28 APRIL 1894

LAST MEETING

LIVERPOOL 0
UNITED 0
PREMIER LEAGUE, 14 OCTOBER 2017

BIGGEST WIN

6-1
FIRST DIVISION, 5 MAY 1928

BIGGEST DEFEAT

1-7
SECOND DIVISION, 12 OCTOBER 1895

FIGHTING FOR SILVERWARE

1965 CHARITY SHIELD
UNITED 2 LIVERPOOL 2 (shared)
1977 FA CUP FINAL
UNITED 2 LIVERPOOL 1
1977 CHARITY SHIELD
LIVERPOOL 0 UNITED 0 (shared)
1983 LEAGUE CUP FINAL
LIVERPOOL 2 UNITED 1 (AET)
1983 CHARITY SHIELD
UNITED 2 LIVERPOOL 0
1990 CHARITY SHIELD
UNITED 1 LIVERPOOL 1
1996 FA CUP FINAL
UNITED 1 LIVERPOOL 0
2001 CHARITY SHIELD
LIVERPOOL 2 UNITED 1
2003 LEAGUE CUP FINAL
LIVERPOOL 2 UNITED 0

OTHER STATS

OWN GOALS SCORED: UNITED 7, LIVERPOOL 4
PENALTIES SCORED: UNITED 23, LIVERPOOL 21
HAT-TRICKS: UNITED 5, LIVERPOOL 6
RED CARDS: UNITED 12, LIVERPOOL 9

24% DID YOU KNOW? Ryan Giggs has appeared in almost a quarter of meetings between United and Liverpool. His 48 outings against the Merseysiders are the most made by any Red – only Pat Jennings (53) and Peter Shilton (58) have ever made more appearances against Liverpool for any club.

*DID YOU KNOW? After stalemates in the last four meetings between United and Liverpool, the fixture is currently amid its longest ever run of successive draws. Will that sequence continue today?

Manchester United v Liverpool • 55

10 MARCH 2018, v LIVERPOOL
Our home game with Liverpool in spring 2018 was the 200th clash between the old rivals, which allowed the programme a reason to crunch the numbers on the story so far. Game no.200 was one to remember too, with Marcus Rashford's double securing a fine win for Manchester's Reds.

13 JULY 2020, v SOUTHAMPTON
The conclusion of the 2019/20 campaign may have been completed behind closed doors, but this didn't affect new signing Bruno Fernandes's performances, with the Portuguese magnifico proving a big hit with the fans in his debut season for United.

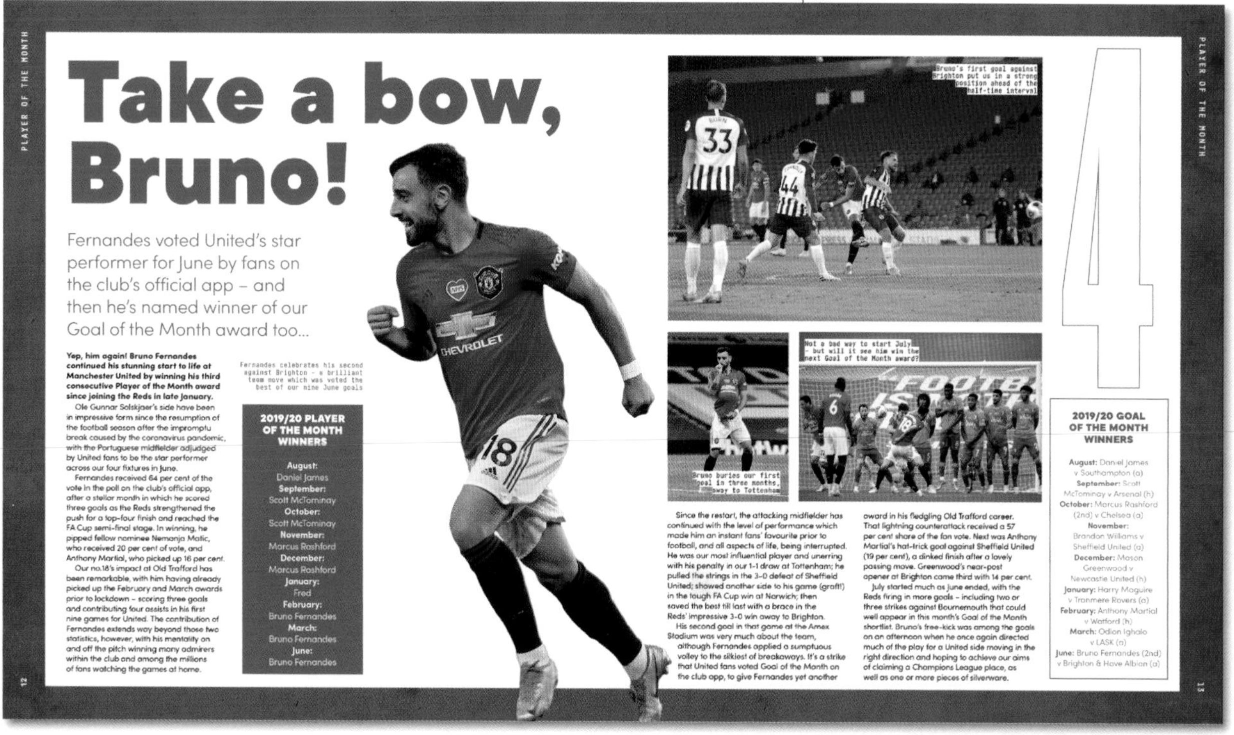

PLAYER OF THE MONTH

Take a bow, Bruno!

Fernandes voted United's star performer for June by fans on the club's official app – and then he's named winner of our Goal of the Month award too...

Yep, him again! Bruno Fernandes continued his stunning start to life at Manchester United by winning his third consecutive Player of the Month award since joining the Reds in late January.

Ole Gunnar Solskjaer's side have been in impressive form since the resumption of the football season after the impromptu break caused by the coronavirus pandemic, with the Portuguese midfielder adjudged by United fans to be the star performer across our four fixtures in June.

Fernandes received 64 per cent of the vote in the poll on the club's official app, after a stellar month in which he scored three goals as the Reds strengthened the push for a top-four finish and reached the FA Cup semi-final stage. In winning, he pipped fellow nominee Nemanja Matic, who received 20 per cent of vote, and Anthony Martial, who picked up 16 per cent.

Our no.18's impact at Old Trafford has been remarkable, with him having already picked up the February and March awards prior to lockdown – scoring three goals and contributing four assists in his first nine games for United. The contribution of Fernandes extends way beyond those two statistics, however, with his mentality on and off the pitch winning many admirers within the club and among the millions of fans watching the games at home.

Fernandes celebrates his second against Brighton – a brilliant team move which was voted the best of our nine June goals

2019/20 PLAYER OF THE MONTH WINNERS

August: Daniel James
September: Scott McTominay
October: Scott McTominay
November: Marcus Rashford
December: Marcus Rashford
January: Fred
February: Bruno Fernandes
March: Bruno Fernandes
June: Bruno Fernandes

Bruno's first goal against Brighton put us in a strong position ahead of the half-time interval

Bruno buries our first goal in three months, away to Tottenham

Not a bad way to start July – but will it see him win the next Goal of the Month award?

Since the restart, the attacking midfielder has continued with the level of performance which made him an instant fans' favourite prior to football, and all aspects of life, being interrupted. He was our most influential player and unerring with his penalty in our 1-1 draw at Tottenham; he pulled the strings in the 3-0 defeat of Sheffield United; showed another side to his game (graft!) in the tough FA Cup win at Norwich; then saved the best till last with a brace in the Reds' impressive 3-0 win away to Brighton.

His second goal in that game at the Amex Stadium was very much about the team, although Fernandes applied a sumptuous volley to the silkiest of breakaways. It's a strike that United fans voted Goal of the Month on the club app, to give Fernandes yet another award in his fledgling Old Trafford career. That lightning counterattack received a 57 per cent share of the fan vote. Next was Anthony Martial's hat-trick goal against Sheffield United (19 per cent), a dinked finish after a lovely passing move. Greenwood's near-post opener at Brighton came third with 14 per cent.

July started much as June ended, with the Reds firing in more goals – including two or three strikes against Bournemouth that could well appear in this month's Goal of the Month shortlist. Bruno's free-kick was among the goals on an afternoon when he once again directed much of the play for a United side moving in the right direction and hoping to achieve our aims of claiming a Champions League place, as well as one or more pieces of silverware.

2019/20 GOAL OF THE MONTH WINNERS

August: Daniel James v Southampton (a)
September: Scott McTominay v Arsenal (h)
October: Marcus Rashford (2nd) v Chelsea (a)
November: Brandon Williams v Sheffield United (a)
December: Mason Greenwood v Newcastle United (h)
January: Harry Maguire v Tranmere Rovers (a)
February: Anthony Martial v Watford (h)
March: Odion Ighalo v LASK (a)
June: Bruno Fernandes (2nd) v Brighton & Hove Albion (a)

12 · 13

CHAPTER 13

Other matches

Away from the regular cut and thrust of first-team football, the Theatre of Dreams has frequently played host to all sorts of special occasions down the years – with the *UR* team on hand to provide a programme...

'The most handsomest, the most spacious and the most remarkable arena I have ever seen,' wrote the *Sporting Chronicle*'s football correspondent, of Old Trafford on its opening day in 1910. 'As a football ground it is unrivalled in the world; it is an honour to Manchester and the home of a team who can do wonders when they are so disposed.'

Such was the splendour of Archibald Leitch's construction, that the small matter of the opening game – a 3-4 defeat to Liverpool – scarcely warranted a mention in comparison. In the ensuing 110 years and counting, through two wartime bombings, the evolution from standing to all-seater and over 2,400 United matches, the Theatre of Dreams has retained its jaw-dropping splendour. As such, it's little surprise that it should be coveted for alternative usage outside its primary function as the Reds' home for competitive matches. From testimonials, youth and reserve games, friendly and invitational fixtures involving the Reds, to huge international encounters and neutral usage for cup finals, Old Trafford has been a versatile and prestigious host to a high number of occasions requiring matchday programmes. As such, the *United Review* team has always been on hand to produce programmes for such showpieces.

Above: Wayne Rooney's 2016 testimonial against Everton was a chance to thank the then-skipper for his service

Aside from Wembley Stadium, Old Trafford is the only venue in England to have hosted finals in the Champions League, FA Cup and League Cup. When UEFA selected the Theatre of Dreams to host the 2003 final of its flagship competition, UEFA's communications director Mike Lee stressed: "In terms of airports, ground capacity, parking, media and supporters facilities, Old Trafford was clearly first choice."

The 1970 FA Cup final required a replay to separate Chelsea and Leeds, so Old Trafford stepped in

United faced Real Madrid in a special club centenary friendly in 1978, with the programme cover befitting the occasion

Such standards have prompted repeated usage by the England national team. Only Wembley played host to more Three Lions fixtures than the 17 held at Old Trafford between 1926-2007. The Football Association also came calling when looking to host non-competitive fixtures, such as an English FA XI friendly encounter against the army, and then against an Italian FA team, both in the space of four years.

Old Trafford had already staged the 1915 FA Cup final between Sheffield United and Chelsea – known as the Khaki Cup final on account of the number of servicemen and servicewomen among the 50,000-strong attendance – when the honour was offered again in 1970. Once again Chelsea were involved, this time finding themselves inseparable from Leeds in the 2-2 final at Wembley, and the replay went the Blues' way with a 2-1 win. Seven years later, *United Review* staff were once more on duty after hours, putting together the programme for the 1977 League Cup final second replay between Aston Villa and Everton, an epic encounter ultimately decided in Villa's favour after extra-time.

All along the Old Trafford timeline, opportunities have arisen to bid farewell to long-serving legendary players. When the stadium hosts the festivities, *United Review* invariably produces a one-off programme to mark the occasion. Since the turn of the millennium alone, testimonials have paid tribute to Denis Irwin, Ryan Giggs, Roy Keane, Gary Neville, Paul Scholes, Rio Ferdinand, Wayne Rooney and Michael Carrick, each requiring an editorial offering to celebrate the players' longstanding efforts on the field.

While falling outside the norm of a set season and requiring extra effort to complete to the requisite standard, such special occasions add to the rich tapestry of the *United Review* back catalogue.

WELCOME TO OLD TRAFFORD

MANCHESTER in general, and Manchester United Football Club in particular are proud to be chosen as the battle ground of this great contest between England and Ireland. The Football Association has few grounds equal to Old Trafford in well-kept field and commodious seating accommodation. The crowd that gathers here is one of the most sportsmanlike in the country and will watch this brilliant galaxy of famous players with interest, keenly enhanced by partisan enthusiasm. Whether the Red Rose or the Shamrock wins is of lesser importance than the quality and sportsmanship of the game. The game is international but between friends used to living and working together. It should increase our respect for each other.

Our one regret is that the honoured President of the Football Association, Mr. W. Pickford, will not be with us. He has answered the Great Call. And yet his passing away at the ripe age of 77 leaves nothing but splendid memories of a great sportsman—one who devoted himself to the cause of Football with a wonderful zeal and progressive mind. Referees owe much to him for clarifying the spirit and the laws of the game.

Manchester United cannot but help feeling gratified that their own trainer, Tom Curry, the "father" of the Manchester United players, is to act as attendant to the English team.

16 November 1938

England v Ireland

British Home Championship

In the 51st edition of the British Home Championship – a four-team competition contested by England, Wales, Scotland and Ireland – Old Trafford played host to the tournament's only fixture on English soil. Having lost to Wales in Cardiff, England met Ireland in Manchester requiring a victory. United goalkeeper Tommy Breen had been set to start for Ireland but had to withdraw beforehand through injury – perhaps no bad thing since England striker Willie Hall duly scored five times, a feat which remains a joint-national record for the Three Lions. England's 7-0 win clawed them back into contention for the trophy, which they ultimately shared with both Scotland and Wales.

An eye-catching cover design, a heartfelt welcome message and pen pics of the two teams were among highlights of an eight-page programme for Old Trafford's second-ever international match

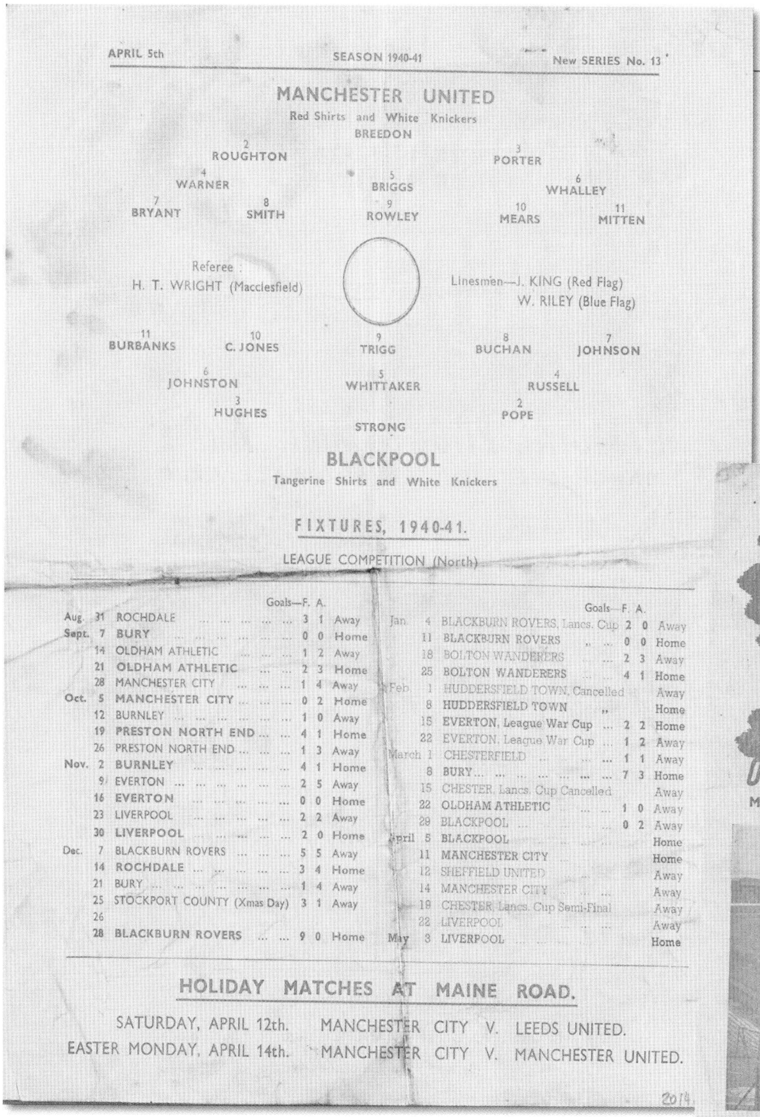

APRIL 5th | SEASON 1940-41 | New SERIES No. 13

MANCHESTER UNITED

Red Shirts and White Knickers

BREEDON

2 ROUGHTON — 3 PORTER

4 WARNER — 5 BRIGGS — 6 WHALLEY

7 BRYANT — 8 SMITH — 9 ROWLEY — 10 MEARS — 11 MITTEN

Referee : H. T. WRIGHT (Macclesfield)

Linesmen—J. KING (Red Flag) W. RILEY (Blue Flag)

11 BURBANKS — 10 C. JONES — 9 TRIGG — 8 BUCHAN — 7 JOHNSON

6 JOHNSTON — 5 WHITTAKER — 4 RUSSELL

3 HUGHES — 2 POPE

STRONG

BLACKPOOL

Tangerine Shirts and White Knickers

FIXTURES, 1940-41.

LEAGUE COMPETITION (North)

			Goals—F.	A.	
Aug.	31	ROCHDALE	3	1	Away
Sept.	7	BURY	0	0	Home
	14	OLDHAM ATHLETIC	1	2	Away
	21	OLDHAM ATHLETIC	2	3	Home
	28	MANCHESTER CITY	1	4	Away
Oct.	5	MANCHESTER CITY	0	2	Home
	12	BURNLEY	1	0	Away
	19	PRESTON NORTH END	4	1	Home
	26	PRESTON NORTH END	1	3	Away
Nov.	2	BURNLEY	4	1	Home
	9	EVERTON	2	5	Away
	16	EVERTON	0	0	Home
	23	LIVERPOOL	2	2	Away
	30	LIVERPOOL	2	0	Home
Dec.	7	BLACKBURN ROVERS	5	5	Away
	14	ROCHDALE	3	4	Home
	21	BURY	1	4	Away
	25	STOCKPORT COUNTY (Xmas Day)	3	1	Away
	26				
	28	BLACKBURN ROVERS	9	0	Home

			Goals—F.	A.	
Jan.	4	BLACKBURN ROVERS, Lancs. Cup	2	0	Away
	11	BLACKBURN ROVERS	0	0	Home
	18	BOLTON WANDERERS	2	3	Away
	25	BOLTON WANDERERS	4	1	Home
Feb.	1	HUDDERSFIELD TOWN, Cancelled			Away
	8	HUDDERSFIELD TOWN ,,			Home
	15	EVERTON, League War Cup	2	2	Home
	22	EVERTON, League War Cup	1	2	Away
March	1	CHESTERFIELD	1	1	Away
	8	BURY	7	3	Home
	15	CHESTER, Lancs. Cup Cancelled			Away
	22	OLDHAM ATHLETIC	1	0	Away
	29	BLACKPOOL	0	2	Away
April	5	BLACKPOOL			Home
	11	MANCHESTER CITY			Home
	12	SHEFFIELD UNITED			Away
	14	MANCHESTER CITY			Away
	19	CHESTER, Lancs. Cup Semi-Final			Away
	22	LIVERPOOL			Away
May	3	LIVERPOOL			Home

HOLIDAY MATCHES AT MAINE ROAD.

SATURDAY, APRIL 12th. MANCHESTER CITY V. LEEDS UNITED.

EASTER MONDAY, APRIL 14th. MANCHESTER CITY V. MANCHESTER UNITED.

2014

The Reds were playing at the home of the Blues by the time of this wartime fixture with Blackpool, Old Trafford having been bombed out, but there were a number of familiar names in United's starting XI

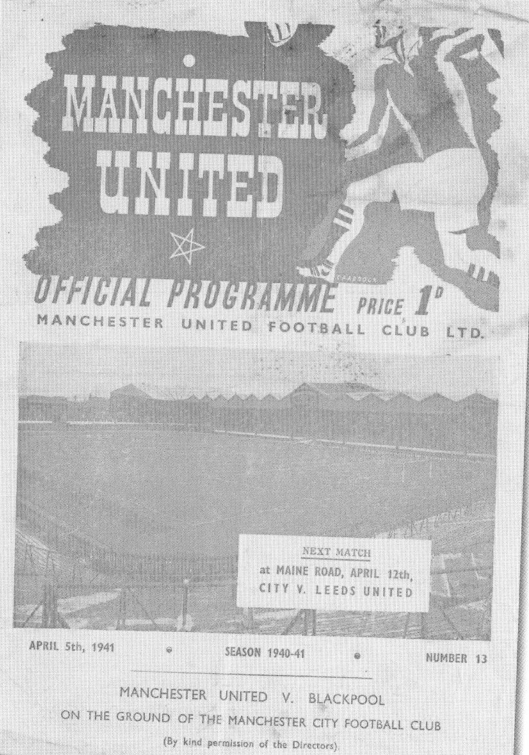

United's programme was little more than a team-sheet during the Second World War, merely listing the two teams and fixtures

5 April 1941

United v Blackpool

Maine Road

With football paling into relative insignificance compared to the small matter of the Second World War, clubs contested non-competitive calendars during the late 1930s and early 1940s. Points hinged not on wins, draws and losses, but on goal averages. Walter Crickmer's Reds were in the North Regional League and enjoyed an undulating run of results best summarised by December's meetings with Blackburn, which ended 5-5 and 9-0. When Old Trafford was bombed in March 1941, Blackpool's visit the following month had to be switched to Maine Road, where United slipped to a 3-2 defeat on course to finishing eighth, between Halifax Town and Lincoln City.

★ ★ ★ **THE RED STARS** ★ ★ ★

Reading left to right—Djajic, Palfi, Tomasevic, Vukosavljevic, Zlatkovic, Ognjanov, Djurdjevic, Kasanin, Zvekanovic, Lovric, Mitic (Captain).

WHO'S WHO WITH THE RED STARS

At the time of going to press it was not possible to print the actual team to be fielded to-day but we give below details of players from whom the selection will be made.

1. **MRKUSIC, SRDJAN.** Age 35. Height 6' 1". Weight 13st. 9lb. Occupation, Engineer. Goalkeeper. Fifteen National Team appearances.

2. **LOVRIC, LJUBOMIR.** Age 30. Height 5' 11". Weight 12st. 5 lb. Occupation, Journalist. Goalkeeper. Twelve National Team appearances.

3. **STANKOVIC, BRANKO.** Age 29. Height 5' 10½". Weight 12 st. 5 lb. Occupation, Student. Right Full-back. Twenty-eight National Team appearances. Played against England at Highbury.

4. **TADIC, DIMITRIJE.** Age 25. Height 5' 8½". Weight 10 st. 5 lb. Occupation, Student. Left Full-back.

5. **KASANIN, MLADEN.** Age 28. Height 5' 11". Weight 12 st. 3 lb. Occupation, Journalist. Left Full-back.

6. **DISKIC, MILORAD.** Age 26. Height 6' 0". Weight 12 st. 12 lb. Occupation, Clerk. Centre Half-back.

7. **ZVEKANOVIC, IVAN.** Age 29. Height 5' 9½". Weight 11 st. 13 lb. Occupation, Clerk. Right Full-back.

8. **PALFI, BELA.** Age 27. Height 5' 6½". Weight 10 st. 7 lb. Occupation, Journalist. Right Half-back. Three National Team appearances.

9. **DJURDJEVIC, MILIVOJE.** Age 30. Height 6' 0". Weight 12 st. 12 lb. Occupation, Clerk. Centre Half-back. Two National Team appearances.

10. **DJAJIC, PREDRAG.** Age 28. Height 5' 6". Weight 11 st. 8 lb. Occupation, Student. Left Half-back. Fifteen National Team appearances. Played against England at Highbury.

11. **OGNJANOV, TIHOMIR.** Age 23. Height 5' 8". Weight 11 st. 4 lb. Occupation, Clerk. Outside Right. Nine National Team appearances. Played against England at Highbury.

12. **MITIC, RAJKO.** Age 28. Height 5' 8½". Weight 11 st. 8 lb. Occupation, Student. Twenty-seven National Team appearances. Inside Right. Played against England at Highbury and captained the team.

13. **TOMASEVIC, KOSTA.** Age 27. Height 5' 6". Weight 11 st. 13 lb. Occupation, Student. Centre Forward. Eleven National Team appearances.

14. **JEZERKIC, JOVAN.** Age 30. Height 5' 9". Weight 10 st. 7 lb. Occupation, Clerk. Wing or Centre Forward. Five National Team appearances.

15. **VUKOSAVLJEVIC, BRANISLAV.** Age 21. Height 5' 9". Weight 11 st. 7 lb. Occupation, Student. Outside Left. Two National Team appearances.

16. **MIHAILOVIC, PRVOSLAV.** Age 29. Height 5' 8". Weight 10 st. 9 lb. Occupation, Clerk. Inside Left. Ten National Team appearances.

17. **ZLATKOVIC, SINISA.** Age 26. Height 5' 10". Weight 11 st. 11 lb. Occupation, Clerk. Inside Left.

18. **ZIVANOVIC, TOSA.** Age 23. Height 5' 9½". Weight 10 st. 5 lb. Occupation, Student. Centre or Inside Forward. Five National Team appearances. Played against England at Highbury and scored the equalising goal.

19. **KUJUNDZIC, LAJCO.** Age 27. Height 5' 10". Weight 11 st. 8 lb. Occupation, Clerk. Half-back.

20. **KOSTIC, BORA.** Age 20. Height 5' 10½". Weight 12 st. 3 lb. Occupation, Student. Inside Forward.

★ ★ ★ ★ ★ ★ ★ ★ ★ ★

PAGE THREE

INTERNATIONAL FOOTBALL

by Sidney F. Wicks, Editor "United Review"

We offer a sincere and warmhearted welcome to our comrades from Yugoslavia, a country distinguished for its fighting qualities in every sphere of life.

This game is one of those planned as a part of the Festival of Britain which is to show to the world that the old British qualities possess unabated strength even though post-war economic problems make the national task a formidable one.

Sport, which plays such a prominent part in British life, is represented in such games as these. It is indeed good that we can meet friends from other nations on the football field which is so rich in comradeship. Here we forget the theories which divide man from man, and pay honour to our ideal of sport. For on the football field there is rivalry without enmity, victory without boastfulness, defeat without dishonour. Here every player fights as an individual yet fights most of all for his team. "The ship is greater than the crew." Here both teams honour and obey the referee, who is the guardian of fairplay and who interprets the rules of the game without fear or favour. The referee is the man whom we honour because without him a disciplined sport would become a jungle struggle. A sportsman is a man who loses without losing his head and who wins without getting a swelled one! If a team plays well and respects the rules then that team, win or lose, is cheered by the crowd.

Our friends from Yugoslavia will give us a splendid game because of their dash and determination and mastery of the art of football. We hope both teams will be happy in the comradeship which a healthy struggle creates. We say "Good Luck" to our comrades now and always; may they take back to their country happy memories of British Sport; and may the friendship between us remain unbroken through the years to come.

Mi upucujemo toplu, srdacnu dobrodoslicu nasim prijateljima iz Jugoslavije, zemlje koja je poznata po svojim borbenim tradicijama i stvaralastvu na svim poljima.

Ova utakmica igra se u okviru Festivala Velike Britanije koji treba da pokaze svetu da drevne britanske vrline imaju neospornu snagu i danas kada su posleratni ekonomski problemi neobicno otezali nas zadatak.

Sport koji u zivotu Velike Britanije igra tako znacajnu ulogu dolazi do punog izrazaja u ovakvim igrama. Mi smo srecni sto nam se daje prilika da na futbalskom polju koje pruza toliko mogucnosti za stvaranje drugarstva sretnemo prijatelje iz drugih zemalja. Tu mi zaboravljamo teorije koje dele coveka od coveka i zajednicki sluzimo velikoj ideji sporta. Na futbalskom polju postoji rivalstvo ali bez neprijateljstva, pobeda bez nadmenosti, postoji i poraz ali castan. Svaki igrac bori se kao pojedinac, ali pre svega za svoj tim. Brod je vazniji nego posada. Oba tima postuju sudiju koji vodi racuna da igra bude fer i primenjuje pravila bez straha i bez pristrastnosti. Sudiju postujemo posto bi bez njega sport postao nekontrolisana borba. Pravi sportista dobija i gubi, ali uvek ostaje na visini. Ako tim igra dobro i postuje pravila njemu aplaudiraju bez obzira da li je pobednik ili pobodjeni.

Nasi pri jatel ji iz Jugoslavije pokazace nam sjajnu igru zahvaljujuci svojoj brzini odlucnosti i futbalskoj vestini. Nadamo se da, ce oba tima uspostaviti srdacno prijateljstvo koje pruza zdrava sportska borba. Mi nasim prijateljima zelimo dobru srecu danas i ubuduce. Neka u njihovu zemlju ponesu najlepse uspomene o britanskom sportu, neka nase prijateljstvo ostane nepomuceno!

12 May 1951

United v Red Star Belgrade

Festival of Britain

Conceived to help celebrate Great Britain's historical achievements and raise spirits during the post-war recovery, the Festival of Britain dominated the summer of 1951 around the Isles. Football made up only a tiny fraction of the event, but the Football Association still invited swathes of foreign sides over to face domestic clubs. United's meeting with Red Star Belgrade was one of 35 friendlies held on 12 May 1951, ranging from Spurs against Borussia Dortmund to Aldershot v National Schifflange (from Luxembourg). An early opener put Red Star ahead to stun a crowd in excess of 40,000, but Jack Rowley's late penalty nabbed a draw for the hosts.

United Review welcomes Red Star to Old Trafford for this post-season friendly, and [above, right] gives the vital statistics of the players in the ranks of the Yugoslav champions

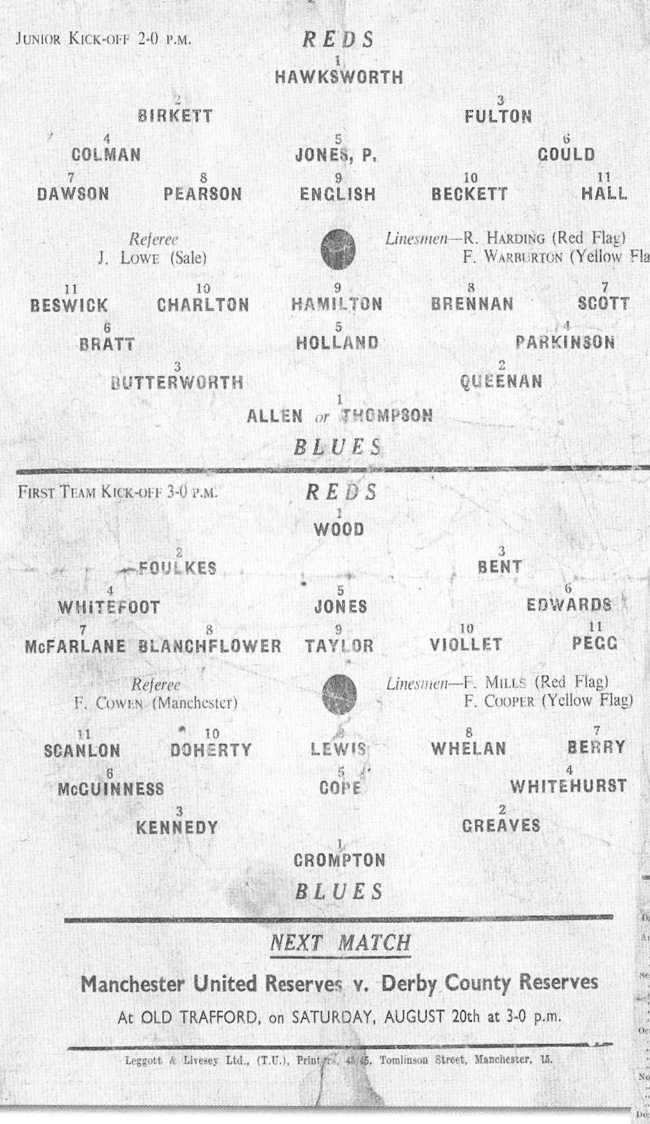

JUNIOR KICK-OFF 2-0 P.M.

REDS

1 HAWKSWORTH

2 BIRKETT — 3 FULTON

4 COLMAN — 5 JONES, P. — 6 GOULD

7 DAWSON — 8 PEARSON — 9 ENGLISH — 10 BECKETT — 11 HALL

Referee J. LOWE (Sale)

Linesmen—R. HARDING (Red Flag)
F. WARBURTON (Yellow Flag)

11 BESWICK — 10 CHARLTON — 9 HAMILTON — 8 BRENNAN — 7 SCOTT

6 BRATT — 5 HOLLAND — 4 PARKINSON

3 BUTTERWORTH — 2 QUEENAN

1 ALLEN *or* THOMPSON

BLUES

FIRST TEAM KICK-OFF 3-0 P.M.

REDS

1 WOOD

2 FOULKES — 3 BENT

4 WHITEFOOT — 5 JONES — 6 EDWARDS

7 McFARLANE — 8 BLANCHFLOWER — 9 TAYLOR — 10 VIOLLET — 11 PEGG

Referee F. COWEN (Manchester)

Linesmen—F. MILLS (Red Flag)
F. COOPER (Yellow Flag)

11 SCANLON — 10 DOHERTY — 9 LEWIS — 8 WHELAN — 7 BERRY

6 McGUINNESS — 5 COPE — 4 WHITEHURST

3 KENNEDY — 2 GREAVES

1 CROMPTON

BLUES

NEXT MATCH

Manchester United Reserves v. Derby County Reserves

At OLD TRAFFORD, on SATURDAY, AUGUST 20th at 3-0 p.m.

Leggott & Livesey Ltd., (T.U.), Printers, 43/45, Tomlinson Street, Manchester, 15.

A two-page programme was on sale at this double-header of warm-up matches, which were inter-squad games played as a curtain-raiser to the 1955/56 season

MANCHESTER UNITED
FOOTBALL CLUB LIMITED

★

Official Programme

★

Price **1d.**

LEAGUE TEAM FIXTURES

Date 1955	Opponents	Ground
Aug. 20	Birmingham City	Away
„ 24	Tottenham Hotspur	Home
„ 27	West Bromwich Albion	Home
„ 31	Tottenham Hotspur	Away
Sept. 3	Manchester City	Away
„ 7	Everton	Home
„ 10	Sheffield United	Away
„ 14	Everton	Away
„ 17	Preston North End	Home
„ 24	Burnley	Away
Oct. 1	Luton Town	Home
„ 8	Wolverhampton Wanderers	Home
„ 15	Aston Villa	Away
„ 22	Huddersfield Town	Home
„ 29	Cardiff City	Away
Nov. 5	Arsenal	Home
„ 12	Bolton Wanderers	Away
„ 19	Chelsea	Home
„ 26	Blackpool	Away
Dec. 3	Sunderland	Home
„ 10	Portsmouth	Away
„ 17	Birmingham City	Home
„ 24	West Bromwich Albion	Away
„ 26	Charlton Athletic	Home
„ 27	Charlton Athletic	Away
„ 31	Manchester City	Home
1956		
Jan. 7	F. A. Cup (3rd Round).	
„ 14	Sheffield United	Home
„ 21	Preston North End	Away
„ 28	F. A. Cup (4th Round).	
Feb. 4	Burnley	Home
„ 11	Luton Town	Away
„ 18	Wolverhampton Wanderers (5th)	Away
„ 25	Aston Villa	Home
Mar. 3	Chelsea (6th)	Away
„ 10	Cardiff City	Home
„ 17	Arsenal (S.F.)	Away
„ 24	Bolton Wanderers	Home
„ 30	Newcastle United	Home
„ 31	Huddersfield Town	Away
April 2	Newcastle United	Away
„ 7	Blackpool	Home
„ 14	Sunderland	Away
„ 21	Portsmouth	Home
May 5	F. A. Cup Final.	

CENTRAL LEAGUE FIXTURES

Date 1955	Opponents	Ground
Aug. 20	Derby County	Home
„ 24	Barnsley	Away
„ 27	Newcastle United	Away
„ 29	Barnsley	Home
Sept. 3	Manchester City	Home
„ 10	Sheffield United	Home
„ 17	Preston North End	Away
„ 21	Everton	Away
„ 24	Burnley	Home
Oct. 1	Leeds United	Away
„ 8	Sheffield Wednesday	Away
„ 15	Huddersfield Town	Home
„ 22	Blackburn Rovers	Away
„ 29	Blackpool	Home
Nov. 5	Bolton Wanderers	Away
„ 12	Chesterfield	Home
„ 19	Liverpool	Away
„ 26	Stoke City	Home
Dec. 3	Aston Villa	Away
„ 10	Wolverhampton Wanderers	Home
„ 17	Derby County	Away
„ 24	Newcastle United	Home
„ 26	Bury	Away
„ 27	Bury	Home
„ 31	Manchester City	Away
1956		
Jan. 7	—	
„ 14	Sheffield United	Away
„ 21	Preston North End	Home
„ 28	—	
Feb. 4	Burnley	Away
„ 11	Leeds United	Home
„ 18	Sheffield Wednesday	Home
„ 25	Huddersfield Town	Away
Mar. 3	Blackburn Rovers	Home
„ 10	Blackpool	Away
„ 17	Bolton Wanderers	Home
„ 24	Chesterfield	Away
„ 30	West Bromwich Albion	Away
„ 31	Liverpool	Home
April 2	West Bromwich Albion	Home
„ 7	Stoke City	Away
„ 14	Aston Villa	Home
„ 21	Wolverhampton Wanderers	Away
„ 28	Everton	Home
May 5	—	

13 August 1955

Reds v Blues

Old Trafford

Before the First World War and leading up to the early 1960s, pre-season inter-squad matches were commonplace at United. A week before the 1955/56 season-opener at Birmingham, Old Trafford hosted two practice matches, firstly made up of those in the junior ranks – including Bobby Charlton and Eddie Colman – then among the first-team squad. Matt Busby used the latter to shape his starting XI for St Andrews, with eight of the 'Reds' team starting a week later. Roger Byrne and Colin Webster also came into the fold despite missing the friendly altogether, while Albert Scanlon was the only 'Blues' player to make the cut, replacing David Pegg.

FOOTBALL IN THE ARMY

By Lt.-Col. G. J. MITCHELL, O.B.E.

Secretary of the Army Football Association

The Army's connection with Association Football goes back a long way. In the early days of the F.A. Cup for example, the Royal Engineers took part in three out of the first four finals, winning the Cup in 1875 on their third appearance in the final. The Army Cup — the Army's own knock-out competition — was first competed for in 1888–9, and has been played for uninterruptedly since then except for the years of the two World Wars. Perhaps the greatest contribution made by the Army to the development of the game has been its missionary work; many places where the game now flourishes owe their introduction to football to overseas garrisons of the Army.

In more modern times the most important representative fixtures for the Army have been the inter-service matches and the games with the French and Belgian Armies for the Kentish Cup. The latter games are a big attraction on the Continent — deservedly so, for they produce fine football of an open sporting variety. Earlier this month the Army F.A. broke new representative ground, visiting Lisbon to play a match against the strong Portuguese Army XI at the newly-constructed Alvalade Stadium.

Since the War some fine players have represented the Army, whose representative side has become something of a forcing ground for future internationals. In the last two years, for example, such stars as Alan Hodgkinson (Sheffield United), Eddie Colman (Manchester United), and the latest under-23 international, Bill Curry (Newcastle United) have all reached the top largely as a result of their play for the Army. This is to make no mention of players like Duncan Edwards, Cliff Jones (Swansea Town), and Alex Parker of Falkirk and Scotland, all of whom were established stars before joining the Army. This year's side is no exception and contains the usual crop of brilliant youngsters.

Apart from its fine representative side the Army also runs a representative amateur side of a quality good enough to test the best in the amateur game. A highlight of this season will probably be a match at Hampden Park, Glasgow, against the famous Scottish Club, Queen's Park.

With the probable ending of National Service in 1962, the Army will be faced with the problem of developing its own players. A start has already been made in this direction. The ready co-operation of Sir Stanley Rous, Secretary of the F.A., and Walter Winterbottom, F.A. Director of Coaching, has allowed a scheme to be introduced by which F.A. coaches are provided for every boys' and apprentice unit in the Army. At the same time a Youth Cup has been introduced for the first time to bridge the gap between boys' and men's football. The results of these progressive measures, which are a typical product of the progressive co-operation between the Army F.A. and its parent association the F.A., will undoubtedly make all the difference to the Army in what is bound to be a difficult transitional stage.

To-night's match is yet another typical example of the unceasing help and support given by the F.A. to sport in the services. Yet the debt is perhaps not entirely one sided, for the Army is one of the leading trainers of referees in the country. There are to-day some 1,500 currently serving, of whom 95 per cent are regular soldiers — truly no small contribution to a class of officials of whom there are never enough and without whom the game would be impossible.

Army football has never been healthier than it is to-day, and it can

Continued on page four

PAGE THREE

30 October 1957

FA XI v Army XI

Representative match

The influence of the military on Manchester United in wartime is not to be underestimated. Matt Busby was stationed in his army regiment in Italy when he received United's job offer (and where he enlisted Jimmy Murphy as his assistant), while Eddie Colman and Duncan Edwards both represented the Army at football. Just over a decade on from the end of the Second World War, Old Trafford gladly played host as the FA continued to support services football with a high-profile friendly, settled 6-3 in the FA XI's favour, with five-goal forward Brian Clough – then of Middlesbrough – at the centre of events.

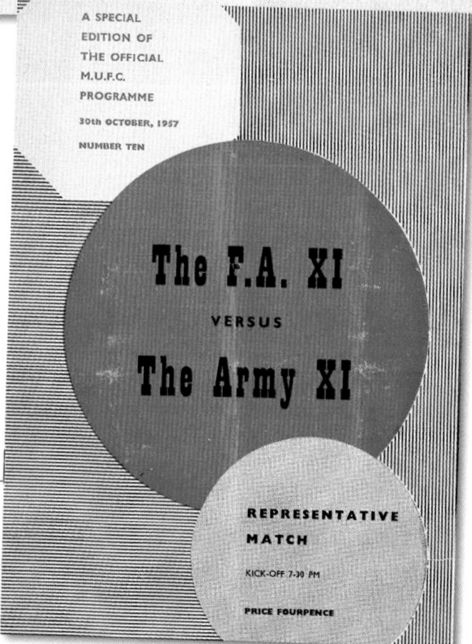

This unusual fixture had a rather familiar looking programme, with the *United Review* team including many of the popular features within this special issue. Bricks and Bokays [above] certainly had some fun!

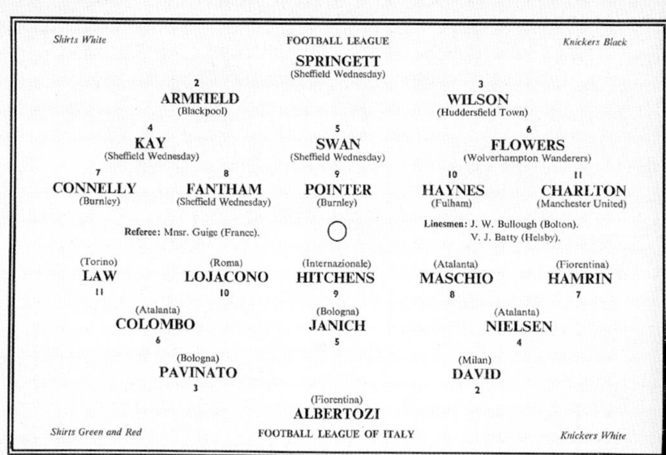

Shirts White — FOOTBALL LEAGUE — Knickers Black

SPRINGETT (Sheffield Wednesday)

2 ARMFIELD (Blackpool) — 3 WILSON (Huddersfield Town)

4 KAY (Sheffield Wednesday) — 5 SWAN (Sheffield Wednesday) — 6 FLOWERS (Wolverhampton Wanderers)

7 CONNELLY (Burnley) — 8 FANTHAM (Sheffield Wednesday) — 9 POINTER (Burnley) — 10 HAYNES (Fulham) — 11 CHARLTON (Manchester United)

Referee: Mnsr. Guige (France).

Linesmen: J. W. Bullough (Bolton). V. J. Batty (Helsby).

(Torino) LAW 11 — (Roma) LOJACONO 10 — (Internazionale) HITCHENS 9 — (Atalanta) MASCHIO 8 — (Fiorentina) HAMRIN 7

(Atalanta) COLOMBO 6 — (Bologna) JANICH 5 — (Atalanta) NIELSEN 4

(Bologna) PAVINATO 3 — (Milan) DAVID 2

(Fiorentina) ALBERTOZI

Shirts Green and Red — FOOTBALL LEAGUE OF ITALY — Knickers White

SUBSTITUTES. A GOALKEEPER SUBSTITUTE WILL BE ALLOWED AT ANY TIME DURING TO-NIGHT'S MATCH. ONE OTHE[R] PLAYER CAN BE SUBSTITUTED UP TO HALF-TIME.

United's Bobby Charlton lined up against Torino's Denis Law, and the two would later become team-mates to help make Matt Busby's Reds kings of European football in 1968. Wales international John Charles also featured in the pen pics but was unable to play

8 November 1961

English FA v Italian FA

Old Trafford

Bobby Charlton was United's sole representative when the cream of the First Division was selected to take on a hand-picked star XI from *Serie A*, but there were ultimately two of the future United Trinity in action at Old Trafford that evening. Denis Law, then of Torino, sported no.11 for the Italian XI, who nabbed a 2-0 victory courtesy of late goals from Argentina and Roma midfielder Francisco Lojacono and former Aston Villa striker Gerry Hitchens, back in England just three months after his move to Internazionale. Matt Busby was among those watching on, and less than a year later he initiated his move to bring 'the Lawman' back to English football.

Denis Law (inside left).
Born Aberdeen in February, 1940, and currently the biggest success in the Italian First Division. A Scottish international, equally skilled as a schemer and goalscorer, Law spent only one season at Maine Road but made more friends in months than most people make in years.

There was plenty of praise for Torino's inside-left in the profiles section of the programme, and eight months later he was back at Old Trafford to sign for the Reds

Friday 3rd March 1967 Number 18 Price sixpence

Souvenir programme

A special edition of the official M.U.F.C. programme to commemorate

THE FIRST FOOTBALL MATCH IN DIVISION ONE TO BE TELEVISED ON CLOSED-CIRCUIT T.V.

ARSENAL v MANCHESTER UTD.

KICK-OFF 7·30 p.m.

DIRECT FROM ARSENAL STADIUM

BY ARRANGEMENT WITH ARSENAL F.C. AND VIEWSPORT LTD.

TALKING SPORT

by **Arthur Walmsley**
of **THE SUN**

It is almost 26 years to the month since I first attended an open-air cinema. It was on a steamy night in Lagos, West Africa, where open-air screening – in the absence of air-conditioning – was a necessity rather than a novelty.

It was a somewhat bizarre experience. The show began with a newsreel and I was astonished to see a small, wriggling object run along Mr. Churchill's cigar and dive off the end.

For almost half an hour interest in the entertainment was distracted by similar darting images then, suddenly, the screen went blank.

It was the first of several planned "breaks" in the programme and solved the mystery of the moving objects. Two Africans with long-handled brooms stepped in front of the screen and began to wipe it clear of lizards, for whom the silver screen seemed to have an even more magnetic attraction than ever it had for the most film-struck youngster seeking Hollywood fame and fortune.

Film critics who say children are the greatest scene stealers have never seen the shattering effect of a lizard apparently disappearing down Clark Gable's throat as he made tender love to Claudette Colbert.

Yet bizarre as that Lagos night was it could not have conditioned me to the wildly improbable prospect that 26 years in the future I would be watching open-air "cinema" at Old Trafford and seeing United play "live" at Highbury.

The prospect is exciting – and if reports of the success of the experiment on other grounds are any guide then we are not going to be disappointed.

But tonight's events have a deeper significance than mere novelty appeal. They mark the first big breakthrough by closed circuit T.V. into Top League football and illustrate that under the right circumstances T.V. and Soccer can work together to mutual advantage.

Indeed, it was the relaying of tonight's Highbury game that sparked the idea of doing the same for the Everton-Liverpool fifth round F.A. Cup-tie at Goodison Park.

With more than 100,000 Merseysiders clamouring to see that game and only 63,000 tickets available, the screening of the match at Anfield to take the 40,000-plus overspill not only offers the chance for nearly twice as many fans to see the game "live" but at prices not inflated by black marketeers.

Just how much T.V. and Soccer will be able to work together without harm to the game as a whole remains to be seen but it is perhaps no exaggeration to say that tonight we could be sitting in on the start of something big.

Let's face it – if watching lizards crawling down Clark Gable's throat 26 years ago didn't open my eyes to the possibilities of tonight's events how can one be dogmatic about what or what not we may be seeing 26 years from now.

One swift and far-reaching consequence of tonight's screening is already planned. A video-tape colour film of the game will be flown to the United States tomorrow morning to help in the development of football in that emergent Soccer nation.

Let's hope that it turns out to be a film worthy of a Soccer "Oscar".

MUSIC

Manchester's leading record specialists, Hime & Addison, 37 John Dalton Street, supply all the records played at Old Trafford.

3 March 1967

Arsenal v Manchester United

Division One

For title-chasing United, this was a historic evening, with the Friday-night trip to Highbury becoming the first game in English football to be televised on closed circuit TV. United supporters who gathered at Old Trafford to watch the 1-1 draw, which moved the Reds closer to a second title in three seasons, could mark the occasion with a special edition of *United Review*, within which *Sun* writer and *Review* columnist Arthur Walmsley presciently penned: 'Tonight's events... illustrate that under the right circumstances TV and soccer can work together to mutual advantage.' Neither party ever looked back.

VOLUME XXVIII No. 18

3rd March, 1967

MATT BUSBY TALKING

This evening – although we will be playing in London and some 200 miles away from Old Trafford – it is my sincere pleasure to welcome all our supporters who have come along to join in this novel venture.

We are, as it were, the "guinea pigs" of the First Division in this respect and your directors and the players too, were delighted to have the opportunity of participating in a closed circuit T.V. experiment.

"Nothing ventured, nothing gained" seems to be the sensible approach. It is exactly what is happening here this evening and we look forward to the result of the project with deep interest.

The League Management Committee has given permission for this "live" screening and we are most grateful to them for the consideration and understanding they have shown us on this occasion.

At the time of writing, closed circuit screening of a number of important games is under consideration and I know many clubs involved in such discussions will be watching events at Old Trafford tonight.

Our game against Arsenal at Highbury is a vital one after our F.A. Cup set-back a fortnight ago with the League Championship commanding our sole attention from now until the end of the season.

I feel quite sure you will continue to give us the benefit of your generous support – vocal and otherwise – in the weeks ahead and this evening the players will be trying that much harder to please you all because of the novelty involved and the knowledge that although they may not hear you they have your encouragement and best wishes for the task on hand.

Matt Busby shared his thoughts ahead of our away game at Highbury, and [above, right] columnist Arthur Walmsley looks forward to a first for football at Old Trafford

29 April 1970

Chelsea v Leeds United

FA Cup final replay

When Chelsea and Leeds played out a 2-2 draw at Wembley in the 1970 FA Cup final, a replay was required to decide the winner for the first time since 1912. Wembley's bedraggled pitch required a switch of venue to Old Trafford where, despite their contrasting styles, little could separate the teams on the field – much as Leeds had required three attempts to overcome Wilf McGuinness's United in the semi-finals. It was no surprise, then, that extra-time was required again at Old Trafford, where the replay became infamous for its violent challenges from both sides. Chelsea ultimately limped to a 2-1 win through David Webb's 104th-minute winner.

This is Old Trafford

Photo by Airviews Ltd

Manchester United's big Cantilever stand on the North side of the ground was completed 4 years ago – the distinctive roof pattern being clearly seen on the right-hand side of the picture. The Stand offers an uninterrupted view for over 10,000 spectators and a row of private boxes with a separate lift spans the width of the Stand. Old Trafford – with a capacity of 63,000 spectators was chosen as a venue for the World Cup games in 1966, an F.A. Cup Semi Final in 1968, the England v. Russia Under-23 International last year and today for the F.A. Cup Final Replay – the first to take place since 1912.

We at Old Trafford join in offering the finalists from Chelsea and Leeds a hearty welcome to Old Trafford.

Edited and Produced by SIDNEY F. WICKS LTD., 21 Newton Street, Manchester M1 1HJ
Printed by DIRECT PRINTING LTD., Ducie Street, Manchester M1 2JW

Fans of Chelsea and Leeds, plus any neutrals, were given an outline of Old Trafford's proud credentials

A greeting from Louis Edwards

Chairman, Manchester United Football Club

It is with feelings of gratification and pride that we at Manchester United play hosts on behalf of the Football Association in staging the replay of the F.A. Cup Final at Old Trafford tonight.

This honour which comes our way is all the more appreciated for the fact that having only just narrowly missed being in the Final ourselves after our three epic semi-final games with Leeds United the final chapter of the 1970 F.A. Cup story is to be played out on our ground.

I need hardly say that no effort has been spared by the staff of Manchester United to ensure that all facilities – both playing and for spectators – will prove worthy of the occasion.

Ground planning at Old Trafford has been concentrated on making the club worthy of the big occasion. We were proud to be honoured as a World Cup centre in 1966 and I am confident that new visitors to Old Trafford tonight will agree that those plans have not been without success.

I am sure we will enjoy another memorable game between two splendid teams tonight and I wish to say "Welcome, to you all" and to express our pleasure in being able to play a part in this historic Final.

At the time of going to press I learn that the Prime Minister the Rt. Hon. Harold Wilson, O.B.E., M.P. intends to honour us with his presence tonight and on behalf of all at Old Trafford I offer him the most cordial welcome.

PAGE TWO

Hosting the FA Cup final replay was a proud moment for the chairman and the club

The Teams

Manchester United	Glasgow Celtic
Alex Stepney	Denis Connaghan
Tommy O'Neil	David Hay
Tony Dunne	Danny McGrain
Martin Buchan	Jim Brogan
Steve James	Bobby Murdoch
David Sadler	Billy McNeill
Willie Morgan	George Connelly
Brian Kidd	Jimmy Johnstone
Bobby Charlton	Ken Dalglish
John Fitzpatrick	Dixie Deans
Denis Law	Lou Macari
George Best	Tom Callaghan
Ian Moore	Vic Davidson
Sammy McIlroy	Harry Hood
Tony Young	Bobby Lennox

Referee

C. Thomas – Treorchy, Glamorgan

Linesmen

E. Blunstone – Crewe

G. A. Myers – York

Tactician Extraordinary

BY SIR ALF RAMSEY

I very much welcome the opportunity to contribute my appreciation of Bobby Charlton in this his Testimonial Match programme as I have been closely linked with this outstanding footballer since my appointment as England Team Manager at the beginning of 1963. My first contact with Bobby was, in fact, when England played France in Paris on February 27th, 1963. I found him a quiet, neatly dressed and likeable young man. By this time he had already obtained some 40 Caps as an England forward but it was obvious that every match was a new challenge for him; his attitude and approach to the game were exactly the same as if it was his first international.

Bobby is probably the best known footballer in the world today. Certainly he is the one player supporters abroad know as well as their own particular national heroes. Wherever I go in my football travels I am asked for photographs and autographs of the England players and it is nearly always "Bobbee" whom they want most of all. He has been a wonderful ambassador for England, not only as a footballer but also in the way in which he has upheld the prestige of his country in every possible sense during his 12 years as an international player, during which time he has visited over 30 countries. He is acknowledged wherever he has appeared as a player of exemplary conduct and of World Class ability and skill; he has emerged over the years as a tactician extraordinary.

Every era has had its outstanding performers on the football field. The 1960s surely belong to Bobby Charlton. Here is a player who has done more than any other over a long period of time to enhance the name of British football. His own particular brand of play is all too rare these days – he has the ability to play equally well as a forward and in mid-field. He can kick the ball accurately and powerfully with both feet. He has an elegant and distinctive style of running which frequently penetrates unprepared defences; he can spot and seize goal-scoring opportunities but he is equally effective at setting up chances for his colleagues by defence splitting passes. He gives 100 per cent effort in everything he does. Perhaps the last remark is the key to Bobby's success. I have been associated with him now for over eight years and I have found in the many training sessions that Bobby sets an example which is second to none. His endeavour, his dedication and his concentration must be an inspiration to any young player coming into the team for the first time and the same qualities are there for all to admire on the field of play. For 90 minutes he has but one thought in mind; to win the ball, to go forward and to score goals.

It is sad to think that after 14 years in senior football Bobby Charlton is now approaching the end of his illustrious career in the game, although I am sure we shall see him in action for many months to come yet. Thank-you, Bobby Charlton, for your efforts for England, which will always be remembered by the thousands of supporters who have flocked to see you, not only at Wembley, but in so many towns and cities at home and overseas.

A E Ramsey

18 September 1972

United v Celtic

Bobby Charlton's testimonial

The end of one of English football's greatest careers required a fitting celebration, and a crowd of over 60,000 supporters set an attendance record for a testimonial which stood until 2001 when, fittingly, Sir Bobby's figure was overtaken by Ryan Giggs. The United and England legend requested a battle of Britain between the Reds and Celtic, both European Cup winners within the previous half-decade. Although neither side could find a way to mark the occasion with a goal, the quality of the scoreless draw pleased the man of the hour, who afterwards reflected: "I wanted all those generous people to see a real game and they got it."

Many greats of the game sent in messages to the match programme on Charlton's big night, among them his former England manager Sir Alf Ramsey [above, right]

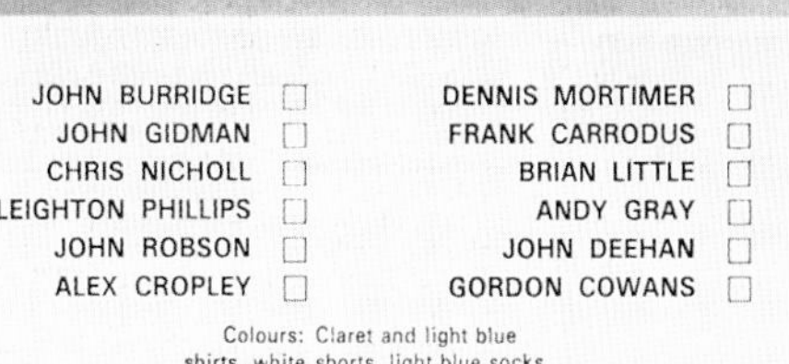

JOHN BURRIDGE
JOHN GIDMAN
CHRIS NICHOLL
LEIGHTON PHILLIPS
JOHN ROBSON
ALEX CROPLEY
DENNIS MORTIMER
FRANK CARRODUS
BRIAN LITTLE
ANDY GRAY
JOHN DEEHAN
GORDON COWANS

Colours: Claret and light blue shirts, white shorts, light blue socks

ASTON VILLA

Team Check

EVERTON

DAVID LAWSON
DAVID JONES
TERRY DARRACOTT
MICK LYONS
KEN McNAUGHT
ANDY KING
BRYAN HAMILTON
MARTIN DOBSON
BOB LATCHFORD
DUNCAN McKENZIE
RON GOODLASS
GEORGE TELFER

Colours: Royal blue shirts and shorts, white socks

It is always a privilege and pleasure to play at Old Trafford and the fact that tonight's match is a Cup Final makes it an extra special occasion for us all.

We have had two sterling battles with Everton so far and we anticipate another this evening. The determination of both teams on the field has been matched by the vocal capabilities of both sets of supporters off it.

It would be remiss of me not to take this opportunity to thank the Aston Villa supporters for their marvellous encouragement on our cup journeys. It has been an expensive business, but our fans have not faltered along the way, and we will be doing everything we can tonight to ensure that their loyalty, encouragement and enthusiasm has all been worthwhile.

SIR WILLIAM DUGDALE,
Chairman, Aston Villa F.C.

To have to play a cup final not once, but THREE times, cannot be any club's idea of the best way to do things, but with the League Cup Final going to a record third meeting Everton are very pleased that the venue is Old Trafford. We've had some memorable games on this great ground over the years and we hope tonight's will be another—with the right result for us!

Some people may feel that our resurgence this season really began with our 3–0 victory on this ground in the fifth round of the League Cup and it would complete the cycle to lift the trophy here as well.

BILL SCOTT,
Chairman, Everton F.C.

13 April 1977

Aston Villa v Everton

League Cup final second replay

Old Trafford completed the double of hosting both major domestic cup finals when Aston Villa and Everton proved inseparable across a goaless draw at Wembley and a 1-1 tie at Hillsborough. It was in Manchester, at the third attempt, that the showpiece really kicked into life as Villa, featuring future Reds defender John Gidman, edged a five-goal extra-time thriller. Everton established a half-time lead through Bob Latchford, but required Mick Lyons's leveller to force an extra period after Chris Nicholl's thunderbolt and Brian Little's clinical finish had put the Villans ahead. Ultimately, it was Little who had the final say, sneaking in to tap home a deflected cross in front of the Stretford End and finally settling matters.

United Review produced the programme for the third instalment of 1977's epic League Cup final, in which both chairmen expressed the hope that Old Trafford would prove to be their lucky ground

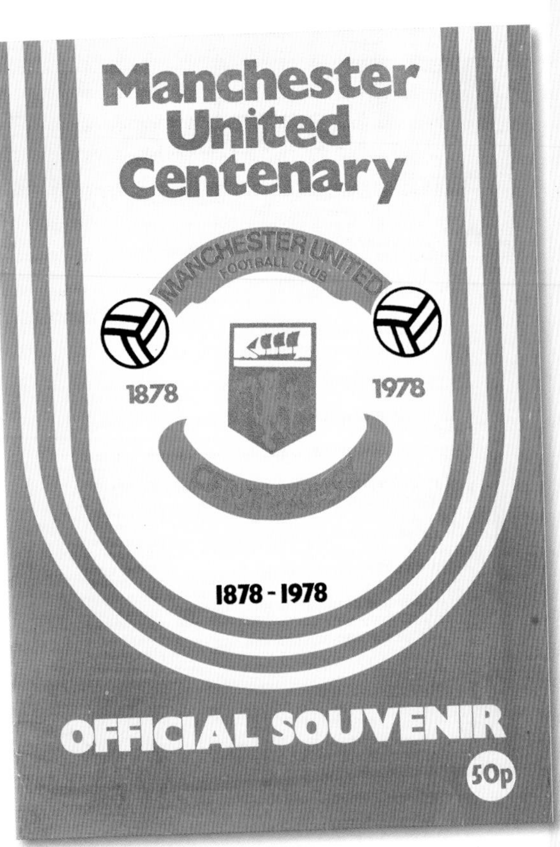

A return to glory?

I hope so

By Martin Buchan

To be captain of United at a time like this is certainly a great honour, you only have to glance back through the club's history and look at the names of the players who have held the position to get some idea of my feelings in this centenary year.

And what will it be like for Martin Buchan to lead Manchester United in their historic centenary game against the great Real Madrid?

Really, after our pre-season tour, and the preparations for season 1978-79, I'll be looking forward to my fourth full term as club captain. My thoughts will be more to the future than the past despite United's long and famous association with the Spanish side.

Because I didn't play in any of the classic encounters between our teams I have no personal memories to recall . . . but I do remember watching the famous European Cup Final of 1960 on television. That was when the masters beat Eintracht Frankfurt 7—3 at Hampden Park, Glasgow in what was probably the most entertaining football match ever seen.

The Real team that night included the great di Stefano, Puskas and Gento, and I'm glad that we won't have to face—or should I say chase—their ghosting figures in this game.

I am sad that the death of Senor Santiago Bernabeau has denied Sir Matt the opportunity of renewing an old friendship, and the players of meeting the man who, like Matt Busby, made his club a national institution.

Like United, Real have found that success is not everlasting, and have experienced bad times as well as good.

Both sets of players would love to give their supporters, and themselves, a return to the heady days of European Cup glory and, as always at the beginning of a new season, we'll be starting off in a mood of optimism to set the scene for a "real" thriller in our centenary game.

Our optimism, I believe, is well founded, as our two new aquisitions, Joe Jordan and Gordon McQueen, settled into the side very well at the end of last season.

Manager Dave Sexton has the benefit of a year's experience, working with the players, and won't have to start this new season in the shadow of another manager, as he did when he came to Old Trafford following Tommy Docherty's F.A. Cup success in 1977.

On reflection, Last season was a difficult time for all of us at Old Trafford, but as I said earlier, my thoughts now are for the future, as United begins its second century.

I enjoy being captain of Manchester United, and hope to lead the team to many more victories especially in this historic year for the club.

18

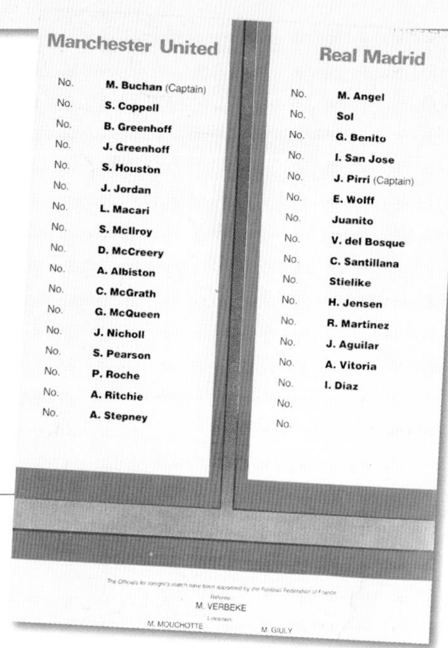

Manchester United	Real Madrid
No. M. Buchan (Captain)	No. M. Angel
No. S. Coppell	No. Sol
No. B. Greenhoff	No. G. Benito
No. J. Greenhoff	No. I. San Jose
No. S. Houston	No. J. Pirri (Captain)
No. J. Jordan	No. E. Wolff
No. L. Macari	No. Juanito
No. S. McIlroy	No. V. del Bosque
No. D. McCreery	No. C. Santillana
No. A. Albiston	No. Stielike
No. C. McGrath	No. H. Jensen
No. G. McQueen	No. R. Martinez
No. J. Nicholl	No. J. Aguilar
No. S. Pearson	No. A. Vitoria
No. P. Roche	No. I. Diaz
No. A. Ritchie	No.
No. A. Stepney	No.

M. VERBEKE

M. MOUCHOTTE M. GIULY

7 August 1978

Manchester United v Real Madrid

Centenary friendly

To mark the 100th anniversary of Newton Heath's formation, a special centenary encounter was arranged against Spanish giants Real Madrid. A suitably snazzy programme marked the occasion and included an upbeat captain's column from skipper Martin Buchan, who foretold: 'We'll be starting off in a mood of optimism to set the scene for a real thriller in our centenary game.' So it proved, with Dave Sexton's side in swashbuckling form against the mighty visitors. Sammy McIlroy helped himself to a brilliant brace in little more than half an hour, and Jimmy Greenhoff headed in a third and rounded off the scoring with a fine curled effort 15 minutes from time.

The special edition programme produced to mark United's centenary was more like a chronicle of the club's history, but it included a look not only at the past but also towards the future [above, right]

Back row (l to r): Mr. D. H. Bushell (Team Manager) R. Wilson, A. Hughes, J. Charlton, J. Thomson, M. Foster, A. Mike, D. Hall, D. Deanus, Mr. D. G. Compton (Assistant Manager).
Front row (l to r): K. Gyamfi, M. Harriott, N. Barmby, M. S. H. Green (ESFA Chairman), J. Foster, A. Marlowe, L. Durrant, D. Brocklehurst.

A smattering of recognisable faces and names in the team photo and squad lists ahead of the England v Scotland clash at Under-15s level

ENGLISH SCHOOLS' FOOTBALL ASSOCIATION

VICTORY SHIELD

UNDER-15 INTERNATIONAL

ENGLAND v SCOTLAND
Friday 21st April
at
MANCHESTER UNITED F.C.
OLD TRAFFORD
(By kind permission of the Directors)
Kick-off 7.00pm

ORGANISED BY MANCHESTER SCHOOLS' F.A.

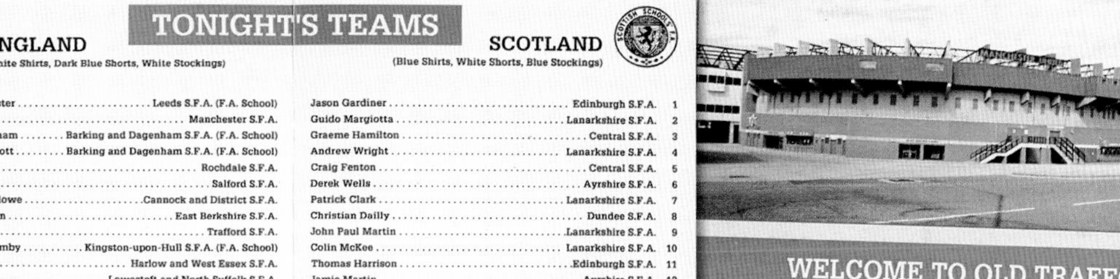

WELCOME TO OLD TRAFFORD

TONIGHT'S TEAMS

ENGLAND
(White Shirts, Dark Blue Shorts, White Stockings)

No.	Player	Association
1	Matthew Foster	Leeds S.F.A. (F.A. School)
2	John Foster	Manchester S.F.A.
3	Michael Basham	Barking and Dagenham S.F.A. (F.A. School)
4	Marvin Harriott	Barking and Dagenham S.F.A. (F.A. School)
5	David Hall	Rochdale S.F.A.
6	Ryan Wilson	Salford S.F.A.
7	Andrew Marlowe	Cannock and District S.F.A.
8	John Charlton	East Berkshire S.F.A.
9	Adrian Mike	Trafford S.F.A.
10	Nicholas Barmby	Kingston-upon-Hull S.F.A. (F.A. School)
11	Paul Read	Harlow and West Essex S.F.A.
12	Lee Durrant	Lowestoft and North Suffolk S.F.A.
13	Darren Gaskey	Basildon and Romford S.F.A.
14	Justin Lee	Vale of Whitehorse S.F.A.
15	David Brocklehurst	Chesterfield S.F.A.
16	Jon Thomson	Chester-le-Street and Washington S.F.A.

Team Manager: Mr. D. Bushell
Assistant Manager: Mr. D. G. Crompton

SCOTLAND
(Blue Shirts, White Shorts, Blue Stockings)

Jason Gardiner	Edinburgh S.F.A.	1
Guido Margiotta	Lanarkshire S.F.A.	2
Graeme Hamilton	Central S.F.A.	3
Andrew Wright	Lanarkshire S.F.A.	4
Craig Fenton	Central S.F.A.	5
Derek Wells	Ayrshire S.F.A.	6
Patrick Clark	Lanarkshire S.F.A.	7
Christian Dailly	Dundee S.F.A.	8
John Paul Martin	Lanarkshire S.F.A.	9
Colin McKee	Lanarkshire S.F.A.	10
Thomas Harrison	Edinburgh S.F.A.	11
Jamie Martin	Ayrshire S.F.A.	12
Levi Smith	Aberdeen S.F.A.	13
Lee Robertson	Edinburgh S.F.A.	14
Graeme McCheyne	Lanarkshire S.F.A.	15
John Hudson	Dumfries and Galloway S.F.A.	16

Team Manager: Mr. W. L. Donaldson
Assistant Manager: Mr. B. McAlindon

TONIGHT'S OFFICIALS

Referee:
Mr. D. B. Allison (Lancashire County F.A.)

Linesmen:
Mr. A. R. Gahan
(Leicestershire and Rutland County F.A.) Red Trim
Mr. I. Cowley
(Birmingham County F.A.) Yellow Trim.

6 7

21 April 1989

England v Scotland

Under-15 international Victory Shield

Managed by long-serving United coach Dave Bushell, England Under-15s were able to name young Welsh-born Ryan Wilson for a Friday-night Victory Shield encounter with Scotland at Old Trafford. Even then, the teenager's reputation within youth football circuits was huge, and he played a starring role as England went on to lift the Shield for the first time in three years. Less than two years down the line, Wilson – now better known as Ryan Giggs – was lining up at Old Trafford again, this time to make his Reds debut against Everton, marking the commencement of the greatest football career in the history of English football.

League football.
RYAN WILSON, Moorside H.S. Salford, plays with the City of Salford S.F.A. as a left winger and with Great Manchester County S.F.A. He has played Rugby for Lancashire. he enjoys most sports and likes to watch T.V. or attend discos. He has signed for Manchester United F.C. and sees his future in a red shirt at Old Trafford.
MICHAEL BASHAM, Bishop Ward R.C. Secondary, Dagenham, is a member of the F.A.

This was the first time – but certainly not the last! – that Ryan Giggs (then Wilson) appeared in the programme for a game at Old Trafford

BRYAN ROBSON
OBE

TESTIMONIAL YEAR 1990-1991

MAIN EVENT

MANCHESTER UNITED
V
CELTIC

OFFICIAL PROGRAMME AND SOUVENIR BROCHURE £3.00

'HE IS MY PLAYER OF THE EIGHTIES'

A tribute from Bobby Robson, England manager 1982-1990

I am glad of this opportunity to say a few words about Bryan Robson, because this summer with England has seen the parting of our ways.

Bryan has been skipper of the international team throughout my eight years as manager and I will always look back on our relationship as one of the most positive and enduring experiences in charge.

His loyalty and commitment to the cause were outstanding and provides one of my happiest memories from the international world as I set about my new job here in Holland.

During our eight years working together we had our highs and lows as a team, but the great thing about him was that even when things looked their blackest, like after the European championships two years ago, he never wavered.

In fact his contribution was much more positive than that, because when we were up against it he tried extra hard. Although injury robbed him of a place in the World Cup semi-finals in Italy this summer, it was Bryan Robson more than any other single player who was responsible for getting us there in such good shape.

He was magnificent after Germany in 1988 and played out of his skin to get us back on the road to success. At a time when it would have been easy for heads to drop, his chin came up. He stood up ready to be counted and stiffened the backbone along with men like Peter Shilton and Terry Butcher in readiness for our good performance at the World Cup in Italy.

But for injuries to the captain at vital times, we might have had even more success, perhaps, at the World Cup in Mexico in 1986.

It was the recurring dislocation of his shoulder which stopped him that time, just as an Achilles tendon problem stopped him in the final stages in Italy.

Bryan has had dreadfully bad luck with injuries, though having said that, he has always been vulnerable because of the fearless way he plays.

Lesser players have won more but none have given as much. He should have had well over a hundred caps by now, but under me he has missed more than 30 through injury.

It's the price he has paid for his committed style.

Of course, you are not taught to play like Bryan Robson, it is in-born. It's a natural characteristic which separates the men from the boys.

Whenever I selected a squad for an England match I always worried about people dropping out, particularly the skipper, for he was always the last one you wanted to be missing.

I think some people probably felt I put too much emphasis on his value to the team and waited too long at times to give him every possible chance of recovering from some injury or other; but it was very difficult to do otherwise because he was simply our best player.

When he ever told me he was injured, my heart used to sink. I used to ask myself who was there to replace him, and the answer was that while we always had excellent players around, nobody quite measured up to Bryan Robson.

He has always been worth his weight in gold to both his country and to Manchester United. He is priceless . . . not just an inspiration but a match-winner.

There hasn't been another midfield player to compare with him, and I have no hesitation naming him my Player of the Eighties.

There have been Peter Shilton, Kevin Keegan and Trevor Brooking, plus a few more, but only one Bryan Robson.

Bobby Robson

20 November 1990

Manchester United v Celtic

Bryan Robson testimonial

Mercifully, one of United's greatest-ever servants was able to squeeze two Premier League titles into the tail end of his Reds career, but not before his 10-year anniversary at the club had been marked with a fittingly feisty testimonial against Celtic. Mark Hughes tapped United into an early lead against the Scots, only for the hosts to trail 1-2 at the interval after a quickfire turnaround. Robson, used sparingly after undergoing an Achilles operation in the preceding weeks, was introduced as a second-half substitute. The visitors quickly scored a third to wrap up the victory, but few home supporters cared while saluting the brilliance of Captain Marvel.

THREE FACES OF BRYAN

United Review editor Cliff Butler and regular contributor David Meek helped out with the production of this 82-page programme for Robbo's big night, with one of its many highlights being a glowing tribute from England manager Bobby Robson to his trusted captain [above, right]

A TRIBUTE FROM ALEX FERGUSON

Just one club could tempt Alex Ferguson across the border from Aberdeen - Manchester United. That was the message on the "bush telegraph" for the directors at Old Trafford when it became clear that Ron Atkinson, despite his achievements, would be leaving.

It was a decision Ferguson will never regret, as he became the second Scot to succeed Sir Matt. "Even as a football-daft kid I knew what Sir Matt had done for Manchester United," says Ferguson.

"He laid the foundations of the club and saw it grow, but his feet never left the ground.

"Some people are afraid of traditions. I have found his influence and history a soothing effect. He is also such a wonderful man physically, and he has that special presence of all great people."

"Most important, perhaps, he has never changed as a person during his life. He is an example to follow. If I ever achieved a modicum of the success Sir Matt gained and then allowed myself to be carried away by it, I would deserved to have my backside kicked."

"It could be easy to have inflated values at this club. But when you realise the length of successful service he has given and yet retained the same personality, it sets a standard anyone would be proud to follow."

"Sir Matt was one huge reason why I was delighted to come to Old Trafford after possibly expecting never to leave Scotland."

by DEREK POTTER

SOUVENIR BROCHURE £5

SIR MATT BUSBY

I wish to thank all concerned who helped organise this special occasion, and to all you wonderful people, both young and old, who have supported the club and myself through the years.

From the bottom of my heart, many thanks and God Bless you all.

Matt Busby

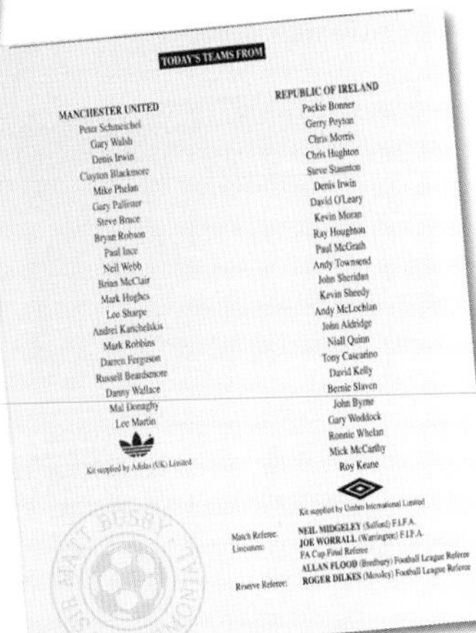

TODAY'S TEAMS FROM

MANCHESTER UNITED	REPUBLIC OF IRELAND
Peter Schmeichel	Packie Bonner
Gary Walsh	Gerry Peyton
Denis Irwin	Chris Morris
Clayton Blackmore	Chris Hughton
Mike Phelan	Steve Staunton
Gary Pallister	Denis Irwin
Steve Bruce	David O'Leary
Bryan Robson	Kevin Moran
Paul Ince	Ray Houghton
Neil Webb	Paul McGrath
Brian McClair	Andy Townsend
Mark Hughes	John Sheridan
Lee Sharpe	Kevin Sheedy
Andrei Kanchelskis	Andy McLochlan
Mark Robbins	John Aldridge
Darren Ferguson	Niall Quinn
Russell Beardsmore	Tony Cascarino
Danny Wallace	David Kelly
Mal Donaghy	Bernie Slaven
Lee Martin	John Byrne
	Gary Waddock
	Ronnie Whelan
	Mick McCarthy
	Roy Keane
Kit supplied by Adidas (UK) Limited	Kit supplied by Umbro International Limited

Match Referee: NEIL MIDGELEY (Salford) F.I.F.A.
Linesmen: JOE WORRALL (Warrington) F.I.F.A. FA Cup Final Referee
ALLAN FLOOD (Bredbury) Football League Referee
Reserve Referee: ROGER DILKES (Mossley) Football League Referee

11 August 1991

Manchester United v Rep of Ireland XI

Sir Matt Busby testimonial

Preceded by a veterans' Manchester derby which featured several 1968 European Cup-winning Reds, a specially arranged meeting between Alex Ferguson's United and Jack Charlton's Republic of Ireland paid tribute to the legendary work of Sir Matt Busby. 'Even as a football-daft kid, I knew what Sir Matt had done for Manchester United,' Ferguson wrote in the programme. Acting as a curtain-raiser to the 1991/92 campaign, the encounter gave supporters a first glimpse of Peter Schmeichel at Old Trafford, and the imperious Dane was beaten only by fellow home debutant Paul Parker's own goal, before Bryan Robson struck after the break to secure a draw.

United's programme team again played a big part in the pulling together of this bespoke issue for Sir Matt's testimonial match, for which the cover [above] was designed by artist Harold Riley

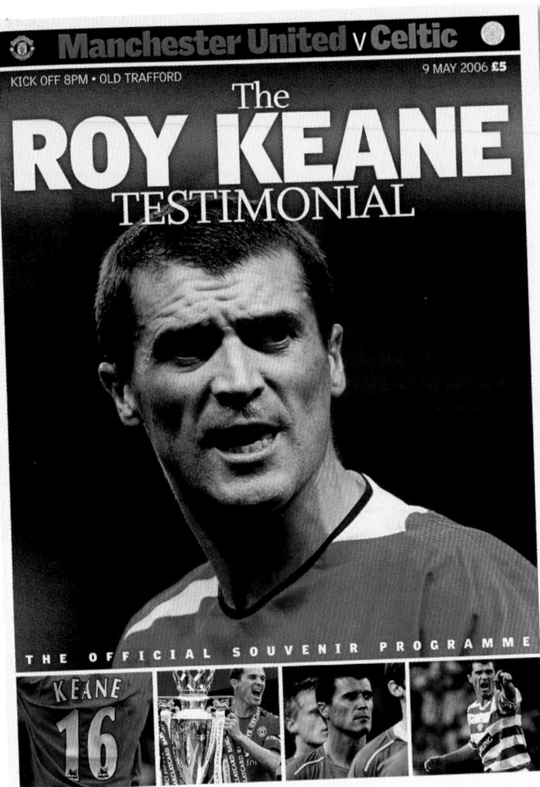

TESTIMONIAL

SIR ALEX FERGUSON ON KEANO

United's heartbeat

Roy Keane's will to win made me proud to be associated with him during his 12 years at Old Trafford

I think this is going to be a testimonial with a difference. It's been a sell-out for over a week and, with 23,000 Celtic fans filling the North Stand this evening, there's sure to be a fabulous atmosphere. And unlike many goodwill friendly matches, I think it is safe to say that there will definitely be a competitive edge both on and off the field!

That's fitting for a game featuring Roy Keane, a player who was always different and who didn't know how to play without a will to win. It was there for all to see in the second leg of our Champions League semi-final against Juventus in Turin in our Treble season. Roy was booked soon after scoring our first goal and, on top of a previous yellow card, it meant he would be ruled out of the final should we get there.

He knew it, of course, but far from allowing it to depress him he raised his game to see us through to a 3-2 win on the night and into the final. It was quite the most selfless display it has ever been my privilege to witness in the game and typical of his total commitment to Manchester United.

Roy's performance in Turin was the most selfless display it has ever been my privilege to witness

Roy left us for Celtic rather abruptly in November and there was a lot of idle chatter into the whys and wherefores. It was not an easy parting of the ways for either of us, but it takes nothing away from a fantastic association I enjoyed as his manager for 12 years. He was one of this club's great captains and I didn't describe him once as the heartbeat of Manchester United for nothing.

Party like it's 1999: United have just won the league

4 Roy Keane Testimonial

The ROY KEANE TESTIMONIAL

9 MAY 2006

Manchester United

1 Tim **HOWARD**
2 Gary **NEVILLE**
3 Patrice **EVRA**
4 Gabriel **HEINZE**
5 Rio **FERDINAND**
6 Wes **BROWN**
7 Cristiano **RONALDO**
8 Wayne **ROONEY**
9 Louis **SAHA**
10 Ruud **VAN NISTELROOY**
11 Ryan **GIGGS**
13 Ji-sung **PARK**
14 Alan **SMITH**
15 Nemanja **VIDIC**
17 Liam **MILLER**
18 Paul **SCHOLES**
19 Edwin **VAN DER SAR**
20 Ole Gunnar **SOLSKJAER**
22 John **O'SHEA**
23 Kieran **RICHARDSON**
24 Darren **FLETCHER**
25 Quinton **FORTUNE**
26 Phil **BARDSLEY**
27 Mikael **SILVESTRE**
28 Gerard **PIQUÉ**
30 Luke **STEELE**
31 David **JONES**
34 Paul **McSHANE**
36 Mark **HOWARD**
38 Tom **HEATON**
40 Sylvan **EBANKS-BLAKE**
41 Floribert **NGALULA**
42 Giuseppe **ROSSI**
44 Adam **ECKERSLEY**
46 Lee **MARTIN**
49 Richard **JONES**
50 Darron **GIBSON**
51 Fraizer **CAMPBELL**

Celtic

1 Artur **BORUC**
2 Paul **TELFER**
3 Mohammed **CAMARA**
4 Adam **VIRGO**
6 Dianbobo **BALDE**
7 Maciej **ZURAWSKI**
8 Alan **THOMPSON**
9 Dion **DUBLIN**
10 John **HARTSON**
11 Stephen **PEARSON**
12 Mark **WILSON**
16 Roy **KEANE**
18 Neil **LENNON**
19 Stilian **PETROV**
22 David **MARSHALL**
23 Stanislav **VARGA**
25 Shunsuke **NAKAMURA**
29 Shaun **MALONEY**
33 Ross **WALLACE**
35 Paul **LAWSON**
37 Craig **BEATTIE**
38 Rocco **QUINN**
41 John **KENNEDY**
42 Michael **MCGLINCHEY**
44 Stephen **MCMANUS**
46 Aiden **MCGEADY**
47 Michael **MCGOVERN**
48 Darren **O'DEA**
49 Scott **CUTHBERT**

9 May 2006

Manchester United v Celtic

Roy Keane testimonial

Though the circumstances of his departure from Old Trafford were far from ideal, Roy Keane was welcomed back with open arms as the end of the 2005/06 campaign. The Irishman returned with his new club, Celtic, in tow, and a huge travelling support ensured a rip-roaring atmosphere as both factions united to salute one of the Reds' greatest leaders. Keane played a goalless first half for Celtic, then ended up on the winning side as he donned a United jersey after the break, prior to Cristiano Ronaldo settling the outcome with a decisive finish.

'One of the club's great captains' has his praises sung by his manager of 12 years (above, right), with one display in April 1999 getting a special mention in a tribute from Sir Alex

Andres Iniesta

"Football is a difficult game, but Paul Scholes made it look easy. I approached him after the final whistle on the pitch at Wembley. I thought it might be his last game and hoped to swap shirts, to shake his hand, to say thank you and "good luck" in English. He said the same to me. In English!

"We swapped shirts and I took mine back home to Spain and put it on display in my house. I explained to my partner about Scholes and how good he's been.

"I've always wanted to play like Paul Scholes. We more or less play in the same position, and so I've been especially interested in how he plays.

"He's an example to every professional footballer, not just young ones who can follow the style of one of the most complete footballers in the world, but experienced players like myself. I've been watching him on television for years and always learned from him.

Scholes' passes are perfectly weighted and his timing is correct when Manchester attack. His vision is such that he always chooses the correct option when he has the ball. That increases the team's chances in front of goal. Attackers must love playing with him behind them.

"Scholes has spent all his career at United. There are very few players in the world who stay at one club, especially a top club for all their career. It's difficult to maintain such a high level for so long, but I'm trying to do it here and Scholes has successfully done it

"Now that he has decided to retire, I'd like to wish him all the best for the future. I've been a fan of his for many years and I have happy memories of watching him. The only bad memory I have of him is in 2008 at Old Trafford, but a great player like him deserved to score that goal."

Edgar Davids

"Every one of us should emulate him. We can all learn from Paul Scholes."

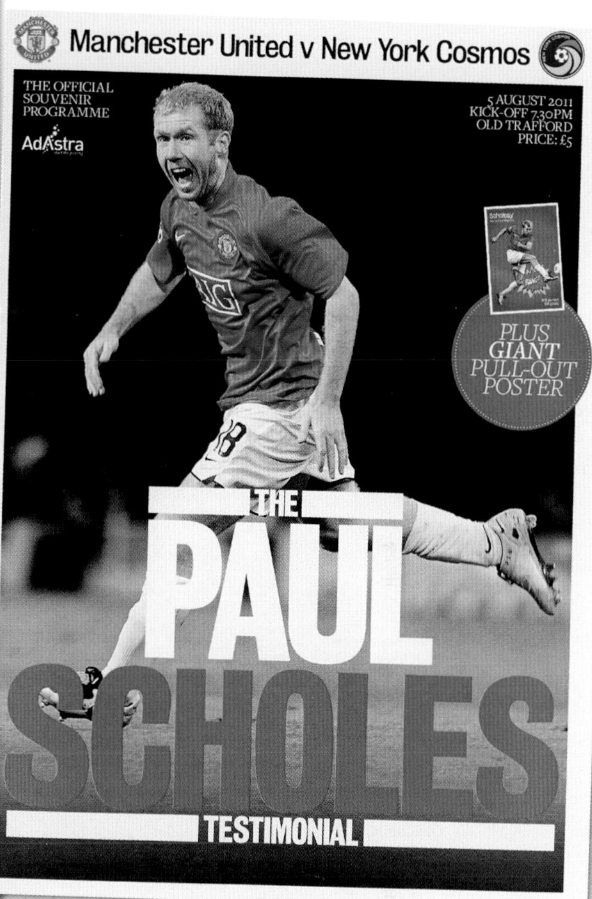

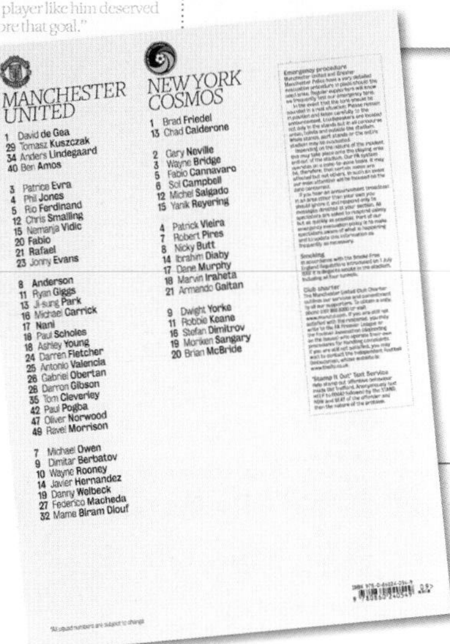

MANCHESTER UNITED

1 David de Gea
29 Tomasz Kuszczak
34 Anders Lindegaard
40 Ben Amos

3 Patrice Evra
4 Phil Jones
5 Rio Ferdinand
12 Chris Smalling
15 Nemanja Vidic
20 Fabio
21 Rafael
23 Jonny Evans

8 Anderson
11 Ryan Giggs
13 Ji-sung Park
16 Michael Carrick
17 Nani
18 Paul Scholes
18 Ashley Young
24 Darren Fletcher
25 Antonio Valencia
26 Gabriel Obertan
28 Darron Gibson
35 Tom Cleverley
42 Paul Pogba
47 Oliver Norwood
49 Ravel Morrison

7 Michael Owen
9 Dimitar Berbatov
10 Wayne Rooney
14 Javier Hernandez
19 Danny Welbeck
27 Federico Macheda
32 Mame Biram Diouf

NEW YORK COSMOS

1 Brad Friedel
13 Chad Calderone

2 Gary Neville
3 Wayne Bridge
5 Fabio Cannavaro
6 Sol Campbell
12 Michel Salgado
15 Yanik Reyering

4 Patrick Vieira
7 Robert Pires
8 Nicky Butt
14 Ibrahim Diaby
17 Dane Murphy
18 Marvin Iraheta
21 Armando Gaitan

9 Dwight Yorke
11 Robbie Keane
16 Stefan Dimitrov
19 Moriken Sangary
20 Brian McBride

5 August 2011

Manchester United v New York Cosmos

Paul Scholes testimonial

In-between his two attempts at retirement, Paul Scholes slotted in a memorable testimonial encounter ahead of the 2011/12 season. The special matchday programme was heaving with glowing tributes to the midfielder, including special tributes from luminaries such as Zinedine Zidane, Xavi and Andres Iniesta. Though the famously bashful Scholes tried to his best to redirect the spotlight by having Pele and Eric Cantona accompany the New York Cosmos to Old Trafford, he duly thundered home a belting long-ranger to set a 6-0 win under way. Little wonder he was out of retirement just five months later.

Barcelona legend Iniesta (above, left) was among the former foes heaping praise on Scholesy on the night of his testimonial against Eric Cantona's (!) New York Cosmos side

News

Get set for a legendary occasion!

United and Real Madrid legends join forces with JLS and co for a great day out

We welcome the Legends from Manchester United and Real Madrid to Old Trafford this afternoon for a very special event designed to raise funds for charity.

Two of the greatest clubs in the history of the game are competing in the second leg of a fund-raising double header after the Spanish giants won 3-2 at the Bernabéu last year in a match that benefited the Real Madrid Foundation and was watched by around 60,000 fans.

The stage is set for the Reds' former stars to bid to overturn that one-goal deficit on home turf with penalties planned if the aggregate scores are level after 90 minutes. Coach Bryan Robson's team includes recently-retired hero Paul Scholes, Edwin van der Sar, Dwight Yorke, Andy Cole and Teddy Sheringham while the prolific Ruud van Nistelrooy will appear for both sides.

The Spanish giants are certain to provide formidable opposition as global superstars Zinedine Zidane and Luis Figo are part of their plans and it promises to be an entertaining clash and an opportunity to watch some of the world's greatest players in action again at Old Trafford.

The Red Heart United day is very much a family affair with all the proceeds going to the Manchester United Foundation to support the local community (read more about the Foundation's activities on p61). Real Madrid director Emilio Butragueno is part of today's visiting squad and has been a big supporter of both charity matches in Madrid and Manchester. "Both Real Madrid and Manchester United are two of the most prestigious clubs in the world," he said at the launch of the game at Old Trafford in March. "We owe our fans a lot, so we set up our foundation in 1977 with the purpose of helping those in need. We have a lot of projects and we are present in 65 countries. The money we raised from the game in Madrid went to 42 projects in 26 countries in Africa. Of course, I would like to thank Manchester United for the help and because of that we are here because we would like to do something in return."

There is also a concert ahead of the match which features some of the cream of British chart talent – JLS, Amelia Lily and Tinchy Stryder. And as well as lots of fun activities in and around the ground, you'll get the chance to say hello to something very dear to all United fans' hearts while celebrating another memorable season. The Barclays Premier League trophy, won in stunning fashion during Sir Alex Ferguson's final season in charge, will be paraded at half-time. It promises to be a very special day at the Theatre of Dreams...

6 MANCHESTER UNITED v REAL MADRID – THE LEGENDS

2 June 2013

Manchester United v Real Madrid

Legends match

Old Trafford's first fixture of the post-Sir Alex Ferguson era pitted together veterans teams from both United and Real Madrid, in a charity fixture arranged to benefit Manchester United Foundation and Unicef. The showpiece acted as the second instalment of the fixture first played a year earlier in Madrid, which the hosts won 3-2. The star-studded line-ups enthralled the 55,000 fans inside the stadium, with Fernando Morientes opening the scoring for the visitors before Ruud van Nistelrooy smashed home a leveller for United. Ruben de la Red rounded off an away victory, but worthy causes proved to be the day's true winners.

RED HEART UNITED

Foundation | Realmadrid

MANCHESTER UNITED

1. EDWIN VAN DER SAR
13. RAIMOND VAN DER GOUW

3. DENIS IRWIN
5. RONNY JOHNSEN
6. JAAP STAM
16. LEE MARTIN
21. HENNING BERG

4. CLAYTON BLACKMORE
7. BRYAN ROBSON
11. LEE SHARPE
15. JESPER BLOMQVIST
18. PAUL SCHOLES
25. QUINTON FORTUNE

8. DION DUBLIN
9. ANDY COLE
10. TEDDY SHERINGHAM
10. RUUD VAN NISTELROOY
19. DWIGHT YORKE

REAL MADRID

1. PEDRO CONTRERAS
13. CARLOS SANCHEZ

2. MICHEL SALGADO
3. FABIO CANNAVARO
4. FERNANDO HIERRO
6. IVAN HELGUERA
19. FERNANDO SANZ
22. FRANCISCO PAVON

5. ZINEDINE ZIDANE
10. LUIS FIGO
11. JOSE AMAVISCA
14. GUTI
16. STEVE MCMANAMAN
18. RUBEN DE LA RED
24. CLAUDE MAKELELE

7. EMILIO BUTRAGUENO
8. ALFONSO PEREZ
9. FERNANDO MORIENTES
17. RUUD VAN NISTELROOY

Referee: Kevin Friend
Assistant referees: Scott Ledger, Matt Wilkes
Fourth official: David Coote

TIMETABLE OF EVENTS

12:00 – Gates open
13:15 – Concert on the pitch
14:00 – Players warm up
14:30 – Match kick-off
15:15 – Half-time activities
15:30 – Second half
16:15 – End of match
16:30 – Trophy presentation

Rolling back the years: United and Real Madrid legends played two matches in aid of the clubs' own charities, with this game at Old Trafford an afternoon of great entertainment

WAYNE ROONEY FOUNDATION

WELCOME

It's a proud night for a grateful Wayne Rooney, who has a message of thanks to all in attendance

Welcome everybody to Old Trafford and a big thank you for coming tonight. It's a proud moment for me to be able to celebrate such an occasion, and hopefully together we can raise lots of money for some fantastic charities.

I signed for Manchester United 12 years ago and never dreamt I would be in this position. It's been an incredible journey so far with lots of trophies and hopefully there are many more to come. It's an unbelievable honour to be part of the history of this special club and my thanks go to everybody who has helped me along the way.

Special thanks, of course, to my family for the amazing support they have given me and the part they've played in my career so far. I can't wait to walk out with my three boys and show them what a special and inspiring place Old Trafford is.

Last, but certainly not least, a huge thank you to the fans for your loyal support over the years. I really appreciate it all. It's an honour to play for you and I look forward to making many more memories together. Let's all enjoy tonight!

BT PRINCIPAL PARTNER OF

WAYNE ROONEY FOUNDATION

MANCHESTER UNITED			EVERTON
DAVID DE GEA	1	1	JOEL ROBLES
ERIC BAILLY	3	3	LEIGHTON BAINES
PHIL JONES	4	4	DARRON GIBSON
MARCOS ROJO	5	5	JOHN STONES
MEMPHIS	7	6	PHIL JAGIELKA
JUAN MATA	8	7	AIDEN McGEADY
ZLATAN IBRAHIMOVIC	9	8	BRYAN OVIEDO
WAYNE ROONEY	10	9	AROUNA KONE
ANTHONY MARTIAL	11	10	ROMELU LUKAKU
CHRIS SMALLING	12	11	KEVIN MIRALLAS
JESSE LINGARD	14	12	AARON LENNON
ADNAN JANUZAJ	15	14	OUMAR NIASSE
MICHAEL CARRICK	16	15	TOM CLEVERLEY
DALEY BLIND	17	16	JAMES McCARTHY
ASHLEY YOUNG	18	18	GARETH BARRY
MARCUS RASHFORD	19	19	GERARD DEULOFEU
SERGIO ROMERO	20	20	ROSS BARKLEY
ANDER HERRERA	21	21	MUHAMED BESIC
HENRIKH MKHITARYAN	22	22	MAARTEN STEKELENBURG
LUKE SHAW	23	23	SEAMUS COLEMAN
TIMOTHY FOSU-MENSAH	24	24	SHANI TARASHAJ
ANTONIO VALENCIA	25	25	RAMIRO FUNES MORI
MAROUANE FELLAINI	27	26	MATTHEW PENNINGTON
MORGAN SCHNEIDERLIN	28	27	TYIAS BROWNING
BASTIAN SCHWEINSTEIGER	31	28	LEANDRO RODRIGUEZ
SAM JOHNSTONE	32	29	LUKE GARBUTT
PADDY McNAIR	33	30	MASON HOLGATE
MATTEO DARMIAN	36	31	KIERAN DOWELL
AXEL TUANZEBE	38	32	BRENDAN GALLOWAY
ANDREAS PEREIRA	44	33	CALLUM CONNOLLY
CAMERON BORTHWICK-JACKSON	43	34	TOM DAVIES
WILL KEANE	48	39	CONOR GRANT

TONIGHT'S OFFICIALS
REFEREE: MICHAEL OLIVER
ASSISTANT REFEREES: SCOTT LEDGER, EDDIE SMART
FOURTH OFFICIAL: BOBBY MADLEY

HUBLOT

thinkmoney

EMERGENCY PROCEDURE

MATCHDAY TEXT SERVICE

£5.00

5 027351 583742

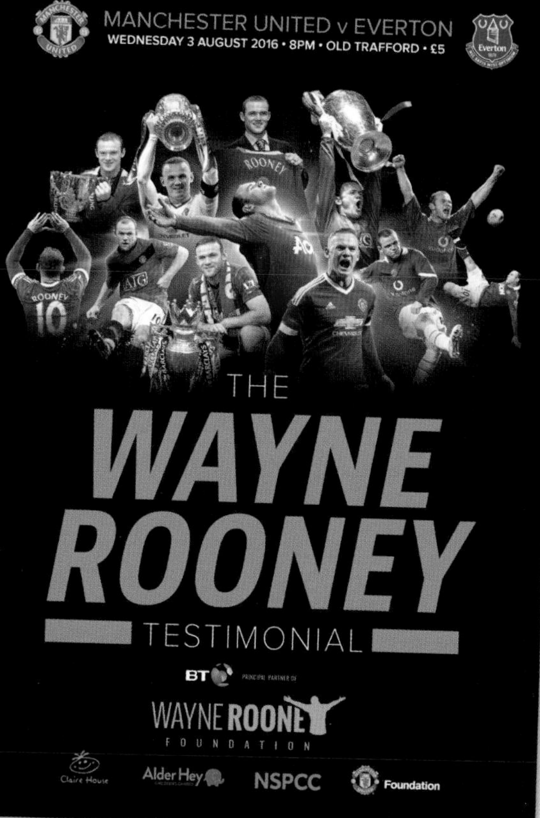

3 August 2016

Manchester United v Everton

Wayne Rooney testimonial

At the start of his final season as a Red, Wayne Rooney's dozen years of service were recognised with a high-profile testimonial against his boyhood club, Everton. Once again, the programme brimmed with tributes from the striker's team-mates from down his gilded Old Trafford years, and the man of the hour welcomed supporters by saying 'it's an unbelievable honour to be part of the history of this special club'. By season's end, Rooney would stand alone as the Reds' all-time top scorer with 253 goals – though unfortunately no goals were forthcoming in his testimonial as the evening finished scoreless!

It was an emotional night for Rooney when the two clubs closest to his heart met for his testimonial, with the money raised going to his chosen charities